THE CENTURY OF THE
HOLY SPIRIT

THE CENTURY OF THE

HOLY SPIRIT

100 Years of Pentecostal

and Charismatic Renewal,

1901–2001

■ ■

VINSON SYNAN

THOMAS NELSON PUBLISHERS

Nashville

Book design and composition by Mark McGarry,
Texas Type and Book Works, Dallas, Texas

Library of Congress Cataloging-in-Publication Data available from Library of
Congress
Synan, Vinson
The century of the Holy Spirit: 100 years of Pentecostal and charismatic renewal,
1901-2001

ISBN 0-7852-4550-2

Printed in the United States of America
5 6 7—06

To my beautiful wife, Carol Lee,
with whom I have shared forty wonderful years
of the century of the Holy Spirit

Contents

Preface

In the midst of the millennial fever that gripped the world in 1999 and 2000, few people realized that the new millennium would actually begin on January 1, 2001. For Christians, this anniversary is special because it marks the 2,000 years of Christian history. But for millions of Pentecostal and charismatic Christians, this anniversary also marks the completion of 100 years of Pentecostal and charismatic renewal.

The title of this book, *The Century of the Holy Spirit*, summarizes what is generally recognized as the most important religious movement of the entire twentieth century. Beginning with a handful of students in Topeka, Kansas, on New Year's Day, 1901, Christians around the world have experienced a renewal of the gifts of the Holy Spirit that dwarfs anything seen since the days of the early church. This movement, which now constitutes the second largest family of Christians in the world (after the Roman Catholic Church), is found in practically every nation and ethnic group in the world. By the end of the century, over 500,000,000 people were involved in this revival which continues its massive growth into the new millennium.

Many readers will wish to learn the distinctions between the Pentecostals and charismatics, which are the subjects of this book. The Pentecostals were the people who pioneered and popularized the idea of a baptism in the Holy Spirit with the necessary sign of speaking in tongues.

In the early days of the century they were expelled from the mainline denominations and forced to found their own churches. Some scholars now call them "classical Pentecostals." The term "charismatic" was first used around 1963 to denote those "neo-Pentecostals" in the mainline Protestant and Catholic churches who also spoke in tongues but who did not see tongues as the necessary evidence of the Pentecostal experience.

Following conventional usage, "Pentecostal" is capitalized throughout this work, while "charismatic" is lowercased. In David Barrett's ground-breaking work in chapter 15, however, an exception is made. Here he makes fine distinctions between Pentecostals and charismatics. These are done for technical reasons that are explained in his notes.

I want to thank Philip P. Stoner, Jim Weaver, Lee Hollaway, and Julia Hoover of Thomas Nelson for their encouragement in bringing this book to life. Their help has been invaluable to me. As usual, my wife, Carol Lee, has been at my side helping with typing, editing, and pushing me to finish the book on time. I also give special thanks to dozens of friends who have contributed photographs to the book. Among these are Wayne Warner, Mike Andaloro, and Harold Hunter. Mark and Virginia Taylor helped me immensely in the area of contemporary charismatic music. I also owe a debt of gratitude to the faculty and staff of the Regent University School of Divinity where I serve as Dean. They have allowed me to take time out of my office in order to complete the job.

Special recognition and thanks are also due to the outstanding writers who contributed several chapters to the book. Two of these, Robert Owens and Susan Hyatt, were my students at Regent University. Ed Harrell, Gary McGee, David Daniels III, Peter Hocken, Everett Wilson, and David Barrett have been friends and colleagues for many years. I have known Pablo Deiros from Argentina from his previous writing and scholarship. These all have added greatly to the literature on global Pentecostalism.

My greatest regret is that space prohibited me from including more information about significant Pentecostal and charismatic movements outside the United States. This subject deserves and awaits a major encyclopedia that can do justice to the vast number of persons and movements that have helped to change the face of Christianity around the world during the past century.

It is my hope that this book will serve as a resource for the average reader, as well as for any professors and students who may choose to use it as a classroom textbook. I have attempted to make it readable as well as scholarly. My thanks to Thomas Nelson for insisting on a book that features so many photographs and vignettes. This should help the reader gain a better grasp and perspective of the story.

In my own lifetime, I lived through two-thirds of the century and have witnessed and participated in many events that I have described. It has been an exciting pilgrimage for me as a Pentecostal preacher, teacher, and historian. In my youth I knew personally some of the old Holiness-Pentecostal pioneers who were active leaders in the late 1890s. In my later years I worked closely with hundreds of important Pentecostal and charismatic leaders around the world. It is my hope that I can pass the torch from these spiritual giants to a new generation who will also tell the story to their children and grandchildren.

Vinson Synan
Regent University
Virginia Beach, Virginia
March 1, 2001

· 1 ·
The Pentecostal Century:
An Overview

Vinson Synan

O N JANUARY 1, 1901, a young woman named Agnes Ozman was baptized in the Holy Spirit at a small Bible school in Topeka, Kansas. A student of former Methodist pastor and holiness teacher Charles Fox Parham, Ozman received a startling manifestation of the gift of tongues and became, in effect, the first Pentecostal of the 20th century.

"I laid my hands upon her and prayed," Parham later recalled of the event. "I had scarcely completed three dozen sentences when a glory fell upon her, a halo seemed to surround her head and face, and she began speaking the Chinese language and was unable to speak English for three days."

According to J. Roswell Flower, the founding secretary of the Assemblies of God, Ozman's experience was the "touch felt 'round the world." As Topeka and the rest of the nation celebrated the new century, few people could have imagined that this humble event would trigger the worldwide Pentecostal charismatic movement, one of the mightiest revivals and missionary movements in the history of the church.

Beginning with only a handful of people in 1901, the number of Pentecostals increased steadily to become the largest family of Protestants in the world by the beginning of the 21st century. With more than two hundred million members designated as "denominational Pentecostals," this group had surpassed the Orthodox churches to become the second largest denominational family of Christians, exceeded in number by only the Roman Catholics.

In addition to these classical denominational Pentecostals, there were millions of charismatics in the mainline denominations and nondenominational churches, both Roman Catholic and Protestant. The combined number now stands at more than five hundred million people. This growth has caused some historians to refer to the 20th century as the "Pentecostal century."

Holiness Roots

Although the Pentecostal movement had its beginnings in the United States, much of its basic theology was rooted in earlier British perfectionistic and charismatic movements. At least three of these—the Methodist holiness movement, the Catholic Apostolic movement of Edward Irving, and the British Keswick "Higher Life" movement—prepared the way for what appeared to be a spontaneous outpouring of the Holy Spirit in America. Perhaps the most important immediate precursor to Pentecostalism was the holiness movement that issued from the heart of Methodism during the 18th century.

John Wesley, an Anglican priest, experienced his evangelical conversion in a meeting at Aldersgate Street in 1738 where, as he said, "my heart was strangely warmed." This he called his "new birth."

From Wesley, Pentecostals also inherited the idea of a crisis "second blessing" subsequent to salvation. This experience he variously called "entire sanctification," "perfect love," "Christian perfection," or "heart purity." Wesley's colleague John Fletcher was the first to call this a "baptism in the Holy Spirit," an experience that brought spiritual power to the recipient as well as inner cleansing.

In the 19th century, Edward Irving and his friends in London suggested the possibility of a restoration of the gifts of the Spirit in the modern church. This popular Presbyterian pastor led the first attempt at "charismatic renewal" in his Regents Square Presbyterian Church in 1831 and later formed the Catholic Apostolic Church. Although tongues and prophecies were experienced in his church, Irving was not successful in his quest for a restoration of New Testament Christianity.

Another predecessor to Pentecostalism was the Keswick Higher Life movement, which flourished in England after 1875. Led at first by American holiness teachers such as Hannah Whitall Smith and William E. Boardman, the Keswick teachers soon changed the goal and content of the "second blessing" from the Wesleyan emphasis on "heart purity" to that of an "enduement of spiritual power for service." D. L. Moody was a leading evangelist associated with the Keswick movement.

Thus, by the time of the Pentecostal outbreak in America in 1901, there had been at least a century of movements emphasizing a second blessing called the baptism in the Holy Spirit. In America, such Keswick teachers as A. B. Simpson and A. J. Gordon also added an emphasis on divine healing.

The first Pentecostal churches in the world originated in the holiness movement before 1901: the United Holy Church (1886), led by W. H. Fulford; the Fire-Baptized Holiness Church (1895), led by B. H. Irwin and J. H. King; the Church of God of Cleveland, Tennessee (1896), led by A. J. Tomlinson; the Church of God in Christ (1897), led by C. H. Mason; and the Pentecostal Holiness

The Regents Square Presbyterian Church

Church (1898), led by A. B. Crumpler. After becoming Pentecostal, these churches, which had been formed as second-blessing holiness denominations, retained their perfectionistic teachings. They simply added the baptism in the Holy Spirit with tongues as initial evidence of a "third blessing." It would not be an overstatement to say that 20th-century Pentecostalism, at least in America, was born in a holiness cradle.

The Origins of Pentecostalism

The first Pentecostals, in the modern sense of the word, can be traced to Parham's Bible school in Topeka, Kansas, in 1901. In spite of controversy over the origins and timing of Parham's emphasis on tongues, all historians agree the movement began early in 1901 just as the world entered the 20th century. As a result of this Topeka Pentecost, Parham formulated the doctrine that tongues were the "Bible evidence" of the baptism in the Holy Spirit.

Teaching that tongues were a supernatural impartation of human languages for the purpose of world evangelization, Parham also advocated that missionaries need not study foreign languages, since they would be able to preach in miraculous tongues all over the world. Armed with this new theology, Parham founded a church movement called the "Apostolic Faith" and began a whirlwind revival tour of the Midwest to promote this new experience. The origins of the movement are elaborated on in chapter 2, "Pentecostal Roots."

It was not until 1906, however, that Pentecostalism achieved worldwide attention. This came through the Azusa Street revival in Los Angeles, led by pastor William Joseph Seymour. Seymour first learned about the baptism in the Holy Spirit with tongues in 1905 at a Bible school Parham led in Houston, Texas.

Charles Parham and Students
Charles Fox Parham is recognized as the theological father of the modern Pentecostal movement.

In 1906, Seymour was invited to pastor a black holiness church in Los Angeles. The historic Azusa meetings began in April 1906 in a former African Methodist Episcopal church building at 312 Azusa Street in downtown Los Angeles.

What happened because of the Azusa Street revival has fascinated church historians for decades and has yet to be fully understood and explained. The Azusa Street Apostolic Faith Mission conducted three services a day, seven days a week, for three and one-half years. Thousands of seekers received the baptism in the Holy Spirit with tongues.

The *Apostolic Faith,* a newspaper Seymour sent free of charge to some fifty thousand readers, spread word of the revival. From Azusa Street, Pentecostalism spread rapidly around the world and moved on to become a major force in Christendom. Chapter 3 provides a detailed account of the Azusa Street revival.

William J. Seymour led the Azusa Street revival in 1906, which spread Pentecostalism around the world. The Azusa Street meetings were notable for interracial harmony.

The Azusa Street movement seems to have been a merger of white American holiness religion with worship styles derived from the African-American Christian tradition, which had developed since the days of chattel slavery in the South. The expressive worship and praise at Azusa Street, which included shouting and dancing, had been common among Appalachian whites as well as southern blacks.

The admixture of tongues and other charisms with southern black and white music and worship styles created a new and indigenous form of

Pentecostalism. This new expression of Christian life would prove extremely attractive to disinherited and deprived people in both America and other nations.

The interracial aspects of Azusa Street were a striking exception to the racism and segregation of the times. The phenomenon of blacks and whites worshiping together under a black pastor seemed incredible to many observers.

William Seymour's place as an important religious figure in the 20th century now seems assured. In his 1972 classic, *A Religious History of the American People*, Sidney Ahlstrom, the noted church historian from Yale University, placed Seymour at the head of the list of American black religious leaders when he said that Seymour's black piety "exerted its greatest influence on American religious history." Seymour and Parham could well be called the "cofounders" of world Pentecostalism. The role and development of the African-American dimension are surveyed in chapter 11.

The Azusa Street Meeting

William Joseph Seymour and the Azusa Street staff

Pentecostal Pioneers

The first wave of Azusa pilgrims journeyed throughout the United States spreading the Pentecostal fire primarily in holiness churches, missions, and camp meetings.

Many American Pentecostal pioneers who received tongues at Azusa Street in 1906 went back to their homes to spread the movement among their own people. One of the first was Gaston Barnabas Cashwell of North Carolina.

Under his ministry Cashwell saw several holiness denominations swept into the new movement, including the Church of God (Cleveland, Tenn.), the Pentecostal Holiness Church, the Fire-Baptized Holiness Church, and the Pentecostal Free-Will Baptist Church.

Charles Harrison Mason journeyed to Azusa Street in 1906 and returned to Memphis, Tennessee, to spread the Pentecostal fire in the Church of God in Christ (COGIC). Mason and the church he founded were made up of African-Americans only one generation removed from slavery. Both Seymour's and Mason's parents had been born as southern slaves.

Although the church split over the question of tongues in 1907, COGIC experienced such explosive growth that today it is by far the largest Pentecostal denomination in North America, claiming almost six million members in more than fifteen thousand local churches.

Another Azusa pilgrim was William H. Durham of Chicago. After receiving tongues at Azusa Street in 1907, he returned to Chicago where he led thousands of Midwesterners and Canadians into the Pentecostal movement. His "finished work" theology of gradual progressive sanctification, which he announced in 1910, led to the formation of the Assemblies of God (AG) in 1914.

E. N. Bell and Joseph Flower led the AG. Because many white pastors had been part of Mason's church, when they left to join the AG the departure was seen partly as a racial separation. In time, the AG was destined to become the largest Pentecostal denomination in the world, claiming by the year 2000 more than two million U.S. members and some forty-four million adherents in 150 countries.

In 1916, a major controversy within the Assemblies of God led to the non-Trinitarian "oneness" Pentecostal movement. This belief taught that Jesus was the only Person in the godhead and that the terms "Father," "Son," and "Holy Spirit" were merely "titles" created by the Roman Catholic Church.

Movement leaders Frank Ewart and Glenn Cook taught that the only valid water baptism was immersion "in Jesus' name" and that speaking in tongues was necessary for salvation. Churches that issued from this movement included the Pentecostal Assemblies of the World and the United Pentecostal Church. Chapters 5 and 6 examine the origin and growth of the holiness Pentecostal and "finished work" churches.

Missionaries of the One-Way Ticket

In addition to the ministers who received their Pentecostal experience at Azusa Street, thousands of others were indirectly influenced by the revival in Los Angeles. Among them was Thomas Ball Barratt of Norway, a Methodist pastor who became known as the Pentecostal apostle to northern and western Europe.

After being baptized in the Holy Spirit and receiving the experience of speaking in tongues in New York City in 1906, Barratt returned to Oslo where, in December 1906, he conducted the first Pentecostal services in Europe. From Norway, Barratt traveled to Sweden, England, France, and Germany, where he sparked other national Pentecostal movements. Under

Barratt, such leaders as Lewi Pethrus in Sweden, Jonathan Paul in Germany, and Alexander Boddy in England were brought into the movement.

From Chicago, through the influence of William Durham, the movement spread quickly to Canada, Italy, and South America. Thriving Italian Pentecostal movements were founded after 1908 in the United States, Brazil, Argentina, and Italy by two Italian immigrants from Chicago, Luigi Francescon and Giacomo Lombardy.

In South Bend, Indiana, near Chicago, two Swedish Baptist immigrants, Daniel Berg and Gunnar Vingren, received the Pentecostal experience. Believing they were called prophetically to Brazil, they embarked on a missionary trip in 1910 that resulted in the formation of the Brazilian Assemblies of God. The Brazilian Assemblies developed into the largest national Pentecostal movement in the world and, with other Brazilian Pentecostals, claimed some thirty million members by 2000.

Also hailing from Chicago was Willis C. Hoover, the Methodist missionary to Chile, who in 1909 led a Pentecostal revival in the Chilean Methodist Episcopal Church. After being excommunicated from the Chilean Methodist Church, Hoover and thirty-seven of his followers organized the Pentecostal Methodist Church, which now has some 1.5 million adherents in Chile.

African Pentecostalism owes its origins to the work of John Graham Lake (1870–1935), who began his ministry as a Methodist preacher but later prospered in business as an insurance executive. In 1898, his wife was miraculously healed of tuberculosis under the ministry of Alexander Dowie, founder of a religious community called Zion City near Chicago.

In 1907 Lake was baptized in the Holy Spirit and spoke in tongues. Zion City produced some five hundred preachers and teachers who entered the ranks of the Pentecostal movement. After his Pentecostal experience, Lake abandoned the insurance business to answer a long-standing call to minister in South Africa. In April 1908, he led a large missionary party to Johannesburg where he began to spread the Pentecostal message throughout the nation.

Lake succeeded in founding two large and influential Pentecostal churches in southern Africa. The white branch took the title Apostolic Faith Mission in 1910, borrowing from the name of the famous mission on Azusa Street (David du Plessis, known to the world as "Mr. Pentecost," came from this church). The black branch eventually developed into the Zion Christian Church, which had six million members by 2000.

Soon after Lake returned to the United States in 1912, the movement reached the Slavic world through the ministry of a Russian-born Baptist pastor, Ivan Voronaev, who received the Pentecostal experience in New

York City in 1919. Through prophecies, he was led to take his family with him to Odessa, Ukraine, in 1922. There he established the first Pentecostal church in the Soviet Union. Voronaev was arrested, imprisoned, and martyred in a communist prison in 1943. The churches he founded survived extreme persecution and have become a major religious force in Russia and the former Soviet Union.

Pentecostalism reached Korea through the ministry of Mary Rumsey, an American missionary who had been baptized in the Holy Spirit at Azusa Street in 1907. At that time, Rumsey believed she was called to bring the Pentecostal message to Japan and Korea. It was not until 1928, however, that she landed in Korea. Prior to World War II, she had planted eight Pentecostal churches there before being forced out of the country by the Japanese.

In 1952 those eight churches were turned over to the Assemblies of God, whose missionaries immediately opened a Bible school in Seoul. One of the first students to enroll was a young convert by the name of Paul Yonggi Cho. After he graduated from Bible college, Cho pioneered a Korean church that became the Yoido Full Gospel Church. The church today claims some 730,000 members, the largest single Christian congregation in the world. Chapter 4, "To the Regions Beyond: The Global Expansion of Pentecostalism," is devoted to the missionary activity of the Pentecostals.

Neo-Pentecostals, Charismatics, and Third Wavers

This first wave of Pentecostal pioneer missionaries produced what has become known as the classical Pentecostal movement, with more than fourteen thousand Pentecostal denominations throughout the world. This phase was followed by organized Pentecostal denominational efforts that produced fast-growing missions and indigenous churches. Some of the most explosive growth coming from these efforts occurred among Hispanics in both the United States and Latin America. Some of the greatest growth also occurred among American blacks as well as in the nations of Africa.

A further phase was the penetration of Pentecostalism into the mainline Protestant and Catholic churches as "charismatic renewal" movements with the aim of renewing the historic churches. It is worth noting that these newer "waves" also originated primarily in the United States. They include the Protestant Neo-Pentecostal movement, which began in 1960 in Van Nuys, California, under the ministry of Dennis Bennett, rector of St. Mark's Episcopal (Anglican) church. Within a decade, this movement had spread to all the 150 major Protestant families of the world, reaching a total of 55 million people by 1990.

Mainline Protestant leaders included: Tommy Tyson and Ross Whetstone (Methodist); Brick Bradford, Rodman Williams, and Brad Long (Presbyterian); Pat Robertson, Howard Conatser, Ken Pagard, and Gary Clark (Baptist); Everett Terry Fullam and Charles Fulton (Episcopal); Gerald Derstine and Nelson Litwiller (Mennonite); and Vernon Stoop (United Church of Christ). Chapters 7 and 8 provide a full treatment of the renewal movement in mainline and major Protestant churches.

The Catholic charismatic renewal movement had its beginnings in Pittsburgh in 1967 among students and faculty at Duquesne University. After spreading rapidly among students at Notre Dame and the University of Michigan, the movement spread worldwide.

Its early leaders were Kevin Ranaghan, Ralph Martin, Steve Clark, and Nancy Kellar. Careful theological leadership was given by Kilian McDonnell and Leon Joseph Cardinal Suenens.

In the 32 years since its inception, the Catholic movement not only has gained the approval of the church but also has touched the lives of over 100 million Catholics in 120 countries. Chapter 9 recounts the major events and people associated with the Catholic renewal movement.

Added to these is the newest category that some called the "third wave" of the Holy Spirit. It originated at Fuller Theological Seminary in 1981 under the classroom ministry of John Wimber, founder of the Association of Vineyard Churches. This "wave" was comprised of mainline evangeli-

cals who experienced signs and wonders but who disdained labels such as "Pentecostal" or "charismatic." The Vineyard was the most visible movement of this category. By 2000 the third wavers, also called "neo-charismatics," were credited with some 295 million members worldwide.

In all these movements, women played leading roles as teachers, evangelists, missionaries, and pastors from the earliest days of the century. Many became effective and even famous for healing ministries

Leon Joseph Cardinal Suenens, Roman Catholic primate of Belgium, gave pastoral direction to the Catholic charismatic renewal while serving as the charismatic liaison to Pope Paul VI.

that attracted multitudes of followers. Among these outstanding women were Agnes Ozman, Maria Woodworth-Etter, Aimee Semple McPherson,

Kathryn Kuhlman, and in more recent times, Marilyn Hickey and Joyce Meyer. Because of the spiritual freedom that abounded in holiness and Pentecostal circles, these women were able to break age-old stereotypes that had hindered women in ministry for centuries. The prominent role of women is treated in chapter 10.

The one area of the world where Pentecostalism spread the fastest from the earliest days was in Latin America. With early beginnings in Chile and Brazil, the Pentecostals grew by leaps and bounds after World War II. By the end of the century, in several Latin American nations the Pentecostals numbered up to 90 percent of all non-Catholics. In some countries Pentecostal growth rates indicated that in a few decades the Pentecostals might have an absolute majority of the population. This was especially true in such countries as Guatemala and Chile. This rapid growth was also seen among Hispanics in the United States and Puerto Rico as well as the countries of Central America. Chapter 12 presents the phenomenal growth within the Hispanic populations of North and South America.

Evangelists and Healers

Throughout this century, Pentecostals produced many evangelists who were known for their mass healing crusades. These included Maria Woodworth-Etter, Aimee Semple McPherson (founder of the International Church of the Foursquare Gospel in 1927), Oral Roberts, Kathryn Kuhlman, Reinhard Bonnke, and Benny Hinn. Beginning in the 1950s with Oral Roberts, the "televangelist" genre appeared, bringing healing, tongues, prophecies, and other spiritual gifts into living rooms across the nation. Some of the most successful include Pat Robertson's Christian Broadcast Network (CBN) and Paul Crouch's Trinity Broadcasting Network (TBN). Two notable television evangelists, Jimmy Swaggart and Jim Bakker, fell into disrepute in the televangelist scandals of the 1980s. Chapter 13 presents a lively account of the major healers and televangelists.

Despite these failures, news of the renewal continued to be carried by most of the religious and secular press. This was paralleled by the publication of millions of books and tapes sold in conferences and crusades internationally. New periodicals spawned by the movement included Dan Malachuk's *Logos* magazine and Stephen Strang's *Charisma* and *Ministries Today* magazines.

In the late 1970s a newer movement of "faith" teachers drew national attention. These included Kenneth Hagin Sr., Kenneth Copeland, and Fred Price. In the 1990s, millions of people tuned in to the teachings of Copeland

The mass healing crusades of Oral Roberts helped to spread Pentecostalism into the mainline churches.

and Price, while others enrolled in Hagin's Rhema Bible College in Broken Arrow, Oklahoma, and a host of other Spirit-filled Bible schools. Overseas, the crusades of the German Pentecostal evangelist Reinhard Bonnke regularly drew crowds of up to one million in cities throughout Africa. The same has been true of other evangelistic crusades throughout India.

Major educational institutions arose during the 20th century as well. Healing evangelist Oral Roberts founded a university under his name in Tulsa, Oklahoma, in 1965, and Pat Robertson founded Regent University in Virginia Beach, Virginia, in 1978. In addition, literally hundreds of Pentecostal universities, liberal arts colleges, and Bible colleges were planted worldwide.

In a sense, the charismatic movement in the United States reached a peak in 1977 when fifty thousand people from all denominations gathered in Arrowhead Stadium in Kansas City, Missouri, for the General Charismatic Conference led by Kevin Ranaghan. Planners for this conference were confronted by the major controversy of the era, which involved the "shepherding" teachings of five charismatic leaders from Fort Lauderdale, Florida: Derek Prince, Bob Mumford, Charles Simpson, Don Basham, and Ern Baxter.

The shepherding-discipleship movement, which taught that every Christian should be under the "covering" authority of a "spiritual leader," fell apart after the five separated in 1986. Other "congresses" in New Orleans (1987), Indianapolis (1990), Orlando (1995), and St. Louis (2000), kept the many streams of Pentecostals and charismatics flowing together.

Times of Refreshing

By 1990, Pentecostals and their charismatic brothers and sisters in the mainline Protestant and Catholic churches were turning their attention toward world evangelization. During the following decade, Pentecostals and charismatics were reinvigorated by new waves of revival that featured such Pentecostal spiritual manifestations as "holy laughter," being "slain in the Spirit," and other "exotic" manifestations. Leading in this new wave was the South African Pentecostal evangelist Rodney Howard-Browne.

Beginning in 1993, many of these manifestations appeared at the Toronto Airport Vineyard Church led by pastor John Arnott. Although Arnott's church was disfellowshipped by John Wimber and the Vineyard movement, the force of the revival continued throughout the decade.

Another wave came in 1995 when a notable revival began at the Brownsville Assembly of God in Pensacola, Florida. Led by pastor John Kilpatrick and evangelist Steve Hill, the Brownsville meetings attracted more than two million visitors and recorded in excess of two hundred thousand conversions.

Revival fires also are sweeping Latin America, particularly Argentina and Brazil, under the leadership of Claudio Freidzon and Carlos Annacondia. Chapter 14, "Streams of Renewal at the End of the Century," updates the growing renewal movement.

All of these movements, both Pentecostal and charismatic, have resulted in a major force in Christianity throughout the world with explosive growth rates not seen before in modern times, as meticulously detailed by David B. Barrett in chapter 15, "The Worldwide Holy Spirit Renewal." These "times of refreshing" show that at the end of the Pentecostal century the movement was far from dead and entered the new millennium with undiminished power. Though renewal and revival have always been a part of Christianity (see "Appendix: A Chronology of Renewal in the Holy Spirit," prepared by David B. Barrett), the 20th century has indeed been the "century of the Holy Spirit."

For Further Reading

The major source for anyone who wants to know more about leading Pentecostal and charismatic persons and movements in the 20th century is Stanley M. Burgess, ed., and Eduard van der Maas, assoc. ed., *New International Dictionary of Pentecostal and Charismatic Movements* (Grand Rapids: Zondervan, 2001). An easy to read but scholarly treatment of the entire century is Vinson Synan's *The Holiness-Pentecostal Tradition: Charismatic Movements in the Twentieth Century* (Grand Rapids: Eerdmans, 1997). A worldwide perspective of Pentecostal growth can be found in Walter Hollenweger's *Pentecostalism: Origins and Developments Worldwide* (Peabody, Mass.: Hendrickson Press, 1997).

A good sociological study of Pentecostal beginnings is Robert Mapes Anderson's *Vision of the Disinherited: The Making of American Pentecostalism* (New York: Oxford Univ. Press, 1979). A valuable biographical source for early Pentecostalism is James R. Goff Jr. and Grant Wacker, eds., *Portraits of a Generation: Early Pentecostal Leaders* (Fayettville, Ark.: Univ. of Arkansas Press, 2001).

The story of the charismatic movement in the mainline churches is given in Kilian McDonnell's excellent *Charismatic Renewal and the Churches* (New York: Seabury Press, 1976). A good book on more recent developments among Protestants is *Pentecostal Currents in American Protestantism* (Chicago: Univ. of Illinois Press, 1999), ed. Edith L. Blumhofer, Russell P. Spittler, and Grant A. Wacker. An engaging account of Pentecostal growth and influence during the century is Harvey Cox's *Fire from Heaven: The Rise of Pentecostal Spirituality and the Reshaping of Religion in the Twenty-First Century* (New York: Addison-Wesley, 1994).

The story of the early Catholic charismatic movement is given in Kevin and Dorothy Ranaghan's *Catholic Pentecostals* (New York: Paulist Press, 1969). An intriguing historical- theological study of charisms in the early church is Kilian McDonnell and George Montague's *Christian Initiation and Baptism in the Holy Spirit: Evidence from the First Eight Centuries* (Collegeville, Minn.: Liturgical Press, 1991).

Those who wish to delve deeper into the sources should consult the library guides written by Charles E. Jones and published by the Scarecrow Press in Metuchen, New Jersey. They are: *A Guide to the Study of the Holiness Movement* (1974); *A Guide to the Study of the Pentecostal Movement*, 2 vols. (1983); *Black Holiness: A Guide to the Study of Black Participation in Wesleyan Perfectionistic and Glossolalic Pentecostal Movements* (1987); and *The Charismatic Movement: A Guide to the Study of Neo-Pentecostalism with an Emphasis on Anglo-American Sources*, (1995). For official church documents relating to the renewal see Kilian McDonnell's monumental *Presence, Power, Praise*, 3 vols. (New York: Paulist Press, 1980).

· 2 ·
Pentecostal Roots

Vinson Synan

O VER THE TWO THOUSAND YEARS of Christian history, there have
been many renewals, revivals, and reforms. Without these occasional
awakenings the church might well have drifted into corruption, dead ritu-
alism, and ultimate insignificance. Some of these renewals offered their enthusiastic followers a spiritual experience or ritual that went beyond the
usual sacraments of the church. For example, among the Montanists in the
second century, the ecstatic utterances of a "new prophecy" brought a
sense of excitement and apocalyptic zeal. Among the Jansenists of 17th-
century France, Catholic reformers spoke in tongues and prophesied and
introduced a new sacrament called the "consolamentum."

In the 18th century, John Wesley offered his Methodist followers a "second blessing," which he called "entire sanctification," an instant crisis experience that he also described as "perfect love" or "Christian perfection."
Radical Wesleyans who left Methodism in the 19th century to join the holiness movement often called this second blessing a "baptism in the Holy
Spirit." Coming from the holiness movement in the early 20th century, a
new enthusiastic movement appeared that emphasized signs and wonders
and the gifts of the Spirit. Followers called themselves "Pentecostals,"
since they looked back to the Day of Pentecost and the outpouring of the
Holy Spirit in the Upper Room as their inspiration. For decades their

growth was slow as they struggled against rejection and persecution. But after World War II their worldwide growth could no longer be ignored. The world began to take notice of a new and vigorous movement that was growing like wildfire around the earth.

In 1958 Henry P. Van Dusen, then president of Union Theological Seminary in New York, stunned the religious world with a prophetic article in *Life* magazine titled "The Third Force in Christendom." With amazing insight, he announced that already a major new force existed in the Christian world alongside traditional Catholicism and Protestantism. Pentecostalism, Van Dusen proclaimed, was destined to change the face of Christianity in the 20th century.[1]

Little did Van Dusen realize that what is now dubbed classical Pentecostalism was shortly to break out in the other two camps. Only two years later, the first Protestant "Neo-Pentecostal" publicly witnessed to his experience, while less than a decade later the movement had entered the Roman Catholic Church. Four years before this, in 1954, a little-known American Pentecostal evangelist named Tommy Hicks had journeyed, without invitation, from California to Buenos Aires, Argentina, seeking an opportunity to preach. He claimed that God had sent him. Without advertising or outside financial support, he conducted the greatest single evangelistic crusade in the history of the church up to that time. His crowds surpassed the records of all evangelists before him, including Finney, Moody, and Billy Graham. In fifty-two days, from May to July of 1954, Hicks preached to an aggregate attendance of some two million, with more than two hundred thousand persons in attendance in a mammoth football stadium for the final service.[2]

The teaching of John Wesley (1703–91) on the "second blessing" made him the theological father of all holiness and Pentecostal movements.

As word spread about the mushroomlike growth of the Pentecostal movement in the United States, Brazil, Chile, Scandinavia, Korea, and Africa, ecclesiastical leaders of the Protestant and Catholic worlds began to take notice of the Pentecostal phenomenon. "What does this mean?" became the question of scholars, pastors, bishops, and laymen alike. By 1964, Charles Sydnor Jr., on learning that the Church of God (Cleveland, Tenn.) had surpassed the Presbyterians as the third largest denomination in Georgia (in the number of local churches), declared that "it is becoming increasingly evident that the Pentecostal movement we are witnessing . . . is an authentic, reformation-revival of historic significance, equal with those other great movements of centuries past."[3]

Clearly a movement of major importance was developing into a major challenge to traditional Christianity. Where did these Pentecostals come from? What did they believe? What were their practices? Were these not the lowly "Holy Rollers" who were dismissed with pity and scorn only a few years earlier? Who was responsible for bringing this major force into being?

Upon closer investigation, it was learned that these Pentecostals emphasized radical conversion, a holy life of separation from the world after conversion, and the "baptism in the Holy Spirit" evidenced by speaking in

JOHN WESLEY'S SECOND BLESSING

In the year 1764, upon a review of the whole subject, I wrote down the sum of what I had observed in the following short propositions:

1. There is such a thing as perfection; for it is again and again mentioned in Scripture.
2. It is not so early as justification; for justified persons are to "go on unto perfection." (Heb. 6:1)
3. It is not so late as death; for St. Paul speaks of living men that were perfect. (Phil. 3:15)
4. It is not absolute. Absolute perfection belongs not to man, nor to angels, but to God alone.
5. It does not make a man infallible: None is infallible, while he remains in the body.
6. Is it sinless? It is not worthwhile to contend for a term. It is "salvation from sin."
7. It is "perfect love." (1 John 4:18) This is the essence of it; its properties, or inseparable fruits, are, rejoicing evermore, praying without ceasing, and in everything giving thanks. (1 Thess. 5:16, &c)
8. It is improvable. It is so far from lying in an indivisible point, from being incapable of increase, that one perfected in love may grow in grace far swifter than he did before.
9. It is amissible, capable of being lost; of which we have numerous instances. But we were not thoroughly convinced of this, till five or six years ago.
10. It is constantly both preceded and followed by a gradual work.
11. But is it in itself instantaneous or not? In examining this, let us go on step by step.

An instantaneous change has been wrought in some believers: None can deny this.

Since that change, they enjoy perfect love; they feel this, and this alone; they "rejoice evermore, pray without ceasing, and in everything give thanks." Now, this is all that I mean by perfection; therefore, these are witnesses of the perfection which I preach.

"But in some this change was not instantaneous." They did not perceive the instant when it was wrought. It is often difficult to perceive the instant when a man dies; yet there is an instant in which life ceases. And if ever sin ceases, there must be a last moment of its existence, and a first moment of our deliverance from it. ■

—JOHN WESLEY
A PLAIN ACCOUNT OF CHRISTIAN PERFECTION

tongues. Following this experience, all the gifts of the Spirit would be experienced in the normal life of the church. Divine healing in answer to prayer was especially emphasized, as was the Second Coming of Christ to "rapture" the church, which could occur at any moment. Also characteristic was joyous and expressive worship, which struck the first-time visitor as emotional and noisy. This included upraised hands, loud praise, messages in tongues, interpretations of tongues, prophecies, prayers for the sick, and the occasional casting out of demons. Fervent preaching from the Bible offered salvation, holiness, healing, and material blessings from the Lord to those who "prayed through" at the altars. The most striking teaching was that the gifts of the Spirit or "charisms" were intended for the 20th-century church as much as for the church of the first century.

The Gifts of the Spirit in History

Many church leaders soon began a crash course on the history of the gifts of the Spirit in the church. Books such as John Sherrill's *They Speak with Other Tongues* and Morton Kelsey's *Tongue Speaking* provided answers for these seekers. What they found was that the church of the New Testament was indeed a charismatic one, according to the reports in the Book of Acts. It was also clear that the early church retained its original gifts and Pentecostal power in the long period of struggle and persecution before the triumph of Christianity in the West under Constantine. After gaining acceptance and power, however, the church began to experience less and less of the miraculous power of the primitive church and turned more and more to ritualistic and sacramental expressions of the faith.

The Montanist renewal movement of the period A.D. 185–212 represented an attempt to restore the charisms to the church. Despite some early successes, in which tongues and prophecy were restored among the followers of Montanus, the movement was ultimately condemned by the church. The major cause of this rejection was not the presence of the charismata, but Montanus's claim that the prophetic utterances were equal to the Scriptures. Many scholars now feel that the church overreacted to Montanism by asserting that the more sensational charisms, though experienced by the apostolic church, were withdrawn after the perfection of the accepted canon of Scripture. This opinion was expressed by Augustine and echoed by scholars in the centuries that followed. On the question of tongues as evidence of receiving the Holy Spirit, Augustine said:

> At the Church's beginning the Holy Spirit fell upon the believers, and they spoke with tongues unlearnt, as the Spirit gave them utterance. It was a sign,

fitted to the time: all the world's tongues were a fitting signification of the Holy Spirit, because the gospel of God was to have its course through every tongue in all parts of the earth. The sign was given and then passed away. We no longer expect that those upon whom the hand is laid, that they may receive the Holy Spirit, will speak with tongues. When we laid our hands on these "infants," the Church's new-born members, none of you (I think) looked to see if they would speak with tongues, or seeing that they did not, had the perversity to argue that they had not received the Holy Spirit, for if they had received, they would have spoken in tongues as happened at the first.[4]

As to all the other extraordinary gifts of the Spirit, Augustine's "cessation theory" was widely influential on generations of subsequent theologians. As he said:

Why, it is asked, do no miracles occur nowadays, such as occurred in former times? I could reply that they were necessary then, before the world came to believe, in order to win the world's belief.[5]

A footnote to Augustine's cessationist theory was the sudden appearance of supernatural healings in public services in his church.

The overreaction to Montanism, which led to a belief that the charismata ended with the apostolic age, continued until modern times. Although the Roman Catholic Church left the door open to miracles in the lives of certain saints (a few of whom were said to speak in tongues and produce miracles of healing), the church tended more and more to teach that the miracles of the apostolic age ended with the early church. With the institutionalization of the church, the less spectacular charisms of government, administration, and teaching came to the fore as the most acceptable gifts available to the hierarchy. The major exception to this acceptance of creeping cessationism was the Orthodox churches of the East. Although the spontaneous manifestation of the charismata also subsided in these churches, Orthodoxy never adopted a theory that the charismata had ceased. Cessationist theology was a creation of the Western church.

The view that the charismata had ceased after the days of the apostles was given classic expression by John Chrysostom in the fourth century in his homilies on 1 Corinthians 12. Confessing his ignorance on the subject, he wrote:

This whole place is very obscure: but the obscurity is produced by our ignorance of the facts referred to and their cessation, being such as then used to occur but now no longer take place. And why do they not happen now? Why look now, the cause too of the obscurity hath produced us again another

question: namely, why did they then happen, and now do so no more? . . .
Well, what did happen then? Whoever was baptized he straightaway spoke
with tongues and not with tongues only, but many also prophesied, and
some performed many wonderful works . . . but more abundant than all was
the gift of tongues among them.[6]

The cessation of the charismata thus became part of the classical theology of the Western church. Augustine and Chrysostom were quoted by
countless theologians and commentators in the centuries that followed.

Gifts such as glossolalia (speaking in tongues) became so rare that the
church generally forgot their proper function in the Christian community.
As the centuries rolled by, speaking in a language not learned by the
speaker was seen as evidence of possession by an evil spirit rather than the
Holy Spirit. In fact, by A.D. 1000 the *Rituale Romanorum* (Roman Ritual) defined glossolalia as *prima facie* evidence of demon possession. It might
have been expected that Reformers such as Luther and Calvin would have
restored the charismata to the church as the common heritage of all believers. Yet this was not to be.

One of the charges leveled against the Reformers by the Catholic authorities was that Protestantism lacked authenticating miracles confirming
their beginnings. To Catholic theologians, miraculous charismata were
seen as divine approval at the beginning of the church. Catholics demanded of Luther and Calvin signs and wonders to attest to their authenticity as true, orthodox Christian churches. Following the lead of
Augustine and Chrysostom, Luther responded with the following view
about the signs, wonders, and gifts of the Holy Spirit:

> The Holy Spirit is sent forth in two ways. In the primitive church he was sent
> forth in a manifest and visible form. Thus He descended upon Christ at the
> Jordan in the form of a dove (Mt. 3:16), and upon the apostles and other be-
> lievers in the form of fire (Acts 2:3). This was the first sending forth of the
> Holy Spirit; it was necessary in the primitive church, which had to be estab-
> lished with visible signs on account of the unbelievers, as Paul testifies. 1 Cor.
> 14:22: "Tongues are for a sign, not for believers but for unbelievers." But later
> on, when the church had been gathered and confirmed by these signs, it was
> not necessary for this visible sending forth of the Holy Spirit to continue.[7]

Through the centuries, then, Christendom, in its Roman Catholic and
Protestant branches, adopted the view that the spectacular supernatural
gifts of the Spirit had ended with the early church and that, with the completion of the inspired canon of Scripture, they would never be needed

again. The Catholic mystical tradition continued to allow for a few saints possessed of "heroic holiness" to exercise some of the gifts, but such holiness was reserved, in the minds of most, for the clergy and religious (bishops, priests, monks, and nuns), not for the masses of ordinary Christians.

This view was the conventional wisdom of the church until the 19th century. Then historical and theological developments caused the beginning of a dramatic change of view in various quarters, notably in England and the United States.

The Reappearance of the Gifts

As Ernest Sandeen has pointed out, the event that caused Christians to take a new look at prophecy and the gifts of the Spirit was the French Revolution. As the revolution advanced in the 1780s the radicals imposed a "reign of terror" that reminded many of the scenes of tribulation in Revelation. The convulsions taking place in France seemed to be signs that the end of the age was near. Once-confusing passages began to have striking contemporary relevance.

In Daniel 7, the prophet spoke of four animals coming up from the sea: a lion, a bear, a leopard, and a fierce beast with ten horns. A "little horn" on the last grew up among the ten and rooted out three of them. This little horn was a ruler who would "persecute the saints of the Most High, and shall intend to change times and law. Then the saints shall be given into his hand for a time and times and half a time" (v. 25). A similar beast was also described in Revelation 13:5 whose time would last for forty-two months. As the French Revolution unfolded, biblical scholars were certain that these passages were literally being fulfilled. The introduction of a new "revolutionary" calendar and the installation of a prostitute in Notre Dame Cathedral as a newly crowned "Goddess of Reason" seemed to underscore the apocalyptic event of 1798 when French troops under General Berthier marched into Rome, set up a new republic, and sent the pope into exile. This was seen as the "deadly wound" marking the end of papal political and spiritual power in the world.

In London, Edward King, a student of biblical prophecy, declared:

Is *not papal power*, at Rome, which was once so terrible, and so domineering at an end? But let us pause a little, was not *their* end, in other parts of the Holy Prophecies, foretold to be, *at the end of 1260 years?*—and was it not foretold by Daniel, to be at the *end* or a *time, times, and half a time?* which computation amounts to the same period. And now let us see;—hear—and understand,

This is the year 1798;—and just 1260 years ago, in the very beginning of the year 538, *Belesarius* put an end to the Empire and Dominion of the Goths at Rome.[8]

To Protestant scholars this interpretation meant they were living in the very last days. The Second Coming of Christ was near: The millennium was shortly to begin; the Holy Spirit would soon be poured out upon all flesh as a further sign that the end was near. The long night of waiting was almost over. At any time the charismata would again be manifested in the earth as on the Day of Pentecost.

The effect of these heady discoveries was the revival of millenarianism in Britain, a new interest in the return of the Jews to Palestine, and a renewed interest in the imminent Second Coming of Christ. Also, there ensued a profound emphasis on the study of biblical prophecy in order to discern "the signs of the times."

Leaders in this new wave of prophetic interest were such British theologians as Lewis Way, John Nelson Darby (founder of the Plymouth Brethren), and Edward Irving. In America, the movement found its greatest champions in the Lutheran scholar J. A. Seiss, and in the "Princeton theology" of Charles Hodge and Benjamin Warfield, both Presbyterians. The search for a renewed outpouring of the charismata was far more pronounced in England than in America. In later times, these Princeton "fundamentalists" and others moved to positions defending the literal inerrancy of Scripture and the any-moment Second Coming of Christ to "rapture the bride," while their English counterparts continued to concentrate on searching for a renewal of the charismata in the church.[9]

Edward Irving

By 1830, some preachers began to investigate all reports of miracles that occurred anywhere in the British Isles. A leader in this effort was Edward Irving, pastor of the prestigious Presbyterian Church on London's Regents Square. When a report was circulated that miraculous healings and glossolalia had occurred in Scotland among a small band of believers, Irving hurried to the small Scottish town of Port Glasgow to investigate. In this small town he was amazed to hear a housewife by the name of Mary Campbell speak in tongues. Two of her friends, twin brothers James and George McDonald, not only spoke in tongues, but interpreted their messages into English as well. On April 20, 1830, in the first recorded tongues message and interpretation in modern times, James gave an utterance in tongues and George interpreted it. The message was "Behold He cometh— Jesus cometh—a weeping Jesus." In fact, it was said that almost all the subsequent interpretations in England centered on the theme "the Lord is coming soon; get ready to meet Him."

From this time onward, Irving taught that tongues were "the standing sign" and the "root and stem" out of which flowed all the other gifts of the Spirit. To Irving, tongues were the "outward and visible sign of that inward and invisible grace which the baptism of the Holy Ghost conferreth." [10]

Irving was one of the most popular preachers of his day. His fashionable church saw crowds of two thousand in attendance to hear his eloquent sermons, which often reflected his views on the renewal of the apostolic gifts—especially the gifts of healing and speaking in tongues. In October 1831 the looked-for restoration began as a woman spoke loudly in tongues in a public service in Irving's church, causing a minor sensation in the city. But London was not at all prepared to accept this phe-

A popular Presbyterian pastor in London, Edward Irving (1792–1834) led a restoration of tongues and prophecy in 1831.

nomenon as the anticipated Pentecostal renewal. The following eyewitness account shows the negative reaction to the sensational utterance that interrupted the Sunday morning service:

> I went to the church . . . and was, as usual, much gratified and comforted by
> Mr. Irving's lectures and prayers; but I was very unexpectedly interrupted

---

EDWARD IRVING ON THE QUESTION OF TONGUES

This gift of tongues is the crowning act of all. None of the old prophets had it, Christ had it not; it belongs to the dispensation of the Holy Ghost proceeding from the risen Christ: it is the proclamation that man is enthroned in heaven, that man is the dwelling-place of God, that all creation if they would know God, must give ear to man's tongue, and know the compass of reason. It is not we that speak, but Christ that speaketh. It is not in us as men that God speaks; but in us as members of Christ, as the Church and body of Christ, that God speaks. The honor is not to us, but to Christ; not to the God-head of Christ, which is ever the same, but to the manhood of Christ, which hath been raised from the state of death to the state of being God's temple, God's most holy place, God's shechinah, God's oracle, for ever and ever. ∎

—EDWARD IRVING,
COLLECTED WORKS

by the well-known voice of one of the sisters, who, finding she was unable to restrain herself, and respecting the regulation of the church (that a woman could not speak in the sanctuary), rushed into the vestry, and gave vent to utterance; whilst another, as I understood, from the same impulse, ran down the side aisle, and out of the church, through the principal door. The sudden, doleful, and unintelligible sounds, being heard by all the congregation, produced the utmost confusion; the act of standing up, the exertion to hear, see, and understand, by each and every one of perhaps 1,500 or 2,000 persons, created a noise which may easily be conceived. Mr. Irving begged for attention, and when order was restored, he explained the occurrence, which he said was not new, except in the congregation, where he had been for some time considering the propriety of introducing it; but though satisfied of the correctness of such a measure, he was afraid of dispersing the flock; nevertheless, as it was now brought forward by God's will, he felt it his duty to submit. [11]

The woman who spoke in tongues was Mary Campbell from Port Glasgow, whom Irving looked upon as a "prophetess." Others felt differently. Thomas Carlyle in his *Reminiscences* spoke caustically of Irving's "dim and weakly flock" and decried the "turmoil" over tongues. He even suggested that a bucket of water should be dumped on the "hysterical madwoman" who had spoken in tongues. Yet, to Irving, Campbell was a holy woman who would make his Presbyterian church an even greater congregation than the church at Corinth.[12]

Although the manifestations of tongues continued for some months in the church on Regents Square, Irving never received the gift of tongues himself, much to his sorrow. In time, the presbytery of London preferred charges against Irving, tried, and convicted him of allowing women to speak in church and also for heresy concerning some of his teachings on the Person of Christ. Many felt that the charges were trumped-up and the trial unfair. At any rate, after Irving left the Presbyterian Church he and his friends organized a new group, which was named the "Catholic Apostolic Church." This group not only taught that all the charismata had been restored, but also that the apostolic office had been restored for the end times. [13]

Even though Irving had founded the church, he was not accorded the rank of apostle, mainly because he never experienced speaking in tongues. In fact he was removed from the leadership of the church and died three years later in Scotland in disgrace. The apostles of the church decided that their order was unique and that there would be no successors. A large body of prophecies was preserved as well as a monumental collection of liturgies that were used in the services. When the last apostle died in 1900, there were no apostles chosen to succeed them. As a result, the church practically disappeared during the 20th century.

C. H. Spurgeon and William Arthur

The unpleasantness of the Irvingite experience did not dampen the enthusiasm or expectancy for a new Pentecost among other devotees of the new prophetic movement. British evangelicals continued to preach and write about the expected charismatic outpouring, which they believed could begin at any time. A typical treatment of the subject was given by the great London Baptist preacher Charles H. Spurgeon in an 1857 sermon titled "The Power of the Holy Spirit:"

> Another great work of the Holy Spirit, which is not accomplished is *the bringing on of the latter-day glory.* In a few more years—I know not when, I know not how—the Holy Spirit will be poured out in far different style from the present. There are diversities of operations; and during the last few years it has been the case that the diversified operations have consisted of very little pouring out of the Spirit. Ministers have gone on in dull routine, continually preaching—preaching—preaching, and little good has been done. I do hope that a fresh era has dawned upon us, and that there is a better pouring out of the Spirit even now. For the hour is coming, and it may be even now, when the Holy Ghost will be poured out again in such a wonderful manner, that many will run to and fro and knowledge shall be increased—the knowledge of the Lord shall cover the earth as the waters cover the surface of the great deep; when His kingdom shall come, and His will shall be done on earth as it is in heaven . . . My eyes flash with the thought that very likely I shall live to see the out-pouring of the Spirit; when "the sons and the daughters of God shall prophesy, and the young men shall see visions, and the old men shall dream dreams." [14]

A year before, a British Methodist preacher, William Arthur, published his influential volume *The Tongue of Fire.* This book, which has remained in print for more than a century, dismissed the traditional view of the cessation and withdrawal of the charismata by saying:

> Whatever is necessary to the holiness of the individual, to the spiritual life and ministering gifts of the church, or to the conversion of the world, is as much the heritage of the people of God in the latest days as in the first . . . We feel satisfied that he who does expect the gift of healing and the gift of

tongues or any other miraculous manifestation of the Holy Spirit . . . has ten times more scriptural ground on which to base his expectation, than have they for their unbelief who do not expect supernatural sanctifying strength for the believer. [15]

Arthur closed this memorable book with the following challenge to all the churches:

And now, adorable Spirit, proceeding from the Father and the Son, descend upon all the churches, renew the pentecost in this our age, and baptize thy people generally—O, baptize them yet again with tongues of fire! Crown this nineteenth century with a revival of "pure and undefiled religion" greater than that of the last century, greater than that of the first, greater than any demonstrations of the Spirit yet vouchsafed to men! [16]

American Holiness Teachers

The language of Pentecost that Arthur popularized became even stronger in America over the next decade. For more than a century before the Civil War, most recipients of the postconversion "second blessing" referred to the experience as "sanctification." Methodist teachers, following the terminology of John Wesley and his colleague John Fletcher, had spoken of "sanctification" and "baptism in the Holy Spirit" as two sides of the same coin. After the war, however, there was a growing tendency to speak of the second work of grace as the "baptism with the Holy Ghost."

This postconversion experience, which began to receive a new emphasis in the 1830s, eventually gained widespread attention as evidenced by the first national holiness camp meeting held in 1867 in Vineland, New Jersey. The Vineland meeting was destined to change the face of American religion. Although it called for a return to holiness living, the call was couched in Pentecostal terms. Those who came were invited to "realize together a Pentecostal baptism of the Holy Ghost" and "to make common supplication for the descent of the Spirit upon ourselves, the church, the nation and the world."[17] This Pentecostal language was the result of the subtle shift that had been taking place among holiness advocates for several years.

Phoebe Worrall Palmer (1807–74), a Methodist teacher and preacher, led a holiness revival from 1839 to 1874 in America, Canada, and England.

In 1839, Asa Mahan, president of Oberlin College, published a book titled *Scripture Doctrine of Christian Perfection.* A defense of the Wesleyan theology of entire sanctification, the theology of the second blessing was presented in strongly Christological terms with little or no emphasis on the Holy Spirit.[18] By 1870, Mahan had published a revision of the same book under the title *The Baptism of the Holy Ghost,* in which a profound shift

PHOEBE WORRALL PALMER

(1807–1874)

Phoebe Palmer was born in New York City on December 18, 1807. Raised as a strict Methodist, she married Walter C. Palmer, a homeopathic physician. Together they shared a deep interest in their Methodist religious roots. Here she taught the Wesleyan "second blessing" experience of "entire sanctification" which she said could be received in an instant by faith, even without any accompanying feeling.

The Palmers had been won to the holiness standard by Pheobe's sister, Sarah A. Lankford, who had begun holding "Tuesday Meetings for the Promotion of Holiness" in her parlor in 1835. By 1839 Mrs. Palmer had not only experienced sanctification, but had become the leader of the meetings. As the "Tuesday Meetings" grew in popularity, hundreds of preachers and laymen from various denominations flocked to her home to hear of the "shorter way" of achieving the perfection and ecstasy that early Christian saints had taken entire lifetimes to acquire. By placing "all on the altar," she taught, one could be instantly sanctified through the Baptism of the Holy Ghost.

The seekers were encouraged to testify to receiving the blessing "by faith" even if they failed to experience any emotional feelings at the moment. Among those who came and found holiness under the Palmers were leading Methodist pastors and bishops. She counted among her friends and followers no less than four bishops of the Methodist Church: Bishops Edmund S. Janes, Leonidas L. Hamline, Jesse T. Peck, and Matthew Simpson. For the next thirty years the Palmers were the national leaders of the movement, traversing the United States and Canada numerous times, and addressing camp meetings and leading churches on their theme of holiness and perfect love.

The year 1839 also saw the beginning of the first periodical in America devoted exclusively to holiness doctrine, *The Guide to Christian Perfection,* later known as *The Guide to Holiness.* Founded in Boston by Timothy Merritt, this monthly paper carried the testimonies of Phoebe Palmer and her husband. In 1865 *The Guide* was purchased by Dr. and Mrs. Palmer themselves and became quite influential within American Protestantism, particularly among Methodists. At its peak, it enjoyed a circulation of 30,000.

Before her death in 1874, the Palmers joined the trend towards pentecostal language to describe the second blessing. Her insistence on an instant crisis experience of what she came to call the "baptism of the Spirit" was an important development in producing the Pentecostal movement in 1901. At her funeral in 1874, T. De Witt Talmadge called Palmer "The Columbus of the Spiritual world." ∎

—VINSON SYNAN
THE HOLINESS-PENTECOSTAL TRADITION

in terminology and exegesis was immediately apparent. In the first, Mahan saw "the blessing" as an ethical experience of cleansing from in-bred sin with references to Ezekiel 36:25; Matthew 5:48; John 17:20–23; and 1 Thessalonians 5:23–24. In the second, his major texts were taken from the Book of Acts (2:4; 19:2, etc.) and from such Old Testament passages as Joel 2:28 and Zechariah 13:1. Pentecostal language permeated the book. The second-blessing experiences of the Wesleys, Madam Guyon, Finney, and Mahan himself were described as "baptism in the Holy Spirit." The effect of this baptism was an "enduement of power from on high" as well as an inner cleansing.[19]

As Donald Dayton has pointed out, "By the turn of the century *every-thing* from camp meetings to choirs are described in the *Guide* as 'Pente-costal.' Sermons are published under the heading 'Pentecostal pulpit'; women's reports under 'Pentecostal womanhood'; personal experiences are reported as 'Pentecostal testimonies,' and so on." In fact, in 1897 the *Guide to Holiness* changed its subtitle from "and Revival Miscellany" to "and Pentecostal Life" in its masthead. This was done, according to the ed-itor, in response to "the signs of the times, which indicate inquiry, research, and ardent pursuit of the gifts and graces, and power of the Holy Spirit." He added further, "The Pentecostal idea is pervading Christian thought and aspirations more than ever before."[20]

The word *Pentecostal* thus took on the aspects of a code word synony-mous with the holiness movement much as the word *charismatic* has be-come fashionable today to refer to all Pentecostals. The term thus became necessary in the title of most holiness books published in the 1890s and early 1900s. A typical example was Martin Wells Knapp's 1898 *Lightning Bolts from Pentecostal Skies, or the Devices of the Devil Unmasked!*[21] The popu-larity of the terms "Pentecostal" and "baptism with the Holy Ghost" soon permeated much of the evangelical world. Melvin Dieter has summarized:

> Pentecost as past proof of God's power, Pentecost as the present pattern for
> the renewal of the churches, and Pentecost as the portent of fulfillment of all
> things in the restoration of God's kingdom among men, became the pervad-
> ing atmosphere of the holiness movement.[22]

In the light of this emphasis, it is not surprising that promotion of a "third blessing" appeared in the ranks of the holiness movement. By the late 1890s some holiness leaders began to promote a separate "baptism with the Holy Ghost and fire" subsequent to the experiences of conversion and sanctification. This was scornfully called "third blessingism." The rapid growth of this movement beginning just before 1900 gave testimony to a hunger on the part of many holiness and evangelical Christians for a more "Pentecostal" experience than they had received under classical holiness teaching.

"Third blessingism" was an important portent of things to come in the holiness movement that produced the later Pentecostal movement. It is not without significance that the first person to speak in tongues in the 20th century, Agnes Ozman, was part of this movement. Such widespread use of Pentecostal terminology had the effect of moving experience-oriented Christians ever closer to modern Pentecostalism.

Keswick Teachers

The Pentecostal emphasis that developed in the holiness movement after 1867 also found expression in the various offshoots of the movement in England and America. This is best seen in the development of the famous Keswick "Higher Life" conferences in England and the Northfield conferences in Massachusetts conducted by D. L. Moody.

The Keswick summer conventions were begun in 1875 as a British counterpart of the blossoming American holiness movement. The Keswick conferences were later dominated by Robert Pearsall Smith, an American evangelist whose wife, Hannah Whitall Smith, also became known as a popular speaker and author. Smith carried the Pentecostal terminology gaining currency among holiness believers to the point of doctrinal change. This new Keswick emphasis displaced the concept of the second blessing as an "eradication" of the sinful nature in favor of a "baptism in the Holy Spirit" as an "enduement of power for service." The experience anticipated by the ardent seekers at Keswick was cast not so much in terms of cleansing as in the anointing by the Spirit. Further, the Spirit-filled life was not a "state of perfection" but a "maintained condition."

This approach caused a rift between the Keswick teachers and the more traditional holiness teachers in America:

> These teachings—the denial of the eradication of inward sin and the emphasis on pre-millennialism, faith healing, and the gifts of the Spirit—opened a wide breach in the holiness ranks. The conflict spread to America when Dwight L. Moody; R. A. Torrey, first president of Moody Bible Institute, Chicago; Adoniram J. Gordon, father of Gordon College, Boston; A. B. Simpson, founder of the Christian and Missionary Alliance; and the evangelist J. Wilbur Chapman began to propagate in this country the Keswick version of the second blessing.[23]

An outstanding example of the Keswick teaching was seen in the work of R. A. Torrey:

> The baptism with the Holy Spirit is an operation of the Holy Spirit distinct from and subsequent from His regenerating work, an impartation of power for service. [Such an experience was] not merely for the apostles, not merely for those of the apostolic age, but for "all that are afar off; even as many as the Lord our God shall call." . . . It is for every believer in every age of the church's history.[24]

Although Torrey and Smith spread the Keswick understanding of the "baptism with the Holy Ghost" from coast to coast, the most influential proponent of the experience in America was D. L. Moody, the most famous evangelist of his day. Even though he already was a powerful preacher, Moody was influenced to seek a deeper experience by two ladies in his Chicago church who prayed constantly for him to be "baptized in the Holy Spirit" for even greater service. At first resistant to any new spiritual experiences, Moody eventually asked the two ladies, both members of the Free Methodist Church, to pray for him. In a dramatic prayer meeting in 1871, Moody reported that he was suddenly baptized with the Holy Spirit. During this experience, Moody testified that he "dropped to the floor and lay bathing his soul in the divine" while his room "seemed ablaze with God."[25]

After his baptism in the Spirit, Moody began to conduct annual Higher Life conferences in Northfield, Massachusetts, to which thousands came to receive their "personal Pentecost." In later years Moody turned his attention to education, founding the Moody Bible Institute in Chicago in 1889. The higher life baptism continued to be taught there even after Moody's death in 1899.

Dwight Lyman Moody (1837–99) was a great evangelist and proponent of the Keswick experience of baptism in the Holy Spirit.

Moody's passing marked an important milestone in the history of the tradition that emphasized a subsequent work of the Holy Spirit after conversion. By this time, the emphasis on a personal Pentecostal experience was no longer considered to be a bizarre teaching on the fringes of mainline evangelical Christianity, but was widely accepted in the mainstream of American and British religious life as an attainable experience for modern times.

Much of the spiritual ferment of the preceding century had centered on the question of the "second blessing" as propounded by John Wesley and his heirs in the holiness and higher life movements. Most Methodists and holiness folk who went down to the mourner's bench were seeking a sanctifying experience of heart purity that was wrought in an instant through a "baptism in the Holy Spirit." By the end of the century, however, Moody and others began to change the definition and content of the much sought-

DWIGHT L. MOODY'S BAPTISM IN THE SPIRIT

Moody continued to hunger for a deepening of his own spiritual life and experience. He had been greatly used of God, but felt that there were greater things in store for him. The year 1871 was a critical one with him. He realized more and more how little he was fitted by personal acquirements for his work, and how much he needed to be qualified for service by the Holy Spirit's power. This realization was deepened by conversations he had with two ladies who sat on the front pew in his church. He could see by the expression of their faces that they were praying. At the close of the service they would say to him, "We have been praying for you." "Why don't you pray for the people?" Mr. Moody would ask. "Because you need the power of the Spirit," was the reply. "I need the power! Why," he said, in relating the incident afterwards, "I thought I had the power. I had the largest congregation in Chicago, and there were many conversions. I was in a sense satisfied. But right along those two godly women kept praying for me, and their earnest talk about anointing for special service set me thinking. I asked them to come and talk with me, and they poured out their hearts in prayer that I might receive the filling of the Holy Spirit. There came a great hunger into my soul. I did not know what it was. I began to cry out as I never did before. I really felt that I did not want to live if I could not have this power for service."

"While Mr. Moody was in this mental and spiritual condition," says his son, "Chicago was laid in ashes. The great fire swept out of existence both Farwell Hall and Illinois Street Church. On Sunday night after the meeting, as Mr. Moody went homeward, he saw the glare of flames, and knew it meant ruin to Chicago. About one o'clock Farwell Hall was burned; and soon his church went down. Everything was scattered."

Mr. Moody went East to New York City to collect funds for the sufferers from the Chicago fire, but his heart and soul were crying out for the power from on high. "My heart was not in the work of begging," says he. "I could not appeal. I was crying all the time that God would fill me with His Spirit. Well, one day, in the city of New York—oh, what a day!—I cannot describe it; I seldom refer to it; it is almost too sacred an experience to name. Paul had such an experience of which he never spoke for fourteen years. I can only say that God revealed Himself to me, and I had such an experience of His love that I had to ask Him to stay His hand. I went to preaching again. The sermons were not different; I did not present any new truths, and yet hundreds were converted. I would not now be placed back where I was before that blessed experience if you should give me all the world—it would be as the small dust of the balance." ■

—JAMES GILCHRIST LAWSON
DEEPER EXPERIENCES OF FAMOUS CHRISTIANS

after experience. However it was defined, the "second blessing" was generally seen as a divine encounter in which the seeker achieved victory over sin and an enduement of Pentecostal power in the same instant.

Camp Meeting Holiness

A major feature of 19th-century spirituality was the rise of the camp meeting movement, which originated on the frontier. Beginning in 1801 in Logan County in Kentucky, America's first camp meeting began spontaneously among Presbyterians and Methodists in a rural setting in the Cane Ridge Presbyterian Church. What began as a communion service erupted into what some called a "frolic of faith." As many as twenty-five thousand people came by wagon train, on foot, and on horseback to witness and experience the "exersizes," as they were called. As thousands experienced conversion, they were often overtaken by such manifestations as "falling under the power," "the jerks," the "holy laugh," and "the holy dance."

America's first camp meeting (1800–1801) was in Cane Ridge, Kentucky, where thousands experienced manifestations of the Holy Spirit.

After the amazing events at Cane Ridge, hundreds of camp meetings were organized across America. Although there were Presbyterians, Methodists, and Baptists at Cane Ridge, most of the new camp meetings were begun by Methodists. The "circuit rider" and the camp meeting were the major techniques that led the Methodist Church to become the largest Protestant church in America by 1900.

After the Civil War, many camp meetings were closed while others fell into a steep decline. But the camp meeting saw a new birth in 1867 with the organization of the "National Camp Meeting Association for the Promotion of Holiness" in Vineland, New Jersey. Led by New York Methodist pastor John Inskip, holiness camp meetings sprang up all over the nation with attendance at some reaching twenty thousand in the 1870s. Although these meetings were led by Methodists, thousands of people from all denominations knelt at the "mourner's bench" to seek and receive the coveted sanctification experience.

PIERCING SCREAMS AND HEAVENLY SMILES
AN EYEWITNESS ACCOUNT OF SIGNS AND WONDERS AT EARLY CAMP MEETINGS

Over his lifetime, Barton Stone witnessed the many bodily "exercises" of frontier revivals. In his 1847 autobiography, he described the forms that religious ecstasy took. A condensed excerpt:

Falling The falling exercise was very common among all classes, the saints and sinners of every age and every grade, from the philosopher to the clown. The subject of this exercise would, generally, with a piercing scream, fall like a log on the floor, earth, or mud, and appear as dead.

At a meeting, two gay young ladies, sisters, both fell, with a shriek of distress, and lay for more than an hour apparently in a lifeless state. At length they began to exhibit symptoms of life, by crying fervently for mercy, and then relapsed into the same death-like state, with an awful gloom on their countenances. After a while, the gloom on the face of one was succeeded by a heavenly smile, and she cried out, "Precious Jesus!" and rose up and spoke of the love of God.

The Jerks Sometimes the subject of the jerks would be affected in some one member of the body, and sometimes in the whole system. When the head alone was affected, it would be jerked backward and forward, or from side to side, so quickly that the features of the face could not be distinguished. When the whole system was affected, I have seen the person stand in one place, and jerk backward and forward in quick succession, their head nearly touching the floor behind and before.

Dancing The dancing exercise generally began with the jerks, then the jerks would cease. The smile of heaven shone on the countenance of the subject, and assimilated to angels appeared the whole person. Sometimes the motion was quick and sometimes slow. Thus they continued to move forward and backward in the same track or alley till nature seemed exhausted, and they would fall prostate on the floor or earth.

Barking The barking exercise (as opposers contemptuously called it) was nothing but the jerks. A person affected with the jerks would often make a grunt, or bark, if you please, from the suddenness of the jerk.

Laughing It was a loud, hearty laughter, but one [that] excited laughter in no one else. The subject appeared rapturously solemn, and his laughter excited solemnity in saints and sinners. It is truly indescribable.

Running The running exercise was nothing more than that persons [who,] feeling something of these bodily agitations, through fear, attempted to run away and thus escape from them. But it commonly happened that they ran not far before they fell or became so greatly agitated that they could proceed no farther.

Singing The singing exercise is more unaccountable than anything else I ever saw. The subject in a very happy state of mind would sing most melodiously, not from the mouth or nose, but entirely in the breast, the sounds issuing thence. Such music silenced everything, and attracted the attention of all. It was most heavenly. None could ever be tired of hearing it. ■

—BARTON W. STONE
CHRISTIAN HISTORY

By the 1880s, the movement began to divide Methodists over the questions concerning creeping legalism, independency, and the very idea of a subsequent instant experience of sanctification. By 1894, the Southern Methodists had not only rejected the second-blessing movement, but had adopted measures to control the evangelists and pastors who promoted the movement. As a result, more than twenty "holiness" denominations were founded by disaffected Methodist "come-outers" who, in the 1890s founded such churches as the Pentecostal Church of the Nazarene, the Pentecostal Holiness Church, and the Fire-Baptized Holiness Church. In 1901, the Pentecostal movement was launched by holiness people whose churches were founded as a result of the camp meeting movement among Methodists.

All of these churches taught the Wesleyan experience of "second blessing" sanctification through what was also called a "baptism of the Holy Spirit." The two aspects of the experience were cleansing (sanctification) and empowering (baptism in the Holy Spirit). These were seen as the two sides of the same coin making up the single "second blessing" experience.

The "Baptism of Fire"

The first revivalist to change this formula was Benjamin Hardin Irwin, founder of the "Fire-Baptized Holiness Church." Irwin was a lawyer from Tecumseh, Nebraska. In 1879, he had a conversion experience in a local Baptist church where he soon became a preacher and then the pastor. In 1891, he was exposed to holiness doctrine through the Iowa Holiness Association.

Switching his allegiance from the Baptists to the Wesleyan Methodists, he became a traveling holiness preacher. In 1895, he experienced what he termed a "baptism of fire." After this new experience his ministry changed as he began to teach the theology of the "third blessing" by which he referred to the baptism in the Holy Spirit. He stated that this was a separate and subsequent experience to both salvation and sanctification, which he retained as the second blessing. Many in the holiness movement condemned this new teaching as heresy, and set out to ostracize people for their beliefs just as they had been ostracized earlier by the Methodists.

Irwin was soon preaching across the continent in tent revivals and establishing fire-baptized holiness associations wherever he went. Starting in Iowa, then traveling widely in the South, Irwin quickly built an impressive organization that covered the United States and was spreading into Canada. The new association was soon taking on all the trappings of a denomination that taught, besides the third blessing, all the tenets of traditional holiness doctrine, plus adherence to the dietary laws of the Old Testament. Irwin began to teach that besides the baptism of fire there were also additional spiritual baptisms, which he called "dynamite," "lyddite," and "oxidite," the explosively emotional nature of which can be inferred from their names.[26]

The fire-baptized movement was noted for the extreme physical manifestations that accompanied these various baptisms. It was claimed that people spoke in tongues in a fire-baptized holiness revival in the Schearer schoolhouse in western North Carolina in 1896. Other signs and manifestations were in evidence as the new movement grew so fast and so far that for a time it appeared that it might draw a majority of the holiness camp into its wake. Then in 1900 their dynamic leader publicly confessed to gross sin and was removed from leadership. This crippling blow shook the nascent denomination and stopped its phenomenal growth.[27]

Irwin's fire-baptized movement was an important bridge to Pentecostalism in that attention was given to the unique empowering action of the Holy Spirit separate from the cleansing work of the Spirit in sanctification. This attention to the Holy Spirit among evangelicals was so intense as the century came to an end that C. I. Scofield, editor of the famous Scofield Bible, stated that more books had been written on the Holy Spirit in the 1890s than in all previous Christian history.

Catholics and the Holy Spirit

A parallel trend toward a new emphasis on the Holy Spirit was also seen among Roman Catholics as the 19th century came to a close.[28] The seeds for this emphasis were planted earlier in the century in the work of two German theologians, Johann Adam Moehler and Matthias Scheeben. Moehler's major work was the 1825 book *Unity in the Church*, which depicted the church as a charismatic body constituted and enlivened by the Holy Spirit. The later work of Scheeben (during the 1870s and 1880s) laid stress on the unique action of the Holy Spirit in the formation of the Christian life. The effect of Moehler's and Scheeben's work was to bring into focus a "theology of the charismata," resulting in a "revalorization" of the gifts of the Spirit, which had suffered a decline among both Catholics and Protestants during the bitter debates of the Reformation.

Even more striking was the story of Elena Guerra. As leader of a group of sisters dedicated to the Christian education of young girls, she became pained at the lack of attention and devotion paid by Catholics to the Holy

Spirit. As a child, Elena had been impressed to pray a novena (a nine-day cycle of special prayer) to the Holy Spirit between the Feasts of the Ascension and Pentecost, to commemorate the days that the apostles waited in the Upper Room for the outpouring of the Spirit. Against the advice of friends, she wrote to Pope Leo XIII, suggesting that the idea of a special novena to the Holy Spirit become a universal observance of the church.

To the astonishment of her friends, the pope not only read her letter, but in 1897 issued an encyclical letter titled *On the Holy Spirit*. In this document, the pope called for such a novena and also directed the church to a new appreciation of the Holy Spirit and the gifts of the Spirit. Millions of Catholics, from theologians to the humble faithful, turned their attention to the Holy Spirit in a way that had not been seen in the church for centuries.

Thus, as the century came to an end, both Catholic and Protestant leaders were calling for a new Pentecost with a restoration of the signs and wonders that had characterized the early church. In a sense, the entire 19th century was like a Pentecost novena—the church waiting in the Upper Room, tarrying for power, and praying for and expecting an outpouring of the Holy Spirit with a renewal of the gifts of the Spirit for the new century that was about to dawn.

For Further Reading

The best starting point for further historical reading on Pentecostal roots is Vinson Synan's *The Holiness-Pentecostal Tradition: Charismatic Movements in the Twentieth Century* (Grand Rapids: Eerdmans, 1997). Two excellent treatments of theological developments that led to the outbreak of Pentecostalism are Donald Dayton's *The Theological Roots of Pentecostalism* (Grand Rapids: Francis Asbury Press, 1987); and Ernest R. Sandeen's *Roots of Fundamentalism: British and American Millenarianism, 1800–1930* (Chicago: Univ. of Chicago Press, 1970). For a good discussion of the origins and development of the cessation of the charismata theory one should consult Jon Ruthven's excellent book *On the Cessation of the Charismata: The Protestant Polemic on Post-Biblical Miracles* (Sheffield, UK: Sheffield Univ. Academic Press, 1993).

Major books outlining the course of the American holiness movement include Timothy Smith's *Revivalism and Social Reform in Mid-Nineteenth-Century America* (New York: Abingdon, 1957); and Melvin Dieter's *The Holiness Revival of the Nineteenth Century* (Metuchen, N.J.: Scarecrow Press, 1980).

Good sources for Edward Irving are Gordon Strachan's *The Pentecostal Theology of Edward Irving* (London: Dartan, Longman & Todd, 1973); and

Wiliam S. Merrick's *Edward Irving: the Forgotten Giant* (East Peoria, Ill.: Scribe's Chamber Publications, 1983). Recent work by David Dorries includes his chapter on Irving, "Edward Irving and the Standing Sign," in *Initial Evidence: Historical and Biblical Perspective on the Pentecostal Doctrine of Spirit Baptism*, ed. Gary B. McGee (Peabody, Mass.: Hendrickson Publishers, 1991).

Much information on this and all succeeding chapters can be found in the excellent and encyclopedic *Dictionary of Pentecostal and Charismatic Movements*, ed. Stanley M. Burgess and Gary B. McGee (Grand Rapids: Zondervan, 1988). Zondervan is slated to release a revised edition titled *New International Dictionary of Pentecostal and Charismatic Movements*, ed. Stanley Burgess and Eduard M. van der Maas.

· 3 ·

The Azusa Street Revival:
The Pentecostal Movement Begins
in America

Robert Owens

O N THE MORNING OF APRIL 19, 1906, readers of the *Los Angeles Times* were shocked to read the banner headline news of the San Francisco earthquake. At 5:18 A.M. the day before, the most powerful earthquake in American history, 8.3 on the Richter scale, had destroyed 514 city blocks in the heart of the city. More than 700 people died from the tremor and the firestorm that followed. The day before, on April 18, readers of the same paper had seen a curious first-page story of a spiritual earthquake that had hit Los Angeles in a little mission church on Azusa Street the night before. The headlines read:

> Weird Babble of Tongues
> New Sect of Fanatics Is Breaking Loose
> Wild Scene Last Night on Azusa Street
> Gurgle of Wordless Talk by a Sister[1]

This is how the world first heard of the Azusa Street revival that was to shake the spiritual world much as the San Francisco earthquake had shaken northern California. Little did the readers know that the after-shocks of the Los Angeles event in a small black holiness church would continue to shake the world with ever greater force throughout the century. A few days earlier a handful of African-American washerwomen and domestic servants had followed the black preacher William J. Seymour as he opened services in an old abandoned African Methodist Episcopal church on Azusa Street. Seymour had arrived a few weeks earlier with a stunning message concerning a "baptism in the Holy Spirit" with the "Bible evidence" of speaking in tongues as the Spirit gave utterance. What happened there on Azusa Street was to change the course of Christian church history forever.

Joseph Smale

As in every great religious revival movement, what appeared to be new and spontaneous was actually the end result of much prayer and preparation. People within the holiness movement were looking in many directions for the next move of God. One person who exemplified this continual seeking for a deeper walk with God was Joseph Smale, pastor of the First Baptist Church of Los Angeles. Smale was born in England and had studied for the ministry at Spurgeon's College in London.

When word reached Los Angeles of the great outpouring in Wales in 1904, Smale took a leave of absence from his pulpit and journeyed to Wales to observe and participate firsthand. While he was there he actually helped Evan Roberts in conducting services.

Returning from Wales, Smale was a changed man. Seeking a revival similar to what he had seen in Wales, Smale entered into a time of deep prayer. Following this time of preparation the newly inspired Baptist preacher started home prayer meetings among the more dedicated of his flock. These home meetings soon led the pastor to start a series of revival meetings at his own church.

The services eventually stretched out into sixteen weeks of continuous intercession for revival. The meetings were marked by spontaneity and freedom of worship. The pastor allowed the Holy Spirit to lead the meetings. Often others would start and lead the meetings before Smale arrived. People from all denominational backgrounds were allowed to preach and testify.

After four months of intense revival services, the elders of the First Baptist Church decided to call their pastor into line. They didn't like the loose way in which the meetings were conducted, the fact that non-Baptists were allowed not only to preach but also to start and even conduct some of the services. They were generally tired of innovation, and wanted to return to the old ways. Pastor Smale decided to quit. Withdrawing with those of the congregation who were united with him in seeking after a revival Smale started the First New Testament Church where the nightly meetings

continued. The view of the holiness people in regard to this split is suc-
cinctly summed up in the words of Frank Bartleman: "What an awful position for a church to take, to throw God out."[2]

Such was the state of the holiness movement in Los Angeles in 1905. It
was a scene filled with ferment and turmoil, blessing and dedication, as
people were willing to divorce themselves from lifelong commitments in
the quest for a new outpouring of the Spirit of God, a second Pentecost.
Old connections were severed and new ones forged as the people of God
sought a fresh anointing. As always, this movement was most pronounced
among the poor and the downtrodden. The lower classes and their leaders
seemed ready to sacrifice their time, their positions, and their reputations
in their longing for the power of God.[3]

The Welsh Revival

Just as the holiness movement set the stage for the birth of modern Pentecostalism, so the Welsh Revival of 1904 clearly demonstrated the worldwide hunger for such a renewal. This revival first set all Wales ablaze, then
London and then all of England, until people from all over the world were
coming to see if this was the new Pentecost.

Unlike so much of independent revivalism in America, the revival of
1904 in Wales was a revival within the churches. It was also a revival of
laymen, a revival of the poor and the outcast. This great revival was led by
a twenty-six-year-old former miner and first-term theology student named
Evan Roberts (1878–1951). This tremendous move of God was marked by a
complete freedom in the Spirit. Observers came away with mixed reactions. Some believed that God was moving among His people and others
saw nothing but hysteria and confusion.

What some observers classified as the ancient Welsh "hywl" others considered speaking in other tongues. Many additional manifestations of ecstatic energy were in evidence during this outpouring, including
prolonged singing, lay preaching, testimonies, united prayer, frequent in-
terruptions of the services by worshipers, a heavy reliance on the inspired
guidance of the Spirit, and an emphasis on the Holy Spirit. Evan Roberts
himself reported seeing many supernatural visions that he accepted as
completely authentic and based upon biblical prophecy. He drew much of
his inspiration and motivation from these visions.

Within weeks of the revival's beginning many people were claiming to
have been baptized with the Holy Spirit. These experiences were accompanied by shouting, laughing, dancing, people falling down under the

power, copious tears, speaking in unknown tongues, and an unusual revival of an old language, as many young people, who knew nothing of the Old Welsh, would during times of spiritual ecstasy speak fluently in that ancient language.[4] The revival soon spread beyond the meetings led by Roberts, though he was the universally proclaimed leader of the movement from beginning to end.

Newspapers spread word of the growing revival far and wide, and people from other parts of Great Britain, as well as from around the world, began searching out Roberts and his meetings.[5] The revival meetings began to take on an increasingly cosmopolitan complexion as citizens of many countries came seeking the power of God. Often during meetings Roberts would "fall under the power" of the Holy Spirit and remain for hours prostrate on the floor.

The effects of the great revival in Wales were tangible and long-lasting. The power of the Holy Spirit as manifested in diverse signs and most especially in conversions and church growth combined with the attendance of many who would later play roles in the Pentecostal revival to make the Welsh revival of 1904 a precurser of the Pentecostal movement.

Charles Fox Parham

The man who is generally recognized as the formulator of Pentecostal doctrine and the theological founder of the movement was Charles Fox Parham (1873–1929).[6] His doctrine of tongues as the "Bible evidence" of the baptism in the Holy Spirit would directly lead to the Azusa Street revival of 1906 and the creation of the world Pentecostal movement.

Parham was born at Muscatine, Iowa, on June 4, 1873. During his youth he was chronically ill and confined to bed for months at a time. During these early childhood infirmities he believed he received a call to the ministry and began reading and studying the Bible extensively. When he was thirteen Parham's mother died, plunging him into a period of turmoil. During this period of crisis, he was "born again" under the ministry of a Brother Lippard of the Congregational House Church.

Believing in his preconversion "call," Parham entered a Methodist-related school, Southwestern College at Winfield, Kansas, in 1889. He had previously decided that he could serve God as a physician just as well as he could by being a minister of the gospel. As he began his studies in medicine he was almost immediately overcome by disease. At this time he experienced a traumatic bout with rheumatic fever. While he was bedfast, he began to study the biblical passages concerning the healings of Jesus.

These studies led Parham to the belief that Jesus would also heal him. He came to believe that the devil had attempted to stop him from entering the ministry by leading him into medicine, and because of this backsliding God had chastised him with rheumatic fever.

When he renounced his intention of pursuing a career in medicine and returned to his original intention of entering the ministry the young preacher did recover from the disease, but not totally. He was crippled in his ankles, and could barely walk, using crutches when he returned to school. Shortly after this, Parham received a revelation telling him that formal education was a hindrance to his ministry, so he immediately quit school. It was at this time, he later reported, that God miraculously healed him completely of the remaining effects of the fever.[7]

Charles Fox Parham (1873–1928), the formulator of Pentecostal theology, was the mentor of William J. Seymour of Azusa Street.

It was Parham who was credited with first advancing the theological argument that tongues are always the initial evidence of a person's receiving the baptism with the Holy Spirit. He was also the first to teach that this baptism, including the resulting tongues, should be seen as a part of every Christian's experience, something to be used in normal life and worship, and not just something that would appear during times of great religious fervor. In addition Parham taught the necessity of being baptized with the Holy Spirit as the only way to escape the coming end-time Great Tribulation,[8] and that speaking with tongues was the only assurance of this. These teachings of Parham's laid the theological and experiential foundations for the later Azusa Street revival and modern Pentecostal practice.

After leaving the Linwood Methodist Church to become an independent holiness preacher, Parham began a career as an itinerant teacher and evangelist. In time, he founded several healing and teaching missions, all of which operated on a faith basis. None of these missions were very successful.[9] By 1898 he had settled in Topeka, Kansas, where he established the Bethel Bible School and Healing Home. In December of 1900, Parham asked his students to search the Scriptures and see if they could discern one special sign of the baptism with the Holy Spirit. While he was away for three days preaching in Kansas City, his students through fasting, prayer, and study of the Scriptures decided unanimously that speaking with other tongues constituted the one and only initial biblical proof of the baptism with the Holy Spirit.

When Parham returned and heard his students' answer to his quest he called for a night-long New Year's watch service on December 31, 1900. During this service one of the students, Agnes N. Ozman, asked Parham to lay hands on her and pray for her to receive the baptism with the Holy Spirit accompanied by the evidence of speaking with other tongues. When he later wrote of this event, Parham said:

> I laid my hands upon her and prayed. I had scarcely repeated three dozen sentences when a glory fell upon her, a halo seemed to surround her head and face, and she began speaking the Chinese language and was unable to speak English for three days. When she tried to write in English to tell us of her experience she wrote the Chinese, copies of which we still have in newspapers printed at that time. [10]

During these meetings, it was later claimed, the students spoke in twenty-one known languages, including Swedish, Russian, Bulgarian,

Japanese, Norwegian, French, Hungarian, Italian, and Spanish. According to Parham, none of his students had studied any of these languages, and they were all confirmed as authentic by native speakers. [11] Parham immediately began teaching that Christian missionaries would have no further need of language training. They needed only to receive the baptism with the Holy Spirit and they would be miraculously empowered to speak whatever language was necessary. This was a teaching Parham would steadfastly maintain throughout the rest of his life, despite ever mounting evidence that this was not substantiated by later events.

Having a doctrine and an experience, Parham closed his faith work in Topeka and started a tour of revivals that lasted for more than four years. Experiencing little success at first, he continued even when most of his followers deserted him. Finally, in Galena, Kansas, the fire he had been attempting to ignite took hold. Fueled by re-

Agnes Ozman's baptism in the Holy Spirit with the expected evidence of tongues "made the Pentecostal movement of the 20th century," according to J. Roswell Flower.

ports of miraculous healings and other miracles, the revival brought fresh followers and large crowds. In 1905 Parham once again established a faith-work Bible school, this time in Houston, Texas. While his school in Houston only had about twenty-five students, one of them, William J. Seymour, was destined later to usher in the Azusa Street revival. [12]

Charles Fox Parham was truly a pioneer in many ways. It was he who coined all three of the common names that have traditionally been applied to modern Pentecostalism including "Pentecostal movement," "Latter Rain movement," and the "Apostolic Faith movement," all of which occur in the title of his first published accounts of the New Year's Day occurrences in Topeka, "The Latter Rain: The Story of the Origin of the Original Apostolic Faith or Pentecostal Movements."[13] He founded what was the first and soon became the model for Pentecostal newspapers when he began publishing the *Apostolic Faith* in 1899. Parham also issued ministerial credentials to Seymour and many others who would later figure prominently in the coming revival.

Los Angeles in 1906

By 1905, spiritual shock waves that had shaken Topeka and Houston began to be felt in Los Angeles. These shock waves reflected the spiritual ferment in the holiness communities, the rapidly growing revelations of the Apostolic Faith movement of Charles Parham, and the continuing reports of the great Welsh revival from people like Frank Bartleman and Joseph Smale. People in the many holiness missions in California began to pray earnestly for an outpouring of the power of God. On November 16, 1905, the words of the holiness preacher and prophet Frank Bartleman were published in the *Way of Faith,* a small holiness newspaper: "Los Angeles seems to be the place and this the time, in the mind of God, for the restoration of the Church." Little did Bartleman know that this longed for revival would not originate in the mainline white churches, but would take place in the Los Angeles African-American community.[14]

The black population of Los Angeles has a history that predates the American conquest in 1848. When the United States assumed control of the city there existed an area known as "Calle de los Negros," a long, narrow street connecting Los Angeles Street to the main plaza.[15] This area was the dwelling place for a population of free African Mexicans who were well represented in the trades and social life of the city. The quiet residential area was increasingly taken over by saloons, brothels, and gambling dens after the Americans and their prejudices arrived.

In 1885, the African-American members of the Fort Street Methodist Church (Northern Convention) separated themselves and founded the Second Baptist Church. This was a church, which, by the early 1900s, had theologically joined the Fundamentalist movement.[16] In the spring of 1906, a member of the Second Baptist Church, Julia Hutchins, began teaching the holiness doctrine of sanctification as a separate work of grace subsequent to salvation after she experienced her own dramatic second-blessing experience. Her teachings were eagerly received by those in the congregation seeking a touch from God. As the growing group of holiness people reached out to more and more of the congregation the pastor asked Sister Hutchins and her followers to leave.

This small band of nine families at first joined themselves to W. F. Manley's Household of God tent meeting. But they were still unsatisfied, seeking the opportunity to teach and preach holiness with greater freedom. In an attempt to find this religious independence they soon established a holiness mission on Santa Fe Street. But independence was evidently not what they had expected it to be, and within two months they became associated with the Southern California Holiness Association. Following the prejudices of the times they believed a man was needed to become the permanent pastor. At the suggestion of Neely Terry, an invitation was sent to Elder William J. Seymour, whom she had met while visiting in the Houston area.

William Joseph Seymour

Born in Louisiana, the son of former slaves, Seymour was a short, stocky African-American man who was blind in one eye and graced by a meek and humble spirit. He began his spiritual odyssey as a child when he made a profession of faith at a Methodist meeting. In his early adulthood he moved to Indianapolis where he joined a local Methodist church. Later he came into contact with the Church of God (Anderson, Ind.), where he eventually received ordination to the ministry. Seymour spent a few years preaching in several churches of that denomination. Called the "Evening Light Saints," these holiness advocates first exposed Seymour to radical holiness teachings. In 1905, after moving to Houston, Texas, in search of lost relatives, he was invited by Mrs. Lucy Farrow to become pastor in her independent holiness mission near Houston. Seymour gained a good reputation among the Christians of the area. Arthur Osterberg, who became a leader at the Azusa Street Mission, described him as "meek and plain spoken and no orator. He spoke the common language of the uneducated class. He might preach for three-quarters of an hour with no more emotionalism than that there post. He was no arm-waving thunderer, by any stretch of the imagination."[17]

Seymour accepted the invitation from Pastor Hutchins as a "divine call" to go to Los Angeles. He was freshly set on fire by Parham's new teaching on evidential tongues, which he had absorbed during his short educational experience at Parham's Houston Bible school. Assuming, from his short acquaintance with Miss Terry, that the people in Los Angeles were eagerly awaiting this message, Seymour set out with Parham's blessing and financial support to spread the message, even though he had not yet received the baptism with the Holy Spirit himself.

For his first Sunday morning sermon Seymour chose as the text Acts 2:4, and boldly preached that unless a person spoke in tongues they had not experienced the true baptism with the Holy Spirit. Following what were the accepted teachings of the holiness movement, Sister Hutchins and the other people at the Santa Fe Mission believed that sanctification and the baptism with the Holy Spirit were the same experience, an experience that most of them claimed to have had. This new teaching of Seymour's required them to renounce their own deeply held belief in a personal experience and seek something more.

The teaching on tongues so upset Sister Hutchins that when Seymour returned for the evening service he found the doors padlocked. And so, one year after they had been expelled from their church for what their pastor considered unbalanced teachings, these Christians were expelling another Christian for the same reason.

Taking seriously her responsibilities as the founder and interim pastor of the Santa Fe Holiness Mission, Sister Hutchins chose to ignore the fact that many of her followers were receptive to what Seymour was preaching. A small group of families subsequently left the Santa Fe Holiness Mission with the rejected pastor, thus launching Seymour on an independent course that was to have such far-reaching repercussions. [18]

Meetings on Bonnie Brea Street

Locked out of his church and nearly penniless, Elder Seymour was a man with a message burning like a fire in his bones. Feeling compelled to carry on despite the reversal at the Santa Fe Holiness Mission, Seymour first began teaching those that followed him at the home of Owen "Irish" Lee, where he initially stayed. Lee was an Irish-American member of one of the Peniel holiness missions. When the Lee home proved inadequate to hold meetings in Seymour accepted the invitation from one of Neely Terry's relatives, Richard and Ruth Asberry, to start holding prayer meetings and worship services in their home at 214 North Bonnie Brae Street. At the time they invited Seymour into their home, the Asberrys were Baptists. They did not at the time personally accept Seymour's teachings, but they had heard what had happened, and they felt sorry for the stranded preacher.

In the beginning, these meetings at the Asberrys were attended mainly by "negro washwomen," and a few of their husbands. Seymour still had one major impediment to his message: He had not yet received the baptism with the Holy Spirit, had not spoken in tongues, and he was having a hard time leading others to the experience.

News of the meetings soon began to spread despite the lack of a breakthrough. The Lees let other members of the Peniel Mission they attended know about the meetings. The McGowans, who had heard Seymour

In this house at 214 Bonnie Brae Street, Pentecost first fell in Los Angeles on April 9, 1906, when several persons spoke in tongues.

preach his one sermon at the Santa Fe Mission, brought the news to their home church, the Holiness Church on Hawthorne Street that was pastored by William Pendleton. Arthur G. Osterberg, the pastor of the independent Full Gospel Church, also heard about the meetings through the well-developed Los Angeles spiritual grapevine, as did Frank Bartleman, the holiness preacher who was always searching for the next "move of God." By late March 1906, these white believers had joined the little group of African-Americans at the house on Bonnie Brae Street and were actively seeking the baptism with the Holy Spirit as evidenced by speaking with other tongues.

But although the numbers were growing, success still alluded Seymour and the other seekers. Almost in despair, Seymour communicated with Parham about the situation in Los Angeles and asked for help. In late March 1906, in response to Seymour's plea, Parham sent April Lucy Farrow and J. A. Warren from Houston to assist Elder Seymour. Although Warren was a tireless worker, he had not yet received the baptism with the Holy Spirit himself, but Sister Farrow had, and she stirred the meetings with her testimonies.

When he was about to leave for the Asberrys' home on the evening of April 9, 1906, Elder Seymour stopped to pray with Mr. Lee for a healing. Owen Lee, who had earlier been discussing spiritual matters with his house guest, related a vision he had had the night before of the twelve apostles coming to him and explaining how to speak in tongues. Lee then asked Seymour to pray with him to receive the baptism with the Holy Spirit. They prayed together, and Lee began speaking in other tongues as he received the baptism. This was the first occasion of anyone receiving the baptism with the Holy Spirit when Elder Seymour prayed for them.

Rushing to the meeting at the Asberry home, Seymour related what had just happened with Edward Lee. This news caused the faith of the people to rise higher than ever before, when suddenly, "Seymour and seven others fell to the floor in a religious ecstasy, speaking with other tongues."[19] When this happened, the young daughter of the Asberrys, Willella, ran out of the house, terrified. Her excitement and fear quickly spread the news of what was occurring in the house to the rest of the area.

When people from the neighborhood gathered outside the home to see what was happening, the participants of the prayer meeting went out on the porch, and began to preach the message of Pentecost. One of the seven recipients of the baptism earlier in the evening was Jennie Moore, who would one day become Seymour's wife. She began to play beautiful music on an old upright piano, and to sing in what people said was Hebrew. Up until this time she had never played the piano, and although she never took a lesson, she was able to play the instrument for the rest of her life. The phenomenon of tongues and the dynamic message was so exciting that the next night even larger crowds gathered in the street in front of the house to hear Elder Seymour preach from a homemade pulpit on the front porch.

The stories of what happened on April 9, 1906, have become legendary among Pentecostals and, as all legends, tend to grow in the passing. The obvious parallels to the Pentecostal experience of the apostles in the New Testament Book of Acts seem to be casually discounted by secular historians.[20] In the absence of any contemporaneous testimony to the contrary, a detailed examination of the surviving testimonies of eyewitnesses makes one thing abundantly clear: Something of extraordinary proportions occurred at the simple four-room house on Bonnie Brae Street on the night of April 9, 1906. One eyewitness relates the occurrences in this way:

> They shouted three days and nights. It was Easter season. The people came from everywhere. By the next morning there was no way of getting near the house. As people came in they would fall under God's power; and the whole city was stirred. They shouted until the foundation of the house gave way, but no one was hurt.[21]

As evidenced by the attendance of people from many denominations and numerous independent churches at the meetings immediately following the April 9 occurrence, the religious segment of the city was indeed stirred. The secular world seemed to take no notice for nine days, or at least the record is bare, until the first newspaper reports appeared April 18, 1906. As corroborated by multiple testimonies after the occurrence of April 9, the meetings at the Bonnie Brae house did indeed run twenty-four hours a day for at least three days. People reported falling under the power of God and receiving the baptism with the Holy Spirit with the evidence of tongues while listening to Seymour preach from across the street.

The crowds grew so large it became impossible to get close to the house, and the press of people who tried to get into the house became so great that the foundation collapsed, sending the front porch crashing into the steep front yard. Miraculously, no one was hurt. Within one week it became necessary to find a larger location for the almost continuous prayer, praise, and worship service that had erupted on April 9, 1906.

The Azusa Street Mission

A quick search of the area turned up an abandoned two-story frame building on a short, two-block-long street in the old downtown industrial district, which was a part of the original African-American ghetto area. This building had originally housed the Stevens African Methodist Episcopal (AME) Church, but the church had followed the migration of its congrega-

From this humble building, the Azusa Street Mission in Los Angeles, Pentecostalism spread around the world.

tion and established itself farther south in a better part of town, changing its name to the First African Methodist Episcopal Church.

Since the church had moved out, the building had served as a wholesale house, a warehouse, a lumberyard, stockyards, a tombstone shop, and had most recently been used as a stable with rooms for rent upstairs. It was a small, rectangular, flat-roofed building, approximately 2,400 square feet (40 x 60) sided with weathered whitewashed clapboards. The only sign that it had once been a house of God was a single Gothic-style window over the main entrance.

In 1906 the building was in an advanced state of disrepair. The doors and windows were broken, and the entire building was filled with debris. Arthur Osterberg, besides being the pastor of the Full Gospel Church, was also the straw boss and timekeeper for the McNeil Construction Company.

THE AZUSA STREET MISSION

A DESCRIPTION FROM 1906

The center of this work is an old wooden Methodist church, marked for sale, partly burned out, recovered by a flat roof and made into two flats by a floor. It is unplastered, simply whitewashed on the rough boarding. Upstairs is a long room, furnished with chairs and three California redwood planks, laid end to end on backless chairs. This is the Pentecostal "upper room," where sanctified souls seek Pentecostal fulness, and go out speaking in new tongues and calling for the old-time references to "new wine." There are smaller rooms where hands are laid on the sick and "they recover" as of old. Below is a room 40 x 60 feet, filled with odds and ends of chairs, benches, and backless seats, where the curious and the eager sit for hours listening to strange sounds and songs and exhortations from the skies. In the center of the big room is a box on end, covered with cotton, which a junk man would value at about 15 cents. This is the pulpit from which is sounded forth what the leader, Brother Seymour, calls old-time repentance, old-time pardon, old-time sanctification, old-time power over devils and diseases, and the old-time "Baptism with the Holy Ghost and fire."

Meetings begin at 10 o'clock every morning and are continued until near midnight. There are three altar services daily. The altar is a plank on two chairs in the center of the room, and here the Holy Ghost falls on men and women and children in old Pentecostal fashion as soon as they have a clear experience of heart purity. Proud preachers and laymen with great heads, filled and inflated with all kinds of theories and beliefs, have come here from all parts, have humbled themselves and got down, not "in the straw," but "on" the straw matting, and have thrown away their notions, and have wept in conscious emptiness before God and begged to be "endued with power from on high," and every honest believer has received the wonderful incoming of the Holy Spirit to fill and thrill and melt and energize his physical frame and faculties, and the Spirit has witnessed to His presence by using the vocal organs in the speaking forth of a "new tongue." ■

—Article in *Way of Faith*, October 11, 1906, possibly by Frank Bartleman

He hired two men from his crew, and personally paid them, to replace the windows and doors in the building. The owner of the construction company, J. V. McNeil, who was himself a devout Catholic, donated lumber and other supplies. [22]

Seymour and a few others cleared the center of the ground floor of trash, spread sawdust on the floor, and placed raw wood planks on some empty nail kegs to provide seating for thirty or forty people. Elder Seymour did something unusual in the arrangement of the seating. In most churches at that time, the pulpit was situated at one end of the building, normally near an altar with the seating arranged from the altar to the opposite end of the building in paired rows. Seymour instead set the platform in the center of the seating arrangement with the pulpit in the center of the platform, and with low prayer altars running all around the platform. Two empty wooden crates (that are always described as shoe boxes) served as the pulpit.

The second floor was emptied of discarded building materials and other junk. It served as a large "Upper Room" where people would "tarry until they were endued with power from on high." The upstairs also did double duty as the sleeping quarters for Seymour and the rest of the full-time staff.

The first secular news reports of the revival appeared, as previously mentioned, on April 18, 1906. The *Los Angeles Daily Times* sent a reporter to an evening service on April 17, and he filed reports that were highly critical of the meetings as well as of the people who attended them. The dramatic new direction in holiness doctrine and practice that became the Pentecostal movement exploded on the secular scene when the paper reported that a "weird babel of tongues," was issuing from the poorer quarters of the city. The writer indicated his opinion of the services from the beginning of the article when he stated that the people at the meetings in question were, "breathing strange utterances and mouthing a creed which it would seem no sane mortal could understand." He went on to say:

> Meetings are held in a tumble-down shack on Azusa Street, near San Pedro Street, and the devotees of the weird doctrine practice the most fanatical rites, preach the wildest theories and work themselves into a state of mad excitement in their peculiar zeal. Colored people and a sprinkling of whites compose the congregation, and night is made hideous in the neighborhood by the howlings of the worshippers, who spend hours swaying forth and back in a nerve racking attitude of prayer and supplication. They claim to have the "gift of tongues" and to be able to understand the babel. [23]

Although the early secular press coverage of the Azusa Street revival was entirely negative, it served the purpose of free advertising and spread word of the outpouring far and wide. By the end of 1906, tracts and articles were being published and circulated as far away as London. While the meetings were still on Bonnie Brae Street and after they moved to the Azusa Street location, the police tried to break them up because they were blocking the streets, causing noise, and a general nuisance. Many eyewitnesses reported seeing a glow from the building that was visible from blocks away. Others reported hearing sounds emanating from the little wooden building like explosions that rocked the neighborhood. Due to these types of phenomena the Fire Department was called out on several occasions when a blaze or explosion was reported at the mission building. The Child Welfare Agency tried to shut down the meetings because there were unsupervised children within and around the building at all hours of the day and night. The Health Department tried to stop the meetings because they said the cramped quarters were unsanitary and a danger to public health.

The religious community came out early and loudly either for or against what was happening, both reactions attesting to the unusual nature of the events. Glenn A. Cook, who was a holiness street preacher in 1906 Los Angeles, said that he originally attended the meetings at Azusa, "thinking he might be able to straighten the people out in their doctrine." He goes on to add: "I was not alone in this effort, as many more preachers and gospel workers began to gather and contend with Brother Seymour."

Since the people who were attending the prayer meetings at the Asberry home, and later at the mission, were from many different churches, the word spread quickly among the religious-minded of Los Angeles. On the first Sunday after she was baptized with the Holy Spirit (Easter Sunday, 1906), Jennie Moore went to her home church, Pastor Smale's First New Testament Church, where she stood up after the sermon and spoke in tongues. This was not well received, and she soon moved her affiliation to the Azusa Street Mission.

Later, shortly after the meetings had moved to Azusa Street, Jennie Moore and Ruth Asberry went to the Peniel Mission where Jennie spoke in tongues as Ruth explained, "This is that prophesied by Joel." The entire congregation followed them to the Azusa Street Mission. Most of the churches, missions, and tent meetings in the area were affected immediately. Some lost so many people to the Azusa Street Mission that they closed their doors and attached themselves to the revival.

This was a disturbing development to many religious workers, and within a short time ministers were warning their flocks to stay away from the Azusa Street Mission. Some called the police and tried to get the meetings shut down. The two most prominent holiness leaders in Los Angeles at the time reacted somewhat differently. Pastor Smale at first supported the work, joining in the revival. But later he pulled back, denounced the Azusa Street Mission, and closed the doors of his church to the tongues-speakers.

Phineas Bresee of the Pentecostal Church of the Nazarene came out strongly against the "tongues movement." Apparently without ever visiting or investigating the Azusa Street Mission himself, he declared it to be a false revival, and told his people to remain separate. Bresee eventually changed the name of his denomination, dropping the word *Pentecostal* in 1919 so that no one would confuse his movement with the tongues-talking followers of Seymour. [24]

The majority of the institutional holiness movement, which had been so instrumental in praying for a new Pentecost, came out vehemently against the revival. The leader of the Pentecostal Union Church, Bishop Alma White, accused the Azusa Street Revival of worshiping the devil while promoting and practicing witchcraft and sexual immorality. These charges were published in a book with the arresting title *Demons Tongues.* Many of the holiness periodicals were quick to caution people that this could be a satanic counterfeit of what they were looking for, and within a short time began to say that the "tongues movement" was of the devil. One holiness leader went so far as to call it the "last vomit of Satan."

In spite of this criticism, people of all types—educated, uneducated, rich, poor, African-Americans, Asians, Hispanics, whites, men, women, native born, recent immigrants, and foreign visitors—prayed, sang, and came to the altar together. In the words of Frank Bartleman, "The color line was washed away in the blood."[25] Early photographs clearly show African-Americans, whites, men, and women, all in leadership roles. The relaxation of then current racial and sexual barriers represented a threat to many who were wedded to the prevailing status quo. This feature of the Azusa Street revival also helped to bring about the persecution of early Pentecostals as well as the widespread denial of the revival's validity.

Prompted by their newfound freedom and by the persecution they engendered, the newly energized Pentecostal believers sought to sweep away what they considered mere human constructions, such as conventional denominational hierarchies. The Pentecostals wanted to replace these structures with divinely inspired governance based upon the model of the Bible. In the tradition of most renewal or revival movements, the early Pentecostals did not view themselves as a separate entity. They saw themselves instead as a movement "within" the Christian church meant by God to once again bring life to an overorganized and spiritless body.

The leaders never encouraged the formation of separate "Pentecostal" denominations. They referred to themselves and their movement as "undenominationalism." On the whole they attempted to remain within their previous affiliations and spread the new Pentecostal theology. This was called "sharing the truth" by the Pentecostals and "infiltration" by their traditional brothers.

These antistructuralist tendencies also surfaced in the worship patterns established by the Azusa Street Mission. Following their belief that the Holy Spirit would guide all believers and not just leaders, everyone was free to speak, even during the services, erasing the lines between clergy and congregation. They also taught that the Holy Spirit and the gospel should not be confined within the four walls of a church building. And so, they took every opportunity to witness, on the job or on the street, and in doing so, erased the lines between sacred and profane space. Further, their belief that the Holy Spirit should be free to direct the services however He wished led to singing and testimonies, preaching, and teaching to be mixed haphazardly throughout the meeting, thus erasing the boundaries between ecclesiastical liturgy and what some claimed was spiritual anarchy.

The ultimate antistructuralist phenomenon associated with the Azusa Street revival was of course the benchmark of the experience, speaking in tongues. Here was an experience that truly cast aside the constraints of human convention and gave free rein to the Spirit. In ecstatic speech the action of human agency was completely denied, and the basic structure of language itself was set aside. In all the varied ecstatic occurrences of the revival, from falling under the power to miracle healings, the transparency of the line between ordinary and extraordinary stands out as the unifying feature. Ultimately it was this blurring of lines, this blending of races and sexes, this routinization of the holy that turned so many religious people into inveterate enemies and brought about the years of persecution and isolation that the descendants of Azusa Street were going to endure. These antistructuralist tendencies continued to surface in a variety of ways, all of which led to deep animosity between the early Pentecostals and other Christians. This animosity in turn led to many of the early Pentecostals being rejected by their original denominations.

Another perspective from which to analyze the world-shaking revival ignited on April 1906 is that of economics. From the beginning, the vast majority of the leaders as well as the followers of the Pentecostal message were drawn from the lower working classes. One of the chief accusations often directed at the adherents of modern Pentecost was that they were illiterate and uneducated, this lack of refinement being used as evidence of their gullibility and foolishness.

News Reports

Exhibiting the religious and racial prejudices of the period, the *Los Angeles Times* and most of the other Los Angeles newspapers had a journalistic feeding frenzy in reporting the Azusa Street meetings. In describing Seymour and his followers, the *Times* said:

> An old colored exhorter, blind in one eye, is the majordomo of the company. With his stony optic fixed on some luckless unbeliever, yells his defiance and challenges an answer. Anathemas are heaped upon him who shall dare to gainsay the utterances of the preacher. Clasped in his big fist the colored brother holds a miniature Bible from which he reads at intervals one or two words—never more. After an hour spent in exhortation the brethren present are invited to join in a "meeting of prayer and testimony." Then it is that pandemonium breaks loose, and the bounds of reason are passed by those who are "filled with the spirit" whatever that may be. "You-oo-po goo-ioo-ioo come under the bloo-oo-oo-boo-ido," shouts an old colored "mammy," in a frenzy of religious zeal. Swinging her arms wildly about her she continues with the strangest harange (sic) ever uttered. Few of her words are intelligible and for the most part her testimony contains the most outrageous jumble of syllables, which are listened to with awe by the company. [26]

Many eyewitnesses gave other accounts, however. "I felt a pulling sensation. I couldn't have turned away if I wanted to." This was how one eyewitness, A. C. Valdez, described his first visit to the mission. He further relates that as he and his mother walked into the building a chill wind touched them, and they were suddenly trembling, in Los Angeles in the summer. Looking around, Valdez noticed that everyone was trembling and he felt as if he was surrounded by God.

There were as many as nine services a day, starting early in the morning and running late into the night. For weeks on end the meetings would blend into one another and last twenty-four hours a day. The building was always open, and the meetings started themselves without a leader to initiate them.

Pentecostal Worship on Azusa Street

At one meeting, which was termed "typical" by a member of the congregation, early in the service an elder opened with the following statement of instruction and warning:

We have no planned program, nor are we afraid of anarchy or crooked spirits. God the Holy Spirit is able to control and protect His work. If any strange manifestations come, trust the Holy Spirit, keep in prayer, and you will see the word of wisdom go forth, a rebuke, an exhortation that will close the door on the enemy and show the victory won. God can use any member of the body, and He often gives the more abundant honor to the weaker members. [27]

The meetings would normally open with prayer, praise, and testimony punctuated by messages in tongues, and a cappella singing in both English and unknown languages. The heavenly quality of the harmonies achieved by the unrehearsed and nonprofessional singers was commented on by supporters and detractors alike. One enthusiastic observer said:

Especially did the enchanting strains of the so-called "Heavenly Choir," or hymns sung under the evident direction of the Holy Spirit both as to words and tune, thrill my whole being. It was not something that could be repeated at will, but supernaturally given for each special occasion and was one of the most indisputable evidences of the presence of the power of God. Perhaps nothing so greatly impressed people as this singing; at once inspiring a holy awe, or a feeling of indescribable wonder, especially if the hearers were in devout attitude. [28]

When someone would receive an anointing for a message, they would stand and preach. If they were acting out of the flesh they were soon convicted and sat back down. The power of God would flow through the room at different times knocking people down in ones, twos, and sometimes by the hundreds. Often masses of people would simultaneously rush to the altar to seek after God. [29]

After the personal testimonies of the locals in attendance, letters were often read from people who had heard of the revival and were inspired to seek the baptism with the Holy Spirit. Thousands of letters attest that many from around the world eventually received the baptism with the Holy Spirit after merely hearing of the Azusa Street outpouring and asking God to touch them where they were. The reading of these letters would generally lead into intense praise as visitors from around the world added personal testimonies that reenforced the spreading character of the revival. Another common topic of the testimonies was how people were drawn to the revival. Some reported first hearing about the revival through visions, some by dreams, and some by unusual circumstances that brought them there with no prior knowledge of what was occurring.

Regarding testimonies of the healings associated with the early Pentecostal movement, Martin E. Marty, the renowned historian of religion, said: "The healing testimonials are so astounding, and recur with such frequency, in so many contexts, one can hardly fail to be awed."[30]

One example that is fairly typical of many concerns a young girl. One night she was baptized with the Holy Spirit, and the next morning she walked into the meeting where she saw a woman who had been crippled for thirty-two years. The young girl walked up to the woman and said, "Jesus wants to heal you." The woman's toes and feet straightened out immediately and she walked out.

There were no hymnbooks or programs, and no collections were taken

AZUSA STREET IN THE LOS ANGELES TIMES

On April 18, 1906, the first news report on the Azusa Street meeting appeared in the *Los Angeles Times*. It was first-page news. According to Bartleman, this "shameful" coverage by the press "only drew more crowds."

The words used to describe the meeting—*weird, fanatical, irreverent, mad, wild*—indicate the utter contempt the secular press held for the early Pentecostals. It was this type of press that Bartleman, as a sympathetic observer and participant, tried to overcome. On their part, the Pentecostals claimed that reporters were converted when they heard Azusa Street worshipers speaking in their native European languages.

In the following story the reporter correctly judged that "the newest religious sect has started in Los Angeles." The prophecy at the close of the article about "awful destruction" was immediately fulfilled. On the next day California was hit by the most destructive earthquake in its history. But although Los Angeles felt the shocks, her sister city, San Francisco, was nearly destroyed. The day after this article appeared, April 19, 1906, headlines in the *Los Angeles Times* proclaimed that the "heart is torn" from San Francisco. The early Pentecostals made much of the earthquake as being a parallel to the "spiritual earthquake" at Azusa Street.

■ ■ ■

WEIRD BABEL OF TONGUES
NEW SECT OF FANATICS IS BREAKING LOOSE
WILD SCENE LAST NIGHT ON AZUSA STREET
GURGLE OF WORDLESS TALK BY A SISTER

Breathing strange utterances and mouthing a creed which it seems no sane mortal could understand, the newest religious sect has started in Los Angeles. Meetings are held in a tumbledown shack on Azusa Street, near San Pedro Street, and devotees of the weird doctrine practice the most fanatical rites, preach the wildest theories and work themselves into a state of mad excitement in their peculiar zeal. Colored people and a sprinkling of whites compose the congregation, and night is made hideous in the neighborhood by the howlings of the worshippers who spend hours swaying forth and back in a nerve-racking [sic] attitude of prayer and supplication. They claim to have "the gift of tongues," and to be able to comprehend the babel.

Such a startling claim has never yet been made by any company of fanatics, even in Los Angeles, the home of almost numberless creeds. Sacred tenets, reverently mentioned by the orthodox believer, are dealt with in a familiar, if not irreverent, manner by these latest religionists.

Stony Optic Defies

An old colored exhorter, blind in one eye, is the majordomo of the company. With his stony optic fixed on some luckless unbeliever, the old man yells his defiance and challenges an answer. Anathemas are heaped upon him who shall dare to gainsay the utterances of the preacher.

Clasped in his big fist the colored brother holds a miniature Bible from which he reads at intervals one or two words—never more. After an hour spent in exhortation the bretheren [sic] present are invited to join in a "meeting of prayer, song and testimony." Then it is that pandemonium breaks loose, and the bounds of reason are passed by those who are "filled with the spirit," whatever that may be.

"You-oo-oo gou-loo-loo come under the bloo-oo-oo boo-loo," shouts an old colored "mammy," in a frenzy of religious zeal. Swinging her arms wildly about her, she continues with the strangest harangue ever uttered. Few of her words are intelligible, and for the most part her testimony contains the most outrageous jumble of syllables, which are listened to with awe by the company.

Let Tongues Come Forth

One of the wildest of the meetings was held last night, and the highest pitch of excitement was reached by the gathering, which continued to "worship" until nearly midnight. The old exhorter urged the "sisters" to let the "tongues come forth" and the women gave themselves over to a riot of religious fervor. As a result a buxom dame was overcome with excitement and almost fainted.

Undismayed by the fearful attitude of the colored worshipper, another black women [sic] jumped to the floor and began a wild gesticulation, which ended in a gurgle of wordless prayers which were nothing less than shocking.

"She's speakin' in unknown tongues," announced the leader, in ah [sic] awed whisper, "keep on sister." The sister continued until it was necessary to assist her to a seat because of her bodily fatigue.

Gold Among Them

Among the "believers" is a man who claims to be a Jawish [sic] rabbi. He says his name is Gold, and claims to have held positions in some of the largest synagogues in the United States. He told the motley company last night that he is well known to the Jewish people of Los Angeles and San Francisco, and referred to prominent local citizens by name. Gold claims to have been miraculously healed and is a convert of the new sect. Another speaker had a vision in which he saw the people of Los Angeles flocking in a mighty stream to perdition. He prophesied awful destruction to this city unless its citizens are brought to a belief in the tenets of the new faith. ■

—*LOS ANGELES TIMES*, APRIL 18, 1906

up. A sign on the wall over an open offering box proclaimed, "Settle with the Lord." There were no prearranged subjects or sermons; everything was left to the spontaneous move of God. The pulpit, as previously stated, was composed of two large wooden "shoe boxes." Elder Seymour would usually sit behind these, deep in prayer with his head buried inside the top box.

When Seymour did preach he emphasized the need to renounce sin and accept Jesus as personal Savior. He did not accentuate tongues or any other manifestation. Many times he told people that if they were to tell others about the revival they should tell them about Jesus, that He was Lord, and of the many people saved. He also encouraged all people to experience the power of God, turn from the world, leave the rigid traditions and legalisms of formal Christianity and instead seek after salvation, sanctification, and the baptism with the Holy Spirit. Two other messages heavily accentuated by all the different preachers at the Azusa Street revival concerned divine healing and the premillennial return of Jesus. [31]

The meetings were attended by members of many denominations and independent churches, some well educated and some quite refined. Pastors, evangelists, and foreign missionaries all came to participate and receive blessings. The personal testimonies from people of foreign extraction who were convicted of sin and sought salvation after hearing someone who did not know their native language exhorting them in that language are very numerous.

The prayer services in the sanctuary were usually short, although prayer was continuous on the second floor. The people would pray as a group for any needs that were brought before them. The worship service consisted of singing, shouting, and ejaculatory prayers. The services were very lively and there was no wasted time. The description of one visitor was that "prayer and worship were everywhere. The altar area was filled with seekers; some kneeling, others were prone on the floor, some were speaking in tongues. Everyone was doing something, all seemingly were lost in God." [32]

Scores of personal and eyewitness accounts attest that many who came to ridicule the meetings were knocked to the floor where they seemed to wrestle with unseen opponents, sometimes for hours. These people generally arose convicted of sin and seeking God. One foreign-born reporter had been assigned by his paper to record the "circuslike" atmosphere in a comic-relief fashion. He attended a nighttime meeting, sitting far in the back. In the midst of the meeting a young woman began to testify about how God had baptized her with the Holy Spirit when she suddenly broke into tongues.

After the meeting the reporter sought her out and asked her where she had learned the language of his native country. She answered that she didn't have any idea what she had said, and that she spoke only English. He then related to her that she had given an entirely accurate account of his sinful life, all in the language of his native tongue.

Immediately the reporter renounced his sins and accepted Jesus as his personal Savior. After this, the young man returned to his newspaper and told them he could not write the false, ridiculing piece they sent him to produce. The reporter then offered to write a truthful story of what had happened to him at the mission. His employers fired him on the spot.

These few examples of the types of events experienced during the meetings at the Azusa Street Mission, according to the literature available, may serve as a synopsis of regularly occurring patterns. The meetings were attended by hundreds and thousands at a time with many more crowded around outside listening at the windows.

The Ebb and Flow of Revival

The massive appeal of the revival had two peaks, from 1906 to 1909 and again from 1911 to 1912. The first peak ran continuously from the initial outpouring on Bonnie Brae Street. After exploding on the religious scene in Los Angeles and gaining worldwide attention, the Azusa Street revival about 1909 entered a period lacking in either spectacular attendance or noteworthy occurrence.

According to Frank Bartleman, this initial phase eventually fell off because of the rise of sectarianism, formality, and ritual. Such things as putting a name on the building, setting up a "throne" for Elder Seymour, and imposing a stricter order on the services caused growing division and slowed the flow of ecstatic manifestations.[33]

Another factor credited with causing the revival to come to an end after 1909 was the nearly unanimous refusal of the majority of the Christian community to accept the revival as genuine. Previous revivals, such as the First and Second Great Awakenings, were widely accepted and greeted initially with great fervor by the general public. This rejection was based on several reasons. First, an antagonism was engendered by the feeling that the Pentecostals saw themselves as a spiritual aristocracy. The Pentecostals acted as if they had received special insights regarding the baptism with the Holy Spirit, the gifts of the Spirit, and the correct method for worship.

The second cause for this failure was one of the distinguishing marks of the Azusa Street revival, the egalitarian quality of the meetings. This feature of the meetings offended many and contributed to the end of the initial phase of the revival. The diverse nature of the ethnic groups, races, and cultures that were brought together at the Azusa Street revival, which was seen as a sign of God's presence, became a source of divisiveness. As other issues based upon theology and practice arose, the underlying differences of the people and other social factors, such as race, class, and previous religious affiliation, acted to influence the depth and duration of the resulting splits and schisms. These racial and other social conflicts eventually led Elder Seymour to feel that his "dream of an interracial Pentecostal movement that would serve as a positive witness to a racially segregated America" was swiftly unraveling. [34]

The most telling blow to the initial peak of the revival may well have been related to racial reasons. Two white women, Clara Lum and Florence Crawford, who had helped publish the Azusa Street Mission's paper, *Apostolic Faith* (which by 1909 had a circulation in excess of 50,000), removed the mailing lists with the agreement of Seymour but without the permission of the board of elders. They then relocated the publication to Mrs. Crawford's Portland, Oregon, headquarters. With the loss of the mailing lists the Azusa Street Mission was effectively cut off from its worldwide base of support and soon lost its resources and its influence. [35]

During the lull, Elder Seymour worked at building the apostolic ministry of the Pacific Apostolic Faith Mission, Inc., which he had incorporated in December 1906. Traveling extensively, Seymour spread the message of Pentecost from Maine to San Diego. He was honored by the Church of God in Christ as an apostle and often addressed their meetings. During the many long periods of absence occasioned by Elder Seymour's preaching missions, his wife, Jennie Evans Moore Seymour, usually led the Azusa Street Mission, which was at the time a small African-American church. Elder Seymour and the young lady, who had miraculously gained the musical skill to play the piano at the prayer meeting in the Asberry home on Bonnie Brae Street on April 9, 1906, were married on May 13, 1908. This marriage was vigorously opposed by both Clara Lum and Florence Crawford, who felt that due to the nearness of the Second Coming there was no time for Seymour to marry. Others suspected that Clara Lum, a white woman, had hoped that Seymour would choose her as his bride.

Also during this lull, the racial problems of the Pentecostal movement were accentuated. Elder Seymour, while honored and sought after by the quickly growing African-American Pentecostal churches, was often ignored by whites. The hostile racial climate and the increasing racial tensions of the times were blamed by many whites for their abandonment of the Azusa Street revival and of Elder Seymour as they either joined or formed racially exclusive denominations and splinter groups.

There was a total lack of newspaper coverage during the lull. Neither the secular nor the religious press reported evidence of miraculous events occurring at the Azusa Street Mission. Between the two peaks, the Azusa Street Mission served as a small local, mostly African-American congregation presided over by Elder Seymour, with nothing to distinguish it from the hundreds of other small African-American Pentecostal churches in the Los Angeles area. Within days of the beginning of the second peak in 1911, the meetings at the Azusa Street Mission were being attended by only a dozen people, all of them African-American.

William Durham and the New Glory Days at Azusa Street

The second peak began in February 1911, when William F. Durham (1873–1912) of Chicago came to the Azusa Street Mission for a preaching mission. Durham was originally from Kentucky, and his first religious affiliation was in the Baptist church, which he joined in 1891. According to his own testimony he did not experience conversion until 1898 when he had a vision of the crucified Christ while traveling through Minnesota. After this life-changing experience Durham immediately devoted the rest of his life to full-time ministry.

In 1901 Durham founded and became the pastor of the North Avenue Mission in Chicago. This holiness mission was located in an area populated by immigrants. As a pastor he preached salvation, sanctification, and healing. Durham also taught that denominational structures were "the greatest hindrance to the advancement of the real cause of Jesus Christ."[36]

When he first heard of the Azusa Street revival, Durham was encouraging and positive in his statements about it. However, within a short time he began to question the theological stance that speaking in tongues was the ever present first initial evidence of baptism with the Holy Spirit. However, when people that he knew began to speak in tongues, he studied the idea further and decided that "all experiences [he] had ever seen, [his] own included, were far below the standard God lifted up in the Acts." Durham eventually visited the Azusa Street Mission in 1907. Later he would say that from his first entrance into the Azusa Street Mission he was aware of God's presence. The pastor from Chicago sought and received the baptism with the Holy Spirit as evidenced by speaking in tongues on March 2, 1907. At the time of Durham's baptism with the Holy Spirit, Elder Seymour prophesied that "wherever Durham preached there would be an outpouring of the Holy Spirit." Upon returning to his church in Chicago, Durham worked tirelessly at spreading the Pentecostal message. The meetings at the North Avenue Mission were soon crowded past capacity as people from throughout the Midwest came to receive the baptism with the Holy Spirit. Many ministers came to hear what Durham had to say and then carried the Pentecostal message home to their own churches. There were also many manifestations of healing reported at Durham's meetings. Aimee Semple, before she married her second husband, Harold McPherson, later reported that she had been healed instantaneously of a broken ankle at one of Durham's Chicago meetings.

Durham and the "Finished Work" Controversy

In 1911 Durham transferred most of his work to Los Angeles. He was experiencing trouble with the leadership of the North Avenue Mission, and he also wanted to center his ministry in the birthplace of modern Pentecostalism. He originally started this new phase of ministry as a preaching mission at the Upper Room Mission in Los Angeles, but they had ejected him over his new theological teaching of the "Finished Work." This teaching repudiated the holiness doctrine of sanctification as a second work of grace and instead declared that everything a believer would ever need was included in the work of Christ on the cross. Durham contended that when Christ said, "It is finished," everything was accomplished—salvation, sanctification, healing, and the baptism with the Holy Spirit. He taught that the only thing required for a believer to access all this was an acceptance of its reality.

This new teaching reenergized the revival and, according to Frank Bartleman, "The fire began to fall at old Azusa as at the beginning." Some called Durham a "pulpit prodigy" who induced his followers into shouting manifestations that critics called "the Durham jerks." The building was once again filled to capacity and people crowded around the windows and doors to hear the revolutionary preacher and his new teaching. Many other missions and churches suspended services and came to hear Durham. The Chicago evangelist stressed salvation by faith alone and his services were marked by reports of mighty miracles and many of the same manifestations of the Spirit that had accompanied the first great peak of activity at the Azusa Street Mission.

These meetings had begun and progressed while Elder Seymour was on a preaching mission back east. As the news of this second peak in attendance spread it was accompanied by the growing controversy over the "Finished Work" theology. When Elder Seymour heard about it he rushed back to combat the perceived heresy. Seymour returned in 1912 and promptly locked Durham out of the Azusa Street Mission. When Durham left the crowds followed him as he started a competing mission in another part of the city, and thus the second peak of the revival passed. [37]

Azusa Street Pilgrims Spread Across America

In the Los Angeles area by 1912, while the Azusa Street Mission was still in operation, the number of churches and missions that directly traced their beginning to the Azusa Street revival was impressive. Each of the following Pentecostal churches was founded and led by people who had received the baptism with the Holy Spirit at the Azusa Street Mission and then moved on to work in other arms of the city.

One of Elder Seymour's original board members, James Alexander, founded two Apostolic Faith missions, one at Seventh and Setous, the other on Fifty-first Street. Another Pentecostal Assembly in Los Angeles was founded by W. F. Manley. A Spanish Apostolic Faith mission was soon flourishing under the guidance of G. Valenzuella. Two other places of worship were founded and directed by William Saxby: the Apostolic Faith Rescue Mission on First Street and the Carr Street Pentecostal Mission. An Italian Pentecostal mission was founded and led by John Perron. The Upper Room Mission was established by Elmer Fisher. Two men, Frank Bartleman and John Pendleton, were the founding pastors of the Eighth and Maple Mission. The Florence Avenue Pentecostal Mission was led by W. L. Sargent. A. G. Osterberg was in charge at the Full Gospel Assembly, and William Durham from Chicago had founded and was preaching at the Seventh Street Mission.

Several leaders of previously existing denominations also came to the Azusa Street Mission, received the baptism with the Holy Spirit, and then returned home to lead their denominations, either partially or wholly, into the Pentecostal ranks. The first of these, Charles H. Mason, founder of the Church of God in Christ, came to Azusa Street for an extended visit in 1907. Upon returning to his headquarters in Memphis, he and the message of Pentecost were rejected by the majority of the church. This led to a split in the church in 1907, when Mason and those who agreed with him reorganized the Church of God in Christ as a Pentecostal denomination. As the only early convert to Pentecostalism who came from a legally incorporated church, Bishop Mason played a vital part in the spread of the movement and its message. Through his practice of ordaining ministers of all races, he acted as a conduit for the fire of the Azusa Street revival to reach all parts of the United States. Between the years 1909 and 1914 there were as many white congregations in the Church of God in Christ as African-American. Today the Church of God in Christ is the largest of all Pentecostal denominations and the fastest growing church in America.

Gaston B. Cashwell (1862–1916), a preacher of the Pentecostal Holiness Church of North Carolina, read the articles by Frank Bartleman in the *Way of Faith* published by J. M. Pike in Columbia, South Carolina. Traveling to Los Angeles in 1907, he was at first repulsed by the noise and emotion in the Azusa Street Mission and initially rejected the movement, mainly because it was led by an African-American. Subsequently, he was convicted of his sin, repented, and received the baptism with the Holy Spirit when several young African-American boys prayed for him.

Returning to his home in Dunn, North Carolina, Cashwell began holding a series of meetings in January of 1907 that developed into an East Coast Pentecostal revival of epic proportions. He is known today as the "Apostle of Pentecost to the South." It was through this spin-off of the Azusa Street revival in North Carolina that the Fire-Baptized Holiness Church, the Pentecostal Holiness Church, and a substantial wing of the Free-Will Baptist Church (which later organized as the Pentecostal Free-Will Baptist Church) were swept into the ranks of the Pentecostal movement.

Leaders of several holiness Bible schools accepted the doctrines espoused by Seymour and the Azusa Street revival as propagated through the ministry of G. B. Cashwell. N. J. Holmes of the Altamont Bible School in Greenville, South Carolina, along with almost the entire student body and faculty, embraced the teachings of Pentecost. From 1907 onward, the Altamont Bible School (later known as Holmes Bible College) became a center for Pentecostal study, ministry, and evangelism.

Other denominations that either joined the Pentecostal ranks or were formed through the Azusa-inspired preaching of G. B. Cashwell were the Church of God (Cleveland Tenn.), the Church of God (Mountain Assembly), and the Pentecostal Association of the Mississippi Valley. Several individual Methodist, Baptist, and Presbyterian churches accepted the Azusa Street message, left their previous affiliations, and joined the newly forming Pentecostal denominations.

The movement of Pentecost following Cashwell's visit to Azusa Street was repeated all over the United States. Florence Crawford, a former board member from the Azusa Street Mission who had been miraculously healed of spinal meningitis, established a flourishing work in Portland, Oregon. Marie Brown carried the Pentecostal flame to New York City, where she and her husband, Robert, founded and pastored the Glad Tidings Tabernacle. William Durham returned to his previously established holiness mission in Chicago and started a series of meetings that became the focal point of the Midwest. Roswell Flower also influenced the Midwest through a successful Pentecostal mission he established in Indianapolis, Indiana. Likewise, Canada was soon set ablaze for Pentecost through the itinerant ministry of A. H. Argue.

The new movement was not confined to North America. Both missionaries from and visitors to Azusa Street quickly spread the Pentecostal message around the world. Not surprisingly, it was the same class of people who accepted the message in the United States—workers, peasants, and generally those at the low end of the socioeconomic scale—who were the most receptive. Once again, as in the United States, it was among those who had previously embraced the holiness message that Pentecostalism found its easiest and largest number of converts.

For Further Reading

The earliest history of the Pentecostal movement in the United States written from inside the movement was Stanley Frodsham's 1926 book *With Signs Following: The Story of the Pentecostal Revival in the Twentieth Century* (Springfield, Mo.: Gospel Publishing House, 1926, 1946). Several other later competent histories include Klaud Kendrick's *The Promise Fulfilled: A History of the American Pentecostal Movement* (Springfield, Mo.: Gospel Publishing House, 1961); John Nichols's *Pentecostalism* (New York: Harper & Row, 1966); and Vinson Synan's *The Holiness-Pentecostal Movement in the United States* (Grand Rapids: Eerdmans, 1971). Synan's book was revised in 1997 under the title *The Holiness-Pentecostal Tradition: Charismatic Movements in the Twentieth Century* (Grand Rapids: Eerdmans).

The first scholar to publish research on the worldwide spread of the movement was the Swiss historian Walter Hollenweger, who in 1966 produced a ten-volume Ph.D. study in German with the title *Handbuch der Pfingstbewegung* (Pentecostal Handbook). A revision and condensation of this monumental work appeared in 1972 under the title *The Pentecostals: The Charismatic Movement in the Churches* (Minneapolis: Augsburg Press). In 1979, Robert Mapes Anderson published a history using a marxist critical approach. It was titled *Vision of the Disinherited: The Making of American Pentecostalism* (New York: Oxford Univ. Press).

The story of Parham's role in Topeka is covered in a book by his wife titled *The Life of Charles Fox Parham: Founder of the Apostolic Faith Movement* (Joplin, Mo.: Tri-State Printing Company, 1944). The major scholarly study of William Seymour is Douglas Nelson's unpublished 1981 Ph.D. dissertation titled "For Such a Time as This: The Story of Bishop William J. Seymour and the Azusa Street Revival" (Univ. of Birmingham, UK). A thorough and readable account of the Azusa Street meetings is Robert Owens's *Speak to the Rock: The Azusa Street Revival, Its Roots and Its Message* (Lanham, Md.: Univ. Press of America, 1998). The worldwide influence of Azusa Street is covered in Cecil M. Robeck's "The International Significance of Azusa Street" in *Pneuma,* Spring 1986.

· 4 ·
To the Regions Beyond: The Global Expansion of Pentecostalism

Gary B. McGee

CHRISTIANITY SAW ITS MOST vigorous advance around the world to date in the 19th century. American and European missionaries evangelized, planted churches, taught school, translated the Scriptures, and operated charitable ministries for the hurting. Despite sending thousands of missionaries and spending millions of dollars, however, the number of converts appeared meager given the investment: only 3.6 million on the foreign fields by 1900. Even so, when the "Great Century" in Christian missions, a term coined by historian Kenneth Scott Latourette, came to an end in 1910 at the World Missionary Conference at Edinburgh, Scotland, confidence in the future knew no limits.

Delegates anticipated that the meeting would awaken a new dawn in missions. China missionary Jonathan Goforth hoped for a "new Pentecost." But when only a few speakers, including him, highlighted the power of the Holy Spirit, his hopes plunged. Having seen the miraculous in his own ministry, he knew that nothing less than the empowerment of God the Holy Spirit could bring closure to the Great Commission. Instead, most of the presenters focused on cooperation and unity, missionary preparation, and communications. "Was there ever such an incomparable opportunity for Christian leaders[?]" he asked. "Alas! It was only a dream," he said with sadness, but then added, "Brethren, the Spirit of God is with us still. Pentecost is yet within our grasp."[1]

Though Edinburgh marked a watershed in several positive ways, Goforth surmised that church and mission leaders had prioritized relationships and mechanics over the pursuit of spiritual dynamics that had propelled early Christian evangelism. Stories of miracles and "spiritual warfare" in faraway places had gripped the imagination of the faithful, but for many they represented exceptions to the normal process of mission work. For example, the Methodist "missionary Elijah," W. J. Davies, commanded rain to fall in a successful encounter with witch doctors in South Africa during a drought. On more than one occasion, enemies of Ludwig Nommensen in Sumatra poisoned his food. Each attempt failed and reminded some observers of Mark 16:18: "And if they drink anything deadly, it will by no means hurt them." In China, the venerable Pastor Hsi adopted the name "Shengmo"—the "demon overcomer"—because of his numerous confrontations with evil spirits.

Over the course of the century, untold numbers of Christians at home and abroad ardently prayed for the outpouring of the Spirit. How else could the mission of the church be accomplished? Some thought the Welsh revival and its tributaries (e.g., India, Korea) might have signaled the beginning of the great end-time revival, except they had run their course by the time Goforth registered at the conference. Now, with the rain clouds already overhead, they wondered when the showers would turn into the promised downpour.

While Edinburgh ended with a triumphant sense of unity and achievement, cracks soon surfaced in the foundation of the mission enterprise. Questions arose over the ultimate claims of Christianity, such as salvation solely through the redemptive work of Jesus Christ, the lostness of humankind, and the authority of Scripture. On the one hand, these disagreements fractured the fellowship and cooperative activities of missionaries; and the reverberations went all the way back to the home base. In America the Fundamentalist/modernist controversy raged through the mainline churches and the results led in part to the long-term shrinkage of their missionary rosters. On the other hand, missionaries with holiness and Keswick "Higher Life" beliefs, along with conservatives in the independent "faith missions" and denominational agencies, maintained their evangelical witness.

Amid the changing scenario, a new pattern of mission appeared, one with an almost unprecedented belief that supernatural demonstrations of power would accompany the preaching of the gospel. To outsiders, it looked like all caution about seeking the charismatic gifts had been thrown

to the wind. Little could the Edinburgh conferees have realized the ultimate magnitude of the Pentecostal revival that had begun just a few years
before, if they were even aware of it. "Signs and wonders" (Acts 5:12) were
a thing of the past for most mission leaders, having ceased in the first century in practice if not by God's sovereign choice. As a radically innovative
movement of the Holy Spirit, Pentecostalism remained loyal to the historic
truths of the faith, but turned the cessationist hourglass upside down by
showing that miracles had not ended with the last of the apostles. Pentecostals pressed to recapture the apostolic dimension of the early church,
especially with their emphasis on speaking in tongues and prayer for the
sick. Not surprisingly, this scandalized other Christians who feared the potential extremes of experiential piety.

Pentecostal periodicals would eventually carry thousands of accounts
of conversions, healings, deliverances from chemical addictions, and exorcisms. Believers would also tell of being guided by visions and dreams as
predicted by the Old Testament prophet Joel (2:28). Indeed, Pentecostals
saw their own initiatives in evangelism as a "last days" restoration of New
Testament Christianity—Acts 29!

Into All the World

Staying at a missionary hostel in New York City in November 1906, four
years before the Edinburgh conclave, the English Methodist pastor
Thomas B. Barratt eagerly waited for news regarding the happenings at
the Apostolic Faith Mission on Azusa Street in Los Angeles, California. De-
siring to be baptized in the Holy Spirit himself, friends laid hands on him
in prayer after which an unusual brightness like a "tongue of fire" came
over his head. He recalled being filled with light, experiencing a newfound
spiritual power, being overcome by a burden for global evangelization,
and preaching and praying in divinely given languages.[2]

His testimony reveals the overriding ethos of Pentecostalism: the urgency to evangelize the world ahead of the imminent return of Jesus
Christ. Pentecostals declared that the Spirit would equip a new breed of
missionaries by dispensing unlearned human languages so they could bypass years of formal study to preach immediately upon reaching their destinations. Though another understanding of tongues-speech would
gradually prevail, this revolutionary agenda sparked an explosion of spiritual energy. This chapter explores the expansion of Pentecostalism from
early revival centers and examines how Spirit-filled believers took the
Good News to the "regions beyond" (2 Cor. 10:16).

THOMAS BALL BARRATT AND ALEXANDER BODDY

Less than six months into the Azusa Street revival, reports of what God was doing had spread far and wide. Many had already made the trek to the small mission in Los Angeles, or they had at least heard about the revival. Many had read about it in the religious press.

Thomas Ball Barratt was among those amazed at the reports coming from the Apostolic Faith Mission. Barratt, an English Methodist minister, was touring the United States in 1907 trying to raise money for his missions work in Norway when he first caught wind of the revival. He promptly began seeking for his own "Pentecost"—the baptism in the Holy Spirit—sometimes praying upward of 12 hours.

"Dear Friends in Los Angeles," Barratt finally was able to announce, "Glory to God. Tongues of fire have descended and His wondrous power has been displayed." He would never forget the night it happened, and he wanted others to know. "I was filled with light and such a power that I began to shout as loud as I could in a foreign language." He did not stop until 4 the next morning.

After receiving the Baptism, Barratt was eager to return to Norway, so he could share the experience with his congregation and with anyone else who would listen. Though some opposed the new teaching, many did not. In Europe, as in America, the Pentecostal message spread like wildfire.

While Barratt was still in New York, he wrote his congregation back home to tell them of his experience, which ignited a spirit of expectancy. When he returned, the field was ripe. In Norway, he began holding meetings in Christiana (present-day Oslo), which were soon packed with eager seekers—as well as curious and skeptical onlookers. Describing the scenes, he wrote: "Several have been in trances and had heavenly visions. Some have seen Jesus at our meetings, and the tongues of fire have been seen again over my head by a free-thinker, convicting him of the power of God." He went on to report that the fire was spreading rapidly, thanks to those who had attended the meetings and had taken the "fire" with them and thanks to the religious press, which covered the events.

One of the more visible visitors was Alexander Boddy, an Anglican vicar. He too was swept up in the revival. In the fall of 1907, Boddy invited Barratt to speak at his church, All Saints, in Sunderland, England, and there, too, revival broke out. It quickly became the movement's center in Great Britain. Another visitor, Lewi Pethrus, returned to Stockholm and became the father of the Swedish Pentecostal movement.

Not only were many visiting revival hot spots, such as Christiana and Sunderland, but many more were reading about the revival in religious periodicals. One paper in England claimed, "Tons of free literature have been sent out from Sunderland to every part of the world." Boddy's paper, *Confidence*, became a mouthpiece for the movement in England. Barratt and Boddy both dedicated themselves to the fledgling movement in northern Europe and became its de facto leaders. From their centers, the revival fanned out across Europe; missionaries took the Pentecostal message to Switzerland, Germany, Holland, Finland, and far beyond. ▪

—ED GITRE
PENTECOSTAL EVANGEL

The diaspora of Pentecostal evangelists and missionaries bore fruit not only in Europe and America, but in other parts of the world as well. Barratt was just one of many pioneers, hardly alone in his efforts. In December 1906 as he left New York City for Norway, a party of missionaries from Azusa Street boarded another ship in the same harbor for passage to Africa. One of them, Lucy Farrow, an American of African descent, had been baptized in the Holy Spirit in 1905 through the ministry of Charles F. Parham. She later spent a number of months assisting her friend William J. Seymour at Azusa Street. Farrow and her colleagues expected the "signs" to follow wherever they preached (Mark 16:17).

Few if any knew with accuracy how many Pentecostal missionaries served abroad (approximately two hundred) or even how far the movement had traveled by 1910. What Pentecostals did know was that the Spirit had raised them up to proclaim Christ to the nations. Pentecostal leader A. J. Tomlinson said in 1913, "My heart is all aflame . . . for this lost world." "Sleep has gone from me," he wrote, because "souls are dropping into hell at the rate of 3,600 every hour—86,400 every day, how can anyone sleep?"[3] Musing on the solution, J. Roswell Flower editorialized in the *Pentecost*, "The baptism of the Holy Ghost does not consist in simply speaking in tongues . . . It fills our souls with the love of God for lost humanity, and makes us much more willing to leave home, friends, and all to work in His vineyard, even if it be far away among the heathen." "When the Holy Spirit comes into our hearts," he added, "the missionary spirit comes in with it; they are inseparable."[4] In due course, Pentecostal missions moved from the margins to a place at center stage in the Christian world mission.

North America

Classical Pentecostalism grew from many sites of renewal. These included Parham's Bethel Bible School in Topeka, Kansas, where the first revival of the century began January 1, 1901. The next came to Swedish-Americans on the border of North Dakota and Minnesota in 1904. One of several in the region that were all apparently unrelated to Topeka, it transpired at a Swedish mission church in Moorhead, Minnesota, pastored by John Thompson.[5] Two and three years later, significant awakenings occurred elsewhere in North America, most notably at the Apostolic Faith Mission on Azusa Street; sundry churches in Chicago, Illinois; an abandoned tobacco warehouse in Dunn, North Carolina; and the Hebden Mission in Toronto, Canada.

To these can be added many other important hubs from which believers departed for ministry at home or abroad, including Spokane, Washington; Memphis and Cleveland, Tennessee; Alliance, Ohio; and Nyack and Rochester, New York. Even the little-known camp meeting at Pleasant Grove, Florida, had an impact well beyond the tabernacle building. Baptized in the Holy Spirit, the Bahamians Edmund and Rebecca Barr returned home to preach the Pentecostal message. Pentecostals put their "traveling shoes" on when they received Spirit baptism. The Puerto Rican Juan L. Lugo left Hawaii and began an evangelistic career that led him to California, Puerto Rico, and New York City.

Pentecostalism became an ever-widening collection of stories about ordinary people who sought the Spirit's infilling, heard the call to mission, and took daring risks to obey heaven's command. One example was Marian Keller. After the death of her first husband to malaria in Tanganyika (now Tanzania), she survived the disease herself only to find that all of her supplies had been stolen. Nevertheless, she carried on until the German colonial authorities arrested her following the outbreak of World War I. Subsequent to her release and trip home to Canada, she returned to Tanganyika. With the help of her second husband, Otto Keller, she continued laying the groundwork for Pentecostalism in that country and neighboring Kenya. Missionaries like the Kellers kept in touch with other Pentecostals through a dizzying array of formal and informal networks linked by letters, periodicals, itinerant preachers, missionary unions and associations, and denominations.

After the Topeka revival, the "Apostolic Faith" movement, as Pentecostalism was originally known, advanced through the south-central section of the United States and upward to Zion City (now Zion), Illinois. Perhaps due to harsh criticisms and other discouraging factors, the Topeka revival did not immediately produce any foreign missionaries. Notwithstanding, awareness in the "latter rain" outpouring of the Spirit increased as Parham and his coworkers traveled as "home missionaries" and evangelized from a new base of operations in Houston, Texas. By the summer of 1906, the Apostolic Faith had become a substantial movement of eight to ten thousand persons, with the large majority living in the Midwest.[6]

Earlier in the year, William Seymour, an African-American student at Parham's Bible school in Houston, had moved to Los Angeles and played a key role in the emergence of what became known as the "Azusa Street revival." Its intercultural and interracial makeup would particularly inspire black Pentecostals in North America as well as oppressed peoples overseas. Living under political and economic exploitation, they saw themselves as the "menservants" and the "maidservants" on whom the Spirit conferred gifts and dignity (Joel 2:29).

Word of Azusa circulated in various ways. Visitors who obtained Spirit baptism went back to their home communities or to other places to share their experiences. Publications kindled interest with accounts of the "latter rain," the "fire falling," and the anointing oil of the Spirit. Azusa Street's *Apostolic Faith* newspaper heralded that "people all over the land have heard that the oil of the Spirit is being poured out in Los Angeles, and they are coming for oil—coming thousands of miles. And they are being filled with the holy oil, the baptism with the Holy Ghost, and wherever they go, it is being poured out."[7] After acquiring a copy and being overjoyed by its contents, Bernt Berntsen packed his bags, boarded a ship to San Francisco, and went to Los Angeles to get his Pentecostal baptism. He then returned to his mission post in China.

As the movement grew, new North American mission agencies came into existence. Representing different groupings of Pentecostals, they included the Assemblies of God, Church of God (Cleveland, Tenn.), International Pentecostal Holiness Church, and the Pentecostal Assemblies of Canada. The Evangelization Society of the Pittsburgh Bible Institute and the grand-sounding National and International Pentecostal Missionary Union were typical of many smaller organizations.

Western Europe

Holiness teachings and also the wide-ranging influence of the Welsh revival blazed the path for Pentecostalism in western Europe. Leaders like Barratt had been deeply impressed by the reports. Arriving home in Oslo (formerly Christiania), he led his congregation into a Pentecostal revival, the results of which would rival those of North American centers in terms of global impact. (Barratt himself toured India, Palestine, and elsewhere promoting Pentecostalism.) The extensive publicity quickly attracted crowds of people. A visitor from South Africa observed, "We . . . had the privilege of visiting Wales at the time when the Revival there was at its height, but we certainly have never seen what we saw at Christiania. That God's Holy Spirit was working in a very marvelous way there can be little doubt."[8] Those drawn to the meetings included Alexander A. Boddy, Anglican rector of All Saints' Church at Monkwearmouth, near Sunderland, England; Jonathan Paul, a holiness leader in Germany; and the Baptist pastor Lewi Pethrus from Sweden.

When Boddy got back to Sunderland, revival followed. It was there that Smith Wigglesworth, destined to become an international evangelist of almost legendary status, received Spirit baptism. From Amsterdam in the

Netherlands came Gerrit R. Polman, a disciple of John Alexander Dowie in America, who laid the foundation for the movement in his country. Boddy began sponsoring the Annual Whitsuntide Pentecostal Conventions that did much to extend the movement in the United Kingdom and beyond. He also published *Confidence,* a monthly publication designed to connect Pentecostals, discuss issues, and provide teaching. Years later another Englishman, Douglas R. Scott, brought the Pentecostal message to France.

Through the inspiration of Barratt, Alexander Boddy, and Cecil H. Polhill (a member of the famous "Cambridge Seven" of athletic fame and past missionary) instituted the Pentecostal Missionary Union in 1909, the first permanent Pentecostal mission agency. William F. P. Burton and James Salter founded the Congo Evangelistic Mission at Preston, England, and Polman, the Dutch Pentecostal Missionary Society, with a number of its personnel going to the Dutch East Indies (now Indonesia) and China.

Alexander Boddy was pastor of All Saints' Anglican church in Sunderland, England. Influenced by Thomas Barratt, he and his wife, Mary, led a Pentecostal revival throughout England before World War I. His magazine, *Confidence,* helped spread the movement throughout northern and western Europe.

The influence of the Oslo revival also extended to Germany, Sweden, and into Finland. Paul returned to the city of Kassel to hold services that led to the founding of the "Mülheim Association." Bitterly attacked by holiness leaders, however, the movement suffered condemnation from the damaging Berlin Declaration of 1909 that pronounced Pentecostalism to be "not from above, but from below." German Pentecostals sent out missionaries in part through the Velbert Mission. Though expelled from the Baptist association in Sweden, Pethrus forged the Pentecostal movement in his country into a major Christian force and superintended its overseas missions. His Filadelfia Church in Stockholm became the largest of its kind in Europe. In the years following Oslo, Scandinavian and British missionaries encircled the globe.

Eastern Europe and Russia

The first hint of activity in eastern Europe and Russia dates to 1907, when Eleanor Patrick, an Englishwoman who had worked with Pentecostals in Frankfort, Germany, reported that a mission had been started in Riga, Latvia. A note later appeared in the *Apostolic Faith* telling of a half dozen peasant girls in adjoining Estonia with manifestations of the "gift of tongues." Someone able to interpret announced the meaning: "Jesus is coming soon! Prepare!"[9] (This sort of prophetic exhortation could be heard in countless Pentecostal congregations in the early decades of the movement.)

In the northern area, women such as Patrick and the German noblewoman Frau von Brasch spearheaded evangelism. They shared this task with A. M. Niblock and William Fetler, among others. Patrick later moved to Saratov in southern Russia where she established a church for the "Volga Germans," an immigrant population with many Mennonites. Within a short time and despite the close scrutiny of the police, the work grew and spread to the outlying settlements.

Pentecostalism in Bulgaria, Ukraine, and Russia got a major boost through the efforts of Ivan Voronaev. Born in central Russia, he had served in a Cossack regiment in the czar's army before becoming a Baptist pastor. But due to persecution from the Russian Orthodox Church, he moved his family by way of Siberia and Manchuria to San Francisco. He accordingly affiliated with the American Baptist Home Missionary Society and shepherded a Russian Baptist congregation. He later relocated to a pastorate in New York City.

Voronaev faced a crisis when his daughter Vera received Spirit baptism at Robert and Marie Brown's Glad Tidings Tabernacle in the city, a Pentecostal powerhouse in the Northeast. The Baptist elders at his church wondered what action he would take. Speaking in tongues and prophecy by members of the controversial Molokon sect in Russia had made Baptists deeply suspicious of anyone who claimed to possess supernatural gifts. As it happened, Voronaev's own spiritual quest caused him to go to Glad Tidings where he, too, acquired the experience. After his congregation split over the issue of tongues, he left with some of his parishioners to found First Russian Pentecostal Assembly.

Lewi Pethrus (1884–1974) was pastor of the Filadelfia Pentecostal Church in Stockholm, Sweden, for many years the largest free church congregation in Europe and until about 1965 the largest Pentecostal church in the world.

Months afterward he decided to leave for the recently created Soviet Union. The call came through a prophetic utterance or an interpretation of tongues, not an unusual means of divine guidance for early Pentecostals. Anna Koltovich declared: "Voronaev, Voronaev, journey to Russia." Initially reluctant, he gained confirmation of this through prayer. In 1920, the family gathered their belongings and sailed for the Black Sea port of Odessa in the Ukraine, assuming the truthfulness of Communist propaganda about a democratic constitution and religious freedom. Entering the Black Sea, the ship stopped at

LEWI PETHRUS OF SWEDEN

In 1907, Lewi Pethrus, pastor of a small Baptist church in rural Sweden, heard of the Pentecostal revival that had erupted in Norway under the Methodist pastor Thomas Ball Barratt. Visiting Barratt in Christiania (now Oslo) in 1907, Pethrus was baptized in the Holy Spirit and spoke in tongues. Upon his return to Sweden, he sparked a national Pentecostal revival that swept far beyond the Baptist churches. In 1911, he became pastor of the Filadelfia Baptist Church in Stockholm, which soon became the epicenter of Swedish Pentecostalism.

In 1913, the Swedish Baptist Convention expelled Pethrus and his entire congregation from the denomination. In short order, the Filadelfia church grew to be the largest free church in Sweden. Pethrus insisted on total autonomy for the local Pentecostal churches in Sweden, although he exercised apostolic control of the movement until his death in 1974.

During his sixty-three-year pastorate, the Filadelfia church helped plant more than five hundred churches in Sweden and sent hundreds of missionaries all over the world. He also established *Dagen*, a daily newspaper, as well as a worldwide radio network known as I.B.R.A. Radio. During the depression, his church became famous for feeding and relief programs that attracted multitudes of the poor and destitute to his services. The church building, which was constructed in 1932, seated four thousand persons.

Pethrus was also influential in world Pentecostal circles, serving as an elder statesman in several world Pentecostal conferences from 1957 to 1974. ■

Varna in Bulgaria where the family stayed for a time. Voronaev used this opportunity to preach and plant churches and thus introduced Pentecostalism to that country.

Circumstances proved more difficult when the family landed at Odessa. The secret police arrested them and seized their possessions. Weeks later they were released sick and starved. To make matters worse, famines and civil war raged in European Russia and the Ukraine. Voronaev discovered the claims concerning human rights in the Soviet Union to be largely untrue. Yet, the atheist government did tolerate the "sects" as a means to undermine the influence of the Orthodox Church. However, the tide ultimately turned against the Pentecostals, Baptists, and other Protestants as well.

When the Baptist churches rejected his message, he traveled extensively and as far north as Leningrad (now St. Petersburg) evangelizing and organizing Pentecostal churches. Voronaev's own congregation in Odessa grew to a thousand members. When the first Pentecostal congress convened in 1927, the pastors elected him to the presidency of the newly formed Union of Christians of Evangelical Faith. During this time, the Russian and Eastern European Mission (REEM), a Pentecostal agency with headquarters in Chicago, sent him financial assistance. It also provided missionary personnel and trained workers at its Bible school in the free city of Danzig (now Gdansk, Poland). By the outbreak of World War II, the Mission recorded eighty thousand believers across the region.

After the declaration of the antireligious decree of 1929, the secret police came to Voronaev's home in the middle of the night and arrested him. A son remembered, "We looked at him as if for the last time and tried to imprint every feature of his face in our memories. His head was bent forward. On his pale face was an expression of utter weariness. The corners of his mouth were twitching slightly. His hair had begun to turn gray. He had grown to be an old man during those last few days."[10] Charged with being a tool of "American imperialists" for receiving money from REEM and allegedly working against the Soviet regime, the authorities sent him to a slave labor camp in Siberia. Reports later told of his death, saying he had been shot and killed in what appeared to be an attempted escape and that his body was torn apart by guard dogs. Though the government closed churches and imprisoned leaders like Voronaev, Baptist, Pentecostal, and other evangelical pastors continued to witness to their faith in the camps.

Ivan Voronaev (1886–1943) was born in central Russia where as a young man he served as a cossack for the czar before his conversion in 1908. He served as pastor of two Baptist churches before fleeing persecution and immigrating to the United States in 1911. In a short time he founded Russian-speaking Baptist churches in San Francisco, Los Angeles, and New York City. He became known as the "Pentecostal Apostle to the Slavic nations" and was martyred in a communist prison.

Another missionary, Nicolai J. Poysti, took the Pentecostal message to Siberia and Manchuria. A native of Finland, he heard the "Macedonian cry" in 1918 as civil war raged in his own country and in neighboring Russia. "Standing in amazement before God," he asked, "do I have to go to this nation which is forcing its way into my country to destroy it?" He then heard the Lord say, "Go tell them that I love them."[11] For years his ministry met danger at almost every turn. In one instance, as he and his wife and daughter sailed by steamer down the Volga River, the ship was caught in a crossfire between Red Bolshevik forces and the White Guards. On a nearby vessel stood the ruthless Leon Trotsky, commander of the Red forces, observing the scene. After a lengthy appeal, he finally gave permission for their boat to move out of the battle zone; perhaps this was his only good deed. Poysti lived long past

Trotsky's assassination to see Russians come to Christ in spite of the antireligious agenda of the Communist regime. His passion for missions
stirred other Finns to action, some of whom eventually went to China,
Manchuria, Thailand, and Borneo.

In southeastern Europe, correspondence between friends contributed to
the introduction of Pentecostalism into Romania. Someone in the United
States sent to Gheorghe Bradin in 1922 a booklet by Aimee Semple
McPherson describing God's power to heal and also wrote to him explaining the baptism in the Holy Spirit. Upon reading it, Bradin prayed for his
wife's healing. "Our joy was great," he remembered. "This healing took
place . . . through faith in Jesus Christ and in His wounds."[12] Romanian
Pentecostalism flourished throughout years of merciless persecution.

Australia

Since John Alexander Dowie had begun his preaching and healing ministry "down under" in Australia prior to moving to the United States,
many of his remaining followers there and in New Zealand warmly
greeted the Pentecostal message. The worldwide network of his Christian
Catholic Apostolic Church from Zion City to Amsterdam, South Africa,
Australia, and New Zealand offered a constituency of people open to miracles and the charismatic gifts. Annual Keswick conventions and the evangelistic crusades of R. A. Torrey and Wilbur Chapman also contributed.

A revival in north Melbourne led by Janet Lancaster, a former
Methodist and mother of nine, spearheaded the movement. Like many
other Pentecostals, she first became interested in divine healing and experienced healing herself. In October 1906, she read a pamphlet from England entitled "Back to Pentecost" and became convinced of the baptism in
the Holy Spirit with tongues. Two years later, Lancaster testified to receiving this baptism and discovered that others in the country had as well. She
and her friends then began conducting services at "Good News Hall."

Stories circulated about people being Spirit baptized, miraculous healings, and even persons being raised from the dead. "For six weeks such a
glorious revival continued night and day that we never entered our home
again," Lancaster reported. "Our furniture was sent for and willing hands
soon adapted various rooms to living purposes."[13] Good News Hall later
sponsored campaigns by Smith Wigglesworth and Aimee Semple McPherson that greatly encouraged the movement. By 1928 one could find Australian missionaries amid the Aboriginal people and in India, China, and
South Africa.

Missionaries

Outside of Europe, America, Australia, and New Zealand, Pentecostals went to the traditional sites of missionary endeavor: Africa, India, China, Japan, Korea, and the Middle East. In contrast to some of their Protestant counterparts who considered that Latin America had been evangelized, Pentecostals with other evangelicals risked persecution from Roman Catholic populations to preach the gospel. Little did they acknowledge, however, how much Catholic Christianity had paved the way for Pentecostalism.

But who were the missionaries and how did they fare? At least four different categories of people ventured abroad. The first was made up of persons who had been called, yet, due to their feelings concerning the urgency of the hour and confidence they had received the necessary languages through Spirit baptism, spent little or no time in gathering financial resources. Their savings or the offerings given by fellow believers probably helped them on their journey. Neither did they study the history and culture of the different peoples they hoped to convert. Ministerial credentials, legal recognition, and mission theory took a backseat to the individual guidance of the Holy Spirit. In numerous cases, their overall impact proved short-lived and disappointing. Disillusionment crept in as harsh realities defied their best efforts. Attempts to evangelize frequently ran aground without awareness of the culture and language, dependable financial assistance to cover their personal expenses or to rent halls for holding services, and without a long-term strategy to achieve success in their new environments. Many returned home heartbroken.

In the second category, hardy souls survived by learning the language, adjusting to different cultural contexts, and adapting to the challenges that confronted them. Even when they discovered that speaking in tongues represented prayer in the Spirit instead of linguistic expertise, they accepted the transition in meaning since they shared in the experience of tongues that had enflamed the disciples with zeal on the Day of Pentecost. They wrote letters to friends and churches to obtain prayer and financial support and worked to train converts for leadership posts in the emerging churches.

Martin L. Ryan provides a valuable case study. After reading a letter describing the Azusa Street revival, he became a Pentecostal. From Spokane, Washington, he escorted twenty members of his congregation to the port of Seattle and then onward to Japan and Hong Kong in September 1907; they became the first missionaries to leave the Pacific Coast for Asia. Assuming they would never see the American shores again since the coming

of Christ lay just days, weeks, or months away, they expected to be reunited with their families in heaven. A member of the party, Cora Fritsch,
wrote home: "Oh! dear ones live closely to Jesus and some happy day I can
see you all again. Oh! dear papa, meet your Cora in Heaven, that is my
dearest wish and prayer."[14] (Fritsch later died in China, never having returned to the United States.) Ryan and his colleagues persevered in spite of
the culture shock and criticisms of the missionary establishment.

The third category consisted of veteran missionaries who brought expertise and a greater level of stability. The majority served in India with a
variety of agencies. For example, Presbyterian missionary Max Wood
Moorhead worked with the YMCA in Ceylon (now Sri Lanka) and Susan
Easton, a Methodist with the Woman's Union Missionary Society of America for Heathen Lands, in Calcutta. Several personnel with the Christian
and Missionary Alliance in China received the Pentecostal baptism including William W. Simpson and Grace Agar.

Finally, Bible institute graduates formed the fourth category. Shorter
than the college and seminary route, the Bible institutes offered an intense
spiritual atmosphere, Bible-centered curriculum, and a speedier entry into
the ministry. What these institutions lacked in providing cross-cultural and
missiological instruction, they made up for in producing committed
women and men who braved the problems of living overseas. Schools such
as the Training Homes of the Pentecostal Missionary Union (London),
Aimee Semple McPherson's Lighthouse of International Foursquare Evangelism (Los Angeles), and Holmes's Bible and Missionary Institute
(Greenville, S.C.) graduated students who served with distinction. Still, college, university, and seminary graduates could also be found in the ranks.

Pioneer missionaries had strong feelings regarding organization, cooperation, faith healing, and church polity. In reference to organization and
cooperative undertakings—"teamwork"—their fierce independence occasionally generated a spiritual elitism. Despite the idealized notion of unity
held by Spirit-filled believers, their penchant for the individual leading of
the Holy Spirit frequently precluded opportunities for joint projects. Nevertheless, collaborative ventures did occur as evidenced in the setting up
of the Interior Mission of Liberia and the relationship between REEM and
the Assemblies of God.

Advocates of faith healing, they usually refused to take medicines with
them or accept vaccinations. Not surprisingly, theory and practice clashed.
Looking back on an almost incredible life story, Grace Agar reminisced:
"Knowing that I was going to the border of Tibet and not expecting to have
any doctors in case of sickness, I definitely took the Lord as my Physician.
He has kept me in health and strength for the past 38 years. He has pro-

tected me from all harm, accidents on ice, slippery roads, from robbers, wild beasts and from epidemics so common in China."[15] Others did not fare so well. During the first twenty-five years of Pentecostal missions in Liberia, one or more missionaries were buried every year.

Generally speaking, the first missionaries structured the churches according to congregational church polity, although increasing numbers preferred mixed Congregational and Presbyterian patterns. In some places they implemented forms of Episcopal polity. Missionaries usually dominated the activities of churches and aspiring leaders, especially in the early years. Ironically for those Pentecostals who encouraged their converts to seek for the gifts of the Spirit, they often limited them in the exercise of leadership gifts (Rom. 12:8). This restriction and the importation of Western modes of church government resulted in the flourishing of independent indigenous churches that retained features of Pentecostal spirituality. Still, as missionaries turned over the reins of leadership after mid-century, national mission churches blossomed.

The locomotion of Pentecostal missions moved on the tracks of pragmatism. Beginning with the assumption that tongues-speech constituted foreign languages, missionaries used every possible means to evangelize unbelievers. Swedish Pentecostals set up Radio I.B.R.A., an international network. Lillian Trasher's Assiout Orphanage in Egypt became well known for its care of thousands of children, many of whom were baptized as Christians in a Muslim context. American missionaries in Upper Volta, French West Africa (now Burkina Faso) translated the Bible into the Mossi language and provided literacy training. When severe economic conditions forced people to search for employment in other countries, Pentecostals carried their Mossi Bibles, songbooks, and Sunday school materials with them and started new churches.

Southern Asia

Movements with charismatic phenomena in British India preceded the development of 20th-century Pentecostalism in Europe and America by at least forty years. News of revivals in the United States and Northern Ireland commencing in 1857 inspired Indian believers to pray for the outpouring of the Holy Spirit. Already influenced by the premillennial eschatology and egalitarian concept of ministry of the Plymouth Brethren, significant revival movements arose in the southern states of Tamil Nadu and Kerala. The records mention the gifts of prophecy and tongues, visions and dreams, the activities of women evangelists, and even the breaking of caste.[16] The longing for indigenous leaders and styles of worship added to their attraction. In due course, the missionary community judged these Indian Christians to have teetered on the brink of heathenism with their misguided spiritual excitement.

By the turn of the century, the leaven of Wesleyan holiness and Keswick "Higher Life" teachings had risen in Protestant communities across the subcontinent. Reports of the Welsh revival prompted similar happenings at mission stations in the spring of 1905. The first stirrings occurred among tribal peoples at Welsh Presbyterian gatherings in the Khassia Hills. Expectancy had also grown at Pandita Ramabai's world-famous Mukti Mission. In one of the most celebrated events of the awakening, the matron of a girls' dormitory hurried to the quarters of Minnie F. Abrams, a former Methodist missionary and now an administrator at the mission, in the middle of the night. Declaring that one of the girls had been baptized in the Holy Spirit and with "fire" (Matt. 3:11), she told how she "saw the fire, and ran across the room for a pail of water, and was about to pour it on her, when I discovered that she was not on fire."[17] This "baptism of fire," signifying to them the purification of sanctification, motivated the other girls to confess their sins and repent.

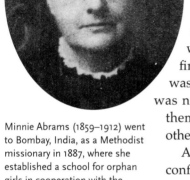

Minnie Abrams (1859–1912) went to Bombay, India, as a Methodist missionary in 1887, where she established a school for orphan girls in cooperation with the famous Indian Christian leader Pandita Ramabai. Abrams was later instrumental in the beginnings of the Pentecostal movement in both India and Chile.

As the revival spread, stories circulated describing confessions of sin, "prayer storms" (hours spent in fervent prayer) that pushed aside traditional Western orders of worship, signs in the heavens, and visions and dreams. Startled missionaries chattered about visible "tongues of fire" on the heads of believers, prophecies, and even miraculous provisions of food. Abrams penned her popular *Baptism of the Holy Ghost and Fire* to urge Christians to pray for the fullness of the Spirit to purify and empower them for mission.

While charismatic phenomena had been present early on, tongues came later as a consequence of Abrams and her "praying band" of women evangelists conducting services at an Anglican mission station. When students who attended returned to their boarding schools, revivals followed, and several spoke in tongues. The most notable instance occurred in Bombay (now Mumbai). Hearing a young girl named Sarah pray in tongues, Canon R. S. Heywood, thinking it might be the same as that experienced on the Day of Pentecost, located someone who could interpret her words. The listener then announced that she was interceding in prayer for the conversion of Libya.

The movement spread as more Indians testified to Spirit baptism. In an early December 1906 issue of the Methodist *Indian Witness*, the editor commented that "no phase of the present revival movement in Asia has received such severe criticism as the unusual and marked physical manifestations which have so often followed its outbreak in different localities." To some they might seem "strange and incredible," but "one should recall similar experience[s] of Bible characters, visions and trances and unknown tongues and that the promise through Joel includes 'all flesh.'"[18] Later that month and inspired by reading the *Apostolic Faith*, Abrams and others at the Mukti Mission experienced speaking in tongues.

Tongues in India caught the attention of the *Apostolic Faith* editors in Los Angeles. Pentecostalism had originated there without the influence of events in North America, thus proving to the faithful the worldwide dimensions of the Spirit's outpouring.[19] Alfred G. and Lillian Garr, the first missionaries to leave Azusa Street, arrived in Calcutta at the turn of 1907. At the close of a missionary conference in the city, Alfred Garr reviewed how the "latter rain" had fallen in America. A revival followed in which some of those present received the Pentecostal baptism. From Calcutta, this next phase of the movement advanced across the country and into Sri Lanka. A notice in 1908 mentioned that more than a thousand people had spoken in tongues, including sixty missionaries associated with fifteen mission societies.[20]

As they did on other mission fields, women made substantial contributions in preaching, charitable undertakings, and in theological and missiological reflection. (In fact, women constituted the majority of Pentecostal missionaries for decades, enjoying privileges and responsibilities in ministry often denied them at home.) Abrams and Alliance missionary Kate Knight became especially well-known. A tourist from England, the Brethren writer G. H. Lang, became so troubled by Knight's insistence on tongues with Spirit baptism and the audacity of a woman preaching that he wrote an entire book to refute her beliefs and those of the Pentecostal movement.[21]

Historian Dana L. Robert proposes that North American "women not only guided the movement's emergence out of holiness, but they founded its first mission-training institutions, acted as its first missionaries, linked healing to missionary commitment, and in Minnie Abrams constructed its first cogent and enduring missiology."[22] The latter did so through her *Baptism in the Holy Ghost and Fire*, which she revised to include the restoration of the gift of tongues.

East Asia

In January 1901, when revival erupted at Bethel Bible School in Topeka, Charles Parham said of Agnes N. Ozman, the first person to speak in tongues: "A halo seemed to surround her head and face, and she began speaking in the Chinese language."[23] Not only that, but "when she tried to write in English to tell us of her experience she wrote in the Chinese language." Hence, on the first day of modern Pentecostalism, the goal to evangelize the most populous nation on earth looked within reach now that in their view the language hurdle had been jumped.

As the first Pentecostal missionaries to reach China, T. J. McIntosh and his wife landed in Hong Kong in August 1907 and immediately went to the nearby Portuguese enclave of Macau. As a result of his preaching, a handful of missionaries and Chinese believers became Pentecostal. A product of the Dunn, North Carolina, revival, McIntosh spoke of a divine summons to go to Macau. However, he quickly departed for Palestine on what would become the first of two world tours. Two more parties of missionaries came to Hong Kong in October: the Garrs, who since January had ministered in India, and Martin Ryan's team from Spokane.

At first Garr held services at the mission compound of the American Board of Commissioners of Foreign Missions (ABCFM) with the assistance of his wife and two women from Spokane. A deacon of the church, Mok Lai Chi, served as interpreter and within a short time acquired the Pentecostal experience himself. Division soon took place within the congregation, and the ABCFM leaders rejected tongues. A new church then formed with Mok as pastor. Taking initiative in evangelism, he began publishing the first Pentecostal paper in China, *Pentecostal Truths*. His activities serve as a reminder that growth in the grass roots happened largely through the efforts of native Christians. Along with the development of classical Pentecostalism, a radical sectarian indigenous group later appeared: the True Jesus Church, whose beliefs revealed a blending of Oneness Pentecostal and Seventh-Day teachings.

Farther inland, Pentecostal revival broke out among Alliance missionaries at Wuchow in 1907: "The Spirit fell in a quiet Saturday night meeting, and without there having been any special exhortation or request in prayer on this line, a number 'began to speak with other tongues.' It was an entirely new experience, but a blessed one to many, both foreign and native brethren and sisters, old and young." Furthermore, "It seems as though the Holy Spirit is falling on the children of God simultaneously in all parts of the world, often without the intervention of a human leader."[24] One notable personality in attendance, Robert A. Jaffray, claimed that Spirit baptism transformed his ministry.

Another Alliance missionary came on the scene a year later: Victor G. Plymire, a graduate of A. B. Simpson's Missionary Training Institute at Nyack, New York. On a furlough home, he received Spirit baptism, joined a Pentecostal denomination, and returned to his work in Tibet, considered by some mission enthusiasts to be the "end of the earth" (Acts 1:8). Despite hardships and personal costs (he buried his first wife and son), he finally baptized his first convert after sixteen years of evangelism.

On the way to Hong Kong from the United States, Ryan and his party stayed for a brief time in Japan. He later returned there from Hong Kong to do permanent mission work. With perhaps the earliest plan of mission by a Pentecostal, he evangelized students, aware that the thousands enrolled in Japanese universities from surrounding countries could potentially go home as witnesses for Christ. There he printed his *Apostolic Light* magazine and had it translated into the Korean language. Since Ryan left Japan in 1909, the extent of his achievements remains unknown.

Life for these "faith" missionaries tested their fortitude when disease struck and funds did not arrive as expected. The young Irish evangelist Robert Semple died from malaria in Hong Kong, leaving his wife, Aimee [Semple McPherson], to care for their infant daughter. Tragedy faced others as well. During their first stay, the Garrs' baby died at childbirth and their two-year-old daughter and a maid both died from an epidemic. On another visit to Hong Kong, Lillian Garr prematurely gave birth to a son who weighed only three pounds. Since Alfred Jr. could not keep milk on his stomach, his death looked near. In desperation his father prayed, "Lord, this is all that I have left. Dear God, please heal my boy, let him take some kind of nourishment." He heard the Lord tell him that the baby would live if they fed him Eagle Brand condensed milk. Unsure where he could find it, he searched from store to store. He finally met a Chinese merchant who told him of getting a shipment of milk that had not been ordered. As Garr examined it, he discovered Eagle Brand milk. In what became a widely known miraculous answer to prayer—with the aid of a "brand name" product no less—the baby digested the milk and grew strong.

Although Pentecostals preferred to hear stories where faith triumphed over difficulties, the stresses on missionary families produced negative outcomes at times. When Rowena Ryan divorced her husband, she complained that she and the five children had lived "in [that] 'heathen country' [Japan] . . . without food and a proper home, and as a last resort . . . she learned the language and finally secured a place as teacher among the . . . children."[25]

The entry of Pentecostalism into Korea began in 1908 through the efforts of two women from California. "Sisters Daniels and Brand" visited with Cora Fritsch in Japan and announced their intention of evangelizing the "Hermit Kingdom" for a few months on their route to Hong Kong and Jerusalem.[26] Years later, in 1928, after the country had been annexed by the Japanese Empire, Methodist evangelist Yong Do Lee began a ministry distinguished by healings and speaking in tongues. Mary Rumsey, who had been baptized in the Holy Spirit at Azusa Street, arrived from America in the same year and established a work that became a beachhead for Pentecostalism.

Along with other destinations, Swedish Pentecostals went to Inner Mongolia. Beginning their work in 1922, they learned the culture and language of the nomadic peoples of this Asian region. One of the best-known, Folke Boberg, had prepared for ministry at the Scandinavian Alliance Mission Bible Institute in Jönköping and Moody Bible Institute in Chicago. The results of his lexicographical labor came to fruition in the highly acclaimed three-volume *Mongolian–English Dictionary*, issued by the Filadelfia Publishing House in Stockholm.

Africa

Pentecostalism has seen its greatest growth in the Southern Hemisphere, principally in Africa and Latin America. The first Pentecostal missionaries, Mary Johnson and Ida Andersson, left Moorhead, Minnesota, in November 1904 for South Africa, following the revival among Swedish-Americans that inspired them to missions. After their ship docked at Durban, they contacted Norwegian and Swedish Christians. Throughout their years in Natal they retained close association with Swedish Holiness Union missionaries.

The next advances into Africa targeted Liberia and Portuguese Angola with a team from Azusa Street that included several African-Americans. To Liberia went the G. W. Batmans, Julia W. Hutchins, and Lucy Farrow. The veteran Methodist missionaries Samuel and Ardella Mead traveled with the Robert Shidelers to Angola. The Meads had originally been part of Bishop William Taylor's "Pioneer Forty" expedition there in 1885. Waiting in New York City for their ship to sail in December 1906, the group met F. M. Cook. In a letter to the *Apostolic Faith*, he said that three years previously he had been called to Africa. Unexpectedly meeting these "Los Angeles saints," Batman and Farrow laid hands on Cook in prayer and "he received his Pentecost and spoke in an African dialect. So now he is one of the Apostolic Faith band for the West Coast of Africa."[27] Early Pentecostals needed only the endorsement of the Holy Spirit before heading for the field.

In 1908, two key figures journeyed to South Africa where their activities met with unusual success: John G. Lake and Thomas Hezmalhalch. A wealthy businessman, Lake had been an elder at John Alexander Dowie's Christian Catholic Apostolic Church in Zion City. He testified to Spirit baptism when Charles Parham held tent services in the city in late 1906. He later reminisced, "I disposed of my estate and distributed my funds in a manner I believed to be for the best interests of the Kingdom of God, and made myself wholly dependent upon God for the support of myself and family, and abandoned myself to the preaching of Jesus."[28] Since Dowie had integrated Zion City and took a forward-looking stance on racial reconciliation, Lake probably sympathized with the interracial dynamics he found on his visit to Azusa Street.

John Graham Lake (1870–1935), known as the "Apostle of Pentecost to South Africa," served only four years in South Africa (1908–12) where he established the two largest Pentecostal churches in the nation. These were the largely white Apostolic Faith Mission (AFM) and the largely Black Zion Christian Church.

Leaving Indianapolis, Indiana, the novice missionaries consisted of the Lakes and their seven children and four adults including Hezmalhalch. As Lake told the story, one financial miracle followed another until they passed customs in South Africa. The foundation for a Pentecostal revival had already been laid in part through the work of Pieter le Roux, a Dutch Reformed missionary who had joined Dowie's organization. By the time a representative came from Zion City, the movement had progressed considerably. As a result of a revival in Wakkerstroom, the total number of "Zionists" reached five thousand. Even though Dowie had highlighted divine healing, the Pentecostal message of the newcomers gained the interest of le Roux.

Lake began his ministry in the Johannesburg area at a black Zionist church in Doornfontein; his preaching attracted whites as well. At the predominantly white Bree Street Tabernacle, members objected to the attendance of the well-known black preacher Elias Letwaba. In his defense, Lake embraced him and kissed him, calling him "my brother." Letwaba's remarkable healing ministry and evangelism did much to encourage Pentecostalism in the black population. His legacy included the founding of Patmos Bible School, the first ministerial training school for his people in the Apostolic Faith Mission.

Unfortunately, Pentecostalism became racially divided, a separation that grew more bitter with the later apartheid policies of the government. Nonetheless, though questions remain in relation to Lake's attitude to-

JOHN G. LAKE

John G. Lake was ordained to the Methodist ministry at the age of twenty-one but chose a career in business rather than the appointment that he was offered. Lake became a very successful businessman, founding a newspaper and then moving into real estate and finally into the insurance business. Although he was offered a $50,000 a year guarantee to be the manager of an insurance trust, Lake felt that God was dealing with him to devote all of his energy to preaching the gospel.

The spiritual breakthrough in Lake's life centered around several remarkable healings in his family, culminating in the instantaneous healing of his wife from tuberculosis under the ministry of John Alexander Dowie in 1898. After experiencing these healings, Lake became associated with Dowie's ministry and served as an elder in the Zion Catholic Apostolic Church. Later, after leaving Dowie, he became involved in ministry at night while continuing his business activities in the daytime. Lake sought God for the baptism in the Holy Spirit, and after nine months of seeking, he felt the power of God come upon him in answer to his prayers.

Shortly after receiving the baptism in the Holy Spirit in 1907, Lake felt God directing him to Africa. He left his job and distributed his funds and set out for Africa in faith that God would supply his family's needs. Lake, his wife and their seven children, and four other adults arrived in South Africa in the spring of 1908. The party of missionaries found that God had gone before them and prepared the way. A lady met them at the boat and provided them with a house because the Lord had spoken to her to provide for his servants. Unfortunately these miraculous provisions did not continue. The people thought that the missionaries were rich Americans, and so while Lake and his party poured all of their resources into the work, they were often without sufficient food to feed themselves.

Mrs. Lake died in December of 1908 while Lake was away on a preaching trip. It has been suggested that she died of overwork and malnutrition. Her death was a severe blow to Lake, and, although he continued to minister in Africa for four more years, he was often stricken with loneliness, which eventually caused his return to the United States. After returning to the States, Lake married Florence Switzer in 1913 and settled in Spokane, Washington, a year later.

It is estimated that during the next five or six years thousands of healings occurred through Lake's ministry. He moved to Portland, Oregon, in May 1920 and started a work similar to his work in Spokane. Lake's health did not allow him to complete his vision of a chain of healing institutions throughout the country, and he died of a stroke in 1935. ■

—JIM ZEIGLER
DICTIONARY OF PENTECOSTAL AND
CHARISMATIC MOVEMENTS

ward segregation, his work influenced the development of the Apostolic Faith Mission of South Africa and the predominantly black independent Zion Apostolic Church, as it was originally known.

The first Canadian missionaries, Charles and Emma Chawner, had been baptized in the Spirit at the Hebden Mission in Toronto. They traveled to the Zulu homeland in South Africa in 1908. Their son Austin and his wife later entered Portuguese-ruled Mozambique to share the gospel. The younger Chawner had been educated at Bethel Bible Training School in Newark, New Jersey. This institution had two important affiliations, one with the sponsoring church—the independent Bethel Pentecostal Assembly; the other with its mission board—the Pentecostal Mission in South and Central Africa (PMSCA).

Minnie T. Draper served as the first board chairperson. A former member of the Christian and Missionary Alliance, she had assisted A. B. Simpson in his healing ministry. The agency operated a field office in South Africa that directed its activities there as well as those in Swaziland and Mozambique. It also sent missionaries to China, India, Venezuela, and Mexico. Wealthy patrons served on the board who understood how to make money work by investing the mission funds on the stock market. At times when the board reached an impasse on a vital decision, they called in Cora O. Lockwood, an older woman in the Newark congregation who had little money but respected spiritual insight. Though not a board member, she would pray to discern God's will and cast the deciding vote.

In West Africa, Pentecostal missionaries from the United Kingdom first entered Gold Coast (now Ghana) and Nigeria in the early 1930s. Classical Pentecostalism grew in both the British and French colonies. Yet, significant indigenous movements with Pentecostal-like phenomena also came into existence. William Wadé Harris, reared in a Liberian Methodist home, led a mass movement to Christianity across Ivory Coast and Gold Coast. Viewing himself as a black "Elijah" in the "last days," thousands were converted. Speaking in tongues, healings, and miracles all had a place in his spiritual vision.

Latin America

World evangelization weighed heavily on the minds of the faithful in Chicago. William H. Durham's North Avenue Mission, in particular, commissioned noteworthy missionaries. An Italian immigrant, the Presbyterian Luigi Francescon, received Spirit baptism there in 1907. Sometime afterward, Durham prophesied that God wanted him to evangelize the Italian community. With his friend Pietro Ottolini, he established Christian Assembly, the first Italian-American Pentecostal church in North America. An associate, Giacomo Lombardi, went to Italy and organized congregations that became the nucleus of the Italian Pentecostal movement. Francescon traveled to Argentina in 1909 to preach to Italians living in that country. But his best success came as an outgrowth of a visit to São Paulo, Brazil. The sizable "Congregação Cristã do Brazil" owes its origin to his ministry.

In the same year in which Francescon went to Argentina, Pentecostalism commenced on the far side of the Andes Mountains in Chile. At Valparaiso, Dr. Willis Hoover pastored the First Methodist Church. He traced the causes of the renewal to a discussion in an adult Sunday school class, interest in the holiness teaching of sanctification, and unusual testimonies of God's power in the lives of church members. During a study of the Book of Acts, a member asked him: "What prevents our being a church like the Early Church?" "Nothing prevents it," he replied, "except something within ourselves."[29] Along with other Christians worldwide, they prayed for the outpouring of the Spirit.

Daniel Berg (1884–1963) and Gunnar Vingren came as immigrants from Sweden to the United States in 1902. They were already Baptists when they arrived but soon came into contact with Pentecostals in the Chicago area. Because of a prophecy to go to an unknown place called "Para," the two journeyed to Brazil in 1910. In 1912 they founded the Assemblies of God of Brazil, which eventually became one of the largest Pentecostal movements in the world.

In 1907, Hoover and his wife, Mary, received a copy of the first edition of Abrams's *Baptism of the Holy Ghost and Fire*. Minnie and Mary had been students together and graduated in the first class of the women's Chicago Training School for City, Home, and Foreign Missions. Although the book did not mention tongues-speech, Abrams had written it to describe the early stages of the Indian revival and the baptism of fire: "We have only a short time left us in which to gather out from these thousand millions of unevangelised people the Lord's portion. If we do not do this work, their blood will be required of us . . . It is time that we seek the fulness of the Holy Ghost, the fire that empowers us to preach the gospel with signs following."[30]

News of speaking in tongues reached the Hoovers with a stopover by Fredrik Franson a year later. Before long Pentecostal revival began among the Methodists of Valparaiso. A mission official in New York City depicted the reports as having "much to compare with the history of the Methodist revival in its primitive times."[31] Nevertheless, the controversial happenings triggered rejection by denominational authorities. Even with the severing of relations, the revival created the fast-growing "Pentecostal Methodist" movement.

By far the most spectacular growth of Pentecostalism anywhere in the world has been in Brazil. The investments of Francescon and the Swedish-Americans Daniel Berg and Adolf Gunnar Vingren paid rich dividends. Raised in a Baptist home, Berg immigrated to the United States in 1902 because of an economic depression in his motherland. He acquired the Pentecostal baptism on a later visit to Sweden. Vingren arrived a year later, worked as a laborer to save money for his education, and then enrolled in the Swedish Department of the University of Chicago Divinity School to prepare for the ministry. They met for the first time at a Pentecostal conference sponsored by First Swedish Baptist Church in Chicago and then attended meetings at the North Avenue Mission. Vingren subsequently became pastor of a Swedish Baptist church in South Bend, Indiana.

At a Saturday night service in 1910, Adolf Uldine, a church member in South Bend, prophesied over Vingren that God wanted him to go to "Para" and preach the Good News. Shortly after, he gave the same prophecy to Berg. Not knowing its location, they went to the Chicago Public Library to consult a world atlas. They discovered it to be the northeastern Brazilian coastal state of Pará and soon embarked for the capital, Belém, the chief port of the Amazon basin. The pastor of a Baptist church welcomed them warmly and invited them to stay in his home. The atmosphere changed, however, when Berg and Vingren began preaching on the baptism in the Holy Spirit. As a result, they left the residence and along with eighteen members of the church started a new congregation.

Like other Pentecostal missionaries who ventured abroad on "faith," they prayed for the Lord's provision, but did not allow this to mean inaction on their part. In true "tent-making" fashion, Berg found a job as a foundryman in a steel mill while his partner handled pastoral responsibilities. His wages supported them and paid for lessons in the Portuguese language. As the movement grew, they registered it with the government under the name "Assemblies of God." In the years that followed, scores of Swedish and American missionaries went to Brazil to assist in what became the biggest Protestant community in the country.

Conclusion

Leaders at the Edinburgh conference looked forward to the fulfillment of the Great Commission through united action. Without doubt, the gathering proved to be a major turning point in church history. As the delegates deliberated, however, a radical new movement was already mobilizing for action. With renewal as its compass, the Pentecostal movement pointed to a largely forgotten dimension of the Spirit's ministry. Through a distinctively charismatic understanding of Spirit baptism and an uncompromising belief in the contemporary availability of the spiritual gifts, Pentecostalism in its various forms has changed the landscape of Christianity and introduced an authentic Trinitarian praxis of mission.

Lacking the education and financial support of the mainline missionaries and facing the rejection of their evangelical and holiness counterparts did not keep the Pentecostals from eagerly accepting the task before them. The leveling effect of the outpouring of the Holy Spirit meant that anyone could be called to preach. In contrast to the stiffly rational piety of much of evangelical Christianity at the turn of the 20th century, the experiential dynamic of Pentecostal faith captured the interest of peoples in the mission lands whose worldviews more closely resembled those of ancient times than post-Enlightenment Western civilization. As the Lord delayed His coming, Pentecostals realized that building Christ's church required more than signs and wonders. As a result, their methods came to closely resemble those of other evangelical missionaries, but with a unique emphasis on the Spirit's activity. Moreover, many endeavored to implement indigenous church principles, though with a distinctly Euramerican twist.

"I am now sailing to the regions beyond where Jesus wants to use me and the glory of God is [surging] through my body again and again," reflected Cora Fritsch as the *Minnesota* pushed out of Puget Sound for the Orient. "Best of all I feel the sunshine of my Savior's face beaming down upon me and the assurance that God is pleased with me."[32] Underneath her youthful exuberance rested a deep-seated commitment. Indeed, she knew that the Pentecostal baptism had empowered her for sharing the Good News.

With the same inspiration and confidence a century later, Korean, Singaporean, Filipino, Indian, Salvadoran, Brazilian, Nigerian, and other Pentecostals and charismatics risked all to go to the ends of the earth to proclaim "this gospel of the kingdom . . . as a witness to all the nations" (Matt. 24:14). Such is the story of "Pentecostal" missions in the global expansion of Christianity in our time.

For Further Reading

The most comprehensive source for the global expansion of the Pentecostal movement is Stanley M. Burgess, ed., and Eduard M. van der Maas, assoc. ed., *New International Dictionary of Pentecostal and Charismatic Movements* (Grand Rapids: Zondervan, 2001). A useful source is Walter Hollenweger's *Pentecostalism: Origins and Developments Worldwide* (Peabody, Mass.: Hendrickson Publishers, Inc., 1997). Another scholarly source is Murray W. Dempster, Byron D. Klaus, and Douglas Petersen, eds., *The Globalization of Pentecostalism: A Religion Made to Travel* (Irvine, Calif.: Regnum Books International, 1999). A fine sociological work is Karla Poewe, ed., *Charismatic Christianity as a Global Culture* (Columbia: Univ. of South Carolina Press, 1994).

Works on European Pentecostalism include: Thomas Ball Barratt, *In the Days of the Latter Rain* (Oslo, Norway, 1909. Reprinted by the Garland Publishing Company in the Higher Life Series, New York, 1985); William C. Fletcher, *Soviet Charismatics: The Pentecostals in the USSR* (New York: Peter Lang, 1985); and David Bundy, "Swedish Pentecostal Mission Theory and Practice to 1930: Foundational Values in Conflict," *Mission Studies: Journal of the International Association for Mission Studies* XIV — 1 & 2 (1997): 147–74.

Latin American sources include Edward L. Cleary and Hannah W. Stewart Gambino, eds., *Power, Politics, and Pentecostals in Latin America* (Boulder, Colo.: Westview Press, 1997); David Stoll, *Is Latin America Turning Protestant?* (Los Angeles: Univ. of California Press, 1990; and David Martin, *Tongues of Fire: The Explosion of Protestantism in Latin America* (London: Oxford Univ. Press, 1990). Willis Collins Hoover, *History of the Pentecostal Revival in Chile,* transl. Mario G. Hoover (Lakeland, Florida). Available through Mario G. Hoover, 4312 Orangewood Loop East, Lakeland, FL 33813-1848. A useful study is Everett A. Wilson's "Identity, Community, and Status: The Legacy of the Central American Pentecostal Pioneers," *In Earthen Vessels: American Evangelicals and Foreign Missions, 1880–1980,* ed. Joel A. Carpenter and Wilbert R. Shenk (Grand Rapids: Eerdmans, 1990), 133–51.

A good source for African Pentecostalism is Allan Anderson's *Bazalwane: African Pentecostals in South Africa* (Pretoria: Univ. of South Africa Press, 1992). A fine book on the movement in Australia can be found in Barry Chant's *Heart of Fire: The Story of Australian Pentecostalism,* rev. ed. (Unley Park, Australia: House of Tabor, 1984).

· 5 ·
The Holiness Pentecostal Churches

Vinson Synan

O VER THE YEARS, the Pentecostals have been called by various names.
Although many of the first Pentecostal churches in the United States
were known as "holiness" churches, the first strictly Pentecostal groups
used variations of the name "Apostolic Faith." This was the name chosen
by Charles Parham for his small group in Topeka, Kansas, when Pentecost
fell in 1901. When Parham's African-American follower and friend William
J. Seymour opened the famous Azusa Street Mission in Los Angeles in 1906,
he also used the name Apostolic Faith.

In the years that followed, other names were used. Some common ones
were "Full Gospel," "Pentecostal," and "Latter Rain." At times, the public
scornfully called them "Holy Rollers," a name universally rejected by adherents of the movement. Many of the new denominations used the word
"Pentecostal" in their names while others adopted more doctrinally neutral names such as Assemblies of God, Church of God, Church of the
Foursquare Gospel, and Church of God in Christ.

For many decades, the Pentecostals were the outcasts of religious society. One reason for this rejection was that most of the first Pentecostal
churches were planted among the poor and disinherited classes. David
Barrett states that "no movement in the 20th century was more harassed,
tormented, persecuted and martyred" for its faith than the Pentecostals.

In spite of being cast out of the mainline churches, the Pentecostals grew, especially in the years following World War II. A fertile ground for growth was found among blacks and poor whites in the South and Midwest. Many Pentecostals mirrored the stereotypes of the Oklahoma families who fled the dust bowl of the 1930s to find new opportunity in California. Indeed, the central family in John Steinbeck's novel *The Grapes of Wrath* was based on a Pentecostal holiness family who joined the trek from Oklahoma to California.

Despite their economic poverty, the Pentecostals soon sent missionaries all over the world and in time began to grow faster than most other Christian denominations. Although they grew especially fast in Third World countries, they also made surprising inroads in Europe and North America.

After World War II, the Pentecostals began to prosper and rise into the middle class. With this new prosperity came greater social acceptance. The skyrocketing growth rates of the Pentecostal churches also forced the major mainline denominations to take a new look at them and what they believed.

There are now well over one hundred Pentecostal denominations in the United States and thousands of smaller fellowships and independent churches. As a rule of thumb, for every congregation that is part of an organized denomination, there exists an independent congregation. Thus the number of unaffiliated independent churches in the United States matches the number of churches in the major denominations, such as the Assemblies of God.

Wesleyan Pentecostal Churches

The first American Pentecostal churches began with deep roots in the Wesleyan holiness movement that had spread across America during the 19th century. For decades holiness teachers and preachers had taught that there were two "blessings" offered to believers. The first, justification by faith, was also called a "new birth." This crisis of conversion was a common understanding and experience for most evangelical believers in America. The Wesleyans, however, claimed a "second blessing," which, using Wesley's language, was called "entire sanctification," an instant experience that gave the believer victory over sin and perfect love toward God and man. Most of the first generation of Pentecostals were from this holiness stream that had its roots in Methodism.

When the Pentecostal movement began, these "holiness Pentecostals" simply added the baptism in the Holy Spirit with tongues as "initial evidence" of a "third blessing" that brought power for witnessing to those who had already been sanctified. With the new tongues experience, sanctification was seen as a prerequisite "cleansing" that qualified the seeker to experience the "third blessing" of baptism in the Holy Spirit. An early prophetic utterance stated ominously that "My Spirit will not dwell in an unclean temple." Seekers were encouraged to abandon all the roots of bitterness and original sin so that nothing would block their reception of the Spirit. In fact, it was told that Seymour would not admit seekers to enter the upper room to seek the baptism until he was satisfied that their sanctification experience had been certified downstairs.

The historic Azusa Street testimony was "I am saved, sanctified, and filled with the Holy Ghost." In addition to the three works of grace, these early Pentecostals stressed instant divine healing "as in the atonement" and the premillennial Second Coming of Christ to rapture the church at the end of the age. This was known as the "fivefold gospel" of Parham, Seymour, Azusa Street, and the first Pentecostal denominations.

These churches also adopted strict "holiness codes," which forbade their members to use tobacco or alcohol or to attend theaters or other places of "worldly amusement." Also outlawed were professional sports, "outward adornments" such as lipstick or "bobbed hair," and immodest dress.

As time passed, there were controversies within the movement that led to a variety of views and changes on the three-blessings doctrinal scheme that had been the universal teaching of the movement for a decade.

The first family of American Pentecostal churches, therefore, could be classified as embracing Wesleyan Pentecostalism due to the basic Arminian perfectionistic theology that was inherited from the holiness movement. Some of the major American churches include the following:

The Church of God in Christ

From the earliest days, the Church of God in Christ has been one of the largest and fastest-growing Pentecostal denominations in the United States. A largely African-American church, it has played a central role in the development of the movement throughout the century.

Chartered in 1897, the Church of God in Christ was the first legally chartered body among the American Pentecostal denominations. With a claimed membership that exceeds five million persons, this church is twice the size of the Assemblies of God in the United States. Though some would debate these claims, the Church of God in Christ is clearly one of the oldest and largest of all the Pentecostal movements in the world—and also one of the fastest growing.

The Roles of C. H. Mason and C. P. Jones

The roots of the Church of God in Christ lie deep in the late 19th-century holiness movement in the southern states. These roots are also grounded in the culture and history of the American blacks. The story of this church in its early years was also largely the biographies of two prominent church leaders: C. P. Jones and C. H. Mason.

Charles Harrison Mason, born in 1866 in Bartlett, Tennessee, was the son of former slaves. He grew up in a Missionary Baptist church and as a young man felt the call to preach. In 1893 he entered Arkansas Baptist College to study for the ministry but was soon grieved by the liberal teachings he heard. He left school after only three months because he felt that there was "no salvation in the schools or colleges." In 1895, while on a visit to Jackson, Mississippi, he met Charles Price Jones, another young Baptist preacher, who was to affect his life greatly and was then serving as pastor of the Mt. Helms Baptist Church of Jackson, Mississippi. [1]

Later that year, Jones and Mason traveled to Lexington, Mississippi, where they preached the Wesleyan doctrine of entire sanctification as a second work of grace. Initiating holiness revivals in local Baptist churches, the two fiery preachers were soon disfellowshipped and forbidden to preach in the churches of the local Baptist associations. They thereupon opened a historic revival campaign in a cotton gin in Lexington in February 1896 and saw the first local congregation formed. [2]

The name for the new group came to Mason in March 1897 as he walked the streets of Little Rock, Arkansas. The Church of God in Christ seemed to be a biblical name for the new holiness church in Lexington. The teachings of the new group were the typical perfectionistic doctrines of the turn-of-the-century holiness movement. Those receiving the sanctification experience were thenceforth holy and known as saints. These holiness people neither smoked tobacco

Bishop Charles Harrison Mason (1866–1961), cofounder of the Church of God in Christ, lived to see his church become the largest Pentecostal denomination in America.

nor drank alcohol. They dressed modestly, worked hard, and paid their bills. They praised the Lord fervently with shouting and spiritual dancing. Among them the poorest sharecropper could become a preacher of the gospel or even a bishop in the church.

In 1897, the Church of God in Christ was legally chartered in nearby Memphis, Tennessee, the first Pentecostal church in America to obtain such recognition. After this, Memphis became the headquarters of the church and the site of the annual convocations that became huge rallying gatherings for the faithful.[3]

The church continued peacefully for several years with dual leadership. Though Jones was the leader of the church, Mason was the dominant

CHARLES H. MASON, 1866–1961

SEEKER OF SLAVE CHRISTIANITY

Charles Mason grew up hearing about the passionate Christianity of the slaves from his parents, both of whom had only recently been freed when Charles was born. He was enthralled even as a child, and constantly prayed, said one family member, "above all things [for] a religion like the one he had heard about from the old slaves and seen demonstrated."

At age fourteen, one year after his father died of the plague in an Arkansas swamp shack, Mason lay dying of tuberculosis. But on a Sunday morning, his wife recounted in his biography, he "got out of bed and walked outside all by himself. There, under the morning skies, he prayed and praised God for his healing, [and he] renewed his commitment to God."

In 1891 Charles was ordained as a Baptist minister. But before he began preaching, he married Alice Saxton, who was so opposed to his plans for preaching that she divorced him two years later. About the same time, Mason struggled with the increasingly liberal Arkansas Baptist College, and dropped out. "I packed my books, arose, and bade them a final farewell to follow Jesus, with the Bible as my sacred guide," he later recounted.

Increasingly interested in Holiness "second blessing" teachings, he joined with Charles P. Jones to form the "Church of God in Christ" (COGIC)—a name he said God gave him while walking down a street in Little Rock, Arkansas. A decade later Mason felt "a wave of glory" while visiting the Azusa Street Revival and began to speak in tongues. When he returned to Memphis to share his experience, Jones "withdrew the right hand of fellowship." But Mason took a large portion of COGIC members and, after a lengthy legal battle, the name of the denomination.

Though the COGIC at one time had as many white ministers as black—it was the only Pentecostal church in America authorized by the government to ordain ministers—Mason continued to seek the "spiritual essence" and "prayer tradition" of the slave religious experience. In 1914 many of the white COGIC ministers broke off to form the Assemblies of God (AG), but Mason continued to work on both sides of the racial divide, speaking at AG conferences and meetings. "The church is like the eye," he often said. "It has a little black in it and a little white in it, and without both it can't see."

Today the COGIC has almost 6 million members in the United States—more than twice that of the Assemblies of God. ∎

FROM
—*CHRISTIAN HISTORY*

personality. They were a fine and harmonious team. Mason was known for his godly character and preaching ability, while Jones was known for his hymns, many of which became popular throughout the nation. Two of his better-known hymns are "Deeper, Deeper" and "Come unto Me."

Pentecost Comes to Memphis

The tranquillity between Mason and Jones was broken, however, when in 1906 word reached Memphis of the new Pentecost being experienced in Los Angeles in a little mission on Azusa Street. The pastor of the mission was a black man, William J. Seymour, who preached that the saints, although sanctified, had not received the baptism in the Holy Ghost until they had spoken in tongues as the initial evidence. It was said that all the gifts of the Spirit were being restored to the church at Azusa Street and that white people were coming to be taught by blacks and to worship together in apparent equality.[4]

The news from Azusa Street met with a divided response in the Church of God in Christ, which by now had spread widely into Tennessee, Mississippi, and Arkansas. Jones was cool to the new teaching, while Mason was eager to travel to Los Angeles to investigate the revival. Mason for years had claimed that God had endowed him with supernatural characteristics manifested in dreams and visions. In the end, Mason prevailed on two fellow leaders to accompany him on a pilgrimage to Azusa Street. In March 1907, Mason, along with J. A. Jeter and D. J. Young, traveled to Los Angeles.

What they saw at Azusa Street was powerful and convincing. In the words of Frank Bartleman, "The color line was washed away by the blood." People of all races and nationalities worshiped together in striking unity and equality. The gift of tongues was matched by other gifts such as interpretation, healing, words of knowledge and wisdom, and exorcism of demons. In a short time, Mason and Young received the baptism, spoke in tongues, and returned to Memphis eager to share their new experience with the rest of the church.

When they arrived, they were surprised to find that another Azusa Street pilgrim, Glenn A. Cook, a white man, had already visited the church and preached the new Pentecostal doctrine. Many of the saints had accepted the message and were speaking in tongues as the Spirit gave them utterance. Everyone did not accept Cook's message, however, most notably C. P. Jones, who in 1907 was serving as the general overseer and presiding elder of the denomination.

A struggle for the future of the church ensued as the new Pentecostal party led by Mason vied with Jones for the leadership of the church. By

August 1907 the issue came to a head in the general assembly of the church as it met in Jackson, Mississippi. After a lengthy discussion that lasted three days and into the nights, the assembly withdrew the right hand of fellowship from C. H. Mason and all who promulgated the doctrine of speaking in tongues "as the initial evidence." When Mason left the assembly, about half of the ministers and laity left with him.

In September 1907, the Pentecostal group gathered another convocation in Memphis where the Church of God in Christ became a full-fledged member of the Pentecostal movement. In 1909, after two years of struggle, the courts allowed the Mason faction to retain the name Church of God in Christ, and a Pentecostal statement that separated the baptism in the Holy Spirit from the experience of sanctification was added to the articles of faith. It stated that "the full baptism in the Holy Spirit is evidenced by speaking in other tongues."

Although tongues were thus welcomed and accepted in the church, other manifestations were also commonly seen as evidence of the indwelling Holy Spirit, such as healing, prophecy, shouting, and "dancing in the Spirit."

Meanwhile, Jones and his non-Pentecostal followers separated to form a new group, which they named the Church of Christ (Holiness) U.S.A.[5]

Growth and Divisions

From its base in Memphis, the Church of God in Christ spread rapidly over the United States. Its first base was in the South where the Pentecostal revival swept through many black neighborhoods like a prairie fire. Mason often organized churches by preaching in the streets. As the Pentecostal movement spread among whites in the South, Mason occasionally visited these churches and was recognized as the outstanding leader among the black Pentecostals. In 1921, he met again with William J. Seymour in New Jersey, where the two black Pentecostal apostles talked about the old Azusa days. Although the two leaders were not in the same denomination, they remained lifelong friends.

As his church grew, Mason demonstrated his organizing genius. Each diocese was led by a bishop who usually served for life. Jurisdictions were divided and subdivided as the church grew so that the church spread into all of the states of the Union by the end of World War II. The church was and remained episcopal in government with great power exercised by the bishops. From 1910 to 1916, Mason began four major departments that aided in the growth of the church. They were the women's department, the Sunday school, the Young People's Willing Workers (YPWW), and the home and foreign missions department.

The basic teachings of the church were also defined in the early years. Basically a holiness church, the denomination continued to teach an experience and life of holiness as the ultimate goal of the Christian life. To this was added the Pentecostal baptism with the Holy Spirit, which brought into the life of the church and the believers all the gifts of the Spirit. When the "oneness" controversy erupted in the Pentecostal world after 1913, the Church of God in Christ remained staunchly Trinitarian. Added to the sacraments of water baptism and the Lord's Supper was the ordinance of footwashing.

An important early teaching of the church was pacifism, or the teaching that Christians should not engage in war. Because of his determined stand on this issue, Mason was jailed in 1918 in Lexington, Mississippi, because he forbade his followers to serve in the armed forces of the nation. While he was imprisoned, a storm blew the roof off the courthouse building, whereupon the magistrates released him the next day.

Throughout his life, Mason was hounded for his pacifist views, even to the point that the FBI kept a file on his activities. Like most of the other Pentecostal bodies in the United States, however, the Church of God in Christ softened this stand during World War II because of the apparent evils of fascism and Nazism.[6]

The "Gentleman's Agreement"

Mason would not accept the separation of Christians on the basis of race. Although he never openly fought the Jim Crow system of racial segregation, he felt keenly the racial separations among Pentecostals that came after the "glory days" in Azusa Street. Indeed, for many years Mason's church was the most integrated denomination in the United States. In the most racist period of American history (1890–1924), the Pentecostals stood out as a glaring exception to the segregation of the times.

In fact, hundreds of white Pentecostal preachers were ordained at Mason's hands and given ministerial credentials from the Church of God in Christ in the years before World War I. One reason for this situation was that the Church of God in Christ was the only incorporated Pentecostal denomination in the nation for many years. In order for a minister to be bonded to perform marriages, to be deferred from the draft, or to obtain clergy permits on the railroads, he had to demonstrate that he was a minister of a recognized religious body. Mason's church had the prized charter of incorporation, which made it attractive for hundreds of white ministers to join his church. Beyond this, however, Mason's powerful preaching, charismatic personality, and brotherly love, despite segregation, attracted thousands of whites.

As time went on, some of the white pastors began to hold separate Bible conferences while keeping their relationship with Mason intact. Finally, a "gentleman's agreement" was struck whereby the whites could issue credentials in Mason's name and that of the Church of God in Christ, the only stipulation being that no credentials would be given to anyone who was unworthy.

Just before the beginning of World War I, a large group of white Pentecostal ministers became dissatisfied with this arrangement and began organizing a new denomination that could also be chartered, thus granting the above benefits to the ministers of the new group. Most of the founders of the Assemblies of God (AG) who gathered in Hot Springs, Arkansas, in April 1914 carried credentials with the Church of God in Christ. Although Mason and his group were nominally invited to attend the Hot Springs conclave, no letters of invitation were sent to the black ministers.

Mason did attend the meeting, however, and was invited to preach on the Thursday night of the convention. His choir sang a special number after which the venerable bishop preached a sermon on the wonders of God as seen in the lowly sweet potato. Despite Mason's appearance, the AG organized a largely white denomination, which soon became the largest Pentecostal church in the country. Thus the organization of the Assemblies of God was at least partially a racial separation from Mason's church.[7]

After 1914, the leaders of the white Pentecostal denominations looked upon the Church of God in Christ as the black Pentecostal movement for the United States. Black converts in white churches were encouraged to join the Church of God in Christ in the light of the segregation practiced at the time.[8]

Some of the church's greatest growth came in the years following World Wars I and II when blacks migrated en masse to the large industrial cities of the North. Millions of southern blacks moved to New York City, Detroit, Philadelphia, Chicago, Boston, Los Angeles, and other urban centers to escape the agrarian poverty that still blighted much of the South.

These migrants brought their churches with them to the cities where they settled. Many of these were members of the Church of God in Christ. Often they settled in storefront buildings or bought the elegant church buildings sold by whites who had fled the inner cities for the suburbs.

The Pentecostal churches proved to be the most successful in serving this mass of humanity that crowded into the urban ghettos. In some cities almost every block boasted a Church of God in Christ—in many cases humble and unostentatious, yet a powerfully redemptive force in the neighborhood. The story of one of these urban migrant churches was powerfully portrayed in James Baldwin's book *Go Tell It on the Mountain*, which was an autobiographical account of his childhood in a storefront Pentecostal church in Harlem. Because of this massive migration and the unquestioned attraction of Pentecostal worship for the disinherited blacks, both rural and urban, the Church of God in Christ experienced massive growth in the middle of the century.[9]

At the time of Mason's death in 1961, his church had entered every state in the Union and numbered some 400,000 members in the United States. This compared favorably with the record of John Wesley, who counted 100,000 Methodist followers when he died in 1791. Before his death, Mason had constructed the massive Mason Temple in Memphis where the faithful gathered annually for the great convocations that became the largest annual gatherings in the city. This temple, which seats almost 10,000, was unable to hold the convocation crowds that annually numbered some 40,000 persons. Upon his death at the age of ninety-five, the church was given permission to bury Mason in the lobby of the temple, the only person so honored in the history of the city.[10]

After Mason's death a power struggle ensued over who would inherit the mantle of the fallen apostle. The temporary winner was O. T. Jones Sr., who served as senior bishop from 1962 to 1968. But in the end it was Mason's son-in-law, J. O. Patterson, who became the heir to Mason's legacy. Elected to lead the church in November of 1968, Patterson was given the title of presiding bishop. He then led the church in a period of great growth and development. His successors, Bishops L. H. Ford, Chandler Owens, and Gilbert E. Patterson, continued the legacy of C. H. Mason. Despite a schism in 1969 in which fourteen Church of God in Christ bishops formed the Church of God in Christ, International (now claiming 200,000 members), the church has continued to grow rapidly.[11]

In 1964 a census was taken of the church in the United States, and the membership was reported at 425,000 members in 4,100 congregations. The next census was not attempted until 1982. As a result of that count, the *Yearbook of American and Canadian Churches* reported an American membership for the church at 3,709,861 persons in 9,982 congregations. By the year 2000, the membership figure stood at 5,499,875 members in 15,300 congregations. This is one of the most explosive records of church growth in the history of the United States. These figures indicate that the Church of God in Christ is the second largest black organization in America, exceeded only by the National Baptist Convention.

Although the Church of God in Christ did not play a major role in the black civil rights movements of the 1950s and 1960s, many Church of God in Christ ministers and members stood at the side of Martin Luther King

Jr. in his nonviolent crusade for equal rights. In fact it was in Memphis's Mason Temple that King preached his famous "I Have Been to the Mountain" message. This, his last sermon, was delivered the night before his assassination. Furthermore, the site of his death was the Lorraine Motel, owned by a leading Memphis lay member of the Church of God in Christ.

In recent years, the charismatic movement has been conspicuous in its apparent lack of success with blacks in the mainline churches. But the Pentecostal movement has positively flourished in the predominantly black Church of God in Christ. In the last decades of the 20th century, the Church of God in Christ continued to serve as a haven for the masses.

A footnote to this story is that the Church of Christ (Holiness) U.S.A., founded by C. P. Jones in 1907 in rejection of the Pentecostal experience, continues until this day. A comparison of the records of the two churches since then is instructive about the power of Pentecost for church growth. In 2000, Jones's church reported only 25,000 members in 146 churches, while the Church of God in Christ had grown to over 5 million members in more than 15,000 congregations. The only difference between the two was the releasing of the power of the Holy Spirit in the Church of God in Christ with signs and wonders following.

The story of Mason and his Church of God in Christ is truly one of the great success stories of church growth in modern America.

The Pentecostal Holiness Church

The Pentecostal Holiness Church was organized as a holiness denomination in 1898, several years before the Pentecostal movement began in the United States. Its roots lie in the National Holiness Association movement, which began in Vineland, New Jersey, in 1867 just after the end of the Civil War. The present church represents the merger of three bodies that were products of that movement.

Founded by Abner Blackmon Crumpler, a Methodist holiness preacher from North Carolina, the church was organized in 1896 as the North Carolina Holiness Association. The name was changed to the Pentecostal Holiness Church when the first congregation was formed in Greensboro, North Carolina, in 1898.

The other major group that flowed into the present denomination was the Fire-Baptized Holiness Church, founded in Iowa in 1895 by former Baptist preacher Benjamin H. Irwin. This group taught a third blessing after sanctification called the baptism in the Holy Ghost and fire. By 1898, this group had organized a national denomination with churches in eight states and two Canadian provinces.

The fire-baptized movement almost disappeared after Irwin backslid and abandoned the church. Before this he had taught several more baptisms including the baptisms of "dynamite," "lyddite," and "oxidite."[12]

The Azusa Street Revival

The 1906 annual conference of the Pentecostal Holiness Church of North Carolina was notable for the absence of Gaston Barnabas Cashwell, one of the leading evangelists and pastors in the new denomination since he left Methodism to join the new church in 1903. Abner Blackmon Crumpler, the leader of the conference, read a letter from Cashwell that greatly interested the delegates. In it he asked forgiveness from anyone he had offended and announced that he was going to Los Angeles "to seek for the baptism of the Holy Ghost."[13]

For several months there had been great interest in the Azusa Street revival throughout the South because of the glowing eyewitness accounts by Frank Bartleman in the *Way of Faith,* a regional holiness magazine. Cashwell was the only minister venturesome enough to take action. He decided to make the long journey to Los Angeles to find out for himself if this was indeed the new Pentecost they had been praying for and expecting for years. Trusting God to supply his needs, he bought a one-way train ticket to Los Angeles and traveled in the only suit he owned.

Once in Los Angeles, Cashwell went directly to the Azusa Street Mission. He was dismayed at what he saw. The pastor, William J. Seymour, was a black man, as were most of the worshipers. When blacks laid hands upon him to receive the baptism, he abruptly left the meeting confused and disappointed. That night, however, God dealt with his racial prejudices and gave him a love for blacks and a renewed hunger to be baptized in the Holy Spirit. The next night, at Cashwell's request, Seymour and several young blacks laid hands again on this southern gentleman, who was baptized in the Spirit and, according to his own account, spoke perfect German. Before Cashwell returned to North Carolina, Seymour and the Azusa mission took up an offering and presented him with a new suit and enough money for the return journey.

The Flame Spreads

Upon arriving in his hometown of Dunn, North Carolina, in December 1906, Cashwell immediately preached Pentecost in the local holiness church. Interest was so great, that in the first week of January 1907, he rented a three-story tobacco warehouse near the railroad tracks in Dunn for a month-long Pentecostal crusade, which became for the East Coast another Azusa Street.

Most of the ministers in the three largest area holiness movements came by the scores, hungry to receive their own "personal Pentecost." These churches included the Pentecostal Holiness Church, the Fire-Baptized Holiness Church, and the Holiness Free-Will Baptist churches of the area. Overnight most of the ministers and churches in these groups were swept lock, stock, and barrel into the Pentecostal movement.

A month later, the general overseer of the Fire-Baptized Holiness Church, Joseph H. King, invited Cashwell to preach at his church in Toccoa, Georgia. Although King had heard of the new baptism accompanied by glossolalia, he was not fully convinced of its validity. Upon hearing one message from Cashwell, however, he knelt at the altar and received the baptism in a quiet but powerful manifestation of tongues. [14]

In the next six months Cashwell completed a whirlwind preaching tour of the Southern states that established him as the "apostle of Pentecost to the South." On a trip to Birmingham, Alabama, in the summer of 1907 he brought the message of Pentecost to A. J. Tomlinson, general overseer of

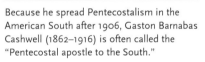

Because he spread Pentecostalism in the American South after 1906, Gaston Barnabas Cashwell (1862–1916) is often called the "Pentecostal apostle to the South."

the Church of God in Cleveland, Tennessee, and to H. G. Rodgers and M. M. Pinson, later founders of the Assemblies of God. [15]

Officially Pentecostal

Though the Pentecostal experience was sweeping his church, Crumpler was one of the few who refused to accept the theory of "initial evidence." Although he accepted the validity of tongues, he did not believe that everyone had to speak in tongues to experience a genuine baptism in the Holy Spirit. For several months Crumpler and the Pentecostal party led by Cashwell and his converts struggled over the issue.

The issue came to a head in the annual conference meeting in Dunn, North Carolina, in November 1908. About 90 percent of the ministers and laity had experienced tongues by this time. On the first day of the convention, delegates reelected Crumpler as president, but the "initial evidence" battle had come to a head. The next day he left forever the convention and the church he had founded. The Pentecostals had won.

The convention immediately added a Pentecostal article to the statement of faith that accepted tongues as the initial evidence. As far as is known, this was the first church body to adopt a Pentecostal statement as the official doctrine of the denomination.

Delegates also selected the *Bridegroom's Messenger,* a magazine published by Cashwell, as the official periodical of the church. A final action was taken in 1909 when the word *Pentecostal* was once again added to the name of the church. It had been dropped in 1903 in an attempt to further identify the church with the holiness movement.

Another citadel to accept Pentecostalism was the Bible college in Greenville, South Carolina, founded by Nickles John Holmes in 1898 as a holiness school. In 1907, Holmes and most of his faculty received the Pentecostal experience and spoke in tongues under Cashwell's influence. By

GASTON BARNABAS CASHWELL, 1862–1916

SOUTHERN APOSTLE OF PENTECOST

When the Pentecostal Holiness Church (PHC) met for its annual conference in Lumberton, North Carolina, in November 1906, one of its most prominent members, G. B. Cashwell, was absent. But he had left a letter: "I realize that my life has fallen short of the standard of holiness we preach; but I have repented in my home in Dunn, North Carolina, and I have been restored. I am unable to be with you at this time, for I am now leaving for Los Angeles, California, where I shall seek for the baptism of the Holy Ghost."

But when the blond, middle-aged, 250-pound Holiness preacher from North Carolina arrived at the Azusa Street Revival, he was very uncomfortable. He found many of the practices "fanatical," and when a young black man laid hands on him for the baptism in the Holy Spirit, he was repulsed. But he soon "suffered a crucifixion" and "died" to his prejudice. He returned to the church and asked the black leaders to lay hands on him and pray. Immediately, he began to speak in tongues.

Cashwell returned to Dunn the next month and began preaching to his fellow Holiness believers about Spirit baptism and speaking in tongues. Though his superior in the PHC opposed his teachings, Cashwell continued to preach across the region. He soon became known as "the apostle of Pentecost in the South."

Only two years later, however, Cashwell left the PHC, apparently frustrated after not being elected its president. But in that time, he had brought four major Holiness denominations— the Pentecostal Holiness Church, the Fire-Baptized Holiness Church, the Church of God (Cleveland, Tennessee), and the Pentecostal Free-Will Baptist Church—into the Pentecostal movement. ∎

FROM
—*CHRISTIAN HISTORY*

1909, Holmes had accepted Pentecostalism, and subsequently his school became an early theological and educational center for the movement. Now officially related to the Pentecostal Holiness Church, Holmes Bible College stands as the oldest continuing Pentecostal educational institution in the world. [16]

Mergers

By the end of 1908, much of the southern holiness movement had entered the Pentecostal fold. In the following months a feeling emerged that those of "like precious faith" should unite to promote the Pentecostal message more effectively. This led to a merger of the Pentecostal Holiness Church with the Fire-Baptized Holiness Church in 1911 in the village of Falcon, North Carolina. The same ecumenical feeling led to the merger of the churches affiliated with the college in 1915. These congregations were located mostly in South Carolina and had roots in the Presbyterian Church.

The Theology of the Church

The Pentecostal Holiness Church has roots in the original teachings of the Azusa Street revival. Already a holiness church before 1906, it taught the Wesleyan theology of instant second-blessing sanctification. After Azusa Street, the church simply added the baptism in the Holy Spirit evidenced by tongues as a third blessing. This was in harmony with the teachings of Irwin and the fire-baptized branch of the church.

Since 1908, the Pentecostal Holiness Church has taught what are known as five cardinal doctrines, that is, (1) justification by faith, (2) entire sanctification, (3) the baptism in the Holy Spirit evidenced by speaking in tongues, (4) Christ's atonement providing for divine healing, and (5) the imminent, premillennial Second Coming of Christ.

Influential books in forming this theology were G. F. Taylor's 1907 book *The Spirit and the Bride* and J. H. King's 1911 volume, *From Passover to Pentecost*. [17]

Over the years the church has gained a reputation for its defense of what its leaders consider the original Pentecostal message. In the "finished work" controversy over sanctification after 1910, the church soundly defended the second work of entire sanctification against the teachings of William Durham. Those who accepted Durham's teachings formed the Assemblies of God in 1914. [18]

The only schism in the church's history came in 1920 when a division came over divine healing and the use of medicine. Some Georgia pastors defended the right of Christians to use medicine and doctors, while most of the church leaders taught that one should trust God for healing without recourse to medicine. Those who advocated the use of medicine withdrew from the denomination to form the Congregational Holiness Church in 1921.[19]

Growing Pains

In the post–World War II era, the Pentecostal Holiness Church, along with other American Pentecostal bodies, experienced tremendous growth. Much of this came during the era of the "divine healing" crusades of the late 1940s and early 1950s. Leading this movement was Oral Roberts, a Pentecostal holiness evangelist from Oklahoma. At first immensely popular with most Pentecostal laymen and church leaders, Roberts's ministry became increasingly controversial after 1953.

For a decade the church was torn by pro- and anti-Roberts factions with some anti-Roberts ministers calling for a schism in the church. In the end, cooler heads prevailed and the threat of division passed. In time, leading churchmen such as R. O. Corvin and Bishop Oscar Moore worked with Roberts in his evangelistic association and in his new university.

By the mid-1960s Roberts had won the support of most of his denomination, including Bishop Joseph A. Synan. Synan, an early Roberts opponent, joined in the dedication of Oral Roberts University in 1967. Despite his acceptance, Roberts joined the Methodist Church in 1968 to the dismay and puzzlement of his many friends in Pentecostal denominations.[20]

The Roberts story illustrates a significant fact about the denomination: the Pentecostal Holiness Church is as famous for the ministers who have left the church as for those who have remained. In addition to Roberts, such leaders as Charles Stanley, former president of the Southern Baptist Convention, and C. M. Ward, former Assemblies of God radio preacher, were born and spiritually formed in the Pentecostal Holiness Church. Others in this category are T. L. Lowery of the Church of God and Dan Sheaffer of the Assemblies of God.

Pentecostal Ecumenism

For many decades there was little contact between the various American Pentecostal bodies except by ministers who transferred from one denomination to another. However, there were cases of proselytism and "sheep stealing" that caused unpleasant feelings between the various groups. This began to change during the dark days of World War II when the first steps were taken to bring Pentecostals into fellowship with one another.

The first contacts were made in 1943 in the lobbies of the newly formed National Association of Evangelicals. Several Pentecostal bodies served as charter members of this group drawn together by the emergency situation brought about by the war. The Pentecostal Holiness Church was one of these groups.

By 1948, several Pentecostal groups formed the Pentecostal Fellowship of North America (PFNA) in Des Moines, Iowa. Preliminary to this organization was a rally in Washington, D.C., where plans for a constitution were formulated. Leading figures in this meeting were Bishop Synan, who helped formulate the constitution, and Oral Roberts, who preached in the final public rally. From those early days, the Pentecostal Holiness Church has taken a leading role in the PFNA meetings as well as the World Pentecostal Conferences that have been held every three years since 1947. [21]

The Church in 2000

In the 1960s the Pentecostal Holiness Church began to branch out beyond the United States by affiliating with sister Pentecostal bodies in the Third World. This was done in addition to its traditional world mission efforts. In 1967 an affiliation was formed with the Pentecostal Methodist Church of Chile, one of the largest national Pentecostal churches in the world. At the time, the Jotabeche Pentecostal Methodist congregation was the largest in the world with more than sixty thousand members.

Today this congregation is in second place despite the fact that it has grown to number 350,000 members. In 2000 the Pentecostal Methodist Church of Chile claimed no less than 1.5 million members and adherents.

A similar affiliation was forged with the Wesleyan Methodist Church of Brazil in 1985. A Pentecostal body with roots in the Brazilian Methodist Church, the Wesleyan church numbered some 100,000 members and adherents in 2000. [22]

With 200,000 adult baptized members in the United States in more than 1,800 local churches and with mission churches and affiliates in 91 nations, the International Pentecostal Holiness Church and its affiliates in 2000 numbered 2.5 million persons around the world. The church headquarters since 1974 has been located in Oklahoma City, a major center for the church. [23]

The leadership of the church is looking at the 21st century as the time of the greatest growth and evangelization in its history. In 1985 a program known as "Target 2000" was launched. The goal of this program is for the church to be able to claim one-tenth of 1 percent of the world population for Jesus Christ by the end of the century. To achieve this goal, new churches are being opened in world-class cities in the United States and other nations each year. [24]

For many decades the Pentecostal Holiness Church was a church that spoke with a Southern accent and was largely a rural denomination ministering in the South and the Midwest. It now wishes to minister and preach the gospel in all the languages and accents of the world.

The Churches of God

Of the two hundred or so denominations in the United States with a variation of the name Church of God, the largest one is a Pentecostal body with headquarters in Cleveland, Tennessee. Because of the many churches with similar names, the major bodies with the name Church of God have added headquarters designations to distinguish them from sister churches. Others such as the Church of God of Anderson, Indiana, sometimes also add the byline "non-Pentecostal" to avoid confusion with the Pentecostals who also boast of a denomination known as the Pentecostal Church of God.

In addition to this, there are at least three denominations headquartered in the small city of Cleveland, Tennessee, with the name Church of God: the Church of God (Cleveland, Tenn.), the Church of God of Prophecy, and the Jerusalem Acres Church of God. Another related group with headquarters in Huntsville, Alabama, carries the name Church of God, World Headquarters. None of these churches are related to the Winebrenner Church of God, which antedates most of the above-mentioned groups.

In August 1986, the Church of God (Cleveland, Tenn.) observed a centennial harking back to what is claimed as the beginning of the Pentecostal movement in the United States. More than thirty-five thousand persons gathered in Atlanta for the Sixty-first General Assembly, the largest gathering in the history of the church.

The Christian Union

What was commemorated was a meeting in 1886 at Barney Creek in Monroe County, Tennessee, under the leadership of R. G. Spurling Sr., where a group known as the Christian Union was formed. Spurling, a Baptist, called for a new reformation in the church since, by his reckoning, all the other churches had fallen into a spiritual dark age. [25]

After some years, new groups appeared around the countryside. Church of God historians such as Charles W. Conn point to the revival in the Schearer schoolhouse in the Coker Creek community of North Carolina as an important root of the church. During a revival in 1896 conducted by evangelists of the Fire-Baptized Holiness Church, William Martin, Milton McNabb, and Joe M. Tipton, some unusual phenomena electrified the community.

This meeting exhibited the doctrines and practices of Benjamin Hardin Irwin's fire-baptized movement, which was spreading rapidly at the time. Such Irwinite fanaticisms as third, fourth, and fifth baptisms of fire, dynamite, and oxidite were taught to the faithful, who were also forbidden to eat pork, drink coffee, or violate any of the dietary laws of the Old Testament.

Because of these extremes, rowdies descended on the meetings, and violence was visited upon the hapless worshipers. It was also reported that some of the people at the Schearer schoolhouse spoke in strange tongues when they received the baptism of fire. After the excitement of the revival died away, Tipton, Martin, McNabb, and R. G. Spurling Jr. continued to preach in whatever schoolhouses and brush arbors they could secure, despite the persecution and rejection of their mountaineer neighbors.[26]

The Role of A. J. Tomlinson

A new beginning came after the turn of the century with the organization of the "Holiness Church at Camp Creek" in western North Carolina on May 15, 1902, in the home of lay preacher W. F. Bryant. The pastor of the church at this time was R. G. Spurling Jr. This church might have existed alone except for the visit in 1903 of a traveling Bible salesman from Indiana by the name of Ambrose Jessup Tomlinson. A Quaker, Tomlinson was in the holiness wing of Quakerism and earned a living by selling Bibles and other religious materials to the pious mountain folk of eastern Tennessee and western North Carolina.[27]

In the summer of 1903, Tomlinson, who had visited the region occasionally since 1896, happened upon the tiny congregation at Camp Creek and was invited to join. His education and knowledge of the Bible were obviously superior to that of the congregation, and so he was looked upon as a prize that could help the struggling group. Before joining, however, Tomlinson spent the night in "prevailing prayer" on nearby Burger Mountain where he received a vision of the Church of God of the last days, which would restore the entire body of Christ to the faith of the New Testament.[28]

The next day, June 13, 1903, the Hoosier salesman joined the church with the understanding that it was the Church of God of the Bible and not a man-made organization. With the winning of Tomlinson, the Camp Creek church gained one of the great organizing geniuses of modern American church history. [29]

In a short time, Tomlinson had planted churches in Union Grove and

A. J. Tomlinson

Drygo in Tennessee and a small congregation in Jones, Georgia. A mission was also established in nearby Cleveland, which became a center of activities for the group. By 1906 these churches were able to call the first general gathering to consider matters of common interest. Thus on January 26 and 27, 1906, the first general assembly convened in the home of J. C. Murphy of Camp Creek, North Carolina. [30]

Since Tomlinson was serving as pastor of the local church, he was selected to serve as the moderator. The new church adopted strict teachings of personal holiness that forbade their members to use tobacco or alcohol. Footwashing as a required ordinance was approved as was the use of Sunday schools. To avoid the errors of denominationalism, Tomlinson wrote into the record that none of the *Minutes*

AMBROSE JESSUP (A. J.) TOMLINSON, 1865–1943

CHURCH OF GOD VISIONARY

"Jesus had started the Church of God when he was here on earth, and a record was kept of its progress and activities for several years after the death of its founder. The period known as the Dark Ages had come after the Church of God had departed from the faith and the church was lost to view."

Understanding it to be the only "True Church of God," in 1903, Tomlinson became the leader of a small band of Holiness believers in Camp Creek, North Carolina, known as the Church of God (though it had recently changed its name to the Holiness Church). By 1909 he was its general overseer.

Tomlinson began teaching Pentecostal doctrines as early as January 1907, but truly brought the denomination into the Pentecostal movement after speaking in tongues at a G. B. Cashwell revival meeting in 1908.

Though he was made "permanent general overseer" in 1914, he was removed from the denomination in 1922. Taking 2,000 members with him, he formed the Tomlinson Church of God, later renamed the Church of God of Prophecy. ∎

—CHRISTIAN HISTORY

should ever be used "to establish a sect or denomination." The congregations represented by the twenty-one delegates who gathered in the living room of the Murphy home were to be known simply as holiness churches.[31]

In the second meeting, which convened in Bradley County, Tennessee, in January 1907, the group chose the name Church of God since it was a name mentioned in the Bible. There seemed to be no connection with any other church in America other than Tomlinson's knowledge of the Church of God (Anderson, Ind.) and the Winebrenner group in Pennsylvania.

The new denomination was typical of the holiness churches formed in America in this period. The second blessing of entire sanctification was sought as a baptism with the Holy Ghost, which freed the seeker from the results of original sin. Also strongly affirmed was the certainty of divine healing for the body in answer to prayer. The Irwinite fanaticisms of 1896 gave way to a more moderate version of the American holiness movement. Under Tomlinson's dynamic leadership, the Church of God planted churches throughout the mountain areas of Tennessee, Georgia, Kentucky, West Virginia, and North Carolina.

Pentecost. In 1906, Tomlinson and other leaders of the church heard the news from Azusa Street about a new Pentecost characterized by speaking in other tongues. The news was welcomed in the environs of Cleveland as another wave of holiness revival that could bless all the churches. Tomlinson was especially interested in the new doctrine and experience. In his diary, he recorded every conceivable spiritual manifestation he saw in his meetings, but never had he recorded a case of glossolalia.[32]

With extreme interest, he visited Birmingham, Alabama, in June 1907 to hear Gaston Barnabas Cashwell, a North Carolina preacher from the Pentecostal Holiness Church who had received the baptism at Azusa Street. Cashwell was on a whirlwind tour of the South explaining the Pentecostal movement to the large crowds of holiness people who gathered to hear the new tongues. Although Tomlinson missed meeting Cashwell, he did meet with M. M. Pinson, a later founding father of the Assemblies of God, and talked with him about the new Pentecostal movement. Although Tomlinson did not receive the tongues experience in Birmingham in 1907, he returned to Cleveland determined that his church would enter into this new spiritual experience.

Calling on the church to pray for a new Pentecost, the general moderator invited Cashwell to preach in the following general assembly to convene in January 1908 in Cleveland. By the time Cashwell arrived, which was after the general assembly officially closed, many of the pastors had already received the baptism and were speaking with other tongues. They were now praying for their leader.

Tomlinson's baptism was one of the most colorful in all the literature of Pentecostalism. While Cashwell was preaching, the general overseer fell to the floor behind the pulpit with his head under a chair. He then spoke in not one, but ten different tongues in succession. With this event, it was a foregone conclusion that the Church of God would be a part of the growing Pentecostal movement. After January 1908, glossolalia appeared in practically every service that Tomlinson observed in the churches. Tongues, interpretations, and prophecies became so prevalent that major decisions of the general assemblies were taken in accordance with charismatic directions brought forth by tongues and interpretations.

The new dynamic brought on by the Pentecostal experience caused fantastic growth in the fledgling church. Almost all of north Cleveland was won to the church by 1909. Communities all over the South were soon visited by itinerant preachers who ministered in mill villages, mining camps, towns, crossroads, and larger cities in the region. In time, the churches followed their migrant members north into the industrial cities of the Northeast and the Midwest. The Church of God indeed began to move like a mighty army across the land. In 1910 some 1,005 members were reported in 27 churches. By 1920 those figures had mushroomed to 14,606 members in 389 congregations.[33]

Divisions. The impetus of these early years was broken after World War I, however, when questions arose over the methods Tomlinson used in running the church. Over the years, he had gathered more power into his own hands and had even led the church in adopting a new constitution in 1914 giving him the overseer's position for life. In 1917 an openly theocratic constitution was adopted, confirming his lifetime appointment. By 1922 dissatisfaction arose over the alleged mishandling of monies. A struggle ensued in the following months between Tomlinson and a council of elders led by Flavius Josephus Lee and I. S. Llewellyn.[34]

In a church trial that took place in Bradley County, Tennessee, in 1923, the council of elders removed Tomlinson from office, whereupon he withdrew from the church. He and his followers then organized another denomination as the Church of God. With monies arriving by mail in Cleveland, the post office was at a loss as to how the mail should be delivered. This led to a protracted lawsuit that eventually was decided by the Supreme Court of Tennessee. The final decision resulted in the two churches being legally known as the Church of God and the "Tomlinson Church of God."

The Church of God of Prophecy

This situation with the Tomlinson Church of God continued until Tomlinson's death in 1943, when a question of future leadership opened between the followers of Tomlinson's two sons, Homer and Milton. Homer, a long-time preacher, had considered himself heir to his father's position. Many pastors, however, felt that Homer was unstable and preferred the younger son, Milton, who had worked as a printer in the White Wing publishing house owned by the church and as a pastor in Kentucky. When Milton was chosen overseer, Homer left to organize yet another denomination known as the Church of God, World Headquarters. Until his death in 1968, his headquarters were in Queens, New York. Over the years he became famous worldwide for his claims of being the king and bishop of the entire world.[35]

The church Milton headed adopted the name "Church of God of Prophecy" in 1952 and pursued a vigorous ministry from a modern headquarters in Cleveland. Both the World Headquarters and Church of God of Prophecy churches continued to teach Tomlinson's eschatological vision of a day when all churches would flow into the Church of God as the founder had envisioned on Burger Mountain in 1903.

The Church of God (Cleveland, Tennessee)

The Church of God, led after 1923 by F. J. Lee, eventually became known as the Church of God (Cleveland, Tenn.) for reasons of identity. This body grew rapidly to become the mainstream of the movement. By 1943, it had joined the National Association of Evangelicals and later was a charter member in the formation of the Pentecostal Fellowship of North America in 1948. It also became one of the largest and fastest-growing Pentecostal churches in the world. Early missions efforts made the Churches of God a dominant force in the Caribbean nations. Later mergers established strong affiliations with national churches in South Africa, Indonesia, and Romania.[36]

As of August 2000, the Cleveland Church of God numbered nearly six million members and adherents in over eighty nations of the world. In the United States, 6,408 churches ministered to a membership of 887,148 members. Since 1910 the *Church of God Evangel* has chronicled the growth and activities of the church.[37]

The Church of God of Prophecy has also grown in America and around the world. In 2000 the American church counted 76,351 members within 1,908 congregations. Church activities are controlled by the general assembly, which each year attracts 20,000 of the faithful to its meetings.[38]

The United Holy Church

The oldest continuing Pentecostal denomination in the United States is the United Holy Church, a largely African-American denomination with roots in North Carolina. The meetings that produced the church occurred in the town of Method, a suburb of Raleigh, North Carolina, in 1886. There a holiness revival broke out in an African-American Baptist congregation where the doctrine and experience of entire sanctification were proclaimed. The holiness revival was led by a Wesleyan prayer group that had its first meetings in 1882. Leading the revival were L. M. Mason, D. S. Freeman, and G. W. Roberts. Baptist officials saw this revival as being contrary to Baptist faith and practice, and, after the revival closed, the holiness faction was asked to leave the church. A new holiness congregation was then organized in May of 1886. Mason was elected to serve as the church's first president. This group, the Providence Holy Church, became the mother church of the denomination.[39]

Other congregations in North Carolina joined the group in the years from 1886 to 1894 when the first convocation was convened in Durham. In 1900 a formal organization was formed and a "manual and discipline for the governing of the churches" was adopted. One of the leaders in this early period was W. H. Fulford from the Fire-Baptized Holiness Church, which was led by the white evangelist Benjamin Hardin Irwin. He served as president from 1903 until 1916. It is probable that under Fulford's leadership the United Holy Church entered the ranks of the Pentecostal movement as hundreds of members were baptized in the Holy Spirit and spoke with other tongues. After 1916, Elder H. L. Fisher became the long-term head of the church. His tenure of office lasted from 1916 until his death in 1947.[40]

The church grew in both the South and the North in the early years of the 20th century as thousands of blacks migrated to the North in search of jobs. Soon the largest local churches were to be found in Philadelphia, New York City, and Chicago.[41]

In 1979, the church was torn by a major division that lasted until the year 2000. One group was led by Bishop W. N. Strobhar of New York and the other by Bishop James A. Forbes. Despite many efforts to avoid division, the church was torn asunder, with Strobhar leading churches in the northern part of the country and Forbes leading a large group located in the southern states. This division was finally healed, and the church reunited in May of 2000 in a great reconciliation convocation in Greensboro, North Carolina, where the main speaker was T. D. Jakes. After the merger, church officials claimed a membership in America of some seven hundred thousand members.[42]

The First Wave of American Pentecostalism

These holiness Pentecostal churches were the first wave of Pentecostalism in the world. Starting with a basic Arminian-Wesleyan theology, they added the Pentecostal baptism in the Holy Spirit evidenced by speaking in tongues to their already highly developed holiness theological system. Representing a radical brand of holiness teaching and experience, it was easier for them to make the transition to Pentecostalism than some of the other more conservative holiness churches such as the Church of the Nazarene and the Wesleyan Methodist Church.

Almost all the founders of the Pentecostal movement, including Charles Parham, William Seymour, and others, were from this stream. The Azusa Street testimony, "I am saved, sanctified, and filled with the Holy Ghost," became the rallying cry of this movement. The "fivefold gospel" of these churches became the first theological manifesto of world Pentecostalism. They were:

1. Justification by faith
2. Sanctification as a second, definite, perfecting work of grace
3. Baptism in the Holy Spirit evidenced by speaking in tongues
4. Divine healing as in the atonement
5. The premillenial Second Coming of Christ

Although some of these teachings were later altered by successive waves of Pentecostals and newer charismatics in the mainline churches, these were the formative teachings that produced the first Pentecostal churches in the world.

For Further Reading

The best narrative source for the background and development of these churches can be found in Vinson Synan's *The Holiness-Pentecostal Tradition: Charismatic Movements in the Twentieth Century* (Grand Rapids: Eerdmans, 1972, 1997). Another major source is Stanley Burgess and Eduard M. van der Maas, eds., *New International Dictionary of Pentecostal and Charismatic Movements* (Grand Rapids: Zondervan, 2001).

The major history of the Church of God in Christ is Ithiel Clemmons's *Bishop C H. Mason and the Roots of the Church of God in Christ* (Bakersfield, Calif.: Pneuma Life Publishing, 1996). For the story of the Church of God (Cleveland, Tenn.), see Charles Conn's *Like a Mighty Army: A History of the*

Church of God, 1886–1976 (Cleveland, Tenn.: Pathway Press, 1955, 1977). The history of the Church of God of Prophecy is given in Charles Davidson's *Upon This Rock,* 3 vols. (Cleveland, Tenn.: White Wing Publishing House, 1973–76).

The latest history of the Pentecostal Holiness Church is Vinson Synan's *The Old-Time Power: A Centennial History of the Pentecostal Holiness Church* (Franklin Springs, Ga.: Life Springs Press, 1973, 1998). The earliest history with much primary material based on personal interviews is Joseph E. Campbell's *The Pentecostal Holiness Church: 1898–1948* (Franklin Springs, Ga.: Publishing House of the Pentecostal Holiness Church, 1951).

The story of the United Holy Church is told in Chester Gregory's well-written book *The History of the United Holy Church of America, Inc.; 1886–1986* (Baltimore: Gateway Press, 1986).

· 6 ·
The "Finished Work" Pentecostal Churches

Vinson Synan

THE HOLINESS PENTECOSTAL CHURCHES were the first organized Pentecostal churches in the world, but as the movement exploded around the nation and the world, thousands of converts were attracted to the movement who did not have roots in the Wesleyan theological stream that dominated American Pentecostalism in the early years. Many of these new Pentecostals were from Baptist, Presbyterian, or other backgrounds. Soon, some of these seekers went directly from conversion to the baptism in the Holy Spirit without the intervening "second blessing" of sanctification.

The first doctrinal variation in the Pentecostal movement was in the place of the "second blessing" in the life of the Pentecostal believer. Many were taken aback by the extreme legalism among some holiness Pentecostals that seemed to border on Pharisaism at best or fanaticism at worst. Also, insistence on a second blessing ran contrary to the theology and experience of many people who entered the movement from non-Wesleyan backgrounds.

The first man to challenge the "three blessing" theology was William H. Durham of Chicago. A longtime holiness preacher of second-blessing sanctification prior to his Pentecostal experience, he stopped preaching instant sanctification as he searched for a new theology. By 1911, he had fashioned what he called the "finished work of Calvary" theology, which denied the necessity of a "second blessing" experience prior to speaking in tongues. For Durham, sanctification was a gradual process that began at conversion and was followed by a progressive growth. This teaching, so revolutionary for the times among Pentecostals, opened a wide theological rift in the Pentecostal movement. Leaders such as Parham, Seymour, and others denounced the "finished work" teaching as a threat to the survival of the movement.

In time, independent Pentecostals who agreed with Durham joined together to form the Assemblies of God in 1914. Most of the Pentecostal churches in the world that were formed subsequently affirmed the Durham view. This reduced the spiritual experiences of these Pentecostals from three to two. Afterward, the "finished work" Pentecostals testified to being "saved and baptized in the Holy Ghost" without reference to sanctification.

The Assemblies of God

With thirty-five million members worldwide, the Assemblies of God (AG) is by far the largest and best-known Pentecostal fellowship in the world. It is also the most influential and visible Pentecostal body, commanding respect in the broader world of evangelical and charismatic Christianity.

The history of the AG is in large part the story of the entire Pentecostal movement, not only in the United States, but also around the world. With roots in the apostolic faith movement, founded by Charles Parham, and the Azusa Street revival, it was the first denomination to be entirely a product of the Pentecostal movement. The other earlier Pentecostal bodies had roots in the holiness movement.

In April 1914, more than three hundred persons gathered in the Grand Opera House in Hot Springs, Arkansas, to create a new national organization for the hundreds of independent Pentecostal assemblies that dotted the cities and towns across the country. This meeting was to be an important turning point for the Pentecostal movement in the United States and ultimately for the world.[1]

Formation

The formation of this new fellowship owed much to men who were not present in Hot Springs and who were never to be a part of the church. Included in this number were Charles Parham, the formulator of the teaching that speaking in tongues was the "initial evidence" of the baptism in the Holy Spirit, a doctrine that became the distinctive of the AG belief concerning the baptism in the Holy Spirit. Another absentee was William J. Seymour, who led the Azusa Street revival in Los Angeles where most of those present accepted the experience. A third person, William Durham, who had passed away in 1912, forged the most distinctive doctrine of the new denomination. His "finished work" theory of entire sanctification distinguished the AG from the older holiness Pentecostal bodies that stressed the "second work" aspect of sanctification. The fourth absentee was A. B. Simpson, founder of the Christian and Missionary Alliance, whose church furnished many of the leaders of the new church as well as its basic theology and world missions thrust.[2]

Another who was present but did not join was Charles H. Mason, head of the Church of God in Christ from Memphis, Tennessee. Though Mason was black and most of the members of his church were blacks, a significant number were whites. Many of those forming the AG were white pastors who had been affiliated with Mason and his church. Many had carried credentials of the Church of God in Christ provided by Mason with the understanding that none would be issued to anyone who was "unworthy."

William H. Durham (1873–1912) is often called the theological father of the Assemblies of God. His "finished work" view of sanctification opened the door to thousands of people from non-Wesleyan backgrounds.

Though the ties between Mason and the white Pentecostals were not strong by 1914, Mason was nevertheless invited to preach at the convention. He did not join the new church, however. In a sense, the organization of the AG was in part a racial separation from Mason's church.[3]

Founding Fathers

Those who were present at the Hot Springs council represented the major elements that formed the church. The chairman and first general superintendent was Eudorus N. Bell, a former Baptist from Texas who was then pastor of a local Pentecostal assembly in Malvern, Arkansas. Bell had been educated in the Southern Baptist Seminary in Louisville, Kentucky, and had studied at the University of Chicago. Many Baptists such as he had entered into the Pentecostal experience despite the lack of teaching in the holiness tradition. Bell represented the large "baptistic" element of the new church.[4]

J. Roswell Flower was elected to serve as general secretary of the church at the youthful age of twenty-six. He was to serve in many positions in the

SANCTIFICATION SCUFFLES

In 1911 as William Durham denounced the "second blessing" doctrine of sanctification, a young woman attacked him with her hat pin to register her "pointed opposition." She was not alone in her contempt for his "demonic" views. The conflict over sanctification had burst forth a year earlier and became the first full-blown controversy of the Pentecostal movement.

The early Pentecostal movement arose from the holiness movement and, like its parent, shared John Wesley's views on sanctification: that it was an instantaneous experience of "entire sanctification" or "Christian perfection" and that it was a separate experience from conversion. Early Pentecostals called it a "second blessing" and regarded it as a necessary preparation for a third experience, the indwelling of the Holy Spirit (that is, the new Pentecostal experience).

In 1910, William H. Durham, pastor of the North Avenue Mission in Chicago, began making waves throughout Pentecostal circles when he denounced these views. "I began to write against the doctrine that it takes two works of grace to save and cleanse a man," he later wrote. "I denied and still deny that God does not deal with the nature of sin at conversion. I deny that a man who is converted or born again is outwardly washed and cleansed but that his heart is left unclean with enmity against God in it."

This wouldn't be salvation, he argued, because salvation "means that all the old man, or old nature, which was sinful and depraved and which was the very thing in us that was condemned, is crucified with Christ." He dubbed his position the "finished work at Calvary" because he believed the work of Christ on the cross was sufficient for both salvation and sanctification. Finished-work Pentecostals slowly also came to stress a gradual process of sanctification, not an instantaneous one, in which the sanctifying work of Christ was "appropriated" over one's life.

Locked Out of Azusa

Durham returned to the Azusa Mission in 1911 (where he had received the gift of tongues in 1906). William Seymour was on a preaching tour, and Durham was invited to preach. His finished-work teaching generated conflict but sparked a fresh revival. Wrote one observer, "The fire began to fall at old Azusa as at the beginning." But when Seymour heard what was going on, he promptly returned and padlocked the church door to prevent the Chicago preacher from speaking further in his pulpit. Undaunted, Durham moved to a rival mission and continued proclaiming his message.

From his home in Kansas, Charles Parham (by then dropping rapidly out of the Pentecostal spotlight) declared, "If this man's doctrine is true, let my life go out to prove it, but if our teaching on a definite grace of sanctification is true, let his life pay the forfeit." When Durham passed away unexpectedly later that year, Parham claimed vindication and remarked to his followers "how signally God has answered."

Despite such ardent denunciation, Durham's interpretation emerged as the preferred theological position for roughly half of all Pentecostals by 1915. Most of the denominations formed as Holiness bodies prior to the Pentecostal outpouring remained staunch supporters of the second-blessing doctrine, while newer organizations, including the Assemblies of God, either left the matter open to individuals or adopted the finished-work view. It is today the view of most American Pentecostals. ∎

—JAMES R. GOFF JR.
CHRISTIAN HISTORY

Assemblies of God until his retirement in 1959, when he was again in the position of general secretary. Flower, along with Noel Perkin and Frank Boyd, had been loosely associated with the Christian and Missionary Alliance before entering the Pentecostal ranks.[5]

M. M. Pinson, an ardent follower of William Durham, preached the keynote sermon at the council on "the finished work of Calvary," the dominant theological theme of the gathering. Pinson had been ordained in J. O. McClurkan's Pentecostal Mission in Nashville, Tennessee, a group that later merged with the Church of the Nazarene. He represented the large number of Wesleyans who joined the Assemblies despite the newer view on sanctification. Indeed, thousands of holiness Pentecostals representing various views of holiness joined with the Assemblies in the next decade. Thus, during these years, one of the most controversial questions in the *Pentecostal Evangel*, the church's official periodical, concerned the second blessing.[6]

Pinson, Flower, and Bell also edited the three periodicals that influenced the call to Hot Springs. Flower's *Christian Evangel* was published in Plainfield, Indiana. Bell's *Apostolic Faith* and Pinson's *Word and Witness*, which had been merged under the latter name in 1912, were published in Malvern, Arkansas.[7]

In their roles of communicating church news and upcoming conventions, these periodicals were vital to the development of the basic organizations that came together in Hot Springs to form the new church. In Alabama, Pinson's group used the name Church of God from 1909 until 1911 when it changed its name to Church of God in Christ. Bell's group in Texas used the name Apostolic Faith until 1911 when it also adopted the name Church of God in Christ and accepted credentials from Mason's church. These two groups joined with Flower in Indiana by issuing the call

The Assemblies of God organized in April 1914 with 356 ministers from all parts of the nation.

for the Hot Springs council in 1914. Others joining them in the call were A. P. Collins, H. A. Goss, and D. C. O. Opperman.[8]

Reasons for Organizing

Five reasons were given for the call to hold the Hot Springs council. The first was to formulate a defensible doctrinal position for the growing number of independent Pentecostal churches, which were often tossed about "with every wind of doctrine." A second reason was the desire to consolidate and conserve the Pentecostal work, which was in danger of dissipating without better mutual support from pastors who were often isolated from one another and lacking in fellowship.

In this building the historic meeting was held in 1914 that produced the Assemblies of God, destined to become the largest Pentecostal denomination in the world.

A third reason was the need for a central foreign missions agency to account for funds being sent abroad to the host of eager Pentecostal missionaries fanning out all over the world with little experience, support, or direction. A fourth reason was the need to establish approved Bible schools to train future pastors and leaders for the churches.

A fifth reason for the council grew out of the first four. A new organization was needed to conserve the fruit of the Pentecostal revival that was moving powerfully throughout the nation and the world. What was produced in Hot Springs was a "new wineskin" for the new wine of the Holy Spirit that was being poured out.[9]

The Teachings of the Church

The name for the new church was fundamental to its success. Since the name common to most of the groups coming together was the Church of God in Christ, the new name conveyed a variation of that name. The word *assembly* comes from the same Greek word that is commonly translated "church." The plural form, *assemblies*, pointed to the congregational nature of the group, which consisted of hundreds of independent assemblies banded together for fellowship and common ministry. The name was suggested by T. K. Leonard, whose local congregation in Findlay, Ohio, had been called Assembly of God for several years before 1914.[10]

There was a common concern that the new church should not be a creedal one and not too tightly organized. Therefore, it was decided that a binding creedal statement of faith would not be adopted. However, the Preamble and Resolution on Constitution contained the basic teachings on which the churches agreed, thus placing them in the non-Wesleyan, evangelical, dispensational Pentecostal camp. The crucial doctrine holding all together was that speaking in tongues was the "initial evidence" of the baptism in the Holy Spirit.[11]

The doctrinal latitude allowed in 1914 was an effort to continue the freedom of the Spirit to move in fresh ways in the churches. Any doctrinal restraints that would inhibit this freedom were to be avoided. This cherished freedom was to be severely tested, however, by the rise of the "oneness" movement in the church during the next two years.

This movement, which supporters called the "Jesus' name" movement and detractors dubbed the "Jesus only" movement, had origins in California in 1913, just one year before the meeting of the Hot Springs council. Led by Frank Ewart and Glenn Cook, the new teaching denied the doctrine of the Trinity and insisted on a unitarianism of the Son. Trinitarians were accused of worshiping "three gods." The oneness view was that the only valid form of water baptism was "in Jesus' name" and that speaking in tongues was necessary to salvation. This teaching spread rapidly from assembly to assembly after 1914 and threatened to engulf the entire church.[12]

The danger was heightened in 1915 when General Superintendent Bell was rebaptized in Jesus' name. The Third General Council, which convened in St. Louis, Missouri, in October 1915, was so divided that no vote was taken on the explosive new issue. In the following months the Trinitarians, led by Flower, Pinson, and John W. Welch, rallied their forces to counter the Unitarians. A crucial victory was the reconversion of Bell to the Unitarian view. By the time the Fourth General Council convened in 1916, the Trinitarians were in control. When the final vote was taken, the new denomination lost 156 of its ordained ministers to the Jesus' name partisans.

Eudorus Bell, the first general superintendent of the Assemblies of God, was one of the few early Pentecostals with formal education. A graduate of the Southern Baptist Theological Seminary in Louisville, Kentucky and the University of Chicago, he served as pastor of Southern Baptist churches for seventeen years before becoming a Pentecostal in 1908.

With this decision behind them, the remaining delegates then adopted a Trinitarian statement of faith, which became the doctrinal standard of practically all the Pentecostal churches formed after that time.[13]

The Church Grows

The growth of the Assemblies of God since 1914 has been phenomenal, both in the United States and around the world. Begun basically as a missionary society, the church developed one of the most aggressive foreign missions programs in the world. Missionaries were sent to the far corners of the globe to spread the Pentecostal message. Sacrificial giving for world missions became the major concern of the churches.

The desire to expand in the mission fields was matched by an equal desire to spread throughout the United States. Assemblies of God churches were soon planted in every state of the union. In large cities where mainline churches were dying, thriving assemblies were organized. In thousands of cities where other denominations failed, the Assemblies of God was able to penetrate.

The greatest growth of the AG came after World War II in the healing revivals that brought the Pentecostal message to the masses of the nation. After a period of slower growth in the 1960s, the church prospered in the period of the charismatic renewal in the traditional denominations. The 1970s and first half of the 1980s saw the church grow to become one of the major denominations in the United States. By 2000 some of the largest congregations in the nation were affiliated with the Assemblies of God. Among them were Karl Strader's Carpenter's Home Church in Lakeland, Florida, with a sanctuary seating about ten thousand persons. Other large Assemblies include the six-thousand-seat Crossroads Cathedral, Oklahoma City, Oklahoma, pastored by Dan Sheaffer; Calvary Temple in Irving, Texas, pastored by Don George; and First Assembly of God in Phoenix, Arizona, pastored by Tommy Barnett.[14]

Leading the world in size and church growth is the Assemblies of God Church in Seoul, South Korea, led by Paul Yonggi Cho. It is known locally as the Yoido Full Gospel Church. With a membership of more than 730,000 in 2000, this congregation is expected to eventually pass the one million mark.[15]

The growth statistics of the AG are impressive indeed. From the 300 members who gathered in Hot Springs in 1914, the church has grown in 2000 to a worldwide following that claims a membership of more than 35 million persons, of which 2.5 million are in the United States. Using a more demographic approach, David Barrett credits the AG with 44 million members and adherents. The American church counts 12,055 local congregations. These Christians worship in a global community of 121,424 churches and outreach centers, including 10,886 in the United States. A total of 1,464 American missionaries work in 118 countries. Around the world, 301 Bible schools train ministers to spread the work of the church.[16]

When the missions program was started, it was decided that the goal of the church was to develop self-governing, self-supporting fields—free of dependence on the church in the United States. Therefore, many national churches carry the name Assemblies of God without direct ties to the American headquarters in Springfield, Missouri. Though all fly the same banner and agree on the same doctrines, throughout the world they are more truly a fellowship of national, independent churches than a single international church body. This is true of the largest national church, the Brazilian Assemblies of God. The Brazilian church was formed in 1910, four years before the one in the United States.

Of all the leaders in the history of the AG, no one has exerted a more far-reaching influence than Thomas Zimmerman, who ended his service as general superintendent in December 1985. During his twenty-six years in office, the church more than doubled in size in the United States. Zimmerman also helped bring the Pentecostals into the evangelical mainstream when he was elected as the first Pentecostal president of the National Association of Evangelicals. After the 1985 general council, he was asked to serve as president of the Lausanne committee.

In the 1980s members of the AG attained high positions in the political world. James Watt, who served as secretary of the interior under President Ronald Reagan, was the first Pentecostal ever to hold a position of cabinet rank. In 1985 John D. Ashcroft was inaugurated as governor of Missouri, the first Pentecostal to be elected governor of a state.

Traveling almost anywhere in the world, one is likely to see congregations of the Assemblies of God in the smallest village or the most densely populated metropolis. By 2000, the AG were winning some ten thousand converts a day around the world. According to Thomas Trask, general superintendent in 2000, if the present growth rates continue, the Assemblies of God will number more than one hundred million members by the time of the centennial celebration of the church in 2014.[17]

The International Church of the Foursquare Gospel

In July 1922 the world-famous evangelist Aimee Semple McPherson stood in the Oakland Civic Auditorium in California and shared a vision that in time became the International Church of the Foursquare Gospel. Preaching from Ezekiel 1:4–28, which describes a creature with four faces, she saw in that passage four major doctrines. They were symbolized in the man, the lion, the ox, and the eagle, and these images became the core of her ministry.

The evangelist went on to tell of the vision she had had that clarified the meaning of the faces. She said they all represented Jesus: the face of the man was Jesus as Savior; the lion was Jesus as baptizer in the Holy Spirit; the ox was Jesus as healer; and the eagle was Jesus as the coming King. She described this revelation as "a perfect gospel, a complete gospel for body, for soul, for spirit, and for eternity." Thus was born the theology and the name for a major Pentecostal denomination that today ministers in fifty-five nations of the world under the banner of the International Church of the Foursquare Gospel.[18]

ASSEMBLIES OF GOD 2000 COVENANT

Having been commanded to take this gospel to all the world,

Knowing we are living in the last days of time,
Recognizing that people without Jesus are eternally lost,
Having received empowerment through the Holy Spirit's baptism to accomplish this task,
Acknowledging that without Christ we can do nothing,
Having the Lord's promise to supply all the resources necessary to fulfill His commands,
Acknowledging that God has recommissioned us with His enabling,

We, the Assemblies of God—part of a great community of believers worldwide—hereby recommit ourselves to obey the Great Commission and to seek a fresh enduement of power to accomplish this task.

We will give sacrificially of our resources and ourselves and will not rest until everyone has heard the gospel both in the United States and in all the world.

"Go ye therefore and teach all nations, baptizing them in the name of the Father, and of the Son, and of the Holy Ghost: teaching them to observe all things whatsoever I have commanded you: and lo, I am with you always, even unto the end of the world."

—*Matthew 28:19, 20*

—THOMAS TRASK, GENERAL SUPERINTENDENT
OF THE ASSEMBLIES OF GOD

It has been said that an institution is the lengthened shadow of a man. In this case, it is the lengthened shadow of a woman.

Aimee Semple McPherson was born in Ingersoll, Ontario, Canada, in 1890. She holds a prominent rank among all religious leaders in the 20th century regardless of sex and may well be the most important ordained woman minister in the history of Christianity. A flamboyant, talented, and attractive woman, she commanded the attention of the world for more than two decades. Her early years were chronicled in her 1927 autobiography, *In the Service of the King.*

Aimee's father was a Methodist, but her early religious training came from her mother, Minnie Kennedy, who served as a leader in the Salvation Army. Despite being raised in the holiness tradition, Aimee was converted as a teenager in 1907 in a revival conducted by a young Pentecostal evangelist named Robert Semple. Soon after that, Aimee was baptized in the Holy Spirit and spoke in tongues. She then left the Salvation Army to become a Pentecostal, and she also fell in love with the evangelist and married him.[19]

The young couple accepted a call to go to the Orient as missionaries. In 1910 they arrived in

Built by Aimee Semple McPherson in 1923, Angelus Temple seated 5,300 people. Some 25,000 persons attended the 21 weekly services conducted by "Sister Aimee" while she served as pastor from 1923 to 1944.

China and were there only a few short months when Semple died. Aimee was then eight months pregnant with her first child. Returning to the United States, she worked in the Salvation Army with her mother in New York City. In 1912, she married Harold Stewart McPherson of Providence, Rhode Island. They had a son, Rolf Kennedy McPherson, who was destined to become president of the church in 1944.

Aimee's marriage to McPherson was an unhappy one since she felt called to hit the sawdust trail while he wished to continue as a businessman. They were later divorced. In 1915, "Sister Aimee," as she was affectionately known, answered the call to evangelize after holding a successful revival crusade in Mount Forest, Ontario. By 1918, after a whirlwind tour of revivals up and down the East Coast, she settled in Los Angeles, where she lived for the rest of her life.

It took several years, however, before the restless evangelist was able to settle on a denominational home in which to minister. Before founding the

Foursquare movement, she joined at least three churches in addition to the Salvation Army in which she was born. In December 1920 she united with the Hancock Methodist Episcopal Church in Philadelphia. In March 1922 Pastor William Keeney Towner ordained her as a Baptist minister in the First Baptist Church in San Jose, California. And for several years afterward she was listed as a minister of the Assemblies of God. All of these affiliations lapsed when she founded her own denomination in 1927.[20]

Angelus Temple

During the latter part of the 1920s, Aimee became a national celebrity as well as a pastor and evangelist. With a national magazine called the *Bridal Call* (now known as *Foursquare World Advance)* and with the financial sup-

---

THE GREAT "I AM" OR "I WAS"?

(AN EXCERPT FROM A SERMON BY AIMEE SEMPLE MCPHERSON)

"Pit-a-pat! Pit-a-pat"—say the hundreds and thousands of feet, surging by the church doors of our land. "Pat! Pat! Pit-a-pat!"—hurrying multitudes, on business and pleasure bent.

From out the church door floats the voice of Pastor and Evangelist in an effort to halt the down-rushing throng in their headlong race toward destruction and attract their attention to the Christ.

"Stop! Stop! Giddy throng, surging by like a river, take your eyes from the bright lights of the gilded way," they cry. "Leave the paths of death, enter our open door and listen while we tell you the sweet though ancient story of 'The Great I WAS.'

"Eloquently, instructively, we will tell you of the wonderful power Christ 'used' to have, the miracles He 'used' to perform, the sick He 'used' to heal. 'Tis a graphic and blessed history of those things which Jesus did almost nineteen hundred years before you were born. They happened far, far away across the sea which you have never sailed, in a country which you have never seen, among people you have never known. Wonderful, marvelous, was the power that 'used' to flow from 'The Great I WAS' . . ."

And out o'er the heads of the people I hear the message ring: "Awake! Thou that sleepest, arise from the dead! The Lord still lives today. His power has never abated. His Word has never changed. The things He did in Bible days, He still lives to do today. Not a burden is there He cannot bear nor a fetter He cannot break.

"Here bring your sins, He'll wash them away. Here bring your sicknesses, He'll heal you today. We serve not a dead but a living God; not 'I WAS,' but 'The Great I AM.'

"Come young, come old; come sad, come glad; come weary and faltering of step; come sick, come well! Come one, come all unto 'The Great I AM.' There is food for the hungry, there is strength for the faint; there is hope for the hopeless, and sight for the blind." ∎

—CHRISTIAN HISTORY

port that came from her continuing salvation-healing crusades, she began construction of the Angelus Temple near Echo Park in Los Angeles in 1921. This sanctuary, the largest church in America at the time with 5,300 seats, became the center of her burgeoning ministry. Its value was $1.5 million (in 1921 dollars!).

During the first year in the temple, more than ten thousand persons answered altar calls to be "born again." For the next twenty years, the temple was usually filled to capacity with persons anxious to see and hear the legendary woman evangelist. Thousands of people were often turned away for lack of seats. In those years, Aimee ministered to more than twenty thousand persons per week. It was truly America's first "superchurch."

Aimee's ministry continued to skyrocket after the dedication of the temple in 1923. She was the first woman to preach a sermon over the radio (1922) and the first pastor to build a radio station owned by a local church. The station went on the air in 1924 with the call letters KFSG (Kall Foursquare Gospel). In 1925, she also opened a Bible school housed in a five-story building constructed next to the church. The school was called L.I.F.E. Bible College (Lighthouse International Foursquare Evangelism), an institution founded with a mandate to train the hundreds of new young leaders who flocked to her church.

The ministries of Aimee Semple McPherson and the Angelus Temple were staggering. In the beginning, she personally conducted twenty-one services per week for the faithful. Her dramatic services captured the imagination and curiosity of the public. She often wrote the dramas, pageants, and oratorios that were presented by the huge staff of the temple. In one typical service, Sister Aimee, dressed as a policeman, drove a motorcycle onto the huge stage, blew a whistle, and shouted, "Stop, you are going to hell!" In another service, the stage was set as a cotton plantation in the Old South with overtones of *Gone with the Wind* modified to proclaim the Foursquare gospel. These extravaganzas made her a celebrity from coast to coast, with her activities gaining press attention equal to that of any Hollywood star. [21]

All was not drama and glamour at the temple, however. In 1926 the Angelus Temple Commissary was opened to feed the hungry and clothe the naked. When the Great Depression hit the nation after 1929, the temple fed and clothed more than 1.5 million needy people in the Los Angeles area. Because of her love for the poor, Sister Aimee won the everlasting love and devotion of the down-and-outers of depressed America.

Among those attracted to the evangelist in those hard times were movie star Anthony Quinn and Richard Halverson, who later served as chaplain of the U.S. Senate. The most famous person ever to "walk the aisles" in

Angelus Temple was a young Quaker boy by the name of Richard Milhous Nixon.[22]

In May 1926, Aimee disappeared from a beach near Los Angeles, and her whereabouts were unknown for several weeks. When she reappeared in June in New Mexico, she claimed to have been kidnapped. Many rumors circulated about "the vanishing evangelist," but in a subsequent court case, she was acquitted of any fraud or wrongdoing. In later years she was also involved in sensational lawsuits with her mother, Minnie, who served as her business manager. The dauntless Aimee, however, survived these crises as well as others and each time went on to even greater victories.[23]

The Foursquare Gospel Church Formed

With her growing and dynamic ministry attracting thousands of faithful followers throughout the United States, Aimee organized her own denomination in 1927. True to her 1922 vision, it was called the "International Church of the Foursquare Gospel" with headquarters at Angelus Temple. The new church was identical to the Assemblies of God in doctrine, while differing in organizational structure and polity. Under Sister Aimee's tight control, the denomination developed a strong centralized structure with all church properties owned by the parent corporation.[24]

The Foursquare doctrinal statement placed it in the mainstream of the American Pentecostal movement. Trinitarian and evangelical, the church adopted the "initial evidence" theory of glossolalia as constituting the first sign of receiving the baptism in the Holy Spirit. The idea of four major doctrinal statements had been used earlier by A. B. Simpson of the Christian and Missionary Alliance, who had spoken of Jesus as "Savior, sanctifier, healer, and coming King." The only difference in the Foursquare statement was the substitution of "baptizer in the Holy Spirit" for "sanctifier." Aimee also compiled a *Declaration of Faith* consisting of twenty-two articles that elaborated on the four fundamental teachings of the church.[25]

The early days of the new organization saw explosive growth as many independent Pentecostal congregations applied to join the movement. By 1928 there were more than fifty Foursquare churches in southern California with scores of others throughout the United States applying to join. Soon missionaries were carrying the Foursquare banner to Canada, Britain, and many other nations. The main reason for this early growth was the magnetic and dynamic personality of the founder.[26]

Aimee often traveled to the mission fields. In 1943, she was on such a trip in Mexico when she contracted a tropical fever. A year later, on September 22, 1944, she died after preaching a sermon in Oakland, California.

Her death certificate indicated she had died from "shock and respiratory failure" after she took an overdose of sleeping capsules prescribed by a doctor.

The Church After Aimee

After her death, leadership passed to her son, Rolf, who has served as president ever since. To carry on the administration of the organization, McPherson relied on a general field supervisor and district supervisors for the United States; they carried out the day-to-day affairs of the denomination. In addition, a director of world missions was given supervision of the church's foreign missionaries. The best known of the general supervisors was Howard P. Courtney, who served the church from 1944 to 1974.[27]

Since 1927, the growth of the church has been steady, though not as spectacular as in the early days. By 1944, the number of congregations in the United States had reached five hundred. After a period of slow growth in the 1950s and 1960s, the church experienced a revival and renewal in the 1970s and 1980s during the time of the charismatic renewal in the mainline churches. Of all the classical Pentecostal denominations, the Foursquare Church has been the most affected by the charismatic renewal. To many outsiders, the worship services of the church are such that charismatics from mainline denominations feel immediately at home.[28]

A great impetus in this development has been the ministry of Jack Hayford, whose Church on the Way in Van Nuys, California, has grown to be the largest Foursquare congregation in the United States. With ten thousand–plus members, Hayford's church is a modern-day counterpart to Angelus Temple. Hayford's influence reaches far beyond the bounds of his denomination, however, since he is a popular speaker for many charismatic conferences.

The greatest American growth for the church in recent years has taken place in the northwestern states where Roy Hicks Jr. led in planting many churches in Oregon and Washington. Other significant growth has taken place in California and the East. By 2000, some of the largest Foursquare churches in America included Jack Hayford's Church on the Way in Van Nuys, California (as mentioned above); Ron Mehl's Foursquare congregation in Beaverton, Oregon; and the Faith Center Church in Eugene, Oregon, pastored by Roy Hicks Jr. At least two Foursquare congregations own television stations. These are operated by the Foursquare churches in Decatur, Illinois, and Roanoke, Virginia.

For most of its history, the American church was larger than the churches on the mission fields. In 1952, for instance, only one-third of the church's members lived outside the United States. By 1960 the numbers were approximately equal. By 2000, however, more than two-thirds of the church membership lived overseas. The figures for that year were 238,000 members and 2,000 churches in the United States and 863,642 in other countries. The grand total of members, affiliates and adherents worldwide in 2000 stood at 1,045,236 persons.

Serving these churches is a ministerium of 4,856 pastors, evangelists, and missionaries around the world. Of these, 737 are ordained women, many of whom serve as pastors. In fact, the 1986 minutes indicate that no less than 41 percent of all the ordained Foursquare ministers in the United States are women, one of the highest proportions of women ministers of any church in the world. This large percentage may reflect the fact that a woman, with roots in the Salvation Army, founded the church.

In recent years, the church has emphasized education more than in the past. In addition to L.I.F.E. Bible College, the Foursquare Church operates the Mount Vernon Bible College in Ohio. Also, there is a greater interest in theology as Foursquare students enroll in major universities and seminaries around the nation. A major theology of the church was published in 1983 by L.I.F.E. Bible College. Written by Guy Duffield and Nathaniel Van Cleave, it is titled *Foundations of Pentecostal Theology.*[29]

The Pentecostal Church of God

The Pentecostal Church of God, which has its roots in the Assemblies of God, was formed in 1919 under the leadership of John C. Sinclair and George Brinkman, who were founding fathers of the AG in 1914. Along with most leaders of the church, they were strong advocates of never adopting a doctrinal statement for the denomination. Sinclair, an executive presbyter of the Assemblies of God and pastor of a large church in Chicago, was known as the first person to receive the Pentecostal experience in that city, while Brinkman was editor of the *Pentecostal Herald*, an influential independent Pentecostal journal.[30]

At its founding in 1914, the AG refused to adopt a doctrinal statement since most of the founders harbored fears of developing into a creedal church with denominational authority exercised from the top. Two years later, the oneness question resulted in a division in which the non-Trinitarians left to form their own associations. In 1916, to clarify its position on the Trinity, the AG adopted a "Statement of Fundamental Truths," which some saw as a dangerous development. Sinclair and Brinkman then led a movement to separate from the AG and form a new church without a doctrinal statement.[31]

In 1919, a new church was born in Chicago with the name "Pentecostal Assemblies of the U.S.A." The new body adopted Brinkman's *Pentecostal Herald* as their official organ and began to plant churches across the nation. Doctrinally, the new denomination was identical to the AG but more loosely organized. At first the church operated essentially as an office to hold ministerial licenses with little ecclesiastical control over churches or ministers. In 1922, the name of the church was changed to Pentecostal Church of God. In 1934, the words "of America" were added to the name. Since that time the church has been known as the Pentecostal Church of God of America.

One of the founders of the Pentecostal Church of God, John C. Sinclair (1863–1936) was so committed to the principle of independency that he later withdrew from the church he had founded.

Over the years, the church has been governed by a general convention that convenes every two years. In the year 1934, the church established the "Messenger Publishing House" in Kansas City.

Although the Pentecostal Church of God began with a promise never to adopt a creed, doctrinal questions and controversies made it necessary to adopt a statement of faith. This was done in 1933. The statement was similar to that of the Assemblies of God, which placed the Pentecostal Church of God in the "Baptistic" stream of American Pentecostalism.[32]

The church spread slowly throughout the United States. An American Indian missions program was begun in 1949. Although the church had maintained a department of foreign missions since 1932, it was not until 1949 that a full-time missions director was named. Since that time the church has sponsored a vigorous missions ministry in more than twenty countries. By the year 2000, the Pentecostal Church of God had 104,000 members in 1,237 congregations in the United States. The global membership stood at 800,000 in more than 8,000 churches and preaching points.[33]

One of the most influential Pentecostal missionary evangelists, T. L. Osborn, came from the Pentecostal Church of God. His healing crusades in many nations helped spearhead the mass evangelistic campaigns of the 1950s. He was particularly successful in preaching to huge throngs in non-Christian cultures of Africa, Asia, and Latin America.

Another famous family from the Pentecostal Church of God was the Tathams of Sallisaw, Oklahoma. This family was the subject of John

Steinbeck's 1939 novel *Grapes of Wrath,* the story of a poverty-stricken Oklahoma family who fled to California in the days of the Great Depression and the horrors of the dust bowl. Coming from a local Pentecostal holiness church, the family went to California in the 1930s. After their arrival, the Tathams joined a local congregation of the Pentecostal Church of God. The hero of the book, Oca Tatham, became an ordained minister in the church and pastored several congregations in California. Some members of the Tatham family eventually became wealthy businessmen in Fresno, California.[34]

In 1951, the general offices and publishing house were moved to Joplin, Missouri, where they remain today. The official church organ, now called the *Pentecostal Messenger,* is published in Joplin.

The Open Bible Standard Church

One of the youngest classical Pentecostal denominations in America is the Open Bible Standard Church with headquarters in Des Moines, Iowa. This church was formed in 1935 by a merger of two Pentecostal bodies, the Bible Standard Church and the Open Bible Evangelistic Association. The history of this church is interesting because of the fact that both merging churches had separated from denominations founded by women ministers.[35]

The Bible Standard Church had its roots in Florence Crawford's Apostolic Faith Church in Portland, Oregon. Crawford had been a prominent member of the pastoral staff at the famous Azusa Street Mission, helping William Seymour in editing the Azusa paper *Apostolic Faith.* She later moved to Portland where she continued to publish the paper. In time, Crawford's church suffered a division led by Fred Hornshuh and A. J. Hegan, who complained about the exclusiveness and strictness of the church. In particular they disagreed with Crawford's rule that divorced persons could never remarry and remain in the church. In 1919 they founded a new church with less-stringent rules on divorce and remarriage.

The Open Bible Evangelistic Association was begun by John R. Richey in Des Moines in 1932 as a division in the International Church of the Foursquare Gospel, which had been founded by another woman preacher, the famous Aimee Semple McPherson. Richey, a dynamic speaker and gifted organizer, was disenchanted by the famous kidnapping incident involving Sister Aimee in 1926. He also objected to the centralized polity of the Foursquare Church, which demanded that all church properties be deeded to the national organization.[36]

The nucleus of Richey's new denomination was the three large Foursquare congregations that were formed after McPherson's sensational evangelistic crusades in Des Moines in 1927 and 1928. By 1932, Richey was able to lead the entire Iowa and Minnesota Districts of the International Church of the Foursquare into a split with the denomination. The churches in these states became the new Open Bible Evangelistic Association in 1932.[37]

As leaders of the two groups met and compared notes, they felt such a kinship over doctrine and church government that a merger was effected in Des Moines in 1935, producing a new denomination, the "Open Bible Standard Churches, Inc." The new church was doctrinally and organizationally similar to the AG, stressing salvation by faith, the baptism in the Holy Spirit evidenced by speaking in tongues, divine healing, and the millennial Rapture of the church. Starting with 210 ministers in 1932, the church had grown to encompass more than 50,000 members in 382 churches by the year 2000.[38]

The Oneness Pentecostals

A third stream of American Pentecostalism is the "oneness" movement, which is non-Trinitarian while remaining basically evangelical and Pentecostal. Often pejoratively called the "Jesus only" movement in the early days, insiders preferred the label "Oneness," "Jesus' name," or "apostolic." While the holiness Pentecostals taught three blessings and the finished-work Pentecostals two blessings, the oneness Pentecostals taught a "one blessing" approach where everything (salvation, sanctification, and baptism in the Holy Spirit with tongues) was received in the waters of baptism by immersion in the "name of Jesus."[39]

According to oneness teaching, the only valid baptism is in "Jesus' name" and not "in the name of the Father, Son, and Holy Ghost." Trinitarian baptism is seen as a Roman Catholic error that was forced on the church in the Nicean Creed in A.D. 325. Therefore, anyone who received Trinitarian baptism was not fully Christian. Also, these were the only Pentecostals in the world who taught that speaking in tongues was necessary to salvation. Without tongues, they taught, baptismal regeneration was impossible.[40]

Born in Australia, Frank J. Ewart (1876–1947) pastored Baptist churches before joining the Pentecostals in 1908. Along with Glenn Cook, he founded the oneness Pentecostal movement in 1914.

Because of this theology, the oneness Pentecostals launched a determined campaign to rebaptize all Pentecostal members using the Jesus' name formula. At first they were spectacularly successful, even rebaptizing the general superintendent of the Assemblies of God, E. N. Bell. In a short time, however, the Trinitarians were able to swing the AG back into the Trinitarian fold. Led by J. Roswell Flower and John W. Welch, Bell returned to the Trinitarian position. The Assemblies of God and the church rejected the Unitarian challenge in 1916.[41]

Garfield T. Haywood (1880–1931) was one of the founders of the Pentecostal Assemblies of the World. He was also noted as a prolific hymn writer.

The separation was costly for the infant Assemblies of God. The entire Louisiana District joined the oneness cause as did hundreds of pastors and churches across the nation. A large church allied with the AG was a congregation in Indianapolis under the leadership of black pastor Garfield Thomas Haywood. When he joined the oneness movement, large numbers of black pastors joined with him to form hundreds of "apostolic" and "Jesus' name" churches across the nation.

DIVIDING OVER ONENESS

The oneness movement pushed Pentecostals to organize.

> Preach in Jesus' Name,
> Teach in Jesus' Name,
> Heal the sick in His Name;
> And always proclaim,
> It was Jesus' Name
> In which the power came;
> Baptize in His name
> Enduring the shame,
> For there is victory in Jesus' Name.

So went one of the hymns of the oneness Pentecostals, for whom *Jesus* was the name of the Father, the Son, and the Holy Spirit. Their desire to recapture the mantle of the apostolic church started with questions over the proper formula to use in water baptism. But they were soon questioning even the doctrine of the Trinity.

In April 1913, a Pentecostal holiness meeting was held in Arroyo Seco, California. Between 1,500 and 2,000 Pentecostals, mainly pastors, attended the meetings each night, with hundreds more filling the camp on Sundays. It was here that Robert Edward McAlister, a respected Canadian minister, observed that though Jesus had told His disciples to "baptize [disciples] in the name of the Father and of the Son and of the Holy Spirit," the New Testament invariably records the apostles baptizing only "in the name of Jesus."

Pentecostal preacher Frank J. Ewart later said, "The gun was fired from that platform which was destined to resound throughout all Christendom."

In fact, by January 1915, the message had spread across the continent. Many of the Pentecostal faithful were rebaptized to follow the ways of the apostolic church. They believed older doctrines, long diseased by generations of unfaithfulness and the inability to heed God's Spirit were being uncovered by this "new light" of the Holy Spirit.

For most of the new adherents, this was just a different formula for baptism, not a conscious rejection of the Trinity. Eventually, however, while oneness Pentecostals worshiped God as Father, Son, and Holy Spirit, the terms "Trinity" and "persons" were rejected as unbiblical.

Two in the Spirit

J. Roswell Flower, later secretary of the Assemblies of God (AG), was anxious not only about the apparent denial of orthodox doctrine but also with the potential this "new issue" had for creating division. He urged other leaders to call a meeting of the General Council to prevent it from spreading.

On October 1, 1915, a total of 525 delegates met in St. Louis, ready for a confrontation. The oneness adherents did not present an aggressive front, so no strong effort was made to censure them. Instead, the council proposed a compromise. It specifically denounced the practice of rebaptism as well as a few other oneness doctrines. But it acknowledged both formulas for baptism as Christian.

The oneness Pentecostals became increasingly vocal after the council, and within a year, the AG delegates were back in St. Louis. They were to decide once and for all whether the denomination was big enough to accept oneness adherents.

Since its formation in 1914, the group had rebelled against formal organization. They wanted to reestablish the church of the New Testament, and the New Testament gave no examples of organization beyond local churches. Creeds, "tradition," and power structures had corrupted the church and stifled the Holy Spirit.

So rather than address the doctrinal issues of the Trinity, the oneness contingent (made up largely of African-Americans) stressed that they did not want to establish a set of doctrinal statements for the AG. In fact, they voted against every proposition that was raised.

Their strategy failed. A "Statement of Fundamental Truths," almost half of which was a repudiation of oneness beliefs, was accepted as the AG standard. More than a quarter of those attending, 156 members, were forced to leave the AG and form new organizations (the most important of these were the Pentecostal Assemblies of the World and—via several future mergers—the United Pentecostal Church). But because of the AG's reaction to the "new issue," the group became solidified as a denomination early in its history.

Many small oneness groups formed after 1916, though many have remained independent. Today scholars estimate there are between 1.5 and 5 million oneness Pentecostals worldwide, and they make up only a fraction of 1 percent of the world's Pentecostals. ∎

—KENNETH GILL
CHRISTIAN HISTORY

The Pentecostal Assemblies of the World

As we have seen, the oneness Pentecostal movement had its origins in the early years of the Assemblies of God and developed as a schism from that church. After the climactic vote in the 1916 General Council in St. Louis, in which the AG officially cast its lot with the Trinitarians, 156 pastors walked out and were forced to search for a new organization. What they found was a loosely organized church, the Pentecostal Assemblies of the World, that had begun in California in 1906 under the leadership of J. J. Frazee. Although begun as a Trinitarian church, the organization quickly adopted the oneness theology and became a home to those Pentecostal Unitarians that had left the AG. The headquarters of the new church was soon moved to Indianapolis since the largest oneness church in the nation was located there. This church was pastored by Garfield Thomas Haywood, a black pastor of a racially integrated but largely African-American congregation. In 1916 a large contingent of white former Assemblies of God pastors, led by Howard Goss and D. C. O. Opperman, merged with the church, making it the major oneness church in the nation.[42]

From the beginning, the Pentecostal Assemblies of the World was racially integrated.The foremost leader was Haywood, who served as presiding

---

WHAT DO ONENESS PENTECOSTALS BELIEVE?

Oneness Pentecostalism (OP) is the third stream of the 20th-century Pentecostal movement (the holiness Pentecostal and "finished work" movements being the first two). Its seeds were sown early in a baptismal sermon at a camp meeting near Los Angeles in 1913. Within a year, a leading Pentecostal pioneer, Frank Ewart, developed the homiletical insight into a systematic doctrine that provided the rationale for baptism in the name of the Lord Jesus Christ.

Two other leading Pentecostal pioneers, Garfield T. Haywood and Andrew D. Urshan, were prominent in developing and promoting the new teaching. The fundamental doctrine has not changed substantially, though variations exist and emphases ebb and flow.

I. The Name of God
The Name of God is the doctrine that undergirds all others. It is the primary means by which one knows God and follows Jesus. The name is not a mere description or label for God but the way in which God reveals Himself and provides salvation. God is present where His name is applied.

II. The Oneness of God
There is a sense in which God is a "trinity," but it is reserved for the threefold way that God reveals Himself and acts in the world. That is, God is radically one in His transcendence, but threefold in His immanence. However different they are in function, these three "manifestations" converge

ultimately in Jesus Christ, the One in whom "dwells all the fullness of the Godhead bodily" (Col. 2:9), which is why the oneness of God and His name are so vigorously defended.

III. The Fullness of God in Jesus

Doctrinally, "Jesus" is the revealed name of God for the dispensation of the New Covenant. This leads to a number of affirmations. First, and unlike other biblical interpreters, Jesus is regarded as the name that points to His *deity*, not His humanity. "Lord" and "Christ" are titles that set Him apart from others that bear the name. Since His name is *God's* proper name for this dispensation, it points to His divine origin. Second, since God is one, His name must be *singular*. The Trinitarian words, being plural, cannot by definition fulfill the promise of being the one name. Further, the "dividing" of God into three Persons diminishes the full force of God's oneness and full revelation in Jesus. Third, the Person of Jesus and His name are *inseparable*. To be saved by Jesus includes taking on His name. This act occurs in water baptism in the name of the Lord Jesus Christ.

Oneness Christology affirms the traditional belief in the two natures of Christ. In His deity He is the incarnation of the one Spirit of God. In His human nature, He is the Son of God. He is preexistent as the "expression" or the "Word" of God, not a distinct person within the Godhead. In His incarnation, Jesus is the embodiment of the Father through the Word. It is only in this limited sense that OP calls Jesus the Father. To deny the Fatherhood of Jesus is to deny His deity! In a word, the deity of Jesus is described as the Spirit of God, who proceeds from eternity through the Word, taking on human flesh in Jesus.

IV. The One Way to Salvation: Acts 2:38

God's way of salvation is through Jesus. Since the name of Jesus is inseparable from His person and work, the believer is to be sealed with this name of salvation. The place for this sealing is in water baptism. For oneness Pentecostals, the charter of salvation is set forth in the triple act of repentance, baptism in the name of the Lord Jesus Christ, and Spirit baptism, according to Acts 2:38.

Jesus' commission (Matt. 28:19) is interpreted as a command, not a formula to repeat. The command is to baptize disciples in the name (singular) of the Father, Son, and Spirit. Since Jesus is now the revelational name of God for salvation, it is the only valid name to be invoked in baptism. The triune words are "titles," not a proper name; and they are plural, not singular. Since the titles all coalesce in Jesus, the only appropriate response to Matthew 28:19 is to turn to the apostolic practice.

The oneness of God, the revelational name of Jesus, and the one way to salvation tend to set OP Christians apart from others. Some adherents teach that while OP represents the full biblical teaching and practice, salvation is accomplished by grace through faith in Christ. Others teach a more exclusive doctrine, that Acts 2:38 represents the new birth and the only biblical warrant for salvation. On the eternal destiny of others, they remain silent. Some extend the birth metaphor to indicate that spiritual life begins at conception, not birth. ■

—David A. Reed, Ph.D.
Wycliffe College, Toronto

bishop from 1925 until his death in 1931. Not only was Haywood a gifted churchman and leader, he was a noted hymn writer as well. Two of his best-known hymns are "I See a Crimson Stream of Blood" and "Jesus the Son of God."

The Pentecostal Assemblies of the World continued as an integrated church body until 1924 when a separation occurred that eventually resulted in the formation of the largely white United Pentecostal Church. This was the last of the major racial separations in a movement that had exploded at Azusa Street, where it was said that "the color line was washed away in the Blood."[43]

The United Pentecostal Church

The problems of running a racially integrated denomination during the era of Jim Crow racial segregation was almost insurmountable in the South. For years the Pentecostal Assemblies of the World were forced to have all their official annual conferences above the Mason-Dixon Line due to the lack of hotel accommodations for blacks in the South. Since most of the churches in the North were African-American while those in the South were largely white, most elections were dominated by black delegates from the northern states since fewer southerners could afford the cost of a trip to the North.

By 1921, the white southerners had begun to conduct a "Southern Bible Conference," which was notable for the absence of blacks. For the next three years the situation deteriorated, until in 1924 there was a final racial separation with most of the whites forming the "Pentecostal Ministerial Alliance" in Jackson, Tennessee, in 1925. A short time later, this group changed its name to the "Pentecostal Church, Incorporated."

Another oneness group that developed at the same time was the "Pentecostal Assemblies of Jesus Christ," which by 1936 had grown to number 16,000 members in 245 churches. Since this church was mostly white, had identical doctrines with the Pentecostal Church, Incorporated, and operated mostly in the same territory, a move began to merge the two bodies. This was accomplished in 1945 in St. Louis, Missouri, where a new church

Born in Persia, Andrew David Urshan (1884–1967) became a Pentecostal missionary to Russia. In 1916, after joining the Oneness Pentecostals, he became an apologist for the movement. His son Nathaniel became well known as a radio speaker and as general superintendent of the United Pentecostal Church.

was born. Called the United Pentecostal Church, this denomination soon outgrew the Pentecostal Assemblies of the World and became the largest oneness church in America and the world.[44]

By the year 2000, the United Pentecostal Church claimed 700,000 constituents in 3,953 congregations in the United States and 2,293,164 members in other nations.[45]

For Further Reading

There are abundant sources of information about the churches in the "finished work" tradition, especially for the Assemblies of God. The most comprehensive recent history of the Assemblies of God is Edith Blumhofer's two-volume *The Assemblies of God: A Chapter in the Story of American Pentecostalism* (Springfield, Mo.: Gospel Publishing House, 1989). Earlier histories include William Menzies, *Anointed to Serve: The Story of the Assemblies of God* (Springfield, Mo.: Gospel Publishing House, 1971); Klaud Kendrick, *The Promise Fulfilled: A History of the Modern Pentecostal Movement* (Springfield, Mo.: Gospel Publishing House, 1961); and Carl Brumback's *Suddenly . . . From Heaven: A History of the Assemblies of God* (Springfield, Mo.: Gospel Publishing House, 1961), which gives an insider's view of the church.

There are many books on Aimee Semple McPherson and the Foursquare church movement. Recent popular biographies include David Epstein's *Sister Aimee: The Life of Aimee Semple McPherson* (New York: Harcourt Brace Jovanovich, 1993); and Edith Blumhofer's *Aimee Semple McPherson: Everybody's Sister* (Grand Rapids: Eerdmans, 1993).

The major history of the Open Bible Standard church is R. Bryant Mitchell's *Heritage and Horizons* (Des Moines: Open Bible, 1982). The history of the Pentecostal Church of God is given in Aaron Wilson's *Our Story: The History of the Pentecostal Church of God* (Joplin, Mo.: Messenger Publishing House, 2001).

One of the first and best histories of the oneness Pentecostals was Fred J. Foster's *Think It Not Strange: A History of the Oneness Movement* (St. Louis: Pentecostal Publishing House, 1965). Frank Ewart's *The Phenomenon of Pentecost:A History of the Latter Rain* (St. Louis: Pentecostal Publishing House, 1947) gives a good firsthand account by a founding father. David Reed did groundbreaking scholarly research in his "Aspects of the Origins of Oneness Pentecostalism," in Vinson Synan, ed., *Aspects of Pentecostal/Charismatic Origins* (Plainfield, N.J.: Logos International, 1975), 143–168.

A major history of the Pentecostal Assemblies of the World is James L. Tyson's *The Early Pentecostal Revival: History of the Twentieth Century Pente-*

costals and the Pentecostal Assemblies of the World (Hazelwood, Mo.: Word Aflame Press, 1992). The best books on oneness theology are David Bernard's *The Oneness of God* (St. Louis: Word Aflame Press, 1983); and *The Oneness of Jesus Christ* (St. Louis: Word Aflame Press, 1994). The definitive history of the oneness movement is Talmadge L. French's excellent book *Our God Is One: The Story of the Oneness Pentecostals* (Indianapolis, Ind.: Voice and Vision, 2000).

· 7 ·

Charismatic Renewal Enters the Mainline Churches

Vinson Synan

For six decades (1901–60) Pentecostalism was considered to be outside the pale of respectable Christianity in America and the world. The Pentecostals were noisy and to many people disorderly. Their worship was beyond understanding to those without knowledge of the inner spirituality that undergirded the movement. On top of this, most Pentecostals were poor, underprivileged, uneducated, and out of touch with the latest theological trends that preoccupied most of Protestantism. Such movements as Modernism and the social gospel were unknown to most Pentecostals, and those few who were aware of these trends vehemently denounced them. In fact, there was a great deal of mutual ignorance on all sides. The popular response to the lowly Pentecostal churches and people was to dismiss them as "Holy Rollers" who, despised as they were, fulfilled a useful function by ministering to the poor and outcast who felt unwelcome and out of place in the increasingly rich and sophisticated mainline churches.

Most Protestants and Catholics were, to be sure, unaware of the growing numbers of the Pentecostals who busied themselves with planting churches in practically every community in America. Such practices as speaking in tongues, prophesying, and exorcising demons were considered to be bizarre by-products of religious ignorance and unbridled enthusiasm. Indeed, for the first half of the 20th century there was a mutual rejection between the Pentecostals and the mainline churches and society at large.

In this situation, the public harbored a deep curiosity about Pentecostal goings-on. People secretly looked in the windows of the crowded Pentecostal churches to watch the shouting and exuberance that characterized the services. At times people who were desperately sick threw caution to the wind and flocked to the healing services of such early Pentecostal healing evangelists as Maria Woodworth-Etter and Aimee Semple McPherson. Many were healed and became ardent Pentecostals. This often meant the severing of normal family relations as the converts were rejected by their families and friends.

After World War II, this situation began to change as Pentecostals prospered along with the rest of American society. With their newfound prosperity, Pentecostals moved up in society and often built large and modern church buildings that caught the attention of the public. After 1948, there was a veritable explosion of interest in the movement in the wake of the healing ministries of such evangelists as William Branham, Oral Roberts, and Jack Coe. With the onset of Oral Roberts's television ministry, divine healing entered the living rooms of the American people. Catholics were especially attracted to Roberts's ministry. Catholic bishops in New York, Philadelphia, and Chicago were concerned about the large numbers of Catholics who attended the healing crusades, and especially about those who also sent offerings to the Oklahoma evangelist. It was inevitable that sooner or later Pentecostalism would spill over into the mainline churches. Before 1960, pastors of mainline churches who spoke in tongues were generally expelled from their churches and forced to join some Pentecostal denomination. There were probably thousands who either left their churches or kept quiet about their brush with Pentecostalism in order to keep their pulpits. Hundreds of thousands of laypersons, however, left their more ritualistic and formal churches to join the exciting worship of the Pentecostals, where miracles were offered in every service and joyful worship filled the air with lusty singing, hand-clapping, and "dancing before the Lord."

Before 1960, several mainline pastors entered into the tongues experience and suffered various reactions from their church leaders. Among these were Harald Bredesen (Lutheran and later Dutch Reformed), Richard Winkler (Episcopal), Tommy Tyson (Methodist), and Gerald Derstine (Mennonite). Like many others before him, Derstine was expelled ("silenced") from the Mennonite ministry, while Tyson and Winkler were subjected to ecclesiastical investigations before being allowed to stay in the ministry.

The major breakthrough into the mainline churches was led by Episcopalian pastor Dennis Bennett at St. Mark's Episcopal Church in Van Nuys, California, in 1960. After speaking in tongues, he was pressured by his congregation and bishop to resign his church. His resolute witness to the validity of his experience led to a sensational media frenzy that ended by creating a new movement whose followers were soon given the tag "Neo-Pentecostals" (New Pentecostals). After leaving St. Mark's, Bennett carried on a successful Pentecostal ministry for two decades in St. Luke's Episcopal Church in Seattle, Washington. Soon afterward an avalanche of pastors and laymen followed Bennett into the movement. Among these were Larry Christenson (Lutheran), James Brown (Presbyterian), Howard Conatser (Southern Baptist), and Nelson Litwiller (Mennonite).

The following sections of this chapter are the stories of the several Protestant renewal movements that began in the two decades following Bennett's successful campaign to make the mainline churches safe for the new Pentecostals.

The Episcopal Renewal

Dennis Bennett

At nine o'clock in the morning on a November day in 1959, Dennis Bennett, rector of St. Mark's Episcopal Church in Van Nuys, California, knelt in the home of some friends and began to pray in tongues. Unknown to Bennett, this experience of being baptized in the Holy Spirit was destined to change his life forever. Furthermore, the major churches of Christendom were to be strangely affected in the years to come as a result of this event.[1]

In a way, Bennett was at the opposite pole of the people called Pentecostals who championed the experience they called baptism in the Holy Spirit. For them this was often a cataclysmic baptism evidenced by glossolalia, or speaking in tongues. Most surveys of American opinion placed Episcopalians at the top of the list of respectable Christians, while the lowly Pentecostals usually occupied the bottom rung on the social ladder.[2]

Episcopalian Dennis Bennett (1917–91) is credited with beginning the Pentecostal movement in the mainline churches in 1960 .

The aftermath of Bennett's experience was remarkable in that many members of his parish also received the Pentecostal experience and saw their lives and spiritual devotion completely changed. In

DENNIS BENNETT'S BAPTISM IN THE HOLY SPIRIT

We were sitting in their front room, our host and hostess on the davenport under the window, I in an overstuffed chair across the room, and the other clergyman to my right. The California autumn sun was shining bright and hot outside, and the neighborhood was fairly quiet for a Saturday, the silence broken only by an occasional car going by. I was self-conscious, and determined not to lose my dignity!

"What do I do?" I asked them again.

"Ask Jesus to baptize you in the Holy Spirit," said John. "We'll pray with you, and you just pray and praise the Lord."

I said: "Now remember, I want this nearness to God you have, that's all; I'm not interested in speaking with tongues!"

"Well," they said, "all we can tell you about that is that it came with the package!"

John came across the room and laid his hands first on my head, and then on my friend's. He began to pray, very quietly, and I recognized the same thing as when Bud had prayed with me a few days before: he was speaking a language that I did not understand, and speaking it very fluently. He wasn't a bit "worked up" about it, either. Then he prayed in English, asking Jesus to baptize me in the Holy Spirit.

I began to pray, as he told me, and I prayed very quietly, too. I was not about to get even a little bit excited! I was simply following instructions. I suppose I must have prayed out loud for about twenty minutes—at least it seemed to be a long time—and was just about to give up when a very strange thing happened. My tongue tripped, just as it might when you are trying to recite a tongue twister, and I began to speak in a new language!

Right away I recognized several things: first, it wasn't some kind of psychological trick or compulsion. There was nothing compulsive about it. I was allowing these new words to come to my lips and was speaking them out of my own volition, without in any way being forced to do it. I wasn't "carried away" in any sense of the word, but was fully in possession of my wits and my willpower. I spoke the new language because it was interesting to speak a language I had never learned, even though I didn't know what I was saying. I had taken quite a while to learn a small amount of German and French, but here was a language "for free." Secondly, it was a real language, not some kind of "baby talk." It had grammar and syntax; it had inflection and expression—and it was rather beautiful. I went on allowing these new words to come to my lips for about five minutes, then said to my friends:

"Well! That must be what you mean by 'speaking in tongues'—but what is it all about? I don't feel anything!"

They said joyfully:

"Praise the Lord!"

This seemed a bit irrelevant and was a little strong for my constitution. It bordered on the fanatical for such a thing to be said by Episcopalians on a fine Saturday afternoon sitting right in the front room of their home! With much to think about, I gathered up my friend, and we took our leave. ∎

—Dennis Bennett
Nine O'Clock in the Morning

April 1960, Bennett shared his experience with the members of his wealthy parish. What followed was almost a riot of rejection. "We are Episcopalians, not a bunch of wild-eyed hillbillies," shouted a speaker from a chair used as a soapbox. "Throw out the damned tongues-speakers," yelled another.[3]

To make a long story short, Bennett did resign shortly, but not before the newspapers as well as *Time* and *Newsweek* magazines gave such national publicity to the event that Bennett became a controversial figure overnight. He also became the leader of a new force in the traditional denominations, which was called the Neo-Pentecostal movement. *Time* magazine reported that "now glossolalia seems to be on its way back in U.S. churches—not only in the uninhibited Pentecostal sects, but even among the Episcopalians, who have been called 'God's frozen people.'"[4]

Although Bennett's case was striking and made headlines around the world, he was not the first clergyman in his church to speak in tongues and remain in the ministry. With varying degrees of success, at least two of his colleagues had preceded him in experiencing Pentecostal phenomena.

In 1907, after the Azusa Street revival had awakened the world to the gifts of the Spirit, Alexander Boddy, vicar of All Souls Anglican Church in Sunderland, England, had fostered a Pentecostal revival in his church. For several years the annual Sunderland conventions became centers for church renewal in England, Europe, and the United States. This "renewal that failed" was ended mainly because of World War I and a lack of able leadership. As Boddy's many followers, among them Methodists, Baptists, Plymouth Brethren, and the Salvation Army, saw that Pentecostalism seemed unlikely to change the British mainline churches, they departed to form new Pentecostal denominations in Britain, notably the Assemblies of God and the Elim Pentecostal Church.

Michael Harper speaks of Boddy as a "prophet few listened to, and most forgot." The first Anglican Pentecostal, Boddy moved from Sunderland in 1922 to become vicar of Pittington, which was located in the same diocese. He remained there until his death in 1929, a man clearly ahead of his time.[5]

Richard Winkler

In 1956, an American Episcopal priest, Richard Winkler, rector of the Trinity Episcopal Church in Wheaton, Illinois, was baptized in the Holy Spirit and spoke in tongues. He was probably the first Episcopal pastor in America to espouse the movement openly. His ministry was so revolutionized after receiving the Pentecostal baptism that healing services were held in his church and many members received the Pentecostal experiences.[6]

Because of Bennett's and Winkler's experiences, the Episcopal Church issued three reports in the 1960s to deal with the growing movement in the church. The first one appeared in April 1960 in response to Bennett's experience. This document adopted the dispensational view that tongues belonged to the infancy of the church and were discarded like scaffolding after the church came to maturity. Winkler's case also elicited a report in December 1960 that warned of diabolic deception and sectarianism. While recognizing that glossolalia could be genuine, the report stated that "reason is supremely the voice of the Holy Ghost." Despite this pronouncement, Winkler was allowed to remain in his church, making it an early center for charismatic activity in the Midwest.[7]

The reaction to Bennett's experience was so explosive that his baptism in the Spirit became a true baptism of fire. Because of his suffering and later vindication, he is widely regarded as the father of the charismatic movement in the mainline churches.

The movement spread rapidly into the Episcopal churches of southern California after Bennett's case became well known. By 1963 *Christianity Today* spoke of a new penetration in which two thousand Episcopalians in southern California were said to be speaking in tongues.[8]

These new Pentecostals were somewhat different from the older classical Pentecostals, explained Jean Stone, an early leader in the movement. They were less emotional and used their gifts more privately as a prayer language. They also violated many stereotypes about Pentecostalism that had been widely held for decades. They were made up primarily of well-educated clergy and lay professionals. Also, their services were quite orderly and paid much attention to Paul's directions about the decent and orderly use of the gifts.[9]

The ecclesiastical response to Bennett's experience was swift and negative. His ecclesiastical superior, Bishop Francis Bloy, not only forbade tongues-speaking in St. Mark's, but banned its use in all the parishes of his diocese. Elsewhere in California, Bishop James A. Pike issued a 2,500-word letter to all 125 parishes of his diocese forbidding glossolalia in the churches. Calling the movement "heresy in embryo," he stated that "this particular phenomenon has reached a point where it is dangerous to the peace and unity of the church." These statements notwithstanding, there was no stopping the move of the Spirit in the Episcopal churches of California and other states.[10]

Despite his prohibition of tongues in the services of his diocese, Pike was occasionally greeted with congregations and priests who would burst out singing in tongues during his regular rounds of the churches. Ironically, this same Bishop Pike later ended his ecclesiastical career in disgrace after a vain search to communicate with the dead through the medium of spiritualism.

Other more friendly voices were heard in the church. After hearing about the plight of Bennett, William Fisher Lewis, bishop of Olympia, Washington, invited him to assume the pastorate of St. Luke's Episcopal Church, a run-down urban parish near Seattle. Since consideration had already been given to closing St. Luke's, Lewis invited Bennett to come and "bring the fire" with him. With this permission to teach and express his Pentecostal modes of worship and praise, Bennett and his church were soon in the midst of a tremendous spiritual renewal.

Centers of Charismatic Renewal

St. Luke's became a center of charismatic renewal, not only for the Episcopal Church, but also for many churches and pastors from various denominations in the northwestern United States. In a short time, Bennett's entire vestry and most of the membership of the church had been baptized in the Holy Spirit. Although the Sunday morning services were quite traditional, the Tuesday night prayer meetings were packed with people and Pentecostal power. For many years, hundreds of persons attended services weekly at St. Luke's, with an average of twenty persons being baptized in the Holy Spirit each week. These were not only Episcopalians; the hundreds also included Baptists, Methodists, Catholics, and Presbyterians.

St. Luke's Episcopal Church in Seattle, Washington, became a center for charismatic renewal under the leadership of Dennis Bennett.

In a short time St. Luke's was the largest Episcopal congregation in the entire northwestern region of the United States. Offerings were multiplied as the church changed from an urban liability to a dynamic spiritual center.[11]

Bennett's experiences were widely publicized in the press, thus drawing attention to the growing Pentecostal movement in the Episcopal Church. His example encouraged hundreds of other clergymen to come out of the closet and testify to their experiences in the Holy Spirit.

These Spirit-baptized clergymen were Pentecostals, to be sure, but they wanted to remain in their churches and lead their coreligionists in a spiritual renewal. They differed from their brothers in the traditional Pentecostal denominations such as the Assemblies of God, yet they shared in the same dynamic experiences in the Holy Spirit. Though many Episcopal pastors such as Winkler, and ministers in other churches such as Harald Bredesen and James Brown, had received the Pentecostal experience before he had, Bennett was recognized as the pioneer of the Neo-Pentecostal movement because of the publicity surrounding his case.

Another important early center for the Episcopal renewal soon developed in the Church of the Redeemer in Houston, Texas. Here Graham Pulkingham led his congregation in an experiment in charismatic parish renewal, an example that served as a model for many other churches. The rapid growth of the parish with its unique community life and social ministries attracted national attention. Many Episcopal leaders as well as pastors from other denominations traveled to Houston to see how Pentecostal worship could be integrated into the full liturgical and sacramental life of the church.[12]

To aid the struggling new movement in the church, a new publication, edited by Jean Stone, appeared in 1961 under the title *Trinity*. This, the first Neo-Pentecostal paper in the United States, featured many Episcopal leaders and writers. It also acted as the voice of the Blessed Trinity Society, a new organization founded to foster the ministry of healing in the church that functioned from 1961 to 1966. This was the first organized charismatic society in an American mainline denomination.[13]

Worldwide Anglican Renewal

Further help came from a 1962 study of the Episcopal bishops that was published in the *Journal of the General Convention*. Referring to new movements in the church, the bishops affirmed that "God's Spirit is ever moving in new ways" and the "new movements have in history enriched the body of Christ." Observing that the church "should not be a sect, but should be spacious," the bishops nevertheless counseled against "self-righteousness, divisiveness, one-sidedness, and exaggeration." The renewal should, therefore, relate itself to the "full, rich, balanced life of the historic church," said the bishops.[14]

This statement became the official policy of the church toward the Neo-Pentecostal movement and opened the door to wide acceptance and participation of charismatics in the church. After 1962, the movement did indeed spread rapidly in the church, not only in America, but around the world.

In England, a group of evangelicals led by Canon Michael Harper established the "Fountain Trust," an ecumenical body of charismatics in all the churches, but mainly led by Anglicans. In other nations, bishops and archbishops became involved, the most important being Archbishop William Burnett of Capetown, South Africa. Other influential leaders were Bishop Festo Kivengere of Uganda, Bishops Chitemo and Madina of Tanzania, Archbishop Manassas Kuria of Kenya, Bishop Derek Rawcliffe of the New Hebrides Islands, and Ban it Chiu, bishop of Singapore. The influence of the movement was widespread and influential.[15]

In Atlanta, Georgia, David Collins, canon of the largest Episcopal parish in the United States, became a national leader in the movement. Other leaders included Bishop William Frey of Colorado, Robert Hawn, Everett (Terry) Fullam, and Charles M. Irish. To coordinate this growing force in the American church, in 1973 these men formed the Episcopal Charismatic Fellowship. This body soon published a journal entitled *Acts 29,* which became a clearinghouse for information about the movement.[16]

By the mid-1970s the Episcopal and Anglican movements, along with most other mainline churches, had abandoned the name Neo-Pentecostal movement for the more neutral term "charismatic renewal." Also, to escape the cultural baggage of classical Pentecostalism, Episcopal leaders began to develop an "organic" theology of the baptism in the Holy Spirit, which emphasized the work of the Holy Spirit throughout the Christian life, as well as in the initial personal experience of being baptized in the Holy Spirit. Charismatic Episcopalians also drew on the ancient creeds of the church for their experiences in the Holy Spirit.

A New Canterbury Tale

With a wide measure of acceptance within the Anglican communion, Anglican charismatics planned an international conference at Canterbury in 1978 to precede the meeting of the Lambeth Conference. Lambeth is the most important gathering of Anglicanism, where all the bishops meet only once every decade. During the week before Lambeth, about five hundred charismatic leaders gathered at the University of Kent at Canterbury. A week of prayer and workshops preceded the closing services in the historic cathedral. In the first service, Archbishop of Canterbury Donald Coggan addressed the delegates warmly.

The closing liturgy was so wondrous that it is still referred to as "a new Canterbury tale." Led by Archbishop Burnett, the three-hour service included tongues, prophecies, prayer for the sick, and great rejoicing. This all took place within the context of a traditional Anglican Communion service.

At the close of this historic gathering, the two thousand worshipers joined in a time of rejoicing as the Spirit was poured out in Pentecostal fullness. Canterbury truly became a new Upper Room. The ancient walls of the cathedral echoed the shouts of praise that swelled from the hearts of the congregation. Thirty-two bishops and archbishops dancing around the high altar in high praise of the Lord were an unforgettable sight.[17]

After 1978, the movement continued to spread among Anglican churches and mission fields around the world. In some cases, entire national churches were swept by the movement. The church in the New Hebrides was one such case. At Canterbury, Bishop Rawcliffe told of all his churches and priests being deeply affected by a revival of the charismatic gifts. In England, David Watson told of overflow crowds at his services in York, which included great crowds filling the cathedral for charismatic services.

Thirty-two Anglican bishops dance before the Lord in Canterbury Cathedral in 1978.

Some African bishops, such as Festo Kivengere, could not recall a time when their national Anglican churches were anything but charismatic. This was especially true of those churches touched by the great East African revivals of the 1930s.

In America, Everett Fullam, vicar of St. Paul's Church in Darien, Connecticut, experienced overflow crowds as the Spirit moved in his regular services. The "miracle at Darien" was repeated at numerous other Episcopal churches in America.[18]

Three northern Virginia parishes experienced extraordinary growth in the early 1980s when they decided to "go the charismatic route." The Falls Church and Truro parishes were two of Virginia's oldest colonial Episcopal parishes. Yet they took on new life as the Holy Spirit was poured out among their members. In the same area, the Church of the Apostles experienced extraordinary growth. Under the leadership of Rector Renny Scott, this church grew from fifty in attendance to more than two thousand in only seven years. Theirs was described as an "exuberant charismatic parish."[19]

By 1994 a survey showed that out of 7,200 Episcopal parishes in the United States, over 400 were involved in the charismatic renewal. Some of these were the fastest-growing churches in the denomination.

The Lutheran Renewal

Harald Bredesen

In 1947 a young Lutheran layman in New York City noticed a growing local Pentecostal congregation where hundreds of people from all denominational backgrounds gathered to receive healing and to experience what they called the baptism in the Holy Spirit. Although he was an official of the World Council of Christian Education headquartered in Manhattan, the young man felt irresistibly drawn to investigate the unusual services that attracted so many people in the big city.

Soon the young Lutheran joined the crowds at the altar seeking the baptism. In a short time he received the Pentecostal experience and arose speaking in a new language he had not learned. The young man was named Harald Bredesen, and the church was an Assemblies of God congregation pastored by P. G. Emmett. [20]

This man Bredesen was destined to be a John the Baptist for the charismatic renewal movement in the mainline denominational churches. He was one of the earliest ministers outside the classical Pentecostal movement to experience glossolalia and continue in the ministry of a traditional non-Pentecostal church.

Harald Bredesen was one of the most widely influential of the early charismatic leaders.

Bredesen had been born and raised a thoroughgoing Lutheran with plans of entering a Lutheran pastorate after his work ended with the staff of the World Council of Christian Education in New York. The son of a Lutheran pastor in Minnesota, he had attended Luther Theological Seminary in St. Paul and had served a pastoral internship in Aberdeen, South Dakota, before coming to his position in New York.

In later years Bredesen was to influence many important Christian leaders to experience the baptism in the Holy Spirit, including Pat Robertson, John Sherrill, and Pat Boone. He was ordained a minister in the Dutch Reformed Church and accepted a call to pastor a Dutch Reformed congregation in Mt. Vernon, New York. In the 1960s he also led many of his parishioners into the Pentecostal experience. In 1963 he was instrumental in leading a sensational meeting at Yale University where many students also spoke in tongues. They were jokingly called "glossoyalies" by the press. [21]

HARALD BREDESEN'S TESTIMONY

Up to this point, I had wanted power for service, power for witness, and power to live the Christian life. Now I had one desire, and that was to satisfy the yearning heart of Jesus with myself. Previously, I had loved God with reservation, had served Him with reservation, and therefore I had assumed that He loved me—with reservation. In that moment it seemed as if all my sins and repeated failures and shortcomings had no more power to shut out His love for me than a flyspeck could shut out the sun. In spite of what I was, in spite of what I was not, in spite of all my reservations, He loved me *without* reservation. I was so overwhelmed, overjoyed, and amazed by the total unreservedness of His love for me that my hands went up in awe. Now I didn't have to ask anybody, "Why do you raise your hands?" It was just involuntary wonder and surrender.

I tried to say, "Thank You, Jesus, thank You, Jesus," but I couldn't express the inexpressible. Then, to my great relief, the Holy Spirit did it for me. It was just as if a bottle was uncorked, and out of me poured a torrent of words in a language I had never studied before. Now everything I had ever wanted to say to God, I could say.

After a long time of praising God and knowing that this experience was real, came the return of the realization that I was going to have to tell my friends. I knew what they would say: "Harald, you have gotten yourself mixed up with a group of hysterical people who whip themselves up into a frenzy of religious excitement and then let off steam in a form of ecstatic gibberish. All this has rubbed off on you."

I prayed, "Lord, if this is a true language, then You can reveal it to me." I went out the door and down one of the many paths that lead into the surrounding woods. As I walked along this path, my new prayer tongue was flowing, an artesian spring within me, of praise and adoration.

Coming up the path was a pretty, flaxen-haired girl of about eleven. When she came to me, she stood and cocked her head and then laughed. "You're speaking Polish."

I wrote on a slip of paper, "Where is there a Polish man? I want to speak to him." I was afraid to start speaking in English for fear I'd never be able to begin again in this tongue. The girl led me to a man who was standing on the front steps of his cabin; he was squat and muscular, maybe a Pennsylvania miner. I thought, "Just think, I've never met this man, but in Christ we are brothers."

He exclaimed, "Bracia, Bracia! You call me Brother." He said, "You are praising God, going from one Slavic dialect to the other."

When I left him, my heart was overjoyed. ∎

—HARALD BREDESEN
YES, LORD

By the 1980s Bredesen was well known as a friend to President Sadat of Egypt as well as an adviser to his old friend and protégé Pat Robertson in his bid for the Republican nomination for the presidency of the United States. In the long run, however, Bredesen may be best known as one of the earliest Neo-Pentecostals who served as a harbinger of things to come in the mainline denominations.[22]

Larry Christenson

Larry Christenson was one of the first Lutherans to experience the baptism in the Holy Spirit in the 1960s. Only a year out of seminary and in his first pastorate, Trinity Lutheran Church (American Lutheran Church or ALC) in San Pedro, California, Christenson had been fascinated by the possibility of divine healing through an earlier reading of Agnes Sanford's book *The Healing Light.*

While attending a revival service in a Foursquare Pentecostal church in San Pedro, he heard about the baptism in the Holy Spirit evidenced by speaking in tongues. The evangelists, Wayne and Mary Westburg, prayed for him, but nothing happened. That night, however, the young Lutheran pastor awakened, "sat bolt upright in bed and found an unknown tongue" hovering on his lips. He spoke a sentence in tongues and then fell back to sleep. This was on Friday morning, August 4, 1961. The next night he returned to the Foursquare church, where he reported that a "great sense of praise and joy began to well up within me, and it spilled over my lips in a new tongue." It was a wonderful experience, he said, "though not a particularly overwhelming one."

Larry Christenson (1928–) led the Lutheran charismatic movement after his baptism in the Holy Spirit in San Pedro, California, in 1961.

Christenson was immediately concerned with the question of whether this experience was Lutheran and about his future as a Lutheran pastor. In a later conversation with David du Plessis, he was advised to stay in the Lutheran Church and spread the renewal among his peers.[23]

The Character of Lutherans

Historically, Lutherans have been primarily concerned with issues coming out of the Protestant Reformation. These include such basic principles as justification by faith and the primacy of the Scriptures.

In many ways Martin Luther was a social conservative while acting as a theological revolutionary. In the Reformation, he went so far and no farther. His opposition to the Peasants' War and the Anabaptist movement indicated his conservatism. He held in special contempt the enthusiasts whom he called the "schwarmerei." He was also quite critical of the claims to miracles, which he regarded as Roman Catholic superstition. Although it has been said that Luther spoke in tongues, there is no credible contemporary evidence to support this claim.

Indeed, Luther heartily subscribed to the cessation theory, which held that the signs, wonders, and miracles of the New Testament ceased after the age of the apostles. Thus, one who spoke in tongues in modern times would probably not be considered a typical Lutheran.[24]

Others Receive the Baptism

Despite Lutheran tradition, the early 1960s saw a veritable flood of Lutherans who received the Pentecostal experience. All the branches of American Lutheranism were affected, including the American Lutheran Church (ALC), the Lutheran Church in America (LCA), and the Lutheran Church, Missouri Synod (LCMS).

An interesting testimony came from Erwin Prange, a pastor who was baptized in the Holy Spirit in the sanctuary of his church on a morning in 1963 just before leading a confirmation class. As he prayed, a voice seemed to say, "The gift is already yours; just reach out and take it." Then, stretching his hands toward the altar, "I opened my mouth, and strange babbling sounds rushed forth. Had I done it? Or was it the Spirit? Before I had time to wonder, all sorts of strange things began to happen. God came out of the shadows. 'He is real!' I thought. 'He is here! He loves me!' . . . every cell and atom of my body tingled with the vibrant life of God." When he went to teach his confirmation class, he talked for ten minutes in a language neither he nor his hearers could understand.[25]

Leading pastors who received the baptism in this period included Herbert Mjorud, who was serving as a full-time evangelist of the ALC in 1962 after visiting Dennis Bennett's Episcopal church in Seattle. Afterward he was amazed to see a healing ministry break out in his evangelistic crusades. In a revival in Anacortes, Washington, in March 1962, more than seventy Lutherans were baptized in the Holy Spirit. As a result of this meeting, Mjorud was accused of heresy by several pastors.

After Mjorud answered the charges before the president of the denomination, all charges were dropped. But his call as an ALC evangelist was not renewed, and he became an independent evangelist. His later years were distinguished by mass healing crusades in many nations of the world.[26]

Mjorud was not alone in being investigated by church authorities. In 1963 the ALC appointed a commission of three to investigate the persons involved with glossolalia in the church. This team consisted of a psychologist, a psychiatrist, and a New Testament theologian. In San Pedro, the team examined Christenson and thirty-two members of his congregation. A control group of twenty tongues-speakers was compared with another group of non-tongues-speakers. Although the team expected the Pentecostals to be "unstable people emotionally" and that the movement would be "short-lived," they were wrong on both counts. The results were published in the book titled *The Psychology of Speaking in Tongues* by John Kildahl (the clinical psychologist in the study).[27]

Throughout the 1960s and 1970s, hundreds of Lutheran pastors and thousands of laypersons entered into the Pentecostal experience. Among these were Donald Pfotenhauer, Erwin Prange, Robert Heil, Rodney Lensch, Delbert Rossin, Herb Mirly, and Theodore Jungkuntz of the Lutheran Church, Missouri Synod. In the American Lutheran Church, Morris Vaagenes, James Hanson, and George Voeks joined Christenson and Mjorud as leaders in the movement.

The Lutheran Church in America was not as deeply affected as the other branches. Yet by 1970, Paul Swedeberg and Glen Pearson were leading charismatic renewal movements in their local churches.[28]

Many of these pastors suffered varying degrees of acceptance or rejection from their ecclesiastical superiors. The most wrenching case of rejection was that experienced by Don Pfotenhauer, pastor of the Way of the Cross Lutheran Church in Blaine, Minnesota. This congregation was part of the Missouri Synod, one of the most conservative Lutheran bodies in America.

After Pfotenhauer received the baptism in the Holy Spirit in 1964, church authorities attempted to remove him from his pulpit. Though Pfotenhauer tried to stay with his church, a great majority of whom supported him, he was finally excommunicated in 1970. His supporters then organized an independent group with the same name, "Way of the Cross." His story made headlines for years in the Minneapolis newspapers.[29]

By the early 1970s, because of this case and other similar ones, Lutheran charismatics began to band together to promote the movement in their churches. By 1972, the idea of a national all-Lutheran charismatic conference gained currency among several leaders.

Sparked by Norris Wogen, the first International Lutheran Conference on the Holy Spirit was convened in the Civic Auditorium in Minneapolis in 1972. To the delight of the organizers, the auditorium, which seated nine thousand persons, was filled to capacity when more than ten thousand persons registered for the sessions. In the years after 1972, this conference grew to be the largest annual gathering of Lutherans in the United States.[30]

A Lutheran Charismatic Theology

In time, Lutheran charismatic pastors felt the need to produce a charismatic theology that would situate the Pentecostal experience and phenomena within the Lutheran theological system. In 1976 a book was published by Larry Christenson titled *The Charismatic Renewal Among Lutherans.* In this volume, Christenson traced the history of the movement and offered what he called an organic view of the baptism in the Holy Spirit (as contrasted to the classical Pentecostal second blessing, initial evidence view).

This book was followed in 1987 with the most ambitious and important theological work yet done within the Lutheran renewal. Edited by Larry Christenson in consultation with forty of his colleagues, it is titled *Welcome, Holy Spirit.* In this work, the International Lutheran Charismatic Theological Consultation leans in the direction of the classical Pentecostal position by recognizing a New Testament distinction between a charismatic sending of the Holy Spirit and the salvific coming of the Spirit at initiation.

In addition to these works, Theodore Jungkuntz has produced some basic works relating the renewal to the theology and sacramental life of the church. These include a booklet titled *A Lutheran Charismatic Catechism* and a theological treatise titled *Confirmation and the Charismata,* both produced in 1983.[31]

While the charismatics were developing their theology, the Lutheran denominations were also studying the movement and issuing reports designed to guide pastors in relating to the movement.

The Lutheran Church, Missouri Synod, ordered a report on the movement in April 1968 when it learned that forty-four of its pastors were involved in the renewal. By the time the report was completed in 1972, the number had risen to more than two hundred pastors. This was to be the most negative Lutheran report of the many that followed around the world. After questioning the possibility of valid manifestations of supernatural gifts and miracles in the modern age, the report declared that "power and renewal are to be sought in the Word and sacraments, not in special signs and miracles."[32]

The *1972 Guidelines* of the ALC was much more positive in tone. While cautioning charismatics concerning the proper place of the gifts in the lives of believers, the report called for an allowance for diversity, which would give the renewal liberty to develop further within the church.[33]

In 1974, the LCA issued the most positive report of all. *The Charismatic Movement: A Pastoral Perspective* stated that "there is no cause for Lutheran pastors or people to suggest either explicitly or implicitly that one cannot be charismatic and remain a Lutheran in good standing."[34]

By the 1980s some resistance remained in certain Lutheran quarters, but in general charismatic renewal was so accepted that it had become part of the Lutheran landscape.

Lutheran Charismatic Organizations

After the 1972 Minneapolis conference, Lutheran charismatic leaders set up permanent organizations to promote the work of the renewal. In 1973 Lutheran Charismatic Renewal Services was formed under the leadership of Larry Christenson and Dick Denny, an ALC layman. By the end of the 1970s the North Heights Lutheran Church in St. Paul, Minnesota, emerged as an important center for Lutheran renewal. Under the leadership of Pastor Morris Vaagenes and W. Dennis Pederson, the International Lutheran Center for Church Renewal was formed in 1980.[35]

By 1983, these two service organizations were merged and offices were located in the North Heights church in St. Paul. The name of the merged group was changed to the International Lutheran Renewal Center with Larry Christenson as the full-time director. Also working on the staff with Christenson were Dick Denny, Betty Denny, Dennis Pederson, and Del Rossin.[36]

Status of Lutheran Renewal

The 1979 Gallup poll conducted for *Christianity Today* estimated that 20 percent of all American Lutherans identified with the charismatic/Pentecostal renewal. This same poll showed that 3 percent of all American Lutherans spoke with tongues. Most estimates are that from 10 percent to 20 percent of all Lutherans were involved in the renewal. These figures would indicate that by 1980 between 1 million and 1.7 million identified with the movement in the United States.[37]

Surveys conducted by Fuller Theological Seminary in 1985 indicated growing participation on the part of Lutheran pastors in the United States. Figures for all the Lutheran denominations in America in the 1970s and 1980s yielded the following results:

	1974	1979	1984	1985
Pastors open	332	466	1000	1295
Pastors charismatic	249	349	751	975
Pastors declared	166	233	501	650[38]

In addition to the American scene, the renewal moved strongly into Lutheran churches around the world. The Scandinavian Lutheran churches were deeply involved in charismatic renewal as were the Lutheran churches of Germany. Reports indicated also that some African Lutheran bishops were moving in the charismatic direction.

In the 1990s more and more Lutheran churches became openly charismatic in their worship services. Several model congregations made headlines as examples of renewal in the Lutheran tradition, including the Resurrection Lutheran Church (Missouri Synod) in Charlotte, North Carolina. Led into the renewal by Pastor Herb Mirly, this church developed a unique form of high Lutheran liturgical worship that was enlivened by charismatic prayer and praise.[39]

Other prominent Lutheran congregations in the renewal during the 1990s included Trinity Lutheran Church in San Pedro, California, pastored by Paul Anderson, and Faith Lutheran Church in Geneva, Illinois, pastored by Del Rossin.

The Presbyterian and Reformed Renewal

From their earliest days in Switzerland and Scotland, the Presbyterians have been rock-ribbed proponents of John Calvin's theology, a system known for its tight Presbyterian ecclesiology as well as its more famous theological propositions. The Presbyterian system that has developed since the 16th century has not been known for innovation and experimentation, but rather for adherence to the strict formulations of its founding father.

It might come as a surprise to many to find that there is a rich and even pioneering history of renewal in the Presbyterian churches. Although Calvin, along with Luther, subscribed to the cessation theory of the charismata, to Calvin it was not because God withdrew these gifts from the church. In his *Institutes*, Calvin explained that they fell into disuse in the churches because of "a lack of faith." He never forbade their use or felt that they should be forbidden. Moreover, because of his extended attention to the Third Person of the Trinity in his writings, he has been called the "theologian of the Holy Spirit" among reformers.[40]

Because of the work of Princeton Presbyterian theologians B. B. Warfield and Charles Hodge, some 20th-century Presbyterians have been noted for a fundamentalist position that excludes both perfectionism and Pentecostalism from the Calvinist tradition. The standard work on the subject was Warfield's stem *Counterfeit Miracles*, a 1918 book that denied that any genuine miracles have occurred in the world since the age of the apostles. Another book in this genre was Ronald Knox's *Enthusiasm*, which took a dim view of all emotionalism in religion.[41]

Despite this strain of thought among some Presbyterians, many American pastors have participated and even pioneered in spiritual renewal in a way that would have displeased Warfield, but would perhaps have been applauded by Calvin. Britain and America have been the setting for many of these spiritual pioneers.

Early Presbyterian Revivalists

In 1800 one of the greatest revivals in American history broke out at Cane Ridge, Kentucky, under the leadership of three Presbyterian ministers: James McGready, William Hodges, and John Rankin. Eyewitnesses reported that the floors of the Red River Presbyterian Church were "covered with the slain" while others cried loudly for mercy. At times the pastors would "dance before the Lord," declaring, "This is the Holy Ghost." Soon as many as twenty-five thousand gathered in the forests to praise the Lord. This began the great camp-meeting tradition in America. The effects of the revival were nationwide.[42]

These demonstrations were not new in American religion. They had all been seen in the 1700s in the revival services of Jonathan Edwards, that great Calvinist theologian and pastor from Northhampton, Massachusetts. It was not unusual for sinners to scream out for mercy or fall out in the aisles under the conviction of the Holy Spirit. Though Edwards was a Puritan minister of the Congregational Church, he stood in the Calvinist tradition of the Presbyterians.[43]

One of the major spiritual movements among American Presbyterians also occurred on the frontier in the years between 1810 and 1840. The major cause of a split between eastern and western Presbyterians was a disagreement over educational requirements for ordination. Because of great revivals and spiritual manifestations, large numbers of converts joined the churches. This led to a lack of ministers. Traditionally, Presbyterians had insisted on a seminary degree for entry into the ministry. The westerners felt that those with less education could also qualify to minister to the masses of new converts.

Because of this educational question, the manifestation of expressive worship, and the manifestations of spiritual joy, the Cumberland Presbyterian Church was formed in 1810 as a separate denomination. It has continued its revivalistic tradition in the mid-South to this day.

Presbyterians also took a leading part in the great holiness revivals that swept America in the middle and late 1800s. For instance, in 1859, William Boardman wrote a book called *The Higher Christian Life*, which interpreted the Methodist teaching on entire sanctification to those in the Presbyterian and Reformed traditions. A former Presbyterian, Charles Grandison Finney, became the greatest revivalist of his day after receiving a vivid experience in the Holy Spirit that radically changed his life and ministry. His powerful evangelistic ministry marked Finney as the first "professional evangelist" in America.[44]

A Presbyterian pastor actually led the first charismatic renewal movement of modern times to penetrate a mainline denomination. He was Edward Irving, who led a gifts movement in the Regents Square Presbyterian Church in London in 1831. After a woman lay leader, Mary Campbell, spoke in tongues and prophesied, Irving was tried by his presbytery and defrocked. Since the English Presbyterian Church refused to accept these extraordinary gifts in their sanctuaries, Irving aided in the beginnings of the Catholic Apostolic Church, which existed until 1901. Although he never spoke in tongues and died soon after the inauguration of the new movement, Irving will always be remembered as an early persecuted pioneer of Pentecostalism among Presbyterians.[45]

Some years later in America, A. B. Simpson, a Canadian-born Presbyterian pastor from New York City, began to teach the possibility of divine healing in answer to prayer. This came after he was instantly healed of a long-standing condition. He also accepted the basic teachings of the holiness movement and received a sanctification experience in 1881. At about the same time, he experienced a tremendous call to send missionaries around the world. After some fifteen years as a Presbyterian pastor, he began an interdenominational agency in 1886 that he called the Christian and Missionary Alliance.

Simpson's alliance soon developed into a separate denomination that sent large numbers of missionaries to many nations of the world. His school at Nyack, New York, became an outstanding institution for training missionaries. In 1907, the school experienced a Pentecostal outpouring that almost brought the Alliance into the Pentecostal movement. Later, in 1914, several former Alliance ministers were instrumental in founding the Assemblies of God.

Another Presbyterian pioneer in this era was N. J. Holmes, pastor of the Second Presbyterian Church in Greenville, South Carolina. In 1896, Holmes journeyed to Northfield, Massachusetts, to attend a "higher life" conference led by D. L. Moody, who had earlier received a powerful baptism in the Holy Spirit. In Moody's meeting Holmes received an experience in the Holy Spirit that he later identified with the Wesleyan experience of entire sanctification. In 1898 he began his school on Paris Mountain outside Greenville. By this time, Holmes had been tried and expelled from the Enoree Presbytery for espousing the new experience and theology.

In 1905 a student in Holmes's school, Lida Purkie, electrified the student body when she spoke in tongues in a prayer meeting. A year later, the entire school, including both faculty and student body, received their personal Pentecost. This revival occurred after Holmes heard the Pentecostal message from G. B. Cashwell, who had visited Azusa Street a few months earlier. Holmes Bible College, the oldest college in the Pentecostal world, continues as a faith school related to the Pentecostal Holiness Church. Several of the earliest congregations in that denomination were first known as Brewerton Presbyterian churches.[46]

Presbyterian Charismatics

When the Neo-Pentecostal or charismatic movement began in the mainline churches in the United States after World War II, the Presbyterians were again in the forefront of renewal. The first well-known Presbyterian pastor to experience tongues and healing and remain in his church was James Brown, pastor of the Upper Octorara Presbyterian congregation near Parkesburg, just outside Philadelphia, Pennsylvania. In the mid-1950s Brown was baptized with the Holy Spirit and began to speak in tongues. This experience helped move him from an extremely liberal theological position to that of an evangelical charismatic Christian.

At first Brown was convinced that he could not remain a Presbyterian with his new experience. Perplexed as to what course of action he should follow, Brown asked David du Plessis for advice. "Stay in your church and renew it" was the word from the famous Pentecostal leader. This Brown determined to do.

His basic decision was to conduct traditional Presbyterian worship in the regular Sunday services, but to have Neo-Pentecostal worship in informal Saturday evening sessions in the sanctuary. This strategy worked for more than twenty years with a minimum of friction. In time the Saturday services attracted hundreds each week, with the little country church often jammed with as many as 750 enthusiastic worshipers. Thousands of both clergy and laity were baptized in the Holy Spirit in these services. With Brown playing the tambourines, the services were joyful and full of praise. People from all denominations came to witness prophesy, tongues, interpretation, and prayer for the sick. All along, Brown was active and accepted in his presbytery.[47]

These events were taking place in the late 1950s before the more famous events in Van Nuys, California, surrounding the ministry of Dennis Bennett. For several years prior to 1960, Brown had the largest charismatic prayer meeting in the United States. In 1977, he retired after thirty-seven years in the same pastorate, an early success story of the renewal movement.

Brick Bradford. The path of the Presbyterian spiritual pioneers became harder after the national news furor created by the Bennett case in California. The Presbyterians became litigious and defensive when Pentecostal phenomena appeared in their midst. An early casualty of a stiffening opposition in the church was George C. "Brick" Bradford, pastor of the First Presbyterian Church, El Reno, near Oklahoma City. Bradford was baptized in the Holy Spirit in 1966 at a CFO ("Camp Farthest Out") meeting in Ardmore, Oklahoma. As he was empowered by the Holy Spirit, Bradford said his "ministry was revolutionized."

When the leaders of the presbytery heard that Bradford was speaking in tongues, they immediately assumed that he needed mental counseling. Accordingly, he was sent to a psychiatrist who had also been filled with the Spirit. He gave Bradford a clean bill of health. Not satisfied with this result, the Washita presbytery sent him to another psychologist who gave them the diagnosis they desired. Despite the fact that he had been a lawyer and held a law degree from the University of Texas, Bradford was removed from his pastorate in December 1967.[48]

A lawyer in Texas before becoming a Presbyterian pastor, Brick Bradford (1923–) led the Presbyterian charismatics after receiving the Pentecostal experience. He founded the Presbyterian Charismatic Communion in 1966.

After this decision, Bradford retained his Presbyterian ordination for three more years and began an itinerant ministry speaking in whatever Presbyterian churches would open their doors. He also spoke in many Full Gospel Business Men's gatherings and Pentecostal churches. Freewill offerings supported his family during these lean years.

In May 1966 Bradford and five other Presbyterian charismatic ministers took an important step. They organized the Charismatic Communion, which later took the name Presbyterian Charismatic Communion (PCC). This was the first charismatic organization to be formed in a mainline denomination. Bradford was chosen as the general secretary. In one year, the new group listed 125 Presbyterian ministers on its rolls, and in a short time hundreds of pastors and laymen joined forces in this well-organized ministry.[49]

The Robert Whitaker Case. Not long after this move, Bradford and the PCC were confronted with a landmark case that tested the place of the gifts of the Spirit in the Presbyterian system. This case arose because of a dispute concerning the ministry of Robert C. Whitaker, pastor of the Chandler Presbyterian Church near Phoenix, Arizona.

In 1962 Whitaker had been baptized in the Holy Spirit and had seen the Holy Spirit slowly but surely revolutionize his ministry and the ministry of the Chandler church. By 1967 a number of his members had spoken in tongues. Also, like James Brown, no tongues or laying on of hands was practiced in the regular services of the church. However, in home prayer meetings revival broke out. The church experienced tremendous growth in a short time, with most of the congregation in full support of the movement.

In 1967, a small group of dissenting elders was able to persuade the presbytery of Phoenix to appoint an administrative commission to investigate Whitaker's ministry and the use of the gifts of the Holy Spirit within the life of the congregation. When Whitaker refused to take a vow to "cease and desist" from speaking in tongues, praying for the sick, and casting out demons, the presbytery removed him as pastor of First Presbyterian Church in Chandler. Rather than accept this decision, he decided to appeal to the synod of Arizona on grounds that the verdict was contrary to Scripture and violated his conscience according to provisions within the Book of Order. [50]

In February 1968, when the appeal from the presbytery of Phoenix to the synod of Arizona failed, Whitaker was faced with accepting or appealing the decision. Giving strong counsel and aid to Whitaker was a leading figure in world Presbyterianism, the late John A. Mackay, president emeritus of Princeton Theological Seminary. Both Mackay and Bradford strongly encouraged Whitaker to continue the fight. Providentially, Bradford had been a lawyer before entering the ministry and offered his services as counsel for the plaintiff.

Bradford added a third reason for appealing to the Permanent Judicial Commission of the General Assembly, the highest court of the United Presbyterian Church. He argued that no lower judicatory (presbytery or synod) could add to the ordination vows already set forth in the church constitution. In May 1968, *Rev. Robert C. Whitaker vs. The Synod of Arizona* was decided in favor of Whitaker. [51]

It was a great moral victory for all charismatics in the mainline churches. But the victory did not end with the successful appeal. As a result of the Whitaker case, every Presbyterian minister was protected from arbitrary removal from his or her parish by a presbytery on grounds of involvement in the charismatic renewal. Because the case did not rule on the theological implications involved in the controversy, the 180th General Assembly (1968) ordered a theological study to be made on the question of tongues, healing, exorcism, and the Neo-Pentecostal movement in general.

The study commissioned by the General Assembly was the first and possibly the most thorough ever conducted by a major denomination. The commission was made up of persons versed in theology, psychology, psychiatry, pastoral ministry, and ecclesiology. The report was so ground-breaking and comprehensive that it served as a model for many other denominational reports in following years. Again, the Presbyterians were pioneers in renewal.

The report of those competent in the behavioral sciences "found no evidence of pathology in the movement." The exegetical sections of the re-

port, while rejecting a separate experience of Holy Spirit baptism, did allow for the exercise of spiritual gifts in the contemporary church as long as they did not lead to disorder and division. Rejecting the cessation of the charismata theory, the report said: "We therefore conclude on the basis of Scripture, that the practice of glossolalia should neither be despised nor forbidden; on the other hand, it should not be emphasized nor made normative for Christian experience."

A set of guidelines was offered for both charismatics and noncharismatics, with a view toward keeping peace in the churches. Over all, the report was positive in its exegetical, psychological, and pastoral sections. The report's guidelines were adopted overwhelmingly, and it was received as a whole by the 182nd General Assembly of the United Presbyterian Church in

Robert Whitaker's trial opened the way for hundreds of Presbyterian clergymen to remain in their churches after being renewed in the Holy Spirit.

1970 and has been the official policy of the church since that time. [52]

Despite this victory, other Presbyterian pastors faced legal difficulties in the churches in the years after 1970. Another classic case was that of Earl W. Morey Jr., pastor of the St. Giles Presbyterian Church of Richmond, Virginia, who was investigated and exonerated three times before the Hanover presbytery would accept his right to exercise the gifts of the Spirit in the prayer meetings of the church.

Growth and Development

None of these legal obstacles, however, could hinder the work of the Holy Spirit in the American Presbyterian churches. Throughout the 1970s the renewal moved with ever increasing force in the churches. In Hollywood's First Presbyterian Church, one of the largest Presbyterian churches in the world, more than six hundred members were said to be speaking in tongues. Other prominent Presbyterian leaders, including Louis Evans of the National Presbyterian Church in Washington, D.C., his wife, Colleen Townsend Evans, and the late Catherine Marshall and her husband, Leonard LeSourd, were openly active in the movement. Mrs. LeSourd, widow of Senate chaplain Peter Marshall, wrote two books recounting her charismatic experiences, *Something More* and *The Helper,* which sold more than eighteen million copies before her death in 1983.[53]

An important addition to the movement came in 1965 when J. Rodman Williams was baptized in the Holy Spirit while serving as professor of systematic theology at the Austin Presbyterian Theological Seminary in Texas. Already an able and well-known theologian among Presbyterians, Williams added serious theological depth to the charismatic movement as a whole. In later years he made great contributions through his books and teaching positions at Melodyland and the school of theology at the Regent University School of Divinity. Especially influential was Williams's book *The Pentecostal Reality.* Presbyterian theologian Charles Farah served the renewal in a similar fashion from his teaching position at Oral Roberts University.[54]

A leading Presbyterian theologian, J. Rodman Williams (1918–) became the most important theologian of the charismatic renewal. He wrote his *Renewal Theology* while serving as professor of theology at Regent University.

In 1974, the Charismatic Communion of Presbyterian Ministers changed its name to the Presbyterian Charismatic Communion. This change was brought about because of the thousands of laymen who wished to join the ministry of the group. Another change was effected in 1984 when the name was again changed, this time to Presbyterian and Reformed Renewal Ministries, International (PRRM).[55]

By 1985 the PRRM counted almost 1,000 clergy members of the 2,500 to 3,000 who had been baptized in the Holy Spirit. The total membership of the group is about 5,000 contributing members. This relatively small group is representative of some 250,000 charismatics in the Presbyterian and Reformed Churches in the United States. The PRRM organization publishes a bimonthly magazine titled *Renewal News,* which serves as an information channel for conferences and developments among Presbyterian charismatics.[56]

Some of the Presbyterian churches that have been renewed in the Holy Spirit are the following: New Covenant Presbyterian, Pompano Beach, Florida (George Callahan, pastor); St. Giles Presbyterian, Richmond, Virginia (Louis Skidmore, pastor); St. Giles, Charlotte, North Carolina (Percy Burns, pastor); Hope Presbyterian, Portland, Oregon (Larry Trogen, pastor); Bethany Presbyterian, Seattle, Washington (Dick Denham, pastor); Silverlake Presbyterian, Los Angeles, California (Bob Whitaker, pastor); Trinity Presbyterian, San Diego, California (Dick Adams, pastor); Our Lord's Community Church (RCA), Oklahoma City (Robert Wise, pastor);

PROFESSOR J. RODMAN WILLIAMS

AND THE HOLY SPIRIT

Then came Wednesday, the day before Thanksgiving—THE DAY! I felt at ease, and began to turn to letters on my desk. One letter was from a pastor who described his experience of recently visiting the seminary and being prayed for by a student to receive the gift of the Holy Spirit. He wrote about how later he began to speak in tongues and praise God mightily. As I read and reread the letter, the words somehow seemed to leap off the page, and I found myself being overcome. I was soon on my knees practically in tears praying for the Holy Spirit, and pounding the chair—asking, seeking, knocking—in a way I never had done before. *Now I intensely yearned for the gift of the Holy Spirit.* Then I stood and began to beseech God to break me open, to fill me to the fullest—with sometimes an almost torturous cry to what was in myself to possess my total being. But for a time all seemed to no avail. With hands outstretched I then began to pray to God the Father, Son, and Holy Spirit—and mixed in with the entreaty was a verse of Scripture I kept crying out: "Bless the Lord, O my soul; and all that is within me, bless His holy name!" I yearned to bless the Lord with *all* my being—my total self, body, soul, and spirit—*all* that was within me. Then I knew it was happening: *I was being filled with His Holy Spirit.* Also, for the first time I earnestly desired to speak in tongues because the English language seemed totally incapable of expressing the inexpressible glory and love of God. Instead of articulating rational words I began to ejaculate sounds of any kind, praying that somehow the Lord would use them. Suddenly I realized that something drastic was happening: my noises were being left behind, and I was off with such utterance, such words as I had never heard before.

Wave after wave, torrent after torrent, poured out. It was utterly fantastic. I was doing it and yet I was not. I seemed to be utterly detached and utterly involved. To some degree I could control the speed of the words—but not much; they were pouring out at a terrific rate. I could stop the flow whenever I wanted, but in operation I had absolutely no control over the nature or articulation of the sounds. My tongue, my jaws, my vocal cords were totally possessed—but not by me. Tears began to stream down my face—joy unutterable, amazement incredible. Over and over I felt borne down to the floor by the sheer weight of it all—and sometimes I would cry: "I don't believe it; I don't believe it!" It was so completely unlike anything I had ever known before.

Finally, I sat down in my chair, but still felt buoyed up as if by a vast inner power. I knew I was on earth, but it was as if heaven had intersected it—and I was in both. God was so much there that I scarcely moved a muscle: His delicate, lush, ineffable presence.

Suddenly, it dawned on me that I had not yet so much as glanced at a Bible. Quickly I opened one up to Acts 2. To be sure, I had read the Pentecostal story many times, but this was incredibly different. *I felt I was there.* As I read the words with my eyes and my mind, and began to do so out loud, I knew I could speak, as I read, in a tongue. This I did, verse after verse—reading the account of the filling with the Holy Spirit, speaking in other tongues, and what immediately followed—reading all this with the accompaniment of my own new tongue! By the time I arrived at the verse, "Being therefore exalted at the right hand of God, and having received from the Father the promise of the Holy Spirit, he [Christ] has poured out this which you see and hear" (v. 33), I was so overwhelmed that I could only stand and sing, "Praise God, praise God," over and over again.

> The whole event lasted about an hour. Then I felt strangely impelled by the Holy Spirit to move around the house, room after room, each time to speak out with a prayer in the tongue. I was not sure why I was doing this, but it was as if the Holy Spirit was blessing each spot, each corner. Truly, as it later turned out, He was preparing a sanctuary for His presence and action. ■
>
> —J. RODMAN WILLIAMS
> *THEOLOGICAL PILGRIMAGE*

and Heights Cumberland Presbyterian Church in Albuquerque, New Mexico (Larry Moss, pastor). [57]

In addition to these congregations in the United States, charismatic Presbyterian churches flourish on the mission fields around the world. Especially powerful renewals are taking place in Brazil, Korea, New Zealand, Nigeria, Kenya, Uganda, Guatemala, Nicaragua, and Taiwan.

Just as Presbyterians have been at the forefront of renewal in the past, one must assume that they will continue to provide leadership for the renewal of the churches in the future. Upon the retirement of Brick Bradford on December 31, 1989, Bradford Long, a former missionary to Taiwan, became the leader of the movement. The record shows that the Presbyterians have truly been pioneers in renewal, a fact that should be appreciated by Christians of all churches.

Starting with a few "Neo-Pentecostal" pioneers such as Dennis Bennett, Brick Bradford, and Larry Christenson, the charismatic renewal became a major force in the historic "mainline" churches by the mid-1970s. This first wave entered the churches that one would least expect to be affected by Pentecostalism. The Episcopalians, Presbyterians, and Lutherans represented the respectable center of American Protestantism.

That highly educated churchmen such as Bennett, Bradford, and Christenson could speak in tongues, call themselves "Pentecostals," and remain in their churches blasted all the stereotypes that had held sway in American religious life for decades.

In a way these men and the movements they created gave an aura of respectability to a movement that many serious Christians had dismissed as part of a bizarre mutation of Christian faith. After suffering for their Pentecostal testimony, these men outlived their critics and brought the movement into the center of church life.

They became models for a multitude of pastors and churches that hungered for revival but were unsure about going the charismatic route. Now that the bridge had been crossed, tens of thousands of charismatics followed them into what became known as the "charismatic renewal." Because of their pioneering efforts, practically every denomination in America and around the world soon experienced their own Pentecostal revival.

For Further Reading

The most accessible source for this chapter is Stanley M. Burgess, ed., and Eduard M. van der Maas, assoc. ed., *New International Dictionary of Pentecostal and Charismatic Movements* (Grand Rapids: Zondervan, 2001). A popular historical treatment is given in Vinson Synan's *In the Latter Days: The Outpouring of the Holy Spirit in the Twentieth Century* (Ann Arbor, Mich.: Servant Publications, 1991). Richard Quebedeaux gives an excellent account of the growth of the movement in *The New Charismatics II* (San Francisco: Harper & Row, 1983). The reaction of the mainline churches is detailed in Kilian McDonnell's *Charismatic Renewal and the Churches* (New York: Seabury Press, 1976).

A good source for the worldwide spread of the movement among Episcopalians and Anglicans is Michael Harper's *As At the Beginning: The Twentieth Century Pentecostal Revival* (London: Hodder and Stoughton, 1965). The Lutheran story is well presented in Christenson, *The Charismatic Renewal Among Lutherans* (Minneapolis: International Lutheran Renewal Center, 1975); and Erling Jorstad, *Bold in the Spirit: Lutheran Charismatic Renewal in America Today* (Minneapolis: Augsburg Publishing House, 1974).

The history and the theology of the Presbyterian renewal are given in J. Rodman Williams, *The Pentecostal Reality* (Plainfield, N.J.: Logos International, 1972); and *The Era of the Spirit* (Plainfield, N.J.: Logos International, 1971). Williams's three-volume *Renewal Theology* (Grand Rapids: Zondervan, 1988, 1990, 1992) is the most comprehensive systematic theology yet produced by the charismatic renewal movement.

Other major sources for Reformed Pentecostalism include Brick Bradford's *Releasing the Power of the Holy Spirit* (Oklahoma City: Presbyterian Charismatic Communion, 1983) and the Report of the United Presbyterian Church titled *The Work of the Holy Spirit* (1970). Henry I. Lederle develops a taxonomy of the views on Spirit-baptism and explores ways to integrate this Pentecostal teaching into a broad, ecumenical framework in his *Treasures Old and New: Interpretations of Spirit-Baptism in the Charismatic Renewal Movement* (Peabody, Mass: Hendrickson, 1988).

· 8 ·

The "Charismatics": Renewal in Major Protestant Denominations

Vinson Synan

O NE OF THE SURPRISES of the renewal was that it came first to the more sacramental and traditional Protestant churches rather than the more evangelical and fundamentalist denominations. Beginning among Episcopalians in 1960, the movement made early inroads among Presbyterians, Lutherans, and most surprising of all, Roman Catholics. Some of the more traditional Protestant churches had already had skirmishes with Pentecostals in the early years of the century and had built-in defenses against the Neo-Pentecostal movement when the movement mushroomed after 1970.

But it was impossible to hold back the charismatic tide that was sweeping the churches of the world. In general, resistance in the more traditional churches was higher than in the "liberal" churches. Yet, in the end, the charismatic movement made huge strides in all the churches during the decade of the 1970s, so much so that a Gallup poll in 1979 estimated that 20 percent of church members from practically all churches identified themselves as "Pentecostal or charismatic" believers. This amounted to some thirty million adults in the United States.

As the movement grew in the mainline churches, several renewal organizations were created to serve and direct the renewal within the various traditions. By the mid-1970s there were thousands of mainline

Protestant pastors and churches that were deeply involved in the renewal. As the decade came to an end there were many ecumenical contacts made between the leaders of the various renewal movements, especially in the United States and Europe.

Also, most of these newer groups adopted the name "charismatic" rather than the earlier designation of "Neo-Pentecostal." This made a clear line of distinction between these renewal movements and the Pentecostals who were still held at arm's length by most mainline churchmen. By 1980 the words "charismatic renewal" became common to describe the new wave of Holy Spirit renewal. In recognition of their pioneering role in the renewal, the historic Pentecostals were now dubbed "classical Pentecostals."

These charismatic renewalists were determined to stay in their churches and bring revival and renewal to their own people. At times they found opposition from denominational officials who were leery of the Pentecostal phenomena that began to appear in their churches. By and large, however, most denominations took a wait-and-see attitude and allowed the various charismatic organizations to flourish in their midst. Perhaps the new acceptance was due to the fact that charismatics in local churches were often the best volunteer workers and tithe payers to be found.

This chapter describes the major charismatic renewal movements that developed in major Protestant denominations in the 1970s.

The Methodist Renewal

In many ways, Methodism is the mother church for the hundreds of holiness and Pentecostal denominations that have arisen in the past century. Founded in 18th-century England by John Wesley and his followers, Methodism arose as a renewal movement in the Church of England of which Wesley was a priest. Although Wesley remained an Anglican until his death, his Methodist Societies became separate denominations contrary to his wishes.

The name Methodist was given in derision to Wesley and his friends in the Holy Club at Oxford University in the 1720s. By following a method of prayer, confession, and frequent Communion, this group of university students attempted to fulfill the admonition of Hebrews 12:14: "Pursue peace with all people, and holiness, without which no one will see the Lord."[1]

In seeking holiness, Wesley developed the theology of the second blessing of entire sanctification, which could be received after conversion. Although he taught that sanctification was a process, Wesley also held out the possibility of an instantaneous experience similar to that of some great Catholic and Anglican mystics.

The idea of subsequence, that is, a second-blessing experience following conversion, is thus the basic theological principle of the holiness and Pentecostal movements. Following Wesley, most of the holiness churches, such as the Church of the Nazarene, have stressed the ethical cleansing aspect of the experience, while the Pentecostals, following Wesley's colleague John Fletcher, have stressed the baptism in the Holy Spirit aspect with their own unique emphasis on accompanying manifestations of the charismata.[2]

Mainline Methodist Churches

When Francis Asbury organized the American Methodist Church in Baltimore in 1784, he read Wesley's direction to the conference: "We believe that God's design in raising up the preachers called Methodists in America is to reform the continent and spread scriptural holiness over these lands." The 19th-century Methodists took Wesley seriously. They spread scriptural holiness over America through circuit rider preachers and the camp meeting, which became a Methodist specialty in frontier America.[3]

The frontier Methodists also became famous for their expressive worship and the demonstrations that often accompanied their revivals. Such exercises as "the jerks," "treeing the devil," being "slain in the Spirit," the "holy dance," and the "holy laugh" were not uncommon in these services. They were often laughingly called "Methodist fits." To the faithful, however, they were seen as signs of God's presence and power. Thus if people fell on the floor "slain by the Spirit" while a Methodist preacher ministered, it was considered the best sign that he was called to be a bishop.

During these years, the number of Methodists grew by leaps and bounds in the United States. They spread from coast to coast and border to border. By the end of the Civil War, Methodists were accounted the largest denominational family in America.

As the church grew in numbers, wealth, and influence, it became increasingly difficult to keep the second-blessing teaching alive and vital among both ministers and laymen. By 1839 a movement to breathe new life into the church and renew the experience of sanctification was begun by Phoebe and Walter Palmer in New York City. Working with Timothy Merritt and his *Guide to Holiness,* which was published in Boston, the Palmers led in teaching an altar terminology whereby one was sanctified instantaneously by placing his "all on the altar."[4]

Another renewal movement was inaugurated after the Civil War by

New York Methodist pastors John Inskip and Alfred Cookman at the suggestion of a laywoman from Pennsylvania, Harriett Drake. Through their efforts, the National Holiness Association was formed in Vineland, New Jersey, in 1867. This loose association soon grew to be a nationwide holiness crusade that gathered huge crowds on old Methodist campgrounds to pray for a return of the old-time power. Although this effort was ecumenical, Methodist preachers and laypersons led the way. [5]

As this movement spread, two tendencies appeared. One was a turn to extreme legalism, which caused a wedge between moderate Methodists and more radical holiness teachers. Another trend was to speak of the second blessing as a baptism of the Holy Ghost for an enduement of power for service. Thus, the Methodist Church, which began as a renewal movement in Anglicanism, became itself the object of a renewal movement within its own ranks similar to Wesley's efforts a century earlier. [6]

By the 20th century, however, the mainline Methodist churches in America largely rejected the holiness renewal efforts as well as the frontier spiritual demonstrations that often accompanied holiness preaching. The church then turned to an emphasis on education and social action. As a result, by the turn of the century, several dozen holiness and Pentecostal denominations went their separate ways in order to emphasize the deeper life that they felt was being abandoned by the mainline Methodist churches.

Tommy Tyson and the "Charismatic" Methodists

The story of Tommy Tyson is that of a 20th-century Methodist pastor and evangelist who returned to his spiritual roots to bring the power of the Holy Spirit back to his church. Coming from a family of Methodist preachers in North Carolina, Tyson had pastored several churches in the North Carolina Conference when he felt a need for a deeper work of God in his life and ministry. In 1952, while serving as pastor of the Bethany Methodist Church in Durham, North Carolina, he was baptized in the Holy Spirit and experienced speaking in tongues. [7]

When he shared this new experience with his parishioners, they shied away from him. He then considered leaving the ministry and working as a layman. Going to his bishop, Paul Garber, he explained, "If no more than I have now is causing this kind of a reaction, there's no telling what will happen if the Lord really gets hold of me." Then he told him, "I am already packed."

The bishop's reply was a welcome relief and an open invitation to begin a charismatic ministry in the Methodist Church: "Now you just go back and unpack that bag. You're not going anyplace. We need you. We want you. But you need us too," said the bishop.

Two years later, in 1954, Tyson was appointed as a conference evangelist and began a worldwide ministry of teaching and preaching that was instrumental in leading thousands of ministers and laymen into the Pentecostal experience. Although his ministry was especially influential in Methodist circles, he also became a leading speaker for Catholic and Episcopal charismatics.

Through his ministry in "Camps Farthest Out" (CFO) he spread the charismatic movement to thousands of others. In the mid-1960s, he became a close friend of Oral Roberts and served as the first director of religious life on the Oral Roberts University campus. His friendship with Roberts helped the charismatic movement to gain a more receptive attitude within the church.

Tommy Tyson (1922–), an early Methodist charismatic, was influential in the founding years of Oral Roberts University.

Other Methodist leaders followed Tyson at ORU and helped to bring the seminary into being. The leading influence in shaping the seminary was Jimmy Buskirk, whom Roberts recruited from Emory University to serve as the founding dean of the graduate school of theology. Working closely with Buskirk was Bishop Mack Stokes, whose support and presence helped the institution gain credibility both in the academic world and in the United Methodist Church. Other "cradle" Methodists who worked at ORU and who were widely known as charismatics were Bob Stamps and Robert Tuttle.[8]

The Adopted Methodist Charismatics

Perhaps the most notable charismatic figure among Methodists is Oral Roberts, an "adopted" member of the church. Born in the home of Pentecostal holiness preachers in eastern Oklahoma, Roberts became known worldwide in the 1950s for his tent divine-healing crusades. During the time his ministry stirred controversy among his own Pentecostal brethren, Roberts was gaining respect in the traditional mainline churches because of his television ministry.[9]

In 1965, when he began his university in Tulsa, the charismatic movement was growing in the mainline churches. In time, Methodists grew to be a major source of the financial support for his ministry. Through the friendship of Finis Crutchfield, pastor of the Boston Avenue Methodist Church in Tulsa, Oklahoma, and Oklahoma bishop Angie Smith, Roberts joined the United Methodist Church in 1968. He was accepted as a local preacher although he vowed to continue preaching the same message he had proclaimed as a Pentecostal. After this, Oral Roberts University became a major training center for Methodist preachers.

Another "adopted" Methodist charismatic leader was Ross Whetstone, who came to the church as an officer of the Salvation Army. Whetstone had been baptized in the Holy Ghost in 1937 as an eighteen-year-old boy. The next year, he joined the Salvation Army, where he was commissioned as an officer in 1939. In 1950 he transferred his ordination to the Central New York Conference of the Methodist Church.[10]

After pastoring several Methodist churches, Whetstone was called to provide leadership for the lay witness movement as an executive on the board of evangelism for the denomination. By the 1970s, Whetstone was looked upon as the leading spokesman for Methodist charismatics and was given increasing responsibility for overseeing the movement in the church. Over the years, hundreds of other holiness and Pentecostal ministers have transferred to the Methodist Church and have carried on forceful Spirit-filled ministries in their assignments. They, like Roberts and Whetstone, have been a leavening influence in the church.

United Methodist Renewal Fellowship

Although thousands of Methodists had been led into a Pentecostal experience by leaders such as Tyson, a charismatic Methodist organization did not exist until 1977 when Whetstone and others joined additional denominations in putting together the Kansas City Charismatic Conference. In Kansas City the Methodist delegation formed the United Methodist Renewal Services Fellowship (UMRSF) to serve as a central rallying force for Methodist charismatics.

In 1980 the UMRSF was given offices in the national headquarters of the United Methodist Church in Nashville, Tennessee. Rather than being another adversary pressure group within the church, the UMRSF is officially recognized by the board of discipleship and enjoys the support of the church at large. An indication of this acceptance is the fact that the board of discipleship charged this group to represent the interests of the United Methodist Church at the New Orleans Congresses on the Holy Spirit in 1986 and 1987.[11]

The UMRSF sponsors many conferences and seminars around the country in its efforts to renew the church. The major annual gatherings are the Aldersgate Conferences on the Holy Spirit, which gather some two thousand to three thousand participants annually. The group also publishes a newsletter entitled *Manna* to keep the members and friends of the Methodist charismatic renewal movement informed.

The theology of the Methodist charismatic movement is similar to that of other mainline Protestant charismatic movements. While not emphasizing the instant second-blessing sanctification teachings of the classical holiness bodies and the initial-evidence doctrine of the classical Pentecostals, the Methodist charismatics see baptism in the Holy Spirit as the actualization of the Holy Spirit and His gifts that were received at initiation. They do stress, however, the continuing manifestation of all the gifts of the Spirit in the ongoing life of the believer and the church.

Despite the Methodist roots of the Pentecostal movement, the American Methodist Church was late in issuing a report on the charismatic movement. When it was issued in 1976, the report pointed to Wesley's mature teaching on the progressive aspect of sanctification and indicated that Methodist charismatics who take over classical Pentecostal theology "are no longer Methodists, at least in the Wesleyan sense." [12]

The Methodist Church has been the site of many schisms resulting in the formation of new bodies. Among the casualties of the past are such holiness churches with Methodist roots as the Church of the Nazarene, the Free Methodist Church, the Wesleyan Church, and the Salvation Army. Many of these bodies adopted doctrinal statements and church structures almost identical with classical Methodist usages.

The Methodists also contributed much to the formation of the classical Pentecostal denominations. The theological foundations of Pentecostalism were laid by former Methodists such as Charles Parham, William J. Seymour, and J. H. King. The basic theology of almost all Pentecostal bodies in the world is essentially the Arminian perfectionistic theology of Methodism with some charismatic and dispensational additions.

Perhaps the most striking event in Methodist charismatic history was the schism in Chile in 1909 that produced the Pentecostal Methodist Church of Chile. Under the leadership of Willis Hoover, an American missionary, a Pentecostal revival broke out in the Methodist churches in Valparaiso and Santiago where simple church members spoke in tongues, prophesied, and "danced in the Spirit." In a short time thirty-seven Pentecostals were tried in a church court for being "irrational and anti-Methodist." At the time there were six thousand Methodists in Chile. The Pentecostals organized the Iglesia Metodista Pentecostal (Pentecostal Methodist Church) later that year.

Now with charismatics accepted in the church, it may be possible for the 1.7 million American Methodists who identify with the charismatic movement to remain in the church and carry out a significant ministry of renewal. Also there may be a growing tendency among Methodist leaders to begin conversations with the "children" of Methodism who have shown more vigorous growth than the mother church.

The Methodist Charismatic Movement Today

Across America many Methodist congregations are involved in charismatic renewal. In most cases they have the cooperation and support of their bishops, although in some areas charismatic pastors have difficulty with their ecclesiastical superiors.

By 2000, the United Methodist Church was moving to integrate the renewal into the structures of the church. Avenues of communication were created by the appointment of charismatic coordinators for the five jurisdictions in the United States. Plans were also made for other consultants and coordinators to be appointed to work with these jurisdictional leaders in interpreting the renewal to the bishops and integrating its dynamic force into the life of the church.[13]

In the 1990s the Methodist renewalists chose Gary Moore, a layman, to lead the movement. Through the ministry of annual "Aldersgate" conferences, Moore led the thousands of Methodist charismatics from a new retreat center in Goodlettsville, Tennessee, a town on the outskirts of Nashville.

The Baptist Renewal

John Osteen

John Osteen was a typical Southern Baptist pastor in 1958 with a grave problem in his family. His daughter, who had been born with cerebral palsy, was given no hope of recovery by her doctors. In desperation, this man, pastor of the Hibbard Memorial Baptist Church in Houston, Texas, began to study the promises of divine healing in the Bible. With an awakened interest in the miracles recorded in the New Testament, he prayed for his daughter, and to his happy astonishment, she was suddenly and miraculously healed.

Shortly after this, Osteen sought the fellowship of Pentecostals in the Houston area. J. R. Godwin, pastor of Houston's First Assembly of God, befriended him and explained to him the baptism in the Holy Spirit. In a short time, Osteen received a powerful Pentecostal experience "with a flow of tongues."

A few months later, the Hibbard Baptist Church conducted a trial charging Osteen with "heresy." During the time of the trial, two deacons who had opposed him also spoke in tongues and "switched sides." At the end of the trial, 82 percent of the congregation voted in Osteen's favor. Although he was free to stay as pastor of the church, he was often heckled by his opponents. Finally, in 1961, he and one hundred of his supporters moved their services to the local feed and seed store where they organized the Lakewood Baptist Church.

After two years in the new location, Osteen heard the Lord tell him to "lift up your voice like an archangel and prophesy to My people in the valley of dry bones." This led to several years of evangelistic crusades in many parts of the world with "amazing results." In 1969, he was led to return to the Lakewood church to resume his pastorate there. Again he started with about 100 people. By 1990, the church had grown to more than 5,000 families and built a sanctuary to seat 8,000, where Osteen ministered to a total of 15,000–plus persons per week.[14]

In many ways, Osteen's story is the story of the charismatic renewal among Baptists. He was one of untold hundreds of Baptist pastors who were renewed in the Holy Spirit during the century and suffered varying degrees of rejection from their denomination.

The Baptist View of the Charismata

Largely absent from modern Baptist doctrinal formulations is any mention of signs, wonders, or the gifts of the Spirit. Some early Baptist statements, however, seem to indicate an openness to manifestations of the Spirit. From England, early American Baptists received a tradition of laying on of hands after water baptism "for a further reception of the Holy Spirit of promise, or for the addition of the grace of the Spirit" since "the 'whole Gospel was confirmed in primitive times by signs and wonders and divers miracles and gifts of the Holy Ghost in general.'" Baptist historian Edward Hiscox points to early records of the Philadelphia association where there are indications that various gifts of the Spirit were in operation in the churches of that area about 1743.[15]

Through the years, however, the doctrine of the laying on of hands fell into disuse in the churches. Though there seems to be evidence of charismatic activity among some early Baptists, in time the vast majority of the pastors and teachers in the churches adopted a "cessation of the charismata" view of the gifts that was common in most churches. By the 20th century, the most common argument heard in Baptist churches was that the signs and wonders of the Bible were meant only for the apostolic age.

Despite this trend, several prominent 19th-century Baptists voiced expectations of a restoration of apostolic signs and wonders to the church. Such well-known Baptist leaders as C. H. Spurgeon in London and A. J. Gordon in Boston often preached about a new outpouring of the Holy Spirit in their day that would radically change the churches and the world. Indeed, Gordon, a leading turn-of-the-century Baptist pastor and teacher, is often cited as a forerunner of modern Pentecostalism because of his forceful teachings on a "baptism in the Holy Spirit" subsequent to conversion and the reality of divine healing in answer to prayer.

These men were the exceptions to the rule, however. Coming from the Calvinist tradition, Baptists have generally been little affected by perfectionistic and charismatic movements, most of which have generally had their roots in the Arminian-Wesleyan tradition. Yet, in the 20th century the Pentecostal churches have probably won more converts from among Baptists than from any other Protestant group in the United States.

Early Baptist Pentecostals

Though Osteen was an early Neo-Pentecostal, he was by no means the first Baptist in America to be numbered among the Pentecostals. That distinction is held by a group of Free-Will Baptists in North and South Carolina who received the "baptism" and spoke in tongues after the Azusa Street outpouring in 1906. Hearing the Pentecostal message in Dunn, North Carolina, in 1907 from the lips of Gaston Cashwell, an Azusa Street pilgrim, many pastors and members of the Free-Will Baptist churches spoke in tongues and led their churches into a thoroughgoing charismatic renewal. These early Baptist Pentecostals were rejected by many of their brothers in the local Baptist associations. As a result, in 1908 they organized the Pentecostal Free-Will Baptist Church, which today numbers about 150 churches and 13,000 members in the Central Atlantic states.[16]

Over the years since the turn of the century, former Baptists have figured largely in the formation of Pentecostal denominations. These include C. H. Mason, founder of the Church of God in Christ, and E. N. Bell, first general superintendent of the Assemblies of God. Most of these early leaders were expelled from their churches when they testified to their Pentecostal experiences.

Independent Baptist evangelists also made news in the 1950s in the heyday of the healing-deliverance crusade movement. Among those claiming Baptist ordinations were William Branham and Tommy Hicks. These men conducted some of the largest healing crusades yet seen. In 1955, Hicks preached to more than 200,000 persons per night in Argentina, at that time the largest attended evangelistic crusade in all Christian history. Although nominal Baptists, these men operated almost totally in Pentecostal environments.[17]

With the advent of the Neo-Pentecostal movement in the 1960s, many Baptist pastors and laymen received the baptism in the Holy Spirit and attempted to stay in their denominations. John Osteen's rejection experience was typical of the 1960s and in many quarters is still typical today.

Among the early Neo-Pentecostals who faced rejection were the well-known writer Jamie Buckingham of Melbourne, Florida; Howard Conatser of Dallas, Texas; Ken Sumrall of Pensacola, Florida; and Charles Simpson of Mobile, Alabama. All were Southern Baptists who encountered stern opposition from their fellow pastors in spite of solid support from their congregations.

The case of Conatser became widely known when his Beverly Hills Baptist Church in Dallas was rejected by the Dallas Baptist Association and the Texas Baptist state convention. Despite this situation, Beverly Hills continued to claim membership in the national Southern Baptist Convention while making every attempt to remain loyal to the denomination.

Overcoming all opposition, the Beverly Hills congregation grew to encompass more than four thousand members in the mid–1970s. Because of its explosive growth, the church was eventually forced to conduct services in a local entertainment center known as the Bronco Bowl to accommodate the crowds. Opposing Conatser at this time was W. A. Criswell, pastor of the nation's largest Baptist congregation, Dallas First Baptist Church. At the height of the controversy, Criswell's own daughter received the Pentecostal experience and spoke in tongues.[18]

The Beverly Hills case was never resolved, however, since after the death of Conatser in 1978, the congregation left the Southern Baptist Convention to become an independent church. This also was the fate of the churches pastored by Simpson, Buckingham, and Sumrall.

The renewal faced less opposition in the American Baptist Churches (the old Northern Baptist Church, also known as the ABC) than from the Southern Baptist Convention. One of the earliest Neo-Pentecostals in this denomination was Howard Ervin of the Emmanuel Baptist Church in Atlantic Highlands, New Jersey. Baptized in the Holy Spirit in 1958, he soon became a proponent of Pentecostalism in the mainline churches. A graduate of Princeton Theological Seminary holding the Th.D. degree, Ervin wrote an early apology for Neo-Pentecostalism in the 1967 book *These Are Not Drunken As Ye Suppose.* In later years he became a professor of theology at Oral Roberts University.

Other outstanding ABC leaders were Ken Pagard of Chula Vista,

California, who pioneered in organizing household groups in his church, and Gary Clark of Salem, New Hampshire. Clark's First Baptist church grew from fewer than one hundred members to more than six hundred before he moved to California in 1986 to pursue a ministry in world missions. For fifteen years Clark's church led all Baptist churches in New Hampshire in growth. Other early ABC charismatics were Charles Moore of Portland, Oregon, and Ray and Margorie Bess of DuQuoin, Illinois.[19]

During these years, Pat Robertson, a young Southern Baptist theology student at Yale University, heard about the baptism in the Holy Spirit from Robert Walker, the editor of *Christian Life* magazine. In 1957, while serving as an assistant pastor to Harald Bredesen at the Reformed Church in Mt. Vernon, New York, Robertson received the Pentecostal experience and spoke in other tongues. In 1960, Robertson returned to his native Virginia where his father had served as a Democratic U.S. senator. In 1960 he started his Christian Broadcasting Network in a broken-down studio in Portsmouth, Virginia. Since that time, Robertson's ministry has become legendary in both American religion and the television industry.

When Robertson entered the 1988 race for the Republican nomination for president of the United States, he gave up his Baptist ordination. Twelve years later, in March of 2000, in celebration of his seventieth birthday, Robertson renewed his ordination vows as a minister of the gospel with a mission to evangelize the world through his many ministries based in Virginia Beach, Virginia. By 2000 these ministries included the *700 Club* and other television programming broadcast in more than seventy nations, Regent University, which was being increasingly recognized as the preeminent Christian university in the world, the Christian Coalition, Operation Blessing, and the American Center for Law and Justice. His world evangelization vision, "World Reach," had as its goal the winning of 500 million persons to Christ. By the year 2000, over 145 million conversion decisions had been registered worldwide.

American Baptist Charismatic Fellowship

The most visible group of Baptist charismatics in America are those associated with the American Baptist Churches (ABC). Through the vision of laypersons Ray and Marjorie Bess, the first national conference on the Holy Spirit was conducted in 1975 at the Green Lake ABC camp in Wisconsin. Early leaders of the group were Ken Pagard and Joe Atkinson. In 1982, Gary Clark was chosen to lead the group, which is now called the American Baptist Charismatic Fellowship.

In addition to the renewal in the United States, important charismatic

PAT ROBERTSON
AND HARALD BREDESEN'S PROPHECY

Together, Harald Bredesen and I watched God open a new chapter of church history—a chapter which today has millions of characters. Now it is called the Charismatic Renewal. Then it had no name. It wasn't quite born. Those of us involved in it were an underground movement, worshiping behind locked doors.

Harald and I and some of my fellow seminary students were doing just that late one night in 1959 in historic First Reformed, the ancient Dutch Reformed church which Harald pastored in Westchester County's Mount Vernon, New York.

We loved that old stone church. With its flying buttresses, graceful arches and jewel-like windows, it was a bit of old Holland in a suburban American setting. Behind its massive walls and locked double doors we felt safe in our newfound freedom of worship.

Then suddenly, through Harald's lips the word came, "I am doing a new thing in the earth. Why will you be bound by fear? Hold nothing back. Hold nothing back!"

The new thing God was doing in our midst would draw the attention of the world and vastly bless scores of millions.

To that very sanctuary would come *New York Times* editor Bob Slosser, to experience the new thing and, in book after book, cogently share it. To that very sanctuary would come CBS: *The World Tonight*, to beam the new thing to the nation.

From that old stone church, what we had done behind locked double doors Walter Cronkite would carry to his twenty million viewers, and *The Saturday Evening Post* to its six millions. *Time*, the Associated Press and the United Press International would carry it to untold millions around the globe.

The very next night (after that word had come through Harald's lips) found Harald, my classmate, Dick Simmons, and I in the Fifth Avenue home of another Dutch Reformed pastor. Around Norman Vincent Peale's dinner table we held nothing back.

Mrs. Peale went from that dinner to an editorial board meeting of *Guidepost*; she held nothing back.

Senior editor John Sherrill interviewed Harald and set out on a quest which led to his receiving the baptism of the Holy Spirit, and his writing a score of books, holding nothing back.

He was in the midst of writing *They Speak With Other Tongues* when Harald brought to him a street preacher named David Wilkerson. Together they wrote *The Cross and the Switchblade*. With twenty million copies in print, *The Cross and the Switchblade* is, next to the Bible, the world's all-time Christian bestseller.

In Kansas City in 1977 as Father Francis McNutt stood to address fifty thousand Catholic and Protestant Charismatics, his first words were, "The Charismatic renewal in the Catholic Church (then numbering thirty million, including the Pope) began with two books, *They Speak With Other Tongues* and *The Cross and the Switchblade*." His words made us glad we had held nothing back. ■

—PAT ROBERTSON
IN HARALD BREDESEN'S *YES, LORD*

growth is being evidenced in ABC mission fields around the world. In 1984, Clark estimated that at least one-third of all the denomination's missionaries had received a "charismatic experience."

The Southern Baptist Explosion

In recent years, there has been a veritable charismatic explosion among Southern Baptists. Although many charismatics have maintained a low profile in order to keep peace in the church, the movement has continued to grow. Despite some advances, there continue to be cases where pastors are forced to leave the denomination when their experiences become known. No one knows how many Southern Baptist pastors and missionaries have received the Pentecostal experience, but their numbers are probably very large. In the late 1980s John Wimber was instrumental in leading thousands of pastors and laypersons into the baptism in the Holy Spirit. It was also rumored that a high percentage of all Southern Baptist missionaries on the field had spoken in tongues.

Several Southern Baptist ministers have also pastored independent charismatic congregations while maintaining their Southern Baptist ordinations. Two of these were Richard Hogue and Clark Whitten of Edmond, Oklahoma's Metrochurch. Hogue, who had been a popular youth evangelist during the era of the Jesus revolution in the 1960s, settled in Edmond in 1975 to begin the Metrochurch ministry. By the mid-1980s the church had grown to more than four thousand members, mostly from Southern Baptist backgrounds.

In 1986 Whitten succeeded Hogue in the Metrochurch pastorate after a remarkable ministry at the Gateway Baptist Church of Roswell, New Mexico, where he led the Southern Baptist Convention in baptisms in 1982–83. Perhaps because Whitten and many of his members spoke in tongues, the Pecos Valley Baptist Association never received the congregation into its fellowship although the congregation remained a member in good standing in the Southern Baptist Convention.

Unlike Hogue and Whitten, other Southern Baptist pastors have given up their church ordinations to follow independent ministries. One example was Larry Lea, former pastor of the Church on the Rock in Rockwall, Texas. Lea, who previously served as youth minister in Conatser's Beverly Hills Church in Dallas, saw tremendous growth in his congregation. Beginning with thirteen members in 1979, his suburban congregation numbered eleven thousand in the mid-1980s. In addition to the pastorate, Lea was named in 1986 to serve as dean of the theological seminary at Oral Roberts University as well as vice president of the university for spiritual affairs.

Other less well known Southern Baptist pastors and churches continued to practice charismatic ministries. A case in point was the Friendship Baptist Church in Mansfield, Texas, pastored by LeRoy Martin. With seventy-five members, Friendship Baptist Church is a member of the largest Southern Baptist association in the world, the Tarrant Baptist Association. Although Martin's church was openly charismatic, he remained in good standing with the association. Some old-timers in the association once told Martin that "if the charismatics ever have to leave the association, about 40 percent of the churches will have to go."[20]

Another example is that of Don LeMaster, pastor of the West Lauderdale Baptist Church near Fort Lauderdale, Florida. After coming to the church in 1967, LeMaster led his church into a deepening charismatic ministry. The church did not hide its identity, since the word *charismatic* was printed on the letterhead of the church's stationery.

Although LeMaster faced some opposition from fellow Baptist pastors in the early 1970s, friendly pastors defended LeMaster's congregational right to local autonomy. In the local Gulfstream Baptist Association, "nobody bothers us," said LeMaster, who was allowed to remain as a member in good standing for over two decades. In 1984, he ministered to a congregation of thirty-five hundred members that he said was "growing like crazy."[21]

The burgeoning ministry of James Robison is also a growing expression of a charismatic presence among Southern Baptists. Although he does not speak in tongues, Robison's crusades feature prayer for the sick and the exorcism of demonic spirits. He openly accepts the support of Pentecostals and speaks often in charismatic and Pentecostal circles. The support he has lost from his fellow Southern Baptists has been more than made up for in support from Pentecostals and charismatics. His theme of restoration reflects the restorationist view of the early Pentecostals.

A large group of Southern Baptists who favored a deeper spiritual life centered their efforts around a magazine titled *Fullness*. Published in Fort Worth in 1977, this magazine was edited by Ras Robinson and a circle of spiritually concerned Southern Baptist friends. *Fullness* served charismatic Baptists and others outside Baptist and charismatic circles. In 1986, at least 64 percent of the readers were Baptist.[22]

Over the years, many pastors with Pentecostal roots have also come to prominence in Southern Baptist churches. Literally hundreds of Baptist pastors were converted and received their spiritual formation in Pentecostal homes and churches. Among these are Charles Stanley, pastor of Atlanta's First Baptist Church and former president of the Southern Baptist Convention, who was born and raised in the Pentecostal Holiness Church, and Gene Garrison, pastor of the First Baptist Church in Oklahoma City, whose roots were in the Assemblies of God.

The American Baptist Churches also claimed as an ordained minister David Hubbard, who served as president of Fuller Theological Seminary in Pasadena, California. Hubbard's parents were Pentecostal preachers in California.

The Future

Although American Baptist charismatics have been organized for more than two decades and find open favor within the denomination, Southern Baptists have thus far been unable to organize a continuing support group. Many Spirit-filled pastors and laypersons are hoping to change this situation soon.

The New Orleans Congresses on the Holy Spirit and World Evangelization featured Baptist sessions in both 1986 and 1987. Baptist participants hoped that these delegates could "establish lines of communication and fellowship" for Spirit-filled Southern Baptists. Their goal was "to bring spiritual renewal to the church while remaining loyal to the local, state, and national conventions." [23]

It is the contention of people like C. Peter Wagner that a new "third wave" of the Spirit is breaking out in the mainstream evangelical churches, including the Baptists. Studies have indicated that about 20 percent of all Baptists in America see themselves as "Pentecostal or charismatic Christians." According to a Gallup poll taken in 1979, at least five million U.S. Baptists feel this way. Some observers, including Wagner, estimate that in 2000 there are between two hundred and three hundred "fullness" congregations in the Southern Baptist Convention.[24]

The Mennonite Renewal

Of all the church families that have been touched by the renewing power of the Holy Spirit in this century, none have been more deeply affected than the Mennonites. The story of the charismatic renewal among Mennonites is the story of hundreds of pastors and bishops, and many thousands of laypersons who have been radically renewed through the baptism in the Holy Spirit.

Like most of the renewals of this century, the Mennonite revival was unplanned and surprising. It all began during a youth "vacation Bible school" in the Loman Mennonite Church in Minnesota where seven churches had sent seventy-six teenagers to study the Bible between Christmas 1954 and New Year's Day 1955. The leader of this special school was Gerald Derstine, pastor of the Strawberry Lake Mennonite Church near Ogema, Minnesota. A "Mennonite of the Mennonites," Derstine's family had roots in his denomination that could be traced to the 18th century in Pennsylvania.[25]

Gerald Derstine and Strawberry Lake

What happened during those five days and in the months that followed would radically change Derstine's world as well as the Mennonite churches of the world. On the first day of the camp, thirteen unconverted youths in the group were born again after a time of fasting and prayer by the seven pastors in charge. Then, to the puzzlement of the pastors, the phenomenal began to take place.

At first, several children reported hearing angels singing. Afterward, a spirit of intercession for unsaved parents and friends led to fervent prayer for their salvation. Then, quite unexpectedly, some of the children fell prostrate on the floor in a state of trembling ecstasy. The pastors, fearful of demonic activity, began to "plead the blood of Jesus" for protection, but things continued to happen. Others fell to the floor and spoke in tongues.

Born into a leading Mennonite family, Gerald Derstine (1928–) was excommunicated from the ministry after an unusual revival in Minnesota in 1955. He was later restored.

In short order, these young Mennonites prophesied about impending world events and about a coming worldwide spiritual awakening. One prophesied that Billy Graham would one day preach the gospel behind the Iron Curtain. (This was in 1954!) Some saw visions of Jesus. At times "tongues, prophecy, and interpretation flowed like a rushing river," according to Derstine. At other times, singing in tongues filled the plain little Mennonite church with "heavenly melodies." Words of knowledge gave astounding evidence of an unusual "visitation" from God.

Upon returning to his pastorate in Strawberry Lake, Derstine was surprised to see the same charismatic phenomena repeated in homes and in the sanctuary of his church. A prophecy stated that this revival would eventually "affect the entire world." Far from opposing these miraculous manifestations, Derstine accepted them as a fulfillment of Joel's prophecy about the Holy Spirit being poured out "on all flesh" in the last days. He also was baptized in the Holy Spirit, spoke in tongues, and experienced many of the same spiritual manifestations himself.

THE FIRE FALLS IN STRAWBERRY LAKE

The little clock in the back of the church was ticking away, into the wee hours of the morning, when our first assurance came that this was indeed a work of God. Skip, the first boy who had come crying to the front, stopped the strange jabbering and began to speak intelligibly. A radiant smile lit up his face as he began to clearly articulate one word at a time. He spoke so slowly and so softly we had to lean close to hear what he was saying. His body was relaxed and peaceful now but his eyes remained closed as he said in a gentle, barely audible voice, "Turn—in—your—Bibles—to Acts 2:17—and—18—and—you—shall—under—stand—."

I quickly reached for my Bible. Thank God, at least he was saying something scriptural. My fingers trembled as I leafed through to the book of Acts, chapter 2, verses 17 and 18. I began reading to the small cluster of people who had gathered around the boy:

"And it shall come to pass in the last days, saith God, I will pour out of my Spirit upon all flesh: and your sons and your daughters shall prophesy, and your young men shall see visions, and your old men shall dream dreams: And on my servants and on my handmaidens I will pour out in those days of my Spirit; and they shall prophesy."

I stared at the words in astonishment. Then I looked at the boy and back at the verses again. Could all this truly be a work of God? In fact, could it be possible that this was the very revival we had been praying and fasting for? I wanted to believe it. Yet it was contrary to our doctrine. We had always been taught that these particular Scriptures had been fulfilled in Bible days. I read over the passage once more. "In the last days—"

"Brother Derstine! Come over here. Connie's saying something." I hurried over to the side of the young girl who was still lying on the floor. She also had a heavenly smile on her face and was talking. She spoke authoritatively, one word at a time, as she told of an "end-time revival" such as the world had never seen. Her friends, hovering over her, leaned close to catch every word. On their faces was a mixture of bewilderment and relief.

By that time the other young people who had been lying on the floor, "speaking in tongues" and trembling, became still and one by one they began to speak. Some of them sang. Others described heavenly scenes complete with elaborate descriptive gestures. Yet they all still lay on the floor, eyes closed, in a trance. There were prophecies of impending world events. (These particularly bothered me. We were only interested in revival for our own community.) There were words of exhortation and passages of Scripture. As each one ended his message almost invariably he would say, "This is my body you see, this is my voice you hear, but this is from the Lord." One word at a time. ■

—GERALD DERSTINE
FOLLOWING THE FIRE

Word spread rapidly in the Mennonite community concerning the strange happenings in Strawberry Lake. Soon bishops and elders of the area began an investigation of Derstine and the events in Loman and Strawberry Lake. By April 1955, the bishops conducted a hearing that resulted in Derstine's being "silenced" from the Mennonite ministry. If only he would admit that some demonic activity had taken place and that some of the manifestations had been "an act of Satan," and if he would promise not to talk about it in the future, Derstine could continue as a Mennonite pastor. This he refused to do.

Later in the year, Derstine met Henry Brunk, a fiery Spirit-filled Mennonite evangelist from Florida who headed the Gospel Crusade Evangelistic Association. By 1959, Derstine had moved to Florida to work with Brunk in developing the Christian Retreat in Bradenton.[26]

The question of the presence of spiritual gifts in Mennonite churches was not settled by the Derstine affair, however. A glance at the long history of Anabaptists and Mennonites is replete with instances of charismatic phenomena similar to those that occurred in Minnesota.

The Mennonite Tradition

The Mennonites arose from among the Anabaptists of the 16th century. These rebaptizers, as they were called by their enemies, constituted the most radical of the Reformation movements. They taught believer's baptism, as well as separation of church and state. Other Anabaptist views included pacifism and refusal to take oaths in court.

Begining in Zurich, the Anabaptist movement spread to Germany and Holland. A moderate leader in Holland was Menno Simons, an ex–Roman Catholic priest, who in 1537 assumed a place of leadership among the Anabaptists. His followers eventually became known as Mennonites whose broad family included such groups as the Amish and the Hutterites. Modern Baptists are also heir to the same Anabaptist vision as the Mennonites.

According to Mennonite writer Terry Miner, the early Mennonites were "thoroughly charismatic in the best sense of the word." The story of the church under persecution included many instances of prophecy, dreams, visions, and even martyrdom. Anabaptists and Mennonites saw themselves as neither Protestant nor Catholic, and as such were persecuted from all sides. Their vision was not simply a reformation of the church, but a restoration of primitive Christianity. As to the gifts of the Spirit, Menno Simons accepted the presence of all the charisms in church but always insisted that they be tested by Scripture.[27]

Mennonite Charismatics

Four centuries later, the Mennonites, like all other Christians, have been profoundly affected by the modern Pentecostal and charismatic movements. In his book *My Personal Pentecost*, Mennonite charismatic leader

Roy Koch has described three phases in Mennonite attitudes toward Pentecostalism: "abomination (pre-1950s), toleration (1960s) and propagation (1970s)." In the first stage Mennonites sternly opposed the Pentecostal movement. Despite a 1906 statement by Oregon Mennonites calling for a new openness to the baptism in the Holy Spirit, most Mennonites joined other Christians in condemning the Pentecostals. In spite of this attitude, many Mennonites received the experience in these years but remained quiet about it.[28]

Bishop Nelson Litwiller's experience was typical of many in his church. As a missionary to Latin America in the 1920s and 1930s, he was turned off by the style and claims of the Pentecostals he met in Argentina. "They claimed that they had the power and that we didn't," he said. Yet he was impressed by the tremendous growth of the movement in comparison to the relatively slow growth of the other evangelical churches.

Derstine's rejection by the church leaders in Strawberry Lake also demonstrated the attitudes of most Mennonites during this period. Nevertheless, during the 1960s and 1970s several thousand Mennonites received the baptism in the Holy Spirit. They were influenced more by the general charismatic awakening in the mainline churches than by Derstine's experiences. The story of Litwiller is a case in point. His acceptance of the baptism in the Holy Spirit came through Spirit-filled Roman Catholics in South Bend, Indiana. Through the influence of Kevin Ranaghan and others, the venerable missionary bishop was transformed through the Holy Spirit and became a national leader in the movement.

Other important Mennonite leaders swept into the movement in the same decade included Roy Koch, Bishop Elam Glick, Herb Minnich, Terry Miller, Allen Yoder, Dan Yutzy, George Brunk, Fred Augsburger, and Harold Gingerich. This period of toleration during the 1960s saw the Mennonite churches accepting the orthodoxy and validity of these charismatic leaders who carefully expressed an inflexible loyalty to their church, despite their Pentecostal experiences.

This phase of toleration soon led into Koch's third stage, that of propagation, or the aggressive promotion of the charismatic movement within the churches with the cautious but clear approval of the ecclesiastical leaders. This period, beginning in the 1970s, saw the inauguration of organized efforts to bring charismatic renewal to the churches.

In 1971, a report was approved by the Lancaster Conference, one of the largest and most traditional regional groups in the nation. This report called for acceptance of "unhindered manifestation of the Spirit's presence through the vibrant expression of praise and the fearless spreading of the good news of the mighty works of God taking place in our time." This report led to a major study of the Holy Spirit and the gifts of the Spirit in the Mennonite Church, the largest of the American Mennonite bodies. This document, which was adopted by the general assembly in July 1977, recognized both strengths and potential weaknesses in the charismatic movement within the church, with the strengths outweighing the weaknesses.[29] The strengths included "a release of spiritual gifts and power; a strong effective ministry of evangelism; great unity and love among the brotherhood; new forms of community and local church life; miracles of healing; winning the active support of many young people who would otherwise be lost to Christ and the church; the rediscovery of tongues; the gift of knowledge and other spiritual gifts; a commitment to work within existing churches rather than to separate from them; a great love for Jesus Christ our Lord, and for His church as His body." Potential weaknesses included the possibility of "religious arrogance" and a "careless use of Scripture."

In this new climate of acceptance, the Mennonite charismatics organized service groups to conduct renewal conferences around the United States and Canada. Although an early consultation of charismatic leaders was held in 1972, the major arm of the renewal emerged in 1975.

Mennonite Renewal Services

The Mennonite Renewal Services (MRS) came into being as a result of letters sent by Kevin Ranaghan to Litwiller and Harold Bauman, inviting the Mennonites to participate in a great ecumenical conference in Kansas City in 1977. Litwiller then invited a group of Mennonite charismatic leaders to meet in Youngstown, Ohio, to consider the invitation. At this meeting the Mennonite Renewal Services was born. The founders of the group included Nelson Litwiller, Dan Yutzy, Harold Bauman, Roy Koch, Herbert Minnich, and Fred Augsburger. From that time until 1996, MRS served as the charismatic arm of the Mennonite Church.[30]

Since 1977, when Mennonites and Baptists joined together in the Kansas City Charismatic Conference, Mennonites have played a leading role in the general charismatic movement in the United States. When he passed away at eighty-eight years of age in 1986, Bishop Nelson Litwiller had grown to be a respected elder statesman to younger leaders from many denominations.

Closely allied with the Mennonites were the charismatics in the various branches of the Church of the Brethren. Their "Brethren Renewal Services" paralleled the work of the Mennonites. For a few years their ministries were entwined under the name Empowered Ministries. The magazine

Empowered carried news of both movements, which often conducted joint conferences.

The growth of the charismatic renewal among Mennonites was spectacular. By 2000, estimates were that 20 percent of all Mennonites in the United States and Canada had received the baptism in the Holy Spirit, including both clergy and laity. In some conferences as many as 35 percent of the churches were active in the renewal. Many Mennonites believe with John Howard Yoder that Pentecostalism "is in our century the closest parallel to what Anabaptism was in the sixteenth."[31]

Throughout the 1980s and 1990s, some local Mennonite churches experienced spectacular growth through the power of the Holy Spirit. The most spectacular church growth in the Mennonite community in recent years occurred in the Hopewell Mennonite Church in Pennsylvania. This congregation, under the leadership of charismatic pastor Merle Stoltzfus, grew from fifty to two thousand members in a few years.

In retrospect, one could say that the experiences of the young vacation Bible school students in Strawberry Lake were not a temporary aberration but were in profound continuity with Mennonite faith and practice. By now, the renewal among Mennonites is one of the major success stories of the charismatic renewal.

A symbol of the acceptance of the renewal was the fact that in 1977 the Mennonite Church officially "restored" Gerald Derstine as an approved minister, thus ending twenty-two years of silence in the church. His work has not been in vain. Today practically all the Mennonite missionaries of the world have received the baptism in the Holy Spirit, and these mission fields are blazing areas of power evangelism.[32]

The Orthodox Renewal

The Eastern Orthodox Church constitutes the third largest family of Christians in the world, numbering some 175 million members worldwide in 2000. More than sixty million of these are members of the Russian Orthodox Church in the Soviet Union. In Greece, nearly nine million people embrace the Orthodox faith, encompassing 98.1 percent of the total population. Millions more live in other Eastern European and Middle Eastern nations dominated by Islam. For centuries, Orthodoxy has been a martyr church, with millions of her faithful slain for professing faith in Christ (it is estimated that over thirty million Orthodox Christians were martyred from 1917 to 1953 in Russia alone). They have kept their faith in Jesus when their own country became for them a foreign land.

In America, the Orthodox Church claims some five million members. These are distributed among a number of jurisdictions: Greek, Russian, Antiochian, Ukrainian, and several others. In 1965, the Orthodox Church in America (OCA) was formed as a self-governing entity with the blessings of the Russian bishops. It now claims one million English-speaking members. Orthodoxy in America is rapidly moving from its initial status as an immigrant church to hold a distinct place in American religious life.

Orthodoxy has always claimed to be charismatic in its worship and piety. At no time has it held to a theory of the cessation of the gifts of the Holy Spirit. Signs and wonders, including prophecy, healing, and miracles, have traditionally been accepted as part of the heritage of the church.[33]

Despite this tradition, no major body of Christians in the world has been less affected by the charismatic movement of recent decades. Even so, against the resistance of many church leaders, several Orthodox priests and laymen have persistently struggled to plant the seeds of renewal.

Eusebius A. Stephanou

An early leader of this charismatic renewal in the Orthodox Church was Eusebius A. Stephanou of Fort Wayne, Indiana. Stephanou, a celibate priest descended from a long line of Orthodox clergymen, brought impressive credentials to his task of charismatic leadership. Educated at the University of Michigan, Holy Cross School of Theology, and the General Episcopal Seminary in New York, he holds the B.A., S.T.M., and Th.D. degrees. He was a professor of theology and sub-dean at Holy Cross and subsequently held a teaching post at Notre Dame University.[34]

In 1968, feeling a need to "bring the Orthodox Church into line with the gospel of Christ," Stephanou launched a magazine entitled the *Logos*. His goal was the "re-evangelization of our people." Stephanou's criticism of the Greek Orthodox hierarchy, however, quickly got him into trouble, and he was suspended from the priesthood for six months for "undermining church authority." For the next several years, Stephanou, his magazine, and his insistent calls for reform proved to be a source of controversy within the Orthodox Church.

In 1972, Stephanou encountered another Orthodox priest, Athanasius Emmert of Huntington, West Virginia, who shared with him about the life-changing power of the Holy Spirit. Emmert laid hands on Stephanou and prayed for the "release" of the Holy Spirit (Orthodox Christians pray to be filled with the Holy Spirit when they are baptized—usually as infants— and look at the charismatic experience as a release of that gift already received). He was filled with the power of God, began to speak in other tongues, and thereby changed the *Logos* into an instrument for serving charismatic renewal in the Orthodox Church.[35]

Orthodox Charismatic Renewal

The following year, the very first Orthodox Charismatic Conference was held in Ann Arbor, Michigan, with about one hundred people in attendance. At that time there were estimated to be one thousand Orthodox charismatics scattered among two dozen prayer groups. Stephanou, Emmert, and a number of other clergy and laymen continued to work for renewal through the Logos Ministry for Orthodox Renewal.

Because of his renewal leadership, criticism of the Orthodox hierarchy, and continued reform activism, Stephanou has suffered several disciplinary actions. In July 1983, he was censured by his bishop and archbishop and placed on indefinite suspension despite hundreds of letters of support from his charismatic friends in the Orthodox Church. Stephanou continued as editor of the *Logos* and was a popular speaker at charismatic conferences in America and abroad.

In 1977 another Orthodox charismatic ministry emerged on the scene: the Service Committee for Orthodox Charismatic Renewal. This committee sought to bring together charismatic leaders from a wide variety of Orthodox jurisdictions to facilitate administration, coordination, and communication in the movement. They have sponsored a number of renewal conferences throughout the United States and Canada and publish a monthly newsletter, *Theosis*. Gerald Munk also served on the steering committee planning the New Orleans Congresses on the Holy Spirit and World Evangelization in 1986 and 1987.

The United Church of Christ Renewal

The United Church of Christ is one of the oldest denominations in the United States, a church that can trace its heritage to the Pilgrim fathers who landed at Plymouth Rock in 1620. These were the Puritans who fled to America to escape persecution from the established State Church of England. Their struggle for religious liberty is a part of the priceless heritage of American freedom.

For more than two centuries the Puritan Church was known as the Congregational Church and was famous for its firm Calvinist theology, its local church autonomy, and its strict Puritan lifestyle. In time, the Congregationalists spread from New England to all parts of the United States. The present United Church of Christ represents the merger of four different denominations over the years. The Congregational Christian Church, with roots in 19th-century Virginia, merged with the Congregationalists in 1931 to form the Congregational Christian churches.

In 1957 this church merged with the Evangelical and Reformed Church, which itself was the merger of two German-American churches with entirely different roots from the Congregationalists. These two churches, the German Reformed Church and the German Evangelical Synod of North America, merged in 1934 to form the Evangelical and Reformed Church in the U.S.

The denomination that resulted from these mergers in 1957 took the name United Church of Christ. This merger was unique in that the Evangelical and Reformed Church had its roots in German Calvinist piety while the Congregational Church came from distinctly English roots. Their governmental forms were also different. The Evangelical and Reformed Church had a more highly centralized government in contrast to the congregational polity seen in the very name of the Congregational Church. The UCC (as it is often called) is famous also for its theology, which has caused it to be referred to as the most liberal denomination in the country. This openness to liberal ideas has ancient roots in the church, going back to the founding of the Unitarian movement in New England. Unitarians, who denied the Trinity, came mostly from Congregational backgrounds. The Unitarian Church was formed in 1825. Famous liberal leaders who remained in the church in the 19th century included Horace Bushnell, Henry Ward Beecher, and George Washington Gladden, a father of the social gospel movement.[36]

In more recent times, the United Church of Christ has been a leader in many social causes that would have been inconceivable to the Pilgrim fathers. This has led to a general decline in the church, with heavy membership losses in recent years. Despite these tendencies, there have always been groups of evangelicals in the church who worked and prayed for a return to the solid evangelical faith of the Pilgrim fathers and the German Reformers.

The FCC/UCC

The Fellowship of Charismatic Christians in the United Church of Christ (FCC/UCC) is the central force in attempting to bring renewal to the church. This group began in the late 1970s under the leadership of J. Ray Thompson, pastor of a UCC congregation in Reno, Nevada. Thompson was baptized in the Holy Spirit in 1972 and spoke in other tongues. After his Pentecostal experience, he hungered to find other charismatics in the church with whom he could share fellowship. The opportunity came in 1977 when the Kansas City Charismatic Conference brought together more than fifty thousand Christians from practically all denominations.[37]

At the suggestion of Reuben Sheares II, a denominational leader, Thompson ran a notice in a church periodical asking for charismatic members of the church to identify themselves. When about forty persons responded, Thompson sent out a series of newsletters suggesting that those interested meet in Kansas City to organize a charismatic group within the church. As a result of these efforts, seventy-three persons gathered in Kansas City on July 22, 1977, to form the Charismatic Fellowship in the United Church of Christ. A temporary steering committee of twelve persons was selected to serve with Thompson, who was elected chairman.

The purpose of this organization was to minister to the lonely and isolated charismatics in the church, establish a Christ-centered voice within the church, and solidify the witness of the movement of the Holy Spirit in the United Church of Christ. The small but determined group left Kansas City with a vision to bring renewal to the church through the power and gifts of the Holy Spirit.

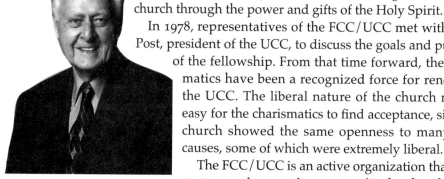

In 1978, representatives of the FCC/UCC met with Avery Post, president of the UCC, to discuss the goals and purposes of the fellowship. From that time forward, the charismatics have been a recognized force for renewal in the UCC. The liberal nature of the church made it easy for the charismatics to find acceptance, since the church showed the same openness to many other causes, some of which were extremely liberal.

The FCC/UCC is an active organization that sponsors several renewal programs for the church. These include the Acts Alive renewal conferences in which teams come to local churches for weekend events stressing lay witness, baptism in the Holy Spirit, and the use of spiritual gifts. A second program called Ecclesia brings renewal services to local churches stressing body life. A third ministry is the King's Kids Camps, which brings hundreds of young people to the Lord each summer.

Vernon Stoop (1927–) served as leader of the charismatics in the United Church of Christ as well as Secretary of the North American Renewal Service Committee.

Vernon Stoop. Since 1979, when the FCC/UCC was restructured, the group has been led by several persons, including David Emmons, Robert Welsh, and Robert Weeden. The director of services is Vernon Stoop, pastor of the Shepherd of the Hills UCC in Bechtelsville, Pennsylvania. Stoop also edits the *Focus Newsletter,* a periodical that serves as a clearinghouse of information for the movement. In addition to these responsibilities, Stoop serves as secretary of the Charismatic Concerns Committee (CCC), and the North American Renewal Service Committee (NARSC), which planned the 1986 and 1987 New Orleans Congresses on the Holy Spirit and world evangelization. Since then Stoop has played a key role in planning the NARSC congresses in Indianapolis (1990), Orlando (1995), and St. Louis (2000).

The Road Ahead

The most successful approach in recent years has been the fostering of charismatic renewal in older congregations in a way that will promote unity and avoid divisiveness. Stoop's Shepherd of the Hills Church in Bechtelsville, Pennsylvania, is a model of this approach. This congregation, which is 150 years old, has been led by senior pastor Stoop for forty years. His goal has been to "bring about a marriage of a traditional noncharismatic congregation and those charismatic elements that have grown up within the fellowship without splitting the congregation." So far, this approach has proved successful at Shepherd of the Hills.

The Wesleyan Charismatics

For decades the words *Wesleyan* and *charismatic* have been seen as mutually exclusive terms. No group of churches has been more negative toward the gifts of the Spirit, especially that of tongues, than historic holiness groups such as the Church of the Nazarene, the Wesleyan Church, and the Church of God (Anderson, Ind.). At best, tongues have been looked upon with suspicion, and at worst they have been dismissed as demonic.

This situation is remarkable in light of the historic fact that the Pentecostal movement originated in America and, indeed, around the world largely among Wesleyan holiness people. In fact, the original Pentecostals held to a basic belief in sanctification as a second work of grace and counted themselves as part of the holiness movement. They simply added a third blessing called the baptism in the Holy Spirit evidenced by speaking in other tongues.[38]

With the organization of the Assemblies of God in 1914, many Pentecostals drifted from the Wesleyan camp, but about half of American Pentecostals today still hold to a fundamentally Wesleyan-Arminian theology. It is generally agreed that classical Pentecostals share a common ancestry with the holiness people and that the two movements are far more similar than they are different from each other.

The Pentecostal Church of the Nazarene

The common roots of the two movements can be seen in the fact that the original name of the Church of the Nazarene was the "Pentecostal Church of the Nazarene." The word *Pentecostal* was dropped from the name in 1919, however, to avoid confusion with the tongues-speakers who had since preempted the name Pentecostal. The Nazarene position on tongues came when the founder of the church, Phineas Bresee, rejected the Azusa Street manifestations as invalid. His view was that the Pentecostal movement had as much effect in Los Angeles as a "pebble thrown into the sea."[39]

Bresee and his colleague J. P. Widney were quite willing to accept differences among early Nazarenes in matters that they considered nonessential to salvation. Their early theme was "in essentials, unity; in non-essentials, liberty; in all things, charity." After Bresee's death, however, tongues were seen as a threat to the church, since so many holiness people departed from their churches to form the first new Pentecostal denominations. The hard-line anti-Pentecostal attitude of many holiness people was summarized in Alma White's 1912 book titled *Demons and Tongues*, which attributed all glossolalia to demonic influence.

Other holiness-type churches that rejected Pentecostalism included the Wesleyan Methodist Church, the Salvation Army, the Free Methodist Church, the Church of God (Anderson, Ind.), and the Pilgrim Holiness Church. Holiness churches that accepted the Pentecostal message included the Church of God (Cleveland, Tenn.), the Pentecostal Holiness Church, the Church of God in Christ, the United Holy Church, and the Pentecostal Free-Will Baptist Church. These became the first organized Pentecostal denominations in America.

John L. Peters and Warren Black. When the Neo-Pentecostal movement began after 1960, it was inevitable that some Wesleyan holiness people would become involved again in the manifestations of the Holy Spirit. An early Neo-Pentecostal was John L. Peters, formerly general secretary of the Nazarene Young People's Society and well-known historian of the holiness movement. Although Peters had left the Nazarene Church in 1948 to become a Methodist, his influence continued among many of his friends in the church. In 1962 Peters received the baptism in the Holy Spirit and spoke in tongues.[40]

In 1963, after hearing the testimony of Peters on one of John Osteen's broadcasts, Warren Black, controller of the Nazarene Publishing House in Kansas City, received the baptism in the Holy Spirit. After several days of prayer and fasting in his home, Black drew a circle on the floor, stepped inside the circle, and promised God that he would seek Him until he was satisfied. "I was seeking God, not tongues," he said. What he received, however, was a powerful Pentecostal experience accompanied by speaking in tongues. At the same time he was instantly healed of a long-standing speech problem.[41]

Although divine healing was taught by the Nazarenes, tongues were still widely considered to be either fleshly or demonic. In 1971, as a result of his testimony before a Nazarene college student body, Black was put out of the church. Believing that his excommunication was done illegally, Black and other like-minded Nazarenes decided to take the charismatic question to the delegates of the highest body in the church, the general assembly. Before this body met in Miami in 1972, all the delegates were sent a packet by mail explaining his position. Black was backed in this action by about twenty-five Nazarene members.

Also presented to this assembly were four "memorials" from Nazarene districts calling on the church to disallow tongues in the churches. The appeals from Black "caused a furor" in the assembly. Many wanted to end the matter then and there by forbidding tongues forever. Others, led by Jack Ford of England, called for a study commission that could deal with the subject more dispassionately. Ford reminded the general assembly that the Calvary holiness denomination in England that merged with the Church of the Nazarene in 1955 had allowed tongues in the churches although the practice was not encouraged.

Nazarenes Take a Stand. The general assembly took no action in 1972, but to the surprise of Black and others, it was learned that the general superintendents had acted on their own the previous year when they issued their interpretation of the *Manual.* Their statement, which lacked the authority of general assembly action, stated that "speaking in tongues either as the evidence of the baptism with the Holy Spirit or as an ecstatic Neo-Pentecostal prayer language is interpreted as inveighing against the doctrine and practices of the churches."[42]

For thirteen years, the church operated under the contradictions engendered by the Calvary holiness precedent in England and the interpretation of the general superintendents. On the basis of the English precedent, Dan Brady, a pastor from Dayton, Ohio, who had been defrocked for speaking in tongues, appealed to be reinstated in the church. In 1985, his appeal was denied on the highest judicial level.

This led the church to add a first-ever official statement on tongues in the *Manual*. This occurred in the general assembly that met in Anaheim, California, in 1985. The statement was placed in the appendix and now stands as the official policy of the church. After affirming that the biblical evidence of the baptism in the Holy Spirit is the "cleansing of the heart from sin" and the "fruit of the Spirit," the article states: "To affirm that even a special or any alleged physical evidence or 'prayer language' is evidence of the baptism with the Holy Spirit is contrary to the biblical and historical position of the church."[43]

This statement, which does not actually forbid tongues, is a disavowal of the initial-evidence theory propounded by the Pentecostals in the early part of the century. Very few charismatics in the mainline churches would disagree with this position as it relates to glossolalia. In effect, the working position of the church now seems to be that tongues will be allowed in private devotions as long as the practice is not propagated in such a way as to support the initial-evidence theory or bring division to the churches. This would include the understanding that tongues will not be manifested in the public worship services of the church.

To many Nazarenes, however, the effect of this statement has been to outlaw tongues in the church. A case in point is the experience of Steve Gustin, pastor of a Nazarene congregation in Azusa, California. By 1986 this church was 90 percent charismatic and made attempts to stay in the denomination. But after the general assembly passed the resolution on tongues in 1985, the Azusa congregation was expelled from the denomination. After leaving, the congregation took the name Berean Christian Center. Whether other pastors or churches leave over the issue seems to depend on how church authorities interpret the language of the 1985 statement.

Other Holiness Churches Speak Out

A position similar to that of the Nazarenes was taken in June 1986 by the general assembly of the Church of God (Anderson, Ind.). For many years local churches of this denomination have added the term "non-Pentecostal" in their advertising to distinguish them from the many Pentecostal groups that use variations of the name Church of God. After a yearlong study, the assembly adopted a special study commission report that in general restated the church's historic position that tongues are not the initial evidence of the baptism in the Holy Spirit.

The report did, however, allow that tongues are one of the authentic gifts of the Spirit for today and did not disallow their use in private devotions. Like the Nazarenes, the Church of God seems willing to accommodate glossolalics who do not publicly display, or promote divisively, the gift of tongues.[44]

In spite of the rigid historical position of these and other holiness churches many pastors and laymen have spoken in tongues over the years. Pastors in such situations have usually been removed from their pulpits immediately when authorities heard of their experiences. Nazarenes who have been excommunicated over the years include Wilbur Jackson, Merrill Bolender, Wayne Buchart, Jerry Love, Robert Mueller, Stan Pulliam, Jep Anderson, and David Alsobrook. Ray Bringham, a well-known charismatic leader from the Church of God, has led a struggle for many years to bring renewal back to his church.[45]

Wilbur Jackson and the Wesleyan Charismatic Fellowship

In recent years, many of these former pastors have met together in conferences sponsored by Wilbur Jackson's King's Mountain Faith Fellowship in Cincinnati, Ohio. Jackson, pastor of the Lockland Nazarene Church in Cincinnati, was separated from the Church of the Nazarene in 1971 after his Pentecostal experience became known. He has become the acknowledged leader of the group that would still like to see a charismatic renewal in the church.

In 1979, in a meeting of like-minded ministers, he formed the Wesleyan-Holiness Charismatic Fellowship for ministry to those who had suffered rejection by the churches. In 1977, a group of these men met in Kansas City to plan strategies for the future. In 1985, the organization was restructured and strengthened. This group also led sessions in the New Orleans Congresses on the Holy Spirit and world evangelization in 1986 and 1987.[46]

A sign of reconciliation for the future was the publication of Howard Snyder's 1986 book, *The Divided Flame: Wesleyans and the Charismatic Renewal*. This volume was a plea for those in the Wesleyan tradition to open their churches to the gifts of the Holy Spirit. Snyder contends that Wesley himself was charismatic and that, indeed, all churches are by definition charismatic or they are not fully Christian. He contends also that holiness churches should enter into dialogue with charismatic Christianity, since each side could learn from the other.[47]

Since the Nazarene statement of 1985 and the Church of God statement of 1986 did not forbid tongues, but only the teaching that tongues constitute the initial evidence of the baptism in the Holy Spirit, the door may be open for Nazarenes and other Wesleyans to pray in tongues and remain in the churches.

For Further Reading

Two books tell the background story of the Methodist tradition, which many see as the mother of the Pentecostal tradition. They are Vinson Synan's *The Holiness-Pentecostal Tradition* (Grand Rapids: Eerdmans, 1997); and Donald Dayton's *Theological Roots of Pentecostalism* (Grand Rapids: Francis Asbury Press, 1987). An annotated collection of official church documents on the renewal are preserved in Kilian McDonnell's *Presence, Power, Praise*, 3 vols. (Collegeville, Minn: Liturgical Press, 1980). A fine survey of the renewal is Russell Spittler's *Perspectives on the New Pentecostalism* (Grand Rapids: Baker, 1976).

The story of Oral Roberts's connection with the Methodist charismatics is given in David Harrell's *Oral Roberts: An American Life* (Bloomington: Univ. of Indiana Press, 1985).

The major Baptist theologian of the renewal is Howard Ervin of Oral Roberts University. His book, *And Forbid Not to Speak in Tongues* (Plainfield, N.J.: Logos International, 1971), was an early classic defense of Pentecostalism among Baptists. Pat Robertson's autobiographical *Shout It from the Housetop*, with Jamie Buckingham (Plainfield, N.J.: Logos International, 1972), gives an exciting account of early charismatic television programming.

The Gerald Derstine story is given in his *Following the Fire* (Plainfield, N.J.: Logos International, 1980). Other sources on Mennonite and Orthodox renewal can be found in Kilian McDonnell's *Charismatic Renewal and the Churches* (New York: Seabury Press, 1976). An attempt to bridge the gap between Pentecostals and Wesleyans is found in Howard Snyder's *The Divided Flame: Wesleyans and the Charismatic Renewal* (Grand Rapids: Francis Asbury Press, 1986).

· 9 ·
The Catholic Charismatic Renewal

Peter Hocken

S ATURDAY, FEBRUARY 18, 1967, was another Day of Pentecost. It was
by God's choice a historic day for the Roman Catholic Church. That
evening the Holy Spirit fell upon a group of Roman Catholics at a retreat
house just north of Pittsburgh, Pennsylvania. Most were students from
Duquesne University. They had not planned a service in chapel, but rather
a birthday party for one of the participants in the weekend retreat. But in
various ways, God led these twenty-five Catholics to the chapel, where
they encountered a tangible presence of the Spirit. Some laughed and
cried, a few fell prostrate to the floor, all spoke in tongues. They prayed
and sang until the early hours of the morning. It was the birth of the
charismatic renewal in the Catholic Church.

One of the students, Patty Gallagher Mansfield, described the meeting
in this way:

> That night the Lord brought the whole group into the chapel.
> . . . The professors then laid hands on some of the students but most of us re-
> ceived the baptism in the Spirit while kneeling before the blessed sacrament
> in prayer. Some of us started speaking in tongues; others received gifts of
> discernment, prophecy and wisdom.
>
> But the most important gift was the fruit of love which bound the whole

community together. In the Lord's Spirit we found a unity we had long tried to achieve on our own.[1]

Another student, David Mangan, described what happened when he entered the room:

I cried harder than I ever cried in my life, but I did not shed one tear. All of a sudden Jesus Christ was so real and so present that I could feel him all around. I was overcome with such a feeling of love that I cannot describe it.[2]

This event, now known as the "Duquesne Weekend," became the first Catholic charismatic prayer meeting and started a chain of events that

---

TONGUES AT DUQUESNE UNIVERSITY

One night at a prayer meeting I sat next to David Mangan who had already received the gift of tongues. I was flabbergasted as I heard David pray in beautiful, flowing French. It sounded like the words of a psalm, praising the kindness of the Divine Child, extolling the streams of living water. The cadence of his French was different, but his pronunciation was perfect. After the meeting I asked David if he knew he had been praying in French; he didn't. I was impressed by the authenticity of this charismatic gift. It was a sign to me that God was at work.

Soon I began to long to praise God more, to go beyond my own limited abilities to extol His goodness. St. Paul advises, *"Earnestly desire the spiritual gifts"* (cf. 1 Cor. 14:1). I asked God for the gift of tongues, but I failed to realize that I needed to move my lips and use my voice in order to yield to tongues. I thought that a prayer language would force its way out of me if I waited in silence long enough.

When I woke up on March 13, 1967, I was excited by the sound of clicking in my throat. I hoped it might be the gift of tongues, but I was afraid to be in the middle of a class when it "overtook me." I cut class and went above the University Chapel to pray in the oratory, one of our favorite places for prayer in those early days. I was determined I would stay there as long as it took until I prayed in tongues. So I knelt with my mouth open . . . waiting.

The clicking became louder; my mouth started to move and then I began to grunt. "Oh no," I thought, "don't tell me the Lord is going to give me an ugly, guttural tongue after I majored in French because of the beauty of the language!" But I kept grunting away until finally I was singing in tongues, a lovely song which flowed from the depths of my being. It was a beautiful language, different from the tongue I pray in now. Although I didn't recognize the words, in my heart I *knew* I was singing the *Magnificat*—the very passage the Lord had given me the night I was baptized in the Spirit. *"My soul magnifies the Lord and my spirit rejoices in God my Savior, for He has regarded the low estate of His handmaiden. For behold all generations will call me blessed."* (Luke 1:46–48). ∎

—PATTY GALLAGHER MANSFIELD
AS BY A NEW PENTECOST

soon proved to be one of the major strands in the charismatic movement of the 20th century. It was a development no one had expected. Who could imagine that a movement with a background in Protestant revivalism and links with Pentecostalism could break out in the Roman Catholic Church?

This is the first time in Christian history that a movement of Protestant provenance had not only entered the Roman Catholic Church, but had also been received and accepted by church authority. This remarkable fact alone suggests that the Catholic expression of the charismatic movement has a major significance and a vast potential.

Patty Gallagher Mansfield not only experienced the Holy Spirit in the "Duquesne Weekend," but also wrote the most vivid accounts of the meetings.

Roots of the Catholic Renewal

While some individual Catholics had been baptized in the Spirit before 1967, the weekend at the Ark and the Dove retreat house near Pittsburgh in February 1967 represented the beginning of a recognizable movement of charismatic renewal among Catholics. Although there was the element of an unexpected theophany at the Ark and the Dove, charismatic Christians of other churches had played a part in its preparation.[3]

The weekend had been organized by four Catholic faculty members at Duquesne University who the previous month had attended a charismatic group led by a Presbyterian woman, Flo Dodge, where two professors, Ralph Keifer and Bill Storey, had been prayed over for the baptism in the Spirit. The students had been encouraged to read *The Cross and the Switchblade* by David Wilkerson. But at the Duquesne Weekend, there were only Catholics present.

The news of this Pentecost event spread quickly to friends at the University of Notre Dame in South Bend, Indiana, and Michigan State University in East Lansing, Michigan. In South Bend a group soon formed around Kevin and Dorothy Ranaghan and quickly made contact with a Pentecostal layman, Ray Bullard, who was president of the local Full Gospel Business Men's Fellowship International (FGBMFI). In East Lansing, Ralph Martin's and Steve Clark's interest had already been aroused by their reading of *The Cross and the Switchblade*. South Bend and Ann Arbor, Michigan, where Martin and Clark soon moved, rapidly became the organizing centers for the Catholic movement as communities were formed of students and recent graduates newly baptized in the Spirit.

These Catholic origins differed from those in the Protestant churches in significant ways. The first Catholic leaders were almost all young university graduates who had none of the anti-intellectual attitudes sometimes found in Pentecostal and charismatic circles. They were young men and women deeply committed to the Catholic faith, already excited by the vision of the Second Vatican Council for the renewal of the Catholic Church. They therefore understood immediately that their new charismatic experience was for the sake of the whole church, and they saw the new movement as an answer to the prayer of Pope John XXIII for a new Pentecost.

Elena Guerra (1835–1914) was an Italian nun whose devotion to the Holy Spirit influenced Pope Leo XIII to declare a novena to the Holy Spirit in 1897.

Other developments in the Catholic Church helped prepare the way for the renewal. One of these, the biblical movement, had been gaining ground among Catholics since the 1940s. All over the world Catholic scholars were delving into biblical studies on a scale never seen in modern times. Catholic laypersons were also encouraged to read the Bible for themselves. After the renewal began, there was a rush among charismatics to read the Scriptures in order to understand the baptism in the Holy Spirit and the gifts of the Spirit that were breaking out in the church.

Another important precurser was the cursillo movement, which had begun in Spain after World War II. From Spain, *cursillo* (which means "short course" in Spanish) spread around the world. It consisted of a concentrated weekend where Catholics, who had been "sacramentalized," were reevangelized to become committed and practicing Christians.

A developing Catholic lay movement was also important in preparing the way for renewal. From the days of Pope Pius X (1903–14), a new emphasis on the role of laymen had been growing in the church. As the 20th century progressed, laypersons were not only seen as "crisis ministers" in the absence of priests, but as those who "share in His priestly function of offering spiritual worship for the glory of God and the salvation of men." Since the Catholic charismatic renewal originated with and was led largely by laypersons, this movement was crucial in opening the door to thousands of laypersons to take leading roles in the renewal after 1967.

The ecumenical movement, which had been growing throughout most of the century, was also a background contributing factor in the developing Catholic renewal. As Kilian McDonnell observed, "Behind every early charismatic stood a classical Pentecostal." Such Pentecostal leaders as David Wilkerson, David du Plessis, and Vinson Synan gave significant input and direction to the renewal in the early days. A most important force in spreading the renewal was the FGBMFI, led by California layman Demos Shakarian. By welcoming Catholics as members and speakers, Shakarian's group provided an important platform for the spread of the renewal throughout the world.[4]

This summary makes clear that the Catholic charismatic renewal came

POPE LEO XIII AND ELENA GUERRA

The most obvious and perhaps the most important preparation for the charismatic renewal within the Catholic Church was the encyclical letter, *On the Holy Spirit*, published by Pope Leo XIII in 1897. In it, the Pope bemoaned the fact that the Holy Spirit was little known and appreciated, and summoned people to renew their devotion to Him. This letter gave a routine summary, precise and authoritative but not otherwise remarkable, of Catholic teaching about the Holy Spirit. It spoke in a general way of the gifts of the Spirit, but said nothing specific about the charismata. Nevertheless, the simple fact of its appearance was important. It was a sign from the highest authority in the Church drawing attention to the actual importance of this article of Christian faith. Millions of people either read the encyclical, or were touched by it indirectly through sermons, books, etc. A considerable number of valuable studies on the role of the Holy Spirit were stimulated in large part by this papal action.

It is natural to wonder what prompted Leo to publish this encyclical, which his more famous writings on the social order, on the restoration of Thomism, and on the divisions among Christians had hardly led us to expect. It seems, in fact, to have been one of the more charismatic acts in the career of this remarkable Pope. It resulted from the suggestion of an obscure Italian woman, Elena Guerra (1835–1914), who had gathered a group of women into a sisterhood devoted to the Christian education of girls. The characteristic feature of Elena's spirituality was an indomitable and all-encompassing devotion to the Holy Spirit. It grieved her that most people thought so little of the Holy Spirit. Inspired by a practice she had learned as a child in her parish church, she used to recommend that the ten days between the yearly feasts of Ascension and Pentecost be spent in prayer and preparation for the gifts of the Spirit, in imitation of the Apostles in the Cenacle. Eventually she had the audacity to write to Pope Leo, urging him to recommend this practice. To the amazement of many people who had tried to dissuade her, the Pope responded promptly by a letter officially endorsing her idea of a "new Cenacle." Although the Pope had not met her, he told his counselors that if she had any other such inspirations for the welfare of the Church, they should be communicated to him.

With this encouragement, Elena wrote again, urging the Pope to establish this practice throughout the Church as a "permanent and universal Cenacle." This he did six months later, by the Encyclical *On the Holy Spirit*, which prescribed that every Catholic church should prepare for the feast of Pentecost by a novena of prayer. ∎

—EDWARD O'CONNOR IN *NEW COVENANT*

into being first through an unexpected move of the Spirit at the "Duquesne weekend" following Protestant charismatic influences in Pittsburgh, with other early influences including the FGBMFI and David Wilkerson. However, from the beginning the leaders of this new movement received it as the Lord's gift to the Catholic Church, and they soon formed new organizations and committees to promote it within the Catholic communion. Furthermore, the Catholic leaders interpreted the significance of the movement in the light of the renewal vision of Vatican II, and particularly as a fruit of the council's opening to ecumenism and the work of the Holy Spirit in the other churches.[5]

The Catholic charismatic renewal (CCR) has clearly been one of the major strands in the charismatic movement of the 20th century. It is also one of the most surprising developments in view of the revivalistic background and character of the charismatic movement.

Characteristics of Catholic Charismatic Renewal

The charismatic elements of CCR have been the same as among the Protestants: the foundational experience of baptism in the Spirit, the appearance and exercise of the spiritual gifts of 1 Corinthians 12:8–10, exuberant praise,

exaltation of Jesus as living Lord, evangelization and testimonies, and hearing the Lord. But in the Catholic context, there were some significant differences in the forms taken and in the style and tempo of celebration.

Especially in the period until 1980, CCR took the form of prayer groups—generally weekly and occasionally ecumenical in makeup—and covenant communities. There were very few parishes that could be described as charismatic parishes. Since 1980, there has been a growth of renewal centers, which particularly in the United States have tended to take the place of the covenant communities as focal points for the promotion of renewal.

Charismatic Catholics have been concerned to integrate the charismatic dimension within the liturgical-sacramental life of their church. This happens especially through the celebration of charismatic Eucharists, with a creative blend of the structured and the spontaneous.

With his wife, Dorothy, Kevin Ranaghan (1942–) was an early leader, writer, and organizer of the Catholic renewal.

Charismatic liturgies of this kind have been an impressive feature of CCR conferences and retreats. There has also been a strong linking of the charismatic and the sacramental in liturgies of healing—either with healing ministry within the Eucharist or sacramental anointing of the sick in a charismatic context. CCR has particularly developed the ministry of inner healing, and a number of priests, nuns, and laypeople have emerged into full-time healing ministries, including in the United States: Francis Mac-Nutt, the Linn brothers, Fr. Ralph di Orio, and Fr. Edward McDonough. At the world level, the best-known Catholics in healing ministry have been Fr. Emilien Tardif, a missionary from Quebec (1928–99), Fr. Mathew Naickomparambil from Kerala, India (1947–), and Sr. Briege McKenna (1946–), a nun from Ireland based in Florida.

Reactions of the Offi cial Church

For a movement that began outside the Roman communion, CCR was received with remarkable equanimity by the Vatican and the Catholic

---

CATHOLICS AND PENTECOSTALS AT NOTRE DAME

We went to Ray's house the following week and met in his basement room with eleven Pentecostal ministers and their wives from all over Indiana. They spent the evening attempting to persuade us that if you were baptized in the Spirit you had to be speaking in tongues. We let them know we were open to praying in tongues, but we held fast to our conviction that we were already baptized in the Spirit because we could see it in our lives. The issue got resolved because we were willing to speak in tongues if it were not seen as a theological necessity to being baptized in the Holy Spirit. At a certain point, we said we were willing to give it a try, and a man explained to us what was involved. Very late that evening, sometime after midnight, down in that basement room, the brothers lined us up on one side of the room and the ministers on the other side of the room, and they began to pray in tongues and to walk toward us with outstretched hands. Before they reached us, many of us began to pray and sing in tongues.

After a time of praying in tongues, Ghezzi says, the students' Pentecostal friends asked them when they would be leaving the Catholic Church and joining up with a Pentecostal Church:

The question actually left us a little shocked. Our response was that we wouldn't be leaving the Catholic Church, that being baptized in the Holy Spirit was completely compatible with our belief in the Catholic Church. We assured our friends that we had a great respect for them and that we would have fellowship with them, but we would be remaining in the Catholic Church.

I think there's something significant about the fact that those of us who were baptized in the Holy Spirit then would never have thought about abandoning the Roman Catholic Church.

Our Pentecostal friends had seen Catholics join Pentecostal churches when they were baptized in the Spirit. Because we did not do that, the Catholic charismatic renewal became possible. ∎

—BERT GHEZZI IN VINSON SYNAN'S *IN THE LATTER DAYS*

hierarchy. In this reception, Leon Joseph Cardinal Suenens of Belgium played a role of exceptional importance. Suenens came into contact with CCR in 1972, and from 1973 he spoke as a participant, encouraging its reception and integration into the life of the Catholic Church. Suenens's influence was immense, not just because he was a cardinal, but because he was respected as one of the major figures of the Second Vatican Council.

The United States bishops responded as early as 1969 with a positive statement from an episcopal committee on doctrine. Pope Paul VI addressed the first International Leaders Conference in Rome in 1973, but the real turning point came with the international CCR conference held in Rome in 1975. The explosive character of the renewal was manifest in charismatic liturgies held in St. Peter's basilica with ten thousand voices raised in exuberant praise and with words of prophecy being pronounced from the high altar of St. Peter's. The pope told them that "the church and the world need more than ever that the miracle of Pentecost should continue in history," saying that the renewal was "a chance" for the church and for the world.

Leon Joseph Cardinal Suenens (1904–96) was appointed as papal liaison to the Catholic charismatic renewal by Pope Paul VI. His "Malines documents" gave pastoral guidance to the movement.

Paul VI appointed Cardinal Suenens as his special adviser to oversee the reception of CCR into the life of the Catholic Church. When Suenens retired from this role in 1982, John Paul II appointed a German bishop, Paul Cordes, the secretary of the Pontifical Council for the Laity, as his personal representative for CCR. This combination integrated CCR more into Vatican structures, a link that continued when in 1995 Cordes was replaced in both jobs by a Polish bishop, Stanislaus Rylko.

Many Catholic hierarchies have issued positive statements on CCR, with the pre-1980 documents being included in Kilian McDonnell's three-volume collection *Presence, Power, Praise*. These statements indicate that the Catholic bishops, unlike many Protestant leaders, had no problem in principle with speaking in tongues or the other spiritual gifts. The difficult area for the Catholic Church was ecumenical: the issues of spiritual sharing with other Christians. The most recent statement from the U.S. bishops on the thirtieth anniversary of CCR (1997) is the most affirmative, saying, "With great thanksgiving and enthusiasm, that in the Catholic Charismatic Renewal and in the grace of baptism in the Holy Spirit we see God's outpouring of a new Pentecost."

Sizing up the Catholic Renewal

The CCR gave rise fairly quickly to more theological reflection and study than in the Protestant sectors of the charismatic movement. Unlike the Protestant reactions, there was little special Catholic focus on glossolalia. A number of scholars and theologians became participants in CCR, of whom the most influential were Fr. Francis Sullivan, SJ, a professor at the Gregorian University in Rome; Fr. George Montague, SM, and Fr. Francis Martin, both biblical scholars; Fr. Albert de Monléon, OP, a theologian in the Emmanuel community in France and later a bishop; Fr. René Laurentin, a French biblical scholar and theologian; and Fr. Paul Lebeau, SJ, a Belgian theologian who became theological adviser to Cardinal Suenens. Also a major contributor to the theological reflection was Fr. Kilian McDonnell, OSB, who grasped the significance of the Pentecostal and charismatic movements.[6]

In 1973, Cardinal Suenens gathered a group of theologians with a view to issuing a series of documents on CCR. In effect, of the "Malines documents," as they came to be known, only the first was the work of this group, *Theological and Pastoral Orientations on the Catholic Charismatic Renewal* (1974). Five further theological documents were issued between 1978 and 1987, all written by Cardinal Suenens.[7]

The first thrust of Catholic theological thought concerned baptism in the Spirit and its relationship to sacramental initiation. All the Catholic writers sought to differentiate a Catholic understanding from the Pentecostal teaching, insisting that the Holy Spirit is given in the sacraments of initiation. The majority, including the first Malines document, distinguished between the actual conferral of the Spirit in the sacraments and coming to an experiential awareness of the gift already received.

By contrast, Father Sullivan understood baptism in the Spirit as a new mission of the Holy Spirit, truly bringing something new. At a much later stage, Fr. Kilian McDonnell and Fr. George Montague produced a biblical and patristic study, *Christian Initiation and Baptism in the Holy Spirit* (1991). This study, which was widely promoted in CCR, aims to demonstrate that baptism in the Spirit was originally an integral element in Christian initiation, with charisms of the Spirit being expected and experienced in the process of sacramental and ecclesial initiation.

As Catholic theology pays more attention than most Protestant theology to creation and the natural order, CCR teaching and theological reflection are uncomfortable with a stark choice between Holy Spirit and demonic causation that excludes the role of natural forces, biological, psychic, and sociocultural. This can be seen particularly in the Malines documents that deal with the controverted subjects of *Renewal and the Powers of Darkness* (1983) and *Resting in the Spirit* (1987).

Phases of the Movement

CCR has certainly seen remarkable growth, but it has also seen marked decline in some countries, especially the United States, Canada, and Ireland. It has sparked many new initiatives, principally from the grass roots. While it is difficult to divide its thirty-four-year history into clear-cut periods, especially when considering the movement as a worldwide phenomenon, it is nonetheless possible to detect certain phases that may be helpful for understanding its evolution.

1970–80: This was the period of rapid growth in the United States, with annual international conferences, mostly held at Notre Dame, attracting ever greater crowds up to the massive interchurch conference held at Kansas City in July 1977. There was a parallel growth in regional confer-

The national Catholic charismatic conference at Notre Dame in 1973 drew more than thirty thousand participants.

ences, of which the largest were the eastern regional conferences in Atlantic City, New Jersey, and those held in southern California. In many ways, these CCR conferences were an astonishing sight, both for Catholics and for Protestants. Vinson Synan has described his amazement at the sight of ten thousand charismatic Catholics praising the Lord and giving testimonies to their experience of the Holy Spirit, and how he wept as he heard them "singing our songs" and "exercising our gifts."[8]

This was the period of the implanting of CCR in other English-speaking countries (England, 1970–71; Australia, 1970; New Zealand, 1971) as well as in Western Europe (France, 1971–72; Belgium, 1972; Germany, 1972; Italy, 1973; Spain, 1973–74; Portugal, 1974). For Eastern Europe in the grip of atheistic Communism, spontaneous movements of faith were forbidden, and only in Poland (1976–77) do the roots of CCR go back to this period. The origins of CCR in Latin America mostly date from the period 1970–74, while other nations where CCR took root in the 1970s include South Korea (1971) and India (1972).

Many of the major charismatic communities were founded during this time. Three countries in particular saw a flourishing of new communities: the United States, France, and Australia. The American and Australian communities mostly sought to be ecumenical communities, respecting the church allegiance of their members but in fact having a Catholic majority. Of the French communities, only *Chemin Neuf* had an ecumenical vision and makeup.

The most influential communities were Word of God, Ann Arbor, Michigan; People of Praise, South Bend, Indiana; Alleluia, Augusta, Georgia; Emmanuel, Brisbane, Australia; *Emmanuel*, Paris, France; *Chemin Neuf*, Lyon, France; and Lion of Judah (later renamed *Béatitudes*), Cordes, France. The communities quickly became the servicing agencies and centers for CCR, organizing major conferences and publishing popular magazines, e.g., *New Covenant* (USA), *Il Est Vivant!* (France), and *Feu et Lumière* (France).

During this initial period, the cross-fertilization between Catholic and Protestant was quite striking. This was shown in the contributions of Protestant teachers (especially such nondenominational leaders as Bob Mumford and Charles Simpson) to Catholic magazines and conferences, in the literature sold under Catholic auspices, and not least in the dissemination of new songs and choruses. It was particularly evident in *Pastoral Renewal*, a monthly magazine for "pastoral leaders of all Christian traditions" published from Ann Arbor beginning in 1976. The impulse for unity and the period of most rapid growth reached their climax in the Kansas City conference on charismatic renewal in the Christian churches in July

1977 attended by more than fifty thousand people. The high-water mark had perhaps been around 1977–78, the years of Kansas City (1977) and the last East Coast gathering at Atlantic City (1978).

During this period, CCR in other countries was largely dependent for materials and inspiration on the numerically larger and more dynamic movement in the United States. Apart from France, where the new communities provided a more solid foundation, the Catholic renewal in the 1970s was relatively small.

1980–90: In general, the 1980s saw a conscious effort on the part of CCR to be more fully integrated into the life of the Catholic Church. While CCR had been welcomed and encouraged by the popes, there was a widespread feeling that it was still on the margins of Catholic life. From the start, the leaders had believed that CCR was for the renewal of the church, and many were experiencing frustration over its apparent relegation to a permissible but exotic spirituality.

This shift of direction was symbolized by the move in 1981 of the International Communication Office from Brussels to Rome and its being renamed the International Catholic Charismatic Renewal Office (ICCRO). By this time, diocesan renewal structures were developing, with liaisons appointed to represent the local bishop often assuming a local leadership role. These changes inevitably represented a lessening in the ecumenical thrust of CCR.

It was also the period of lessening influence from the covenant communities, many of which went through major crises from the late 1980s. The crises mostly focused on the exercise of authority, with some diocesan bishops expressing concern about authoritarian patterns, insistence on male headship, and inadequate accountability by the leadership.

The points of contention often included the ecumenical dimension, in which it was proving more difficult than expected to combine a firm attachment to one's church with a commitment to a community that overarched the church divisions. The Word of God community in Ann Arbor, Michigan, had pioneered a model for denominational fellowships within an ecumenical covenant community, forming Catholic, Lutheran, Reformed, and nondenominational fellowships. Difficulties arose with some clergy leading church fellowships not being part of the main leadership of the overall community. Another difficulty in such ecumenical communities concerned the church formation and identity of the children of parents who were committed community members.

The crisis with the most far-reaching effects was in the Word of God community and its progeny, the international community known as the Sword of the Spirit. After growing internal tensions, a split in the leadership occurred in 1990 with a separation between Ralph Martin, who took over a smaller and more loosely structured Word of God community, and Steve Clark and Bruce Yocum. These two continued the covenant community vision in the Sword of the Spirit, forming a new community in the Ann Arbor area called the Washtenaw Covenant Community. The split led to *New Covenant* magazine being sold to a Catholic publisher and to the demise of *Pastoral Renewal*. The conflict in Ann Arbor severely weakened the model of covenant community that had so influenced the early years of CCR.

As the influence of the communities diminished in the 1980s, greater roles of responsibility were assumed by diocesan and regional leaders. The shift in the membership in the National Service Committee from leaders of the major communities to leaders of the movement within dioceses signified a change in the nature of the movement itself in the United States. From one centralized movement around the communities with one large national conference, the CCR moved to becoming a networking of Diocesan Service Committees with some forty conferences throughout the states.

In 1984 Fr. Ken Metz of Milwaukee became the first noncommunity chair of the NSC (1984–87). The NSC with the vision of diocesan leaders including Fr. Sam Jacobs, Sr. Nancy Kellar, David Thorp, and Fr. Chris Aridas began working to strengthen the local renewal while networking diocesan groups with one another and with the NSC.

It was seen that the renewal was strongest where there were Diocesan Renewal Centers, therefore the NSC began a yearly gathering of Renewal Centers to strengthen existing centers and foster the development of new ones. By the late 1980s some eighty Diocesan Renewal Centers were serving the CCR in their regions.

The cry of the local renewal for leadership training was responded to by the NSC with the development of a "Traveling Timothy" program, which provided for national leaders traveling from state to state providing leadership formation. The demand became so great that the NSC developed a series of Leadership Formation videotapes that have been used throughout the world in the Catholic and even the Episcopal renewal movement.

A further significant move away from the influence of the communities over the national Catholic renewal in the United States was the move in 198(?) of the national office from South Bend, Indiana, to Virginia just outside Washington, D.C. The move close to Washington, D.C. (where other renewal movements have their offices) also reflected the desire of the NSC to move the renewal to the heart of the church. In 1991 the NSC began to move the national conference around the United States to various dioceses in an effort to further strengthen the local renewal and to give greater visibility on the local level to national leaders.

During the 1980s the Catholic charismatic renewal grew rapidly among various ethnic groups—Hispanic, Haitian, Korean, and Filipino. During that time leaders of these groups met with the English-speaking NSC and had "tracks" in their language at the national conference. By the beginning of the 1990s they were strong enough to have their own National Service committees and conferences.

Following the lead of Paul VI, John Paul II (1920–) gave his approval and offered pastoral care to the Catholic charismatic movement.

A strong affirmation by Pope John Paul II of the Catholic charismatic renewal in the United States was the naming in 1989 of Fr. Sam Jacobs, who had become chair of the NSC in 1987, as a diocesan bishop. The CCR had other bishops, outstandingly Bishop Joseph McKinney, who had become active in the charismatic renewal; but Bishop Sam was the first priest in the United States deeply committed to the CCR to be named bishop.

The fruit of the work of the NSC throughout the 1980s was manifest at the 25th Anniversary National Conference in 1992. The theme "Return to

THE POPES ON CATHOLIC CHARISMATIC RENEWAL

How then could this "spiritual renewal" not be a "chance" for the church and for the world? And how, in this case, could one not take all the means to ensure that it remains so? It ought to rejuvenate the world, give it back a spirituality, a soul, a religious thought; it ought to re-open its closed lips to prayer and open its mouth to song, to joy, to hymns, and to witnessing. It will be very fortuitous for our times, for our brothers, that there should be a generation, your generation of young people, who shout out to the world the greatness of the God of Pentecost.

—POPE PAUL VI, ROME, 1975

The vigor and fruitfulness of the Renewal certainly attest to the powerful presence of the Holy Spirit at work in the Church in these years after the Second Vatican Council. Of course, the Spirit has guided the Church in every age, producing a great variety of gifts among the faithful. Because of the Spirit, the Church preserves a continual youthful vitality. And the Charismatic Renewal is an eloquent manifestation of this vitality today, a bold statement of what "the Spirit is saying to the churches" (Rev. 2:7) as we approach the close of the second millennium. ∎

—POPE JOHN PAUL II, ROME, 1987

the Upper Room" brought eighteen thousand Catholics back to Pittsburgh where the move of the Spirit had begun.

Parallel to the new development of the NSC in the eighties was a growing networking of diocesan liaisons appointed by the bishops to represent the CCR to the local bishop, and the local bishop to the CCR . The liaisons organized their own annual conference, as well as sponsoring an annual theological conference addressing major issues in CCR.

As the covenant communities became less central, other institutions and groupings flourished. Of particular importance has been the influence of the University of Steubenville in Ohio, led by Fr. Michael Scanlan. Father Scanlan promoted Steubenville as a site for large summer conferences for priests and for youth as well as developing the college as a Catholic educational institution integrating dynamic spiritual life with a quality education.

Some new celibate communities have also emerged, in particular the Companions of the Cross, founded around 1985 by Fr. Bob Bedard in Ottawa, Canada, and the Franciscan Friars of the Renewal, begun by Frs. Benedict Groeschel and Stan Fortuna in New York City in 1987. The Companions of the Cross specialize in evangelization, giving parish missions and retreats, with a particular concentration on youth, the poor, and alienated Catholics. The Franciscan Friars of the Renewal seek to go back to the Franciscan roots of poverty and preaching, working particularly with the homeless and the poor, as well as giving youth retreats.

The lessening number of participants in CCR received various interpretations. The most optimistic was that the Catholics who had flocked to big conferences in the 1970s were now bringing their new charismatic life to their parishes. The more pessimistic was that the new life in the Spirit had not taken deep root, evaporating as the initial enthusiasm waned. The truth is probably in between: while there was some falling away, it is remarkable how many full-time Catholic layworkers in the United States have come from a CCR background.

In Europe, the 1980s saw the growing influence of the major French communities (Emmanuel, Chemin Neuf, Béatitudes, Pain de Vie), all of which were expanding into other European countries and especially into French-speaking Africa. Unlike the American communities, which had mostly sought to consolidate in one major location, the French communities quickly formed new branches, first all over France and then elsewhere.

This pattern was facilitated by the new communities frequently being offered the use of ancient monasteries and convents that the religious orders could no longer fill. The French communities had stronger links with the Catholic past than their American counterparts, and several developed new forms of use for traditional sites of pilgrimage. The Emmanuel community was asked to run the shrine and basilica at Paray-le-Monial, the historic origin of the Catholic devotion to the Sacred Heart of Jesus, which is now a major center each summer for teaching conferences. Chemin Neuf established close connections with the shrine in Ars, and the Béatitudes animated for some years a major pilgrimage to Lourdes.

In Italy, the main officially organized section of the renewal became known as *Rinnovamento nello Spirito Santo* (RnS, Renewal in the Holy Spirit). Their annual spring conference at Rimini soon became the largest CCR gathering in Europe. From Italy also came one of the most valued teachers in the CCR, Fr. Raniero Cantalamessa, a Capuchin priest-scholar who in 1984 was appointed preacher to the papal household.

During the 1980s, CCR began to pay more explicit attention to evangelization. Evangelization had been brought to the Catholic agenda by the letter *Evangelii Nuntiandi* of Pope Paul VI in 1975, and the charismatic Catholics were among the most motivated to respond to this call. One of the first Catholic responses came in Mexico City, where the Fellowship of Communities of Evangelization in the Holy Spirit was formed and soon spread to other Latin American countries with the backing of the Catholic hierarchy.

In Malta, the Glory of God Covenant Community was impacted by the YWAM model for discipleship training schools. This led in early 1985 to a Catholic training school for evangelization, out of which grew the Malta-based International Catholic Programme of Evangelization (ICPE). Also in Mexico, the lay leader José Prado Flores in 1985 launched the *Kekako* program (Ke for *Kerygma*, Ka for *Karisma*, and Ko for *Koinonia*).

In the last half of the 1980s, key renewal leaders became concerned to recover the ecumenical dynamism of the early years. As a result new international and continental bodies were formed: the North American Renewal Service Committee (NARSC, 1987), the European Charismatic Consultation (ECC, 1988), and the International Charismatic Consultation on World Evangelization (ICCOWE, 1988). The ICCOWE initiative dated back to a 1983 meeting in which Fr. Tom Forrest took part.[9]

In the 1980s the forward thrust of CCR shifted from North America to the Third World. While renewal was receding in North America, it was continuing to grow in Africa, Asia, and Latin America. In the less affluent areas of the world, CCR was not simply another item in the religious supermarket, one among many competing options for the spiritually inclined.

Third World bishops are closer to their people, and many saw that God was transforming the lives of their people through CCR. A sign of this was the international CCR retreat for priests held in the Vatican in 1984, in which a significant section of the Filipino hierarchy took part. In fact, the Philippines experienced a sharp growth in CCR following the political revolution of 1986. More details on CCR in the Third World as the movement continued to grow are given below.

1990–2000: The last decade of the 20th century witnessed a significant shift in perception of CCR within the Catholic Church. This had two principal causes: the setting aside of the 1990s as a Decade of Evangelization, and Pope John Paul II's encouragement of the new movements in the Catholic Church.

The idea that the 1990s should be set aside as a Decade of Evangelization was proposed to the pope by Fr. Tom Forrest and an Italian leader of another movement. As a result, the Evangelization 2000 office was set up in Rome in 1986, with Father Forrest as director. One of the main thrusts of this work has been to set up Catholic schools of evangelization. The Decade of Evangelization gave new impetus to the evangelistic initiatives of the 1980s, and brought them more into the heart of the church's response to the pope's call.

In 1971, while serving as a Redemptorist priest in Puerto Rico, Tom Forrest (1927–) was baptized in the Holy Spirit. He later became a popular speaker in both Catholic and ecumenical circles.

ICPE has steadily developed, opening new centers in Germany, Ghana, India, New Zealand, the Philippines, and Poland. A Nigerian bishop, impressed by ICPE on a visit to Malta, formed the Emmaus School of Evangelization as a pilot project for all Nigeria that has since influenced neighboring African countries. By 1998, there were three hundred *Kekako* schools of evangelization in thirty-seven countries.

During the 1990s, José Prado Flores worked closely for a time with the *Koinonia Giovanni Battista*, a community of Italian origin founded by Argentinian priest Fr. Ricardo Arganares, developing several formation courses named after New Testament figures; for example, the Philip course, the Paul course, and the John course.

The Catholic understanding of evangelization has consistently emphasized the need for the primary proclamation of the gospel and initial conversion to lead to a transformation of society and culture. Outstanding examples of Catholics brought alive in the Spirit developing effective social programs come from Colombia and the Philippines. In Colombia, *El Minuto de Dios* community, led by Frs. Diego Jaramillo and Camillo Bernal, practices the "preferential option for the poor" in a charismatic way, empowered by the Holy Spirit. They help with education, housing, health care, community development, and disaster relief, as well as running a radio station with an evangelistic message.[10]

In the Philippines, God's Little Children community, founded and led by Fr. Bart Pastor in Tacloban City, has elaborated a twelve-stage program for the insertion of the gospel into the physical, economic, social, political, cultural, and environmental dimensions of human life. In France, the *Pain de Vie* community has a strong orientation toward the poor and the marginalized.

The growing CCR attention to evangelization being made a church focus for the 1990s contributed to CCR being more fully received as an integral element within the Catholic Church. Particularly in Africa, Asia, and Latin America CCR was increasingly seen by the Catholic hierarchies as one of the most effective instruments for winning people to Jesus Christ.

Further, Pope John Paul II has consistently encouraged the "new movements" within the Catholic Church, some of which are also deeply committed to evangelization such as *Communio e Liberazione*, *Neo-Catechumenate*, and the Community of *Sant' Egidio*. Regular meetings have been held for leaders in the movements, encouraging their collaboration and mutual respect.

The pope's desire for the new movements to be fully integrated into the Catholic Church has led to the drawing up of official statutes leading to

canonical recognition by the church authorities. Statutes were approved in September 1993 for the international CCR organization that was renamed ICCRS. Charles Whitehead of England served as president of ICCRS at this time and Fr. Ken Metz of the United States as director from 1987 to 1994. In 1994 Sr. Nancy Kellar, SC, was elected the first woman director of ICCRS.[11]

Similarly, the Vatican had encouraged the new charismatic communities in CCR to come together in one overarching organization. As a result, the Catholic Fraternity of Charismatic Covenant Communities and Fellowships (CFCCCF) was formed in November 1990 and received full canonical status with approved statutes in November 1995. New communities can apply for an interim "underway" status in CFCCCF, during which they are helped and mentored by larger and more experienced communities.

Sister Nancy Kellar (1940–) is a popular speaker and ecumenical leader in the Catholic charismatic renewal.

Particularly important was the vast gathering in Rome at Pentecost 1998, to which the pope invited all the participants in the "new movements." The pope gave a major address, stating that during the Second Vatican Council "the Church rediscovered the charismatic dimension as being essential to her identity." It was from this rediscovery that there had been "a remarkable development of ecclesial movements and new communities." "I want to cry out," the pope said: "'Be open and docile to the gifts of the Spirit.'" He remarked that the movements had passed through a time of testing, but now a new stage was opening of "ecclesial maturity." So the pope himself was treating the new movements, including CCR, as valued parts of the church needed for the fulfillment of her mission. It was an official statement that CCR and other movements had come of age.[12]

One immediate consequence of the Rome meeting has been the coming together of some other movements with CCR. The pope had emphasized to the movements the necessity of welcoming and recognizing one another's gifts. So since Pentecost 1998 there have been several gatherings linking CCR leaders with those from the *Focolari* movement and the Community of *Sant' Egidio*.

While the pope's emphasis has been on the necessary correlation of the institutional and the charismatic, and on mutual communion of collaboration—communion of the new movements with the bishops and with each other—there have also been centralizing tendencies at work within the Vatican and the Catholic hierarchy. The most recent Catholic Code of Canon Law (1983) recognizes for the first time the right of Catholic laypeople to form associations within the Catholic Church. Thus, a number of CCR communities chose not to join CFCCCF, but rather to obtain official recognition from their local bishops.

In Italy, most of the new charismatic communities did not belong to RnS, the officially approved form of CCR, and in 1996 formed their own association, *Iniziativa di Comunione nel Rinnovamento Carismatico* (Initiative for Communion within the Charismatic Renewal). The legitimacy of this initiative has been recognized by the Catholic authorities and by RnS, which is an important example of a healthy balance between organizational coordination and structural diversity.

CCR's most rapid growth in the 1990s was in Africa, Asia, and Latin America. The most extraordinary growth has occurred in Brazil and India. In Brazil there are now more than sixty thousand CCR prayer groups, and an estimated eight million Catholics involved in CCR, up from four million in 1994. CCR broadcasts dominate the 181 Catholic radio stations in Brazil, and Catholic charismatics own the Century XXI Production Center in Sao Paolo, which has four television studios. The preacher with the highest audience ratings is a young priest in CCR, Fr. Marcelo Rossi. In India, there has been strong growth, especially in Kerala, where the Divine

Retreat Center at Muringoor attracts massive crowds, averaging fifteen thousand a day, to the evangelistic-healing ministry of Fr. Mathew Naick-omparambil and his team. Sometimes diocesan CCR conventions attract over ten thousand people.

Mexico has a flourishing CCR with several dynamic new communities, and showed a strong outreach to youth with fourteen thousand at their National Youth Gathering in 1998. In the Philippines there are several million charismatic Catholics, with the El Shaddai movement drawing hundreds of thousands to massive open-air, nationally televised rallies in Manila. Couples for Christ is another movement that developed out of CCR in the Philippines, and has since spread to many other countries. The Filipino CCR communities have formed their own Federation of Transparochial Covenant Communities.[13]

In English-speaking Africa, the republics of Ghana, Tanzania, and Uganda have experienced the biggest growth in CCR, these being the countries with full-time leaders. Though several of the French-speaking African nations have been ravaged by war, CCR has grown faster than in most English-speaking nations due to the involvement of the French communities, especially *Emmanuel* and *Chemin Neuf*. In most Eastern European countries, CCR as a Catholic movement really dates only from the collapse of Communism. Bishop Cordes in the Vatican specifically asked some of the French communities to set up centers in the former Communist nations. Lithuania and Slovakia are two nations where the development of CCR has been much helped by U.S. leaders, particularly Ralph Martin, Peter Herbeck, and Dave Nodar.

During the 1990s the charismatic movement as a whole became less clearly defined. As it has increasingly influenced the wider church, there are more and more people whose faith-life is stronger due to the renewal, but who would not call themselves charismatics. This tendency had become more marked in the Protestant sector through the influence of John Wimber, and also through the rise of healing ministries not identified as charismatic. It was magnified in the 1990s first by the "Toronto blessing" and then by the Alpha course.

The CCR would seem to be one of the charismatic sectors least affected by the Toronto phenomenon, that is, the wave of "renewal" variously called the Father's blessing or the new wine, which was accompanied by a great variety of physical manifestations. However, even if few Catholic leaders visibly identified themselves with the Toronto stream that spread from the Airport Church beginning in January 1994, it has probably influenced more ordinary participants than most CCR leaders imagine.[14]

One reason for this is the wide dissemination of enthusiastic charismatic literature that abounds in reports of the latest charismatic happenings. Awareness of this was evidently a factor in the theological commission for CCR in Germany issuing a document on the subject in 1995. One country where the Catholic Church has been deeply impacted by the Father's blessing is Uganda, under the leadership of a German missionary named Fr. Ernst Sievers.[15]

The Alpha course originated from an Anglican Evangelical parish in London and soon attracted Catholic participants. As a result, the English NSC set up a Catholic office for Alpha in St. Albans in 1997, an initiative soon followed in the United States, where a Catholic office for Alpha was established in Baltimore. While Alpha presents itself as an evangelistic course to reach the unchurched, suitable for use by all Christians, it contains a charismatic component. The Holy Spirit weekend, held about a third of the way through the course, gives teaching on the spiritual gifts and encourages participants to seek the gift of tongues. So, while Alpha does not directly recruit for charismatic groups, it is leading many Christians into charismatic experience. In England, Alpha is providing a new breath of life for CCR, giving many prayer groups a new sense of mission, and this boost can be expected in other countries as Catholics there take up the Alpha course.

Alpha can also stand as a symbol of a resurgence of the ecumenical component in charismatic renewal. The new interchurch charismatic bodies formed in the late 1980s all supported the Decade of Evangelization and made evangelization a major theme of their big conferences: NARSC at Indianapolis and ECC at Bern, Switzerland, both in 1990, followed by ICCOWE with a worldwide gathering of leaders in Brighton, England, in 1991. Orlando 95, organized by NARSC, followed the Brighton pattern of including a theological track within a popular conference. All these conferences had a strong Catholic participation, often approaching 50 percent of the attendance. CCR international leadership has strongly supported the ecumenical thrust of the Holy Spirit, especially Charles Whitehead, the president of ICCRS until early 2000, whose wife is Anglican, and Fr. Raniero Cantalamessa, who has often preached on Christian unity and whose message at Brighton was a highlight of the conference.

While the United States, Great Britain, and the Netherlands had long had annual meetings of charismatic leaders with Catholic participation, and France followed suit from the mid-1980s, new meetings began in Germany (1993) and Ireland (1997) bringing together Catholics, mainline Protestants, and new church (nondenominational) leaders.

In Italy, a strong impulse for ecumenical reconciliation has been given by Matteo Calisi (Catholic) and Giovanni Traettino (Pentecostal), who hold a joint Catholic-Pentecostal conference each autumn. In 1995, Calisi and Traettino led a striking footwashing ceremony at the CCR Rimini conference, when an African cardinal and other prelates washed the feet of Traettino. Calisi and Traettino also ministered together at the 1997 ICCOWE-ECC conference in Prague, Czech Republic. With the theme "Building Bridges, Breaking Barriers," this conference aimed to spread the spirit of interchurch reconciliation to Eastern Europe, where ecumenical relations were less developed, and CCR has related much less to the renewal in other churches. A national interchurch conference in Nuremberg at Pentecost 1999, again with Father Cantalamessa, gave a new ecumenical impetus to CCR in Germany.

A development in the Roman Catholic Church of the highest spiritual significance for church renewal and Christian unity has been the pope's expression of repentance for the sins of Catholics through the ages against unity and against love. The liturgy of repentance in St. Peter's, Rome, on March 12, 2000, was quickly followed by the pope's historic visit to Israel at the end of March and his renewed expression of sorrow for the sins committed against the Jewish people. It would seem that CCR has not been a major contributor to this process, despite the spiritual sensitivity toward Israel and the Jewish people in much of the Pentecostal and charismatic worlds. Also, the contribution of Protestant charismatic leaders such as John Dawson led to the ministries of reconciliation through the promotion of "prayer journeys of repentance." However, the Béatitudes community of France has done much to provide a deeper biblical understanding of Israel and love for the Jewish people. Father Cantalamessa has also preached strongly on the necessity of repentance for the sins committed against the Jews and its relationship to the healing of the wounds of Christian division.

Conclusion

Despite some disappointments and some areas of decline, CCR has been overall a remarkable success story. It has undoubtedly exercised an influence in the Roman Catholic Church much wider than its visible constituency. The Roman Catholic Church has a much higher awareness of the Holy Spirit in the year 2000 than in the mid-1960s. While this is due to a number of causes, including biblical and liturgical renewal, CCR has surely been a major influence, being perhaps the most effective instrument for getting ordinary Catholics to read their Bibles and cherish the Word of God.

Catholic worship has in many ways become more joyful, with songs of charismatic origin being widely sung, often with little idea of their origin.

CCR has probably played an even bigger role in the Catholic Church's becoming more evangelistic, with the majority of Catholics entering into evangelistic ministries coming from the ranks of CCR or having trained at CCR schools of evangelization. In the United States, many young laypeople becoming directors of religious education or youth ministers in the Catholic parishes are graduates of Steubenville.

Another area of Catholic life where there has been a significant influence from CCR is that of healing. While the Vatican II decision to make the sacrament of anointing a ministry to the sick, and not simply to the dying, did not owe anything to Pentecostal or charismatic influences, this change has opened the door to a new Catholic appreciation for the ministry of healing. The development in CCR of the ministry of inner healing has also introduced a new element into the ministry of Catholic priests in the hearing of confessions.

Finally, CCR has undoubtedly effected a major change in the openness of ordinary Catholics to Christians of other Christian churches. The charismatic renewal is the first grassroots movement to span virtually all the Christian churches and traditions. Many lay Catholics had their first experience of ecumenism in CCR, which brought alive in their hearts what the Second Vatican Council had said about spiritual ecumenism and the Lord's will for Christian unity. CCR represents an interesting blend of reshaping the Catholic heritage and of opening to Protestant gifts, all in the melting pot of the Holy Spirit.

For Further Reading

Kilian McDonnell has been the primary theologian, historian, and adviser to the Catholic charismatic renewal from the beginning. His major works include: *Charismatic Renewal and the Churches* (New York: Seabury Press, 1976); *Presence, Power, Praise*, 3 vols. (Collegeville, Minn.: Liturgical Press, 1980); and, along with George Montague, *Christian Initiation and Baptism in the Holy Spirit* (Collegeville, Minn.: Liturgical Press, 1991).

Early histories of the movement include Kevin and Dorothy Ranaghan, eds., *Catholic Pentecostals* (Paramus, N.J.: Paulist Press, 1969); and Edward O'Connor, *The Pentecostal Movement in the Catholic Church* (Notre Dame, Ind.: Ave Maria Press, 1971). A good later history is Francis A. Sullivan's *Charisms and the Charismatic Renewal* (Ann Arbor, Mich.: Servant Publications, 1982). An extremely important book for its theological and ecclesiastical insights is Leon. J. Suenens's *A New Pentecost?* (New York: Seabury Press, 1975).

Official papal statements on the renewal are collected in *Then Peter Stood Up . . . : Collection of the popes' addresses to the CCR from its origin to the year 2000* (Rome: ICCRS, 2000). A good contemporary source for Catholic charismatic thought in the 1970s is contained in *Theological and Pastoral Orientations on the Catholic Charismatic Renewal* (Ann Arbor, Mich.: Word of Life, 1974). A full treatment of worldwide developments can be found in Peter Hocken's article "Charismatic Movement" in Stanley Burgess and Gary McGee's *Dictionary of Pentecostal and Charismatic Movements* (Grand Rapids: Zondervan, 1988), 130–60.

· 10 ·
Spirit-Filled Women

Susan C. Hyatt

FROM THE VERY FIRST DAY in modern Pentecostal history, January 1, 1901, women have played leading and often pivotal roles in the growth and development of the movement. On this first day of the 20th century a woman was the first person to usher in the "Century of the Holy Spirit." This lady was Agnes Ozman, a humble thirty-year-old holiness preacher, whose baptism in the Holy Spirit accompanied by speaking in tongues has become a major landmark in church history.

According to J. Roswell Flower, founding secretary of the Assemblies of God, Ozman's experience "made the Pentecostal movement of the 20th century." The reason Ozman was accorded this honor, according to Flower, was that she was the first person in history to receive the Holy Spirit baptism expecting that tongues would be the "Bible evidence" of the experience. Many persons before Ozman had claimed to be baptized in the Holy Spirit and many others had spoken in tongues, but this was the first time the two were linked together.

Was it mere coincidence that a woman—Agnes Ozman—would be the first person to usher in the century of the Spirit? Many writers and scholars have seen her role as the fulfillment of biblical prophecies that God would "pour out His Spirit on all flesh" and that His "sons and daughters" would prophesy and so become witnesses for Him. Others saw the fulfillment of

Joel's prophecy (2:28–29) that He would pour out His Spirit on both "menservants and maidservants."

The leading role of Agnes Ozman presaged a century in which women were to minister in ways never before seen in church history. In a sense, she stood between a long line of women preachers that preceded her in the 19th century and an even longer line of Pentecostal women ministers who would startle the world in the 20th century.

Preparation in the 17th and 18th Centuries

Historically, women have always found greater freedom in Spirit-oriented renewal movements of Christianity than in the more traditional institutions. In these movements, those who possessed the experience and gifting of the Spirit were recognized as leaders rather than those authorized by the traditional institution. This was especially true in the early Pentecostal revival due, in part, to the presence of Quaker and Methodist ideals that had permeated much of 19th-century America, improving the lot of women generally. Indeed, the prominence of women, especially in leadership in the early Pentecostal revival, can be adequately understood only in light of this influence.

Women of Early Quakerism

The early Quakers (1650–90), also known as Friends, represented the most significant historic turning point for women since the time of Jesus. Arising in England about 1650, these missions-minded people, many of whom were women, spread the gospel, at great risk for their lives, from Turkey to the English colonies in the New World. By 1660, they had become the fastest-growing movement in the Western world. These charismatic believers enjoyed the manifestations of the Spirit, divine healing, and all the spiritual gifts, including singing in the Spirit. Edward Burroughs, one of the early members of the Society of Friends, wrote, "Our tongues were loosed and our mouths opened, and we spake with new tongues, as the Lord gave utterance."[1]

The early Quakers emphasized the Scriptures and the interior life of the Spirit over and against the outward forms and rituals of the institutional church. They were preoccupied with a Christian lifestyle reflecting the compassion of Jesus and renouncing any dependence on outward religion. This ideal carried over into their concept of ministry, which, for them, was synonymous with Christian living. Men and women were equally and individually responsible to walk in intimacy with the Lord and in utmost respect for others. The gifting of the Spirit was considered the qualifying factor for leadership responsibility and missionary activity. They recognized no separate clerical class.

Because of this, Quaker women such as Margaret Fell (1614–1702) came to the forefront. In 1666, while in prison for her faith, she wrote *Women Speaking Justified,* the first book by a woman giving a biblically based theology for female public ministry. A former Anglican gentry, Fell was instrumental in helping women learn to exercise their equality in the Society. (This rich heritage is one reason the Quaker women were so competent in leading social change in America in the 1800s.) Countless Quaker women in 19th-century America made a significant difference, equipping women in such a way that they were ready for leadership responsibility in the Pentecostal revival.

An important fact often overlooked about the early Pentecostal revival was the direct influence of Quaker thinking. The initial great outpouring occurred in Bethel Bible College in Topeka, Kansas, operated by Charles Fox Parham (1873–1929). Although Bethel is commonly considered a holiness school, it should be remembered that Sarah Thistlethwaite-Parham (1877–1937) and her sister Lillian Thistlethwaite (1873–1939) were birthright Friends who never renounced Quakerism and that Parham himself had spent many hours modifying his Methodist holiness theology in dialogue with his wife's Quaker grandfather. While the Parham-Thislethwaite influence prevailed, gender equality typical to the Friends characterized the revival. Was it perhaps this dignity and equality afforded women in the early Pentecostal revival that infused it with exceptional dynamism?

Women of Early Methodism

Another major element that brought women to prominence in the early Pentecostal revival was the holiness movement that had emerged from Methodism. The Methodist revival in England (1739–60) had been, like the early Friends' revival, charismatic in nature. It demonstrated, as well, an important inclusivism of women, giving them unusual respect, recognition, and freedom to minister. In fact, one scholar has noted, "Emancipation of womanhood began with John Wesley."[2] Three main elements account for this elevation of women: Wesley's central theology of holiness; Wesley's emphasis on the "inner witness" or "warmed heart"; and Wesley's mother, Susanna.

Wesley's central theme was holiness of life. His scriptural point of reference was Hebrews 12:14: "Pursue peace with all people, and holiness, without which no one will see the Lord." Because this, he believed, was the responsibility of every believer, he rejected the notion that holiness was reserved for a clergy class, insisting instead that holiness is to be the life-long pursuit of every believer. This was a socially leveling concept.

One vital requirement of early Methodist teaching about holiness was the importance of giving public testimony to the experience of sanctifica-tion in the believer's heart by God. This responsibility was to be fulfilled by women as well as by men. Thus, suddenly but subtly, the centuries-old silence barrier for women was shattered in socially acceptable religion. It was a short step, indeed, from testifying to teaching and preaching.

After Wesley's conversion-sanctification experience at Aldersgate in which he had felt his heart "strangely warmed," he increasingly empha-sized the importance of the experiential element of faith. This led to an in-creasing openness to Methodist women whose hearts had also been "strangely warmed" by the Spirit, and this openness eventually led to the sanctioning of women to preach. When challenged as to why he would commission women to preach and lead, Wesley replied, "Because God owns them in the saving of souls, and who am I to withstand God?"[3]

Perhaps the most influential of the Methodist women was Wesley's mother, Susanna Annesley Wesley (1669–1742). In fact, some scholars con-sider Susanna to be the true founder of Methodism.[4] This highly intelli-gent, self-educated woman established the format for Methodism with her popular family devotions. Susanna, nurtured in theology as a child by her father, the "St. Paul of nonconformists," believed in the activity of the Spirit in the believer's life to be authoritative above the dictates of the in-stitutional church.

Preparation in the Early 19th Century

The preeminence of the interior life in the theological formulations of the Friends and Methodists was strategic in the long process of restoring the biblical status of women. Merging with other elements in 19th-century America, they loosened—and in some cases, shattered—the cultural re-straints that had chained women for centuries. In fact, during that era peo-ple and movements worked for the participation and leadership of women in the church and in society at large. These included American revivalism and America's sense of divine destiny that broke the back of slavery in America.

The Revivalism of Finney and Mahan

The revivalism of Charles Finney (1792–1875) and Asa Mahan (1799–1889) emphasized a subsequent empowering of the Spirit, which they identified as the baptism of the Holy Spirit. Their belief system, like that of the early Quakers and Methodists, precipitated social reforms that included the elevation of women. In fact, one of the most controversial of Finney's "new measures" during the Second Great Awakening (1800–1840) was his practice of allowing women to pray aloud and testify in mixed gatherings. In addition, Finney and Mahan helped establish Oberlin College (1833), the first coeducational college in the world, for the purpose of perpetuating Finney's "blend of revivalism and reform." Mahan, who participated in the Keswick movement with Hannah Whittal Smith, was a strong supporter of women. He suggested the following epitaph for his gravestone: "The first man, in the history of the race, who conducted women, in connection with members of the opposite sex, through a full course of liberal education, and conferred upon her the high degrees which had hitherto been exclusive prerogative of men."

A Sense of Divine Destiny

America's special sense of divine destiny helped produce a social conscience that called for an end to social sins, especially slavery. This led to the abolition movement, which culminated in the Civil War (1861–65). Abolition was an important movement, not only in cleansing culture of the sin of slavery, but also in terms of the possibilities it could bring to women. For example, it brought women into the public arena with a voice and a cause. It strengthened the public speaking skills of those women who were bold enough to preach, speak, and debate on behalf of the slaves. It challenged the idea of predestined roles based on skin color, thereby opening the possibility that God did not, in fact, have predestined social roles dictated either by skin color or gender.

It also called forth an approach to biblical interpretation that led to a more accurate reading of the text, an approach that helped advance the biblical truth of woman's place of equality in God's economy. In this approach, proof-texting lost credibility as a means of establishing doctrine. Instead of throwing isolated scriptures like stones at one another in the debate, abolitionists began arguing on the basis of scriptural principles. This method required that passages be understood only in their legitimate contexts, and the theological starting point for liberation of the slaves was

Galatians 3:28, which states that in Christ "there is neither . . . slave nor free, there is neither male nor female." This was good news for both slaves and women.

Preparation in the Late 19th Century

Following the Civil War, several interwoven movements further advanced the status of women, mobilizing more women and helping develop their leadership and ministry skills for participation in the coming Pentecostal revival. These included the holiness movement, the Woman's Christian Temperance Union, the missionary movement, the Women's Suffrage Movement, and the healing movement. In addition, the status of women continued to advance through the Keswick movement and the changes precipitated through Finney-Mahan revivalism. These movements were grounded in Scripture and motivated by the Spirit. They emphasized the inner experience of the Spirit and an outward, corporate effort to improve particular aspects of life for women. Together these provided considerable momentum for women to move into leadership and public ministry.

The Holiness Movement

Biblical Themes. The holiness movement was an attempt begun among Methodists to experience the spiritual dynamism of first-generation Methodism, and it eventually spread to affect every denomination in America. The holiness movement provided three important biblical themes that strengthened women's right to public influence.

1. *The Galatians 3:28 theme of biblical equality.* This became the battle cry for the liberation of women. In 1891 William B. Godbey wrote, "It is the God-given right, blood-bought privilege, and bounden duty of the women, as well as the men, to preach the gospel."[5]
2. *The redemption argument for biblical equality.* The point is this: If women were under a curse through the Fall, now, by virtue of re-demption, the curse associated with that event is broken by the work of Jesus Christ.
3. *The Pentecostal theme for biblical equality.* This theme, based on Joel 2:28 and Acts 2:17–18, points to the outpouring of the Spirit on men and women alike, empowering both equally for end-time ministry.

The Influence of Phoebe Palmer. One of the most prominent leaders of the holiness movement was Phoebe Worrall Palmer (1807–74). Never ordained, Phoebe was a reluctant but highly gifted preacher. A devout Methodist from childhood, she married fellow Methodist and New York City physician Walter Clarke Palmer (1804–83), who graciously underwrote her many ministry travels and eventually closed his medical practice to "carry her suitcases." He also opened a publishing company to extend her influence through her writing.

Simple obedience to God's call resulted in Phoebe's far-reaching influence. She was its dominant theologian emphasizing a baptism of the Holy Spirit subsequent to conversion. The movement's foremost Bible teacher and most prominent evangelist before the Civil War, she recorded at least twenty-five thousand conversions and sanctification experiences in her meetings. Through her books and the *Guide to Holiness* periodical (1864–74), she became its most influential writer. One of her books, the 421-page *The Promise of the Father* (1859), articulates a biblical theology validating woman's right and responsibility to obey the call to public ministry, with Acts 2:17–18 as its starting point for discussion. *The Way of Holiness* (1843) shifts the terminology of the holiness movement to the language of Pentecost, and *Four Years in the Old World* (1867) documents her revival meetings in England.

Despite her effectiveness in public ministry, Phoebe endured biting criticism and ridicule from those who opposed women in ministry. Unhindered, she forthrightly debunked her critics. She also mourned such attitudes toward women, saying,

> The church in many ways is a sort of potter's field, where the gifts of woman, as so many strangers, are buried. How long, O Lord, how long before man shall roll away the stone that we may see a resurrection?
>
> > Daughters of Zion, from the dust
> > Exalt thy fallen head;
> > Again in thy Redeemer trust.—
> > He calls thee from the dead.[6]

Phoebe's example inspired many other women, including such stalwarts as Catherine Booth and Amanda Smith.

Catherine Mumford Booth (1829–90) was "an unfailing, unflinching, uncompromising champion of woman's rights." Cofounder of the Salvation Army with her husband, William Booth (1829–1912), she worked tirelessly for equal authority, equal rights, and equal responsibilities for

Amanda Berry Smith (1837–1915) won her freedom from slavery as a result of her preaching ability. Her autobiography is a classic in holiness literature.

women on the basis of redemption and Pentecost. In the marriage relationship, she staunchly refused to be considered or treated anything but equal with her husband. She wrote a thirty-two-page tract titled *Female Ministry* in which she laments the inequality of women as "a remarkable device of the devil," but she triumphantly proclaims, "the time of her deliverance draweth nigh."[7]

Amanda Matthews-Berry Smith (1837–1915) was born to slaves in the state of Maryland. She began preaching in 1870 and continued with tremendous success despite cruel racism and barbarous sexism. Although she had only three months of formal schooling, Smith was both highly articulate and wonderfully anointed. Her gift indeed made room for her, and she gained remarkable respect in all quarters of society. She ministered with great success throughout America, the British Isles, Liberia, Sierra Leone, Burma, and India where she was commended by Methodist bishop Thoburn.

Hannah Whittal Smith

One woman in particular seems to have been a common factor in several movements leading up to the Pentecostal revival. The imprint of Philadelphia Quaker Hannah Whittal Smith (1832–1911) is everywhere. Perhaps her influence in Pentecostalism came most directly through the Keswick movement, in which she shared the platform with such well-known leaders as Asa Mahan, William Boardman, Amanda and Robert Pearsall Smith, and others.

The WCTU. Hannah also worked closely with Frances Willard (1839–98), the most influential leader of the Woman's Christian Temperance Union (WCTU). Through Willard's administrative gift and dependence on God, this Christian women's movement for the protection of the home quickly became the largest women's organization in the world with works in fifty nations. In America, its local halls became favorite meeting places of Parham's nondenominational Pentecostal meetings.

Frances Willard had grown up on Finney revivalism and experienced sanctification in one of Phoebe Palmer's meetings. She wrote, "[Only] as I come close to God and through Christ's blood am made a new creature, am I ready for this work so blessed and so high." Willard called on Whittal-Smith to be the first superintendent of the Evangelistic Department and on Dr. Katherine C. Bushnell (1855–1946) to be the organization's national evangelist for the advancement of social purity.

Katherine Bushnell was a highly intelligent woman whose devotion to the gospel first led her to China as a Methodist Episcopal missionary doctor and later to the Wisconsin lumber camps as an activist exposing the sex slave trade. Perhaps her single most important work and ongoing contribution to the Pentecostal charismatic movement is her book *God's Word to Women*. Initially released as one hundred Bible study lessons on woman's place in the divine economy, it was published in book form in 1923. After fading into obscurity for several years, it was discovered and republished by Pentecostal preacher Ray B. Munson. It subsequently gained favor among Spirit-filled women in the closing decade of the century and is now regarded as a classic.

Women's Suffrage. Hannah Whittal Smith's work extended beyond the Keswickians and the activists such as Willard and Bushnell. An ardent suffragette, she was a close ally of Susan B. Anthony (1820–1906) and many of the other Quaker men and women who led the long and arduous battle for women to receive the right to vote in America. She entered this arena "by the way of the gospel," knowing that "women were made free by the working out of the principles of Christ who had declared there is neither male nor female in Him."[8] Anthony prayed "most earnestly and constantly, for some terrific shock to startle women of the nation into a self-respect." Perhaps the Pentecostal revival was, at least in part, a positive answer to her prayer.

Women in the Missionary Movement

The missionary movement was the largest of the mass women's movements of the 19th century. This meant that hosts of women were already mobilized in missions when the Pentecostal revival arrived on the scene. Missions, of course, was the heartbeat of Quakerism from the beginning, and it was also an important concern of the holiness people as the 20th century dawned. On the field, women were free to function in all aspects of ministry, while at home, women's missionary societies provided every kind of support and literature, and held missionary conventions and institutes. Groups such as A. B. Simpson's Christian and Missionary Alliance trained and supported women in missionary activity, and many CMA women became leaders in the early Pentecostal revival. Surely the consecration and mobility of women missionaries became a main channel for the dispersion of the Pentecostal message around the world.

Women in the Healing Movement

The healing movement was another important arena in which women gained prominence prior to the Pentecostal revival. By 1887, the practice of divine healing and the concept of faith homes had become so popular in America that more than thirty such centers were in operation. The leading figure in this movement was Boston physician Charles Cullis. The blending of the healing movement with other movements that elevated women is clear. In 1862, for example, Cullis had received his sanctification experience through the ministry of Phoebe Palmer. Counted among his close friends were Hannah Whittal Smith, A. B. Simpson, and Dr. A. J. Gordon. Dr. Gordon (1836–95), a Boston pastor of great intellectual and spiritual stature, was an ardent holiness advocate and supporter of the advancement of women. His 1894 work, *The Ministry of Women,* remains an important statement of support for women. Both Gordon and Simpson facilitated the development of strong women leaders who became influential leaders in the early Pentecostal revival.

Maria Woodworth-Etter (1844–1924) conducted mass tent healing revivals as a holiness preacher before becoming a Pentecostal in 1912.

Carrie Judd Montgomery (1848–1946) was the first woman to itinerate across America. A colleague of A. B. Simpson, Carrie had been active in the healing movement since her healing in 1879 through Elizabeth Mix's ministry. During the 1880s she operated Faith Rest Cottage, a healing home in Buffalo, New York. In 1890, when she married George Montgomery, she moved with him to Oakland, California, where she opened the Home of Peace in 1893, the first West Coast healing home. In 1908, she was baptized in the Spirit and became a charter member of the Assemblies of God in 1914. Nevertheless, she retained close ties with her non-Pentecostal friends in groups such as the Christian and Missionary Alliance, of which she had been a founding member in 1887.

Maria Woodworth-Etter (1844–1924), an itinerant holiness evangelist, began preaching in the early 1880s and by 1885 was drawing crowds of twenty-five thousand, with as many as five hundred per week making commitments to Christ. Unusual signs and wonders characterized her meetings.

People were healed, slain in the spirit, and some experienced visions that went on for extended periods. In 1912, she joined the Pentecostal movement through the efforts of F. F. Bosworth and was warmly embraced by the Pentecostals.

The Early Pentecostal Revival of the 20th Century

The Holy Spirit, working through the interwoven movements of the 19th century, significantly advanced the status of women. By the turn of the century, women were well positioned to flow with the Spirit in whatever capacity He would choose. The stage was set so that women and men together would advance the Pentecostal outpouring around the world in the new century.

The Thistlethwaite-Parham Factor

The Parhams, Charles and Sarah, together with Sarah's sister, Lillian, benefited from a unique blend of elements from the holiness, Methodist, Quaker, Missionary, and healing movement influences. The Thistlethwaite sisters had experienced "the old-fashioned, mourner's bench conversion experience" through the summer evangelistic ministry of Charles Fox Parham, who at the time was a teenage ministerial student (1889–93) at Southwest Kansas Methodist Conference College in Winfield. From 1893 to 1895, while Parham was pastoring the Methodist church in Eudora, Kansas, he also conducted meetings in Tonganoxie on Sunday afternoons. It would appear that he accepted some of the ways of the Friends, for he gave up the opportunity to advance in Methodism when he resigned the pastorate after much soul-searching, prayer, and fasting. In 1896, he and Sarah, whom he affectionately called "Nellie," wed in a Quaker ceremony, a rite based on mutuality and equality.

After a brief period of holiness-type evangelistic ministry, Charles and Sarah, together with Lillian, opened Bethel Home in Topeka in 1898. Here they carried out the usual social services to the needy, cared for the sick and dying, taught the Bible, and published the biweekly periodical the *Apostolic Faith* magazine. Hungry to see Holy Spirit revival that would culminate in world evangelization, they opened Bethel Bible College on the outskirts of Topeka, and it was there that the 20th-century Pentecostal revival began in the 1900-1901 New Year's Eve watchnight service. For nearly the next five years, the pioneers of Pentecost were Parham disciples either directly or indirectly.

Women of the Parham Era. In addition to the Thistlethwaite sisters, a number of dynamic women ministered and led in various ways during the early years of the revival (1901–7). Agnes Ozman (1870–1937), of course, continued her ministry. Maude and Howard Stanley, also present at the Bethel outpouring, became well known in the Assemblies of God.[9]

At the Parham meetings in Lawrence, Kansas, in 1901, a Mrs. Waldron received the Pentecostal message and power. She was probably the first person to take the message to Dowie's Zion City, Illinois, church. Although Zion City generally rejected the message, several, including John G. Lake, listened with much interest. No doubt Mrs. Waldron's work laid the groundwork for Parham's most influential revival in Zion City in 1906 and 1907. As a result of this revival, at least five hundred consecrated, missions-minded, and Spirit-baptized workers, many of them women, went forth in America and the world. This vast infusion of Zion Pentecostals so early in the revival assured the integration of the doctrine of divine healing into the fabric of Pentecostalism.

Gordon P. Gardiner, in his excellent series of articles "Out of Zion . . . into all the World," published in *Bread of Life* magazine from October 1981 through October 1985, tells the stories of many of the Zion Pentecostal pioneers. Martha Wing Robinson (1874–1938) founded the influential Zion Faith Homes. Marie Burgess Brown (1880–1971), who, along with F. F. Bosworth and John G. Lake, was baptized in the Spirit on October 18, 1906, in one of Parham's home meetings in Zion City, went on to found and pastor Glad Tidings Tabernacle in New York City. In 1961, while she was still pastoring Glad Tidings, it was described as "a church with the largest missionary budget in the missionary-minded Assemblies of God."[10] Jean Campbell Hall Mason, baptized in the Spirit on October 18, 1906, had a powerful ministry throughout Canada and the United States until her death in 1964. Bernice C. Lee, baptized in the Spirit on October 30, 1906, went to India where she raised up local congregations and trained hundreds of national leaders. Dr. Lillian B. Yeomans, a medical doctor from Canada, was a missionary and writer whose works are still read today. They include *Healing from Heaven* and *Balm of Gilead*. Dr. Yeoman spent her latter years as a teacher in Aimee Semple McPherson's L.I.F.E. Bible College.

Prior to going to Zion City, however, the Thistlethwaite-Parhams held healing meetings in Nevada and El Dorado Springs, Missouri, in 1903. Many people heard the message and were saved, healed, and baptized in the Holy Spirit. Sarah Parham writes, "Our home was continually filled with the sick and suffering seeking healing and God manifested His mighty power."[11] These people must be added to the unheralded but ever

he Holiness Camp Meeting in Falcon, North Carolina, in 1905. It became Pentecostal in 1907.

"Praying Hands" at the entrance of Oral Roberts University in Tulsa, Oklahoma.

The building locally known as "Stones Folly" in Topeka, Kansas, where the Pentecostal movement began in 1901.

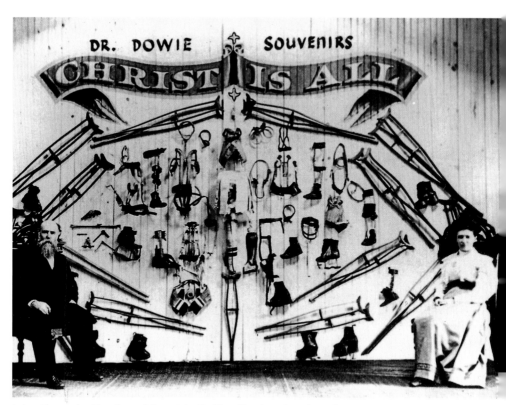

John Alexander Dowie and "trophies" of healing in a booth at the Chicago World's Fair in 1894.

Smith Wigglesworth from England who rose from poverty and illiteracy to become one of the most powerful Pentecostal preachers of his day.

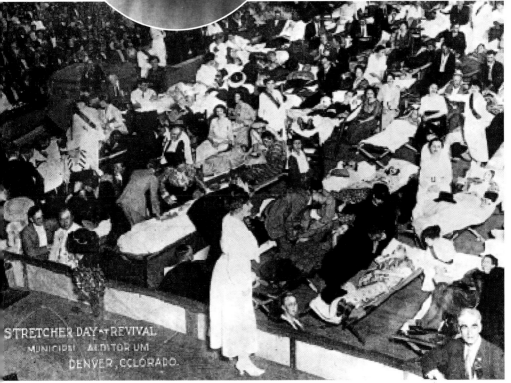

Aimee Semple McPherson on "Stretcher Day" at a Denver crusade in 1927.

Four televangelists—1979. Left to right: Demos Shakarian, Billy Graham, Rex Humbard, and Pat Robertson.

The choir in a Pentecostal Church in Lutsk in the Ukraine, which has 1,500 members.

Catholic charismatic scholars in Rome—1974.

Pentecostal worship in the Spirit.

Leaders of the International Charismatic Consultation on World Evangelization (ICCOWE) in England. Left to right: Father Tom Forrest, Sr. Kim Kollins, Kriengsak Wonsak, Michael Harper, Vinson Synan, and Larry Christenson.

The "Memphis Miracle" in 1994. Don Evans of the Assemblies of God washes the feet of Bishop Ithiel Clemmons of the Church of God in Christ.

Dancing before the Lord in the "Celebrate Jesus 2000" Congress in St. Louis, Missouri, June 2000.

Washington for Jesus—1988 led by John Giminez, pastor of the Rock Church in Virginia Beach, Virginia.

Filadelfia Church in Stockholm, Sweden, which was built by Pastor Lewi Pethrus in 1932. For decades this was the largest free church in Europe and one of the largest Pentecostal churches in the world.

Claudio Freidzon addresses a mass healing crusade in Argentina.

A Reinhard Bonnke African crusade in 1999.

15,000 charismatics celebrating in St. Louis, 2000.

Seekers praying in the altar in the Brownsville Revival in Pensacola, Florida, in 1996. Over 2,000,000 persons attended these services.

World-renowned choir of Christ Church in Nashville, Tennessee.

Pastor Tommy Barnett preaching in the First Assembly in Phoenix, Arizona.

First Assembly of God, Phoenix, Arizona, a church with 12,000 members.

John Arnott leads prayer in the "Toronto Blessing" revival.

Persons "Slain the Spirit" in Toronto.

Pentecostal expressive worship and praise.

Bethany Christian Center Pentecostal Holiness Church, Oradea, Romania.

Pastor David Yonggi Cho preaches in one of seven Sunday services in the Yoido Church in Seoul, Korea.

The Yoido Full Gospel Church (Assemblies of God) in Seoul, Korea. With 730,000 members, it is the largest local church in the world.

Reinhard Bonnke ministers healing before 1,600,000 persons in Nigeria in November, 2000. This was the largest crusade ever conducted in the history of Christian evangelism, with over 10,000,000 attending six services. Over 4,000,000 signed conversion cards.

An Indian Pentecostal Church conference in the State of Kerala, South India.

The staff of Pat Robertson's "700 Club," the longest running Christian television program in existence. From left to right are: Terry Meeuwsen, Lee Webb, Lisa Ryan, Gordon Robertson, and Pat Robertson.

The Benny Hinn Crusade in Nairobi, Kenya, in April 2000.

increasing numbers of men and women who carried the Pentecostal testimony throughout the land. One of these was Mary Arthur of Galena, Kansas.

Through Mary Arthur's influence, the Thistlethwaite-Parhams went to Galena in 1904 and conducted the first area-wide Pentecostal revival of modern times. It embraced all social classes throughout the region, and in a three-month period more than 800 people were saved, 500 were sanctified, and 250 received the baptism in the Spirit. Hundreds were healed. Out of this influential revival, Mary Arthur and Francene Dobson founded the first mission begun as a direct result of Pentecostal preaching.[12]

In 1905 the Parhams conducted meetings in and around Houston as well as a short-term Bible school in 1906. The bands of workers ministering with Parham in these meetings were composed of men and women alike. They were colaborers with no sense of women being secondary or subordinate. The names of two women are recorded again and again, Mabel Smith and Lucy Farrow. Both of these women were sent by Parham in response to William J. Seymour's pleas for help in the opening days of Azusa Street. Smith also helped in the Zion City revival, and her name appears frequently in early Pentecostal reports.

Lucy Farrow deserves special mention. Born in slavery in Virginia, she was serving as a holiness pastor in Houston by the time Parham arrived there in 1905. She worked closely with the Parhams, serving as governess to the children and preaching and ministering in the meetings.[13] Farrow had introduced Parham and Seymour by this time, encouraging Seymour to attend the Bible school. Although Seymour is universally acclaimed as the leading figure of the Azusa Street revival (April 1906–9), Mother Cotton reported that "no one experienced the Pentecostal baptism until Lucy Farrow arrived and began praying for people to receive it."[14] In August 1906 she preached in Parham's Houston camp meeting and, according to a participant, demonstrated "an unusual power to lay hands on people for the reception of the Holy Spirit."[15] Later that month, she conducted a Pentecostal revival in Portsmouth, Virginia, during which 200 were saved and 150 were baptized in the Spirit. From there, she journeyed as one of the first Pentecostal missionaries to Liberia, West Africa.

Women also figure prominently in the early administrative tasks of the revival. By the close of 1905, with the groundswell of Spirit-baptized believers becoming so great and with at least fifty full-time men and women working in the field, people started pressuring Parham to organize the revival. The loose fellowship he formed, known as the "apostolic faith movement," was officially formed in May 1906, with men and women equally represented. Of the four shouldering responsibility in addition to Parham, two were men and two were women, including Rilda Cole, state director for Kansas, and Lillian Thistlethwaite, who was the general secretary. All workers and evangelists, men and women, were equally issued credentials, and many of these helped form the nucleus of the Assemblies of God in 1914.

Women of the Azusa Street Revival

In important respects, women were instrumental in initiating the famous Azusa Street revival. After visiting Parham's Houston Bible school, a woman named Neely Terry suggested to her home church in Los Angeles that William Seymour be invited to be their pastor. However, when the leadership did not receive the Pentecostal message Seymour preached, Richard and Ruth Asberry invited him to hold meetings in their Bonnie Brae Street home. As attendance and enthusiasm increased, at Seymour's request Parham dispatched Lucy Farrow to help. Upon her arrival, she prayed with people and immediately they began being baptized in the Spirit with the evidence of tongues-speaking. The revival was under way.

Jennie Evans Moore (1883–1936) was the first woman baptized in the Spirit at Bonnie Brae Street through Lucy Farrow's ministry. After itinerat-

One of the first persons to receive the Pentecostal experience in Los Angeles in 1906, Jennie Evans Moore (1883–1936) married William J. Seymour and pastored the Azusa Street mission after Seymour's death in 1922.

ing as a Pentecostal evangelist, she returned to Los Angeles and married Seymour on May 13, 1908. Following his death in 1922, she became the pastor of the Azusa Street Mission until her own passing in 1936.

Many other women also carried out leadership tasks at Azusa Street. When Seymour decided to form a board of elders to guide the affairs of the Azusa Mission, he chose seven women and four other men. The women included Jennie Evans Moore, Sister Price, Mrs. G. W. Evans, Clara Lum, Phoebe Sargent, Rachel Sizelove, and Florence Crawford. As editor of the *Apostolic Faith* paper, Clara Lum spread the exciting news of the outpouring far and wide. Florence Crawford (1872–1936) was anointed to preach, a fact that was obvious by the tremendous response to meetings she conducted in the northwestern United States and

Canada between August and December 1906. With Mr. and Mrs. Evans and Clara Lum, she left Azusa and went to Portland where she established the Apostolic Faith Church in the Northwest. From Portland, with the Azusa mailing list of several thousand in hand, they continued to publish *Apostolic Faith,* much to the consternation of Seymour and the faithful Azusa people.

The women in the early days of the Pentecostal revival were empowered, both experientially and theologically, in their leadership activities. However, as the years passed and the revival spread, the support for and confidence of women generally diminished. Although experience and anointing continued to be reasons for promotion, the theological underpinnings were weakened and replaced by less favorable theologies. This led, both overtly and subtly, to some limitations being placed on women and to men being promoted over women. Nevertheless, in various fields, women continued to be

Florence Crawford (1872–1936) helped Seymour edit the *Apostolic Faith* paper at Azusa Street. After moving the paper to Portland, Oregon, in 1909, she founded another apostolic faith denomination.

prominent for a time. They founded new denominations, swelled the missionary ranks, and established the first permanent Bible schools of the Pentecostal movement.

Women in the Early Pentecostal Bible Schools

Teachers and Bible schools have been vital from the beginning of the Pentecostal revival. A Bible school birthed the revival, Bible schools nurtured future leaders, and Bible schools provided the venue for fresh outpouring that injected new life into the movement.

Women founded the first permanent Pentecostal Bible schools. In these schools, women also served in all capacities, including those of administration and teaching. Often they were unnamed catalysts for revival and faithful equippers of the men who became leaders of the movement.

The Duncan Sisters. In November 1894, Elizabeth Duncan Baker (c. 1849–1915) and her four sisters began a missions-oriented faith ministry in Rochester, New York. Their impressive ministry center included Elim Faith Home (est. 1895), Elim Publishing House, Elim Tabernacle Church, and Rochester Bible Training School (est. 1906–24). At the June 1907 convention,

Elim Tabernacle experienced a Pentecostal outpouring and the Training School became the first permanent Bible school of the 20th-century Pentecostal revival.

Elizabeth, especially, influenced the character of the work. Of Methodist stock and a recipient of divine healing, she had been infused with courage as a woman by her association with the Woman's Christian Temperance Union. She was inspired by George Mueller and had sat at the feet of Dr. A. J. Gordon in Boston. She came to emphasize the "deepening of spiritual life and . . . healing of the body" through her close friend Elizabeth Sisson (1843–1934), a missionary, writer, evangelist, and church planter who eventually moved to California to work with Carrie Judd Montgomery.

The Duncan sisters always held a special place in their hearts for missions. Elizabeth's 1888–90 visit to Pandita Ramabai's (1858–1920) work in India served to intensify this interest. Elizabeth and Ramabai became fast friends, and she was instrumental in Ramabai's establishment of a mission to temple prostitutes. She raised money in both England and the United States for the Indian ministry.

Mother Moss. Virginia E. "Mother" Moss (1875–1919) was an educator and pastor. A third-generation woman in ministry, Mother Moss was baptized in the Spirit at the 1907 Pentecostal revival at A. B. Simpson's Nyack Missionary Training Center in New York. In 1910, she moved her ministry center to North Bergen, New Jersey, where she merged her mission and healing home to become the Beulah Heights Assembly. A strong proponent of missions, she saw the need to equip those going to the field. Consequently, she established Beulah Heights Bible and Missionary Training School in 1912.

Minnie Tingley Draper. Minnie Tingley Draper (1858–1921) was another educator in the early Pentecostal revival on the East Coast. Draper had a powerful healing evangelist ministry, and as an administrative executive with the Christian and Missionary Alliance she worked closely with A. B. Simpson. She founded Bethel Pentecostal Assembly in Newark, New Jersey, in 1907, and in 1910 she incorporated the Executive Council of the Bethel Pentecostal Assembly. She presided over the earliest Pentecostal missionary agency in the United States, an agency that became known as the South and Central African Pentecostal Mission. She published the *South and Central African Pentecostal Herald,* which later adopted the title *Full Gospel Missionary Herald.* In 1916 Draper established Bethel Bible Training School as part of the Newark ministry center.

Aimee Semple McPherson (1890–1944), whose story is a tale of tragedy and exploits, was born in Ingersoll, Ontario, Canada, to a Methodist father and Salvation Army mother. Her marriage to Pentecostal evangelist Robert

Semple on August 12, 1908, ended in China exactly two years later when he died of malaria. After her daughter was born the following month in Hong Kong, she returned to the United States, wounded and bewildered, only to be cast off by her Pentecostal friends as a failure.

Just over a year later, she married Harold McPherson and moved to Rhode Island where her son, Rolf, was born. When her sense of God's call exceeded her need for earthly security, she returned to Canada to reenter ministry. Her husband joined her in ministry for a time, but the lifestyle took its toll on both and McPherson left the evangelistic party, returning to Rhode Island, and the couple divorced in August 1921.

Meanwhile, Aimee's ministry was flourishing. In 1917 she began monthly publication of the *Bridal Call*. In 1919, she received ordination papers from the Assemblies of God as an evangelist; however, she returned these credentials in January 1922. Her divorce, together with the construction and ownership of Angeles Temple, precipitated an incompatible relationship with that organization. On January 1, 1923, she opened the 5,300-seat Angeles Temple where for three years she preached every night and three times on Sundays to crowds of 5,000 and more. A month later she opened the Lighthouse for International Foursquare Evangelism, known as L.I.F.E. Bible College, "a training center to equip men and

women to become the evangelists, missionaries, pastors, and teachers so desperately needed to bring people to Christ and to ground people's faith in God's Word." In 1924 she began operating her own radio station, KFSG in Los Angeles, and in 1927 she opened the Angeles Temple Commissary. The same year she incorporated the International Church of the Foursquare Gospel. In spite of ongoing turmoil in her personal life, she continued an effective ministry until her death on September 26, 1944. Sister Aimee, as she was affectionately called, was buried in Forest Lawn Cemetery in Glendale, California, on October 9, 1944, in one of the largest funerals ever held in Los Angeles. Some believe she was the most prominent woman leader of Pentecostalism.

Aimee Semple McPherson (1890–1944) was the best-known woman preacher in modern times. The church she founded, the International Church of the Foursquare Gospel, now spans the globe.

Christine Amelia Eckman (1879–1955) was born in British Guiana, where she was converted at the age of twenty-one. She and her sister Alice joined the Full Gospel Mission and after two

AIMEE SEMPLE MCPHERSON

Aimee Semple McPherson was born in October 1890, to James and Minnie Kennedy, a Methodist and a Salvation Army devotee respectively, in Ontario, Canada. As a teenager, Aimee was introduced to Pentecostalism through the preaching of Robert Semple. Much to the alarm of her parents, she began praying for the baptism of the Holy Spirit.

Her prayers were eventually answered, and she quit high school to give more time to the local Pentecostal mission. When Robert proposed, she promptly accepted. She was 17 when they married, but two years later, in Hong Kong, just as the couple began a missions career, he died.

Aimee returned from Hong Kong to join her mother and to don the Army uniform. She also married a young businessman named Harold McPherson, who loved her enough to try to go her way after her hospital experience. For a few years, they shared a hand-to-mouth existence. They lived in a gospel car plastered with Bible verses and slogans—WHERE WILL YOU SPEND ETERNITY? and JESUS SAVES—and loaded with religious tracts.

In the summer of 1917 Aimee began issuing *The Bridal Call*, a monthly magazine that mobilized her scattered following into a network of supporters and began attracting the attention of the press.

But neither adoring crowds nor a friendly press could heal a growing rift between husband and wife. After a short preaching stint, Harold McPherson quietly filed for divorce.

Still Aimee was on the upswing. In 1918 she accepted an invitation to preach on the other side of the country. The automobile trip to Los Angeles was an adventure only a handful of intrepid women had undertaken before her. All along the way, she preached, distributed tracts, and visited small congregations.

From Los Angeles in 1919, McPherson launched a series of meetings that catapulted her to fame. Within a year, the largest auditoriums in America's largest cities could not hold the crowds that flocked to hear her. She acquiesced to popular demand that she pray for the sick, and "stretcher days" became hallmarks of her campaigns.

Reporters marveled at her oratorical skills: "Never did I hear such language from a human being. Without one moment's intermission, she would talk from an hour to an hour and a half, holding her audience spellbound." Pastors from many denominations threw their support behind her city-wide campaigns. In 1922, her ministry took her to Australia, the first of a number of trips abroad.

Motherly Pastor

On January 1, 1923, McPherson dedicated Angelus Temple, which held up to 5,300 worshipers. The ceremonies included hundreds of colorfully clad gypsies (who had named her their queen), a roster of prominent Protestant preachers, and thousands of adoring fans. With a permanent pulpit, new possibilities quickly became realities: a church-owned radio station was launched in 1924, and her Bible school moved into its own building in 1925.

"Sister" (as she was fondly referred to) was a citizen of note in a burgeoning city. Angelus Temple floats won prizes in Rose Bowl parades, and the Temple itself became a tourist attraction. Sister's comings and goings from the city's Union Station drew more people than had the visits of presidents and other visiting dignitaries.

Well-advertised illustrated sermons offered the faithful who shunned nearby Hollywood entertainments a taste of theater. Parades, uniforms, award-winning bands, catchy music, and programs for all ages enlisted people's participation. Ambitious programs to feed the hungry and respond to natural disasters gained goodwill.

Popular demand quickly overwhelmed her. People stood in line for hours for seats. A prayer room was open around the clock, and daytime services accommodated those who wanted to "tarry" for baptism in the Holy Spirit.

Kidnapped?

But hints of problems lay just beneath this flourishing façade. Some complained about Minnie Kennedy exercising too much financial control; others, about her theology (not distinctly Pentecostal; too ecumenical). But the storm that left permanent damage broke in May of 1926.

As Sister later told it, she was kidnapped on Tuesday afternoon, May 26, from the beach near Santa Monica and spirited away to a cabin were she was held prisoner.

That evening, Minnie Kennedy appeared in Sister's place, led the lively singing, and narrated the slide show. Only at the end of the service did she say that Sister had gone for a swim, failed to return, and was presumed drowned. "Sister is gone," she concluded. "We know she is with Jesus."

For the next few days, Los Angeles talked of little else. Thousands walked aimlessly on the Ocean Park Beach where Sister had last been seen. Police devised contingency plans for crowd control if Sister's body were retrieved. An elaborate memorial service was held for McPherson on June 20.

Three days later, Sister reappeared in Douglas, Arizona, with a tale of having escaped from kidnappers. The crowds that had mourned her loss prepared a lavish welcome home. On Saturday, June 26, 150,000 lined the route from the train station to Angelus Temple, cheering and wishing Sister well.

But some law enforcement officials challenged her kidnapping story. Charges and countercharges swirled until December when the Los Angeles district attorney acknowledged that he had no case against McPherson. On her daily radio shows, she presented herself as victim—of kidnappers, of a corrupt law enforcement system, of the press, and of hostile clergy.

Popular Even in Decline

Sister continued her ministry, but her appeal was less universal and more tied to her version of Pentecostalism. Discontent among some of the Temple faithful erupted into bitter quarrels that the local press turned into media events. She lent her name to various business schemes that failed. Serious illness also plagued her through much of the 1930s. A disastrous third marriage lasted less than two years.

Sister's most notable public achievement in the 1930s was a social program. The Angelus Temple's Commissary provided food, clothing, and other necessities to needy families—no questions asked. When the Depression hit, she added a Free Dining Hall, which supplied over 80,000 meals in its first two months of operation. (Today Angelus Temple is home to five ethnic Foursquare congregations, and the Commissary still distributes free meals.)

In the 1940s, she began barnstorming again, though she continued to battle illnesses. In September 1944, she felt well enough to address 10,000 people in the Oakland Auditorium. The next morning, her son Rolf found her unconscious in her room. Shortly before noon, Sister died of complications of kidney failure and the effects of the mixture of prescription drugs she had been taking. Sister's funeral took place on her fifty-fourth birthday, October 9, 1944. Though her popularity had shrunk significantly since the 1920s, the day before her funeral, 50,000 people filed past her coffin. ∎

—EDITH BLUMHOFER
CHRISTIAN HISTORY

years as a successful missionary in the interior of her homeland, Christine was stricken with malaria. In the fall of 1905 she accepted an invitation to rest in the United States where she became involved in ministry at the Holiness Faith Home in East Providence, Rhode Island. Through the kindness of friends, she attended a missionary conference at God's Bible School in Cincinnati, Ohio, and from there preached in various churches in the Midwest, always hoping to receive enough in offerings to return to British Guiana. She never did.

In 1907, news of the Pentecostal revival reached Sister Eckman while she was pastoring the Church of the Firstborn in East Providence. Persuaded of its authenticity, she called for a week of prayer meetings at the church and most of the congregation moved into the revival. Christine herself received the baptism of the Spirit later while visiting Elizabeth Baker and the Duncan Sisters in Rochester, New York.

She married Reuben A. Gibson in 1910, a Christian and Missionary Alliance minister who worked with her in ministry until his death in 1924. Sister Gibson opened the "School of the Prophets" that fall, and in 1936, the name of the school was changed to Zion Bible Institute. Succeeding Gibson was Leonard Heroo, followed by Mary Campbell Wilson, another influential Pentecostal educator. Sister Esther Rollins was a faithful Pentecostal pioneer who taught at Zion for fifty years and educated hundreds of Pentecostal pastors and missionaries. In 1985 Dr. Benjamin Crandall took the reins of the growing school. Himself a 1945 graduate of Zion, he is the son of a Pentecostal pioneer to New York City, Mary Crandall.

Nora Chambers. Perhaps not so well known yet a strategic link in the advancement of Pentecostalism were scores of women Bible teachers. Nora I. Chambers (1883–1953), for example, was an early evangelist, scholar, and teacher who inspired and instructed future leaders, especially in the Church of God (Cleveland, Tenn.). Charles Conn, Church of God superintendent and historian, described her as "a woman of rare intelligence, ability, and, for that early day, education." This remarkable woman was the first teacher in the school that today is Lee College.

Post–World War II Opportunities for Women

Following the Second World War, the latter rain revival and the healing revival gave new impetus to Spirit-filled women. Whereas the former revival reinstated the prophetic gift into languishing Pentecostalism, the second revived the emphasis on divine healing. Both prophesying and healing had been integral parts of early Pentecostalism, but with time they had seriously diminished. The 1930s and 1940s have been described as a time when "the depth of worship and the operation of the gifts of the Spirit so much in evidence in earlier decades was not so prominent."[16] With revival, however, came emphasis on the inner life of the Spirit and anointing as the criterion for service, as well as a resurgence of women in positions of influence. Also, because these revivals occurred primarily outside the established Pentecostal denominations, those gifted women were not bound by institutional restraints. Nevertheless, because the social concerns and theological elements that had advanced women at the turn of the century had subsided or vanished, women were not as prominent as they had been in the first and second decades of Pentecostalism.

Women of the Latter Rain Revival. The latter rain revival started in Sharon Bible School in North Battleford, Saskatchewan, Canada, as a result of spiritual hunger aroused in faculty members who had attended the healing crusades of William Branham in Vancouver in the fall of 1947. By February 1948 the heavens had opened and a mighty revival had began. From the outset, prophecy was the chief feature of the revival. Among those at the forefront was Myrtle D. Beall (1896–1979), pastor of Bethesda Missionary Temple in Detroit, which in 1948 became the center of revival. Joining Mrs. Beall were Ivan and Minnie Spencer, who brought Elim Bible Institute in Lima, New York, into the movement. As fruit of the revival, hundreds of women, anointed and loosed to minister by the Spirit, once again came to the forefront, some preaching and teaching under their own gospel tents. As the revival waned, many of these women faded into obscurity.

Women of the Healing Revival. The healing revival also brought women to center stage, albeit on a limited scale. Initially the awakening revolved around the phenomenal healing ministry of William Branham and was orchestrated by Gordon Lindsay through the *Voice of Healing*. As the revival waned, an emphasis on missions surfaced, and the name was changed to Christ for the Nations. In 1973 when Lindsay died, his widow, Freda Lindsay (b. 1914), came to the helm of the ministry. She remained one of the most influential, Spirit-filled women of the latter part of the century, overseeing one of the largest Pentecostal missionary organizations in the world. Also strategically involved in teaching at Christ for the Nations Institute for several years was Pauline E. Parham (b. 1909), daughter-in-law of Charles and Sarah Parham.

Freda Lindsay (1914–) preached along with her husband, Gordon Lindsay, until his death in 1973. Afterward she edited the *Voice of Healing* magazine and headed the Christ For the Nations Institute in Dallas, Texas.

T. L. and Daisy Osborn. A prominent ministry couple who emerged as leaders of this revival were T. L. and Daisy Osborn. Although T. L. was the dominant member of this team during the initial twenty-five years, Daisy was the chief administrator and innovator of the ministry. She organized mass crusades in more than seventy nations and introduced the missionary motion picture as a tool to educate American Pentecostals about missions.

In the mid-seventies Daisy noticed that Spirit-filled women were not as involved in ministry and leadership as she had once known them to be. Consequently, as a highly anointed administrator and preacher, she pioneered efforts to elevate the status of women through offering interpretive approaches to difficult passage in the Bible. With the enthusiastic support of her husband, Dr. Daisy proclaimed the "Jesus message" in national and international crusades throughout Africa, Asia, and North and South America until her death in 1995. During this period, she also wrote *Woman Without Limits, The Woman Believer,* and *5 Choices for Women Who Win.*

Through her example and encouragement of women in emerging nations, Daisy reinvigorated Spirit-filled women around the world, including Margaret Idahosa in Benin City, Nigeria, who chairs Christian Women's International Fellowship, one of the largest Spirit-filled women's groups in the world. It mobilizes women in ministry.

Women of the Charismatic Renewal

Evidence of a major Spirit-oriented revival became increasingly apparent in the late 1960s and throughout the 1970s. This revival ignited an interest in things of the Spirit in mainline Protestant denominations, gave new dynamic to the Roman Catholics, and rejuvenated the languishing Pentecostals. The 1977 Kansas City Conference provided some indication that women were again accepted in aspects of leadership. Among those addressing plenary sessions was Dr. Pauline E. Parham. In most cases, however, the prominence women had known in early Pentecostalism was all but absent.

This relative absence of women in strategic leadership was no doubt due to several factors. The charismatics tended to come from the established, traditional denominations that had not experienced the gradual elevation and liberation of women during the previous 250 years. Nevertheless, anointed women were accepted because of the respect for the Holy Spirit's anointing obvious on their lives and ministries. They were, however, normally relegated to "laity" status under supervision in patriarchal structures, perhaps because, as in most revival movements, the new, reviving experience of the Spirit was simply added to the existing theological perspectives. In the structures of traditional Christianity, women simply were not promoted. An additional element that restricted women during this era was the theological emphasis of the discipleship movement, which included teaching on "covering," authoritative male "headship," and strict submission and subordination of women.

Nevertheless, hosts of Spirit-filled women constituted a tremendous groundswell in the charismatic movement. These women greatly enlarged the churches dominated by male leadership, with some starting women's organizations. In a few cases, the anointing was sufficiently strong to thrust women through the normal restraints, enabling them to minister to general audiences. In other cases, mature women from the Pentecostal revival were comfortable in positions of leadership and saw their established ministries take on wider significance.

Dr. Cho's Encounter with God

The largest church in the world in the closing days of the 20th century was Yoido Full Gospel Church, pastored by Yongii Cho in Seoul, South Korea. Following the devastating war of the 1950s a Pentecostal revival flowered, bringing hope and prosperity to the nation. As Cho's congregation began to grow, he sought the Lord about how to manage it. He had a conversation with God that forever changed his attitude about women. He writes,

The Lord began to speak to me: "Yongii Cho, from whom was I born?"

"From a woman, Lord," I responded.

"And on whose lap was I nurtured?"

"Woman, Lord."

"And who followed me throughout my ministry and helped to meet my needs?"

"Women," I said.

"Who stayed until the last minutes of my crucifixion?"

"Women."

"And who came to anoint my body in the tomb?"

"The women."

"Who were the first witnesses to my resurrection?"

"Mary Magdalene, a woman."

"To all my questions you have answered, 'Woman.' Then why are you afraid of women? During my earthly ministry I was surrounded by dear, wonderful women. So why shouldn't my body, the Church, be surrounded and supported by women as well?"

"What else could I do? The Lord had made it clear to me that it was His will to use women in the Church."[17]

Thus to his surprise and to the dismay of the men of the congregation, Cho announced that he would mobilize the women as cell-group pastors. This was the spark that ignited the phenomenal explosion. At the close of the century, 90 percent of the more than fifty thousand cell leaders were women, and 90 percent of the phenomenal church growth was coming through the cell groups.

Women of the Prayer Movement

In addition to the cell-group ministry that facilitated women, Cho's ministry birthed the prayer movement of the closing days of the 20th century. This must, in fact, be credited to Cho's mother-in-law, Jashil Choi, who conceived the now-popular idea of Prayer Mountain. Her retreat center for prayer and fasting on the edge of the buffer zone between North and South Korea has served not only as a bastion of prayer, but also as a prototype for similar ministries around the world.

The prayer movement in the 1990s found many leaders among Spirit-filled women. Teacher and writer Billie Brim, for example, operates Prayer Mountain near Branson, Missouri. Cindy Jacobs, another prominent leader in prayer, is cofounder with her husband of Generals of Intercession in Colorado Springs, Colorado. She is also the U.S. coordinator of C. Peter Wagner's Spiritual Warfare Network.

Women's Aglow Fellowship International

In the charismatic era, many gifted women started groups in which women could encourage and strengthen one another in the faith. Perhaps best known of these is Women's Aglow Fellowship International, which began in 1967 as a "women's version of the Full Gospel Business Men's Fellowship." According to Aglow literature, its purpose is to lead women to Jesus Christ and to provide opportunity for Christian women to grow in their faith and minister to others. Respectful of the prevailing doctrine of male authoritative headship, Aglow developed a structure that gave women freedom under the direction of male advisers. This gave Aglow favor with the charismatic leaders and churches while giving women an opportunity for leadership growth and development. According to international president Jane Hansen, in the closing decade of the century, "God gave the organization three mandates: reconciliation, reaching the Islamic world, and evangelizing the inner city."[18]

Women in the Healing Ministry

Some Spirit-filled women in the charismatic era experienced an unquestionably powerful anointing for public ministry and had the administrative skills to develop their own ministries. Best-known of these renowned ministers was Katherine Kuhlman (1907–76), whose tremendous healing crusades filled the largest arenas in the land, especially after 1965.

Another highly anointed woman who came to prominence with a public healing ministry in the charismatic renewal was Vicki Jamison-Peterson (b. 1936). Grounded in the word of faith message and blessed with an evangelistic anointing, she continues to be remarkably effective in igniting revival, particularly in the "hard ground" of New England. There her meetings have led to the establishing of several new congregations.

Kathryn Kuhlman (1907–76) became the first woman healing evangelist to command a nationwide television audience. Her crusades later influenced younger evangelists such as Benny Hinn.

Women of Wisdom and Experience

Outstanding women leaders with roots in various aspects of classic Pentecostalism experienced fresh impetus during the charismatic era. Since then, their influence has increased, in part due to their wisdom and staying power, in part due to their unquestionably powerful anointing, and in part due to their natural gifts and talents. Their influence now stretches deep into the nations.

Gwen Shaw. The most influential of these is Sister Gwen Shaw (b. 1924), founder of End-Time Handmaidens and Servants (est. 1973) and the first woman to speak in the famous Baptist Church in Moscow in 1966. Sister Gwen, as she is fondly called, is a Canadian-born, birthright Mennonite who experienced Pentecost in 1942. God called her to China while she was a young student at Eastern Pentecostal Bible College, Toronto, Canada, in January 1944. By 1947, she was ministering in Inner Mongolia to her "first love," the Chinese people. After barely escaping the advancing Communist forces of the revolution, Gwen continued to minister in the Orient for twenty-three years from her base in Hong Kong. God has used this humble yet distinguished woman of faith and compassion to light revival fires

KATHRYN KUHLMAN (1907–76)

THE WORLD'S MOST WIDELY KNOWN FEMALE EVANGELIST
AFTER WORLD WAR II

After completing the tenth grade—all that was offered—Kathryn Kuhlman began her ministry at age sixteen, assisting her sister and brother-in-law. She was soon on her own, itinerating in Idaho, Utah, and Colorado, finally settling down in Denver in 1933 in the Kuhlman Revival Tabernacle. By 1935 she had built the 2,000-seat Denver Revival Tabernacle. She effectively used the media and established an influential radio ministry. Her marriage to an evangelist, who divorced his wife to marry Kuhlman, destroyed her Denver ministry. They continued to evangelize, but apparently after about six years—she was silent on the subject—she left him and started over again on her own.

In 1946 in Franklin, Pennsylvania, a woman was suddenly healed of a tumor during one of Kuhlman's services. This was to develop as a characteristic phenomena of the "miracle services." Kuhlman would call out the specific disorder that was being cured in a certain area of the auditorium, and it would be received by the appropriate individual. She again developed a daily radio ministry. In 1948 she moved to Pittsburgh, which remained her headquarters as she held regular services in Carnegie Hall and the First Presbyterian Church. She was catapulted toward national fame by a seven-page laudatory article in *Redbook* magazine.

From California in 1965 came the insistent invitation of Ralph Wilkerson of Anaheim Christian Center (later Melodyland). She began services at the Pasadena Civic Auditorium, which seated 2,500, but later moved to the Los Angeles Shrine Auditorium, where she regularly filled the 7,000 seats for ten years. She also continued the Pittsburgh meetings while expanding into television, producing more than five hundred telecasts for the CBS network. In 1972 she received the first honorary doctorate awarded by Oral Roberts University.

It was not until the mid-1960s that Kuhlman became particularly identified with the charismatic movement. The older Pentecostals out of the holiness tradition found her twice suspect: She was a divorcee, and she did not satisfy them by giving testimony in her ministry to any personal experience of speaking in tongues. She did not permit tongues in the regular course of the miracle services.

Kuhlman objected to the appellation "faith healer" and gave the credit to the power of the Holy Spirit. Believing that gifts of healing were for the sick, the only gift she claimed, if any at all, was that of "faith" or "the word of knowledge" (1 Cor. 12:8–9). She had no explanation of why some were healed and some not, but she emphasized that the greater miracle was the regeneration of the new birth and always referred to herself as an evangelist.

Apart from the well-documented healings, the most sensational phenomena associated with Kuhlman was "going under the power" (sometimes referred to as being "slain in the Spirit") as people fell when she prayed for them. This sometimes happened to dozens at a time and occasionally hundreds.

Kuhlman was an incessant worker and gave meticulous attention to every detail of her services; everything had to be first-class. Conducting them herself, she was on her feet for four to five hours at a time. She was very dramatic in gesture and consciously deliberate in speech. She was a strikingly tall redhead and dressed elegantly. Her friend and biographer Jamie Buckingham admits: "She loved her expensive clothes, precious jewels, luxury hotels, and first class travel." She was a star, even until her death just short of her seventieth birthday. ∎

—D. J. WILSON IN *DICTIONARY OF PENTECOSTAL AND CHARISMATIC MOVEMENTS* in nation after nation for the past forty-five years. Particularly, beginning in 1973 she experienced a specific assignment from the Lord to encourage women in their callings. She cried out to God in prayer for ten thousand women who would totally surrender to Him and reach the world for Jesus in the power of the Holy Spirit. As a result, her annual summer convention is attended by thousands of men and women from countless nations. A well-educated, prolific writer, publisher, songwriter, and preacher, Sister Gwen continues to go to the world from her base in Engeltal, Jasper, Arkansas.

Fuschia Pickett. The influx of new believers and biblical illiterates during the charismatic renewal provided an unlimited opportunity for Pentecostal/charismatic teachers. Among these were mature, gifted women who, from a vast wealth of knowledge and experience, could teach and write. An outstanding example of this is Dr. Fuschia Pickett (b. 1918), a well-educated theologian, administrator, teacher, and writer with thirteen books to her credit. At the height of the charismatic renewal, Dr. Pickett founded Fountain Gate Bible College (est. 1974) and Church (est. 1971) in Plano, Texas. In 1988, she passed her mantle to Dr. Sam Sasser and began to travel throughout the nation as a "Mother in Israel," helping churches and ministers. Dr. Pickett began to develop Christian leadership on a wider scale through existing Bible schools, writing, and involvement with Strang Communications. Through this prestigious charismatic publishing company, she helped launch *Spirit Led Women* magazine during the final years of the century.

Spirit-Filled Women in the Media

Radio. Perhaps no other factor gave prominence to Spirit-filled women in the 20th century like the media, especially radio, television, and satellite technology. The first license for a Christian radio station was issued by the Federal Communications Commission in 1924 to Aimee Semple McPherson for KFSG (Los Angeles). Suddenly a woman's voice was preaching the gospel publicly and yet within the privacy of the home. This was a small but significant beginning for women in Christian media.

Television. Women such as Tammy Fay Bakker (b. 1940) of the PTL Television Network (est. 1974) and Jan Crouch, cofounder of the Trinity Broadcasting Network (est. 1973), have been pioneers in this field. Other highly esteemed women leaders who have gained international fame and favor through this media are Marilyn Hickey (b. 1931) and Joyce Meyer. In addition to their daily telecasts, they sell countless books and other teaching tools. Marilyn founded Word to the World College in Denver in 1981.

She regularly ministers overseas to the masses and to heads of state. Joyce, with ministry headquarters in Fenton, Missouri, ministers extensively in churches and hosts large conferences in major cities of America.

Video and Satellite. The technological revolution that became popular around 1980 opened a whole new way of reaching and teaching. Word of Faith Bible College (est. 1979) in Dallas, Texas, was the pioneer in video Bible schools. By videotaping the lessons at its home base, the school was able to reproduce and provide them in a packaged curriculum for local churches who otherwise could not provide high-quality Bible teaching on a regular basis for their hungry constitutents. The first and only woman to participate as a regular Bible teacher in this school was Valarie Owen. Through this media, she taught thousands of students in hundreds of schools around the globe, and when the Bible school switched to live satellite communication in 1983, Valarie was the first and only woman to teach Bible school regularly via satellite across America and Canada.

By the end of the century, Joyce Meyer's teaching telecasts were broadcast around the nation and the world. She also filled the largest arenas in the nation.

Women at the Close of the 20th Century

The Internet

As the Internet became a primary means of communication in the latter 1990s, Spirit-filled women were ready. Many women and women's groups, once isolated by geography, took advantage of the unlimited freedom to teach and minister via Web sites, chat rooms, and E-mail without the restraints of time or space. Of particular note is God's Word to Women (www.godswordtowomen.org), operated by three Texas women who are encouraging and teaching women around the world on a personal level. Barbara Collins (b. 1935), former dean of student affairs and faculty member at Dr. Pickett's Fountain Gate Bible College, joined forces with Patricia Joyce (b. 1938) and Gay Anderson (b. 1933) to provide a comprehensive yet personal communications link for Spirit-filled women. This innovative site draws its name and much of its theological position from Dr. Katherine Bushnell's classic book *God's Word to Women*. As a result, the classic work of Dr. Bushnell is now reaching the nations.

Women and Revival Fire

As a "third wave" of Spirit-filled revival swept the world in the final decade of the 20th century, the Spirit again lifted many women to prominence. A revival broke out in January 1994 in the Vineyard congregation of John and Carol Arnott of Toronto, Canada. Known as the "Toronto Blessing," the revival meetings soon became the leading tourist attraction of Toronto, and almost immediately the "blessing" spread around the world. In this revival, Carol Arnott is equally prominent with her husband and commands equal respect from revivalgoers. Other parts of the ministry and revival also reflect this respect for women. Fred Wright, coordinator of Partners-in-Harvest, the loose ministerial fellowship arm of Toronto Airport Christian Fellowship, has publically apologized to the women of the revival for the abuse and mistreatment of the historic church through the centuries. TACF Women's Director and founder of Releasers of Life Ministries, Mary Audrey Raycroft, now teaches around the world on a regular basis. She is helping raise up a confident, healed, biblically literate, end-time host of revival women in the nations of the world.

Spirit-Filled Women Scholars

During the last decade of the century as well, women began attending and graduating from seminaries in record numbers. Spirit-filled women found open doors at such accredited institutions as Oral Roberts University, Regent University, Assemblies of God Theological Seminary, the Church of God Graduate School of Theology, and Fuller Theological Seminary. Leading women scholars include Drs. Edith Blumhoffer, Cheryl Bridges-Johns, Rebecca Patten, and Priscilla Benham, who have also taken leadership responsibilities in the Society for Pentecostal Studies. Another academic society specifically encouraging educated women as well as confronting the domestic abuse crisis in Christian homes is Christians for Biblical Equality. Although primarily an evangelical society, a large number of Pentecostal and charismatic women became an integral part of this rapidly growing organization in the closing days of the century.

Problems and Solutions for Spirit-Filled Women

In the final decade of the 20th century, many Spirit-filled women struggled with the discrepancy between the experiential call of the Spirit to leadership and the restraining elements of existing structures. Consequently, many educated, Spirit-filled women began to uncover the activity of the Spirit in history, which repeatedly and consistently brought women to liberty, equality, and confidence in Christ. Others diligently studied the Scriptures and the culture of New Testament times to uncover accurate renderings of difficult passages in an effort to harmonize the experience of the Spirit and their understanding of the Word. Spirit-filled women believe that the Word, accurately interpreted, and the activity of the Spirit agree. It appears that a century has brought Spirit-filled women full circle; they found themselves having to recover in 1999 what they had in 1901.

God's Women

At strategic times in salvation history, God has chosen women and empowered them with His Spirit to carry out His will in extraordinary ways. He chose Mary to give birth to the Savior. He chose another Mary to be the first apostle to proclaim the Good News of His resurrection. And He chose women in the early church to pastor, teach, and proclaim the gospel. Women were coworkers with the apostle Paul and joint-heirs together with Christ and their brothers in the faith. And at the dawn of the greatest revival since the Day of Pentecost, He bestowed on a humble woman— Agnes Ozman—the privilege and responsibility of being the first to experience and proclaim the Pentecostal baptism of the Spirit in the 20th century. Throughout the century, He called countless women and empowered them to fulfill both humble and high-profile assignments. In the 20th century, Spirit-filled women began to discover that these women were not exceptions to God's plan, but instead were His prototypes for God's woman.

For Further Reading

A good starting place for the story of women in the Pentecostal tradition is Edith Blumhofer's *Pentecost in My Soul* (Springfield: Gospel Publishing House, 1989). A more comprehensive treatment can be found in Susan C. Hyatt's *In the Spirit We're Equal: The Spirit, The Bible and Women—A Revival Perspective* (Dallas: Hyatt Press, 1998). For the beginnings of a holiness theology of women in ministry see Phoebe Palmer's *The Promise of the Father* (Boston: Henry V. Degen, 1859).

Many women are featured in Stanley M. Burgess, ed., and Eduard M. van der Maas, assoc. ed., *New International Dictionary of Pentecostal and Charismatic Movements* (Grand Rapids: Zondervan, 2001). Histories that deal with Pentecostal women ministers include: Carl Brumback, *A Sound from Heaven* (Springfield: Gospel Publishing House, 1977); Edith Blumhofer *The Assemblies of God: A Chapter in the Story of American Pentecostalism,* 2 vols. (Springfield, Mo.: Gospel Publishing House, 1989); and Vinson Synan, *The Holiness-Pentecostal Tradition* (Grand Rapids: Eerdmans, 1997).

Books on Aimee Semple McPherson include: Edith Blumhofer's *Aimee Semple McPherson: Everybody's Sister* (Grand Rapids: Eerdmans, 1991; and Daniel Epstein's *Sister Aimee: The Life of Aimee Semple McPherson* (New York: Harcourt Brace Jovanovich, 1993). A sympathetic book on Kathryn Kuhlman is Jamie Buckingham's *Daughter of Destiny: Kathryn Kuhlman . . . Her Story* (Plainfield, N.J.: Logos International, 1976). A more balanced biography is Wayne Warner's *Kathryn Kuhlman: The Woman Behind the Miracles* (Minneapolis, Minn.: Fortress Press, 1994).

· 11 ·
African-American Pentecostalism in the 20th Century

David Daniels III

Throughout the 20th century, black Pentecostalism has been a vital movement within American Pentecostalism and Christianity. It has been instrumental in creating new options in religious music, social ethics, community ministry, preaching, and theology. As a tradition it has undergone three distinct phases. It erupted as a renewal movement alongside the black holiness movement with a vision of reforming the black church. This initial phase was followed by the marginalization of Pentecostalism within the black church and black Pentecostalism attracting adherents from the marginalized communities of the black poor and working class.

During the last quarter of the 20th century, black Pentecostalism found prominence as a religious preference of the members within the new black middle class. This era also marked black Pentecostalism's garnering of a popular image as a fresh spirituality and worship style. Across the United States, black Pentecostal congregations are counted among the largest churches as well as the most numerous set of congregations in myriad suburban and inner-city communities. Black Pentecostalism has entered its second century as a major tradition within the black church and American Christianity.

Black Pentecostalism counts within its ranks denominations and fellowships whose leadership reflects a cross section of perspectives on politics, religious culture, gender relations, theology, and ministry. Black Pentecostalism is constituted by this diversity. This diversity is a product of the African-American movements that participated in the construction of Pentecostalism itself as well as black Pentecostalism. These different trajectories intersected within black Pentecostalism, creating various denominational streams with a common focus on Scripture, conversion, the baptism in the Holy Spirit, and other themes. While the diversity within black Pentecostalism encompasses many variations, this chapter will explore only the two major competing positions for the sake of brevity.

Pentecostalism emerged during the 20th century as a major presence within the African-American community that created a host of new congregations and denominations as well as transformed the religious life of historic black denominations. Pentecostalism remains distinct among Christian movements in the United States for being a major community in which African-American Christian movements intersected with white American Christian movements along with Hispanics and others in constructing Pentecostalism as a religious tradition. From its origins Pentecostalism has been an interracial and multicultural expression of Christianity.

The Black Holiness Movement

African-American Pentecostalism started as a movement basically within the black holiness movement, a movement that paralleled and intersected with the larger white holiness movement in the United States. Black holiness leaders, holiness prayer and Bible groups, and congregations formed their holiness movement during the aftermath of the Civil War. The precursors to the movement were leaders who espoused the holiness doctrine and experience at the advent of the 19th century. Jarena Lee, a member of Richard Allen's congregation and an early African Methodist female preacher, testified to receiving the holiness experience as early as 1808. She identified William Scott, an African-American, as the person who introduced her to the holiness message. Other antebellum African-American female preachers were Zilpha Elaw, Julia Foote, and Sojourner Truth, the abolitionist. Daniel Alexander Payne, Joseph C. Price, and Isaac Lane led the ranks among African-American clergy, and Amanda Berry Smith led among women evangelists.[1]

The black holiness movement consisted of interlocking regional movements clustered around Virginia, Pennsylvania, Missouri, North and South Carolina, the mid-South (Mississippi, Tennessee, Arkansas, Alabama), and the Michigan-Ohio area. These regional movements attracted adherents from Methodist and Baptist churches. Methodists led the movement in the North and Southeast for the most part, while Baptists dominated the movement in the mid-South.

One source for nondenominational congregations being introduced into the black church were African-American leaders within the Church of God (Anderson, Ind.), a biracial holiness movement led by Daniel Warner. African-Americans began founding their own holiness denominations in 1867 with the establishment of the Zion Union Apostolic Church in Virginia under the leadership of James R. Howell, a minister in the African Methodist Episcopal Zion Church (AMEZ).[2]

The Philadelphia revival of 1877 secured a place for the black holiness movement within the black church of the 19th century. This revival started at Bethel African Methodist Episcopal Church, the historic pulpit of Richard Allen, during the pastorate of George C. Whitfield. Whitfield inaugurated his pastoral appointment to Bethel in June of 1877, preaching holiness sermons and scheduling an all-day holiness conference for the twentieth of that month. The all-day conference exemplified the tenor of the Philadelphia revival by being biracial, interdenominational, and affirming female religious leadership.

Represented at the conference were African-Americans from the local Episcopal, Baptist, Presbyterian, and Methodist churches. Whitfield invited as conference speakers prominent local African-American clergy, such as Redding B. Johns, pastor of First African Presbyterian Church, and Theophilius Gould, former pastor of Bethel AMEC.

Also invited were white holiness clergy of national stature, such as John S. Inskip, president of the National Camp Meeting for the Promotion of Holiness; E. I. D. Pepper, editor of the *Christian Standard;* and William MacDonald. The key congregations of the revival besides Bethel AMEC were First African Presbyterian Church, pastored by Redding B. Johns, and Union American Methodist Episcopal Church, pastored by Lorenzo D. Blackstone.[3]

Among AMEC (African Methodist Episcopal Church) ministers in the Philadelphia vicinity the holiness message became the norm. At the August session of the local AMEC Preachers Association in 1877, the holiness experience became the topic of discussion. Each of the twelve ministers present defined himself in reference to the holiness doctrine. These ministers included some of the leading AMEC clergy within the nation, including Jabez P. Campbell, Benjamin Tanner, Henry McNeal Turner, and Levi Coppin. Nine ministers testified to having the holiness experience: R. Barney, Jabez P. Campbell, W. H. Davis, Theophilus Gould, H. H. Lewis, L.

Patterson, W. H. Stiles, Benjamin Tanner, and J. S. Thompson. The two dissenters from the group were Henry McNeal Turner and Levi Coppin. C. C. Felts shared that he was seeking the holiness experience. Turner defined the holiness experience as a "gradual work" in contrast to the majority who defined it as instantaneous. Coppin acknowledged only the experience of conversion and "nothing else."

The involvement of Campbell, Tanner, and Whitfield gave the movement strong institutional support within AMEC in Philadelphia, given Campbell's status as a bishop, Tanner's influence as editor of the national weekly the *Christian Recorder*, and Whitfield's position as pastor of historic Bethel Church. Holiness meetings were held in AMEC congregations in Chester, Germantown, and other areas around Philadelphia as well as in western Pennsylvania.[4]

The Philadelphia revival lasted from 1877 to 1879, the year when George Whitfield died. In addition to Whitfield's death, the leadership of the Philadelphia holiness movement suffered with the removal of Blackstone from his pastorate and the resignation of Johns from his position. Holiness meetings sponsored by these congregations ceased as suddenly as they had begun. Even Bethel's holiness meetings were discontinued after being banned by the congregation's officers. Holiness meetings in Philadelphia continued only in homes or at street rallies while leadership shifted from prominent pastors to the laypeople.

Eventually, public holiness meetings started to reappear within congregations and other venues. Under Whitfield's successor at Bethel, Levi Coppin, holiness meetings were again permitted at the church. Zion Wesley AMEC initiated its first holiness meeting ever with semimonthly meetings. Holiness meetings were being sponsored weekly at Benezeb Hall, a public auditorium. The Philadephia revival of 1877 had advanced the holiness movement within the African Methodist Episcopal Church more than any other event.[5]

The second major event evolved during the bishopric of T. M. D. Ward. The North Missouri AMEC Conference by 1881 "resolved to go out and preach the gospel of holiness." Besides Ward, leaders in this campaign included James Taylor and A. W. Talbert. Rev. James W. Taylor and Bishop T. M. D. Ward led the holiness movement within the AMEC in Missouri by 1881. Taylor had received the holiness experience at a camp meeting in 1877, and Ward publicly announced his support of the holiness message in 1880. A. W. Talbert pastored a congregation in the Washington, Missouri, area.

While George Whitfield was the most prominent AMEC pastor to promote holiness, Amanda Berry Smith was the most prominent individual to cultivate interest in holiness within the AMEC. Her ministry took her around the world. She preached in Europe, Asia, and Africa in addition to the United States during the late 19th century.

Other women leaders were Sister Callund, Emma Williams, and Emily Calkins. A Sister Callund who had attended the school at Bethel AMEC in Philadelphia and preached a holiness message to the congregation in 1878 conducted an evangelistic tour in the western United States. Emma Williams, an AMEC holiness preacher who relocated from the North to the South, returned north as part of a building fund campaign for a congregation in the South; she had already completed three church-building projects. Thus these women intersected their holiness ministries with the Philadelphia movement. Emily Calkins Stevens, a native of New Jersey, began serving as an AMEC evangelist in North and South Carolina in 1882. Stevens received the holiness experience in 1853 and began preaching in 1868.[6]

The holiness message also spread to black congregations in Virginia and North Carolina during the early 1880s. The Boydton Institute in Boydton, Virginia, a town near the Virginia–North Carolina state line, served as a center for the promotion of holiness. In 1881 nearly the entire student body of 104 African-Americans sought the holiness experience and large numbers received it. These students became schoolteachers and ministers throughout the region.

During the late 1880s and the early 1890s, North Carolina black holiness congregations formed in the Raleigh, Wilmington, Durham, and Clinton areas. According to Henry Fisher, a later participant, in 1886 a holiness revival began in a home in Method, located outside of Raleigh. A small but devoted number of African-Americans embraced holiness. In Wilmington during November 1892, Elijah Lowney of Cleveland, Ohio, an ex–Methodist minister, conducted a holiness revival at First Baptist Church. Lowney attracted a biracial and interdenominational following.

The holiness revival outgrew First Baptist and moved to the Sam Jones Tabernacle, accommodating about four thousand people. From the revival a black holiness congregation was formed. At this place, a local AMEC preacher received the holiness experience and became the leader. By 1895, C. J. Wilcox, a member of the Lowney team, formed another black holiness congregation in the area. A few years later, W. H. Fulford, who belonged to the biracial Fire-Baptized Holiness Church, conducted a successful holiness revival in Wilmington to a biracial audience. During the 1890s, black holiness congregations were also formed in Sampson County, around Clinton and Turkey. During October 1894 the Raleigh group joined with a Durham group to sponsor a convocation.[7]

In September 1900, C. J. Wilcox, Joseph Silver, and John Scott, holiness ministers in the Wilmington area, organized the Union Holiness Convention. By September 1900, P. N. Marable of Clinton and W. C. Carlton of Turkey, both local clergy and schoolteachers, organized the Big Kahara Holiness Association, although some people in holiness circles advocated that holiness people remain in congregations of established denominations, opposing forming separate congregations. On October 13, 1900, the Raleigh and Durham groups united to organize a holiness denomination, the Holy Church of North Carolina. On October 15, 1900, the holiness groups clustered around Raleigh, Wilmington, and Durham united to form the Holy Church of North Carolina and Virginia, with W. H. Fulford serving as president from 1901 to 1916.

Among the Colored Methodist Episcopal churches (later renamed the Christian Methodist Episcopal Church or CME), Bishop Lucius Holsey and others preached holiness sermons in the late 19th century. During 1897 there were CME institutes in Missouri, Kentucky, and Arkansas that advertised discussions of the holiness experience. In 1903 two separate groups withdrew from the CME Church to form a holiness association and congregation, respectively. At West Lake, Louisiana, a faction organized Christ's Sanctified Holy Church. And at Jackson, Tennessee, a group withdrew under Robert E. Hart, the former pastor of Liberty Temple CME, the CME mother church. In the African Methodist Episcopal Zion Church (AMEZ), Bishop Alexander Walters preached holiness messages during the 1890s and was involved in the Christian Holiness Association. D. J. Young, an AMEZ minister, joined the holiness movement in the early 1890s and participated in events sponsored by the Burning Bush, officially known as the Metropolitan Christian Association.[8]

Independent Holiness Fellowships and Black Restorationism

Historian Charles Edwin Brown recorded that during 1886 Jane Williams and other African-Americans embraced the holiness message in Charleston, South Carolina. They were instrumental in introducing the holiness message, under the auspices of the Church of God (Anderson, Ind.), to African-Americans in other parts of South Carolina and in Michigan and Alabama. Charles Oglesby, an African-American holiness preacher, licensed Beatrice Sapp in 1891 as an evangelist in the Church of God. Sapp moved from South Carolina to Alabama afterward and was instrumental in establishing holiness congregations among African-Americans throughout the state. In 1895 she pastored a small congregation of thirty-five members in Bessemer.[9]

During the late 1890s, William E. Fuller also organized black holiness congregations in South Carolina. Fuller served on the executive committee of the biracial Fire-Baptized Holiness Church, which was organized in 1898 in Anderson, South Carolina, by Benjamin Irwin.[10]

In 1902 a faction withdrew from the major black restorationist fellowship, the Church of the Living God (Christian Fellowship for Christian Workers) founded by William Christian, and formed the Church of Living God (Apostolic Church). In 1903 another group led by Magdalena Tate separated from William Christian, organizing in Nashville, Tennessee, the Church of the Living God, the Pillar and Ground of the Truth. William Christian, who was ordained as a Baptist preacher in 1875 and led a Baptist congregation in Ft. Smith, Arkansas, established in 1888 the Church of the Living God (Christian Fellowship for Christian Workers) near Wrightsville, Arkansas.

After Christian received a revelation in 1888 that "he was preaching the doctrine of men and not of Christ," he embraced the restorationist themes of Alexander Campbell. This revelation changed Christ-

William E. Fuller (1875–1958) was a founding executive of the biracial Fire-Baptized Holiness Church in 1898.

ian's theology and preaching. It set him on a course of evaluating the Baptist faith and practice with the Scriptures as the criteria, critiquing denominational Protestantism as a corrupted religion. Christian asserted that naming churches as Baptist, Methodist, or Presbyterian was unbiblical; he felt that the church names selected should be taken from the Scriptures. He critiqued the conversion process in revivalistic churches, proposing to substitute biblical repentance for the emphasis on godly sorrow and "getting religion." Christian withdrew from the Baptist communion to form his Bible-based fellowship, which by 1898 had approximately ninety congregations or ministries in eleven states, including the Indian Territory.[11]

Christian's new biblical preaching included race consciousness. In response to the theory that Africans descended from beasts and not from the biblical Adam, Christian defended the humanity of African peoples on biblical grounds. He taught that Adam was the father of the Hebrews, the Hebrews were the original black peoples, and that from these black people Jesus Christ descended. He argued that Europeans and Asians were humans who came from another moment in creation. Christian also advocated an implicit critique of capitalism. He contended that the earth belonged to God, and land should be held in common under the control of the government, which should lease land to individuals.[12]

Within the Kentucky and Tennessee area, George and Laura Goings were instrumental in spreading the holiness message to African-Americans. The Goingses, an African-American pastoral team affiliated with a holiness church based in California, began their ministry to the region in 1897 in Slaughterville, Kentucky. There they discovered a significant holiness movement that emphasized ecclesial fellowships and opposed the formation of congregations or denominations. They also discovered a small black holiness congregation in Slaughterville, which was organized by four African-Americans in 1892 and pastored by James A. Biglow.[13]

George Goings's holiness theology included a social dimension. He rebuffed ministry to African-Americans that skirted the devastation of slavery and the injustice of their contemporary experience. He argued that the structures of the society systematically undermined all efforts of racial uplift. Furthermore, in his perspective the terrorism white Americans employed to control African-Americans deepened the crisis. The paucity of resources used to improve the plight exposed the lack of commitment of the society to African-American progress, according to Goings.[14]

The Black Holiness Movement in Baptist Churches

The dominant holiness movement among African-Americans in the mid-South emerged during the mid-1890s under the leadership of Charles Price Jones and Charles Harrison Mason. The movement took a variety of institutional forms: conferences, revivals, publications, itinerant evangelists, holiness congregations, and associations of congregations and clergy. While Mason was initially a Baptist itinerant evangelist when he embraced the holiness message, Jones was already an established Baptist pastor with pastoral experience in Arkansas and Alabama. Jones began his pastorate in 1895 at Mt. Helm Baptist Church, a prestigious college church in Jackson, Mississippi, preaching holiness sermons and conducting holiness revivals. He sponsored his first holiness convention in June 1896 at Mt. Helm. By 1897, the conference attracted a strong regional audience with participants from Mississippi, Arkansas, Louisiana, Tennessee, Alabama, Missouri, Illinois, North Carolina, and Georgia.[15]

Various Baptist congregations identified with the movement during the late 1890s. Originally two established congregations joined the movement: the most prominent congregation to embrace the holiness doctrine was Mt. Helm; the other leading congregation was Damascus Baptist Church in Hazelhurst, Mississippi, a pastorate of Walter S. Pleasant. The other congregations associated with the movement were established as holiness congregations. By 1905 ten established Baptist congregations were joined by twenty-nine new church developments to form a regional association with congregations scattered throughout the mid-South.

Within the established congregations there were often ecclesial struggles. In October 1901 Charles Price Jones and the majority of Mt. Helm lost possession of the church property to the antiholiness faction within the congregation in the courts. The legal defeat did not end Jones's ministry. In the aftermath of the loss, Jones organized Christ Temple as an independent congregation. By 1906, Christ Temple had built an edifice with a seating capacity of two thousand. On Sundays during this era, eight hundred to a thousand people worshiped at the church.[16]

The black holiness movement entered the 20th century with approximately two hundred congregations dotted across the United States. In addition to these congregations were prominent individuals like AMEC evangelist Amanda Berry Smith, Baptist home missionary Virginia Broughton, and the AMEZ Bishop Alexander Walters, who were leaders in the movement but remained in their original denominations.

The black holiness movement formed the core of black Pentecostalism with the majority of the seven major denominational families having their origins within black holiness fellowships and denominations of the late 19th century. For the most part, the first black Pentecostal denominations can be clustered into these seven denominational families:

1. United Holy Church of America
2. Church of the Living God
3. Church of God in Christ family
4. Church of God (Apostolic)
5. Fire Baptized Holiness Church of the Americas
6. Apostolic Faith Church of God
7. Pentecostal Assemblies of the World

Only the last two denominational families are in the minority, tracing their origins to the Azusa Street revival. The black holiness movement participated in the construction of American Pentecostalism and was a major source of black Pentecostalism.[17]

William J. Seymour and the Azusa Street Revival

Out of a congregation associated with the black holiness movement erupted the Azusa Street revival, the center for the emergence of Pentecostalism as a

national and international movement. In 1906 a small black holiness congregation, headed by Julia Hutchins, sponsored a revival led by William J.
Seymour. It was at this revival that the black holiness movement began to
participate in the construction of Pentecostalism and
that Pentecostalism became an international movement. Hutchins invited Seymour to Los Angeles
from Houston after he was highly recommended by
Lucy Farrow, a niece of the late Frederick Douglass.
According to historian Cecil R. Robeck, Hutchins
and the other members formed the new congregation after withdrawing from the black Second Baptist Church, which refused to embrace the holiness
message.

After hearing Seymour, Hutchins barred him from
her pulpit because of his Pentecostal interpretation of
the holiness message. However, other members of
the congregation, first Edward Lee and later Richard
Asberry, invited Seymour to resume preaching at
their respective homes. The audience continued to
outgrow the sites until Seymour secured facilities at
312 Azusa Street, the former makeshift sanctuary of
St. Stephen's AMEC (later renamed First AME). Seymour's meeting at Azusa Street, the Apostolic Faith
Mission, attracted the attention of local whites,
blacks, and Latinos, especially those involved in the
holiness community. Soon afterward representatives
of local and regional holiness groups throughout the
United States converged on Azusa Street to examine
the new teaching.[18]

William Joseph Seymour (1870–1922)
was pastor of the Azusa Street
Mission during the "glory days" of
1906 to 1909. He established
Pentecostalism as a world force.

Within twelve months, the Azusa Street revival spawned an international movement and published a monthly newspaper, the *Apostolic Faith*.
From 1906 to 1908, Seymour, the Apostolic Faith Mission, and the *Apostolic
Faith* gave the movement a major center and crucial early leadership. Like
its holiness counterpart, the Pentecostal movement was basically local and
regional with varied leaderships by women as well as men. In various
places Pentecostalism took over entire African-American holiness congregations and institutions. The Azusa Street revival defined Pentecostalism
nationally and globally, shaped its interracial relations, and gave it its multicultural character.[19]

Seymour was introduced to the Pentecostal interpretation of the holiness
message by Charles Parham. Parham popularized the linking of glossolalia

WILLIAM JOSEPH SEYMOUR

Of all the outstanding black American religious leaders in the twentieth century, one of the least recognized is William Joseph Seymour, the unsung pastor of the Azusa Street Mission in Los Angeles, and catalyst of the worldwide Pentecostal movement. Only in the last few decades have scholars become aware of his importance, beginning perhaps with Yale University historian Sidney Ahlstrom, who said Seymour personified a black piety "which exerted its greatest direct influence on American religious history," placing Seymour's impact ahead of figures like W.E.B. Dubois and Martin Luther King, Jr.

William Joseph Seymour was born in Centerville, Louisiana, on May 2, 1870 to former slaves Simon and Phyllis Seymour. Raised as a Baptist, Seymour was given to dreams and visions as a youth. At age 25, he moved to Indianapolis, where he worked as a railroad porter and then waited on tables in a fashionable restaurant. Around this time, he contracted smallpox and went blind in his left eye.

In 1900 he relocated to Cincinnati, where he joined the "reformation" Church of God (headquartered in Anderson, Indiana), also known as "the Evening Light Saints." Here he became steeped in radical Holiness theology which taught second blessing entire sanctification (i.e., sanctification is a post-conversion experience that results in complete holiness), divine healing, premillennialism, and the promise of a worldwide Holy Spirit revival before the rapture.

In 1903 Seymour moved to Houston, Texas, in search of his family. There he joined a small Holiness church pastored by a black woman, Lucy Farrow, who soon put him in touch with Charles Fox Parham. Parham was a Holiness teacher under whose ministry a student had spoken in tongues (glossolalia) two years earlier. For Parham, this was the "Bible evidence" of the baptism in the Holy Spirit. When he established a Bible school to train disciples in his "Apostolic Faith" in Houston, Farrow urged Seymour to attend.

Since Texas law forbade blacks to sit in classrooms with whites, Parham encouraged Seymour to remain in a hallway and listen to his lectures through the doorway. Here Seymour accepted Parham's premise of a "third blessing" baptism in the Holy Spirit evidenced by speaking in tongues. Though Seymour had not yet personally experienced tongues, he sometimes preached this message with Parham in Houston churches.

In early 1906, Seymour was invited to help Julia Hutchins pastor a Holiness church in Los Angeles. With Parham's support, Seymour journeyed to California, where he preached the new Pentecostal doctrine using Acts 2:4 as his text. Hutchins, however, rejected Seymour's teaching on tongues and padlocked the door to him and his message.

Seymour was then invited to stay in the home of Richard Asberry at 214 Bonnie Brae Street, where on April 9, after a month of intense prayer and fasting, Seymour and several others spoke in tongues. Word spread quickly about the strange events on Bonnie Brae Street and drew so much attention that Seymour was forced to preach on the front porch to crowds gathered in the street. At one point, the jostling crowd grew so large the porch floor caved in.

Seymour searched Los Angeles for a suitable building. What he found was an old abandoned African Methodist Episcopal church on Azusa Street that had recently been used as a warehouse and stable. Although it was a shambles, Seymour and his small band of black washerwomen, maids, and laborers cleaned the building, set up board plant seats, and made a pulpit out of old shoe box shipping crates. Services began in mid-April on the church, which was named the "Apostolic Faith Mission."

[CONTINUED . . .]

What happened at Azusa Street during the next three years was to change the course of church history. Although the little frame building measured only 40 by 50 feet, as many as 600 persons jammed inside while hundreds more looked in through the windows. The central attraction was tongues, with the addition of traditional black worship styles that included shouting, trances, and the holy dance. There was no order of service, since "the Holy Ghost was in control." No offerings were taken, although a box hung on the wall proclaimed, "Settle with the Lord." Altar workers enthusiastically prayed seekers through to the coveted tongues experience. It was a noisy place, and services lasted into the night.

In September, Seymour began publishing his own paper titled *The Apostolic Faith*. At its height, it went free to some 50,000 subscribers around the world.

After the "glory years" of 1906 to 1909, the Azusa Street mission became a small black church pastored by Seymour until his death on September 28, 1922, and then by his wife, Jennie, until her death in 1936. It was later sold for unpaid taxes and demolished. Today, a Japanese Cultural Center occupies the ground.

By the year 2000, the spiritual heirs of Seymour, the Pentecostals and Charismatics, numbered over 500 million adherents, making it the second largest family of Christians in the world. Today, practically all Pentecostal and charismatic movements can trace their roots directly or indirectly to the humble mission on Azusa Street and its pastor. ▪

—VINSON SYNAN
CHRISTIAN HISTORY

with the biblical Pentecost event of Acts 2 and described this experience as the baptism of the Holy Spirit subsequent to the sanctification experience. He began preaching this new doctrine in 1901 within holiness circles in the midwestern United States. In 1905, William J. Seymour "enrolled" in Parham's school in Houston, although Parham's enforcement of segregation prevented him from sitting with the students. In 1906 Seymour took this new message to Los Angeles.[20]

African-American holiness leaders who embraced Pentecostalism along with all or some of their associated congregations included William Fuller, W. H. Fulford, Magdalena Tate, Charles Harrison Mason, Thomas J. Cox, and F. W. Williams. Among the black holiness leaders who opposed the Pentecostal addition were Amanda Berry Smith, Bishop Alexander Walters, George and Laura Goings, William Christian, Charles Price Jones, and Virginia Broughton. While some black holiness leaders severed relationships with the new black Pentecostal leaders, others remained colleagues in ministry.

The Interracial Ideal

Seymour's Apostolic Faith Mission provided the model of race relations. From 1906 to 1908, blacks, whites, Latinos, and Asians worshiped together at the mission. White Pentecostal leaders such as Florence Crawford, Glenn Cook, R. J. Scott, and Clara Lum worked alongside Pastor Seymour and other African-Americans such as Jennie Evans Moore, Lucy Farrow, and Ophelia Wiley. Early Pentecostalism struggled with its interracial identity during an era in American Christianity and society when most institutions and movements espoused racial segregation. Frank Bartleman, an Azusa Street revival participant, marveled: "The color line was washed away in the blood [of Jesus Christ]."

While Baptist, Methodist, Presbyterian, and holiness communions marched into racially segregated congregations, associations, and denominational structures from 1865 to 1910, black and white Pentecostals together pastored and preached, fellowshipped and worshiped between 1906 and 1914. In general, independent white Pentecostal ministers declined to join the emerging white-led Pentecostal denominations before 1914, yet many affiliated with the predominantly black Pentecostal holiness group, the Church of God in Christ. The Pentecostal leadership was strongly anti–Ku Klux Klan and were often the targets of Klan terrorism because of the Pentecostal interracial ethic. Yet racism also tempered the interracial ideal within early Pentecostalism. Parham exhibited racist behavior and a patronizing attitude toward his black counterparts, especially Seymour.

In 1908 blacks withdrew from the Fire-Baptized Holiness Church (later renamed Pentecostal Holiness Church). In 1913, the Pentecostal Holiness Church allowed the remaining black congregations to form their own separate church. In 1914 a large group of whites withdrew from the Church of God in Christ. In 1924 the majority of whites withdrew from the 50 percent black Pentecostal Assemblies of the World. While segregation among Pentecostals followed the pattern of American Protestantism after the Civil War, there were exceptions. All whites did not withdraw from the Church of God in Christ or the Pentecostal Assemblies of the World. Blacks and whites continued to struggle together to structure their interracial relationships during the height of segregation in the United States.[21]

Within black Pentecostalism ensued a struggle for constructive interracial relations. In 1924 the Church of God in Christ adopted a Protestant model of establishing a minority conference, specifically a white conference, to unite the congregations across the United States that belonged to the mostly black denomination. This development was in response to the argument of the clergy who questioned the anomaly of white congregations in a black denomination as being a racial minority with the larger system, but sought to maximize their presence by uniting under a common administrative unit. The conference existed until the early 1930s when the predominantly black leadership abolished the conference, accusing the leadership of forming a denomination.

From 1919 to 1924 the Pentecostal Assemblies of the World was an interracial denomination. It experienced a drastic increase in African-American membership due to the appeal of Garfield Thomas Haywood, an African-American minister who was elected by his interracial denomination as the general secretary in 1919 and executive vice-chairman in 1922. Between 1924 and 1937, the denomination first lost a large group of whites, later merged with another group of whites, and eventually reorganized as a largely black denomination that slotted representation of the white minority at all levels of the structure.[22]

Theological and Political Controversies

During the 1910s the Pentecostal movement split into two theological camps—Trinitarian and apostolic ("oneness")—over the interpretation of the doctrine of the Godhead. The oneness doctrine critiqued as polytheistic the classic Christian doctrine of the Trinity. Apostolics, as they called themselves, claimed that consistent monotheism required the existence of only one God, not three Persons-in-one as espoused by the doctrine of the Trinity. They argued that Jesus was the name of God and that while God expressed Godself in the form of the Father, Son, and Holy Spirit, these were expressions or "titles" of God, not distinct persons. However, most of the black Pentecostal denominations that were established in the late 19th century remained Trinitarian, such as the United Holy Church; the Church of the Living God, Pillar and Ground of Truth; Fire-Baptized Holiness Church of America; and the Church of God in Christ.

Only the Christian Band (later renamed Church of God [Apostolic]) and the Pentecostal Assemblies of the World embraced the oneness doctrine. Black Pentecostal congregations within the circle of Garfield Thomas Haywood in the Midwest constituted the majority that formed the nucleus of black apostolics in the Pentecostal Assemblies of the World. These congregations often identified with fellowships that espoused progressive sanctification instead of instantaneous sanctification advanced by the holiness wing of black Pentecostalism.[23]

Garfield Thomas Haywood's denomination, the Pentecostal Assemblies of the World, is the parent body of the major black apostolic denominations in the United States. A significant leader of the black oneness movement who originally served in the Pentecostal Assemblies of the World was Robert C. Lawson, who organized the Church of Our Lord Jesus Christ of the Apostolic Faith in 1919. From Lawson's denomination some of the prominent apostolic ministers emerged: Sherrod C. Johnson, the founder of the Church of the Lord Jesus Christ of the Apostolic Faith in 1930, and Smallwood Williams, the founder of Bible Way Churches of Our Lord Jesus Christ Worldwide in 1957. From a separate trajectory initiated by the Church of God (Apostolic), another cluster of apostolic denominations developed. The black oneness movement has become a major stream within black Pentecostalism and in some cities constitutes the most influential black Pentecostal congregations.[24]

Garfield Thomas Haywood (1880–1931) left the Assemblies of God in 1914 to found the Pentecostal Assemblies of the World, the first major oneness church.

During the late 1910s, some key black Pentecostal leaders challenged the United States' entry into World War I by adopting pacifism and engaging in antiwar preaching. According to historian Theodore Kornweibel Jr., the Church of God in Christ and the Pentecostal Assemblies of the World articulated their opposition to the war. The most prominent Pentecostal pacifist was Charles Harrison Mason.

According to a federal agent, Mason preached throughout the United States that World War I was "a rich man's war and a poor man's fight." Mason based his objection to the war on the biblical injunction against "shedding human blood or taking human life." After Congress passed the draft act, Mason directed his assistants to apply for conscientious-objector status for draft-age males in the Church of God in Christ. Federal agents placed Mason and others under surveillance and had them arrested for obstruction of the draft in various states for their pacifist activities.[25]

Also during this time, the black religious nationalism of the late 19th century espoused by holiness leaders such as William Christian, George Goings, and Alexander Walters found expression in the pan-Africanist movement of Marcus Garvey and the Universal Negro Improvement Association (UNIA). Among the black Pentecostal clergy who supported the UNIA were E. R. Driver of the Church of God in Christ, Sidney Solomon of the Pentecostal Church, and Elias Dempsey Smith of the Triumph the Church and Kingdom of God in Christ. In 1919 Elias Dempsey Smith hosted Marcus Garvey at the national meeting of his denomination.

Black religious nationalism within black Pentecostalism also shaped the mission emphasis of the movement. Liberia was the mission site for a number of missionaries from Seymour's Apostolic Faith Mission. The J. R.

Ledbetters represented the Pentecostal Assemblies of the World in Liberia from 1914 to 1924. Around 1918 the United Holy Church raised funds to sponsor its first foreign missionaries, Isaac and Annie Williams, who were assigned to Liberia. In 1919 a group of African-Americans organized the United Pentecostal Council of the Assemblies of God to support missionaries to Liberia; their first missionaries, Rev. Alexander and Margaret Howard, arrived in Liberia in 1920. In the 1920s members of the Church of God in Christ went as missionaries to predominantly black countries: Ms. January to Liberia in the early 1920s; Mattie McCauley to Trinidad in 1927; and Joseph Paulceus, a Haitian, to Haiti in 1929.

Black Pentecostals Reroute the Black Holiness Movement

Within its first decade black Pentecostals outnumbered their black holiness adherents. Instead of defining themselves in contrast to the black holiness movement, black Pentecostal leaders expanded the contours of the black holiness movement to include non-Pentecostal holiness believers and Pentecostal holiness believers. These leaders refer to their congregations as holiness or "sanctified" churches rather than Pentecostal churches. Thus the holiness identity encompassed the Pentecostal experience.

These Pentecostals also espoused a "church against the world" sentiment. Their Christian orientation and practices reflected more of the religious ethos of the 19th century than the 20th. "Tarrying" at the altar became a Pentecostal counterpart to the Baptist mourner's bench, both of which defined their experience of the Christian faith. Through tarrying, a form of contemplative prayer, black Pentecostals experienced conversion, sanctification, and Spirit baptism by the sovereignty of God. Tarrying became the framework out of which black Pentecostal culture evolved with its cluster of musical and worship practices: call-and-response song and patterns, improvisational style, an array of musical instruments, rhythmic sounds and beats, religious dancing, prayer chants, and key worship responses of hallelujah, glory, praise God, thank you, and yes, Lord.

As the "sanctified Church," black Pentecostals incorporated elements from the late 19th-century prayer and healing movements. From Elizabeth Mix, the first black female serving full-time as a healing evangelist in the 1870s and 1880s, a healing movement within the black holiness movement became central to black Pentecostalism. Charles Harrison Mason, W. H. Fulford, Lucy Smith, Rosa Artemus Horne, and Saint Samuel built ministries as healing evangelists. In Chicago, Mattie and Charles Poole began a cluster of congregations modeled after their Bethlehem Healing Temple that stressed the healing ministry.

Often prayer ministries served as the context for healing ministries as well as intercessory prayer. Charles Harrison Mason, Elizabeth Dabney, Samuel Crouch, and Elsie Shaw were known for their commitment to prayer. All-night prayer vigils called "shut-ins" and consecrations, three- to four-hour prayer meetings, and twice a week fastings along with peri- odic forty-day fasts were the core elements of prayer ministries. Vital to these prayer ministries would also be the practice of a tarrying service, a prayer rite that prepared individuals for conversion, sanctification, and the baptism in the Holy Spirit. The prayer and healing tradition was a uni- fying force in black Pentecostalism, a counterbalance to the divisive ten- sions over interdenominational conflicts and doctrinal controversies.[26]

The debates about women's ordination and ministry within the black holiness movement during the late 19th century shaped the decisions about women's ordination among black Pentecostals. While the Church of the God in Christ approved women as evangelists and restricted ordained ministry to males, the Church of the Living God and United Holy Church stream ordained women. Even though various denominations ordained women, women pastors came under constant rhetorical attack from vari- ous quarters for "usurping authority over men." In spite of this tendency, in various cities women pastored or headed the only black Pentecostal congregations that existed.

These congregations often evolved from women-led prayer bands. In Brooklyn there was only Eva Lambert's St. Mark Holy Church until the mid-1920s. In Harlem women pastored the existing black Pentecostal con- gregations until the arrival of Robert Clarence Lawson in 1919. While the United Holy Church and the Pentecostal Assemblies of the World or- dained women as ministers and authorized them to pastor, they excluded women from the office of bishop. Consequently, black Pentecostal women have adopted the model established in 1903 by Magdalena Tate of women founding and heading denominations that promoted full male-female equality in the church.

A case in point was Ida Robinson, who in 1924 withdrew her congrega- tion from the United Holy Church because it denied women the office of bishop and founded the Mt. Sinai Holy Church to rectify the inequality. In 1944 Beulah Counts, the pastor of the Brooklyn congregation within the Mt. Sinai Holy Church, withdrew from her denomination and organ- ized the Greater Zion Pentecostal Church of America. The same year, Magdalene Mabe Phillips, pastor of a United Holy Church congregation in

Baltimore, withdrew from her denomination to organize the Alpha and Omega Pentecostal Church.

In 1947, Mozella Cook resigned from the Church of God in Christ and established the Sought Out Church of God in Christ and Spiritual House of Prayer in Brunswick, Georgia. During the next year, Florine Reed established the Temple of God, with her first congregation in Boston, Massa-

Bishop Ida Robinson (1891–1946) left the United Holy Church in 1924 to found the Mt. Sinai Holy Church, which continued under female leadership after her death.

chusetts. The House of the Lord founded by Alonzo Austin Daughtry in 1930 in Augusta, Georgia, was one of the few denominations not organized by women that elected a woman as presiding bishop. Inez Conroy succeeded Daughtry in 1952 and served until 1960. Even in male-dominated denominations, black Pentecostal women played critical and progressive roles in women's departments.[27]

Black Pentecostal women and men were also instrumental in the development of a forerunner of gospel music called "sanctified music." Sanctified music became the major carrier of black religious folk music associated with slave and West African culture, which was noted for its call-and-response, improvisation, polyrhythms, and diatonic harmonies. According to Anthony Heilbut, a gospel music historian, the black Pentecostal movement was critical to the development of gospel music. Together with Thomas Dorsey, a Baptist and the recognized father of the gospel music movement, Sallie Martin traveled across the country, individually and with Dorsey, organizing gospel choirs in black congregations. Sallie Martin attended black Pentecostal conventions to present the new songs.

Established black Pentecostal recording artists like Sallie Sanders, Ford McGee, and Arizona Dranes added the new gospel songs to their repertoire. In their recordings of the 1920s black Pentecostal recording artists introduced to the broader religious community their musical culture, which incorporated the New Orleans jazz style and ragtime-styled piano accompaniment and was impervious to distinctions between sacred and secular music. This musical culture prepared the black religious community for Dorsey's choral and solo compositions that he began distributing in the late 1920s. Finally, during the 1930s, the radio broadcasts of Eva Lambert in New York City, along with Lucy Smith's and William Roberts's in Chicago, introduced the new gospel compositions to thousands of homes.[28]

During the 1950s, the black Pentecostal movement received its first major internal challenge with the rise of the African-American deliverance movement with its focus on exorcism and miracles popularized by William M. Branham and A. A. Allen. Deliverance ministries were touted as being more in touch with the power of God than the average black Pentecostal congregations. Most of these ministries reinforced the sanctified church identity with their emphasis on consecration, demonstrative expressions, jubilance, and religious dancing. By 1956, Arturo Skinner was a key figure with his founding of the Deliverance Evangelistic Centers, with headquarters in Newark, New Jersey.

While deliverance ministries emerged in traditional Pentecostal congregations, such as Chicago's Faith Temple Church of God in Christ under Harry Willis Goldsberry and Berkeley's Ephesians Church of God in Christ under E. E. Cleveland, new independent congregations arose in urban centers that competed with black classical Pentecostalism. These included the Deliverance Evangelistic Center in Philadelphia founded by Benjamin Smith in 1960 and the Monument of Faith Evangelistic Center founded by Richard Henton in Chicago in 1963. The deliverance movement of the 1950s and early 1960s was the first national interracial experiment within American Pentecostalism since the interracial experiments of early Pentecostalism that ended by the 1930s.[29]

Black Ecumenism and Social Witness

Urban black Pentecostal congregations by the 1930s began to cooperate with local and national black ecumenical organizations. Black Pentecostal denominations, according to historian Mary Sawyer, slowly joined the National Fraternal Council of Negro Churches. The council was the major ecumenical thrust among black denominations of the early 20th century. It was founded in 1934, under the initiative of AMEC clergyman Reverdy Ransom, by various black denominations: the African Methodist Episcopal Church; the African Methodist Episcopal Zion Church; the National Baptist Convention, USA, Inc.; the National Baptist Convention of America; the Union American Methodist Episcopal Church; and delegates of community, congregational, holiness and Methodist Episcopal congregations. The black Pentecostal denominations that joined the council were the Church of God in Christ, Church of Our Lord Jesus Christ of the Apostolic Faith, and the Pentecostal Church.

Unfortunately, when white Pentecostals organized the Pentecostal Fellowship of North America in 1948, they denied membership to black Pentecostals. Nonetheless, on the global level, black Pentecostal denominations participated in the 1947 founding of the Pentecostal World Conference, a triennial, multiracial, international assembly. In more recent years, the Church of God in Christ became a charter member of the Congress of National Black Churches, the major black ecumenical organization of the late 20th century.

Black Pentecostals such as William Bentley and George McKinney were active members of the National Association of Evangelicals as well as the National Black Evangelical Association. During the 1980s, J. O. Patterson Sr., under the auspices of the Church of God in Christ, convened the first national assembly of black Pentecostal denominations to begin the process of cooperation among black Pentecostals. Finally, in 1994, black and white Pentecostal denominational leaders organized the Pentecostal and Charismatic Churches of North America, the first national interracial ecumenical council among Pentecostals.[30]

Black Pentecostal leaders also joined the ranks of Christian social activists who engaged in campaigns for better race relations and racial progress of African-Americans. William Roberts was a member of the delegation from the National Fraternal Council of Negro Churches that went to Washington, D.C., in 1941 to demand economic justice for African-Americans. Robert Clarence Lawson joined Baptist pastor Adam Clayton Powell Jr. and other Harlem clergy in job campaigns for blacks. Arenia C. Mallory, a leader in the Church of God in Christ, was a member of Eleanor Roosevelt's Negro Women's Cabinet, which advised the First Lady on issues from the black woman's perspective.

In the 1950s, Smallwood Williams led a legal battle against segregated public schools in Washington, D.C., and J. O. Patterson Sr. participated in the local civil rights campaign in Memphis, Tennessee. During the 1960s, Arthur Brazier and Louis Henry Ford were active in the civil rights efforts in Chicago, while Ithiel Clemmons and Herbert Daughtry were similarly involved in civil rights campaigns in New York City. Included among the churches bombed during the civil rights movement were black Pentecostal congregations in Winnsboro, Louisiana; DeKalb, Mississippi; and Plainview, Texas.[31]

The Transforming of the Sanctifi ed Church Identity into the New Black Pentecostal Church

An emerging black Pentecostal leadership thus ushered in a new era within black Pentecostalism. They advanced new images of black Pentecostalism to supplant its half-century identification as a sanctified or holiness church. There were progressive black Pentecostal leaders who built upon the black Pentecostal trajectories that promoted education, ecumenism, and social justice. They challenged black Pentecostal parochialism by seeking a dual identification with the black church and American Pentecostalism. Clearly rejecting their parochial past, these leaders searched for a more relevant ecclesial context for black Pentecostals. The dual identification succeeded in breaking black Pentecostalism of its parochialism due to its marginalization and isolation from the major and secondary centers of American Protestantism.

While the sanctified church had little public visibility or recognized significance outside poor black neighborhoods, Pentecostalism, specifically middle-class white Pentecostalism, was gaining visibility through national figures such as Oral Roberts and Kathryn Kuhlman and movements such as the charismatic renewal and the Jesus people. The black church gained prominence and earned moral capital through its pivotal role in the civil rights movement and projected a unity among African-American Christians that crossed denominational and theological lines.[32]

Within the new emerging leadership, they debated whether identification with the black church would have precedence over the identification with white Pentecostalism. The situation was complicated because of white Pentecostalism's identification with mainstream evangelicalism. Some leaders argued that African-American Protestantism with its theological and social agenda was more compatible with the black Pentecostal ministry than evangelicalism. These leaders proposed a redefinition of black Pentecostal denominations as black churches with a Pentecostal perspective rather than being black evangelicals with a Pentecostal experience.

In the 1970s a number of black Pentecostal theologians began conversations with the black theology movement associated with James Cone, Jacquelyn Grant, and Gayraud Wilmore, who dominated the theological scene within the black church. Different writers began to engage black theology from a Pentecostal perspective. William Bentley and Bennie Goodwin Jr. sought to incorporate the social critique of black theology within black Pentecostalism and infuse black theology with Pentecostal spirituality and evangelical themes. Leonard Lovett, James Forbes, and James Tinney sought to interject the liberationist agenda of black theology in black Pentecostalism. Within these quarters, black Pentecostals participated in a serious dialogue with liberation theologians. During subsequent decades, black Pentecostal and Neo-Pentecostal theologians such as Robert Franklin, William Turner, Anthea Butler, Alonzo Johnson, and H. Dean Trulear continued this dialogue from their posts as professors at colleges and theological seminaries.[33]

During the 1970s, the "Word of Faith" movement intersected with black Pentecostalism and advanced the break with the sanctified church tradition. Frederick K. C. Price emerged in 1973 as the "word of faith" pioneer among black Christians after establishing Crenshaw Christian Center in Los Angeles. This movement rejected the antimaterialism of the sanctified church and interpreted financial prosperity as a Christian birthright along with salvation and healing. These leaders also introduced a new preaching style that countered the homiletic practices of the sanctified church model in which they stressed instruction rather than inspiration. While black Pentecostals often stressed Christian instruction in various Bible studies during an average week, the sermon had to embrace a different aim. The word of faith preachers specialized in introducing their audiences to the ways to access God's promises of health and wealth.

Frederick Kenneth Cercie Price (1932–) gained fame as a television faith teacher after founding the Crenshaw Christian Center in Los Angeles in 1973.

The Eruption of Black Neo-Pentecostalism

In this post–sanctified church era, Pentecostalism attracted clergy and members within the historic black denominations, especially the African Methodist Episcopal Church and the Baptist Church. By the 1970s Neo-Pentecostal ministers began occupying pastorates of the African Methodist Episcopal Church. The focal point for the movement during the early 1970s was St. Paul AMEC in Cambridge, Massachusetts, under the pastorate of John Bryant. By the 1980s Neo-Pentecostal AMEC congregations were among the largest in the denomination: St. Paul in Cambridge, Bethel in Baltimore, Allen Temple in Queens (New York), and Ward in Los Angeles. Two Neo-Pentecostals, Vernon Byrd and John Bryant, were elected bishops of that denomination.

Within the African Methodist Episcopal Zion Church during the 1980s and 1990s, John A. Cherry and his congregation were at the center in the Full Gospel AMEZ in Temple Hills, Maryland, a suburb of Washington, D.C. In 1999 Cherry withdrew from AMEZ and established a new denomination called "Macedonia Ministries."

The focus points for Neo-Pentecostalism among black Baptists were Roy Brown and his Pilgrim Baptist Cathedral in Brooklyn along with Paul Morton and St. Stephen Full Gospel Baptist Church in New Orleans. During the

BISHOP IDA BELL ROBINSON

(FOUNDER, MOUNT SINAI HOLY CHURCH OF AMERICA, INC.)

She was born Ida Bell on August 3, 1891, in Hazelhurst, Georgia. She first consecrated herself to Christ in 1903 at the age of twelve. In 1908 at the age of seventeen, while attending a street revival in Pensacola, Florida, conducted by members of the Church of God, the future lady bishop accepted a call to a life of holiness. She responded to God's call by holding frequent prayer meetings in her home and witnessing on the streets of Pensacola. Many times, she preached to congregations made up of whomever she could gather around her on street corners.

Ida Bell married Oliver Robinson in 1910 and in 1917 they moved to Philadelphia in search of opportunity. She regarded her marriage as very sacred and solemn, giving her husband, who acted as her driver throughout her ministry, the respect that was his due. She never gave birth to any children of her own, but during her lifetime many claimed her as spiritual mother. She eventually adopted her brother's daughter, Ida, who had been named after her. Oliver Robinson always praised his wife highly, realizing that she used her exceptional ability and talents for the work of God. He was ever supportive of her spiritual efforts.

In 1917, at the time of their move to Philadelphia, many women were being allowed to preach and pastor because of the widespread acceptance of women in the Pentecostal/holiness movement. Through these movements, the call from God on one's life and the yielding to the Holy Ghost for the unction conferred the ability to preach, was more important than a formal education.

In Philadelphia, Ida joined a small Church of God congregation and at times would fill in for Pastor Benjamin Smith. It is not known whether this church was an affiliate of a specific Church of God denomination or whether it was one of the myriads of independent Church of God congregations that dotted the religious landscape at that time. Her popularity increased quickly among the membership due to her outstanding preaching and singing. What exactly occurred at the church where Sister Robinson served as a relief preacher is not known. However it is recorded that because of an uncomfortable situation which developed between the young lady preacher and the pastor, Sister Robinson sought fellowship elsewhere.

After leaving the Church of God, she then began her affiliation with the United Holy Church of America. In this relatively new African-American denomination, she was ordained to the ministry. Her ordination occurred in a public ceremony celebrated by Bishop Henry L. Fisher. Her ministry was accepted by the other officials of the United Holy Church, and she soon became a well-recognized gospel preacher.

Then, in 1919 she was chosen as the leader of a small group of saints when she accepted the pastorate of a United Holy Church mission church located at 505 S. Eleventh Street. After five years she began feeling that God had something special for her to do. Seeking after a divine revelation of the nature of this special work, she began a ten-day fast. During the time of fasting, Elder Robinson believed she received a word from God. This word was, "Come out on Mount Sinai." Consequently, on May 20, 1924, the Mount Sinai Holy Church of America, Inc. petitioned for and received its official charter from the state of Pennsylvania and Robinson became its presiding bishop. From that time until the present, the Mount Sinai Holy Church of America, Inc., has remained under female leadership. ∎

—ROSALEE OWENS

BISHOP T. D. JAKES

Where did Thomas D. Jakes come from? He was born in 1957 in Charleston, West Virginia, the son of Ernest and Odith Jakes. His father was the owner of a janitorial service and his mother was a schoolteacher. At the age of ten he saw his father struck down with a kidney disease that slowly killed him. Instead of rejecting God because of his father's suffering Jakes pursued the Lord: "I sought solace and answers in the Bible. I can never forget where I came from. The sense of time and life ticking away is an undercurrent of my message." Raised a Baptist, he became a Pentecostal, a member first of the Apostolic Church, and later part of the Higher Ground Always Abounding Assemblies. From the age of twenty-two he pastored small storefront churches, and by 1990 he moved to South Charleston, West Virginia, where his church grew from 100 to 300 members.

In 1992 Jakes gave a teaching on "Woman, Thou Art Loosed!" to a Sunday school class in his own church. He expected to be rejected for bringing up painful subjects, i.e., child and spousal abuse. Instead the women in the class asked for more. In a short time Jakes was traveling to other churches and auditoriums around the country with this message. He spoke at the Azusa Conference in Tulsa, sponsored by Rev. Carlton Pearson, in 1993, and from there launched a television ministry on TBN at the invitation of Paul Crouch. Swiftly outgrowing his home base in West Virginia—his staff remembers that people coming to his conferences had to be housed in four states—Jakes in 1996 moved to Dallas, Texas, where, with his family and fifty members of his ministry team, he founded the Potter's House, a local church that in four years grew to twenty-six thousand members.

Jakes soon had a substantial television ministry in Europe and in Africa. After a recent meeting in Soweto, South Africa, he made a commitment to enlarge this ministry overseas. He travels about a dozen times a year to hold meetings and to attend speaking engagements. In the year 2000 this included trips to London, England, and Lagos, Nigeria.

Meanwhile, Jakes moved aggressively to expand his home base of operations in south Dallas, dedicating a new $35 million church building seating more than eight thousand people in October 2000, and starting a major community development initiative valued at $135.2 million called "Project 2000." The latter is planned to include a K–12 school, an education/recreation facility, a performing arts center, a business incubator, an executive retreat center, a golf course, office buildings, a mall, and more, all designed to enhance the quality of life in a part of the city suffering from urban blight.

Much more can be said about Jakes—he has published twenty-four books, and his tape series are widely marketed. Three times a year T. D. Jakes Ministries puts on large conferences, "Woman, Thou art Loosed," "Manpower," and a Pastor's & Leadership Conference. He also has ties to pastors that he provides with some oversight and encouragement.

As the famous preachers of the 20th century pass from the scene, people speculate on their successors. Even the *New York Times* published an article listing Jakes as a candidate for the role of national spiritual leader for the new century. Time will tell what the reach of his ministry will be. ▪

—DR. HUGH MORKEN
REGENT UNIVERSITY

1980s, Brown organized the Pilgrim Assemblies denomination, and Morton spearheaded a Neo-Pentecostal Baptist fellowship, the Full Gospel Baptist Fellowship.[34]

By the 1980s, according to Horace Boyer and Anthony Heilbut, black Pentecostals such as Andrae Crouch, Edwin Hawkins, Walter Hawkins, Shirley Caesar, the Clark sisters, and the Winans would dominate the gospel music movement. During the 1960s, black Pentecostals created a new sound within gospel music that later would be called contemporary gospel music, in contrast to traditional gospel music associated with Thomas Dorsey and Sallie Martin and their successors James Cleveland and Roberta Martin.

The younger generation of black Pentecostal musicians would borrow freely from the soul music of the sixties, a style originally influenced by traditional gospel music. Andrae Crouch composed ballads and incorporated the melodies of soul and pop music, while Edwin Hawkins wrote gospel choral music that borrowed from a variety of jazz and calypso sounds. Impervious to distinctions between sacred and secular music like their Pentecostal predecessors, Crouch and Hawkins ushered in a new phase within black religious music and the black church. By the 1990s black Pentecostals such as Ron Kenoly would shape the praise music movement with sounds drawn from the musical culture of black Pentecostalism and introduce the sounds of African-American music to Pentecostals across the races.

Women's ministry and national ministries became features of black Pentecostals during the last two decades of the 20th century. Ernestine Cleveland Reems served as the model of a black female preacher for hundreds of African-American clergy women. Her E. C. Reems ministry sponsored a major Christian women's conference that gathered black clergy and laywomen from across the United States. Other significant black Pentecostal and Neo-Pentecostal clergy women with national reputations include Juanita Bynum, Claudette Copeland, Barbara Amos, and Jackie McCullough.

During the 1990s black Pentecostal and Neo-Pentecostal males also gained prominence as heads of national ministries. The most phenomenal was T. D. Jakes, pastor of Potter's House Church in Dallas, Texas. Jakes

T. D. Jakes (b. 1957) rose from obscurity to become the most dynamic pastor in America in the 1990s. His Potter's House Church in Dallas was recognized as the fastest-growing American congregation of the 20th century.

created a new moment within black Pentecostalism with his multifaceted ministry of conferences, books, tapes, music, film, and plays. In addition to Jakes, other heads of national ministries included Frederick K. C. Price, Creflo Dollar, and Gilbert E. Patterson.

Black Pentecostalism at Century's End

By the year 2000 black Pentecostalism had escaped the religious periphery and entered the center of American Protestantism. Black Pentecostals had joined Methodism and the Baptist Church as one of three dominant denominational traditions in the black church. In various communities across the nation black Pentecostal pastors and leaders functioned as key spokespersons and community leaders. While there still existed pockets within black Pentecostalism that remained committed to the ethos of the sanctified church era, black Pentecostalism in general was embracing the new era. Among the most significant turns in black Pentecostalism was its participation in the renewing of spirituality and ministry within the black church through the black Neo-Pentecostal movement.

The diversity within black Pentecostalism during the 20th century pointed to the strengths of the tradition. While this diversity clearly expanded rapidly during the century's last decades, the diversity created space for black Pentecostalism to make the transition from its initial parochial phase to its more ecumenical phase. Although over the decades black Pentecostalism has experienced changes in its theological perspectives, worship style, class orientation, and political views, it has retained its strong commitment to Scripture, conversion, Spirit baptism, evangelism, healing, prayer, and its African heritage.

For Further Reading

Segments of the story of black Pentecostalism can be found in Stanley M. Burgess, ed., and Eduard van der Maas, assoc. ed., *New International Dictionary of Pentecostal and Charismatic Movements* (Grand Rapids: Zondervan, 2001). Charles Jones gives exhaustive sources in his two-volume *Guide to the Study of the Pentecostal Movement* (Metuchen, N.J.: Scarecrow Press, 1983), and in his *Black Holiness: A Guide to the Study of Black Participation in Wesleyan Perfectionistic and Glossolalic Pentecostal Movements* (Metuchen, N.J.: Scarecrow Press, 1987). A major source for all African-American churches is J. Gordon Melton and Gary Ward, eds., *Encyclopedia of African American Religions* (New York: Garland Reference Library of Social Science, 1993).

A book that gives the C. P. Jones story is Otho B. Cobbins, ed., *History of the Church of Christ (Holiness) U.S.A.* (New York: Vantage Press, 1966). The most comprehensive history of the Church of God in Christ is Ithiel C. Clemmon's *Bishop C. H. Mason and the Roots of the Church of God in Christ* (Bakersfield, Calif.: Pneuma Life Publishing, 1996). An early treatment of American black Pentecostalism is found in Vinson Synan's *The Holiness-Pentecostal Tradition: Penteccostal and Charismatic Movements in the Twentieth Century* (Grand Rapids: Eerdmans, 1997), 167–86. The story of the United Holy Church is written in Chester W. Gregory's *The History of the United Holy Church of America, Inc., 1886–1986* (Baltimore: Gateway Press, 1986).

The story of black women ministers is given in William A. Andrews, ed., *Sisters of the Spirit: Three Black Women's Autobiography of the Nineteenth Century* (Bloomington: Indiana Univ. Press, 1986). Black women are also studied in Cheryl J. Sanders's *Saints in Exile: The Holiness-Pentecostal Experience* (New York: Oxford Univ. Press 1996).

The only biography of William J. Seymour is Douglas Nelson's dissertation "For Such a Time as This: The Story of Bishop William J. Seymour and the Azusa Street Revival" (Ph.D. dissertation, Univ. of Birmingham, U.K., 1981). A good account of the Azusa Street revival is found in Robert Owens, *Speak to the Rock: The Azusa Street Revival: Its Roots and Message* (Lanham, Md.: Univ. Press of America, 1998).

· 12 ·
Hispanic Pentecostalism in the Americas

Pablo A. Deiros and Everett A. Wilson

THE GROWTH OF PENTECOSTALISM among Spanish- and Portuguese-speaking people of North and South America has been phenomenal. This is especially true of Latin America, the region that despairing Protestant missionaries once termed the "forgotten continent." This unexpected development has caught the attention even of secular students of social change, leading David Stoll to title his investigation of evangelicals in Latin American politics *Is Latin America Turning Protestant?*[1] British sociologist David Martin named his similar study *Tongues of Fire: The Explosion of Protestantism in Latin America.*[2] These and other students of Latin America have asked what could have provoked such a wave of grassroots religious enthusiasm among the neglected and largely voiceless common people of the region. Given the enormous size and the vitality of the movement, its emergence requires some explanation.

It is inescapable that Pentecostalism has spread most rapidly among peoples caught in disruptive social transition. Adherents are in large measure people who have left behind many of the time-honored traditions of the village to adopt the bewildering ways of contemporary life in the city. As a result, Pentecostalism has functioned as a social and spiritual bridge for millions of men and women; in the terminology of some writers, Pentecostalism is a "survival vehicle." David Martin refers to it as a "protective social capsule" that renews the broken ties of family, community, and religion in an atmosphere of hope and anticipation.

> A new faith is able to implant new disciplines, re-order priorities, counter corruption, and destructive *machismo*, and reverse the indifferent and injurious hierarchies of the outside world. Within the enclosed haven of faith a fraternity can be instituted under firm leadership, which provides for release, for mutuality and warmth.[3]

Pentecostalism has energized many distressed populations, it has adapted culturally to the popular tastes of its devotees, and it has addressed the pressing social and spiritual needs of the common people. Some critics have complained that Pentecostals are reactionary, retiring from the political struggles around them while they hang on to a religion that promises personal salvation but not social redemption.[4] Numbers of observers agree with Martin, however, and see Pentecostalism in a positive light, as an assertive effort on the part of the poor to take command of their own lives.

Jeffrey Gros, a Roman Catholic ecumenist, recognizing that Pentecostals indeed are slow to join political reform efforts, has commented that "Pentecostals don't *have* social programs, they *are* a social program."[5] Similarly, Elizabeth Brusco, a sociologist who studied Pentecostal women in Bogotá, Colombia, surprised the academic world with her conclusion that this form of evangelical Christianity was extensively undercutting "machismo," the sexual double standard that denigrates women and is disruptive of families.[6]

Ultimately, despite its effectiveness in mobilizing and giving hope to the masses, Pentecostalism is essentially an individual, subjective matter, a personal experience that provides spiritual resources, a community of faith, and confidence to face an uncertain future. Some writers see in the movement the deep roots of medieval Catholic mysticism, or African and Native American longings for freedom and restoration, while still others see in the movement help for the emerging middle classes that feel spiritually disoriented, frustrated, and denied.[7] The movement is obviously heterogeneous and versatile. Despite the many features it has in common with Pentecostals everywhere, it has become acclimated to any context in which it is found. Accordingly, one finds subspecies of Latin American Pentecostalism, each sustained by the culture of its own nation, ethnic group, region, social class, or age set. Despite their generic similarities, there are distinguishable Brazilian, Argentine, Mexican, and Puerto Rican varieties, as well as several forms that have emerged among North American Hispanics.

The first section of this chapter treats the movement as it has emerged among Hispanic peoples in the United States and in Puerto Rico. The second section is a review of Pentecostalism in Latin America, the sixteen Spanish-speaking republics (exclusive of the Spanish Caribbean) of Mexico, Central America, and Portuguese-speaking Brazil. The great cultural divide that has separated Anglo North America—including the United States, Canada, and some islands of the Caribbean—from Latin America—southward from Mexico to Central and South America—is culturally coming together. Although Pentecostalism is only one small part in this drama, it is nevertheless a strategic episode that has played a disproportionate role in bridging the gap.

North American Hispanic Pentecostalism

Although closely related to the movement as it developed in Latin America, Hispanic Pentecostalism in the United States has its own history and character. While Pentecostals in Latin America derive little help from a social system where the Roman Catholic Church often receives preferential treatment, Hispanic Pentecostal groups in the United States have developed in a society where Protestant values are usually dominant. Moreover, many large Pentecostal groups in Latin America are not closely related to any multinational organization, while Hispanic Pentecostals in the United States for the most part have come into existence as integral parts of larger Anglo denominations. As well, while Latin American Pentecostals have often emerged from among the poorest and most traditional social sectors and ethnic groups at the margins of national life, many U.S. Hispanic Pentecostals have come into these churches with the aspiration to become part of the North American main stream. These several U.S. movements, however, like their counterparts in Latin America, are expressive, assertive, and often audacious, despite the often quite different challenges they face. Together, they make up what *Time* magazine once referred to as the "Fastest Growing Church in the Hemisphere."[8]

Like their Latin American counterparts, North American Hispanic Pentecostals tend to form small, family-like congregations where the individual is recognized and accepted and is usually assigned a responsible task. Often congregations are essentially made up of two or three extended families that may be further related by intermarriage, or may have come from the same country or region in Latin America, or are persons who share a loyalty to a particular leader. Accordingly, the Pentecostal congregation is not merely a passive institution where worshipers gather, but a dynamic organism where all of the members contribute in some concrete way. Financial support, faithful attendance of services, and active participation in the group's many activities, usually including aggressive evangelism, are taken for granted, even, some critics charge, to the neglect of the members' other social obligations.

Observers also point to the strategic part played by strong leaders and the distinctive lifestyles of Pentecostals. Dr. Eugene Nida of the American Bible Society, an anthropologist, sees much of the strength of the movement in the identification of a "natural elite" made up of men and women who may not have much formal education, but are born leaders. They have charisma or at least persuasiveness; they inspire confidence and display mature judgment. Because there have been few opportunities for such people to exert their influence elsewhere, Pentecostals, according to this line of reasoning, have frequently benefited from the emergence of gifted leaders.[9]

As well, membership in a Pentecostal congregation usually imposes a clear-cut witness of the believer's faith and values, referred to by sociologists as "boundary maintenance." In small communities or barrios where everyone sees everyone else's behavior, the rules are legalistic and members who lapse are subject to discipline. This kind of intimate, demanding, cell-like organization was almost universal in Latino churches for many years. Only more recently, since the 1980s, have new kinds of churches come into being. The discussion of Neo-Pentecostal groups, sometimes forming mega-churches and more readily accommodating the larger society, is dealt with in the section on Latin America.

Origins

Like the movements elsewhere, the North American Pentecostal churches trace their beginnings to the Azusa Street revival of 1906. While early Pentecostal missionaries took the message abroad and some expatriate nationals carried it back to their homelands, communities of Spanish-speaking Pentecostals were influenced directly from the humble mission in downtown Los Angeles, where, reportedly, they were among the "Ethiopians, Chinese, Indians, Mexicans, and other nationalities" who gathered for worship. Soon congregations began to take form, often following a network of extended families and associates in labor camps and urban missions. By 1912 there were reports of Mexican congregations in several California towns: San Diego, Colton, San Bernardino, Riverside, Los Angeles, and Watts.[10] Alice Luce, a pioneer of the Hispanic Pentecostal effort, in 1918 reported that:

The summer time has been a special opportunity for "scattering" as the Mexicans of this state move around to the various fruit-picking centers; and in the case of our Christian families we trust it has been true that "they that were scattered abroad went everywhere preaching the Word." They certainly have been testifying for Jesus wherever they went, distributing numbers of Spanish tracts and Gospels, and from one place they sent to me for some hymnbooks that they might hold meetings.[11]

Without anyone to direct them, communities of hardy Pentecostal believers improvised with the resources at their disposal. Dr. Manuel J. Gaxiola has described this early process. "There were no ministerial requirements and anyone who felt called could start a church, either in his own home or in the home of another family."[12] Spanish-speaking churches appeared in northern California in San Jose, Niles, and San Francisco. Eastward along the Mexican border, the work spread to Houston, Pasadena, San Antonio, and, by 1917, to a total of at least seventeen towns in Texas.

The compatibility of Pentecostal beliefs with Latin culture was evident early in the emergence of these churches. Expatriate Hispanics were often deeply religious, attached to their families, given to hospitality, hardworking, and aspiring. Some people who had a sense of religious vocation earlier in life apparently renewed it in their Pentecostal experience. One of the earliest accounts of the formation of a new congregation was a report of a convert in southeast Texas who returned to his own settlement just below the border and soon had a thriving congregation. Without extensive training, external support, or much doctrinal orientation, the young, inexperienced pastor sent a request for help to baptize and catechize his growing flock. This spontaneity and initiative, if not universal in the founding of new churches, has been repeated so frequently that it may be recognized as a basic formula in the success of Hispanic Pentecostalism.[13]

But the populations among which the movement began to take root were often unstable and financially insecure. Many converts to the movement were migrant laborers or were frequently forced by economic circumstances to change their places of residence. Some individuals periodically returned to their country of origin. Congregations had few resources to support a pastor, who also was usually employed, and they had little surplus for acquiring property for a suitable place of worship. Moreover, they often felt ostracized by their own primarily Roman Catholic ethnic communities as well as by the English-speaking Anglo society. Their persistent—sometimes heroic—efforts to share their faith with their families, friends, and work associates make up important chapters of the historical record.

A Profi le of U.S. and Caribbean Pentecostalism

The extension of the Hispanic churches generally followed the regional distribution of Spanish-speaking populations, with the new churches reflecting the local community in respect to concentrations and national origins. Mexicans initially predominated in California and the Southwest, Puerto Ricans in Metropolitan New York and the adjacent urban states, and Cubans since 1959 in south Florida. During the 1980s several hundred thousand Central Americans, Guatemalans, Salvadorans, and Nicaraguans entered the United States. In some cases these immigrants brought the nucleus of a congregation with them, but, more often, they simply presented an opportunity among displaced peoples for other Hispanic Pentecostals to gain new converts.

Meanwhile, the growth of Pentecostalism in Puerto Rico has been especially notable. Pentecostal members on the island number 350,000, equal to the combined total of all the Hispanic adherents found in mainland Pentecostal churches. These denominations include some religious organizations that began within another church before separating to become administratively independent. Most non-Pentecostal evangelicals in Puerto Rico have even acquired the styles and many of the practices of the Pentecostals. In any event, the initiative, leadership, resources, and methods are clearly Hispanic, just as they have been on the mainland.

The growth of the Hispanic Pentecostal groups has more or less reflected the growth of the Latino population through both natural increase and immigration. The census reported almost 2 million Hispanics in the United States just after World War II (although estimates of undocumented immigrants reported an additional one-half million), and 3.8 million Hispanics in the United States in 1960, about half of whom were born in Latin America. By 1970 the number had grown to about 5.5 million before jumping dramatically to 22 million in 1990 and increasing by 30 percent during the nineties to now exceed 30 million. It is expected that the number will continue to grow to 35 million in five years and 40 million by 2010. Latinos already make up 12 percent of the population nationally and will soon be the nation's largest minority. At this rate of growth, one person in four in the United States will be Hispanic by the year 2050.[14]

Since religious conversion is most likely to occur among peoples in transition, especially young people, it is notable that a third of all Hispanics are under eighteen years of age. While the median age for the white population is thirty-eight years and for African-Americans thirty years, the Hispanic median age is twenty-seven years. Almost all whites and African-American citizens living in the United States were born there, but almost 40 percent of all Mexicans and Puerto Ricans were not, and two-thirds of the Cubans and other Latinos were born outside the United States. Almost half of all Latinos live in just six metropolitan areas, three of them in California: Los Angeles, San Francisco, and San Jose; and New York, Miami, and Chicago. Ten states account for 85 percent of the Hispanics: California (34 percent), Texas (19 percent), New York (9 percent), Florida (7 percent), Illinois (4 percent), New Mexico (3 percent), Arizona (3 percent), New Jersey (3 percent), Colorado (2 percent), and Massachusetts (1 percent).

Understandably, the origins and present concentrations of Hispanic Pentecostal churches are in these states. Nevertheless, Latino Pentecostal churches are now found in virtually every part of the country: in Pocatello, Idaho; Ogden, Utah; and Laramie, Wyoming in the West; and in Boston, Hartford, and Providence in New England. Large Central American populations in Arkansas, recruited for the poultry industry, have their own Pentecostal churches, as do Puerto Ricans in Hawaii and Latin Americans of various origins in Washington, D.C.

An index of the Hispanics' assimilation into American life is provided by the proportion that feels comfortable speaking Spanish. According to polls, about 60 percent indicate this preference, down sharply from 90 percent in the 1980s. About 20 percent indicate that they have equal ease in both languages.[15] This cultural marginality reflects the relative poverty and lack of education of many Latinos. While a third of American families have an annual income below $25,000, the statistic for Latinos is one half. Meanwhile, 60 percent of white Americans have at least some college education, but only 34 percent of Hispanics. Thirty percent of whites have completed the bachelor's or an advanced degree, while only 11 percent of Latinos are college graduates or have completed graduate studies.

Studies show that Hispanics have a higher regard for religion than the general U.S. population. They are more traditional in their values, have greater respect for their elders, and see the importance of religion in their lives. Latinos have been proselytized in substantial numbers by Jehovah's Witnesses and Mormons, and are credited with having brought new life to the Roman Catholic Church in the United States, despite a shortage of Spanish-speaking priests. As with other immigrant populations, however, their religious beliefs and practices are formed not only by their cultural heritage but also by their experience in their new homeland.

Among all of the Pentecostal denominations, Hispanic congregations have usually assumed the same general characteristics. Where there are concentrations of Latinos, the Pentecostal churches eventually assimilated individual families or created denominational, Spanish-language divisions to reach them. While these churches have often been paternalistic, they have usually offered enough encouragement and support to make the relationship constructive and amicable. Hispanic churches, in turn, gave new life to congregations that were losing membership and introduced entirely new populations to Pentecostalism. Experiencing the transition of their own members, especially the loss of Latino young people to English-speaking congregations, the mutuality of the two ethnic groups is less lopsided than might initially appear. Not only have Hispanics created their own compatible approaches and leadership styles, but one finds in them indispensable initiative, energy, and vision. Increasingly, Anglo congregations are employing Latino staff members and adding Spanish language services to their programs, while Hispanic congregations conduct services that are bilingual or entirely in English. For many Hispanic Pentecostals, their church membership is more a matter of cultural preference than linguistic necessity.

The Pentecostal Denominations: Their Origins and Features

The relative effectiveness of North American Hispanic Pentecostals may be demonstrated by comparing their efforts with those of the historic Protestant denominations. A study published in 1930, when the Hispanic population was less than two million, found a combined denominational membership of 28,000 within fourteen Protestant denominations. The largest grouping, the Methodists, had 10,000 members, and the Baptists and Presbyterians together totaled 13,000. Thomas Coakley, the author, concluded that the Hispanic sector was "not adequately cared for either religiously or socially. The whole area is practically untouched."[16] Victor De Leon, the historian of the largest of the Pentecostal denominations, the Assemblies of God, titled his 1979 M.A. thesis "The Silent Pentecostals" because they were for so many years overlooked, both by other Pentecostals and by the Hispanic community.[17]

Nevertheless, the Latin Pentecostal churches had already gained a strong foothold before 1930, with organizations, church properties, a network of associations, and training schools in Texas and California. The Assemblies of God Hispanic churches took root along the Texas border where little distinction was made between the Mexicans and Anglo Pentecostals. According to Robert Anderson, early Pentecostals turned to the Latinos when it was clear that Pentecostals were not well received by the prevailing culture. "The Lord told us, 'The white people have rejected the gospel and I will turn to the Mexicans,'" reported one evangelist.[18]

Leadership was given to this work by the young Henry Ball in 1914, when, as an aspiring Methodist minister, he established a modest mission in Ricardo, Texas. He received the encouragement of several neighboring pastors and the help of various associates, including for a time Alice Luce, a British-born former Anglican missionary to India, and her companion, Florence Murcutt, a medical doctor who had vision for reaching Mexico with the gospel. Four years after the Assemblies of God was organized in 1914, the group reported Hispanic churches in fifteen towns. By 1922, when the Latin ministers held their own Fourth Annual Mexican Convention in Dallas, there were registered 50 congregations with 1,500 members.[19]

After attempting unsuccessfully to establish a mission in Monterrey, Mexico, in 1918, Luce, Murcutt, and their companion Sunshine Marshall returned to continue the work among Mexicans in the United States. Marshall married Henry Ball, who for almost forty years remained an important figure among Hispanic Assemblies of God churches. His younger colleague, Demetrio Bazán, succeeded him as the superintendent of the Assemblies of God Latin American District in 1939.[20]

Luce and Murcutt, meanwhile, returned to California where by 1923 Luce had organized a ministerial training school in San Diego and had assisted in the spread of Pentecostal churches throughout the state. After a trip to her homeland, she reported that the church in Los Angeles had tripled in size during her absence. The next year, despite an internal conflict that severely reduced the size of the work, the Seventh Annual Convention of Latin American Pentecostal (Assemblies of God) Churches reported forty congregations.[21] In 1935 there were two hundred ministers on the Assemblies of God roster, and the number of churches by 1939 totaled 170, with 125 more in Mexico.[22]

The schools formed in 1923 contributed importantly to the formation of the church. The Latin American Bible Institute in Texas produced a number of outstanding leaders, including several superintendents of the denomination's work in Mexico, which was totally independent by 1929, as well as many leaders of the U.S. Latin American District. Political figure Reyes Tijerina, who undertook a campaign to restore traditional lands to Hispanics in

Henry Cleopas Ball (1896–1989) spent most of his life developing the Hispanic churches and districts of the Assemblies of God.

New Mexico for a brief time, attended LABI in Texas. The sister school, LABI in southern California, helped train evangelist Robert Fierro, the

Teen Challenge convert Nicky Cruz, and Sonny Arguizoni, founder of Victory Outreach.

When Demetrio Bazán was named the superintendent of the Assemblies of God churches in 1939, the administrative district that had covered all of the churches from Puerto Rico to California was divided in two. The Latin American District was to oversee the churches in the western states and the Spanish Eastern District those on the East Coast. Subsequent reorganizations created a total of eight districts, including Puerto Rico, with a total of 140,000 adherents and 1,300 churches.

As early as 1923, however, the Assemblies' Hispanic work lost its strongest leader and produced a new organization, the *Asamblea de Iglesias Cristianas*, the creation of Francisco Olazábal. Failing to appreciate the strong leadership of the Mexicans themselves, the Assemblies kept the Hispanic work under its tutelage until it lost not only Olazábal, but, in 1953, almost the entire Puerto Rican church. The Assemblies of God had organized in Puerto Rico as the *Iglesia de Dios Pentecostal* (Pentecostal Church of God) at the outset to avoid using the term "asamblea" that had a political connotation. Although the Assemblies of God went on to reestablish itself, the *Iglesia de Dios Pentecostal* remains the largest Pentecostal organization in Puerto Rico. Meanwhile, the congregations of the *Iglesia de Dios Pentecostal* in New York and neighboring states became independent of the Assemblies of God under the name of the Spanish Christian churches.

Francisco Olazábal was a Mexican-trained Methodist minister who became Pentecostal through his association with George and Carrie Judd Montgomery. A businessman from Oakland, California, Montgomery operated mines in the Mexican state of Sonora, among other profitable ventures. After he had married Carrie Judd, a protégée of A. B. Simpson, the couple brought her healing ministry into the ranks of the Pentecostals. Olazábal was associated with Henry Ball in Texas and, in 1918, with Alice Luce when the evangelist conducted a meeting for her in Los Angeles. "God has used Olazábal's faithful messages to bring the light on Pentecost to many," Luce wrote, "especially to those who had known him here before in the Methodist Episcopal Church when he used to criticize and persecute 'this way.'"[23]

Francisco "El Azteca" Olazabal (1886–1937) pioneered Hispanic churches for the Assemblies of God before organizing the Latin American Council of Christian Churches.

In 1923 Olazábal led a group of Mexican pastors to form their own Hispanic denomination, the *Asamblea de Iglesias Cristianas,* which under Olazábal's leadership prospered throughout the 1920s and 1930s. Olazábal's untimely death in an automobile accident in 1937 was a crushing blow to the organization, which soon broke into its component movements in Texas and California on the East Coast, and in Puerto Rico. An extremely capable and well-educated leader, Olazábal has been acclaimed the strongest Pentecostal figure ever to emerge from the Hispanic movement. A reported total of fifty thousand people attended services in his honor in several cities at his death. His churches in Puerto Rico and the work he began on the East Coast remain significant.[24]

Still another stream of Hispanic Pentecostal churches began with independent Mexican Pentecostal congregations that never came under the

FRANCISCO OLAZABAL

Olazabal was converted in California at the turn of the century after receiving a tract from George Montgomery. George and his wife, Carrie Judd Montgomery, taught him basic Christian doctrines. Olazabal felt God's call on his life and returned to Mexico to prepare for the Methodist ministry. After a brief pastorate in El Paso, he attended Moody Bible Institute. In 1917 he became reacquainted with the Montgomerys in California. He was startled to learn that they had become Pentecostals and spoke in tongues. He attended a prayer meeting at their home, along with Alice E. Luce (a significant contributor to early Hispanic ministries) and others, where he was baptized in the Spirit. As a result, he became a Pentecostal preacher credentialed with the Assemblies of God.

Olazabal's new ministry soon bore fruit as young people who were Spirit-baptized in his services entered full-time ministry, many joining the Assemblies of God. In 1918, he moved to El Paso, Texas, staying long enough to plant a church before traveling across the United States holding revival campaigns. As more Spanish-speaking people were converted and joined the Pentecostal ranks, more of their ministers joined the Latin American Convention of the Assemblies of God, founded in 1918 under the leadership of Henry C. Ball.

In 1923 Olazabal and other ministers met in Houston, Texas, and formed the Latin American Council of Christian Churches. Although he had held credentials with the Assemblies of God for only five years, his labors added to the growth of Hispanic congregations in the council.

Considered the most effective Hispanic Pentecostal minister to that time, Olazabal was referred to as the "great Aztec" by a contemporary biographer. His work in New York and Chicago led to the establishment of dozens of new churches, as did his campaigns in Los Angeles and Puerto Rico. His emphases on evangelism and healing were combined with concern for the social needs of the Hispanic communities. By the late 1930s, his organization had fifty churches and an estimated fifty thousand adherents. Olazabal was apparently at the height of his ministry when he was killed in an automobile accident in Texas in 1937. ∎

—EFRAIM ESPINOZA
THE PENTECOSTAL EVANGEL

leadership of any Anglo group. According to Clifton Holland, these groups had adopted the oneness (Unitarian) position even before the doctrine was accepted by many Pentecostals at the time of the Arroyo Seco camp meeting in 1913.[25] By 1949 the group had its own training center in Hayward, California, and by 1970 had organized the North American churches into thirteen districts, each administered by a bishop.

With an episcopal hierarchy, a sister denomination in Mexico, and a conservative, authoritarian structure that forbade the credentialing of women as ministers, the *Asamblea Apostólica de la Fe en Cristo Jesús* apparently came

---

THE SILENT PENTECOSTALS

From the very beginning, Latinos flocked to the Azusa Street Mission in search of the transcendent God and a better life. For reasons that are not entirely clear, their unbridled enthusiasm and desire to testify prompted the leader to "ruthlessly crush" the Latino contingent in 1909.

This conflict gave birth to the Latino Pentecostal movement as scores left the mission and began preaching the Pentecostal message throughout the barrios and farm labor camps in the U.S., Mexico, and Puerto Rico. As early as 1912, Latinos organized their own completely autonomous and independent churches in California, Texas, and Hawaii.

Like a wax museum, the history of Latino Pentecostalism is full of dynamic characters like Chonita Morgan Howard who preached the Pentecostal message on horseback in northern Mexico and Arizona. Domingo Cruz, a fiery, illiterate one-legged was legendary for his persuasive preaching among the migrant farm labor camps of northern California. Still others like Robert Fierro, a.k.a. the "burned over Irishman," and A. C. Valdez thrilled thousands of Latinos and Anglos with their powerful evangelistic services throughout the country.

The work that these silent Pentecostals (their story is rarely told) pioneered prior to World War II is spreading like wildfire throughout the U.S. and Latin America today. Although often only averaging 60 to 100 members, these Pentecostal *templos* and *iglesias* are attracting 30,000 to 40,000 Latinos annually from Roman Catholicism.

"Their minister," one scholar of Latino Pentecostalism stated, "is likely to be a factory worker himself, secure in the Pentecostal belief that 'a man of God with a Bible in his hand has had training enough.' Many Pentecostals attend church every night for a two-hour service. Loud Bible readings and spontaneous testimonials are part of every service, punctuated by shouts of 'Aleluyah' and 'Gracias a Dios [thanks be to God].' The hymns well up with rhythmic clapping, generally accompanied by a guitar, drums, tambourines, and bass fiddle, piano or small combo."

Their call to a "born-again" Spirit-filled life has, unfortunately, resulted in tremendous conflict and persecution in their families and barrios, where they are derisively labeled the "Aleluyas."

The Pentecostal movement, along with a host of other religions, is shattering the stereotype that to be Latino is to be Roman Catholic. Today an estimated 1 million Latinos have embraced the Pentecostal/charismatic movement and attend one of the 10,000 congregations and prayer groups in 40 Latino Pentecostal/charismatic traditions throughout the U.S. and Puerto Rico. ∎

—GASTON ESPINOSA
CHRISTIAN HISTORY

closer than most of the Pentecostal groups to preserving the attitudes and practices of traditional Mexican culture. Sociologist Leo Grebler found this group to be the "predominant Mexican-American Pentecostal sect," on the basis of its being self-contained and operated by Mexican Americans. All of these Pentecostal groups, according to Grebler, have a distinctive familistic quality. "The atmosphere is one of total acceptance: Personal and family troubles are made public for congregational help through prayer; embraces between pew neighbors at the close of the service enhance the sense of a warm and all encompassing community. Pentecostal groups," he concludes, "tend far more than the classic denominations to reach the hard-to-reach in a meaningful fashion."[26]

All of the Pentecostal denominations and many independent congregations are characterized by more or less the same approaches. Substantial growth has been registered by the other major Pentecostal denominations, including the Church of God (Cleveland, Tenn.), whose churches are organized into regional administrative districts, for a total of 640 congregations and 45,000 members. The largest is the northeastern group consisting primarily of Puerto Ricans, but increasingly with many Central Americans and peoples from elsewhere in Latin America. For all denominational groups the southeastern region is essentially Cuban, although there are also many Central Americans. Even the Southwest and California, once largely Mexican, have congregations that are made up largely of Central Americans.

Similarly, the Pentecostal Holiness denomination, the Church of the Four Square Gospel, and the Church of God of Prophecy all now have substantial numbers of Hispanic congregations. Increasingly, figures given by these groups also report the numbers of Hispanics in essentially Anglo Pentecostal congregations, indication of the tendency for these groups to adapt rapidly to the dominant culture. But renewed by recent immigration and even sometimes by imported Latin American leadership, these churches continue to have a distinctive life of their own. They maintain their own programs, reach their own communities, and deal with their own internal issues. The commitment most have made to addressing the issues of gang violence, their inconspicuous but significant assistance to the emotionally and economically distressed, and concern for undocumented persons who attend their churches indicate that contrary to some assessments, they indeed have social programs.

What is the future of such groups? At the present their rapid growth has made them important both to the Latino communities and to the several denominations with which they are affiliated. They have in some cases acquired positions of power within these denominations, where they are receiving increasing recognition and respect. A recent conference held in the United States provided instant translation for the persons in attendance who spoke a language other than English. Nevertheless, the address of each of the major speakers was interpreted live into Spanish (doubling the time required for presentation) in deference to the Hispanics within the denomination.

Hispanic churches that are sometimes filled with young people and even adults who are as comfortable speaking English as Spanish face major challenges to maintaining their identity. While the increasing numbers of recent immigrants will keep alive the love for conducting worship in Spanish, and nostalgia and appropriateness will make the Spanish-speaking congregations effective means of preserving Hispanic culture, the decline in the use of the Spanish language and modification of some traditions appear inevitable. Larger churches, especially, employ all the contemporary methods of church operation found in their Anglo counterparts, and their reasons for being distinctively ethnic congregations sometimes seem to be dissipating.

But the day when Spanish-language congregations lose their significance may be delayed indefinitely. The Pentecostal churches in Latin America continue to experience rapid growth, the world's economies are still undergoing globalization, and the popularity of Latin recording artists and Mexican cuisine continues unabated, helping to close the cultural chasm that has long divided the peoples of the hemisphere. As Pentecostal musicians and composers, evangelists, teachers, and church development experts exert their influence with equal facility on both sides of the border, and Brazilian Pentecostal groups open branch churches in many North American cities, new levels of hemispheric cooperation emerge. Thomas Weyr is among those observers who believe that North American Latinos are more likely to renew their religious institutions, Catholic and Protestant, than they are to restore other social institutions. If he is correct, Hispanic Pentecostalism may in the future play an even larger role among people who are looking with anticipation toward the future.[27]

Pentecostalism in Latin America

Of all the manifestations of Latin American Protestantism, Pentecostalism has been the one that most deeply developed an indigenous model. During the 20th century, Pentecostalism has experienced an unprecedented growth in the continent. In general, it is the fastest-growing Christian movement in Latin America, a fact attributable in part to its adherents' characteristic attitude of constant testimony and religious militancy that translates into a zeal for winning souls.[28] Latin American Pentecostalism represents a very rich combination of independent Pentecostal strains that emerged from the historical evangelical denominations, and movements that originated in the missionary work of European and American Pentecostals in the first decades of the 20th century. In this sense, Pentecostalism has emerged from diverse backgrounds and assumes quite different forms in Latin America.

A more recent development within the broader Latin American Pentecostalism is noted by the term "charismatic movement" or "charismatic renewal movement," which has drawn members from classical Pentecostalism as well as from both the historical and missionary churches. This charismatic renewal is in fact quite distinctive from its classical Pentecostal expression in its adaptability and willingness to include believers of different doctrinal and ecclesial persuasions.

Unlike classical Pentecostalism, many of these churches show, for various reasons, an openness to ecumenical dialogue and thereby exert a powerful intra-ecclesiastical influence. Beneath its impressive heterogeneity, however, Latin American Pentecostalism presents important tendencies and traits common to most of its expressions. Although it is very difficult to draw a single and precise line of identity that could account for the dynamics of religious and ecclesiastical reality, there are significant common denominators to be distinguished.

Most Pentecostal groups are characterized by a mode of religious behavior and belief best described by the general term "evangelical."[29] Apart from their distinctive understanding of some aspects of the doctrine of the Holy Spirit, Latin American Pentecostals share with their non-Pentecostal evangelical counterparts the same doctrinal and ethical convictions and, more important, the abiding sense of the meaning and necessity of a personal experience of redemption.

Roman Catholicism continues to be the religious background and most influential factor in the definition of the Latin American culture. Before the arrival of any Pentecostal testimony, the continent had been under the exclusive dominion of the Roman Catholic Church, as the exclusive expression of the Christian faith. With the entry of Pentecostalism, a new way of understanding the Christian faith and life appeared. Since then, in the religious field, Pentecostal churches have been in a struggle with Roman Catholicism for the soul of Latin America.

Latin American Pentecostalism belongs to that branch of Christianity that places a personal experience of the Holy Spirit as a necessary sign of being a Christian. While Roman Catholics consider that the Holy Spirit works through the priest and the sacraments, and Protestants in general see His manifestation through the understanding and exposition of the Word, Pentecostals conceive the action of the Spirit in a direct manner upon the personal experience of the believer. The doctrinal tenets of most Pentecostals in Latin America are modeled according to the historical Christian tradition. An essential point of their convictions is the belief in the baptism of the Holy Spirit, which is generally understood to be accompanied by the exercise of the gift of tongues as its characteristic sign. Evangelism through the operation of the gift of healing is also a key element in the Pentecostal expansion in Latin America. Their worship is enthusiastic with a deep sense of joy and hope.

The growth of the various Pentecostal denominations has been phenomenal. As early as 1984, Penny Lernoux reported that "every hour 400 Latin Americans convert to the Pentecostals or other fundamentalist or evangelical churches." She also predicted that by the end of the 1900s, in the countries most susceptible to Pentecostal mission activity, such as Guatemala, half of the population would belong to the spectrum of the Pentecostal churches.[30] Her predictions have proved to be true.

Probably the largest missionary presence in Latin America is represented by the Assemblies of God, based in Springfield, Missouri. By 1980 this large Christian community had already disseminated its own vision of the evangelical worldview through 67,375 ministers serving 81,836 churches and another 25,715 students training for the ministry in 145 Bible schools. With 10 million members in the region in 1984 (6 million in Brazil), the Assemblies of God accounted for approximately 1 of every 4 evangelicals in Latin America.[31] Amid El Salvador's wasteland of violence the Assemblies of God presence grew in the 1980s. It had an estimated 100,000 members in both missionary and national churches, or almost half of the Protestant population. In only five years (1980–85) the number of Assemblies churches grew from 20,000 to 80,000.[32]

Throughout Central America in the 1980s and 1990s, scores of Pentecostal organizations were dedicated to full-time evangelism. Guatemala is a case in point as the first country to have at least half the population evangelical today. In one year the Assemblies of God in Guatemala grew 44 percent. For the past twenty years the Church of God (Cleveland, Tenn.) has planted on the average one church in Guatemala every five days, and they have been doing the same in Costa Rica for the past fifteen years.[33]

The Pentecostal churches are a 20th-century phenomenon in Latin America. The estimated proportion of the Pentecostal community today on the continent accounts for 35 percent of all the Pentecostals in the world. In 1995, in Brazil alone, the Assemblies of God numbered 13 million; the Universal Church of the Kingdom of God, 7 million; the Christian Church, 3.4 million; God Is Love, 3.2 million; and Brazil for Christ, 2.6 million. This meant that in 1995, almost 20 percent of the population of that country was Pentecostal, 1 person in 5. More than 30 million Pentecostals in Brazil today account for 80 percent of all the Pentecostals in Latin America. To put the situation in a startling perspective, Brazil has the largest population of Catholics in the world (150 million) while at the same time counting the largest Pentecostal population in the world (30 million).

Beginnings and Development

The origin of Pentecostalism in Latin America is almost as old as its beginnings in the United States and Europe. This means that Latin American Pentecostalism began very early in the history of the movement in the world. It has expanded to all the Latin American republics and the Caribbean to become the most influential expression of the Christian testimony outside the Roman Catholic Church. Its development has been particularly impressive in Chile, where it has been self-governing from the beginning; in Mexico, where it was taken by missionaries from the United States; and in Brazil, where it made its major advances thanks to both independent progressive growth and missionary initiatives.

Chile. The small Methodist community of Valparaiso was the starting point of a pioneer Pentecostal movement in this Roman Catholic country and the first in Latin America.[34] A powerful spiritual revival began in 1902 under the leadership of Willis C. Hoover (1856–1936), a Methodist missionary from Chicago. Versatile in his methods, he was aware of recent revivals in other parts of the world, including the healing emphasis of leading revivalists of his days. In 1895, Hoover had visited the holiness community in Chicago led by William H. Durham. He was especially impressed by an account of a 1905 revival in India where tongues appeared in a girls' school. But it was not until 1907 that he came in contact with the Pentecostal doctrine through his correspondence with Pentecostals in various parts of the world. After numerous prayer vigils beginning in 1907, Hoover and his group experienced the "baptism of the Holy Spirit" in 1909.

Both spiritually sensitive and pragmatic, this Methodist pastor became the father of this almost unique phenomenon in the continent, directed by and for the common people. When Pentecostal phenomena appeared in his meetings in 1909, he permitted spiritual demonstrations and displays that were considered by his critics to be unseemly and unbiblical. Due to his spiritual experiences and growing Pentecostal convictions, Hoover was finally separated from the Methodist Church in 1910. The reasons given were mostly of a doctrinal character.[35]

The movement soon extended to Santiago and thrived against a backdrop of urban migration and social deterioration. In 1910 Hoover and his followers organized *La Iglesia Metodista Pentecostal* (the Pentecostal Methodist Church). It was begun with only three congregations by Pentecostal people who had been rejected by the Methodists. Growth was rapid. By 1911 there were ten churches; by 1929 there were twenty-two. Hoover, with the title of bishop, was the undisputed leader of these congregations until a schism occurred in 1932. At this time, Manuel Umaña, who represented the Chilean nationalist feelings against the "gringo" Hoover, assumed the leadership of the church in Santiago. This congregation, which was called the "Jotabeche" Church (after the street on which it was located), continued to function under the name *Iglesia Metodista Pentecostal*. Hoover and his supporters (among them Víctor Pavez) established the *Iglesia Evangélica Pentecostal* (Pentecostal Evangelical Church). These two churches became the largest Pentecostal communities in Chile. Out of them emerged more than thirty different groups, mostly during this period.[36]

Methodist missionary turned Pentecostal, Willis C. Hoover (1856–1936) led one of the most revolutionary Pentecostal outbreaks in Chile in 1909. His followers now number more than two million persons in Chile.

The *Iglesia Metodista Pentecostal* took twenty years in reaching a membership of 10,000 people. However, even when statistics are not precise, by the middle of the last century it was estimated that the members of the Pentecostal Methodist Church stood at at least 200,000 persons. The *Iglesia Evangélica Pentecostal* had by then some 150,000 members, and also had missions in Argentina, Bolivia, Peru, and Uruguay. In 1929 Chilean Pentecostals constituted one-third of the total Protestant community of 62,000 members.[37] By 1961 it was estimated that the Pentecostal churches were four times more numerous than the rest of the Protestant communities in Chile, with a membership that was calculated between 400,000 and 800,000 persons. This means that between 1929 and 1961 the Pentecostal community in Chile grew by approximately twenty-four times.

Chilean Pentecostalism was characterized by long pastorates and very popular leaders. Hoover himself was the pastor of his congregation for more than a quarter of a century. This Pentecostalism was also distinguished by being the inheritor of the Methodist Episcopal power, an authoritarian leadership, a wide participation of laypeople, autonomy with regard to the foreign control of the work, the populist attitude inherited from Roman Catholicism, and an extraordinary motivation to evangelize the masses. Due to all of these factors, by the 1960s, the Jotabeche congregation, with some 40,000 members, was recognized as the largest Protestant church in the world.

Since its inception and through a marked tendency to split and divide, a continuing feature of Chilean Pentecostalism, the movement has grown and reproduced in amazing ways. In 1946 the *Iglesia Metodista Pentecostal* suffered again a new division when P. Enrique Chávez founded the *Iglesia Pentecostal de Chile*. Other branches of the Pentecostal movement were born as a result of American missionary activity such as the Assemblies of God after 1941.

By 2000, however, about 50 percent of the Chilean Pentecostal movement belonged to the original *Iglesia Metodista Pentecostal,* while another 38 percent belonged to the *Iglesia Evangélica Pentecostal*. Most of the rest belonged to the other diverse expressions of Chilean Pentecostalism. Pentecostals in Chile now make up scores of organizations with an aggregate adherence of as much as one-fifth of the national population. The movement has proved to be divisive as well as dynamic and has appealed primarily to the lower strata of the population. Today it is self-supporting, strongly missionary, and steadily growing.

The Jotabeche Methodist Pentecostal Church in Santiago, Chile, was for many years the largest Protestant church in the world.

Brazil. In Brazil the Pentecostal movement emerged almost simultaneously among local Presbyterian and Baptist communities. In 1910 the Italian-American Luigi Francescon (1866–1964) arrived in Sao Paulo. He had been a tile maker who had founded Chicago's first Italian Presbyterian church in 1892. In 1907 he experienced the baptism of the Spirit and speaking in tongues in the church pastored by William Durham. With other likeminded friends in the Italian community, he established the first Italian Pentecostal church in Chicago, the *Assemblea Cristiana*. Through various trips to Brazil, he founded a Latin American version of his American movement which he called the *Congregação Cristã*. Until 1930 the church was almost totally Italian, but from then on it was Portuguese speaking.[38]

The growth of this congregation during the 1930s was impressive, and reached its peak after the 1950s. By 1936 the *Congregação Cristã* had 36,600 members, and by 1962 the total number was 264,000. The church grew to

305 congregations by 1940, 815 by 1951, and nearly 2,500 before the death of its founder.

In 1910, Francescon said he had received a special revelation from God, which he shared with a small group of believers in São Paulo. The Lord revealed to him that there would be a great harvest of people in the capital city and throughout Brazil if believers remained faithful and humble. This prophecy became a reality. In just half a century this church grew to more than a quarter of a million people. Today the denomination is one of the largest in Brazil.

Another important Pentecostal community in Brazil is the Assemblies of God.[39] This denomination began with the work of two Americans of Swedish origin: Daniel Berg (1884–1963) and A. Gunnar Vingren (1879–1933). They first met at a Chicago conference. Both of them received a prophecy that they were to be missionaries to someplace in the world called "Para." At a local library they discovered that Para was a state in northern Brazil. After a service of confirmation led by William H. Durham of Chicago, the two men began their work in Belem, the capital city of

Luigi Francescon (1866–1964) and his Italian Pentecostal friends from Chicago founded flourishing Pentecostal churches in the United States, Italy, Argentina, and Brazil.

Para, in 1910. The first services were conducted in cooperation with the local Baptist congregation.

After being rejected by the local pastor, they were permitted to hold prayer meetings in the basement of the Baptist chapel where they fasted and prayed for revival. In 1911, after five days of prayer, Celina de Alburquerque was baptized in the Holy Spirit. Some other members of the small group began to speak in tongues as the manifest evidence of the baptism in the Holy Spirit. This led to controversy with the Baptist missionaries, and they were soon cut off from that congregation because of their Pentecostal teachings.

With seventeen adult members and their children, they moved to Albuquerque's home, where, according to Berg, "the first Pentecostal religious service was officially performed in Brazil." The first Brazilian Assemblies of God church was founded on June 18, 1911. After seven more years of work, the new congregation was officially registered as the *Assembleia de Deus*.[40] From Belem they moved to the Amazon region. In 1913 they began to send missionaries to Portugal, then to Madagascar and France. During 1930 and 1931 they went to the south of the country, where they founded large congregations in Rio de Janeiro, São Paulo, Porto Alegre, and other cites.[41]

Today the Assemblies of God constitutes the largest Protestant church in Brazil and in Latin America. Its growth was slow during the first twenty years. In 1930 their membership totaled only 14,000 persons. In a second period of growth, from 1930 to 1950, the membership reached 120,000 people. During this period a better national leadership emerged. Since 1950 growth has been incredible. The Assemblies of God spread widely throughout the country with the development of vigorous and enormous congregations. From 1949 to 1962 the church multiplied its membership by five. By 1965 there were more than 950,000 baptized members. Today the Assemblies of God are the largest Pentecostal church in Brazil.[42]

A third expression of Brazilian Pentecostalism is the church *Brasil para Cristo* (Brazil for Christ) founded by the missionary Manoel de Mello. This dynamic preacher began as an evangelist at the end of the 1940s in Pernambuco and São Paulo. About 1950, de Mello moved to São Paulo as preacher and pastor in the *Carpa Divina* (Divine Tent), where he collaborated with American missionaries of the Foursquare Gospel Church. De Mello attracted large multitudes to his tent crusades. Because of his very particular leadership style and his popularity, de Mello also created controversy. However, his influence continued growing with the years, especially due to his radio programs and political contacts.

From 1955 on his movement operated under the name *Brazil para Cristo* (Brazil for Christ) and since then its growth has been impressive. In 1965 it had more than 1,100 organized churches in Brazil, with some 1,600 ordained pastors and candidates for ordination in the process of training. There were 87 temples under construction in different places of Brazil. In 1963 de Mello estimated that *Brasil para Cristo* had more than 500,000 adherents and that every year there was an average increase of some 80,000 new members. By the year 2000, they constituted the fifth largest Pentecostal denomination in Brazil with some 2.6 million members.

Mexico. Pentecostalism began early in the 20th century in this country. The first Pentecostal missionary to arrive in Mexico was Cesareo Burciaga. Burciaga was converted in Houston, Texas, in 1918, and founded the first church of the Assemblies of God in Musquiz in 1921. By the 1930s the church was registered and experienced great growth, especially during the decade of the 1940s.[43]

Mexican Pentecostalism, however, experienced one of its most important moments in 1932 when María W. Rivera Atkinson (1879–1963) was appointed as missionary of the Church of God (Cleveland, Tenn.) and laid the foundations of that denomination in Obregón and Hermosillo. Atkinson had a deep spiritual experience in 1907, while still a Roman Catholic, and between 1915 and 1920 founded several prayer groups in Sonora, Mexico. In 1924 she was healed of cancer and baptized in the Holy Spirit. She was then appointed as a preacher of the Assemblies of God, ministering in Arizona and Mexico. From 1926 on she resided permanently in Mexico.[44]

The Pentecostal Holiness Church began its American Hispanic and Mexican missionary work in 1931 under the leadership of Esteben Lopez of Weslaco, Texas. Known in Mexico and Texas as "La Iglesia Santa Pentecostes," the church grew from its Texas base of thirty-two churches to encompass four hundred Spanish-speaking congregations in the United States and Mexico by the year 2000.

Mexican Pentecostalism accounts for numerous factions but is the largest Protestant branch in the country. One of the most powerful churches is the *Iglesia Cristiana Independiente Pentecostés* (Pentecost Independent Christian Church). Its foundation goes back to Andrés Ornelas Martínez, a miner who was converted in reading a copy of the Proverbs that came into his hands when he was in Miami. In coming back to his country, he was interested in reading the New Testament and in 1920 returned to Miami to get a Bible. In 1922 he was baptized by a Methodist missionary who introduced him to the doctrine of the baptism in the Holy Spirit and with whom he founded a Pentecostal church. Because of the fusion of both congregations the new church grew. In 1941 Ornelas separated from the foreign missionaries. In 1953 he succeeded in gathering two hundred communities under one organization, the *Iglesia Cristiana Independiente Pentecostés*. Very soon, they sent missionaries to Colombia and Puerto Rico and developed an authentic national Pentecostalism.

Characteristics of Latin American Pentecostalism

A Popular Movement. Interpretations of Latin American Pentecostalism have differed, but they seem to agree in pointing out the new social class of marginalized people produced by the migration of people, particularly from rural areas to the cities. These thousands of migrant workers, both in Mexico and the United States, became the soil from which Pentecostal growth was nurtured. Latin American Pentecostalism has flourished among the popular social classes, even when its adherents held to the values of the middle class or at least aspired to them. Sociologically speaking, some researchers see it as a "Westernization" of the indigenous culture, others as a product of the transition between traditional society and modernity, and even others as a need of sociological identity in a massive society.

Since the 1960s Pentecostal churches have been most successful in identifying themselves as the true "churches of the disinherited." Unlike the historical churches, the Pentecostal churches are class-based organizations and are often protest movements against the existing class structure. These "havens of the masses" have often been at variance with the surrounding social structure in terms of organizational rules and traditional symbols, which they consider as belonging to the upper classes. They refuse to accommodate themselves to traditional Latin American political and social values.

Moreover, Latin American Pentecostals have flourished in places where there is rapid cultural change, in the aimless life of the urban areas, and in the rural districts where economic change has resulted in the disturbance of traditional relationships. Pentecostal advances have usually been made among sectors of the working population of the lower strata—especially in areas or groups of marked social dislocation. In these circumstances Pentecostalism has appeared as a "lower-class solidarity movement."

A Latino Cultural Movement. Pentecostalism in various forms has met with success in Latin America in part because it compares favorably among the lower classes and with both traditional Catholicism and historical Protestantism. Much has been written about "the Latin American character," whose traits include innate warmth and hospitality, resignation in the face of periodic natural calamities, a flexibility of spirit producing tolerance, enchantment with charismatic personalities, individualism, and a distinct turn to emotionalism and mysticism. Particularly in Pentecostalism, these traits have found channels of expression.

In contrast with the Pentecostal type of service, the average meeting of historical Protestant churches is often decried as colorless, tasteless, and boring. In place of the Catholic Church's technical-theological language, which only the clergy understands, Pentecostals have a highly significant system of communication. All may receive the gift of tongues—a more ecstatic experience than reciting the abstract phrases of a specialized language. Much of Pentecostal liturgical dancing and group participation in prayer is a form of folk drama.

Pentecostals do not have the miraculous wafer to offer the people, but they can offer the promise of miraculous healing, not only as the gift of God but as proof of a measure of their faith and of the fact that God has responded to the people's attempt to communicate with Him. There is great emphasis upon group participation in prayer and singing, and the sermons are generally on the intellectual level of the people, with plenty of opportunities for men and women to respond, not only verbally but by signs of the indwelling of the Spirit as well.

A Socially Uplifting Movement. Most converts to Latin American Pentecostal churches have often been drawn from a rootless and disconnected subculture, from people whose extended family networks disintegrated in the rush to the cities and who therefore had lost much of the social infrastructure needed to survive in the hostile urban environment. Sociologists have said that Pentecostals find in their faith a sort of compensation for their social alienation.

An example of these trends is found in the growth of Pentecostal churches in northeastern Brazil. Common to all of them is the fact that the followers constitute part of an underprivileged mass of people, many of them former Catholics, whose socioeconomic situation has made them receptive to the message of local preachers. The message invariably contains the promise of a better life predicated upon immediate conversion. Usually this involves the adoption of an ascetic way of life.

Buoyed by emotional exaltation and messianic expectations, they are eager to proclaim their spiritual rebirth by engaging in forms of behavior intended to repudiate the weaknesses and sins of their former lives. The members of such churches have proved capable of remarkable success in reordering their lives socially and to some extent economically. The pastors of local Pentecostal churches facilitate these personal and social transformations, often acting as public representatives of the unemployed and dispossessed seeking honest work.

CARLOS ANNACONDIA

After observing the ministry of Carlos Annacondia for several years, I am prepared to offer a hypothesis: Annacondia may well be the most effective citywide interdenominational crusade evangelist of all time. If this turns out to be only approximately true, his approach to winning the masses of the cities to Christ deserves close scrutiny.

Annacondia was the committed Christian owner of a prosperous nuts and bolts factory in Quilmes on the outskirts of Buenos Aires when he was called into evangelistic ministry. It was probably no mere coincidence that the day he launched his first public crusade was the day the British sank the Argentine battleship General Belgrano in the 1982 Falkland Islands war. He was 37 years old at the time.

When I use the term "effective evangelism" I follow the lead of Donald McGavran and the Church Growth Movement in arguing that biblical evangelism involves bringing unbelievers to a simultaneous commitment to Christ and also to the body of Christ. Making disciples involves bringing men and women to faith in Jesus and into responsible membership in a local church.

Carlos Annacondia is highly successful in seeing this happen. On a recent visit to Argentina I worked with pastors of four cities. Without any leading questions on my part, in each of the four cities I heard Christian leaders in a matter-of-fact way refer to recent trends in their cities as "before Annacondia" and "after Annacondia." In more than 20 years of studying urban crusade evangelism I have never heard such consistent testimonials of one evangelist across the board. Single instances of effective evangelistic crusades such as Tommy Hicks in Buenos Aires and Stanley Mooneyham in Phnom Penh have been recorded. But Annacondia's ministry seems to be unique.

Several pastors showed me new sanctuaries they had constructed to contain the growth after Annacondia's crusade in their city. One showed me a basketball stadium they had been leasing for six years. Another church now holds 17 services a week in five rented theaters. Another pastor reports "a notable change of attitude among the people of our city as a result of Annacondia's ministry."

What Is Different?

What is Carlos Annacondia doing that other urban evangelists do not usually do? Annacondia has a great deal in common with traditional crusade evangelists. He preaches a simple gospel message, gives an invitation for people to come forward and receive Christ as their Lord and Savior, uses trained counselors to lead them to Christ and give them literature, takes their name and address and invites them to attend a local church.

Like Billy Graham and Luis Palau, Annacondia secures a broad base of interdenominational support from pastors and other Christian leaders in the target area. Like Dwight Moody and Billy Sunday he has had no formal academic theological training. Like Reinhard Bonnke and T. L. Osborne he features miracles, healings and deliverance from evil spirits in his meetings. He is not the only one who preaches in the open air, conducts three-hour services, or has on-the-spot intercessors praying for the ministry. If I am not mistaken, the major difference is Carlos Annacondia's intentional, premeditated, high-energy approach to spiritual warfare.

A permanent fixture of Annacondia's crusades is what has to be one of the most sophisticated and massive deliverance ministries anywhere. Under the direction of Paolo Bottari, a wise, mature and gifted servant of God, literally hundreds of individuals are delivered from demons each of the 30 to 50 consecutive nights of a crusade. The 150-foot deliverance tent, erected behind the speaker's platform, is in operation from 8:00 p.m. to 4:00 a.m. each night. Scores of teams whom Botari has trained do the actual hands-on ministry.

I have never observed a crusade evangelist who is as publicly aggressive in confronting evil spirits as Annacondia. With a high-volume, high-energy, prolonged challenge he actually taunts the spirits until they manifest in one way or another. To the uninitiated the scenario might appear to be total confusion. But to the skilled, experienced members of Annacondia's crusade ministry teams, it is just another evening of power encounters in which the power of Jesus Christ over demonic forces is being displayed for all to see. Many miraculous healings occur, souls are saved, and so great is the spiritual power that unsuspecting pedestrians passing by the crusade meeting have been known to fall down under the power of the Holy Spirit. ■

—C. PETER WAGNER
THE AWESOME ARGENTINA REVIVAL

An Anti-intellectual Movement. The anti-intellectualism of certain segments of Latin American Pentecostalism is one expression of a pervasive, fundamentalist anti-elitism. This is often a reaction against the higher learning of the elites in government and religion. Reason is set in unflattering contrast to revelation, and the arcane matters of modern science juxtaposed to the clear truths of the Bible. In Chile, for example, among some Pentecostals higher formal education for both ministers and laity is frowned upon. Schisms have occurred in some denominations when some members have tried to introduce Bible schools. The preference for the poor, ignorant, and uneducated has wide and indisputable currency among the Chilean Pentecostal churches. Any kind of learning beyond the literacy needed to read the Bible is frowned upon, and educated members who show intellectual interests or ambitions are watched with considerable suspicion.

There is in Latin America a somewhat general impression that to be a good and pious minister, theological education is not necessary, and that an intellectual pastor is deficient in piety. Besides, because of a general attitude of retreating from the "world," Pentecostals have become indifferent to social issues and staunch opponents of political involvement until more recent times. By nature, Pentecostalism is strongly individualistic (in regard to social issues) and intensively emotional. But, as in any religious movement, there are exceptions to the general attitude of its members. In the 1980s and 1990s there were signs of change among the younger leadership of Latin American Pentecostalism.

Claudio Freidzon (1955–) is marked by the same signs and wonders of the early church. Sick bodies are healed and lives are transformed as the Holy Spirit breathes a powerful anointing on all those who receive.

An Urban Movement. Pentecostalism expansion during

THE MINISTRY OF REVEREND CLAUDIO FREIDZON

The year 1992 marked a new stage in Pastor Claudio's ministry when a well-respected friend of his, Pastor Werner Kniesel, paid him a visit. Werner Kniesel is the pastor of the largest congregation in Europe, "Christliches Zentrum Buchegg" (Christian Center Buchegg) in Zurich, Switzerland. Kniesel had known Claudio since his student days at seminary. When Claudio told him of his many ministerial activities, Kniesel asked him a question, "How much time do you take to listen to the Holy Spirit?"

It was during that visit that Kniesel shared the book *Good Morning, Holy Spirit* written by Pastor Benny Hinn. Pastor Claudio felt this book was written just for him. "God greatly blessed me when I read Pastor Benny's book, so I decided to visit the United States in order to meet and pray with him. This pastor's testimony, and his relationship with the Holy Spirit, were a great inspiration for my own life."

During this search, the Holy Spirit came upon Claudio in an extraordinary way. A glorious atmosphere filled the services, and the presence of God began to manifest itself in the church as never before.

Without inviting anybody, or promoting anything, the news spread that something was happening at King of Kings Church. The pastors came on their own to receive this fresh anointing. It transformed their lives and took them back to their first love. The Holy Spirit operated with such power, that many would lie on the floor under the presence of God for hours, some laughing with joy, some crying brokenly, and others as if they were "drunk," in the presence of God.

God showed Reverend Claudio Freidzon that this was His powerful hand working sovereignly, producing fruit in many lives and a renewal in the consecration and the surrender of lives of Christians. The evangelization and edification work spread over the radio and television. Over the course of time, hundreds of pastors came to the King of Kings Church to receive the fresh anointing of the Holy Spirit.

Many came with their whole congregations. For weeks, on occasions, there were lines hundreds of meters long of people waiting to get into the church. People from faraway places came by hired buses to receive more from God.

One of the largest crusades in Argentina with more than 65,000 people packed the "Velez Sarfield" soccer stadium. Brothers and sisters from all denominations, from many different places in our country, came to seek the face of God on a memorable Good Friday. The ministry of the Reverend Claudio Freidzon began to spread outside the borders of Argentina. Pastors and Christian leaders from all over the world, some in teams, started to come to receive God's touch in their lives.

Since the Lord revolutionized Claudio Freidzon's life and ministry, he has traveled extensively, receiving invitations to various parts of the world, to conduct large crusades. These crusades have been characterized by the unity of the pastors in each city where he was invited, by the evangelistic fruit, and by the spiritual renewal for the churches.

In 1998 he held a revival crusade in Ecuador. The event was held in the national stadium of Guayaquil, which seats over 50,000 people, and was completely full every night. Around 1,500 pastors and Christian leaders united to organize and develop this important event. The power of God made an impact on thousands of people. Transformed lives, healing miracles, deliverance, and deep renewal have been the result of this mighty move of God. Approximately 160,000 people attended the different meetings, which has caused a great impact since on the Ecuadorian society.

Pastor Freidzon has written a book called *Holy Spirit, I Hunger for You*, which has now been translated into nine languages. Many Christians around the world have been inspired by this book to develop a deeper and more personal relationship with the Holy Spirit.

More than three and a half million people to date have been reached by his ministry in a personal way, through crusades, conferences, special events, and meetings in churches.

Everywhere Claudio Freidzon has ministered, there have been testimonies of revival, growth, and transformed lives due to the fresh anointing of the Holy Spirit. ∎

—SAM RODRIGUEZ

these years was mainly produced in urban areas under development. The speed of urban growth in Latin America has been truly explosive. The annual demographic growth rate has been above 3 percent. In 1950, three-fourths of the population lived in cities of less than 20,000 people, but by 1975 half the Latin American population was urban. In 1960, only six or seven cities had more than half a million people. A decade later there were already thirty-six cities with more than 500,000 inhabitants.

This phenomenon was due to urban demographic growth and to migration from rural areas to the cities. Those moving to the huge cities had to confront the conditions of a social vacuum marked by the absence of norms or social values. This generally is the factor that produces the possibility of a religious change. The weakening of traditional social controls in a situation of aimlessness, a characteristic of modern urban life, favors the development of an acute crisis in personal identity in many of the urban migrants. This explains why many of them abandon their traditional Catholic beliefs and practices to become Pentecostals. In Latin America there has been a close relationship between the processes of industrialization and urbanization and the growth of Pentecostalism in the cities.[45]

A Diverse Movement. Latin American Pentecostalism has emerged from diverse backgrounds and in many places assumes quite different forms. Brazilian and Mexican Pentecostals fix the Azusa Street revival in 1906 as the start of such works in their countries. In a short time, however, all Latin American countries had developing Pentecostal denominations. Some of them were offshoots of North American groups, but many from the beginning were completely autonomous national movements. Most of these groups were in fact very different from their classical North American expressions in their adaptability and willingness to include believers of different doctrinal and ecclesial persuasions. Besides, as an independent movement or as a movement with scarce dependency from foreign missionary support, Latin American Pentecostalism has been characterized by its diversity.

There are at least three different types of Pentecostals in Latin America. On the one side are those who could be named as classical Pentecostals, having their origins at the beginning of the 20th century. These have constituted their own denominations and have reached a higher level of ecclesiastical institutionalization. They are linked to the major Pentecostal denominations in Europe and North America. A second group, and probably the most dynamic and growing, is that of independent "renewed" Pentecostals, who, together with other charismatics are critical of traditional and institutionalized Pentecostalism.

The fastest-growing churches in Latin America today belong to this sort of independent Pentecostalism. A third expression is what I call "popular Pentecostalism." These groups are inheritors of classic Pentecostalism, but they have acquired the traits of a popularized religiosity. Some of them are borderline expressions of the Christian faith mixed with elements of Pentecostalism.

It is possible to distinguish in the Latin American Pentecostal movement diverse theological lines. On one side, there are those Pentecostals who, theologically, ecumenically, and sociopolitically, are conservatives. Although these Pentecostals have taken an important religious leap in accepting and integrating their respective ecclesial traditions to the Pentecostal experience, they maintain the theological tenets of classic fundamentalism. Basically, they keep a strong pre-millennial eschatology and biblical literalism along with an inerrancy view of the Scriptures. They also have rejected any form of relationship between Catholics and Protestants, and have supported a definite right-wing ideology.

On the other side, there are those who can be described as open to interdenominational or ecumenical relationships. They are more open to progressive theological and sociopolitical currents. Finally, there is a sector in Latin American Pentecostalism that, although identifying with Pentecostalism, keeps a critical attitude towards its theological conclusions, its worldview, and its sociocultural vision.

A Movement of Strong Leaders. In Latin American Pentecostalism, the charismatic leader, unfettered by traditional ecclesiastical structures, easily commands an enthusiastic band of followers. Individualism also finds fulfillment in the Pentecostal understanding of the Christian faith. In many Pentecostal churches, at the top of the ecclesiastical structure is either a group of men or a single strong personality who dominates the group. The strength of this structure is, however, the full participation of almost everyone and a gradation that depends largely on function rather than background. Since the people come largely from the same general socioeconomic class, there is not the tendency for the rich or well-educated to stifle the development of the more humble people, as is the case in many churches of the more historical denominations.

A Growing Movement. Pentecostals account for 75 percent of the evangelical population in Latin America. In some countries this rises to 90 percent of all non-Catholics. They are exploding in numbers. This means that they are the most visible evangelical force in the subcontinent. There are a cluster of reasons for the Pentecostal growth. These include: spiritual factors (the free action of the Spirit); anthropological reasons (hunger for God); sociological elements (they provide a sure sense of shelter, security, identity, and community in the hostile world); pastoral methodology (lay participation); and psychological and cultural factors (freedom of worship and emotion, use of folk music and instruments). According to Mortimer and Esther Arias, "The fact is that they are large, self-supporting, self-governed, and self-multiplying churches, rooted among the poor masses, while the historical Protestant churches are confined to middle-class enclaves. Pentecostals do not lack problems of leadership, education, division and social alienation, but there is no doubt that they have a significant place in the future of Christianity in Latin America."[46]

Pentecostals will continue to grow in numbers and influence in Latin America. It will be so because it is proving itself capable of responding to the immediate concerns of the lower-class masses. This is true of both the continuing activity of missionaries and the rise and growth of independent local churches of the Pentecostal type. In this sense, some predictions made in the past continue in effect. Lalive d'Epinay said years ago that "if the possibilities for social and political participation open to popular classes are reduced, opportunities for the diffusion of Pentecostalism will grow in the same proportion."[47]

The Dutch social scientist Juan Tennekes came to the same conclusion in his study of Chilean Pentecostalism after the 1973 coup d'état. "Now that all legal opposition has been proscribed, the only avenue open is that of religious protest; now that there are no other organizations that may operate as communities, the search for religious community will be greater than ever," he wrote. "Pentecostalism, therefore, will be strengthened . . . For the Chilean people, crushed in fire and blood by its own armed forces, religion will become the only legally accepted form of expressing its problems, doubts and hopes."[48]

For Further Reading

Major recent studies of Latin American Pentecostalism include David Stoll's *Is Latin America Turning Protestant? The Politics of Evangelical Growth* (Berkeley: Univ. of California Press, 1990); and David Martin's *Tongues of Fire: The Explosion of Protestantism in Latin America* (Cambridge, Mass.: Basil Blackwell, Inc., 1990). Much information on Latino Pentecostalism both in the United States and other countries can be found in Stanley M. Burgess, ed., and Eduard M. van der Maas, assoc. ed., *New International Dictionary of Pentecostal and Charismatic Movements* (Grand Rapids: Zondervan, 2001).

Issues related to Roman Catholics and Pentecostals are addressed in Brian H. Smith's *Religious Politics in Latin America: Pentecostal v. Catholic* (South Bend, Ind.: Univ. of Notre Dame Press, 1998), 3–9.

An influential book on North American Pentecostalism is Victor De Leon's *The Silent Pentecostals: A Biographical History of the Pentecostal Movement among the Hispanics in the Twentieth Century* (self-published). A good study of oneness Pentecostalism in Mexico is Manuel J. Gaxiola's *La Serpiente y la Paloma* (Pasadena, Calif.: William Carey Library, 1970).

Firsthand reports of the birth of Chilean Pentecostalism are graphically presented in Willis C. Hoover's *History of the Pentecostal Revival in Chile,* transl. Mario Hoover (Santiago, Chile: Imprenta Eben-Ezer, 2000). This is a translation of the original Spanish edition of 1936. The story of Brazilian Pentecostal beginnings is described in Daniel Berg's autobiography *Enviado por Deus: Memórias de Daniel Berg,* 3rd ed. (Rio de Janeiro: Casa Publicadora das Assembléias de Deus, 1973).

· 13 ·
Healers and Televangelists After World War II

David E. Harrell Jr.

A POWERFUL REVIVAL erupted in the American Pentecostal subculture immediately after the end of World War II. It was led by a group of gifted healing evangelists who built large independent ministries. During the late 1940s and the 1950s, these evangelists held thousands of healing revivals, leaving behind a legacy of hundreds of thousands of testimonies of miraculous healings as well as other supernatural occurrences. The huge crowds attending these revivals provided a base of financial support for the evangelists, making it possible for them to build independent ministries that came to rival the Pentecostal denominations in size and worldwide influence.[1]

American Pentecostalism was poised for a revival in the wake of World War II. A new generation of denominational leaders wanted to put behind them the doctrinal bickering that had splintered Pentecostalism during the early 20th century; they sought to break down the walls that had separated those who shared the baptism of the Holy Spirit. This new irenic spirit was institutionalized in 1948 with the founding of the Pentecostal Fellowship of North America, a union of eight major Pentecostal denominations of the continent. It also opened the way for the eruption of pan-Pentecostal, city-wide revivals that would have not been possible a few years earlier. In addition, Pentecostal churches at the end of the war were bulging with a new generation that craved its own miraculous outpouring of the Holy Spirit. Reared on tales of Azusa Street and the miracles of earlier years, they yearned to witness the power of God in their own day.[2]

Leaders of the Early Healing Revival

The post–World War II healing revival in America dates from a series of meetings held in 1946 by William Branham, a mystical and enigmatic preacher who was then pastoring a small Independent Baptist church in Jeffersonville, Indiana.[3] Branham began a healing and prophetic ministry after attending a "Jesus only" camp meeting during the depression. In early June 1946, Branham preached and prayed for the sick in a small United Pentecostal church in St. Louis and reports of sensational miracles soon circulated throughout that church. News of the miracles spread like wildfire, and in late 1946 Branham was invited to hold a series of meetings in Arkansas. As he traveled from town to town, crowds swelled into thou-

sands, and reports of resurrections from the dead and other miracles resounded through the Pentecostal subculture. In his meetings, Branham displayed an extraordinary gift of the "word of knowledge," which became the trademark of his subsequent evangelistic career. Claiming to minister with an angel at his side, he amazed audiences by discerning the illnesses of people called from the audience.

In the eyes of his devotees, Branham was a "seer as were the Old Testament prophets."[4] Branham remained a legendary figure in the revival into the mid-1950s, although his teaching became increasingly extremist and by 1950 his popularity had been eclipsed by other healing evangelists. When he died in an automobile accident in 1965, he had become a marginal figure among Pentecostals.

William Marrion Branham (1919–65) helped spark the post–World War II healing revival with incredible healing claims accompanied with "words of knowledge."

Seeking to extend Branham's influence beyond the boundaries of the Oneness Pentecostal community, in 1947 Branham's managers secured a widely respected Oregon Assemblies of God pastor, Gordon Lindsay, to arrange the healer's future schedule.[5] Sensing that something extraordinary was afoot, Lindsay soon became the most important coordinator of the healing revival. Lindsay was a talented organizer and publicist; in 1947 he began publishing a magazine, the *Voice of Healing*, which first reported on the activities of William Branham and soon thereafter on the meetings of a growing coterie of other evangelists who had launched independent healing ministries.

By the early 1950s scores of healing evangelists filled tents and auditoriums around the country, attracting tens of thousands of people, reporting thousands of healings and other miracles, and collecting millions of dollars in contributions from supporters. Nearly all of the early evangelists worked under the umbrella of the Voice of Healing organization; among the most celebrated in the 1950s were the bold and flamboyant Jack Coe and the erratic and sensational Amos Alonzo Allen, both of whom pushed claims of divine healing to the uttermost boundaries. Lindsay's magazine also published reports describing scores of extraordinary foreign revivals led by evangelists such as Tommy Hicks and Tommy L. Osborn. A few of the healing evangelists specialized in foreign evangelism, but all of the independent ministers of the 1950s conducted crusades outside the United States, attracting hundreds of thousands to healing revivals in Latin America, Africa, and Asia.[6]

Through his *Voice of Healing* magazine, Gordon Lindsay (1906–73) helped to promote the healing crusades of many evangelists after 1948.

The Voice of Healing group of evangelists was the most coherent center of the healing revival, but some highly successful healing evangelists were never associated with Lindsay's organization. Kathryn Kuhlman, for instance, established a successful healing ministry in Pennsylvania in the 1950s that owed little to the forces that had created the Pentecostal healing revival. During her long career on television she both borrowed from and contributed to the media techniques used by other evangelists, but she maintained a discreet distance from other ministries. In a general way, she did identify with the surging healing revival, and late in life formed a close personal relationship with evangelist Oral Roberts, but her story, like that of some other healers of the period, ran parallel to the revival rather than being a part of it.[7]

Oral Roberts, who also never formally associated with the Voice of Healing group of evangelists, became the preeminent leader of the healing revival in the 1950s.[8] Roberts was a minister in the Pentecostal Holiness Church, as his father had been before him. In 1947, he made a bold decision to give up his pastorate in Enid, Oklahoma, in order to launch an independent healing ministry. Talented, handsome, and well versed in the nuances of Pentecostal theology, Roberts was respectful of the other healing evangelists, particularly of William Branham, but he carefully guarded his independence, and he quickly became the most popular celebrity in the rampant revival. Roberts's crusades featured a healing line in which the evangelist laid his hands on and prayed for the sick. He personally laid hands on perhaps a million people before stopping his crusades in 1968. At the same time, Roberts's meetings were models of decorum (speaking in tongues was discouraged) and his long and entertaining sermons exuded Pentecostal orthodoxy.

Roberts's moderation made him a favorite among Pentecostal denominational leaders. Most Pentecostal leaders cautiously welcomed the outbreak of the revival in 1947. They were as captured by the gifts of the healers and the reports of miracles as were their church members. Symbolizing the importance of the revival, as well as his standing with denominational leaders, Oral Roberts was invited to deliver the closing address at the inaugural meeting of the Pentecostal Fellowship of North America in Des Moines, Iowa, in October 1948.

The son of a poor Oklahoma Pentecostal holiness preacher, Granville Oral Roberts (1918–) became an outstanding healing televangelist in the 1950s after which he founded Oral Roberts University in 1965.

Pentecostal church leaders soon cooled to the healing revival. Many became wary of the excessive claims of the healing evangelists and were troubled by their insatiable appetite for money.[9] While most of the healing evangelists tried to maintain cordial relations with the Pentecostal denominations during the first years of the revival, by 1950 they had created a

ORAL ROBERTS

Granville Oral Roberts, America's premier healing evangelist, was born in Pontotoc County, Oklahoma. Roberts was reared in abject poverty, the son of a Pentecostal Holiness preacher. At age seventeen he was diagnosed as having tuberculosis and was bedridden for more than five months. In July 1935, under the ministry of evangelist George W. Moncey, he was healed of both tuberculosis and stuttering. The following two years he served an apprenticeship under his father in evangelistic ministry. Ordained by the Pentecostal Holiness Church in 1936, he quickly became one of the outstanding ministers in the denomination. Between 1941 and 1947 he served four pastorates.

In 1947 Roberts launched a healing ministry with his first city-wide campaign in Enid, Oklahoma. The same year he published his first book on healing, If You Need Healing—Do These Things!; took the message of healing to the radio airwaves; started his own monthly magazine, Healing Waters; and established his ministry headquarters in Tulsa, Oklahoma. The following year he began crisscrossing America with the largest portable tent ever used to promote the gospel. Eventually his "tent cathedral" would seat crowds of over 12,500.

Roberts' success in healing evangelism thrust him to the leadership of a generation of dynamic revivalists who took the message of divine healing around the world after 1947. His ecumenical crusades were instrumental in the revitalization of Pentecostalism in the post–World War II era. He was also influential in the formation of the Full Gospel Business Men's Fellowship International in 1951 as well as a leading figure in laying the foundation for the modern charismatic movement.

Roberts' most significant impact upon American Christianity came in 1955 when he initiated a national weekly television program that took his healing crusades inside the homes of millions who had never been exposed to the healing message. Through this program the healing message was literally lifted from the Pentecostal subculture of American Christianity to its widest audience in history. By 1980 a Gallup Poll revealed that Roberts' name was recognized by a phenomenal 84 percent of the American public, and historian Vinson Synan observed that Roberts was considered the most prominent Pentecostal in the world.

Between 1947 and 1968 Roberts conducted more than three hundred major crusades, personally praying for millions of people. By the mid-1950s his healing message was broadcast on more than five hundred radio stations, and for almost thirty years his Sunday morning television program was the number one syndicated religious program in the nation. His monthly magazine, renamed Abundant Life in 1956, reached a circulation of over a million, while his devotional magazine, Daily Blessing, exceeded a quarter million subscribers and a monthly column was written for 674 newspapers. By the 1980s there were more than 15 million copies of his eighty-eight books in circulation, and his yearly mail from supporters exceeded five million letters.

Indicative of his growing acceptance by mainline denominations, Roberts was invited in 1966 to be a participant in Billy Graham's Berlin Congress on World Evangelism, transferred his religious affiliation to the United Methodist church in 1968, and began an ambitious television outreach in 1969 with prime-time religious variety shows. The success of the prime-time programming was remarkable, reaching as many as 64 million viewers. This led Edward Fiske, religious editor of the New York Times, to declare that Roberts commanded more personal loyalty in the 1970s than any other minister in America.

In 1965 Roberts opened a coeducational liberal arts college in Tulsa. Receiving regional accreditation in a record six years, Oral Roberts University (ORU) became a major institution when seven graduate colleges were added between 1975 and 1978: Medicine, Nursing, Dentistry, Law, Business, Education, and Theology. The $250 million university, with its ultramodern architecture and facilities, grew to an average enrollment of 5,000 students. The university was dedicated in 1967 by Billy Graham. Adjacent to the university, Roberts established a 450-resident retirement center in 1966.

A high point of Roberts' ministry came with the opening in 1981 of the $250 million City of Faith Medical and Research Center. The complex consisted of a thirty-story hospital, sixty-story medical center, and twenty-story research facility. The philosophy of the center was to merge prayer and medicine, the supernatural and natural, in the treatment of the whole person. Unfortunately the City of Faith never attracted the numbers of patients that Roberts anticipated. It was closed in 1990.

Theologically Roberts is basically a classical Pentecostal, who maintains that speaking in tongues is normative for every believer. His trademark, however, has been essentially an upbeat message of hope. The whole thesis of his ministry has been that God is a good God and that He wills to heal and prosper His people. ∎

PAUL CHAPPELL IN *DICTIONARY OF PENTECOSTAL AND CHARISMATIC MOVEMENTS* network of independent institutions beyond denominational supervision and discipline, indeed, beyond any supervision. By the mid-1950s, most of the independent evangelists who held ministerial credentials with the Assemblies of God had either withdrawn from the denomination or been expelled. Some, including Jack Coe and A. A. Allen, had sharp and widely publicized clashes with the denomination.

Despite losing the support of denominational leaders, Coe, Allen, and scores of other independent healing evangelists continued to attract thousands of people to their meetings in tents and auditoriums. Coe died in 1957, and over the next decade the radical cutting edge of healing revivalism was occupied by the meteoric A. A. Allen, who had been forced to withdraw from the Assemblies of God and the Voice of Healing organization after facing drunk-driving charges during a 1955 revival in Knoxville, Tennessee. Allen survived crisis after crisis and remained popular until his death in 1970. Scores of lesser-known healing evangelists continued to attract large crowds to their meetings, including two of Allen's assistants and protégés, Robert W. Schambach and Don Stewart.

Oral Roberts remained the superstar of the healing revival throughout the fifties and sixties, maintaining a cordial if uneasy relationship with the Pentecostal denominations until he stopped holding campaigns. In the two decades reaching from 1947 to 1967 Roberts held hundreds of revivals in the United States and abroad. He was a skilled organizer and administrator with a facile and innovative intellect. As the family of "partners" supporting his ministry grew, Roberts pioneered new uses of computerized direct mail. He hired the former editor of the *Pentecostal Holiness Advocate*, G. H. Montgomery, to help him develop sophisticated literature, including a magazine that was mailed to more than a million supporters. By the early 1950s, Roberts had carefully put together a radio network that included more than four hundred stations.

Roberts's influence permeated the Pentecostal world. His support was critical in the founding of the Full Gospel Business Men's Fellowship International (FGBMFI) in 1951, the brainchild of California dairyman Demos Shakarian.[10] The FGBMFI became a critical venue for promoting the ministries of the healing evangelists, who were usually featured speakers at its early meetings. Shakarian and Roberts remained close friends through the years and each contributed to the growth of the other's ministry.

Television and Foreign Evangelism

More than anything else, television changed the face of healing revivalism in the late 1950s and early 1960s. During a 1954 Oral Roberts tent crusade in Akron, Ohio, Rex Humbard persuaded Roberts to film three of his evening services for television. The filming posed tough technical challenges because of the poor lighting under the tent, but Roberts was ecstatic when he viewed the results. The programs included not only his sermons but also the "altar calls, healing lines, actual miracles, the coming and going of the great crowds, the reaction of the congregations."[11] Roberts believed that he had found a way to introduce the nation to the remarkable healing revival that had stirred the Pentecostal subculture. He painstakingly pieced together a television network in the mid-1950s; by 1957 his program was being aired on 135 of the nation's 500 television stations, reaching 80 percent of the potential American television audience.

At every turn Roberts met resistance to his aspirations for a television ministry. When his program first aired in New York City, *New York Times* columnist Jack Gould protested: "If Brother Roberts wishes to exploit hysteria and ignorance by putting up his hands and yelling 'Heal,' that is his affair. But it hardly seems within the public interest, convenience and necessity, for the TV industry to go along with him."[12] The *Christian Century* warned that "the Oral Roberts sort of thing" would harm the "cause of vital religion" and throughout 1956 the National Council of Churches lobbied Congress, seeking legislation to ban the sale of television time for religious purposes. While these restrictive efforts were ultimately unsuccessful, Roberts often had difficulty persuading local stations to air his program.[13]

Producing a national television program was very expensive, but the rewards were enticing. Roberts's mail nearly doubled after one month on television; his mailing list grew to more than a million names by the end of the fifties. By that time, every up-and-coming evangelist dreamed of launching a national television program to broaden his or her evangelistic ministry. "The people that's on radio and television," mused old-timer W. V. Grant, "is the ones that's getting the crowds."[14] But most of the healing evangelists who preached under the tents had neither the financial backing nor the technical skills to come close to creating a television empire that rivaled the network put together by Oral Roberts.

By 1960 the American healing revival was changing and slowing down. Healing evangelists still abounded in the sixties, making repetitious visits to virtually every city and village in America, but the crowds were smaller and enthusiasm was diminishing. Some old-timers continued to draw large crowds. Until his death in 1970, A. A. Allen drew thousands to his tent revivals and had limited television exposure. After his death, his young assistant Don Stewart kept the ministry alive for a while and in the 1990s continued to air television programs. Other evangelists such as Ernest Angley conducted large healing revivals and were regional celebrities. Old-timer H. Richard Hall of Cleveland, Tennessee, and scores of others like him, continued to offer healing in modest tents in virtually every small town in the country. Perhaps the most enduring remnant of the original healing revival was Robert W. Schambach, one of Allen's early assistants who left with his mentor's blessing in 1959 to establish his own ministry. Schambach continued to tour the nation in a big tent into the 1990s, providing an enduring glimpse of the ambience and aura of the healing revival. A dynamic and talented preacher who kept his reputation and ministry free from all taint of scandal through the years, Schambach was a favorite celebrity on the Trinity Broadcasting Network in the 1990s, linking old-time healing revivalism to the glitzy media healing ministries that had appeared by the end of the century.

Equally important in the long run, though less visible to most Americans in the 1950s, was the impact that the healing revival had outside the United States. Most American healing evangelists also conducted massive crusades abroad. In perhaps the single most famous crusade of the period, in 1954 evangelist Tommy Hicks reportedly preached one evening to an audience of 400,000 people in a stadium in Buenos Aires, Argentina. During the revival, Hicks reported, President Juan Peron and his wife visited him at his hotel and "there they were both saved."[15]

As the field of aspiring evangelists became more and more crowded, several independent ministers directed their attention, and their appeals for funds, to extending the healing revival around the world. Two ministries that had dramatic and long-lasting influence abroad were T. L. Osborn's World Evangelism and Gordon Lindsay's Christ for the Nations. Osborn and his talented wife, Daisy, conducted hundreds of campaigns in Asia, Africa, and South America, leaving behind tales of thousands of miracles and a generation of native evangelists who aspired to build similar ministries. Lindsay in the 1960s changed the name of his organization from the Voice of Healing to "Christ for the Nations" and began emphasizing the building of indigenous churches around the world. These promoters of healing revivalism abroad were celebrities in the Pentecostal world, but, unlike the television ministers, they gained little visibility outside of the subculture that supported them.

T. L. and Daisy Osborn had spent a discouraging year as missionaries in India in 1946, and returned to America just as the healing revival was exploding. They became convinced that healing and miracles would provide the key to taking the gospel to "the heathen masses everywhere dying without Christ."[16] Encouraged by other evangelists and by Pentecostal denominational leaders, Osborn conducted a series of impressive crusades around the world. He reported thousands of healings and other miracles and his accounts were widely publicized in the United States. At first Osborn was supported financially by other independent ministers, such as Oral Roberts, but he soon built an efficient organization and became adept at soliciting funds by direct mail. In the mid-1950s he began publishing a magazine to promote his work, *Faith Digest,* and in the 1960s the paper's circulation reached 670,000. Osborn's organization became a model of efficiency within the healing revival. "We have won a soul for each 10 cents to 24 cents invested," boasted Osborn in 1961.[17]

Osborn also formulated a surprisingly sophisticated mission philosophy. Searching for a way to follow up the massive revivals he and other healing revivalists conducted abroad, Osborn became convinced that "natives . . . would be the best missionaries . . . They speak the language, they don't need a furlough, they don't need food, they don't get sick."[18] In 1953, he formed the Association for Native Evangelism to encourage the establishment of indigenous churches. The association's original board included representatives from the Assemblies of God, the Church of God, and the International Church of the Foursquare Gospel, but Osborn never allowed the Pentecostal denominations to control the association, and the Pentecostal churches became less and less supportive of his activities.[19] But Osborn

With his wife, Daisy, at his side, Tommy L. Osborn (1923–) pioneered Third World healing crusades to largely non-Christian populations. His ministry paved the way for many other healing evangelists around the world.

pursued his independent path, convinced that success in missions came not to "those who must wait for organization sanction," but rather "to the courageous men and women of faith who advance and do exploits in His name."[20] In 1958, Osborn began a program of "co-evangelism," essentially supporting native evangelists who used his films and distributed his literature.[21]

Osborn's ministry flourished in the 1960s. By the end of the decade Osborn had held crusades in more than forty countries, and his organization had "underwritten over twelve thousand Native Missionaries." During the 1960s Osborn budgeted nearly $50,000 a month to support native missionaries. Typically, he supported a native missionary for only one year, training him or her to build self-supporting congregations. These missionaries, boasted Daisy Osborn, "carried the gospel into nearly fifty thousand villages and areas." As a result, she reported in 1971, more than one new church a day is established and becomes self-supporting through this one outreach to total "over 400 per year."[22] In addition, Osborn supplied vans, loudspeakers, and other equipment for native missionaries and shipped more than a ton of printed materials and films to the mission field every day. His messages and booklets were translated into sixty-seven languages. In 1992, the Osborns estimated that they had trained and supported more than thirty thousand indigenous preachers.[23]

A second important independent missions organization produced by the healing revival was Christ for the Nations, headquartered in Dallas Texas. Until the healing revival began to lose coherence in the 1960s, Gordon Lindsay stood squarely at its center.

Christ for the Nations was initially a "native church building" program. Indigenous Christians left in the wake of the hundreds of healing crusades, particularly those not affiliated with any Pentecostal denomination, applied to Christ for the Nations for funds to build church buildings. In the fifties and sixties, grants of $250 went far toward the construction of crude buildings in the Philippines or Korea; in later years, Christ for the Nations' grants rose to as much as $20,000. Lindsay's monthly magazine featured pictures of the crude buildings funded by the organization; by 1991 the Christ for the Nations had aided in the construction of 8,716 churches in 120 countries.[24]

After Gordon Lindsay's death in 1973, Christ for the Nations was managed by his wife, Freda Lindsay. Under her leadership, the organization expanded in scope and size, while maintaining its interest in foreign evangelism. Gordon Lindsay's books, and those of other Pentecostal writers, were translated into seventy-two languages and the organization distributed more than forty million pieces of literature abroad. Christ for the Nations Institute, established in Dallas in 1970 to train evangelists, claimed twenty-six thousand alumni by the end of the century, including graduates from nearly every nation in the world. By 1990, Christ for the Nations Institute had branches in six foreign countries, had helped fund the establishment of similar Bible schools in twenty-one other countries, and was affiliated with thirty similar Bible schools around the world.[25]

New Ministries and New Directions

New winds were blowing by the beginning of the sixties in America, taking some of the ministries created by the healing revival to new heights and in stunningly different directions. The unexpected outbreak of tongues-speaking in mainstream Protestantism and Roman Catholicism in the 1960s created vast new opportunities for those independent ministers who were sufficiently flexible and innovative to market the Holy Spirit to this vast new audience of seekers.

No one was more successful than Oral Roberts in making that transition from the Pentecostal subculture to the new free-flowing charismatic movement of the 1960s. Roberts had long been aware that his crusade audiences and healing lines included large numbers of people from mainstream churches, and he carefully positioned himself to influence what he saw on the horizon. In 1962, Roberts announced that he would establish a university. Oral Roberts University, opened in 1965, through the years influenced thousands of Pentecostal and charismatic young people. By 2000 the school's enrollment surpassed five thousand students, and it had won a solid reputation within and without religious circles.

The most important single force in the reshaping of independent Pentecostal and charismatic evangelism in the 1960s was the transformation of religious telecasting. Some changes were driven by technology. In the decade of the sixties, independent UHF stations proliferated, and these struggling business ventures were quite willing to provide low-cost time to religious customers. One such station, WYAH, was a shoestring operation begun by young Pat Robertson. In 1961 it became the first all-religious television station in the country. Robertson's Christian Broadcasting Network (CBN) barely survived the early 1960s, but by 1968 CBN had built a new headquarters building and was in the early stages of an incredible upward spiral that paralleled the secular broadcasting success of Ted Turner.[26]

As technology opened new doors for religious broadcasters, the most creative evangelists experimented with new ways to use the medium. CBN contributed much to the transformation of religious television. Robertson began using telethons to raise financial support in 1963, but his most important breakthrough came with the revising of the *700 Club* format in 1965. Young Jim Bakker joined CBN in that year and began hosting a talk show modeled on the *Tonight Show,* which evolved into the *700 Club.* The talk-show format proved to be capable of attracting audiences far different from those who tuned in to crusade services.[27]

Roberts continued to broadcast his healing crusades into the early sixties, but was increasingly dissatisfied with the results. His audiences declined, and he was keenly aware that tent revivalism was a vanishing phenomenon. Television had brought huge increases to his ministry in the 1950s, but in the 1960s the growth had stopped. Perhaps more than any other healing evangelist, Roberts knew that a powerful new interest in the Holy Spirit was spreading in traditional Protestant churches and in the Roman Catholic Church. In 1967 and 1968 Roberts made a series of stunning decisions: He canceled his television program, ended his crusade ministry, and left the Pentecostal Holiness Church to become a Methodist.

Oral Roberts had a plan, a strategy that would dramatically influence the course of modern religious television. By the fall of 1968, he was preparing to return to television in prime-time specials produced in an entertainment format, featuring wholesome and talented student singers from Oral Roberts University and recognizable Hollywood guest stars. The scheme was a high-stakes gamble "to move religion out of the Sunday morning religious ghetto." Roberts aired four specials in prime time in 1969 at a cost of $3 million. The artistic team that put the programs together was headed by Ralph Carmichael, a talented musical writer, and Dick Ross, who had produced specials for Billy Graham and Kathryn Kuhlman, as well as for secular artists. The early programs claimed audiences of around ten million viewers (a 1973 special had an estimated audience of more than thirty-seven million) and after each program the ministry received around a half million letters. Roberts's media gamble paid off handsomely.

The most important legacy of the Oral Roberts media revolution at the end of the 1960s was the introduction of professional production techniques and entertainment content aimed at competing with secular programming. In a conversation with Merv Griffin at the end of 1974, Roberts reflected on his decision: "Merv, when we went on television about seven years ago, we had methods of choreography and so on that turned a lot of church people off, but now there are 111 religious shows or programs on television that came on since we went on and most of them have adopted many of our methods."[28] In many ways, the modern electronic church was born with the airing of Roberts's first prime-time special in March 1969.

A new generation of television evangelists soared to ever loftier heights in the 1970s who owed much to the pioneering of Robertson and Roberts. Kathryn Kuhlman began broadcasting in 1967 with Dick Ross as her producer. Robert Schuller aired his first program in 1970 and Jimmy Swaggart in 1972. In the 1970s Robertson's booming CBN was joined by the TBN network, formed in the late sixties by Jim Bakker and Paul Crouch, and by PTL, a network established by Jim Bakker in Charlotte, North Carolina, in 1974 after he broke with Paul Crouch. While some non-Pentecostal/charismatic evangelists used television effectively, most notably Billy Graham and Jerry Falwell, by the 1970s the medium was dominated by Pentecostals and charismatics.

The reasons were partly organizational. The healing revival of the 1950s and 1960s left behind scores of independent ministries large enough to fund television programs. But the medium itself also did much to determine winners and losers. Pentecostal evangelists had several advantages in the new world of mass communication. First, many were talented musicians with deep roots in the music of the common people. They were ready and willing to become entertainers on television. Second, Pentecostal evangelists brought a clear-cut, simple theology to a medium that demanded concise communication. Oral Roberts's key theological insights—"God is a good God," "something good is going to happen to you," and "expect a miracle"—were memorable television slogans. Furthermore, the upbeat message of hope and, increasingly, of success and prosperity preached by the evangelists appealed to the aspirations of millions of upwardly mobile people around the world. Hundreds of talented and daring evangelists heard the voice of God telling them to reach the world through the miracle of television. Only a few succeeded, but those who did reaped incredible riches and influence.[29]

The Rise of Teaching Ministries

Both the growing charismatic movement and the changing nature of religious television contributed to the rise of a generation of teachers as leaders of the movement, replacing the gifted healing evangelists of the early 1950s. Healing evangelists continued to preach and offer miracles in the auditoriums and tents into the 1990s, but many people hungered for a deeper understanding of the message of the Holy Spirit. By the 1970s, several talented teachers such as Kenneth Copeland and Kenneth Hagin Sr. created large independent ministries based on teaching rather than on revival services. Both Hagin and Copeland had been participants in the early stages of the healing revival, but they vaulted to fame as teachers, emphasizing the miraculous power available to every Christian through faith. Both were skilled teachers who presented their messages in a homey Texas twang. Hagin and Copeland took the healing message, as well as a growing emphasis on God's promise of prosperity for all of His children, beyond the lines seeking miracles under the tents in the fifties. Copeland built a large television ministry in the 1980s and remained an important figure in the world of independent revivalism at the end of the century.

Faith teacher Kenneth Copeland (1937–) and his wife, Gloria, became household names through their telecast the *Believer's Voice of Victory*, which began in 1973.

Kenneth Hagin Sr. established an independent ministry in 1963, but his fame as a teacher accelerated in the 1970s. Joined by his son, Kenneth Hagin Jr., in the 1970s, Hagin built a large following as a radio preacher. The two Hagins authored more than

KENNETH COPELAND (1937–)

Along with his wife, Gloria, Kenneth Copeland was converted in 1962. Just months later the couple were exposed to the charismatic message and both were Spirit-filled and spoke in tongues. However, according to Gloria, for the next five years they just "plodded along spiritually without knowing how to use [their] faith." It was only in 1967, when the Copeland family moved to Tulsa in order for Kenneth to attend Oral Roberts University and instead ended up as Roberts's copilot, that he was exposed to Kenneth Hagin's faith teachings. Copeland was given several of Hagin's teaching tapes; after he listened to them for a month in his garage, he emerged "a changed man."

The Copeland family returned to Fort Worth after a year where Kenneth established his own ministry. In 1973, he initiated his own newsletter, Believer's Voice of Victory, which today is circulated around the globe. Through his radio broadcasts, television ministry, and satellite communications, Copeland's influence has literally been felt worldwide. He has international offices in North America, Europe, Africa, Asia, and Australia. ■

—GEIR LIE

125 books that by the end of the century had sold more than 50 million copies. In 1974, Hagin founded the Rhema Bible Training Center, now in Broken Arrow. In the school thousands of ministers and church workers from around the world were trained in the message of faith as taught by Hagin. The huge Rhema Camp Meeting in the Tulsa Convention Center each July drew thousands of people to celebrate the faith message. In the 1980s the Hagins established Rhema Bible Training Centers in South Africa and Australia, and in 1999 they announced the founding of eleven new branches in Europe, South America, and Asia.[30]

The Heyday of the Television Ministries

During the 1970s and 1980s television seemed to open doors to limitless growth on the part of the independent ministries. Oral Roberts continued to be a dominant force in religious programming. In the mid-1970s he announced a broad expansion of Oral Roberts University into graduate education, including a medical school. The medical school opened in 1978 after Roberts announced plans to build a huge medical complex on campus, including a 777-bed hospital. Tens of millions of dollars flowed into Tulsa to fund these expensive ventures, illustrating again the extraordinary financial reach of the television ministries.

Several other evangelists built television ministries in the 1980s that came to rival or surpass that of Roberts in cash flow, including newcomers such as Robert Tilton, an audacious "faith teacher" whose ministry in 1990 was reportedly generating more than a million dollars a week in contributions. But the most influential and successful television evangelist of the 1980s was Jimmy Swaggart of Baton Rouge, Louisiana.

By the middle of the decade of the eighties, Jimmy Swaggart was probably the most widely known Protestant in the world. An immensely talented musician and a formidable preacher, Swaggart was a loyal member of the Assemblies of God who cultivated a close relationship with that church's leaders. The swelling membership of Assemblies congregations around the country provided a base of support for Swaggart's campaigns, and he, in turn, contributed liberally to the denomination's missions program. For the first time since the expulsion of the independent healing revivalists during the 1950s, Swaggart's ministry lessened tensions between the independent ministries and a major Pentecostal denomination. By the middle of the eighties, Swaggart's meetings had reached a staggering level of exposure. A weekly television audience of ten to fifteen million people viewed his program in the United States and an estimated three hundred million worldwide. His network of 3,200 stations in 145 countries was larger than the three major American networks combined. His ministry's income soared to more than $150 million per year. With this money, Swaggart built a huge Family Worship Center and Bible College in Baton Rouge, founded an extensive overseas children's relief work, supported more than 600 missionaries in 117 countries, made grants to 110 Bible colleges in developing countries, and funneled more than $6 million each year into programs supported by the Assemblies of God. In addition, Swaggart conducted scores of crusades around the world that were broadcast on his television programs.[31]

The 1970s and 1980s also witnessed the continued growth of religious television networks. The Christian Broadcasting Network, guided by Pat Robertson's business skills, became one of the most spectacular media successes of the last half of the 20th century. At the same time, CBN went through a series of transformations that made it appear less and less a religious network. By the end of the eighties, renamed the "Family Channel," CBN had lost much of its earlier religious identity, though the network continued to featured Robertson's *700 Club*. Robertson did not lose his personal commitment to furthering the Pentecostal/charismatic revival. In 1978 he began building Regent University, a graduate university in Virginia Beach, Virginia. Regent became a training ground for a new generation of specialists within the charismatic movement. In a symbolic act in 2000, Robertson reaffirmed his ordination vows as a minister of the gospel in a ceremony presided over by a number of prominent Christian leaders.[32] He had resigned his Southern Baptist ordination during his presidential race in 1988.

Beginning in Portsmouth, Virginia, in 1959, Marion Gordon "Pat" Robertson (1930–) established the first Christian television station in America. This led to the popular *700 Club* and the establishment of Regent University in 1978.

In addition to Robertson's television empire, Trinity Broadcasting Network was launched in 1969 in California by Jim Bakker and Paul Crouch. Crouch was a cautious builder, and in 1973 Bakker moved to Charlotte, North Carolina, where he began building an immensely successful new network, PTL (Praise the Lord or People That Love). Featuring a talk show starring himself and his wife, Tammy Faye, Bakker displayed extraordinary creativity and a seemingly unerring talent for raising money. As funds poured in, Bakker announced a plan to build "Heritage USA," which would include a state-of-the-art television studio, a hotel, campsites, condominiums, and a water park. In 1986 Heritage USA reported more than six million visitors.[33]

By the 1980s, the world of independent Pentecostal and charismatic revivalism had changed much from the healing ministries of the 1950s. While healing was still a featured part of most of the glitzy television ministries of the eighties, the message and the style of the television programs often seemed more focused on success and entertainment. Beginning in 1987, the seemingly unstoppable expansion of televangelism suffered a series of jolts. The unraveling began with reports of a

PAT ROBERTSON (1930–)

Religious broadcaster, politician, businessman, and the founder of the Christian Broadcasting Network (CBN). Born March 22, 1930, in Lexington, VA, Pat Robertson is the son of the late U.S. senator A. Willis Robertson and the late Gladys Churchill Robertson. He is a graduate of Washington and Lee University (B.A., 1950), Yale University Law School (J.D., 1955), and New York Theological Seminary (M.Div., 1959). He served as a first lieutenant in the U.S. Marine Corps (1950–52). Robertson married Adelia ("Dede") Elmer in 1954. They have four children: Timothy, Elizabeth, Gordon, and Ann. He was an ordained Southern Baptist clergyman (1961–87).

The turning point in Robertson's life, according to his own testimony, was a day in New York in 1956 when he accepted Jesus Christ as his Savior ("I passed from death into life"). Later, while in seminary, Robertson was baptized in the Holy Spirit and for a time served as associate to Harald Bredesen, charismatic pastor of the Reformed Church in Mount Vernon, NY.

Robertson moved from New York to Portsmouth, VA, in 1959, and with initial capital of seventy dollars bought a defunct UHF television station. Since that time Robertson has built the worldwide CBN. His flagship weekday television program, The 700 Club, has been on the air continuously since 1966 and is viewed daily by approximately one million people. This program currently airs three times a day on the Fox Family Channel cable network. In a year, viewers of The 700 Club log some 2.4 million prayer calls (over 56 million by year 2000) with 225 prayer counselors manning phones to pray for callers. Since 1982, CBN's Middle East Television station in southern Lebanon has provided daily outreach to Israel and surrounding countries. It is estimated that more than ninety countries around the world are being touched regularly by CBN. CBN is now a sprawling complex of Williamsburg-style buildings on approximately 700 acres in Virginia Beach and Chesapeake with an annual operating budget of more than $200 million and more than 1,000 employees worldwide.

In 1977 Pat Robertson founded CBN (now Regent) University on the CBN campus. Beginning with a graduate School of Communications, the university now also includes the graduate Schools of Education, Government, Counseling, Business, Divinity, Communication, Law, and the Center of Leadership Studies. Regent has been given full accreditation by the Southern Association of Colleges and Schools. The stated mission of the university is to bring biblical truth to bear on every discipline in every area of life.

Another outreach of CBN is Operation Blessing International (OBI), which, beginning in 1978, has become one of America's largest private organizations helping those in need. OBI provides short-term medical, hunger, and disaster relief and development assistance to economically challenged people in the U.S. and overseas.

In September 1986 Robertson announced his intention to run for the presidency of the U.S. if three million registered voters signed petitions by September 1987 to support his candidacy financially and with prayer. That intent was realized in 1988, when Robertson unsuccessfully sought the Republican nomination. At the time of his run for the presidency, Robertson gave up his ordination to avoid possible church/state conflicts. He was re-ordained in 2000 as a sign of his fuller commitment to religious activity.

Robertson is the author of ten books, including The Turning Tide, The New Millennium, The New World Order, and his most recent release, a book of fiction, The End of the Age. The Secret Kingdom was on the New York Times bestseller list in 1983 and, according to Time magazine, was the number one religious book in America in 1984. Robertson is past president of the prestigious Council on National Policy. In 1982 he served on President Ronald Reagan's Task Force on Victims of Crime.

CBN's international mission is to spread the Gospel throughout the world by means of mass media, primarily television broadcasts. CBN's most recent international project, World Reach, was launched in the Fall of 1995. The goal of CBN World Reach is to see 500 million new believers into God's Kingdom as we enter the new millennium ∎

—J. RODMAN WILLIAMS IN THE *NEW INTERNATIONAL DICTIONARY OF PENTECOSTAL AND CHARISMATIC MOVEMENTS* sexual and financial scandal that wrecked the PTL ministry and resulted in the imprisonment of Jim Bakker and other PTL executives. By 1988, a media feeding frenzy was under way. The Bakker debacle was followed by a highly publicized sex scandal involving Jimmy Swaggart. Swaggart's ministry survived at a much diminished level, but he was forced to leave the Assemblies of God and his worldwide influence quickly evaporated. In addition, in the mid-eighties Oral Roberts, bogged down in efforts to fund his ultimately unsuccessful venture into medical education, resorted to fund-raising techniques that caused him once again to become a favorite target of media ridicule.[34]

Old and New Ministries in the Post-Scandal Era

Many institutions survived the scandals little scathed, perhaps none more successfully than Oral Roberts University (ORU). Although Roberts's ambitious effort to build a medical school ended in 1990, Oral Roberts University continued to flourish and serve as a symbol of success in the world of independent Pentecostalism. Richard Roberts succeeded his father to the presidency of ORU in 1993 and proved himself to be a capable and respected administrator. In 1999, the university celebrated its thirty-fifth year with record enrollments that passed 4,200 credit students, and the school was widely acclaimed for the quality of education it offered. Richard Roberts maintained a successful television and evangelistic ministry, and the Oral Roberts Evangelistic Association sponsored an annual International Charismatic Bible Ministers Conference that drew large audiences and typically featured Oral, Richard, and such leading independent evangelists as Kenneth Copeland, Creflo Dollar, Benny Hinn, Marilyn Hickey, and Joyce Meyer.

The collapse of PTL and the changing focus of CBN opened the door for Paul Crouch to turn his TBN network into the most stunning success story of the last decade of the 20th century. Reorganized by Paul and Jan Crouch in 1973 in rented studios in Santa Ana, California, by the end of the century TBN had become a billion-dollar enterprise that included more than eight hundred broadcast and cable outlets. Crouch's ministry included a headquarters in Costa Mesa, California, a state-of-the-art International Production Center in Irving, Texas, and Trinity Music City in Nashville, a complex that included a two-thousand-seat Trinity Music City Church Auditorium and a Virtual Reality Theater. Crouch had deep roots in the healing revival, and TBN provided an outlet for evangelists preaching the old-time revival themes of healing and prosperity.

Among the most visible promoters of the network in the 1990s was R. W. Schambach; his presence and style linked the network to the glories of the earlier revival. The Crouchs' own program, *Praise the Lord*, had a clear Pentecostal aura replete with tongues-speaking. The network also promoted the work of the new generation of healing evangelists such as Benny Hinn. By the end of the century, Crouch's vast media empire was valued at hundreds of millions of dollars (Crouch reported that he had been offered $2 billion for the network) and reported annual donations of around $80 million per year. Early in his career Crouch was an Assemblies of God minister, but as his independent ministry grew he resigned his membership in the denomination and in 1990 severed relationship with the National Religious Broadcasters, signaling his identification with the independent ministers who worked outside the boundaries of organized religion.[35]

The highly publicized scandals of 1987–88 blunted the expansion of the chaotic world of independent ministries, and almost surely drastically cut the flow of money into independent ministries for a time, but adverse publicity did not kill the revival that had begun in the 1950s. Many of the older generation of evangelists continued to have successful television ministries, including Kenneth Copeland, John Osteen, a highly successful Houston pastor and evangelist, pioneering black televangelist Fred Price of Los Angeles, and a widely respected woman faith teacher, Marilyn Hickey.

The scandals also opened the way for new evangelists to stake their claims to a share of the television audience. Robert Tilton vaulted to prominence in the late 1980s and early 1990s. At its peak in 1992, Tilton's *Success-N-Life* broadcast was aired on 235 television stations, and his ministry reportedly generated revenue of around $100 million a year. Beginning in 1992, Tilton's television ministry and his Word of Faith Church in Farmers Branch, Texas, went into a severe decline after an unfavorable exposé on ABC television charged him with mail fraud. At the same time, the evangelist endured two messy divorces within a period of a few months. Tilton tried without success to recoup at the end of the nineties. He, along with other old-time healing evangelists such as Peter Popoff and Don Stewart, purchased time on the BET (Black Entertainment Network) in an effort to restart their ministries.[36]

Other new superstar televangelists burst on the scene in the 1990s. Perhaps the most sensational new superstar of the 1990s was Benny Hinn.[37] The flamboyant Hinn began holding healing campaigns in 1977; in style and demeanor he was a throwback to the early days of the healing revival. His services included healing lines and stunning miracle claims that rivaled those of earlier decades. In 1999 Hinn announced that he was moving his headquarters from Orlando (where he had built a megachurch with twelve thousand members) to Dallas. In a gesture filled with symbolic meaning, Hinn was welcomed to Dallas by eighty-one-year-old Freda Lindsay, whose husband had been the coordinator of the healing revival in the 1950s. "Benny Hinn is the kind of Christian a person ought to be," Mrs. Lindsay told a local reporter.[38] By 1999 Hinn had built a large television network and was one of the most coveted guest stars on TBN.

In addition, Hinn conducted massive overseas crusades; in 1999 he claimed to have preached to audiences of more than a million people in single evening services in Kenya and the Philippines. At one evening service during the Kenya campaign, Hinn reported, 250,000 people "signed cards saying they were making first-time commit- ment of their lives to Jesus Christ."[39] By the end of the century Benny Hinn had become the leading American celebrity in the healing revival.

Lebanese-born Benny Hinn (1952–) drew huge crowds to his healing crusades in America during the 1990s. By 2000 he was preaching to audiences of more than one million persons in Africa and India.

Another bright new star of the 1990s was Joyce Meyer. A direct-spoken, bold, and hu- morous speaker, Meyer had a powerful presence on television. She vaulted to fame in the 1990s. By the end of the decade Meyer was manag- ing a multimillion-dollar independent ministry. Her television program was aired on approximately 350 stations, having the potential to reach one billion people in 150 nations through international, terrestrial, and satellite networks. In the late 1990s Meyer added approximately fifteen thousand names per month to her mailing list. Joyce Meyer Ministries constructed ministry headquarters in Fenton, Missouri, at a cost of more than $20 mil- lion. Millions of her books, tapes, and videos were sold annually and she was a headliner at charismatic conferences.[40]

Equally notable at the end of the decade of the nineties was the rise of a generation of black television preachers. The pioneer black televangelist was Fred Price. Price began pastoring a small Christian and Missionary Al- liance church in Los Angeles in 1973 before launching his independent ministry in the late seventies. Inspired by the faith teaching of Kenneth Hagin Sr., by the end of the century Price had built Crenshaw Christian Center in Los Angeles, a church with more than seventeen thousand members. Price's "Ever Increasing Faith Ministries" included a widely viewed television program and a large publication ministry. In the late 1990s Price preached a controversial series of lessons widely circulated in a packet of seventy-six videotapes, which scolded the church for not taking a stand against slavery and racism, thus contributing to the "conditions that still affect black Americans today."[41]

Following the trailblazing success of Fred Price, other black evangelists were among the most visible televangelists of the 1990s. Creflo A. Dollar Jr., who pastored a church with more than twenty thousand members in Atlanta, had also been mentored in the "word of faith teaching" by Kenneth Hagin Sr. and Kenneth Copeland. In the nineties, he built a large television following and created a multimillion-dollar independent ministry.[42]

Another highly visible black television evangelist was T. D. Jakes of Dallas. His Potter's House Church claimed more than twenty thousand members, and his television program was aired on both the TBN and BET networks. Church-growth specialists proclaimed that Jake's Dallas church was the "fastest-growing American church of the century." Dollar and Jakes were among the most visible conference speakers and popular preachers in the nation at the end of the century.[43]

Finally, in many ways, the cutting edge of the healing revival at the end of the century had moved outside the United States. The legacy of the foreign campaigns of earlier decades had given impetus to the booming growth of indigenous Pentecostal churches abroad and the rise of a new generation of foreign healing evangelists who modeled themselves on the healing evangelists of the 1950s. The largest healing revivals in the world at the end of the 20th century were being conducted by evangelists such as Reinhard Bonnke of Wiesbaden, Germany; Yongii Cho of Seoul, Korea, who had built the huge Yoido Full Gospel Church, which claimed 730,000 members in 2000; and D. S. Dinakaran of

Reinhard Willi Gottfried Bonnke (1940–) from Germany began as a mediocre missionary in Lesotho, Africa. In 1975 he founded the Christ for All Nations (CFAN) ministry after which he consistently preached to the largest crowds in the history of Christian evangelism.

Madras, India. All of these foreign evangelists owed much to the American healing revival. Dinakaran's "Jesus Calls" ministry conducted huge crusades throughout the subcontinent and elsewhere in Asia, often attracting crowds of more than 100,000 people to hear messages of divine healing.

Inspired to launch a healing ministry during a T. L. Osborn campaign in India in 1956, Dinakaran's Jesus Calls ministry looked much like that of an American healing revivalist of the 1950s.[44]

Conclusion

The spontaneous healing revival that erupted in the American Pentecostal subculture after World War II had a dramatic influence on Christianity around the world. While no single force can account for the explosive growth of Pentecostalism in the 20th century, the thousands of crusades conducted by American evangelists all over the world and their support of indigenous churches and evangelists undoubtedly contributed to the phenomenon. In addition, the huge independent ministries created by the revival were largely responsible for the revisioning of modern religious television programming.

The scores of independent ministries spawned by the revival grew and changed dramatically in the last half of the 20th century in cadence with the transformation of Pentecostalism itself and with the rapid advances in communications technology. At the same time, on television and in auditoriums in the United States and around the world, the legacy of the healing revival is still quite visible to all those who remember its beginnings after World War II.

For Further Reading

The only in-depth history of the post–World War II healing evangelists is David Edwin Harrell Jr.'s *All Things Are Possible: The Healing and Charismatic Revivals in Modern America* (Bloomington: Indiana Univ. Press, 1975). Information on more recent evangelists can be found in Stanley M. Burgess, ed., and Eduard van der Maas, assoc. ed., *New International Dictionary of Pentecostal and Charismatic Movements* (Grand Rapids: Zondervan, 2001). Much information on the healing evangelists' relations with the FGBMFI can be found in Vinson Synan's *Under His Banner: History of the Full Gospel Business Men's Fellowship International* (Costa Mesa, Calif.: Gift Publications, 1992).

Many fine biographies have been written on the major healing evangelists. A good biography of William Branham is C. Douglas Weaver's *The Healer-Prophet, William Marrion Branham* (Macon, Ga.: Mercer Univ. Press,

1987). An early autobiography of Lindsay is his *Gordon Lindsay Story* (Dallas: Voice of Healing Publishing Co., n.d.).

The definitive biography of Oral Roberts is David Edwin Harrell Jr.'s excellent *Oral Roberts: An American Life* (Bloomington: Indiana Univ. Press, 1985). Oral Roberts's last and most complete autobiography is *Expect a Miracle: My Life and Ministry* (Nashville: Thomas Nelson, 1995). The best biography of Pat Robertson is David Edwin Harrell Jr.'s *Pat Robertson: A Personal, Political and Religious Portrait* (San Francisco: Harper & Row, 1987). Robertson's story up to 1972 is given in his autobiographical *Shout It from the Housetops* (with Jamie Buckingham) (Plainfield, N.J.: Logos International, 1972).

For books on such televangelists as Jimmy Swaggart, Jim and Tammy Bakker, Bob Tilton, and Fred Price, see Quentin J. Schultze's *Televangelism and American Culture* (Grand Rapids: Baker, 1991); and Jeffrey K. Hadden and Anson Shupe's *Televangelism: Power & Politics on God's Frontier* (New York: Henry Holt and Company, 1988).

· 14 ·

Streams of Renewal
at the End of the Century

Vinson Synan

T HROUGHOUT the entire 20th century the church world witnessed so
many bewildering streams of charismatic renewal flowing in so many
directions that it was almost impossible to describe them all. In view of the
vast sweep of the movement into practically every church in Christendom,
Fr. Tom Forrest spoke of the charismatic renewal as "a stream that flows
everywhere." As the century came to an end, there was evidence that some
streams had peaked and were experiencing decline, while others continued to grow rapidly. Also, newer streams were constantly coming on-line,
contributing to ever-larger growth and worldwide expansion.

The contrast between the older charismatic renewal movements in Europe and America and the more vigorous movements in the developing
nations became more visible as the century came to an end. Although classical Pentecostal churches continued to grow rapidly in most places, most
of the mainline charismatic organizations and conferences experienced a
decline in registrations for major conferences and in financial income. Part
of this was the dispersion and regionalization of the renewal movements
in America and Europe. In the 1970s and early 1980s there were only a few
national events for participants to attend. By 1990, there were hundreds of
regional conferences offered throughout the nation. The Episcopal renewal, for instance, moved from one annual conference to more than forty

regional conferences by 1995. The same was true for the Catholics. Instead of one massive conference at Notre Dame as in the early 1970s, there were by the 1990s more than one hundred regional American conferences, some of which, like the Hispanic and Anglo annual conferences in Los Angeles with over twenty thousand attendees, continued to draw huge crowds.

The novelty and curiosity engendered in the early days became old news by 1990. In the 1960s the fact that Catholics spoke in tongues was headline news; by the 1990s this phenomena was old-hat and hardly news-worthy. The regionalization of the renewal meant that renewal was now much closer to the grass roots with more local input and control. There were also many internal twists and turns within the various renewal movements that at times led to new growth and at other times to division and decline.

As the movement approached the centennial mark in its history, plans were laid to conduct a special conference in Los Angeles in 2001 where the movement came to the attention of the world at Azusa Street in 1906. In preparation, Pentecostals and charismatics from around the world were invited to join in a large celebration scheduled to convene in the Crenshaw Christian Center, a church led by well-known African-American TV evangelist Fred Price. As the movement approached the end of its first century, the situation within the various constituencies was as follows:

Classical Pentecostals

The Pentecostal stream that began as a small group of religious outcasts had matured during the century to become the largest family of Protestants in the world with over two hundred million adherents in the various Western and indigenous Pentecostal churches that appeared during the century. In America the movement developed out of great persecution and rejection to become a respected part of the religious scene.

Part of the move toward respectability was what some pundits call the "evangelicalization" of the Pentecostal movement after 1948, when the Pentecostals joined forces with the National Association of Evangelicals (NAE). Although some evangelicals such as Carl McIntire and Donald Gray Barnhouse rejected the application of the Pentecostals, others such as John Ockenga welcomed them. After their acceptance, the Pentecostals eventually grew to constitute more than 50 percent of the membership of the organization.

Many Pentecostal scholars, historians, and theologians felt that the Pentecostals paid a steep price by becoming so close to the mainline evangelicals. In order to gain acceptance, they charged, the Pentecostals changed their original theological base to include many features that were not native to the Pentecostal theological culture and tradition. As a result, there was a slow decline in the manifestation of the gifts of the Spirit in many Pentecostal churches and a closer alliance with the political positions advocated by the Christian right. By the 1990s, however, there seemed to be a parallel "Pentecostalization" of mainline evangelicals as charismatic worship became more and more acceptable in all churches.

The Pentecostals also moved to consolidate their relations among themselves after World War II. As a result of joining the NAE, the American Pentecostals discovered one another in a new way. Old divisions of the past were overcome as the Pentecostals organized the Pentecostal Fellowship of North America (PFNA) in Des Moines in 1948. This effort at Pentecostal ecumenism was limited to the white and Trinitarian denominations, leaving out the predominantly black and oneness churches. This situation persisted until 1994 when the black and white Pentecostal churches met in Memphis to create a new and racially inclusive fellowship. In what became known as the "Memphis Miracle," the old all-white PFNA, which had existed since 1948, was replaced by a racially inclusive organization called the Pentecostal and Charismatic Churches of North America (PCCNA). The first chairman of the new group was Bishop Ithiel Clemmons of the Church of God in Christ. Assisting Clemmons in creating the new grouping was Bishop Bernard Underwood of the Pentecostal Holiness Church. The old divisions between the Trinitarian and oneness Pentecostal churches continued after 1994 and awaited further study for possible future dialogue.[1]

Nondenominational Pentecostals

Throughout the century, Pentecostalism spawned thousands of independent and nondenominational congregations in the United States and around the world. A rule of thumb was that for every local denominational Pentecostal congregation, there would be at least another one or more independent congregations that had split from the original church over the years. This meant that by the year 2000 there were well over 100,000 autonomous Pentecostal churches in the United States that were not included in the statistics of the Pentecostal denominations.

With the advent of the charismatic movement after 1960, thousands more of these churches appeared in practically every community in the United States and Europe, particularly in Great Britain. These churches often used the word *charismatic* in their names, which gave rise to some confusion over the use of the word. In the 1960s the word *charismatic* was adopted by mainline Protestant and Catholic renewalists to distinguish themselves from the classical Pentecostals. By 1980 the term could mean anything as it began to be co-opted by independent churches. As a result, several denominational renewal groups, including Presbyterians, Methodists, Baptists, and Episcopalians, began to drop the word *charismatic* from their names. The only large renewal movement to continue use of the name was the Catholic charismatic renewal.

The Full Gospel Business Men

One of the most influential nondenominational movements during the last half of the century was the Full Gospel Business Men's Fellowship International (FGBMFI) founded by Demos Shakarian in 1952 in Los Angeles,

California. Shakarian, a wealthy dairyman of Armenian descent, felt the need of starting a ministry for businessmen who were reluctant to attend Pentecostal churches. With the help of Oral Roberts, William Branham, Tommy Hicks, and other healing evangelists, Shakarian was able to make the FGMBFI a major religious force in America and the world in the last decades of the century. At its height, the Full Gospel "merchants of salvation" ministered to some four million persons a month in hotels, restaurants, and cafeterias where businessmen could gather under their own leadership, since women and clergymen could not join as full voting members.

A California dairyman, Pentecostal layman Demos Shakarian (1913–1993) founded the Full Gospel Business Men's Fellowship International (FGBMFI) in 1951. This organization introduced millions of Protestant and Catholic businessmen to the charismatic movement.

The FGBMFI organized over 3,000 local chapters in 117 nations where men could gather to sing hymns, eat good food, speak in tongues, and evangelize their friends. Chapter meetings featured testimonies of successful businessmen, sermons by leading evangelists and pastors, and music from leading Spirit-filled musicians. The annual international conferences of the organization gathered thousands of people from all over the world. In addition, the FGBMFI sponsored dozens of "airlifts" to major cities around the world. Characterized by Oral Roberts as "God's Ballroom

Saints," the Full Gospel Business Men introduced the Pentecostal experience to millions of men who became the nucleus of the many charismatic renewal movements in the mainline churches.[2]

Women's Aglow Fellowship

Following in the footsteps of the Full Gospel Business Men was a similar organization created to minister to the particular needs of women in the renewal. In Seattle, Washington, in 1967 a small local group of Spirit-filled women gathered to hear Rita Bennett speak to the special ministry needs of women. Soon the group began to meet weekly for prayer, lunch, and fellowship under the direction of Ellen Olson of Seattle. In time the organization grew to become a worldwide force. The group grew exponentially after Jane Hansen became president in 1980. By 1990 there were 1,700 chapters in the United States with an additional 900 chapters in 103 nations of the world. At that time more than fifty thousand women gathered each month in Aglow meetings. The organization's monthly magazine, *Aglow,* helped to promote raising funds for Bible distribution and reading materials that were sent around the world.

The stated purposes of Women's Aglow are: to share worship, witness for Christ, work for unity among believers, foster fellowship, and to encourage women to participate fully in the local church.[3]

The Shepherding/Discipleship Movement

Perhaps the most controversial movement to arise within the charismatic renewal took place under the aegis of a nondenominational ministry in Fort Lauderdale, Florida, known as Christian Growth Ministries (CGM). Led by five men, Bob Mumford, Charles Simpson, Derek Prince, Don Basham, and Ern Baxter, these teachers conducted influential seminars and evangelistic meetings around the nation after 1970 that emphasized "discipleship" and "shepherding" to the masses of Protestant and Catholic charismatics that were looking for spiritual direction in the heady days of massive charismatic growth in the 1970s. Modeled after the tradition of "spiritual directors" in the Catholic Church, the Fort Lauderdale teachers called for every believer to have a spiritual adviser as a "covering" for advice and counsel.

The movement was popularized in the monthly magazine *New Wine,* which was edited by Don Basham. Through this magazine as well as millions of books, newsletters, and audiotapes of teaching missions, they spread the central message of the movement, that everyone should be connected to a leader above themselves and in turn disciple others. This "shepherding" system was considered to be an answer for the thousands of charismatics who were drifting from conference to conference and at times receiving questionable teaching and leadership. To these rootless and wandering masses, the Fort Lauderdale teachers offered "covenant relationships" between a "shepherd" or "covering" who would direct the spiritual lives of his "disciples." As the movement developed into a pyramid of authority, it became apparent that the top shepherds in Fort Lauderdale would ultimately have control over the lives and fortunes of thousands of people under their influence. Criticism was sure to follow.

The Fort Lauderdale Shepherds. In 1975, five men: Bob Mumford, Charles Simpson, Derek Prince, Don Basham, and Ern Baxter, established "Christian Growth Ministries" in Fort Lauderdale, Florida. They spread their "discipleship and shepherding" teachings through *New Wine* magazine.

By 1975 the movement's teachings were soundly rejected by many influential leaders, including Demos Shakarian and Pat Robertson. Soon the shepherding teachers were banned from speaking at FGBMFI functions as well as appearances on Robertson's *700 Club*. The popular healing televangelist Kathryn Kuhlman went so far as to brand them as "heretics." Robertson accused them of "controlling the lives of their followers with the overuse of spiritual authority." An abortive meeting of the shepherding teachers and their critics in Minneapolis in August 1975 failed to resolve the issues. Despite this stalemate, the movement continued to grow. In the massive general charismatic conference in Kansas in 1977, the shepherding track attracted twelve thousand registrants, second only to the Catholic charismatic delegation.

After 1977 the movement began to wane as the charismatic renewal movements organized their own programs to train and disciple their followers. By 1983, Derek Prince had detached himself from the other leaders. With the folding of *New Wine* magazine in 1986, the movement practically came to an end. A symbolic closure to the controversy came in 1989 when Bob Mumford issued a public apology for his role in spreading the movement.[4]

THE SHEPHERDING, DISCIPLESHIP CONTROVERSY

Charismatic patriarch Dennis Bennett, Christian broadcaster Pat Robertson, and 27 other key leaders from the Catholic, Protestant, and Independent sectors of the Charismatic Renewal gathered in August 1975 to address the most significant controversy of the burgeoning neo-pentecostal movement. In a small, dimly lit, basement conference room in Minneapolis the men met to try to settle a growing furor over the teachings on "Shepherding and Discipleship." The dispute threatened to completely divide the Renewal that had been distinguished by its ecumenical character. The "summit meeting" that came to be known as the "shoot-out at the Curtis Hotel" made little progress in quieting the storm. Tempers flared, charges went back and forth and most left the meeting in frustration. The media soon picked up on the controversy and headlines only heightened the tensions that focused on the teachings of the "Shepherding Movement."

The movement, also known as the Discipleship movement, was an influential and controversial expression of the Charismatic Renewal in the United States that emerged as a distinct, non-denominational movement in 1974. The movement developed in response to the increasing independence among many Charismatic Christians who were leaving their denominational churches and joining independent churches and prayer groups. The movement taught that every believer needed to submit to a "shepherd" or pastoral leader. This relationship was seen as essential for developing spiritual maturity and required a definite commitment to a pastor. The movement also taught that all pastors and leaders needed to be personally submitted to another leader to foster accountability. These emphases were seen by critics as an attempt to create a kind of "takeover" of the independent Charismatics, creating a pyramid-like chain of command with Shepherding leaders at the top; a charge which the movement's leaders always denied.

The movement grew out of the association in October 1970 of four popular Charismatic Bible teachers: Don Basham, Bob Mumford, Derek Prince, and Charles Simpson. Canadian Pentecostal Ern Baxter joined the four in 1974. The five Bible Teachers were involved with *New Wine Magazine*, which at one time was the most widely circulated Charismatic publication in the U.S. The five were regulars at national and international teaching conferences that became so typical of the neo-pentecostal explosion of the 1960s and 1970s. All the men were also a part of the "cassette tape revolution" that was another feature of the Renewal that saw a proliferation of teaching tapes by noted Charismatic leaders.

Three annual "Men's Shepherds" conferences in 1973-75 helped catalyze that emerging movement that developed into a network of churches under the leadership of the five teachers. The churches in this network were nontraditionally structured with an emphasis on small cell groups or house churches. Lay shepherds led these cell groups.

The five teachers' popularity and *New Wine Magazine*'s broad influence in the Charismatic Renewal gave rise to heated controversy in 1975-76 over the movement's teaching on authority and submission, and translocal pastoral care. While the controversy never entirely abated, it did quiet down by 1980 and the Shepherding movement grew and consolidated until it peaked in 1982 with 100,000 adherents and 500 associated churches. Internal struggles and external pressures eventually caused the movement's dissolution in 1986 that coincided with the cessation of the publication of *New Wine Magazine*. Today a smaller movement continues, called the Covenant movement, for the most part associated with the leadership of Charles Simpson. ∎

—DAVID MOORE

The Charismatic Communities

Closely allied with the shepherding leaders was the movement to create charismatic communities where initiates could separate themselves from the world and live in a "covenant community" led by Spirit-filled leaders who would lead members into a life of devotion and separation from the world. The first of these communities was organized by Pastor Graham Pulkingham's parish of the Holy Redeemer Episcopal Church in Houston, Texas, in 1965. This was followed in 1967 by the "Word of God Community," which was organized in Ann Arbor, Michigan, by Ralph Martin and Steve Clark as an ecumenical community with mostly Catholic leadership and membership. In time, this became the most influential of the early communities, with a majority of the early Catholic charismatic books, music, and teaching materials being produced by community members. This community also published *New Covenant*, the magazine that became the major publication serving the Catholic renewal.

The Word of God Community was organized into "households" of many varieties. For instance, there were households for university dormitory students, for married couples, and for single men and single women. Daily life was organized around prayer sessions, teaching missions, and worship. Weekly public evangelistic services were held to attract new converts while social uplift services were offered to the poor and underprivileged. Community leaders reviewed and approved such major lifestyle decisions as job placement, courtship and marriage, and areas of ministry.

The Word of God was soon joined by the "People of Praise Community" in South Bend, Indiana, led by Kevin Ranaghan and Paul DeCelles. This grew to prominence through the huge Catholic charismatic conferences that convened on the campus of Notre Dame University in the early 1970s. To organize these conferences, members of the People of Praise organized "Charismatic Renewal Services," a corporation that was created mainly to administer charismatic conferences. By 1973, no less than thirty-three thousand Catholics gathered in the football stadium of Notre Dame University in a massive show of charismatic strength.

Other American communities were organized during this period. Among them were the Mother of God Community in Gaithersburg, Maryland, led by Judith Tydings and Edith Difato; the "Community of Jesus" in Cape Cod, Massachusetts, led by Peter Marshall Jr.; and the Alleluia Community in Augusta, Georgia, led by Bill Beatty. Others included the Servants of the Light Community in Minneapolis led by Virgil Vogt; an American Baptist community in Chula Vista, California, led by Ken Pagard; and Jim Ferry's "New Covenant" Community in New Jersey.

The communitarian movement took root in Europe at the same time. France took an early lead in developing charismatic communities. The Catholic Emmanuel Community in Paris, which was organized in 1972, specialized in street-preaching evangelism, while the *Chemin Neuf* in Lyons experimented in ecumenical relationships. Other communities around the world included the Maranatha Community in Brussells and the Emmanuel Community in Brisbane, Australia.

By the mid 1970s, there was a growing interest in joining these communities into an alliance for the sharing of experience and vision. Accordingly, in 1975 a short-lived "association of communities" was formed but soon disbanded due to a lack of common goals. This was succeeded by a new ecumenical association led by the Word of God in Ann Arbor called the "Sword of the Spirit." By 1987 this group numbered twelve "branches," twenty-five "affiliated groups," and six "associated" communities from several nations. After this, the People of Praise in South Bend organized another fellowship of communities that was more loosely structured than the "Sword of the Spirit" grouping. Still another organization called the International Brotherhood of Communities was organized in 1983 under the leadership of the God's Delight Community in Dallas, Texas, and led by Bobby Cavnar.

One of the great contributions of the charismatic communities was the training of dedicated volunteers to serve the wider renewal. Disciplined members of the Word of God and People of Praise Communities served as the "shock troops" and volunteers to help man the massive charismatic conferences that convened in Kansas City (1977), New Orleans (1987), and Indianapolis (1990). The communities also provided places of refuge for scholars and other charismatic leaders. This was especially true of the Mother of God Community in Gaithersburg, Maryland, which became the home base for such Catholic scholars as Francis Martin and Peter Hocken.

By the end of the 1980s controversies and divisions began to break the unity of the communitarian movement in the United States and among affiliates around the world. The major division was between the Word of God's "Sword of the Spirit" communities and those led by People of Praise. Some communities were also investigated by Catholic Church authorities for being too exclusive and restrictive over the private lives of the members.[5]

The Faith Churches

As the charismatic movement grew in the mainline churches, a parallel movement began to grow rapidly among independent Pentecostals called variously the "faith movement" or the "positive confession" theology. The roots of this movement lay deep in classical Pentecostalism and in the healing crusades of the 1950s. Generally seen as a precursor of the movement was Essek William Kenyon, whose "finished work" theories had influenced the early theology of the Assemblies of God. Essentially the faith teaching emphasized "positive confession" as a literal "bringing into existence what we state with our mouth, since faith is a confession." What most people confessed was healing for the body and financial prosperity. This also became popularly known as a "prosperity gospel," which offered its followers health and prosperity in answer to "the prayer of faith."

The theological principles of Essek William Kenyon (1867–1948) became basic teachings of the faith movement led by Kenneth Hagin, Kenneth Copeland, and Fred Price.

Much of the faith message had been foreshadowed in the ministry of Oral Roberts in his healing crusades of the 1950s and in the teachings of Demos Shakarian and the Full Gospel Business Men. In contrast to the general poverty of most Pentecostals, the faith and prosperity teachings amounted to a new "gospel of wealth" for Pentecostals that paralleled the Protestant prosperity teachings of the "gilded age" in the last quarter of the 19th century. For the rising middle class of newly prosperous Pentecostals and charismatics, the teaching held an irresistible attraction.

The faith message achieved movement status in the late 1970s under the leadership of Kenneth Hagin, Kenneth Copeland, Fred Price, and Charles Capps. With a distinctive theology that distinguished between the "Logos Word " (the unchangeable Scriptures) and the "Rhema Word" (tongues, prophecy, etc), the faith teachers offered their followers physical healing, inner healing, freedom from demon oppression, and prosperity in response to the "word of faith," which often was a verbal confession of biblical phrases that the Lord was bound to honor. In time critics branded the teaching as a "name it and claim it" teaching that ignored the realities of unavoidable sickness and poverty in the world. Sometimes, critics claimed, sick people confessed to healings although the "symptoms" might remain. Others, it was claimed, refused to take medicine with disastrous results. Many were turned off by some faith teachers' contention that Christians become "little gods" since they are "born-again children of God."

In spite of these theological squabbles, the faith movement grew exponentially during the 1980s and 1990s. By 1974, Kenneth Hagin had established the Rhema Bible Institute in Broken Arrow, Oklahoma (near Tulsa), and inaugurated a worldwide radio ministry called the Faith Seminar of the Air on 180 stations. By 1988, more than ten thousand students had graduated from his Bible school. The television and crusade ministries of Kenneth Copeland and Frederick Price brought the faith message into the living rooms of mainstream America.

One reason for the growth of the faith movement was the widespread acceptance of the faith teachers among charismatics in all churches. In the 1970s Hagin was a favorite speaker at Full Gospel Business Men's meetings as well as Catholic charismatic conferences. Their influence also spread worldwide through the burgeoning ministries of Reinhard Bonnke and Ray McCauley in South Africa, as well as Ulf Eckman in Sweden.[6]

The Holy Spirit and Mainline Evangelicals

In 1983, Peter Wagner, professor of church growth at Fuller Theological Seminary, proposed the existence of a "third wave of the Holy Spirit" that was entering wholesale into historic evangelical churches. In his view, the first wave consisted of the Pentecostals while the second wave were the charismatics in the mainline churches. Using himself as a paradigm for this movement he said, "I see myself as neither a charismatic nor a Pentecostal." Although he spoke in tongues and was a leading advocate of signs and wonders, he said, "I myself have several theological differences with Pentecostals and charismatics, which don't mar any kind of mutual ministry, but keep me from saying I'm a charismatic." He further noted that he saw the 1980s as a time of opening among "straightline evangelicals and other Christians to the supernatural work of the Holy Spirit that the Pentecostals and charismatics have experienced but without becoming charismatic or Pentecostal."

Pentecostal evangelist Kenneth E. Hagin (1917–) founded the Rhema Bible Training Center in Broken Arrow, Oklahoma, in 1974. He is seen as the father of the faith movement among Pentecostals and charismatics.

Although an organized and well-defined third wave failed to materialize, Wagner's description fitted thousands of pastors and congregations in the United States and around the world. By the 1990s the Pentecostal style of worship had entered into many mainstream evangelical churches with services featuring contemporary music, raised hands, and prayer for the sick. Visitors to some churches would have difficulty distinguishing the worship from a full-blown Pentecostal congregation. In fact many evangelical churches experienced not only tongues and interpretations, but also holy laughter, falling in the Spirit, dancing before the Lord, and singing in tongues.

KENNETH ERWIN HAGIN (1917–)

Hagin was born and raised among Southern Baptists in McKinney, Texas, but is reported to have pastored an interconfessional country church in nearby Roland during 1936–38. One year prior to his first pastorate, however, he was introduced to Pentecostal practices in tent meetings in McKinney conducted by Assemblies of God minister Albert Ott. Two years later Hagin received Spirit baptism. Although holding five pastorates among the Assemblies of God during 1938–49, Hagin did not receive ordination from this denomination until 1942.

After resigning his last pastorate in 1949, Hagin crisscrossed the country as an itinerant evangelist. He received inspiration from the post–World War II healing evangelists, but still didn't meet the movement's coordinator, Gordon Lindsay, until 1953. Two years later Hagin joined the latter's Voice of Healing network of healing evangelists. Through Lindsay's assistance Hagin had his first minibook, *Redeemed from Poverty, Sickness, and Death,* published in 1960. During this period the healing revival was declining and was succeeded by the charismatic renewal.

Through Demos Shakarian's FGBMFI conventions, Hagin's teachings on faith healing now found a receptive audience among non-Pentecostal charismatics. During this same period the formal ties between Hagin and the Assemblies of God were severed as he established the Kenneth E. Hagin Evangelistic Association in 1962.

In 1966 Hagin moved from Garland, Texas, to Tulsa, Oklahoma, where his first radio broadcast, "Faith Seminar of the Air," was initiated. Two years later Hagin produced his own newsletter, the *Word of Faith.* Then in 1974 he established the Rhema Bible Training Center, now located in nearby Broken Arrow, which has produced more than ten thousand graduates who have founded additional faith congregations both within and outside of the United States. Through the Rhema Ministerial Association International, established in 1985, some one thousand local faith congregations are formally connected with the Hagin ministry. In addition to that, influential ministers such as Ken and Gloria Copeland, Jerry Savelle, Norvel Hayes, and Frederick K.C. Price look to the elder Hagin as their mentor. ▪

—Geir Lie

As the movement spread from church to church, there often followed conflicts between the traditionalists and those who longed for the miraculous and more emotionally satisfying services. As some traditional churches rejected the newer style of worship, members wandered off to Pentecostal or independent charismatic congregations to satisfy their longings. This sometimes led to charges of proselytism or "sheep stealing." By the year 2000, some such as David Barrett were calling third wavers "neocharismatics" and assigning them huge numbers of followers. In fact, by 2000 Barrett estimated that there were some 295 million members in the world that fit the description of "third wave" as proposed by Wagner.[7]

Ecumenical Streams

Without intending to do so, the Pentecostal/charismatic movement became the largest and most dynamic grassroots ecumenical force in the Christian world in the last decades of the 20th century. The first Pentecostals were not ecumenical due to their rejection by the mainline churches and society at large. In fact the penetration of Pentecostalism into the mainline churches was not something planned by the Pentecostals but came as individuals received baptism in the Holy Spirit. To be sure, as Kilian McDonnell observed, "behind every Neo-Pentecostal stood a classical Pentecostal." In fact, Pentecostals had barely begun talking to one another when the charismatic movement brought into the picture a whole new generation of Spirit-filled Christians in the mainline churches. Before Pentecostals could adjust to the fact that mainline Protestants were speaking in tongues, the Catholic charismatic renewal began and brought with it a whole new perplexing set of ecumenical problems.

The first Pentecostal to extend the olive branch to the mainline churches was David du Plessis, who eventually became known as "Mr. Pentecost." In his early years as an official of the Apostolic Faith Mission (AFM), a major Pentecostal denomination in South Africa, du Plessis felt called to bring Pentecostalism to all the churches. This was confirmed through a personal prophecy by Smith Wigglesworth in 1936 that proclaimed, "You will bring the message of Pentecost to all churches." After this, du Plessis was instrumental in organizing the first world Pentecostal conference in Zurich, Switzerland, in 1947. Serving as organizing secretary for the world Pentecostal conferences from 1949 to 1958, he worked tirelessly to bring all Pentecostal believers together into a worldwide fellowship.

A South African Pentecostal, David Johannes du Plessis (1905–87) moved to the United States in 1948 where his ecumenical ministry to Protestants and Catholics earned him the nickname "Mr. Pentecost."

Coming to America from his native South Africa in 1948, du Plessis taught at Lee College in Cleveland, Tennessee, before joining the Assemblies of God, while maintaining his ministerial credentials with the AFM in South Africa. In 1951, while pastoring an Assemblies of God congregation in Stamford, Connecticut, he contacted the National Council of Churches in New York City. Resulting friendships with Alexander Mackay, president of Princeton University, and W. A. Visser t'Hooft of the World Council of Churches opened the door for du Plessis to represent the Pentecostals in ecumenical circles. As a result, he became the only Pentecostal who would openly dialogue with the National and World Council of Churches.

DAVID DU PLESSIS: "MR. PENTECOST"

The one person, above all the others, who served as catalyst and spokesman for the Pentecostals after World War II was David J. du Plessis, a South African descendant of exiled French Huguenots who was converted in a South African Pentecostal church known as the Apostolic Faith Mission. According to du Plessis' testimony, the inspiration for the ecumenical work he was destined to perform came to him in the form of a prophecy given in 1936 by the evangelist Smith Wigglesworth. One morning about 7:00 o'clock Wigglesworth burst into du Plessis' office and:

> laying his hands on his shoulders he pushed him against the wall and began to prophesy: "you have been in 'Jerusalem' long enough. . . . I will send you to the uttermost parts of the earth. . . . You will bring the message of Pentecost to all churches. . . you will travel more than evangelists do. . . . God is going to re-vive the churches in the last days and through them turn the world upside down. Even the Pentecostal movement will become a mere joke compared with the revival which God will bring through the churches.

This vision remained unfulfilled for ten years, until the end of World War II made it possible for du Plessis to travel extensively. In 1947, he took a leading role in convening the first Pentecostal World Conference in Zurich, Switzerland, and in 1949 served a short term as General Secretary of the World Conference. His zeal for ecumenism, however, soon cost him his job.

Although stung by the rejection of the Pentecostal leaders, du Plessis was still consumed by Wigglesworth's prophetic vision. In 1951, while pastoring an Assemblies of God congregation in Connecticut, he felt inspired to make contact with the World Council of Churches in nearby New York City. Although he had sternly opposed the Council in its formative stages, he now saw the mainline churches as an evangelistic opportunity. During a trip to the headquarters of the National Council of Churches (NCC), he was astounded by the "warm reception" accorded him. A later meeting with President John MacKay of Princeton Theological Seminary convinced him that the mainline churches were greatly interested in making contact with the Pentecostal churches. After joining the NCC as an individual member in 1954, du Plessis was seated as an unofficial representative of the Pentecostal churches at the second plenary session of the World Council of Churches that met in Evanston, Illinois. This action, and the fact that he attended Vatican II as the only Pentecostal observer, brought down upon his head the ire of his denominational officials. He was excommunicated in 1962 by the Assemblies of God, whose leader viewed him as a maverick without portfolio.

In a short time, du Plessis became the leading figure in spearheading the charismatic movement in the traditional churches. His work as chairman of the Roman Catholic-Pentecostal Dialogue team and as a leading speaker at hundreds of Pentecostal-charismatic meetings around the world eventually earned him the unofficial title of "Mr. Pentecost." In 1974 a group of reporters named du Plessis as one of the eleven "foremost theologians of the twentieth century." Also, for his work in the dialogue and other contributions to the Catholic charismatic movement, he was given, in 1983, the golden "Good Merit" medal by Pope John Paul II for excellent "service to all Christianity." He was the first non-Catholic in history to receive this honor. Though his work has often been controversial, du Plessis' place is secure as one of the most important Pentecostal figures in history. His influence was pivotal in shaping the charismatic movement in the historic churches. ∎

—VINSON SYNAN, IN *HOLINESS PENTECOSTAL TRADITION*

He was invited to represent the Pentecostals in the 1954 assembly of the World Council of Churches in Evanston, Illinois. After this, he was the only accredited Pentecostal observer at the Vatican II sessions in Rome (1962–65), although he served without the official approval of the Pentecostal churches.[8]

All of this ecumenical activity did not sit well with the American Pentecostal leaders who were deeply suspicious of the liberalism of the conciliar movement as well as of the developing charismatic movement among Roman Catholics. As a result, du Plessis was defrocked by the Assemblies of God in 1962. From then until his reinstatement in 1980, he ministered as a local preacher in the First Assembly of God of Oakland, California. Until the end of his life in 1987, du Plessis served as an unofficial Pentecostal "ambassador-at-large" to the major Christian denominations of the world. In this capacity he traveled around the globe on endless missions to churches, conferences, and gatherings, however large or small, to tell the story of the Pentecostal movement.[9]

One of his greatest achievements was the inauguration of a long-running dialogue between the Pentecostals and the Roman Catholic Church. Working with Catholic scholar Fr. Kilian McDonnell of St. John's University in Collegeville, Minnesota, du Plessis led Pentecostals and charismatic teams from 1972 to 1982 in annual sessions where areas of concern were openly discussed and confronted. Serving with him on the Pentecostal/charismatic teams were such scholars as Dr. J. Rodman Williams, Dr. Russell Spittler, Dr. Vinson Synan, and Dr. Cecil Robeck.

From the beginning, the Pentecostals and charismatic Christians crossed denominational barriers to share in teaching, worship, and fellowship. Indeed, by 1980 the movement had become the largest grassroots ecumenical movement in the history of Christendom. In the huge healing crusades of Oral Roberts and Kathryn Kuhlman, Catholics and Protestants, blacks and whites, men and women, young and old, mixed together without apparent regard to the many theological and cultural backgrounds composing the crowds. In time, it was not unusual to see a Catholic priest, an Episcopal pastor, and a Pentecostal evangelist sharing the same platform at Full Gospel Business Men's dinners or the thousands of other conferences, revivals, crusades, and missions sponsored by a multitude of churches and para-church organizations.

The first ongoing ecumenical group to emerge from the renewal was born in the passions raised by the shepherding/discipleship controversy of the late 1970s. As the crisis grew between the Fort Lauderdale teachers and other nationally known figures, a call was sent out to several leaders to meet in Minneapolis to attempt a basis of reconciliation. Attending this meeting were Mumford, Prince, Basham, Simpson, and Baxter from the Fort Lauderdale group, while critics such as Pat Robertson, Dennis Bennett, and others came from the other side. Attempting to moderate the sessions were Brick Bradford and Jamie Buckingham. Although this "shootout at the Curtis Hotel" solved nothing, in the long run it spawned an informal annual meeting of leaders whose aim was to moderate and solve problems that might arise in the future. Because many of these sessions convened at the Marianist Retreat Center near the town of Glencoe, a suburb of St. Louis, the group was known for years as the "Glencoe meeting."

The first Glencoe leaders were Larry Christenson and Kevin Ranaghan, who invited leaders from all the streams of renewal to gather for informal and low-profile meetings every summer to help serve the renewal and keep important leaders in contact with one another. Many problems were actually solved in these sessions. One of them was the criticism raised when Prince and others began to hold public exorcisms. Because these often became messy and disorderly, much disapproval was leveled at the methods of "deliverance" practiced by these leaders. After some dialogue, an agreement was forged whereby everyone abandoned public exorcisms in favor of private individual-deliverance sessions as the need arose. This type of problem solving was low key, out of the public eye, and based on mutual trust and respect.

In the middle 1970s, as the movement moved ever upward in America, there arose a widespread desire to call all Pentecostals and charismatics together for a common witness to what was happening among them. By this time the Catholics were drawing upward of thirty thousand people to their annual conferences in South Bend, while the Lutherans drew more than twenty thousand to their conferences in Minneapolis, the largest annual gathering of Lutherans in the United States. Others, such as the Episcopalians and the Presbyterians, drew increasingly large crowds to their charismatic events. The Full Gospel Business Men seemed to fill any auditorium or arena reserved for their multifarious events. The convention bureaus took note of the fact that the FGBMFI meetings regularly filled more hotel rooms than any other organization in the country.[10]

In the annual Glencoe meeting in 1974, it was suggested by Vinson Synan and others that it was time for all these groups to gather for a "conference of conferences" that would bring together all elements of the renewal at the same time and place. An article in *New Covenant* magazine by Ralph Martin identified three streams of renewal that needed to stay in touch. They were the Pentecostals, the mainline Protestants, and the Catholic charismatics. The idea of an ecumenical general conference soon caught fire and spread across the land. In a short time the Catholic charismatics in South Bend offered to call such a conference, with their conferencing arm of Charismatic Renewal Services providing the seed money and leadership. In several preliminary planning sessions an ecumenical "Planning Committee" representing the streams of renewal was formed under the leadership of Kevin Ranaghan.

The city chosen for the first "General Conference on Charismatic Renewal" was Kansas City, on the banks of the Missouri River. The format was for each separate movement to conduct its own morning "denominational track" followed by common workshops in the afternoons. At night everyone was to gather as one in the huge Arrowhead Stadium, originally built for the Kansas City Chiefs football team. There was great excitement as some fifty thousand Pentecostals and charismatics from many streams gathered in the stadium for an old-fashioned "charismatic camp meeting." For four nights speakers addressed the mass crowd on the moving of the Spirit that seemed to be breaking out everywhere. Tongues, healings, and prophecies were manifested by a carefully assembled "word gift unit," which alone had access to the microphones. The praise was awe-inspiring as tens of thousands of Spirit-filled Christians sang new songs, danced before the Lord, and shouted for joy.

A highlight of the conference was the sermon by Bob Mumford, which resulted in a twenty-minute roar of praise that seemed to never end. The most solemn moment came when a prophecy came forth lamenting the divisions in the body of Christ. Many wept aloud as they heard the haunting words:

Come before me, with broken hearts and contrite spirits
For the body of my Son is broken.
Come before me with tears and mourning,
For the body of my Son is broken.
The light is dim, my people are scattered,
The body of my Son is broken.
I gave all I had in the body and blood of my Son,
It spilled on the earth,
The body of my Son is broken
Turn from the sins of your fathers,
And walk in the ways of my Son.
Return to the plan of your Father.
Return to the purpose of your God.
The body of my Son is broken.
The Lord says to you: stand in unity with one another,
And let nothing tear you apart.

And by no means separate from one another,
Through your bitternesses,
And your personal preferences,
But hold fast to one another.
Because I am about to let you undergo
A time of severe trial and testing,
And you'll need to be in unity with one another.
But I tell you this also,
I am Jesus, the Victor King.
And I have promised you victory.[11]

Sitting together on the platform were an unlikely group: Rev. Thomas Zimmerman, general superintendent of the American Assemblies of God; Leon Joseph Cardinal Suenens, Roman Catholic primate of Belgium; Bishop J. O. Patterson, presiding bishop of the predominantly black Church of God in Christ; and Anglican archbishop Bill Burnett of South

Africa. On the night that Forbes and Burnett spoke, one of the most remarkable prophecies of recent times was given by Lutheran Larry Christenson. He spoke of a future time of racial struggle in South Africa that would end in a miraculous peace without bloodshed as a "white man and a black man" reached out to each other in Jesus Christ, bringing the nation together and avoiding race war. This prophecy came years before anyone had heard of Nelson Mandela or President F. W. de Klerk. The releasing of Mandela from prison, his election to power, and the amazing bloodless transfer of power from whites to blacks in 1994 seemed to be a direct fulfillment of the Kansas City prophecy.

The "Congress on the Holy Spirit and World Evangelization" in New Orleans in 1987 called on all charismatics and Pentecostals to become evangelists during a "decade of world evangelization" in the 1990s.

Reporters in Kansas City were dumbfounded by what they saw. Unable to describe the event in conventional terms, an article in *Time* magazine reported simply that "everyone had a charismatic time." In future years, many people who were in Kansas City felt that this conference marked an early high-water mark of the renewal in America.[12]

For several years, the charismatic movement continued to develop in America within the separate streams in ever increasing power. In 1978, the Full Gospel Business Men held their largest annual conference with more

BILLY GRAHAM ON THE CHARISMATIC RENEWAL

I rejoice with you at the goals of your North American Congress on the Holy Spirit and World Evangelization. And I thank God for the vital role that your movement is having in bringing about a spiritual awakening in this country.

Today it is encouraging to see the Holy Spirit moving in His church across North America and in other parts of the world toward the goal of bringing others to a saving knowledge of Jesus Christ. ∎

—BILLY GRAHAM, 1987

than twenty-five thousand persons attending. Huge crowds continued to attend the Notre Dame and Minneapolis conferences. It seemed that anyone could announce a conference anywhere in the country with any slate of speakers and multitudes would drive, fly, or hitchhike to attend. If there were not enough hotel rooms, many charismatic young people would bring their backpacks and sleeping bags and create their own accommodations.

By 1984 there was increasing pressure to convene another Kansas City-type conference to keep the charismatic ecumenical flame alive. In the Glencoe leaders conference, Vinson Synan and Vernon Stoop were chosen as leaders and soon the vision of another "Kansas City" consumed the group. In order to plan the next conferences, a new legal entity was formed in 1985 called the North American Renewal Service Committee (NARSC) with Vinson Synan as chairman. The steering committee represented over fifty Pentecostal denominations, mainline charismatic renewal groups, and other para-church organizations. In short order, a major leaders conference was scheduled to convene in New Orleans in 1986. At the suggestion of John Wimber, the conference emphasized the theme "The Holy Spirit and World Evangelization." More than seven thousand leaders from all streams gathered in the Superdome in New Orleans where conferees heard such speakers as Dr. Paul Yonggi Cho, Oral Roberts, David du Plessis, Demos Shakarian, and Fr. Tom Forrest.

Billy Graham

The leaders conference was followed the next year by a massive "General Congress," which again met in the Superdome. Here some forty thousand attendees heard Tom Forrest call for the 1990s to be a "Decade of

World Evangelization" with the goal of winning over half the population of the world to Christ by the year 2000. A highlight of the congress was the healing ministry of German evangelist Reinhard Bonnke, who demonstrated his dynamic ministry that was attracting millions of converts in his African crusades. This conference also featured twenty-five blocks of marchers in a parade that was second in size only to the Mardi Gras in New Orleans history.

The New Orleans Congress was followed by similar congresses in Indianapolis in 1990 (25,000 persons), Orlando in 1995 (10,000 persons), and St. Louis in 2000 (15,000 persons). In all of these congresses, the charismatics were encouraged to bring a Christian witness to their neighbors and friends in all parts of the world. According to Synan, these congresses "brought world evangelization into the thinking of the charismatic renewal." They also spawned several new charismatic organizations including the Methodist Aldersgate movement, which brought a powerful charismatic witness to the United Methodist Church.[13]

Other mass gatherings during this period included the "Washington for Jesus" rallies, which met on the Mall in the nation's capital. In 1988 John Geminez, a Hispanic pastor of the Rock Church in Virginia Beach, Virginia, called for a mass meeting to pray for the presidential election. A crowd estimated at five hundred thousand persons filled the mall for the largest Christian gathering in Washington up to that time. When the election was over and Ronald Reagan had won the White House, Geminez and his friends claimed credit for helping change the course of the nation's politics.

International Ecumenical Organizations

As the charismatic movement spread throughout the world, important ecumenical gatherings became common after the Kansas City conference of 1977. Fast-growing charismatic movements among Catholics and Lutherans in Germany along with booming movements in Ireland and France caused European leaders to call for a continental ecumenical charismatic conference to meet in Strasburg, France, in 1982. More than twenty thousand people attended this conference, which was dubbed "Pentecost Over Europe." This was followed by another major conference in Birmingham, England, in 1986 with the name "Acts '86." Leaders in these initiatives were Thomas Roberts, a French Pentecostal, and Anglican charismatic leader Michael Harper.

Following the Strasburg and Berlin meetings, a European ecumenical committee was formed under the leadership of Harper. This group soon suggested that a global organization be formed that would encompass, as much as possible, all the Pentecostal and charismatic movements in the world. This resulted in the creation of the International Charismatic Consultation on World Evangelization (ICCOWE) under the leadership of Harper and an international board of directors from the many streams of the renewal. In 1989 a meeting of leaders gathered in Jerusalem to plan for a strategy of world evangelization. This resulted in a major conference in Brighton, England, in 1991, which drew four thousand leaders from many worldwide charismatic constituencies. Addressing the conference was the newly elected archbishop of Canterbury, George Carey, who was himself a charismatic Anglican whose life and ministry had been changed by the renewal.[14]

Political Renewal in America

As the Pentecostal/charismatic renewal continued to grow in America, political engagement became inevitable due to the sheer numbers of voters involved. Gallup polls commissioned in 1979 by the evangelical magazine *Christianity Today* indicated that no less than twenty-nine million adult Americans considered themselves to be "Pentecostal or charismatic Christians." This was generally true of the major mainline denominations; about 20 percent of all Catholic, Lutheran, Baptist, Episcopalian, and Methodist members declared themselves to be in some way connected with the movement. Added to the publicity engendered by the "born-again" Christianity highlighted during the tenure of President Jimmy Carter was the growing bloc of voters who were not only "born again," but also baptized in the Holy Spirit.

There is little doubt that charismatics were at the core of the voting constituency that elected Ronald Reagan in 1980 and 1984. In fact, the first known Pentecostal to serve at the presidential cabinet level was James Watt, a member of the Assemblies of God who was Reagan's first Secretary of the Interior. With the completion of Reagan's eight years in the White House, the election of 1988 meant that the "religious right" had to choose between supporting Vice President Bush and turning to a candidate of their own. When Pat Robertson entered the race for the Republican nomination in 1988, the Christian conservatives were presented with a viable possibility of controlling the White House itself.

Robertson soon left his day-to-day duties as host of the popular *700 Club* and hit the campaign trail. In response, Vice President Bush called leading evangelical and charismatic leaders to his home to ask for their support. As the presidential primary race heated in 1988, Robertson surprised the pundits by winning the Iowa caucuses and giving Bush a vigorous challenge.

After losing the South Carolina primary, however, Robertson's campaign came to a sudden end short of victory. He was, nevertheless, the first "Spirit-filled" (i.e., tongues-speaking) person ever to run for the highest office in the land.

In the years that followed, Robertson organized the "Christian Coalition" as a mass movement of concerned citizens who supported the positions and candidates of the religious right. In addition to this movement, Robertson in 1990 created the American Center for Law and Justice (ACLJ) to counter the actions and influence of the liberal ACLU. Through lawsuits and court actions ACLJ lawyers fought legal issues dear to the hearts of conservative Christians, sometimes winning cases before the Supreme Court. At the time of the presidential election in 2000, Robertson and his Christian Coalition acted as a swing bloc that helped nominate George W. Bush as the Republican candidate. Robertson thus became a king-maker rather than a king.[15]

The Holy Spirit at the End of the Century

A major public setback for the Pentecostals and charismatics in the late 1980s came in the wake of the televangelist scandals that occurred between 1986 and 1990. These involved Jim and Tammy Bakker of the PTL Network in Charlotte, North Carolina; Jimmy Swaggart, the flamboyant evangelist from Baton Rouge, Louisiana; and to a lesser extent Oral Roberts of Tulsa, Oklahoma. At one time, these three ministries attracted millions of dollars in contributions from their TV audiences. Their influence drew multitudes of curious seekers to Pentecostal and independent charismatic churches.

The downfall of Bakker and Swaggart in 1987, which commanded media headlines for months on end, centered on scandals involving sex and money. On the other hand, the media attacked Oral Roberts for his fund-raising techniques in support of his new medical center in Tulsa known as the City of Faith. The other major televangelist, Pat Robertson, was never involved in the controversies that swirled around the other three. Both Roberts and Robertson had turned their vision and energies toward founding universities as carriers of their legacies to future generations.

In 1965 Roberts chartered his Oral Roberts University in Tulsa, where "teaching, preaching, and healing" would be emphasized in all classes. Robertson started classes in his new Christian Broadcasting Network University (CBNU), an all-graduate school of communications, in 1978. By the end of the century these schools were growing rapidly and gaining intellectual respect throughout the nation. In 1990, the name CBNU was changed to "Regent University" and plans were made to make it the "pre-eminent Christian university" in the world.[16]

Growth at the End of the Century

Despite the media setbacks suffered by the Pentecostals and charismatics in the 1980s due to the televangelist scandals, there was a continuing trend toward growth around the world and a new and more positive tone in the press. By 2000 several major publications in the United States heralded the continuing dynamic growth of the movement. For instance, in June 1998, *Christian History* magazine, which is owned by *Christianity Today*, ran a special issue titled "The Rise of Pentecostalism." It called Pentecostalism "the most explosive Christian movement of the twentieth century." Furthermore, it referred to the Azusa Street revival as the "American Pentecost," and "the most phenomenal event of twentieth century Christianity."[17]

Also in June, the *Los Angeles Times* and the *Philadelphia Enquirer* ran a major story by Mary Rourke titled "Redefining Religion in America," which claimed that "with almost no fanfare the United States is experiencing its most dramatic religious transformation in this century." Among the fastest-growing faiths were Buddhism, Hinduism, and Islam, but among Christians the growth of the unaffiliated "mega-church" is "the biggest story of the 1990s." It said that "no invention poses a greater challenge to mainstream Protestant religion than the nondenominational mega-church." The article went on to say, "Religion is a word they hate . . . They like spirituality because it represents something that culture has sucked out of them." This movement amounts to "reinventing Protestantism." While Pentecostalism was seen as a "subculture of the Protestant church," it has now grown to include millions of people in the mainline Protestant and Roman Catholic Churches.[18]

An even more arresting media event was the cover story in *Newsweek* magazine on April 13, 1998, by Kenneth Woodward titled "Living in the Holy Spirit." It featured the "Brownsville" revival in Pensacola, Florida. Here, as elsewhere, "Spirit-led worship is a body-shaking, soul-stirring experience for millions of Charismatic believers." In a 1998 *Newsweek* poll, 47 percent of Christians said that they have "personally experienced the Holy Spirit." Among evangelical Protestants the figure rose to 75 percent. Also during the year, audiences were mesmerized with Robert Duvall's amazing portrayal of a flawed backwoods southern Pentecostal preacher in his highly acclaimed and highly criticized movie, *The Apostle*.[19]

Major Trends at the Year 2000

Great Growth Continues

All the studies and media reports continued to comment on the explosive growth of Pentecostalism around the world. In his ongoing demographic studies, Dr. David Barrett of Regent University reported even stronger growth than most experts suspected. He is currently working on a new edition of his highly acclaimed *World Christian Encyclopedia*. Based on his estimates for 1999 and my own research, I offer the following figures on world Christianity at the dawn of the new millennium:

World Population 2000	6,010,779,000
Christians	1,990,018,000
Roman Catholics	1,040,020,000
Pentecostals/charismatics	530,000,000
Anglicans	73,200,000
Baptists	59,600,000
Lutherans	57,700,000
Presbyterians	49,800,000
Assemblies of God	35,000,000
Methodists	33,000,000
Pentecostals/Charismatics	
Denominational Pentecostals	215,000,000
Catholic charismatics	92,000,000
Protestant charismatics	71,000,000
Mainline third wavers	110,000,000
Chinese Pentecostals	52,000,000
Total Pentecostal and Charismatic Christians in 1999	530,000,000 [20]

The continuing explosive growth of Pentecostalism indicates that the renewal will continue with increasing strength into the next millennium. Not only was growth occurring in eye-catching mega-churches, but also in the tens of thousands of small local churches that were planted each year in big cities and remote villages around the world. This was highlighted by comparisons of the growth of a major Baptist mission and the Assemblies of God missions in Indonesia since World War II. Since Indonesia is predominantly Muslim, this is a most difficult field. Both Baptists and Assemblies of God missionaries entered Indonesia at about the same time (in the mid-fifties) with missionary staffs similar in size.

Since that time the Baptists have experienced solid growth, to over 30,000 members. The Assemblies of God, however, grew ten times more to about 300,000 members in 1998. Mainline missionaries have commented on the fact that wherever they went to plant a new church in any village in the country, no matter how small, there was already a Pentecostal church there. How they got there we do not know, but the major story of Pentecostalism in this century may well be the one million or more churches that have been planted in almost every city and village of the world.

Worship Becomes More Charismatic

In the last decade of the century the Pentecostal style of worship entered wholesale into the major non-Pentecostal Christian churches of the world. Many of these churches describe themselves as "Charismatic," while others describe themselves as "third wave"–type churches that encourage and experience the gifts of the Spirit without labeling themselves as "Pentecostal" or "charismatic." In such churches spiritual choruses inspired by Pentecostals are sung to the accompaniment of "music ministries" from various instruments. Hand-clapping, raised hands, and dancing before the Lord to rhythmic songs characterize the worship in such churches.

Many even "sing in the Spirit" (in tongues), have public prophecies, lay hands on the sick, and cast out demons. Others experience all the phenomena of the "Toronto Blessing" such as falling out, shouting, exotic noises, and so on. Yet they strongly insist that they are neither Pentecostal nor charismatic. Most often, they are self-described as "evangelical." Yet, to outside observers, they appear to be more akin to an even more traditional and radical type of Pentecostalism.

The Rise of the Mega-Church

In recent years free-standing mega-churches have become the fastest-growing churches in the world. Although some of these are noncharismatic, as typified by Bill Hybel's Willow Creek Church near Chicago, most are of the Pentecostal or, as many observers call them, "independent charismatic" churches—although a high percentage of them were pioneered by Pentecostal pastors. Most of them are deep into the "cell group" movement under such teachers as David Yonggi Cho and Ralph Neighbour. A rather large number of them are members of such classical

Pentecostal denominations as the Church of God in Christ, the Assemblies of God, the Church of God, the Pentecostal Holiness Church, and the International Church of the Foursquare Gospel. Though they are loyal to their denominations, they often operate as independent churches, and in some cases, like mini-denominations.

In America the "independent charismatic" churches include John Hagee's Cornerstone Church in San Antonio, Texas (16,000 members); T. D. Jakes's Potter's House Church in Dallas, Texas (25,000 members); John Osteen's Lakewood Church in Houston, Texas (10,000 members); Billy Joe Daugherty's Victory Christian Center in Tulsa, Oklahoma (10,000 members); Fred Price's Crenshaw Christian Center in Los Angeles (15,000 members); and Rod Parsley's World Harvest Church in Akron, Ohio (8,000 members).

Classical Pentecostal "mega-churches" include Jack Hayford's Church on the Way in Van Nuys, California (Foursquare, 10,000 members); Tommy Barnett's First Assembly of God in Phoenix, Arizona (12,000 Members); Paul Walker's Mt. Paran Church of God in Atlanta (12,000 members); Bishop Charles Blake's West Angeles Church of God in Christ in Los Angeles (15,000 members); and Ron Dryden's Cathedral of Praise in Oklahoma City (Pentecostal Holiness, 5,000 members). According to John Vaughn, the fastest-growing church of the century in America is probably Jakes's church in Dallas. It grew from zero members to over 25,000 within only three years.[21]

Throughout the world, most of the largest congregations are clearly Pentecostal in doctrine and worship style. According to mega-church specialist John Vaughn, the four largest churches in the world in 1998 were:

Church—City—Pastor—Members

1. Yoido Full Gospel Church —Seoul, Korea—David Yonggi Cho —730,000
2. Jotabeche Methodist Pentecostal—Santiago, Chile—Javier Vasquez —350,000
3. Anyang Assembly of God—Seoul, Korea—Yong Mok Cho—150,000
4. Deeper Life Bible Church—Lagos, Nigeria—William Kumuyi—145,000[22]

Cultural Accommodation

Many questions often arise about the growth of these huge churches. Are Pentecostals lowering their holiness standards to attract ever larger followings? Are these churches experiencing mostly transfer growth by pros-elytizing from other churches, or are they winning new converts from the pagan population pool? Are they changing the world, or is the world changing them?

Although some churches and pastors in America and Europe may be softening their standards on such things as movies and the use of tobacco or alcohol, almost all stand firmly for biblical standards on such questions as abortion, pornography, illegal drugs, and homosexuality. The younger Christian churches in the developing nations are pained beyond belief at the attempts of some Western non-Pente-costal churches to ordain practicing homosexuals and to perform same-sex weddings. To my knowledge, there are no Pentecostal churches in the world that condone such outrages against biblical Christianity.

David (Paul) Yonggi Cho (1936–) built the largest church in history in Seoul, Korea. Beginning as a poverty-stricken Assemblies of God pastor in 1958, he saw his Yoido Full Gospel congregation grow to more than 700,000 members.

In the United States there is a powerful countercultural trend to recon-cile the historic and scandalous racial divide between black and white churches. The Pentecostals have led the way in America since 1994 when the "Memphis Miracle" reunited North America's black and white churches in a new organization called the Pentecostal and Charismatic Churches of North America (PCCNA). In July of 1998 the PCCNA issued its first official periodical, titled *Reconciliation,* and edited by Mel Robeck and Harold Hunter.[23]

Convergence Movement

For decades church leaders have recognized that Pentecostalism has be-come one of the three major divisions of Christianity. The idea was first mentioned by Lesslie Newbigin of South India. In his pioneering 1953 book, *The Household of God,* Bishop Newbigin notes three major types of C   h   r   i   s the body of Christ. The first was the Catholic tradition, which emphasized continuity, orthodoxy, and the importance of the sacraments to the life of the church. The Protestant tradition, on the other hand, emphasized the centrality of the Scriptures and the importance of the proclaimed Word of God. The Pentecostals added to these first two historic expressions of the faith an emphasis on the present action of the Spirit in the church through the gifts of the Holy Spirit. According to Newbigin, the church needed all three emphases in order to be a powerful force in the modern world.[24]

The same point was made by Michael Harper in his 1979 book, *Three Sisters*. An early leader in the Anglican charismatic movement in England, Harper stated that "one sister (evangelical) taught me that the basis of

Christian life is a personal relationship with Jesus Christ. A second (Pentecostal) helped me experience the spiritual dynamic of the Holy Spirit. Yet another (Catholic) ushered me into a whole new world where I began to see the implications of Christian community."[25]

In 1992, a group of Episcopal leaders formed the first American denomination to use the word *charismatic* in its name. The Charismatic Episcopal Church was founded by Bishop Randy Adler, a former Pentecostal minister, who wanted to combine "charismatic Christianity with high church style." By 1996, the Charismatic Episcopal Church had grown to number 180 congregations, several of which transferred from the mainline Episcopal Church.[26]

Beginning as an Anglican pastor, Michael Claude Harper (1931–) pioneered the British charismatic movement before becoming an Orthodox priest in protest over the ordination of women in the Anglican communion.

Also making news was the occasional case of a Pentecostal congregation joining the Episcopal Church en masse. The most celebrated case was the five-hundred-member Evangel Assembly of God Church in Valdosta, Georgia, which in 1990 followed its pastor, Stan White, into the Episcopal Church. White, whose father and grandfather were Assemblies of God ministers, said that "Pentecostalism, despite its insistence upon the gifts of the Spirit from the Acts of the Apostles, had not fully appropriated the richness of worship in the early church."[27]

The examples of the Charismatic Episcopal Church and the Valdosta congregation pointed to a growing phenomenon in the 1990s involving Pentecostal churches and individuals returning to the historic mainline churches in search of deeper Christian "roots" and a sense of ritual and decorum that some felt was lacking in the free-flowing worship of their former churches. By 1990, like-minded pastors were banding together in what they called a "convergence movement" designed to bring the three streams together in a new and powerful spiritual configuration.

Even more striking were the cases of charismatic ministers, priests, and congregations joining the ranks of Orthodoxy. In 1993, Pastor Charles Bell led his San Jose, California, Vineyard Christian Fellowship into the Antiochian Evangelical Orthodox Mission. As an Orthodox church, the congregation changed its name to St. Stephen Orthodox Church while its pastor changed his name to "Father Seraphim Bell." Soon "rock music, public prophesying, and speaking in tongues gave way to liturgical readings, lit candles, and kissed paintings of the Virgin Mary." Bell had been influenced by Franky Schaeffer and Peter Gillquist, who earlier had pioneered a movement of evangelicals and charismatics toward orthodoxy.[28]

Meanwhile in England, Michael Harper, the noted Anglican charismatic pioneer, joined the Antiochian Greek Orthodox Church in 1995, taking with him no less than nine fellow Anglican priests on a "journey to Orthodoxy." Harper's action was triggered by the Anglican vote to ordain women priests in 1992. This was done despite the fact that the archbishop of Canterbury, George Carey, was an acknowledged charismatic who had earlier been influenced by Harper's ministry.[29]

The "New Apostolic Church" Movement

In May 1996, Peter Wagner convened a conference at Fuller Theological Seminary in Pasadena, California, with the intriguing name National Symposium on the Postdenominational Church. After years of studying church growth in the "postmodern" age, Wagner concluded that the day of the denomination was rapidly coming to a close while a new generation of "postdenominational" churches was dawning. Before the conference could convene, however, many critics of the idea, including Jack Hayford, forced Wagner to choose a new name. He finally settled on the term "New Apostolic Churches" to describe a "New Testament model of leadership," or indeed "new wineskins" for a new church age.

These new churches, which many think are really "predenominational" movements, would have the following "new" features:

1. New name ("New Apostolic Reformation")
2. New authority structures (the leaders are called "apostles")
3. New leadership training (no seminaries; volunteers, homegrown staff, local Bible colleges, etc.)
4. New ministry focus ("vision driven" [toward the future] rather than "heritage driven" [toward the past])
5. New worship style (keyboards, music ministry teams, lifted hands, loud praise, overhead projectors, etc.)
6. New prayer forms (concert prayer, singing in the Spirit, etc.)
7. New financing ("finances are abundant, giving is expected . . . beneficial . . . cheerful")
8. New outreach (church planting . . . compassion for the poor," etc.)

9. New power orientation (openness to the Holy Spirit and gifts of
   the Spirit . . . healing, demonic deliverance, prophecy, etc.)[30]

In his book describing this movement, *The New Apostolic Churches*, Wagner listed eighteen pastors (or "apostles") who represent the new movement. Of these, only three, Bill Hybels, Michael Fletcher, and David Kim, do not appear to have Pentecostal or charismatic backgrounds. Most, such as Billy Joe Daugherty, Roberts Liardon, and William Kumuyi, are openly Pentecostal or charismatic. Others have been equally identified as part of the Pentecostal/charismatic renewal for years. Clearly most of the "New Apostolic" churches have their roots in classical Pentecostalism, and their distinctive features were pioneered by Pentecostals through the years.

It is interesting that the first name adopted by Charles Parham and the first Pentecostals in 1901 was "Apostolic Faith." Only time will tell if Wagner's attempt to bypass the baptism in the Holy Spirit and the Pentecostal emphasis on tongues as an essential part of the experience will change the direction of the World Pentecostal movement. At the very least, almost every feature of the "New Apostolic Church" movement that Wagner describes was given to the body of Christ by Pentecostals and charismatics.

Youth Explosions

Throughout the century, young people have been among the most enthusiastic of the Pentecostals and charismatics. Beginning with the "Teen Challenge" ministry of David Wilkerson in 1958 and continuing with the "Jesus revolution" in California under the leadership of Chuck Smith, young people deserted conventional mainline churches to join forces with other youth who had been delivered from the drug culture. Coming a little later was the "Maranatha" campus ministry led by Bob Weiner, which carried a potent version of Pentecostalism to the college and university campuses of the nation. Most of these youth ministries offered powerful Christian solutions to youth who had lost their way as radical political protesters and drug abusers.

Most of these "Jesus people" spoke in tongues at some point in their spiritual odyssey from being rebellious "flower children" to becoming born-again Christians. By the time the charismatic movement began among Catholics in the late 1960s and early 1970s, many of the first converts were refugees from the rebellious hippy culture. As the charismatic movement moved toward its climactic years, the most striking feature to outsiders was the extreme youth of its leaders. For instance, the major leaders of the early Catholic charismatic movement were youngsters just out of college, most in their early twenties.

Catching the youthful revival tide was Loren Cunningham, who in 1961 formed a world-encompassing youth missions organization called Youth with a Mission (YWAM). Coming from an Assemblies of God background, Cunningham welcomed youth from all churches into his group. By the 1990s, YWAM counted more than six thousand full-time workers who directed the missions activities of no less than fifty thousand short-term missionaries.

During the 1970s a new "contemporary Christian music" style began to emerge. Christian artists such as Larry Norman, Barry McGuire, Keith Green, and the 2nd Chapter of Acts introduced rock music to the church. The relatively small Christian music business began to explode.

By the end of the 1980s, the charismatic youth culture had produced an entirely new generation of Christian music, to the extreme discomfort of the older generation. Such contemporary Christian music stars as Michael W. Smith, Amy Grant, Carman, and DC Talk were performing artists who filled the nation's largest stadiums for concerts that attracted multitudes of youth to the thunderous music performed by the musicians on the stage.

During the 1990s the musical borders of the young generation expanded to embrace praise and worship music. This new "Generation X" worship style produced volumes of recordings, many of which were "live" at mass youth worship services and conferences. When they returned to their churches, these young people demanded more lively and rhythmic music than most older people were able to tolerate.

Taking a lead in this new era of gospel music was Hosanna-Integrity, a company that produced millions of recordings that influenced popular Christian music around the world. In the end, this new genre of gospel music created a revolutionary charismatic style of worship that challenged the more staid and conservative hymnody of most traditional churches.

Revival Manifestations

Perhaps the most striking revival among Pentecostals in the past fifty years seemed to take place in the very last years of the century. Beginning about 1992 waves of revival with distinctive "manifestations" swept over the church world. The first of these was the "laughing revival" led by South African Pentecostal evangelist Rodney Howard-Browne. The "holy laugh" had been experienced by holiness and Pentecostal people as far back as the Cane Ridge camp meetings in 1800–1801. This movement in turn sparked the "Toronto Blessing" revival under Vineyard pastor John Arnott in 1993. In Toronto, in addition to laughter, many persons experienced falling in the Spirit and various "exotic manifestations" including "animal noises." This movement quickly spread to England where Toronto-like manifestations broke out in London's Holy Trinity Church Brompton (Anglican). By 1996, however, John Wimber expelled the Toronto Vineyard from his movement and drew a line excluding such "exotic" blessings from the Vineyard movement.

While these events were transpiring, another revival broke out in the Brownsville Assembly of God in Pensacola, Florida, under the leadership

of Pastor John Kilpatrick and evangelist Steve Hill. Here the feature was not strange manifestations, but old-fashioned repentance for sin and strong altar calls for deliverance and holiness. Although baptism in the Holy Spirit and evidential tongues were not greatly stressed in Brownsville, the revival tide seemed to reflect the intensity of the early Pentecostal revivals at the beginning of the century.

In contrast to the Toronto story, the leadership of the Assemblies of God provided direction and support to the Brownsville revival. At last count (August 27, 1998), the numbers that had attended the Brownsville meeting stood at 2,425,203 persons. Of these 135,447 had made "decisions for Christ." On a smaller scale, similar revival services shook the small town of Smithton, Missouri, in meetings that also made national headlines.[31]

After a 1993 revival led by John Arnott began in the Airport Vineyard Church in Toronto, controversial "exotic" manifestations resulted in the congregation being expelled in 1996.

The Toronto and Brownsville gatherings were well-publicized Western examples of revivals, but there were countless others breaking out in cities and towns all over the world. In fact, in many Third World nations, there were thousands of charismatic revivals that transformed communities and, at times, entire nations. By 2000, such evangelists as Reinhard Bonnke and Benny Hinn were drawing crowds of more than one million persons to their healing crusades in Africa, India, and other parts of the world.

At the end of the century of the Holy Spirit, newer "Azusa Streets" were popping up in many nations that were spawning mass movements of the Holy Spirit among the masses. Although they did not make headlines in the Western press, they were no less transforming and important revival movements in their own cultures as those so sensationally covered in the media.

Indeed, as the "century of the Holy Spirit" came to an end, there was every indication that the next thousand years could indeed be the "millennium of the Holy Spirit."

· 15 ·
The Worldwide Holy Spirit Renewal

David Barrett

THE 20TH-CENTURY Pentecostal/charismatic renewal in the Holy
Spirit has not entered the world scene on one single, sudden clear-cut
occasion, nor even gradually over a hundred years. It has arrived in three
distinct and separate surges or explosions sufficiently distinct and distinctive for us to label them the first wave (the Pentecostal renewal), the second
wave (the charismatic renewal), and the third wave (the neo-charismatic renewal). All three waves share the same experience of the infilling power of
the Holy Spirit, Third Person of the Triune God. The Spirit has entered and
transformed the lives not simply of small numbers of heroic individuals
and scattered communities (as has always been the case throughout Christianity's twenty centuries of history), but of vast numbers of millions of
Christians across the world today.

The Three Waves of Renewal

The two tables that follow trace the expansion of this renewal across ten
decades and two centuries, and also across seven continents and the entire
world. Historically, the renewal can be seen to have arrived in three massive surges or waves whose origins are traced in Table 1 to the years 1886,
1907, and 1949 respectively. The first wave is known today as Pentecostalism or the Pentecostal renewal (line 1), the second wave as the charismatic
movement or the charismatic renewal (line 9), followed by a third wave of

non-Pentecostal, noncharismatic but neo-charismatic renewal (line 18). (References are to numbered lines in the tables plus their related numbered footnotes.) The Pentecostals, charismatics, and neo-charismatics who make up this renewal today number 27.7 percent of organized global Christianity. They are here classified under 60 different categories (8 relating to Pentecostals, 9 to charismatics, 18 to neo-charismatics).

The whole renewal is excitingly new and photogenic. All three waves are extensively illustrated by photographs in this present book, as well as in the *World Christian Encyclopedia*, 2000, and the *New International Dictionary of Pentecostal and Charismatic Movements*. Readers wanting the full documentation, with lists of all the denominations involved in the world's 238 countries, should consult those works.

The Waves Are Simultaneous

Let's consider an analogy: You are at the beach of a great ocean. If you are standing on the seashore looking at the sandy beach as three large waves come in, they do not hit the beach at the same time; the first breaks on the beach, then the second, then the third. But if you look out to sea well beforehand, you will see all three waves clearly defined and moving together toward the beach, gaining in momentum and size all the time. This is exactly what has happened in the renewal (see column 3 of Table 1 for the relevant historical dates).

Each New Wave Dwarfs the Last

All three waves have burst on the worldwide Christian scene with explosive force. The first wave has spread rapidly across the world of missions, resulting in 65 million Pentecostals today, of whom 63 million are widely called classical Pentecostals. The second wave has swept through all the major non-Pentecostal denominations, to reach 175 million charismatics today. But the third wave has now reached 295 million neo-charismatics, bigger than the two previous waves combined.

Separate Waves but One Single Tide

Pursuing the seashore analogy, it is clear that the waves all consist of and use the same identical mass of water and hit the same beach. In the same way, the three waves are different but closely related phenomena. In fact, they are simply different manifestations of the one overall renewal in the Holy Spirit. Even with these three waves and sixty categories, an underlying unity pervades the movement. This survey views the renewal in the Holy Spirit as one single cohesive movement into which a vast proliferation of all kinds of individuals and communities and cultures and languages have been drawn in a whole range of different circumstances. This explains the massive babel of diversity evident today.

Multiplicity and Diversity

These members are found in 740 Pentecostal denominations, 6,530 non-Pentecostal mainline denominations with large organized internal charismatic movements, and 18,810 independent neo-charismatic denominations and networks. Charismatics are now found across the entire spectrum of Christianity. They are found within all 150 traditional non-Pentecostal ecclesiastical confessions, families, and traditions. Pentecostals/charismatics (our shorthand generic term preferred here for the whole third-wave phenomenon) are found in 9,000 ethnolinguistic cultures, speaking 8,000 languages covering 95 percent of the world's total population.

The sheer magnitude and diversity of the numbers involved beggar the imagination. Table 1 and its footnotes document an A.D. 2000 total of 523 million affiliated church members (line 37). The long-term trends show that by A.D. 2025 this total is likely to have grown to 811 million. Of these, 97 million will be Pentecostals (93 million classical Pentecostals), 274 million will be charismatics, and 460 million will be neo-charismatics.

Today, some 29 percent of all members worldwide are white, 71 percent non-white. Members today are more urban than rural, more female than male, more children (under 18) than adults, more Third World (66 percent) than Western world (32 percent), more living in poverty (87 percent) than affluence (13 percent), more family-related than individualist.

795 Million Believers Since 1900

These totals of believers today are not, however, the whole story. They do not include believers who died yesterday, or last month, or last year, or earlier in the 20th century. A complete tally of all renewal believers throughout the century must therefore include the 175 million former Pentecostal/charismatic/neo-charismatic believers who are no longer alive. The total of all renewal believers throughout the 20th century since A.D. 1900 can thus now be seen to amount to 795 million (see lines 52 and 53 in Tables 1 and 2, and their footnotes).

Persecution and Martyrdom

Members are more harassed, persecuted, suffering, martyred than perhaps any other Christian tradition in recent history. They have been protected to some extent by the fact that their multiple cultures and vast diversity have made it virtually impossible for dictators, tyrants, archenemies, and totalitarian regimes to track them down and find them in order to liquidate them.

When we begin to write down the names and numbers of Pentecostal/charismatic believers who have been murdered for their faith in Christ, the full magnitude and horror stuns us. The totals are as follows. In the three waves of renewal, we know of eight million Pentecostals/charismatics/neo-charismatics who have been killed as martyrs. (For full details and names, see *World Christian Encyclopedia,* 2000, Part 4.)

100 Varieties, One Single Renewal

The incredible variety and diversity in this renewal can be seen from the fact that to do justice to this diversity we have had to create a whole variety of neologisms and new statistical categories. Those described in the tables include: pre-Pentecostals, quasi-Pentecostals, indigenous Pentecostals, ethnic Pentecostals, isolated radio Pentecostals, post-Pentecostals, non-Christian believers in Christ, post-denominationalists, neo-apostolics, oneness apostolics, indigenous charismatics, grassroots neo-charismatics, post-charismatics, crypto-charismatics, radio/TV charismatics, and independent charismatics. Of these sixteen categories only the last two have been universally recognized up to now as genuine Pentecostals/charismatics. In this survey we are taking the position that all of these categories need to be recognized and enumerated as part of the one great renewal.

The Tide Continues to Surge In

All three waves are still continuing to surge in. Massive expansion and growth continue at a current rate of 9 million new members a year, or over 25,000 a day. Two-thirds of this is purely demographic (births minus deaths in the Pentecostal/charismatic community); one-third are converts and other new members. In the early days of all three waves, annual rates of growth were enormous; now they have declined gradually to 2.7 percent per year for Pentecostals, 2.4 percent for charismatics, 3.0 percent per year for neo-charismatics, and 2.1 percent per year for the renewal as a whole (line 53). These overall figures hide a number of situations of saturation, some spheres of decline, and many situations of explosive, uncontrollable growth.

Charismatics greatly outnumber Pentecostals in numbers and in annual converts worldwide. They do, however, have a growing dilemma in that charismatics in the non-Pentecostal mainline Protestant and Catholic churches experience an average intense involvement of only two or three years—after this period as active weekly attenders at prayer meetings, they become irregular or nonattending, justifying our term post-charismatics (line 15). This revolving-door syndrome results in an enormous annual turnover, a serious problem that has not yet begun to be adequately recognized or investigated.

Permeation of Global Christianity

Table 1's lines 39–45 show the geographical spread of the renewal today. Large numbers exist on every continent and in 236 countries. This table suggests the reason why Europe has always had the lowest response to Pentecostalism of any continent (less than 1 percent). Europeans rejected the first wave because they were not prepared to leave the great state churches to become Pentecostals; since 1970, however, they have responded enormously as charismatics *within* those churches. With 21 million charismatics and 24 million neo-charismatics, Europe now has the highest ratio (6.6) of charismatics to Pentecostals of all continents across the world.

At the other end of the spectrum from rejection to acceptance is Asia, whose Christians have become massively Pentecostalized (line 41). This is due mainly to the phenomenal spread of the renewal in Korea, India, the Philippines, Indonesia, and in mainline China.

All state churches and national denominations, with their myriads of agencies and institutions, are now rapidly becoming permeated with charismatics. In addition, roughly 14 percent of charismatics in these mainline churches have seceded or become independent each year since 1970. Altogether, white-led independent charismatic churches across the world number over 100,000 loosely organized into 3,700 or so major denominations or networks in 210 countries (line 33). This must be one of the most staggering sudden surges in the whole history of foreign missions.

Renewal as a Massive Global Force

The enormous force of the renewal can be observed in many ways. One is that a majority of the fifty or so mega-churches—the world's largest single congregations, each with over fifty thousand members—are Pentecostal/charismatic/neo-charismatic.

Another indication of its dynamic is the disproportionately high Pentecostal/charismatic penetration of the media (see footnote to line 63). Charismatics in particular have seized the global initiative in radio, television, movies, audio, video, publishing, literature, magazines, citywide evangelistic campaigns (800 each year), and so on. Virtually all varieties of ministries engaged in by institutionalized Christianity worldwide have now been penetrated by stalwarts of the renewal.

Finance, stewardship, and giving also have risen well above the global Christian average (lines 89–90). Personal annual income of church members in the renewal has grown from $157 billion in 1970 to $1,550 billion by A.D. 2000 (line 60). Of this, $30 billion is donated to Christian causes (line 61). This means that the rank-and-file of the renewal do not need to be further exhorted regarding stewardship. Its lay members are doing all they should, and more. There is, however, an almost universal failure by leaders of the renewal to garner and organize these vast sums coherently for mission and ministry at the world level. In consequence, giving to global foreign missions per member per week is stuck at the paltry figure of 15 U.S. cents.

Here is another illustration of the permeation of global Christianity: the huge numbers of ordained pastors, priests, ministers, bishops, and other church leaders involved (lines 64–66). Over one-third of the world's full-time Christian workers are Pentecostals/charismatics/neo-charismatics.

Penetrating the World

Over the years throughout the history of the Renewal, leaders have summoned members to the task of world evangelization. A favorite theme has been the saying of Jesus: "The fields are white unto harvest." The unharvested or unreached harvest field today consists of 1.6 billion unevangelized persons, who have never heard of Jesus Christ (line 72), in 5,700 unevangelized population segments (cities, peoples, countries). It includes 4,000 unreached ethnolinguistic peoples, 175 unreached megapeoples (of over 1 million population each), 140 unevangelized megacities, 300 unevangelized Islamic metropolises. The harvest force, or harvesters committed to harvesting, consists of 5.5 million full-time Christian workers: Of these, 2.1 million are Pentecostals/charismatics/ neo-charismatics (38 percent; line 64).

The Renewal Plans for Closure

And here is yet another indicator of the magnitude of this penetration of the world's populations: global plans to evangelize the world (line 73). Of the world's 1,500 such plans since A.D. 30, some 12 percent have been definitively Pentecostal/charismatic. Probably 20 percent altogether—300 plans—have had significant charismatic participation. In the last twenty years, this percentage has risen markedly. Of the world's 24 current megaplans launched since 1960, 16, or 67 percent, are Pentecostal/charismatic. So are 9 (64 percent) of the 14 current gigaplans (global plans to evangelize the world each spending over U.S. $1 billion) launched since 1960.

The Tide Engulfs the Globe

Moreover, new bodies are continually emerging. Over 100 new charismatic mission agencies have recently been formed in the Western world, and over 300 more neo-charismatic agencies in the Third World. Many are taking on the challenge of unevangelized population segments in restricted-access countries by appointing nonresidential missionaries.

We can sum up this extraordinary phenomenon as follows. With Pentecostals/charismatics/neo-charismatics now active in 80 percent of the world's 3,300 large metropolises, all in process of actively implementing networking and cooperation with Great Commission Christians of all confessions, a new era in world mission would clearly appear to be under way.

Methodological Notes on Tables 1 and 2

This pair of Tables, 1 and 2, presents a descriptive survey of the phenomenon usually known as the Pentecostal/charismatic renewal, or, by participants, as the renewal in the Holy Spirit. It takes in the somewhat expanded boundaries of the movement that most leaders now understand it as inhabiting. At the same time, the renewal recognizes the existence and reality of

Table 1. The global expansion of the Pentecostal/Charismatic/Neocharismatic Renewal in the Holy Spirit, AD 1900–2025.

Ref (1)	Category (2)	Begun (3)	Totals in AD 2000: Countries (4)	Denoms (5)	PARTICIPANTS in: 1900 (6)	1970 (7)	2000 (8)	2025 (9)
1.	**FIRST WAVE: PENTECOSTAL RENEWAL**							
2.	Pentecostals	1886	225	740	20,000	15,382,330	65,832,970	97,876,000
3.	Denominational Pentecostals	1910	225	740	20,000	15,382,330	65,832,970	97,876,000
4.	Classical Pentecostals	1906	220	660	20,000	14,443,480	63,064,620	93,583,000
5.	Holiness Pentecostals	1886	170	240	15,000	2,322,430	6,315,790	9,644,000
6.	Baptistic Pentecostals	1906	210	390	5,000	11,415,390	54,973,310	81,272,000
7.	Apostolic Pentecostals	1904	29	30	0	705,660	1,775,520	2,667,000
8.	Oneness Pentecostals	1914	130	80	0	938,850	2,768,350	4,293,000
9.	**SECOND WAVE: CHARISMATIC RENEWAL**							
10.	Charismatics	1907	235	6,530	12,000	3,349,400	175,856,690	274,934,000
11.	Mainline active Charismatics	1960	225	6,990	12,000	3,349,400	114,029,250	179,969,000
12.	Mainline Postcharismatics	1973	150	3,540	0	0	61,827,440	94,965,000
13.	Anglican Charismatics	1907	163	130	1,000	509,900	17,562,110	25,470,000
14.	Catholic Charismatics	1967	234	236	10,000	2,000,000	119,912,200	194,973,000
15.	Protestant Charismatics	1959	231	6,460	1,000	824,100	35,200,000	50,156,000
16.	Orthodox Charismatics	1970	25	140	0	15,200	3,167,300	4,295,000
17.	Marginal Charismatics	1980	15	130	0	200	15,000	40,000
18.	**THIRD WAVE: NEOCHARISMATIC RENEWAL**							
19.	Neocharismatics (Independents, Postdenominationalists)	1549	225	18,810	949,400	53,490,560	295,405,240	460,798,000
20.	(a) In 2 kinds of wholly Third Wave networks	1656	220	17,125	949,300	36,854,370	253,936,540	401,173,000
21.	Non-White indigenous Neocharismatics	1783	210	13,425	919,300	29,379,360	203,270,400	327,515,000
22.	African indigenous pentecostals/charismatics	1864	60	9,300	890,000	12,569,300	65,310,530	99,263,000
23.	Black American pentecostals/charismatics	1889	20	90	15,000	2,820,540	7,634,850	11,647,000
24.	Black American Oneness Apostolics	1886	10	150	0	559,120	2,960,900	4,962,000
25.	Brazilian/Portuguese grassroots neocharismatics	1656	20	460	0	2,512,200	23,022,770	39,115,000
26.	Filipino indigenous pentecostals/charismatics	1913	25	380	0	1,818,020	6,776,800	10,909,000
27.	Han Chinese indigenous pentecostals/charismatics	1905	58	180	2,000	310,240	49,749,200	82,948,000
28.	Indian indigenous pentecostals/charismatics	1911	25	580	1,000	1,421,310	16,613,400	29,274,000
29.	Indonesian indigenous pentecostals	1920	5	170	0	2,649,780	6,761,240	10,187,000
30.	Korean indigenous pentecostals/charismatics	1910	30	170	500	100,700	3,338,700	6,037,000
31.	Latin-Hispanic grassroots believers	1909	24	990	0	2,988,090	11,915,560	17,355,000
32.	other indigenous neocharismatics	1948	40	130	100	153,780	1,153,050	1,986,000
33.	White-led Independent Postdenominationalists	1805	210	3,700	30,000	7,475,010	50,666,140	73,658,000
34.	(b) as % of 7 kinds of non-Third-Wave denominations							
35.	Independent neocharismatics	1549	200	925	100	16,636,190	41,468,700	59,625,000
36.	doubly-counted First/Second/Third Wavers (see footnote 36)	1925	80	30	0	10,000	1,716,000	2,321,000
37.	**Global affiliated Pentecostals/Charismatics/Neocharismatics**		236	21,080	981,400	72,223,000	523,767,390	811,551,600

No.							
38. RENEWAL MEMBERS ON 7 CONTINENTS							
39. Renewal members in Africa	60	1830	9,990	901,000	17,049,020	126,010,200	227,819,720
40. Renewal members in Antarctica	1	1980	0	2	0	400	600
41. Renewal members in Asia	50	1870	2,690	4,300	10,144,120	134,889,530	217,550,600
42. Renewal members in Europe	48	1805	1,870	20,000	8,018,180	37,568,700	47,179,500
43. Renewal members in Latin America	46	1783	2,680	10,000	12,621,450	141,432,880	202,277,880
44. Renewal members in Northern America	5	1889	3,520	46,100	24,151,910	79,600,160	110,204,580
45. Renewal members in Oceania	28	1917	330	0	238,240	4,265,520	6,519,300
46. Renewal members as % global church members	238	–		0.2	6.4	27.7	32.5
47. PERIPHERAL CONSTITUENTS							
48. Quasi-Pentecostals (Prepentecostals, Postpentecostals)	110	1739	2,700	2,500,000	4,824,000	17,800,000	51,800,000
49. Unaffiliated believers professing Renewal	230	1950	2,000	210,000	5,300,000	78,327,510	120,000,000
50. WIDER GLOBAL TOTALS OF RENEWAL							
51. Total all Renewal believers alive at mid-year	236		26,565	3,691,400	82,346,270	619,894,900	961,000,000
52. Renewal believers dying since AD 1900	236		11,565	–	34,657,900	175,728,800	270,000,000
53. Total all Renewal believers ever, since AD 1900	236		29,500	3,691,400	117,004,170	795,623,700	1,231,000,000
54. CHURCHES, FINANCE, AGENCIES, WORKERS							
55. Pentecostal churches, congregations (1st Wave)	225		740	10	94,200	480,000	1,080,000
56. Mainline Charismatic prayer groups (2nd Wave)	235		4,450	0	35,000	550,000	1,450,000
57. Catholic Charismatic weekly prayer groups	234		239	0	2,185	160,000	245,000
58. Anglican & Protestant Charismatic groups	231		3,700	0	32,815	250,000	500,000
59. Independent congregations, house churches (3rd Wave)	–			15,000	138,970	591,000	1,296,000
60. Personal income of all Renewal members, $ p.a.	–			250 million	3 billion	1,550 billion	2,400 billion
61. Renewal members' giving to all Christian causes, $ p.a.	–			7 million	157 billion	30 billion	46 billion
62. Renewal service agencies	–			20	600	4,000	7,000
63. Renewal institutions	–			100	1,300	14,000	19,000
64. All pentecostal/charismatic full-time workers	–			2,010	240,790	2,100,000	4,300,000
65. Nationals: pastors, clergy, evangelists, et alii	–			2,000	237,000	1,933,000	3,900,000
66. Aliens: foreign missionaries	–			100	3,790	167,000	400,000
67. THE CONTEXT OF WORLD EVANGELIZATION							
68. Global population	238			1,619,626,000	3,696,148,000	6,055,049,000	7,823,703,000
69. Christians (all varieties)	238			558,132,000	1,236,374,000	1,999,564,000	2,616,670,000
70. Affiliated church members (baptized)	238			521,576,500	1,130,106,000	1,888,439,000	2,490,958,000
71. Non-Christians	238			1,061,494,000	2,459,774,000	4,055,485,000	5,207,033,000
72. Unevangelized persons	230			879,672,000	1,641,245,000	1,629,375,000	1,845,406,000
73. World evangelization global plans since AD 30	160			250	510	1,500	3,000

Table 2. Codes and characteristics of each of the 95 generic categories and ministries of Pentecostals/Charismatics/Neocharismatics.

Ref / Column 1	Category / Column 2	Definitions, characteristics, examples of major significant bodies / Column 5	Main country / Column 6
	FIRST WAVE: PENTECOSTAL RENEWAL		
1.	Pentecostals	Oldest part of Renewal, claiming name, history, experiences, and theology of Pentecostalism	usa
2.	Denominational Pentecostals	Churches of White origin (now 70% Non-White) requiring initial evidence of tongues-speaking	braz
3.	Classical Pentecostals	Members in the older, larger, more traditional Pentecostal denominations	cana
4.		Self-designation of older White denominations, usually excluding Black Pentecostals	usa
5.	Holiness Pentecostals	Those holding 3-fold Wesleyan experience of conversion, sanctification, infilling; IPHC	chil
6.	Baptistic Pentecostals	Emphasizing 2-fold Pentecostal experience of conversion, Spirit-baptism: AoG, COG, ICFG	arge
7.	Apostolic Pentecostals	Denominations emphasizing Pentecostal church government by living apostles: ACG	ghan
8.	Oneness Pentecostals	Denominations emphasizing baptism in name of 'Jesus Only'; anti-trinitarian: UPCI	colo
	SECOND WAVE: CHARISMATIC RENEWAL		
9.	Charismatics	Members of nonpentecostal mainline churches who experience Pentecostal phenomena	ital
10.		All who have experienced Spirit-baptism but remain within nonpentecostal mainline churches	mexi
11.	Mainline active charismatics	All in nonpentecostal churches regularly attending Renewal activities	phil
12.	Mainline postcharismatics	Charismatics who no longer attend Renewal activities but still regard selves as Charismatics	fran
13.	Anglican Charismatics	Total Anglicans in Renewal, past and present, including children and infants	brit
14.	Catholic Charismatics	Total baptized RCs in CCR, past and present, including children and infants	braz
15.	Protestant Charismatics	Total Protestants in Renewal, past and present, including children and infants	aust
16.	Orthodox Charismatics	Total Orthodox in Renewal, past and present, including children and infants	arme
17.	Marginal Charismatics	Total marginal Christians in Renewal, past and present, including children and infants	usa
	THIRD WAVE: NEOCHARISMATIC RENEWAL		
18.	Neocharismatics (Independents, Postdenominationalists).	Spirit-led Independents rejecting White Pentecostal/Charismatic denominationalism	
19.		All baptised in the Holy Spirit in new churches independent of historic Christianity	
20.	(a) In 2 kinds of wholly Third-Wave networks	(1) Non-White and (2) White-led Neocharismatics in wholly Third-Wave networks/churches	chin
21.	Non-White indigenous Neocharismatics	Spirit-baptized Non-Whites in 26 varieties of indigenous, independent, apostolic churches	
22.	African indigenous pentecostals/charismatics	Most AICs are Zionist, Apostolic, Spiritual: ZCC, CCC, AICN, DLBC, AACJM, EJCSK	zimb
23.	Black American pentecostals/charismatics	Black Pentecostalism: Church of God in Christ, UHCA, Full Gospel Catholic Ch	usa
24.	Black American Oneness Apostolics	PAOW, AWCF, Bible Way Churches of Our Lord Jesus Christ WW, COLJCAF	usa
25.	Brazilian/Portuguese grassroots neocharismatics	OBPC (Brazil for Christ Ev Ch), IURD/UCKG, CCB, IPF, IPDA	braz
26.	Filipino indigenous pentecostals/charismatics	Jesus is Lord Fellowship, CDCC, March of Faith, Ecclesiae Dei	phil
27.	Han Chinese indigenous pentecostals/charismatics	True Jesus Church, NBM/BAM, AHC(Little Flock), Han Chinese house churches	chin
28.	Indian indigenous pentecostals/charismatics	Indian Pentecostal Church of God, Believers' Chs of India, Christ Groups, IPA, MFGCM	indi
29.	Indonesian indigenous pentecostals	Indonesia Pentecostal Church (GPI), GBI, GBIS, GPPS, GBT, GUP	indo
30.	Korean indigenous pentecostals/charismatics	Yoido FGC, Grace & Truth Ch, FGlGM, Korea Full Gospel Chs of America	souk
31.	Latino-Hispanic grassroots believers	Autochthonous grassroots (GR) churches, IMPC, IPP, IOAP, IEMP, IEPC	mexi
32.	Other indigenous neocharismatics	Other Asian Churches: Hope of God Churches of Thailand, Latter Rain Ch of Malaysia	thai
33.	White-led independent postdenominationalists	Spirit-baptized Whites in non-Pentecostal/Charismatic apostolic networks	brit
34.	(b) as % of 6 kinds of non-Renewal denominations	Neocharismatics in non-pentecostal/charismatic (even anti-Renewal) denominations	brit
35.	Independent neocharismatics	Neocharismatics within non-pentecostal/charismatic Independent Anglican bodies	brit
36.	doubly-counted First/Second/Third Wavers	Neocharismatics who join Pentecostal bodies; Charismatics who become Neocharismatics	souk
37.	**Global Pentecostals/Charismatics/Neocharismatics**	Total all church members in the Pentecostal/Charismatic/Neocharismatic Renewal	
	RENEWAL MEMBERS ON 7 CONTINENTS		
38.		Renewal (which is 28% of globe) is: 12% Pentecostals, 33% Charismatics, 55% Neocharismatics.	
39.	Renewal members in Africa	12% Pentecostals, 25% Charismatics, 63% Neocharismatics.	
40.	Renewal members in Antarctica	1% Pentecostals, 95% Charismatics, 4% Neocharismatics.	
41.	Renewal members in Asia	5% Pentecostals, 16% Charismatics, 79% Neocharismatics.	
42.	Renewal members in Europe	8% Pentecostals, 56% Charismatics, 36% Neocharismatics.	
43.	Renewal members in Latin America	23% Pentecostals, 52% Charismatics, 24% Neocharismatics.	
44.	Renewal members in Northern America	7% Pentecostals, 28% Charismatics, 65% Neocharismatics.	
45.	Renewal members in Oceania	14% Pentecostals, 63% Charismatics, 24% Neocharismatics.	
46.	Renewal members as % of global church members.	Rising rapidly at first to 6% by 1970 and to 28% by AD 2000.	

47.	**PERIPHERAL CONSTITUENTS**	
48.	Quasi-Pentecostals (Prepentecostals, Postpentecostals)	Defined above for lines 2 and 3, not counted here as Renewal members but as Renewal believers.
49.	Unaffiliated believers professing Renewal	Individual believers experiencing Holy Spirit gifts but remaining unrelated to Renewal bodies.
50.	**WIDER GLOBAL TOTALS OF RENEWAL**	
51.	Total all Renewal believers alive at mid-year	Total of lines 66, 77, and 78.
52.	Renewal believers dying since AD 1900	Former members of Renewal who have died by the year indicated.
53.	Total all Renewal believers ever, since AD 1900	Total of lines 80 and 81.
54.	**CHURCHES, FINANCE, AGENCIES, WORKERS**	
55.	Pentecostal churches, congregations (1st Wave)	Mainly Assemblies of God buildings and properties.
56.	Mainline Charismatic prayer groups (2nd Wave)	These groups' regular weekly attenders are known as the 'shock troops' of the Renewal.
57.	Catholic Charismatic weekly prayer groups	Massive growth since origin in 1967, to 2,185 groups (1970), 12,000 (1980), 90,000 (1990), 160,000 (2000).
58.	Anglican & Protestant Charismatic groups	Large-scale lay and clerical leadership from 1960 onwards.
59.	Independent congregations, house churches (3rd Wave)	A huge number of smaller house groups, over half a billion.
60.	Personal income of all Renewal members, $ p.a.	Enormous wealth but no organized finance or central bank accounts.
61.	Renewal members' giving to all Christian causes, $ p.a.	Low at 2% of personal income given to Christian causes but higher than global Christian rates.
62.	Renewal service agencies	A huge and variegated number of agencies (listed here in footnote).
63.	Renewal institutions	Vast variety (listed here in footnote).
64.	All pentecostal/charismatic full-time workers	Full-time church workers of all kinds: total of next 2 lines, 94 and 95.
65.	Nationals: pastors, clergy, evangelists, et alii	Mostly well-documented by the major denominations and networks.
66.	Aliens: foreign missionaries	Large and rapidly growing numbers serving abroad for shorter or longer terms.
67.	**THE CONTEXT OF WORLD EVANGELIZATION**	
68.	Global population	Populations are shown at mid-year (30 June) for the years 1970, 1995, 2000, 2025.
69.	Christians (all varieties)	Professing plus crypto-Christians; affiliated plus unaffiliated; Great Commission plus latent Christians.
70.	Affiliated church members (baptized)	Baptized or other members of all the churches.
71.	Non-Christians	Now over 4 billion and growing rapidly.
72.	Unevangelized persons	All persons unaware of Christianity, Christ, and/or the gospel.
73.	World evangelization global plans since AD 30	Distinct plans and proposals for completing world evangelization.

large numbers of other branches or segments of global Christianity, to
which it is related in varying degrees of closeness. This means that these tables do not claim to be describing a tradition of Christianity distinct and
separate from all other traditions but a contemporary movement that over-
laps with the rest of the Christian world to a large degree (6 percent in 1970,
rising to 27 percent by A.D. 2000). By 1985, in fact, the renewal had penetrated, and had secured committed representation in, every one of the
Christian world's 156 distinct ecclesiastical confessions, traditions, and
families. By A.D. 2000 this had risen to all 250 traditions. The tables enumerate the progress of all branches of the renewal across the century, with projections from A.D. 2000 to A.D. 2025 based on current long-term trends.

Defi nitions and Additional Data

(Referring to numbered lines.) Each line in Tables 1 and 2 above refers to the
global (total, worldwide) situation, in which pentecostals/charismatics are
found in 99 percent of the world's total of 238 countries (in which 99 percent of the world's population is found). A number of subjects are shown
on the left broken down into divisions and subdivisions or components
listed below them, indented. All indented titles in the tables therefore form
part of, and are included in, unindented or less-indented categories above
them. Basic data and bibliographies on the Pentecostal/charismatic renewal may be found in C. E. Jones, *A Guide to the Study of Pentecostalism*
(1983, 2 vols. 9,883 entries); also C. E. Jones, *Black Holiness: A Guide to the
Study of Black Participation in Wesleyan Perfectionism and Glossalalic Pentecostal Movements* (1987); and with W. J. Hollenweger, ed., *Pentecostal Research in Europe: Problems, Promises and People* (1986), culminating in
Hollenweger's 1997 magnum opus, *Pentecostalism: Origins and Developments Worldwide.*

Columns 1–10 in Table 1

1. Reference number of lines (same as in Table 2).
2. Usual current terminology for all major components and categories of the renewal.
3. Year when first manifestations began.
4. Number of countries where category is in evidence in A.D. 2000.
5. Number of distinct denominations (including networks, par denominations, quasi-denominations) in 2000.
6-9. Number of participants (total community or affiliated) at 1900,
   1970, 2000, with projections to A.D. 2025 based on current trends.

Columns 1–4 in Table 2

1. Reference number of lines (same as in Table 1).
2. Usual current terminology for all major components and categories of the renewal (identical to listing in Table 1).
3. Definitions, characteristics, examples of major significant bodies within each category.
4. Main country where each category is involved (4-letter country code being its first 4 letters).

The Renewal as a Single Movement

The tables above view the 20th-century renewal in the Holy Spirit as one single cohesive movement into which a vast proliferation of all kinds of individuals and communities have been drawn in a whole range of different circumstances over a period of 450 years. Whether termed pentecostals, charismatics, or third wavers, they share a single basic experience. Their contribution to Christianity is a new awareness of spiritual gifts as a ministry to the life of the church. The case for this thesis could be made by listing historical, missiological, theological, sociological, and other data. It could also be made by drawing attention to the fact that in the 1900, 1904, and 1906 revivals, news of these events traveled throughout the globe (by rail, by ship, by telegraph) in a few days and weeks; while today, news of such happenings—conversions, blessings, healings, movements—travels worldwide within a few seconds by telephone, radio, television, electronic mail, Internet, World Wide Web, etc. Such rapid communication across time, space, and all varieties of the renewal reinforces its underlying unity.

The case for the statistical presentation of the renewal as a single interconnected movement can, however, best be made by considering how the movement starts off and spreads in any area, from the days of the earliest pentecostals to those of current charismatics and third wavers.

The start of the movement anywhere has always been an unexpected or unpredictable happening rather than any result of human planning or organization. First individuals (at random across the existing churches), then groups, then large numbers in organized movements become filled with the Spirit and embark on the common charismatic experience. All of them originally can collectively and correctly be termed charismatics. All these charismatics find themselves living within existing mainline non-pentecostal churches and denominations. There, over the last two hundred years they have been termed or labeled as charismatics, revivalists, enthusiasts, spirituals, or pentecostals; and often have been dismissed as cranks, fanatics, sectarians, heretics, schismatics, or worse. However, all of them initially attempt to stay within, and work within, those churches. But before long evictions begin, and ejections, withdrawals, and secessions occur in varying degrees. First, various individuals, then groups, then whole movements are forced into schism or opt for it and so begin separate ecclesiastical structures and new denominations.

From its beginnings, in this way, the renewal has subsequently expanded in three massive surges or waves. We can further divide these waves into a typology of nine stages.

A TYPOLOGY OF THE EVOLUTION OF CHARISMATICS WITHIN CHURCHES

Notes on the nine columns below: 1 = stage in evolution of new charismatic developments
2 = first year of start of new stage
3 = main or majority race involved in stage, either Whites or Non-Whites
4 = fate of charismatics in their existing parent churches
5 = percent of charismatics evicted from parent churches
6 = percent of charismatics who voluntarily secede from parent churches
7 = percent of charismatics lost to parent churches (= columns 5 + 6)
8 = percent remaining in parent churches (- 100 – column 7)
9 = new organizations or developments resulting

Stage	Start	Race	History of charismatics	Fate, %				Resulting Organizations
1	2	3	4	5	6	7	8	9

FIRST WAVE: Rejection, eviction, secession, new denominations/communions = PENTECOSTAL RENEWAL

1.	1741	Non-White	Immediate eviction	100	0	100	0	Black/Non-White denominations
2.	1900	Whites	Eventual secession	90	6	96	4	White-led denominations

SECOND WAVE: Friction, toleration, renewed parishes, mainline groups = CHARISMATIC RENEWAL

3.	1783	Non-Whites	Majority eviction	80	10	90	10	Isolated mainline prayer groups
4.	1907	Whites	Minority eviction	40	30	70	30	Isolated healing ministries
5.	1940	Whites	Partial eviction	10	15	25	75	Large-scale mainline networks
6.	1960	Whites	Few evictions	4	10	14	86	Denominational charismatic agencies

THIRD WAVE: Power evangelism, new structures, networks, megachurches = NEOCHARISMATIC RENEWAL

7.	1980	Whites	Occasional evictions	2	8	10	90	Postdenominational structures
8.	1990	Non-Whites	Rare evictions	1	1	2	98	New denominations and communions
9.	2000	Non-Whites	No evictions	0	0	0	100	New global mission

These nine stages and categories are approximate and descriptive, not watertight or exclusive. For instance, as a result of the global influenza pandemic of 1918, large numbers of blacks in Anglican churches in Africa (Nigeria, Kenya, Uganda, South Africa) became charismatics and formed charismatic prayer groups within Anglican parishes. The majority, however, were soon evicted (and so are enumerated here in Tables 1 and 2 becoming what we now refer to as black pentecostals); only a minority (10 percent) remained within Anglicanism as charismatics in what later became known as the Anglican charismatic renewal.

Having described the renewal as a single movement, we shall next describe its component elements.

Three Waves of 20th-Century Renewal

The tables classify the various movements and types under the following three consecutive waves of the renewal in the Holy Spirit, defining its three key terms as follows.

1. **Pentecostals.** These are defined as Christians who are members of the major explicitly Pentecostal denominations in Pentecostalism or the Pentecostal movement, or the Pentecostal renewal, whose major characteristic is a rediscovery of, and a new experience of, the supernatural with a powerful and energizing ministry of the Holy Spirit in the realm of the miraculous that most other Christians have considered to be highly unusual.

This is interpreted as a rediscovery of the spiritual gifts of New Testament times, and their restoration to ordinary Christian life and ministry. Pentecostalism is usually held to have begun in USA in 1901 (although the present survey shows the year of origin as 1886). For a brief period it was a charismatic revival expecting to remain an interdenominational movement within the existing churches without beginning a new denomination; but from 1909 onward its members were increasingly ejected from all mainline bodies and so forced to begin new organized denominations. (See explanatory note no. 1, below, "First Wave: Pentecostal Renewal," for distinction between use of capital versus lowercase *p* in Pentecostal, etc.)

Pentecostal denominations hold the distinctive teaching that all Christians should seek a postconversion religious experience called baptism in the Holy Spirit, and that a Spirit-baptized believer may receive one or more of the supernatural gifts known in the early church: instantaneous sanctification, the ability to prophesy, to practice divine healing through prayer, to speak in tongues (glossolalia), or to interpret tongues, singing in tongues, singing in the Spirit, dancing in the Spirit, praying with upraised hands, dreams, visions, discernment of spirits, words of wisdom, words of knowledge, emphasis on miracles, power encounters, exorcisms (casting out demons), resuscitations, deliverances, signs, and wonders. From 1906 onward, of explicitly Pentecostal denominations, by comparison with holiness/perfectionist denominations, has been the single addition of speaking with other tongues as the "initial evidence" of one's having received the baptism of the Holy Ghost (or Holy Spirit), whether or not one subsequently experiences regularly the gift of tongues. Most Pentecostal denominations teach that tongues-speaking is mandatory for all members, but in practice today only from 5 percent to 35 percent of all members have practiced this gift either initially or as an ongoing experience. Pentecostal denominations proclaim a "full" or "fourfold" or "fivefold" gospel of Christ as Savior, Sanctifier, Baptizer with the Holy Spirit, Healer, and Returning King. Collectively, all these denominations are sometimes referred to as the "first wave" of this whole 20th-century movement of Holy-Spirit-centered renewal. In the USA, Pentecostals usually name the entire body of these denominations founded before 1940 by the blanket term "classical Pentecostals" to distinguish them from the subsequent "Neo-pentecostals" or "charismatics" in the nonpentecostal denominations.

2. Charismatics. These are defined as Christians affiliated to non-Pentecostal denominations (Anglican, Protestant, Catholic, Orthodox), who receive the experiences above in what then became termed the charismatic movement whose roots go back to 1907 and 1918 but whose rapid expansion has been mainly since 1950 (later called the charismatic renewal), usually describing themselves as having been renewed in the Spirit and experiencing the Spirit's supernatural and miraculous and energizing power, who remain within, and form organized renewal groups within, their older mainline nonpentecostal denominations (instead of leaving to join Pentecostal denominations). They demonstrate any or all of the *charismata pneumatika* (Greek New Testament: gifts of the Spirit) including signs and wonders (but with glossolalia regarded as optional). The whole movement is sometimes termed the "second wave" of the 20th-century renewal. Concerning the key word, note that "in the technical Pauline sense *charismata* (AV, gifts) denote extraordinary powers, distinguishing certain Christians and enabling them to serve the church of Christ, the reception of which is due to the power of divine grace operating in their souls by the Holy Spirit" (*Thayer's Greek-English Lexicon of the New Testament*, 1886, 1977: 667).

3. Neocharismatics (or Third Wavers). Since 1945 thousands of schismatic or other independent charismatic churches have come out of the charismatic movement; these independents have throughout the 20th century from 1900 to the present day numbered more than the first two waves combined. They consist of evangelicals and other Christians who, unrelated or no longer related to the Pentecostals or charismatic renewals, have become filled with the Spirit, or empowered or energized by the Spirit and experiencing the Spirit's supernatural and miraculous ministry (though usually without recognizing a baptism in the Spirit separate from conversion), who exercise gifts of the Spirit (with much less emphasis on tongues, as optional or even absent or unnecessary), and emphasize signs and wonders, supernatural miracles and power encounters, who leave their mainline nonpentecostal denominations but also do not identify themselves as either pentecostals or charismatics. In a number of countries they exhibit pentecostal and charismatic phenomena but combine this with rejection of pentecostal terminology. These believers are increasingly being identified by their leadership as independent, postdenominationalist, restorationist, radical, neo-apostolic, or the "third wave" of the whole 20th-century renewal, the terms "third wave" and "third wavers" having been coined by a participant, C. Peter Wagner, in 1983. (See his articles "A Third Wave?" in *Pastoral Renewal* 8, no. 1 July-August 1983, 1-5; and "The Third Wave," in *Christian Life*, September 1984, 90; and his 1988 book *The Third Wave of the Holy Spirit: Encountering the Power of Signs and Wonders Today*. Because they constitute a major new revitalizing force, in this table we also term the movement the neo-charismatic renewal.

Layout of lines below. The explanatory notes below have numbers referring to the numbered lines in Tables 1 and 2. They are set out with each line's title in Table 1 column 2 being given below in boldface type.

Notes on Lines 1–36

Total Christian community affiliated to (on the rolls of) denominations, churches, or groups, including baptized members, their children and infants, catechumens, inquirers, attendees, but excluding interested non-Christian attendees, casual attendees, visitors, et al. Many Pentecostal denominations enumerate their children and infants, and a number are paedobaptist (infant-baptizing). Most, however, ignore their children's statistics, which has led to serious undernumeration of the spread of the renewal. Whenever statistics of church members are compared to total population figures (which almost always include children and infants), such membership figures must also include its children and infants. Like must always be compared with like.

1. First Wave: Pentecostal Renewal

Pentecostals are defined here as all associated with explicitly Pentecostal denominations that identify themselves in explicitly Pentecostal terms (see definition of *Pentecostals* near the beginning of these footnotes), or with other denominations that as a whole are phenomenologically pentecostal in teaching and practice. Current practice in the USA is to analyze the phenomenon as basically an American one, and as one distinct from Neo-pentecostalism (the charismatic movement), and so to label the whole of denominational Pentecostalism worldwide by the parallel or synonymous term "classical Pentecostalism." In the present table, however, we are concerned more to see the entire phenomenon as a global one requiring a different set of descriptive terms. We therefore divide the movement into two major streams as shown by two different spellings: (1) the term "Pentecostal" with a capital *P* denotes what we are terming classical Pentecostalism (which is mainly white-originated), whereas (2) the term "pentecostals" with a lowercase *p*

refers to the huge phenomenon of black/non-white/Third World indigenous pentecostalism unrelated to Western classical Pentecostalism (see notes
below on line nos. 3–8). To avoid excessive repetition of the comprehensive
adjective *Pentecostal/pentecostal* the adjective *pentecostal* is often used below
to denote the whole. Historically, the first wave developed out of black slavery in the USA, the Evangelical (Wesleyan) revival from 1738 in Britain, and
the holiness (perfectionist) movement took off on a massive universal scale
with widespread tongues and other pentecostal phenomena. Other scholars
cite 1904 (the Welsh revival) or 1906 (Azusa Street), for the same reasons.

2. Pentecostals
(This line's statistics are computed as the sum of line nos. 4–8.) These totals of
all associated with explicitly Pentecostal denominations as elaborated above
are derived from Country Tables 2, in *World Christian Encyclopedia, 2000.*

3. Denominational Pentecostals
In 740 major recognized, clear-cut, wholly Pentecostal denominations of
Pentecostal theology or practice or stance, committed as denominations to
Pentecostal distinctives; these include many minor or very small denomi-
nations in 225 different countries. (This line is the same as no. 2.)

4. Classical Pentecostals
As explained above, in this global classification we define this as a blanket
term for those in 660 traditional Western-related denominations that identify themselves as explicitly Pentecostal; almost all of white origin in USA,
but now worldwide with adherents in all races, found in 220 countries
(sum of line nos. 5–7). USA Pentecostal spokespersons use a somewhat
wider definition, which identifies "classical Pentecostals" (a term that dates
from 1970) with all denominational Pentecostals in contrast to Neo-pentecostals (charismatics); they therefore include under this term the major
early black pentecostal denominations in the USA, notably the Church of
God in Christ with its 6 million members today (which, however, we here
classify under line no. 23). In essence, our procedure is saying that the
whole phenomenon of denominational Pentecostalism/pentecostalism is
best understood when classified into the two subdivisions, (a) black-origi-
nated pentecostalism and (b) white-originated Pentecostalism. As the bet-
ter-organized and better-articulated form, category (b) then better merits
the appellation "classical" Pentecostalism.

There has been a certain amount of blurred boundaries and movement
between Pentecostalism and the charismatic movement. Thus in 1948 the

latter rain revival (New Order of the Latter Rain) erupted among classical Pentecostals in Saskatchewan, Canada, and spread rapidly to Europe, USA, and across the world. It emphasized laying on of hands with prophecy, and government by an order of living apostles; it began Global Missions Broadcast (over radio); but from 1965, it merged into the charismatic movement.

5. Holiness Pentecostals
Also known as Wesleyan Pentecostals, or Methodistic Pentecostals, this was the universal Pentecostal position until the 1910 Northern USA change, and still remains the major southern USA position. It is found today in 240 denominations worldwide, teaching a three-crisis experience (conversion, sanctification, baptism in the Spirit). First claimed glossolalia manifestations: 1896 Fire-Baptized Holiness Church, 1907 Pentecostal Holiness Church, 1907 Church of God in Christ, 1908 Church of God (Cleveland). Total countries involved: 170.

6. Baptistic Pentecostals
Mainline classical Pentecostals teaching "finished work" or two-crisis experience (conversion, baptism in the Spirit); in 390 denominations in 210 countries. Scores of Pentecostal denominations trace their origin to the 1906–9 Azusa Street revival in Los Angeles, USA, under Bishop W. J. Seymour et al., at which thousands first spoke in tongues; but the "finished work" teaching (combining conversion with sanctification or "second blessing") of W. H. Durham in 1910 shifted many northern USA Pentecostals out of the Wesleyan three-crisis teaching into the two-crisis position now known as Baptistic Pentecostalism. The first new denomination to hold this position was the Assemblies of God, founded in 1914, which with its foreign mission work now in 118 countries is by far the largest Pentecostal worldwide denomination. Its meticulously kept annual statistics for each country form Pentecostalism's most solid body of statistical data and hence the main documentation for the renewal's phenomenal growth.

7. Apostolic Pentecostals
The 1904 Welsh revival under Evan Roberts, which is often regarded by European writers as the origin of the worldwide Pentecostal movement, prepared the way for British Pentecostalism, especially apostolic-type teaching resulting in 1908 in the Apostolic Faith Church (Bournemouth), from which a schism in 1916 formed the Apostolic Church (HQ in Wales). Apostolics are now found worldwide in thirty denominations, stressing complex hierarchy of living apostles, prophets, and other charismatic offi-

8. Oneness Pentecostals

In 80 denominations in 130 countries; termed by outsiders Unitarian Pentecostals or Jesus-only Pentecostals, but calling themselves oneness Pentecostals or Jesus' name Pentecostals; baptism in name of Jesus only; widely accepted ecclesiastically as evangelicals but theologically as modal monarchians; since 1920 they have included 25 percent of all Pentecostals in the USA. The major denomination is the United Pentecostal Church, a 1945 union of the Pentecostal Assemblies of Jesus Christ (1913) and the Pentecostal Church (1916). In contrast to this emphasis within denominational Pentecostalism, the charismatic movement has remained explicitly Trinitarian throughout.

Many third-wave denominations (True Jesus Church, etc.) also hold oneness theologies, but are listed not here but under line nos. 22–32 as they occur.

9. Second Wave: Charismatic Renewal

Charismatics (or, until recently, Neo-pentecostals) are usually defined as those baptized or renewed in the Spirit within the mainline nonpentecostal denominations, from its first mass stirrings in 1918 in Africa on to the large-scale rise from 1950 of the charismatic movement (initially also termed Neo-pentecostalism to distinguish it from classical Pentecostalism) who remain within their mainline nonpentecostal denominations. The movement was later called the charismatic renewal. The exact definition used here is given above near the beginning of these footnotes. Note that many individuals and groups in the mainline churches had already received baptism in the Spirit without publicity for many years before the usually quoted beginning dates of 1900, 1907, 1924, 1950, 1959, 1962, 1967, etc. Note also that column 5 "Denominations" for the charismatic renewal means totals of nonpentecostal noncharismatic bodies with organized renewal agencies within them: total is 6,530 denominations in 235 countries.

10. Charismatics

(This line's statistics of members are computed as the sum of line nos. 11–12, or 13–17). These totals of all associated explicitly with the charismatic renewal in the mainline nonpentecostal denominations are derived from detailed surveys summarized in Country Tables 1 and 2 in *World Christian Encyclopedia 2000*, and given in full in *World Christian* database.

11. Mainline Active Charismatics

Active members regularly (weekly, monthly, annually, including members' children) involved in prayer groups within the charismatic renewal in the older mainline denominations. During the period 1906–50, many thousands of mainline clergy and hundreds of thousands of laity received the pentecostal experience and spoke in tongues, but many were ejected and later joined the Pentecostal denominations. By 2000 the renewal had penetrated every one of the Christian world's 250 distinct ecclesiastical confessions, traditions, and families, with charismatics within every tradition, and in the 6,530 denominations.

12. Mainline Postcharismatics

Self-identified charismatics within mainline nonpentecostal denominations who are no longer regularly active in the charismatic renewal but have moved into other spheres of witness and service in their churches. There are three major categories here. (1) Protestant Postcharismatics are charismatics formerly active in renewal, now inactive but in wider ministries; these inactive persons are much fewer than inactive Catholics because of the more developed teaching, pastoral care, and ministry opportunities offered by the ten or so organized denominational renewal fellowships in the USA and their counterparts in Europe. An indication of the rapid turnover in membership is the fact that 25 percent of the 12,000 attendees at the Lutheran ILCOHS annual charismatic conferences in Minneapolis (USA) are first-timers, which implies an average four-year turnover. (2) Catholic Postcharismatics are charismatics formerly active in the Catholic charismatic renewal (for average turnover period of two to three years of active involvement in officially recognized Catholic charismatic prayer groups), now in wider ministries; inaccurately called "graduates" or "alumni" of renewal; in the USA, these consist of 4.6 million inactive in addition to active Catholic charismatic community including children. Added to active persons this means that in 1985 Catholic charismatics worldwide numbered 63.5 million (7.3 percent of the entire Roman Catholic Church), rising to 11.3 percent by A.D. 2000. A number of Catholic theologians hold that Spirit baptism is as irreversible as water baptism. Lastly, (3) Anglican Postcharismatics likewise are charismatics formerly active in the Anglican charismatic renewal, often as far back as 1953, but who are now not actively involved though usually involved in foreign mission or other ministries.

13. Anglican Charismatics

Anglican pentecostals, begun 1907 with clergyman A. A. Boddy (Sunderland, England); then from 1918, due to the global influenza pandemic, numerous prayer and healing groups in the Anglican churches of Nigeria and Kenya, inter alia; then from 1925 the Spirit Movement (Aladura), which was then expelled and seceded as today's African indigenous churches (with total membership of 50 million, have enumerated in line no. 22); subsequently numerous isolated clergy and groups in several countries up to U.S. Episcopalian Agnes Sanford's healing ministry from 1953, Priests R. Winkler in 1956 and D. Bennett in 1959, Blessed Trinity Society (1961), and Church of England clergyman M. C. Harper in 1962 (who then founded Fountain Trust in 1964); in 18 countries by 1978, expanding to 95 countries by 1987 (with 850,000 active adherents in UK served by Anglican Renewal Ministries (ARM); 520,000 (18 percent of all Episcopalians) in USA served by Episcopal Renewal Ministries; with branches of ARM in other countries also); with by A.D. 2000 rapid increase to 17.5 million in 130 denominations in 163 countries. Much of this expansion is due to uniquely structured international charismatic ministry body, SOMA (Sharing of Ministries Abroad), begun 1979, which now covers 27 of the 37 Anglican provinces worldwide and partially covers more, working by 1987 in 70 countries.

14. Catholic Charismatics

Known at first as Catholic pentecostals or neo-pentecostals, then as the Catholic charismatic renewal, begun with early stirrings in Third World countries (Africa, Latin America), then definitively in 1967 in USA; in 1985, 60,000 prayer groups in 140 countries worldwide (in USA 10,500 English, Vietnamese, Korean, Filipino, Haitian, Hispanic, and several other language groups), rising to 143,000 by 1995. Since 1978 there have been National Service Committees in over 120 countries uniting Catholic charismatics. Streams of different emphasis in the USA and several other countries: (a) that centered on Word of God Community (Servant Ministries, University Christian Outreach, *New Covenant* magazine, in Ann Arbor, Michigan, with overseas communities and work in Belgium, Honduras, Hong Kong, India, Indonesia, Lebanon, Nicaragua, Northern Ireland, Philippines, South Africa, Sri Lanka) with cohesive, authoritarian leadership, which originated ICCRO in Brussels, Belgium; and (b) that centered on People of Praise Community (South Bend, Indiana), ICCRO after its relocation in Vatican City in 1987, and a wide international network of covenant communities, with a less authoritarian structure and leadership style. Priests. Since 1974 some 4 percent of USA priests have been active in the renewal, including 2 percent now Postcharismatics. Priests worldwide (now 9,470) are less involved than bishops (now 450); foreign missionaries are more involved than home clergy.

A full interpretation of the methodology of this survey of the Catholic charismatic renewal is given in *World Christian Encyclopedia 2000*.

15. Protestant Charismatics

Origins: 1909 Lutheran prayer groups in state churches (Germany), 1918 charismatics in African countries evicted or secede to form AICs (African Indigenous Churches), 1931 reformed groups related to 1946 Union de Priere (south of France), 1932 charismatic revival in Methodist Church (Southern Rhodesia) leading to massive AACJM schism, 1945 Darmstadt Sisters of Mary (Germany), 1950 Dutch Reformed Church (Netherlands); 1950 origins of Protestant neo-pentecostals in USA; 1958 large-scale neo-pentecostal movements in Brazil's Protestant churches (Renovacao); in 38 countries by 1978, in 130 by 1987, and in 6,460 denominations in 231 countries by 2000. Some representative figures: East Germany, 500,000 participants (7 percent of all members) in state Lutheran church.

16. Orthodox Charismatics

Contemporary successors of scores of charismatic movements within Russian Orthodox Church dating from Spiritual Christians (A.D. 1650); also charismatics in Greek Orthodox Church in Greece, and Eastern and Oriental Orthodox churches in USA (1967, Fr. A. Emmert, who by 1987 had become a Melkite Catholic convert), Canada, Australia, Lebanon, Uganda, Kenya, Tanzania, Egypt, and some thirty other countries. Agency: Service Committee for Orthodox Spiritual Renewal (SCOSR). A recent significant development is the rapid spread of the Brotherhood of Lovers of the Church, a charismatic renewal within the Armenian Apostolic church in the former USSR. Despite these stirrings, Orthodox authorities have generally harassed charismatics relentlessly, this hostility being due to the Orthodox assertion that they never lost the Spirit or the charismata.

17. Marginal Charismatics

There has always been a small nucleus of practicing charismatics within the various heterodox organizations in the marginal Christian mega-bloc.

18. Third Wave: Neo-Charismatic Renewal

These terms describe a new wave of the 20th-century renewal in the Holy Spirit gathering momentum in the 1960s to 1990s with no direct affiliation with either Pentecostalism or the charismatic renewal. Note that large numbers of phenomenological charismatics (in Korea, East Germany, Poland, et al.) do not identify themselves as either pentecostal or charismatic, and instead exhibit a marked rejection of pentecostal terminology.

19. Neo-charismatics (Third Wavers, Independents, Postdenominationalists, Neo-Apostolics)

Persons in mainline nonpentecostal denominations, recently filled with or empowered with the Spirit but usually nonglossolalic, who do not identify themselves with the term "pentecostal" or "charismatic." Because they demonstrate the charismata and the phenomena of pentecostalism, they are also being termed (by outside observers) "quasicharismatics." Totals in A.D. 2000: 295,405,240 members in 18,810 denominations or networks, in 225 countries. Neo-charismatics can be divided into two categories: (a) those in networks entirely (100 percent); neo-charismatics (see line no. 20); and (b) neo-charismatic individuals in independent but nonpentecostal/charismatic denominations (see line no. 34).

20. (a) In Two Kinds of Wholly Third Wave Networks

These 100 percent neo-charismatic bodies have 253,936,000 members in 17,125 denominations/networks in 220 countries.

21. Non-White Indigenous Neo-Charismatics

Apparent/seemingly/largely pentecostal or semipentecostal members of this 250-year old movement of churches indigenous to Christians in non-white races across the world, and begun without reference to Western Christianity; estimated in 1970 as 60 percent (rising by 1985 to 75 percent) of all members of the over 1,000 non-white/Third World indigenous denominations, which, though not all explicitly pentecostal, nevertheless have the main phenomenological hallmarks of pentecostalism (charismatic spirituality, oral liturgy, narrative witness/theology, dreams and visions, emphasis on filling with the Holy Spirit, healing by prayer, atmospheric communication [simultaneous audible prayer], emotive fellowship, et al.). These denominations are found in A.D. 2000 in 210 different countries on all continents, in 13,425 denominations, numbering 203,270,000 persons. The case for enumerating adherents of these movements as pentecostals has been fully made by W. J. Hollenweger in his writings, most recently in "After Twenty Years' Research on Pentecostalism," *International Review of Mission* (April 1986), and *Pentecostalism* (1997). Note that the term "indigenous" as used here refers to the auto-origination of these movements, begun among non-white races without Western or white missionary support.

This whole category can be divided into various subcategories. Indigenous holiness-pentecostals are found in some 60 denominations, teaching three-crisis experience (conversion, sanctification, baptism in the Spirit); in 35 different countries. Indigenous baptistic-pentecostals exist in 70 denominations, teaching two-crisis experience (conversion, baptism in the Spirit); in 45 different countries. Indigenous oneness-pentecostals are widespread in 60 denominations practicing baptism in name of Jesus only; the major such body with missions worldwide is the True Jesus Church (begun in China, 1917). The first such new denomination, a schism from the (mainly white) Assemblies of God (USA), was the Pentecostal Assemblies of the World (1916). These bodies are found in 38 countries today. Indigenous pentecostal-apostolics have over 60 denominations in 18 countries; stress on complex hierarchy of living apostles, prophets, and other charismatic officials. Indigenous radical-pentecostals are found in over 100 deliverance-pentecostal denominations in at least 40 countries and expanding rapidly. Most of the mushrooming new youth churches, hotel churches, theater churches, cinema churches, store churches, and open-air churches are in this category. This category is also known as perfectionist-pentecostals, free pentecostals, deliverance-pentecostals, revivalist-pentecostals, teaching four-crisis experience including deliverance/ecstatic-confession/ascension/perfectionism/prophecy; in over 40 denominations, in over 30 countries and rapidly expanding.

22. African Indigenous Pentecostals/Charismatics

In 60 countries and 9,300 denominations with 65 million members, 92 national councils of AICs, and the continent-wide Organization of African Instituted (formerly independent) Churches, based in Nairobi, Kenya. Origins: 1864.

An important historical note must be added here. In the year 1900 the mainline mission bodies in Africa (Catholic, Anglican, Protestant) regarded these believers as, at best, "nominal" Christians or "unaffiliated" Christians, and this is how they appear in WCE 2000 Country Tables 1 (for Nigeria, South Africa, et al.). Today they are classified, as here, as independent neo-charismatics.

23. Black American Pentecostals/Charismatics

Black Christians in explicitly pentecostal denominations in twenty countries, indigenous to non-white races in that they were begun without outside Western or white missionary assistance or support. The largest is the Church of God in Christ (begun 1895). Most Pentecostal spokespersons in the USA define this variety as an integral part of classical Pentecostalism, although in this table we give this term a more restricted definition (see line no. 4). Our reasoning is that, seen in the total global perspective, this variety is far more accurately located as the archetype of global non-white pentecostalism. Furthermore, many black pentecostals regard the terms "Pentecostal" and "charismatic" as largely white in origin, and have traditionally preferred the term "sanctified." Denominations: 100, with 9 million members.

24. Black American Oneness Apostolics

Some 150 denominations in 10 countries with 3 million membership. Most belong to the Apostolic World Christian Fellowship (150 denominations).

25. Brazilian/Portuguese Grassroots Neo-Charismatics

There were numerous early movements in Portuguese Africa (Angola): Two prophet movements, Nkimba and Kimpasi, had broken from Jesuit missions by 1656; later, prophetess Fumaria; Donna Beatrice's attempt to found an independent Catholic church, for which King Pedro IV had her burned alive in 1706; 1872 Kiyoka; 1904 Epikilipikili; et al. By A.D. 2000 independent pentecostal bodies in Portuguese-speaking countries on 5 continents numbered 460 denominations with 23 million members in 20 countries; including IURD, OBPC, CCB, IPDA, MC (Portugal).

26. Filipino Indigenous Pentecostals/Charismatics

6.7 million members in 380 denominations in 25 countries; the earliest began in 1913.

27. Han Chinese Indigenous Pentecostals/Charismatics

A strong tradition beginning in 1905, widespread by 1955, expanding rapidly throughout mainland China by 1982; by 1985, almost 25 percent of all Protestants were tongues-speakers; estimates of the proportion of all Chinese Christians who are phenomenologically pentecostals/charismatics range from 50 percent to 85 percent in large numbers and networks of de facto independent pentecostal or charismatic churches. Total: 49 million members in 180 denominations in 58 countries.

28. Indian Indigenous Pentecostals/Charismatics

With 16.6 million members in 580 denominations in 25 countries including Europe and the USA.

29. Indonesian Indigenous Pentecostals

Over 6.7 million members in 170 major denominations in 5 countries including the Netherlands.

30. Korean Indigenous Pentecostals/Charismatics

Begun in 1910, there are now 170 denominations with 3.3 million members in 30 countries worldwide.

31. Latino-Hispanic Grassroots Believers

There are 11.9 million believers in 990 denominations or networks in 24 countries. "Grassroots" churches is the name given in preference to Western terminology.

32. Other Indigenous Neo-Charismatics

1.1 million believers in 130 denominations in 40 countries (Thailand, Malaysia, Vietnam, Afro-Caribbean, Japan, Pacific, Amerindian, Messianic Jews, et al.).

33. White-Led Independent Postdenominationalists

Independent charismatic and neo-charismatic churches that either have separated from the charismatic renewal in parent mainline denominations (thus 50 percent of all Presbyterian charismatics in USA are known to have left to join these new churches), or have recently been founded independently (though from out of the same milieux), all being either independent congregations or in loose networks, and all being mainly or predominantly of white membership (Europeans, North Americans) or under overall white leadership or initiative. Total: 50 million members in 3,700 denominations in 210 countries. Examples: house church movements in England (Restoration, and 5 other major groupings), Scotland, Norway, Sweden (many, including Rhema Fellowship), Denmark, Hungary, Poland, France (several communities), Switzerland, Spain (Witnessing), Netherlands (many), New Zealand, South Africa (many, including International Fellowship of Charismatic Churches, with 300 churches, Hatfield Christian Centre [162 churches], etc.), former Soviet Union/USSR (in Central Russia, Northern Russia, Ukraine, Baltic, Georgia, et al.), and USA (60,000 recently formed churches in several major groupings or networks, with some overlap; International Fellowship of Faith Ministries (2,000 churches), International Convention of Faith Churches and Ministries (495 churches in Tulsa), Faith Christian Fellowship International (2,000 ordained ministers), Melodyland Christian Center, People of Destiny, International Communion of Charismatic Churches (former classical Pentecostals, very large, fastest-growing network in 1988), Network of Christian Ministries (latter rain emphasis), Fellowship of Christian Assemblies (101 churches), Maranatha Christian Churches (57 churches), Fellowship of Covenant Ministers & Churches (250 churches), Association of Vineyard Churches (200 churches, founder John Wimber; note that he and the churches have regarded themselves as third wavers rather than charismatics, though most observers hold the reverse is truer), National Leadership Conference, Charismatic Bible Ministries (1,500 ministers), Word

Churches (Word of Faith Movement), Calvary Ministries International (200 churches), Local Covenant Churches (Shepherding), Rhema Ministerial Association (525 churches), International Ministers Forum (500 churches), Full Gospel Chaplaincy (3 million independent charismatics), Christ for the Nations (600 churches), Abundant Life Community Churches (25 churches), et al.). This category also includes quasidenominational networks such as Full Gospel Fellowship of Churches and Ministers International (begun 1962, 425 churches). There are thus similar movements, related and unrelated, in 84 percent of all the countries of the world.

34. (b) as Percent of Seven Kinds of Non-Third-Wave Denominations
This category summarizes neo-charismatic individuals who are members of Independent denominations or networks that are nonpentecostal/noncharismatic or even antipentecostal/anticharismatic. As shown in the *World Christian* database, each such body is assigned a percent figure estimating the size of its neo-charismatic members. Total in A.D. 2000: 41,468,700 in 925 denominations in 200 countries.

35. Independent Neo-Charismatics
This line refers to the relatively small numbers of neo-charismatics in independent denominations uninterested in or hostile to any ties with historic Christianity. Their neo-charismatics number 1.7 million in 30 denominations in 80 countries since 1925, all claiming to have no roots or relationship with any of the four historical mega-blocs (Anglican, Orthodox, Protestant, Roman Catholic).

36. Doubly Counted First/Second/Third Wavers
This category numbering several million persons is difficult to assess because of differences in definition and enumeration procedures. An estimate may be obtained as the totals of line nos. 1–35 minus line no. 37. The category enumerates the growing number of believers and congregations who are enumerated as either Pentecostals (within the first wave) or charismatics (within the second wave), but who also are regarded or regard themselves as neo-charismatics within the third wave. Many Methodist, Baptist, Assemblies of God, and other congregations are in this position and thus are counted twice in our enumeration. The grand total on line no. 36 is therefore best shown as a negative quantity to arrive at accurate overall totals. Examples include many African, Asian, and Latin American believers; this category includes many large, widely known or outstanding Third World churches and congregations belonging to nonpentecostal denominations founded by nonpentecostal or even antipente-

costal mission boards from Europe and North America. Among the most prominent of such congregations are four from Korea: Sung Rak Baptist Church, Seoul (at 25,000 members the largest Southern Baptist-related congregation in the world until its secession in September 1987); Central Evangelical Holiness Church, Seoul (at 6,000 members the largest holiness congregation in the world); and the world's two largest Methodist congregations, in Inchon and Seoul (25,000 members each). All of these congregations exhibit charismatic and pentecostal phenomena.

37. Global Pentecostals/Charismatics/Neo-Charismatics (Affiliated)

Sum of lines nos. 2, 10, 19 minus line 36 (the three waves of renewal).

38. Renewal Members on Seven Continents

Ranked by size: (1) Latin America, (2) Asia, (3) Africa, (4) Northern America, (5) Europe, (6) Oceania, (7) Antarctica.

39. Renewal Members in Africa

Total 126,000,000: 12 percent Pentecostals, 25 percent charismatics, 63 percent neo-charismatics.

40. Renewal Members in Antarctica

Total 400: 50 percent Catholics, 30 percent Protestants.

41. Renewal members in Asia

Total 134,890,000: 5 percent Pentecostals, 16 percent charismatics, 79 percent neo-charismatics.

42. Renewal Members in Europe

Total 37,569,000: 8 percent Pentecostals, 56 percent charismatics, 36 percent neo-charismatics.

43. Renewal Members in Latin America

Total 141,433,000: 23 percent Pentecostals, 52 percent charismatics, 24 percent neo-charismatics.

44. Renewal Members in Northern America

Total 79,600,000: 7 percent Pentecostals, 28 percent charismatics, 65 percent neo-charismatics.

45. Renewal Members in Oceania

Total 4,266,000: 14 percent Pentecostals, 63 percent charismatics, 24 percent neo-charismatics.

46. Renewal Members as Percentage of Global Church Members
Computed as line no. 66 divided by line no. 99, times 100.

47. Peripheral Constituents
Not counted as renewal members, but clearly related to it or close to it are two more categories.

48. Quasi-Pentecostals
This first category consists of Prepentecostals (of whom John Wesley is the archetype), notably the Salvation Army, and Postpentecostals (former members of Pentecostal denominations who have left to join such nonpentecostal mainline bodies as Anglicanism, Catholicism, Lutheranism, etc.).

49. Unaffi liated Believers Professing Renewal
This use of the term "believers" refers to persons with pentecostal gifts or experience who are professing pentecostals/charismatics but who do not, or do not yet, belong to pentecostal or charismatic or third-wave organized churches or groups or communities or denominations. Large numbers become pentecostals/charismatics in personal experience several weeks, months, or even years before they find a church or group and get enrolled and therefore enumerate. They can be estimated, as here, by careful comparison of polls of those professing with those affiliated (enrolled).

50. Wider Global Totals of Renewal
Living persons associated with renewal consisting of (a) column 37, (b) column 50, and column 49.

51. Total All Renewal Believers Alive at Mid-Year
It is important to remember that virtually all Pentecostal or charismatic or neo-charismatic statistics collected, published, or quoted by members or observers are of living believers only and do not include believers who have just died or just been martyred. To balance this bias, line number 52 has been added here.

52. Renewal Believers Dying Since A.D. 1900
These figures give a much truer picture of the size of renewal if one is speaking about the whole of the 20th century. The formula used is: Dead believers = death rate (averaging 1 percent per year/100x(P2-P1)/P2/P1) 1/1 2-42-1 where P1 = total live believers initially at year t1, and P2=total live believers at end of year t2.

53. Total All Renewal Believers Ever, Since a.d. 1900
Calculated as column 51 plus 52. By mid A.D. 2000 this total had passed 795 million.

54. Churches, Finance, Agencies, Workers
All distinct organized local congregations, worship centers, parishes, fellowships, or groupings of all kinds, which are explicitly identified with or attached to the renewal. Mega-churches. A majority of the 150 or so largest mega-churches (the world's largest single congregations, each with over 50,000 members) are pentecostal/charismatic. The largest Protestant church is Full Gospel Central Church, Seoul, Korea, with 600,000 members by 1988, and 800,000 by 1998.

55. Pentecostal Churches, Congregations (First Wave)
Largest grouping, Assemblies of God (USA and overseas): churches excluding outstations (1985) 77,976; (1986) 92,355 (15.6 percent per year increase). All denominations: 480,000 congregations.

56. Mainline Charismatic Prayer Groups (Second Wave)
Growth of weekly groups: (1960) 10,000, rising to (A.D. 2000) 550,000.

57. Catholic Charismatic Weekly Prayer Groups
Growth of weekly groups: (1970) 2,185; (1980) 12,000; (1990) 90,000; (2000) 160,000.

58. Anglican and Protestant Charismatic Groups
Some 250,000 regular prayer groups were meeting by A.D. 2000.

59. Independent Congregations, House Churches (Third Wave)
Around 591,000 by A.D. 2000.

60. Personal Income of All Renewal Members, $ p.a.
Defined as in article "Silver and Gold Have I None," in *International Bulletin of Missionary Research* (October 1983), 150. By 2000 personal income of all renewal members U.S. $1,550 billion per year.

61. Renewal Members' Giving to All Christian Causes, $ p.a.
By A.D. 2000 this amounted to at least $30 billion per year.

62. Renewal Service Agencies
National, countrywide, regional or international bodies, parachurch organ-

izations and agencies that assist or serve the churches but are not themselves denominations or church-planting mission bodies. Among the most significant categories are (a) Pentecostal agencies (missions, evangelism, publishing, etc.), (b) denominational charismatic agencies: Anglican Renewal Ministries (UK), Episcopal Renewal Ministries (USA), International Catholic Charismatic Renewal Services (Vatican City), National Service Committees for the Catholic Charismatic Renewal (in over 120 countries), and 100 more such bodies, (c) global mission agencies: SOMA, Advance, AIMS, and other missionary bodies serving the charismatic renewal, and (d) Third World mission agencies: over 500 locally organized and supported charismatic sending bodies. One of the fastest-growing varieties of renewal agency is TV production organizations, numbering over 500 by 1987 and 1,000 by A.D. 2000. Grand total by A.D. 2000: 4,000 agencies.

63. Renewal Institutions
Major pentecostal/charismatic church-operated or related institutions of all kinds, i.e., fixed centers with premises, plant, and permanent staff, excluding church buildings, worship centers, church headquarters or offices; including high schools, colleges, universities, medical centers, hospitals, clinics presses, book shops, libraries, radio/TV stations and studios, conference centers, study centers, research centers, seminaries, religious communities (monasteries, abbeys, convents, houses), etc. Many of these have been originated by Pentecostal bodies, a growing number by mainline charismatics, and a vast mushrooming of new institutions have been begun by Third Wave networks and churches. But in countries where new initiatives have been prohibited or repressed (e.g., before 1989 East Germany, Poland), thousands of traditionally Christian institutions have been infiltrated and virtually taken over by charismatics.

Charismatic covenant communities. Since 1958 (Community of Jesus, Cape Cod, Massachussetts, now with 900 members) and 1965 (Episcopal Church of the Redeemer, Houston, Texas), residential communities committed to intentional corporate charismatic life, service and mission, mainly ecumenical or interdenominational, with married couples and families as well as celibates, have arisen in 50 countries across the world. Size varies from under 20 persons each to 4,000 (Emmanuel Community, Paris, France, begun 1972). Total communities in 1987: some 2,000 with over quarter of a million members; rising to treble that number by 1998. A very detailed survey is given by P. Hocken, "The Significance of Charismatic Communities," in P. Elbert, ed., *Charismatic Renewal in the Churches* (1990). Grand total by A.D. 2000: 14,000.

64. All Pentecostal/Charismatic Full-Time Workers

Full-time church workers, pastors, clergy, ministers, evangelists, mission-aries, executives, administrators, bishops, moderators, church leaders, et al. This line is the sum of the next two, nos. 65 and 66. Grand total by A.D. 2000: 2,100,000.

65. Nationals: Pastors, Clergy, Evangelists, et al.

Some representative statistics: (1) Pentecostal renewal. Assemblies of God (USA and overseas) credentialed ministers 11,788 (1985), 121,425 (1986), annual increase 8 percent per year. (2) Charismatic renewal. Percentage of charismatics among clergy (some representative figures): (East Germany) Bund der Evangelische Kirchen in der DDR (state Lutheran church): 500 pastors (10 percent of all clergy) are charismatics. (UK) Church of England: 25 percent of all 17,000 clergy. (USA) Episcopal Church in the USA: 21 per-cent of 14,111 clergy are involved, and 64 percent receive ERM periodicals. Lutheran Church Missouri Synod: 400 out of 6,000 clergy are charismatic; several clergy have been unfrocked since 1970. Many ecumenical and evangelical parachurch agencies have 20-60 percent charismatics on staff. In the 2,000 or so Pentecostal agencies, virtually all staff are Pentecostal. Grand total by A.D. 2000: 1,933,000.

66. Aliens: Foreign Missionaries

These include Pentecostals, and the following varieties of charismatics and neo-charismatics (renewed in the Spirit): (1985) 25 percent of all Anglican foreign missionaries, 20 percent of all RCs, 40 percent of all Protestants (60 percent of WEC, 42 percent of ABCIM, etc.); by A.D. 2000, these figures are likely to have increased at least to 50 percent of Anglicans, 25 percent of RCs, 50 percent of Protestants, and 90 percent of Third-World missionaries. Grand total by A.D. 2000: 167,000.

67. The Context of World Evangelization

This last section is added to illustrate what has always been the focus and goal of the renewal as a whole.

68. Global Population

In mid-2000: 6,055,049,000.

69. Christians (All Varieties)

In mid-2000: 1,999,564,000.

70. Affi liated Church Members (Baptized)

Persons (adults and children) on the rolls of the churches and so of organized Christianity: in mid-2000, 1,888,439,000.

71. Non-Christians

In mid-2000: 4,055,485,000.

72. Unevangelized Persons

Total persons in the world who have never heard the name of Jesus Christ and remain unaware of Christianity, Christ, and the gospel. Total in mid-2000: 1,629,375,000.

73. World Evangelization Global Plans Since A.D. 30

Grand total of all distinct plans and proposals for accomplishing world evangelization made by Christians since A.D. 30. Most of these are each described in *World Christian Encyclopedia 2000,* Part 24, "GeoStrategies," with their historical context in Part 2, "CosmoChronology." All 770 global plans by 1987 rising to 1,500 by A.D. 2000 are listed, enumerated, described, analyzed, and interpreted in Part 24 also.

Appendix
A Chronology of Renewal
in the Holy Spirit

David Barrett

The Spirit Empowers the Biblical Era

2000 B.C.   Old Testament refers frequently to activities of the Holy Spirit ("Holy Spirit," 3 times in New International Version Bible; "Spirit of God," 11 times; "Spirit of the Lord," 12 times; "Spirit" or "My Spirit" 42 times); often portrayed as a mighty wind or force.

1225 B.C.   Israel after death of Joshua is ruled for 185 years by judges (charismatic military or civilian warriors/heroes/prophets): 1200 Othniel, Ehud; 1150 Shamgar; Deborah and Barak (1125 Battle of Megiddo); 1100 Gideon (40 years); 1075 Abimelech (3 years); Tola (23 years); Jair (22 years); 1050 Jephthah (6 years); Ibzan (7 years); Elon (10 years); Abdon (8 years); Samson (20 years); Eli (40 years); Samuel (30 years); Joel, Abijah, until monarchy instituted in A.D. 1030.

A.D. 33   New Testament refers often to activities of the Holy Spirit (Gospels 48 times, Acts 58 times, in English New Revised Standard Version Bible).

A.D. 33   Day of Pentecost in Jerusalem: the Spirit creates the church as the body of Christ, as 3,000 are converted among Diaspora Jews and Gentiles from "every nation under heaven," from North Africa to Persia.

A.D. 33   Apostle Peter and the Eleven proclaim to Jerusalem crowds: "Repent . . . and you will receive the gift of the Holy Spirit"; widespread manifestations begin of sudden conversions, tongues (glossolalia), miracles, exorcisms, signs, and wonders.

A.D. 35   Proliferation of "signs and wonders" among early believers (listed 9 times in Acts); miracles and healings at this time an everyday occurrence and an essential part of proclamation of the gospel; "power evangelism" thus one of the normal kinds of evangelism in the early church.

The Spirit Renews Scattered Groups Throughout Eighteen Centuries

A.D. 70 After the apostolic age, many small or local renewals or revivals occur, with scores of isolated charismatic believers (often in monasteries) but no global renewal until the 20th century.

A.D. 79 "Signs and wonders" (miracles demonstrating kingdom of God) do not cease with end of apostolic age, nor with later closing of New Testament canon, but continue throughout church history as minor background waves of prophecy, healing, deliverance, and tongues.

c. 100 Decline of miracles and deaths of last of the Twelve give rise to spreading view that exercise of charismatic gifts ceased after the apostolic age.

c. 150 Justin Martyr (c. 100–165) founds disciple-training school over a house in Rome, documents current "signs and wonders" (exorcisms, healings, and prophesyings), and writes: "The first Apostles, twelve in number, in the power of God went out and proclaimed Christ to every race of men"; and "There is not one single race of men, whether barbarians, or Greeks, or whatever they may be called, nomads, or vagrants, or herdsmen dwelling in tents, among whom prayers and giving of thanks are not offered through the name of the Crucified Jesus"; teaches that all orthodox Christians believe in a resurrection of the flesh and in a millennial reign in the New Jerusalem; martyred at Rome.

c. 155 Other influential apologists write extensively on the Holy Spirit: Tatian, Athenagoras, Theophilus of Antioch, Irenaeus (130–202), Tertullian, Clement of Alexandria (155–215), Origen (185–254), Cyprian (200–258), Hippolytus of Rome.

c. 156 Phrygia: rise of Montanism under new convert Montanus (c. 120–c. 175), a puritanical, prophetic, charismatic, millennial, apocalyptic movement claiming to be a new age of the Holy Spirit; 156, call for Christians to come to Phrygia to await Second Coming; in village of Ardabau, Montanus with Priscilla and Maximilla begins to prophesy that heavenly Jerusalem will soon descend to Earth at Pepuza, a neighboring town in Phyrgia, thus inaugurating kingdom of God; 206, Tertullian joins; 230, movement excommunicated by Synod of Iconium; continues underground until A.D. 880.

c. 251 Novatian (c. 200–258), first learned Roman theologian to write in Latin, emerges as second antipope in papal history, founding rigorist (anti-lapsi) Novatian schism; documents contemporary charismata (prophesyings, tongues, healings, miracles, powers); martyred 258, but his sect spreads across empire and lasts until after A.D. 600.

c. 270   Rise of monasticism in Egypt, as direct challenge to lifestyle of the rich: (1) eremitical (Anthony of Egypt, c. 251–356), (2) cenobitic (Pachomius, c. 287–346); widespread over next two centuries, with many documented healings, exorcisms, miracles, signs, and wonders; Egyptian monks travel widely, evangelizing in Europe, Britain, Ireland, et al.

328   Many post-Nicene Greek Fathers publish expositions on the Holy Spirit: Eusebius of Caesarea (265–339), Cyril of Jerusalem (310–86), Athanasius (296–373), John Chrysostom (347–407), Basil, Gregory of Nyssa.

328   Ascetic Egyptian monk Hilarion of Gaza (291–371), missionary to idolatrous pagans of Palestine, introduces monasticism and establishes first monastery, conducts widely attested ministry of signs and wonders (healings, exorcisms).

374   A layman, Ambrose of Milan (c. 339–97) acclaimed bishop by crowds; in his writings, documents current healings and glossolalia; later teaches Second Coming of Christ will be proceded by destruction of Rome and appearance of Antichrist on Earth.

378   Jerome (c. 345–419) writes: "From India to Britain, all nations resound with the death and resurrection of Christ" (Isaiam cliv, Epistol. Xiii ad Paulinum); estimates 1.9 million Christians to have been martyred since A.D. 33 (out of 120 million Christians, i.e., 1.6 percent or 1 in 60); documents numerous current "signs and wonders" (healings, exorcisms, miracles).

380   Latin theologians write expounding doctrine of the Holy Spirit: Hilary of Poitiers, Ambrose (339–97), Augustine.

381   Council of Constantinople 1 (wnd Ecumenical Council); creed of Nicaea reaffirmed; Macedonianism and Apollinarianism condemned; divinity of Holy Spirit clarified.

426   Augustine (354–430) bishop of Hippo completes in 13 years his treatise *The City of God* (De Civitate Dei), against background of Visigoth invasion of Rome; propounds allegorical millennialism, but also teaches that future final Antichrist will arise as Nero Redivivus; opposes emerging theory of cessation of charismatic gifts as overreaction to excesses of Montanism et al. with the teaching that miracles and charismata ended with the apostolic age; documents numerous recent miracles, exorcisms, healings, and resuscitations.

431   Jewish messiah Moses appears on Crete ready to lead remnants of Israel dryshod to land of Israel; date 440 widely believed for final coming of Messiah; over next 1,500 years, scores more Jewish charismatic claimants arise, attracting widespread followings, fanaticism, violence, and martyrdoms, especially in 1087, 1117, 1127, 1160, 1172, 1295, 1502, 1528, 1648.

Expounding the Spirit in the Middle Ages

500   Throughout the Middle Ages (A.D. 395–1500), scores of apologists, theologians, mystics, bishops publish expositions on the person and work of the Holy Spirit: Gregory the Great, Bede (673–735), Anselm (1033–1109), Peter Abelard (1079–1142), Bernard of Clairvaux (1090–1153), Bonaventure (1217–74), Thomas Aquinas (1225–74).

540   Persia: revival of Christian monasticism throughout Persian Empire under monk Abraham of Kaskar (c. 491–586), who founds Great Monastery on Mt. Izla; disciples Dadyeshu and Babhai found or control 60 monasteries throughout empire; numerous monasteries and missions begun, with special concern for physical and spiritual needs of people; through persecution, spreads across Asia to Yemen, South India, Ceylon, Samarkand, China.

541   Monophysite revival in Syria and the East: organizing genius Jacob Baradaeus (c. 500–578) appointed missionary bishop of Edessa, organizes West Syrian (Jacobite) church, becomes Monophysite apostle to Asia; for 35 years (542–78) eludes spies and soldiers of empire, keeps constantly on the move, plants trail of churches across Asia to India, ordains 100,000 clergy, 27 bishops, 2 patriarchs including Sergius of Antioch, sends lay evangelists throughout Asia; rapid expansion of Syrian Orthodoxy.

544   6th General Synod of Church of the East (Synod of Mar Aba), convened by catholicos Mar Aba the Great; synod begins thoroughgoing reorganization of church, extension of theological education, spiritual and moral revival, revival of monasticism, and work of reunion.

c. 580   Writer, historian, and bishop Gregory of Tours (c. 538–94) gives many accounts of contemporary miracles, healings, and exorcisms.

594   Roman Pope Gregory the Great (540–604) initiates reforms in liturgy and church administration, enhances power and prestige of papacy; publishes Dialogues describing contemporary Christian miracles, visions, prophecies, supernatural awareness, and other spiritual gifts; places detailed planning of organized missions to all heathen among his major objectives, in view of imminence of Last Judgment.

c. 650   Samuel the Confessor, Coptic hermit and prophet of the end times, foresees revival of monastic vocation with vast numbers of young people flocking to enter monasteries.

926   Revival of Western monasticism under Odo (879–942) abbot of Cluny, France.

1096   Islamic theologian Abu Hamid Mohammed al-Ghazali (1058–1111) begins his book *The Revival of the Religious Sciences*, which helps make Sufi mysticism part of Islamic orthodoxy; some parallels with Christian mysticism.

1112   Wandering ex-monk Tanchelm begins preaching across Low Countries, claiming to possess Holy Spirit and to be God as Christ was; announces new Kingdom of the Saints, attacks church and clergy; attacks multitudes of followers, holds magnificent banquets in imitation of wedding banquet in Revelation.

1122 Eastern prelate named John visits Rome, lectures on miracles occurring every year in India on feast of St. Thomas; 20 years later rumors circulate of a Christian king in India, Prester John, said to have inflicted major defeat on Muslim rulers.

1150 Numerous Catholic women mystics or charismatics write extensively on the Holy Spirit: Hildegard of Bingen (1098–1179), Gertrude of Helfta (1256–1301), Birgitta of Sweden (1302–73), Catherine of Siena (1347–80), Julian of Norwich (1342–1420).

1151 Waldensian movement begins following Poor Men of Lyons and reformer Peter Waldo, develops evangelistic and charismatic ministries (visions, prophecies, healings, exorcisms).

c. 1180 Joachim of Fiore (c. 1130–1202), Italian Cistercian abbot and mystic, divides all history into three 40-generation ages or periods (Old Testament, New Testament, future age), writes *Vaticini del Vangelo Eterno* (Prophecies of the Eternal Gospel) and *Expositio in Apocalypsim* describing imminent crisis of evil, apocalyptic symbols of Antichrist, and his 3rd or Final Age of the Spirit (Love) coming by 1260 after Age of the Father (Law), and Age of the Son (Grace), for spiritual men through pilgrimage and great tribulation in a spiritualized Johannine Church replacing carnal Petrine Church; Joachimism spreads widely over next three centuries

1209 Francis of Assisi (1182–1226) founds traveling preachers (Franciscans), largest of the mendicant orders (OFM); widespread healings, signs, and miracles reported; 1270, missionaries in almost every part of the known world; by 1400, missions from Lapland to Congo and Azores to China; soon reaches a medieval peak of 60,000 Franciscans by 1400; 77,000 by 1768; falling to 14,000 by 1900; rising to 40,000 by 1970; by A.D. 2000, 35,200 priests and brothers and 57,300 sisters (nuns).

1254 Sensational Introduction to the Eternal Gospel of abbot Joachim issued by ardent spiritualist Gerard of Borgo San Donnino, claiming its prophecies have been fulfilled by Franciscan order, and insisting Age of the Spirit will begin in 1260.

1282 Stigmatic nun Guglielma of Milan dies, followers identify her as third Person of Trinity and expect her to return in 1300 to supervise a worldwide pentecostal conversion to the Church of the Holy Spirit; 3 followers are executed in 1302, and her remains are exhumed and burned.

1340 German Dominican mystic Johann Tauler (1300–1361) of the Friends of God (Gottesfreunde) initiates major revival in Rhine Valley, whose influence lasts until 1450.

1399 Catalan Dominican wandering preacher Vincent Ferrer (c. 1350–1419) reevangelizes and transforms Christendom throughout Europe;

brings Jews to dialogues, converts 25,000 across Europe; preaches 6,000 apocalyptic sermons each three hours long, with glossolalia, healings, miracles widely reported; writes of future coming of Antichrist, predicts world will end after 2,537 more years in A.D. 3936 (based on number of verses in Book of Psalms); continues to incite torture and forced conversion of Jews; 1403, claims Antichrist has been born this year.

The Spirit at Work Through European Reformers

1517   Three major Reformations begin, with clear teachings on the Holy Spirit: (a) Protestant Reformers Martin Luther (1483–1546), Ulrich Zwingli (1484–1531, John Calvin (1509–64), (b) Catholic Reformers Ignatius Loyola (1491–1556), John of the Cross (1542–91); and (c) Radical Reformers Thomas Muntzer (1488–1525), Menno Simons (1496–1561).

1523   Revival of millennialism by left-wing Protestant Anabaptists, Bohemians, Moravian Brethren, Zwickau Prophets, et al.

1557   France: 33 percent of population reputed to be Protestants (known as Huguenots); 1559, create Reformed Church (73 congregations, 400,000 adherents); widespread manifestations of glossolalia, trances, prophecies, et al.

1628   Revival in Ireland under Blair and Livingstone.

1689   Student revival in Leipzig, Germany.

1700   Wittgenstein revival movement in Germany (till 1750).

1703   Spiritans (CSSp, Holy Ghost Fathers) founded by Claude Francois Poullart des Places (1679–1709) for "Evangelizzazione degli infedeli"; by 1983, 857 houses with 3,671 missionaries.

1716   Irish Presbyterian educator William Tennent (1673–1746) evangelizes in American colonies; 1735, trains men for revivalist ministry in "Log College"; 1741, in old side/new side schism, he supports latter.

The Spirit at Work as Revivals Escalate

1717   A. H. Francke, Lutheran professor of Hebrew, holds revivals and evangelistic campaigns in Germany, based on Halle.

1720   Origins of Great Awakening in America: German evangelist T. J. Frelinghuysen (1692–1747) arrives from Pietism in Europe to Dutch Reformed churches in New Jersey; 1726, guides Irish Presbyterian minister and revivalist G. Tennent (1703–64) and others in revival ministry evangelizing among Scottish and Irish in Philadelphia, New Jersey and beyond.

c. 1720   Camisards prophesy in ecstatic trances and speak in tongues fore-telling imminent destruction of Roman Catholic Church in France; later they flee to England and America as predecessors of Shakers.

1723   Schism of Utrecht: separation from Rome of Little Church of Utrecht or Jansenist Church of Holland; 1889 Declaration of Utrecht rejects Council of Trent; Union of Utrecht unites church with Old Catholic churches of Germany and Switzerland; Jansenist worldview holds "signs and wonders" (miracles, healings, supernatural signs) still widespread.

1725   The Great Awakening revival spreads in New England and through-out the Thirteen Colonies; mass conversions of dechristianized Euro-pean populations in North America, led by revivalist Jonathan Edwards (1703–58), who expounds progressive millennialism (later called postmillennialism), envisaging establishment of Christ's mil-lennial kingdom on Earth around year 1990, with Second Advent at close of millennium; Edwards calls for "concerts of prayer" for world revival; Awakening lasts until 1770.

1738   Conversion of John Wesley (1703–91) at Aldersgate (UK); beginning of 18th-century Evangelical Revival and rise of Methodism under the Wesleys; outreach largely urban, concerned with neds of the poor, un-educated, unemployed, orphans, et al.

c. 1750   Wales: revivals under Howell Harris (1714–73), Daniel Rowland (c. 1713–90), William Williams (1717–91).

1773   Virginia: revival breaks out as first instance of a pentecostal-type reli-gious revival in North America; followed by recurrence in 1787.

1781   USA: revivals break out in several colleges including 1781 Dartmouth, 1783 Princeton and Yale, also Williams, Hampden-Sydney; 1785, na-tionwide "revival of 1800" fixes pattern of denominational life, lasts until 1812.

1782   Concerts of Prayer (for revival and world mission), as envisaged by Jonathan Edwards, spread in Britain, then from 1790 in USA; basis for subsequent worldwide missionary advance.

1783   Native Baptist Church, first Jamaican Afro-Christian movement, begun by ex-slave George Lisle; church plays a significant political role 80 years later; precursor of later end-time pentecostal renewal across world.

1785   Evangelical awakenings (revivals) spread throughout Wales: 1785 Brynengan, 1786 Trecastle, 1791 Bala, 1805 Aberystwyth, 1810 Llangei-tho, 1817 Beddgelert, 1821 Denbighshire, 1822 Anglesey, 1828 Car-marthenshire, 1832 Caernarvonshire, 1840 Merionethshire, 1849 South Wales, et al.

1788   Allgauer revival among Bavarian Catholics, led by Johann Sailer (1751–1832), Michael Feneberg, Martin Boos (1762–1825), Johannes Goszner (1773–1858), Ignatius Lindl (1774–1834).

1796   Norwegian revival under Hans Nielsen Hauge.

1800   Beginnings of local awakenings (revivals) in Scotland: Lewis, Harris, Perthshire.

1800   Widespread evangelistic camp meetings begin in USA; Kentucky revival awakening, with crowds of up to 25,000, sweeps over Kentucky, Tennessee, and the Carolinas.

1806   Britain: revivals secede from Methodism: 1806 Independent Methodists, 1810 Camp Meeting Methodists, joining in 1812 as Primitive Methodists.

1810   Evangelical awakenings (revivals) in Switzerland (Robert Haldane, 1764–1842), France, Low Countries, Germany.

1810   Revival in Russian Orthodox Church; 1813, Russian Bible Society founded, printing in 30 languages (17 new) with 600,000 copies; 1827, disbanded.

c. 1810   Wales: revivals under Christmas Evans (1766–1838), John Elias (1774–1841).

1815   *The Spirit of British Missions* (London: by an Anglican clergyman of the Church Missionary Society) appeals for workers: "The supply of Labourers in the great work of evangelizing the world is a most important topic."

1816   Elberfeld revivals in western Germany: 1816 first revival, 1820 second.

1820   Revival in Pomerania, Germany.

1826   Missionary renewal in western Siberia under Eugene Kazancev, metropolitan of Tobolsk; best epoch of Russian Orthodox missions begins.

1827   Siegen-Dillkreis revival, western Germany.

c. 1830   France: revivals under F. Monod (1794–1863), A. Monod (1802–56).

c. 1830   Switzerland: revivals under Robert Haldane, C. Malan (1787–1864), F. Gaussen (1790–1863), J. H. M. D'Aubigne (1794–1872).

1832   Catholic Apostolic Church founded in London through Edward Irving; charismatic manifestations.

1835   Finland: the Osterbottenvackelse, evangelical awakening in the West, active for 15 years; also revival under Lutheran pastor L. L. Laestadius (1800–1861).

1837   Board of Foreign Missions, Presbyterian Church in the USA established "to aid in the conversion of the world . . . every member of this church is a member for life of said society and bound to do all in his power for the accomplishment of this object"; 1958, becomes Commission on Ecumenical Mission and Relations, for which "the supreme and controlling aim of the Christian Mission to the world is to make the Lord Jesus Christ known to all men . . . in which Christians of all lands share in evangelizing the world and permeating all of life with the spirit and truth of Christ."

1837   Great Awakening in Hawaii, a remarkable revival with mass conversions until 1843: 27,000 Protestant adult converts (20 percent of population).

1838   Turkey: small-scale revivals among Armenians in Nicomedia and (1841) Adabazar, through ABCFM (USA); and later in Aintab and Aleppo.

1842   Revival spreads through state church of Norway; Norwegian Mission Society (Stavanger) begun.

1843   Hermannsburg revival in western Germany.

1844   Persia: revival among Nestorians around ABCFM station Urumiah; other revivals in 1849, 1850.

c. 1860   Netherlands: revivals under G. van Prinsterer (c. 1800–1867), A. Kuyper (1837–1920).

c. 1860   Revival in South Africa erupts under Dutch Reformed moderator Andrew Murray (1828–1917), sweeping Afrikaner churches.

1860   Revival in Ukraine; 1884–1904, persecution of Evangelicals.

1861   Cornish Revivals, in Britain for two years.

1861   Great Christian Revival (Great Awakening) in Jamaica, resulting in rapid spread of Native Baptist Church (now Revival Zion); wild dancing, trances.

1863   Apostles and clergy of Catholic Apostolic Church die off but no replacements allowed.

1863   Universal Catholic Church (later renamed New Apostolic Church) founded in Germany by excommunicated German prophet H. Geyer of Catholic Apostolic Church (UK), emphasizing a successional apostolate subject to a chief apostle with quasi-papal powers, and the gifts of the Holy Spirit including prophecy, tongues, miraculous healing, sacraments, hierarchy of 48 living apostles; by 1988, has 1.7 million members worldwide (mainly Germans) in 45 countries; secretive, cooperates with no other church; 1995, suddenly reveals full church details on World Wide Web; by 2000 has mushroomed to 9.6 million members in 180 countries.

1865   Christian Revival Association (1878, renamed Salvation Army) founded by Methodist evangelist William Booth in England for urban social outreach and street evangelism; 1985, 4,226,900 Salvationists in 75 countries, with vast social service and evangelistic activities and institutions; overriding first agenda defined in 1987 by SA general as "To emphasize the supremacy of evangelism in fulfilling the Lord's great commission . . . To work to the end that every man and woman and child has the opportunity to hear the good news of the gospel."

1870   Punjab: mass movement begins of 50 percent of Hindu Chuhras in Sialkot to American Presbyterian mission; continuing revival up to 1912.

1871   Revivals in Japan, also 1883, following waves of persecution in 1865, 1867, and 1868 ending in 1872 decree of religious liberty.

1875   Theosophical Society founded in New York City under anti-Christian writer Helena Blavatsky (1831–91), combining Gnosticism, mysticism, and occultism of Egypt, India, and China; 1909, young Brahmin Jiddu Krishnamurti (1895–96) claimed as Ascended Master, Christ Spirit, Reincarnate Buddha, Guilding Spirit of the Universe.

1876   Guinea (French). First mission (French Holy Ghost priests).

1880   Thirty Years' Revival in Germany (till 1910); several hundred thousand converted in state churches.

1883   2nd General Conference of Protestant Missionaries of Japan; several revivals; "Japan is now embracing Christianity with a rapidity unexampled since the days of Constantine . . . will be predominantly Christian within 20 years."

1883   Swami Vivekananda (1862–1902) Hindu missionary to the West and leader of Hindu revival in India, wins many in West to Vedantism.

1886   The United Holy Church founded in Method, North Carolina. The Christian Union organized in Tennessee by R. J. Spurling, Sr.

1890   Lynchings of blacks in South of USA average 3 each week during decade; many are Pentecostal preachers.

1894   Soatanana revival begins among Lutheran and LMS churches in Madagascar, lasting over 100 years (Fifohazana, Revivalists).

1895   Association of Pentecostal Churches in America (1919, renamed Church of the Nazarene) formed, 1897 begins foreign missions; by 1987, World Mission Division has 617 foreign missionaries in 84 countries, with two A.D. 2000 programs: Thrust to the Cities ("maximizing holiness evangelism in key cities") and Two Million Adherents by 1995.

1895   Church of God in Christ formed in USA; later become black Pentecostals.

1895   Fire-Baptized Holiness Church under B. H. Irwin teaches a third blessing, a separate "baptism with the Holy Ghost and fire" subsequent to conversion and sanctification; but unconnected with glossolalia or charismata.

1897   Encyclical letter "On the Holy Spirit" issued by Pope Leo XIII, directing attention to the sevenfold gifts of the Spirit (Isaiah 11:2) and promoting universal novena (9-day cycle of prayer) to Holy Spirit before Pentecost Sunday each year; millions influenced.

1899   By end of century, most of the world's 960,000 pentecostals/charismatics are found in black Africa, mostly in independent churches in South Africa or West Africa; rejected by mainline Catholic and Protestant missions and denominations as, at best, unaffiliated semi-pagan crypto-Christians; or as, at worst, separatist, syncretistic, heretical, fanatical schismatics.

1899   Iconographic renewal of the 20th century: Orthodox icons as liturgical art expressing christological truth.

The Spirit Empowers the Pentecostal Renewal

1900   Great worldwide outpouring of the Holy Spirit begins.

1900   In England, J. H. Smyth-Pigott, moved by the death of H. J.Prince, final messenger of the Holy Ghost, announces himself as Christ returned.

1900   Origins of Pentecostalism in USA: British-Israelite holiness preacher Charles F. Parham (1873-1929, Methodist) opens Bethel Bible School near Topeka, Kansas, with 40 students; 1901, they receive baptism of Holy Spirit; 1903 revival spreads through Kansas, 1905 Houston, 1906 to Los Angeles and thence across world (1906 Norway, 1907 Chile, 1908 China, 1909 Korea, 1910 Brazil, and so on).

1901   Latter-rain teaching: after 1,800 years of apparent cessation of large-scale charismata and 100 years of expectancy and teaching in USA on gifts of the Spirit, "restoration of all things" begins with Spirit-baptism and glossolalia, as pentecostal power is restored to the church; thousands of seekers travel to revival centers in USA, Europe, Asia, South America; expounded upon in D. W. Myland, *The Latter Rain Pentecost* (1910).

1904   Welsh revival through ministry of Evan Roberts (1878–1951) in Glamorganshire, Anglesey, Caernavonshire, with 100,000 converts in Wales in 6 months; short-lived (1904–6), but literally sweeps the world; worldwide publicity from the press; leads into worldwide Pentecostal movement including 1905 Switzerland and Germany, 1907 England.

1905   India: Pentecostal revival in Mukti Mission, Poona, under Anglican teacher Pandita Ramabai (1858–1922).

1906   C. F. Parham teaches that missionaries need only to receive the baptism with the Holy Ghost and can then, through the gift of glossolalia, be immediately understood in native languages to the farthest corners of the world; but Pentecostal missionaries abroad try this only to report failure.

1906   First recorded pentecostal meeting in continental Europe; Methodist prophet T. B. Barratt (1862–1940), a Cornishman, preaches to 1,000 in Christiana (Oslo); by 1910 Italy honeycombed with Pentecostal churches; Russian Empire reached 1911 in Helsinki, 1914 St. Petersburg, 1915 Moscow.

1906   Evolution of concepts of fivefold and fourfold full gospel theology: 1906, Azusa Street mission propagates as normal steps or stages in a

Christian's life these five steps: (1) his/her Salvation (Conversion), (2) his/her Entire Sanctification (Wesleyan holiness pattern), (3) his/her Baptism in the Holy Spirit with initial evidence of speaking in tongues, (4) his/her involvement in Divine Healing, and (5) his/her awaiting of Premillennial Second Coming of Christ; 1914 Assemblies of God formed reducing this to fourfold (foursquare) gospel on grounds that the finished work of Christ on the cross covers steps (1) and (2) and combines them into one single step; 1914, rise of the one-ness movement teaching that everything in steps 1 to 4 including tongues comes at the one first stage of Water Baptism in the Name of Jesus.

1906   USA: Pentecostalism achieves nationwide publicity under black holi-ness preacher W. J. Seymour (1870–1922) with revival in Azusa Street, Los Angeles, which lasts from 1906 to 1909; thousands of seekers travel from Europe to seek their personal pentecost with glossolalia; 1906–8, whole pentecostal movement in USA teaches three-stage way of salvation.

1907   First pentecostal movement within Church of England, at parish in Sunderland under clergyman A. A. Boddy (1854–1930).

1907   Massive revival in Korea beginning in Pyongyang; Protestants mush-room by 1914 to 196,389 (73 percent Presbyterians, 27 percent Methodists); phenomenal growth of churches, spreading also into Manchuria and China.

1907   USA: first major sweep of pentecostalism traverses southern holiness movement; in month-long meeting in Dunn, North Carolina ("Azusa Street East"), hundreds receive tongues-attested baptism in the Spirit; several holiness denominations become pentecostalized.

1908   Manchurian Revival, at Changte under Jonathan Goforth (1859–1936).

1908   USA: first schisms as black Pentecostals split from other black Pente-costals, withdrawing or being expelled from black-dominated Apos-tolic Faith Mission (Azusa Street); whites then develop two-stage way of salvation, and in 1914 form Assemblies of God.

1909   "Berlin Declaration" by German Evangelicals rejects Pentecostal claims of restoration of charismata, condemns all pentecostalism as a diabolic manifestation; as a result, Pentecostalism spreads only slowly in German-speaking nations.

1909   Pentecostal movement organized in Chile; USA Methodist missionary W. C. Hoover and 37 charismatics are excommunicated, form Iglesia Methodista Pentecostal.

1909   First charismatic prayer groups form within mainline state churches of Europe: German Pentecostal leader J. A. A. B. Paul (1853–1931) re-mains a Lutheran minister until his death.

1914   Uganda: mass revival, Society of the One Almighty God (KOAB), or Malakite Church, secedes ex-CMS with 91,740 Ganda adherents by 1921.

1915   Anti-Trinitarian or "Jesus only" doctrine introduced into USA Pentecostalism by F. J. Ewart.

1915   Elim Foursquare Gospel Alliance and Revival Party begun in Britain by Pentecostal healer G. Jeffreys (1889–1962); 1935, founds World Revival Crusade.

1917   Apparition of Virgin Mary at Fatima, Portugal, bringing about religious renewal reinforcing conservatism of Portuguese Catholicism; "3rd prophecy of Fatima" never published by Vatican but held to predict global holocaust and annihilation of church.

1917   True Jesus Church (Chen Ye-Su Chiao Hui) begun in Peking, a charismatic schism ex–apostolic faith movement; by 1975, a Chinese world mission with missionaries serving in Hong Kong, India, Indonesia, Japan, Korea, Malaysia, Singapore and USA.

1918   Fundamentalism/modernism controversy erupts within USA Protestantism, until 1931, splitting every major denomination; premillennialism now a major part of all revivalist preaching.

1918   Worldwide Evangelism, a vision of Pentecostal evangelist Aimee S. McPherson (1890–1944), who then in 1922 broadcasts first radio sermon, and in 1923 founds Angelus Temple, Los Angeles, and the International Church of the Foursquare Gospel.

1920   USA: term "fundamentalist" coined to mean a militant or angry conservative evangelical; mostly dispensationalist-premillennialist; after 1925, fundamentalists have difficulty gaining national attention; 1930 fundamentalism loses its initial national prominence within mainline Protestant churches and begins to fragment into small denominations; by 1960s term means ecclesiastical separatists; now almost all are separate Baptist dispensationalists; term excludes holiness and Pentecostals.

1921   General Council of the Assemblies of God USA appoints committee on worldwide cooperation for "the calling of a conference for the formation of an ecumenical union of Pentecostal believers for the more perfect and rapid evangelization of the world"; committee proves unable to meet and the effort collapses by 1923.

1921   International Pentecostal Conference convened in Amsterdam in spite of opposition.

1921   Origins of global electronic church: first broadcast of a church worship service (Calvary Episcopal Church, Pittsburgh, USA), first Baptist broadcast, 1922 first Pentecostal broadcast (Aimee S. McPherson); by 1988, regular listeners/viewers of Christian programs number 1.2 billion (24 percent of the world).

1921   Oxford Group formed in Britain (1921–38), later renamed Moral Re-Armament (MRA); as evangelical renewal centering on personal devotion to Christ, the 4 Absolutes, personal evangelism, and "drawing-room evangelism," spreads rapidly through major denominations and across world; by 1950 no longer solely Christocentric, embracing renewal among Buddhists, Hindus, et al.

1921   Simon Kimbangu (1889–1951) preaches leading to charismatic revival in Lower Congo, resulting in mass conversions, persecutions, jailings, deportations, and by 1960 a massive indigenous church (EJCSK); by A.D. 2000, has 9 million members baptized in Holy Spirit.

1922   USSR: Pentecostalism introduced by I. E. Voronaev (1892–1943), who aids growth in a few months to 20,000 in Ukraine alone; founds 350 congregations by 1929; 1932 imprisoned, 1943 shot in Leningrad.

1923   After Pentecostal evangelist Aimee Semple McPherson (1890–1944) broadcasts first radio sermon in 1922, she magnetizes millions in her 5,000-seat Angelus Temple, Los Angeles, from 1923 to 1944; founds International Church of the Foursquare Gospel and its missions.

1924   USA: white ministers all withdraw from interracial Pentecostal Assemblies of the World (oneness Pentecostals) to form a separate white denomination, explaining that "the mixture of races prevents the effective evangelization of the world"; becomes the Pentecostal Church, Incorporated.

1925   Era of large evangelistic healing campaigns in Europe and USA under first generation of Pentecostal evangelists, including Smith Wigglesworth (1859–1947) who preaches to large crowds in most of world's largest capitals.

The Spirit Empowers the Charismatic Renewal

1925   Spirit Movement (Aladura) in Nigeria; charismatic revivals within Anglican Church lead to major indigenous churches: Cherubim & Seraphim, Christ Apostolic Church, Church of the Lord (Aladura).

1927   China: rapid expansion continues of two charismatic indigenous groups: Watchman Nee's Little Flock, and Preaching Bands of John Sung (Song Shangje).

1927   East African revival movement (Balokole, Saved Ones) emerges in Ruanda, moves rapidly across Uganda, East Africa, Zaire, later to Sudan and Malawi, with cells in Europe and America; from 1931 to 1985, some 80 mass revival conventions are held across East Africa, including 1931 Gahini, 1936 Mukono (Uganda), 1937 Kabete (Kenya), 1939 Katoke Otanganyika), 1945 Kabale ("Jesus Satisfies"), 1949 Kabete (15,000 attenders), 1964 Mombasa (20,000), 1970 Thogoto (40,000), 1978 Tumutumu (45,000), 1979 Thogoto (50,000), and irregularly up to 1997 Mbarara (Uganda).

1927   Origins of latter rain revivals and return to primitive pentecostalism, in South Africa (Blourokkies) and (c. 1930) Germany.

1928   Pentecostalism formally rejected by World Fundamentalist Association as "fanatical and unscriptural"; 1944, rejected also by American Council of Christian Churches who label glossolalia as "one of the great signs of the apostasy."

1931   Charismatic renewal begins in Reformed churches of France; its theologian L. Dalliere (1897–1976) opens dialogue with Catholic and Orthodox churches, also with Jews.

1932   Charismatic revival ex–American Methodists in Southern Rhodesia, led by Johane Maranke, forms massive indigenous church: African Apostolic Church of Johane Maranke (AACJM), with 1,400,000 followers right across Tropical Africa.

1933   Germany: Catholic biblical renewal results in founding of Catholic Bible Association (Katholisches Bibelwerk, KBW), in Stuttgart; by 1980, members number over 30,000 catechists, teachers, priests, and scholars.

1933   Pentecostal preacher W. M. Branham (1909–65) offends mainline Pentecostal denominations by prophesying that 1906–77 is the Laodicean Church Age, followed immediately by mass apostasy, Second Advent of Christ, and the Millennium in 1977; Branhamites (followers) claim him as Last Prophet with messianic attributes.

1933   USSR: intensive forced collectivization and resultant famine kill 10 million kulaks and peasants, mainly Christians in the Ukraine; tens of millions of peasants brutally collectivized through police terror; Pentecostal-Zionists and other denominations virtually liquidated.

1934   Biblical Research Society publishes a seven-volume *Messianic Series* by D. L. Cooper, printing 6 million copies, distributed through 150 branches to Jews worldwide; "These books will remain behind after the Rapture and will be read during the Tribulation by the 144,000 Jewish evangelists of Revelation 7 who will then produce worldwide revival."

1935   World Revival Crusade founded by Pentecostal leader G. Jeffreys.

1936   Vision received by Korean Presbyterian youth Sun Myung Moon to begin Holy Spirit Association for Unification of World Christianity (T'ongil Kyohoe); 1954, begins Unification Church as indigenous church movement in Korea; by 1970, movement has become heterodox in its stance of superseding Christianity as the latter supersedes Judaism.

1937   Ethiopia: after expulsion of missionaries by Italian invaders, widespread revival erupts among Protestant (SIM) churches in the south.

The Spirit Empowers the Neo-Charismatic Renewal

1937   Although first third-wave manifestations erupted in 1656 and 1783, by 1937 large numbers of neo-charismatic churches are being started every year across the world.

1937   Japan's largest indigenous Christian church, Spirit of Jesus, formed as split from Assemblies of God.

1938   Anglican apologist C. S. Lewis (1898–1963) writes best-selling trilogy *Out of the Silent Planet* (Earth ostracized because its ruling spirit Satan has become evil; Mars a perfect planet without original sin), *Perelandra* (1943: Venus ripe for invasion by Satan), *That Hideous Strength* (1947: Satan manipulates scientists to create dystopia on Earth).

1939   European Pentecostal Conference organized at Stockholm (Sweden), result of Donald Gee as prime mover: first attempt to gather representatives of all varieties of European Pentecostalism to discuss doctrinal and theological issues; Scandinavians prove to be vehemently opposed to any and all denominational or centralized organization.

1939   USA: *Old Fashioned Revival Hour* under C. E. Fuller broadcasts over 152 radio stations to 12 million listeners a week, rising to 20 million by 1960; renamed *The Joyful Sound.*

1941   Extensive mass revival in Orthodox churches in German-occupied USSR.

1942   USA: National Association of Evangelicals (NAE) organized; invites several Pentecostal denominations to become affiliated for its 1943 convention.

1943   Timor: intense adventist spirit movement while under repressive Japanese occupation; mainly around Nunkolo in Atoni territory with leading prophetess Juliana Mnao; 1965, a similar resurgence.

1944   USA: Assemblies of God begin *Sermons in Song* radio broadcast, in 1954 renamed *Revivaltime* on over 600 radio stations in USA and 100 more across world.

1945   United Penecostal Church International begun in USA; by 1985, Foreign Missions Division has 212 foreign missionaries in 50 countries.

1947   1st Pentecostal World Conference, Zurich, Switzerland; 250 leaders present, from 23 countries; first attempt to found an ongoing World Pentecostal Fellowship fails (May).

1947   Nagaland, India: two major revival movements erupt: (1) from 1947 to 1952, and (2) from 1976 for over 20 years; hostility and military persecution result.

1947   Oral Roberts Evangelistic Association founded (Tulsa, Okla., USA), with own foreign missions program; 1953, begins Pentecostal television preaching; becomes massive ministry with worldwide healing crusades. Oral Roberts University, City of Faith, Charismatic Bible Ministries.

1947   Pope Pius XII declares in Rome: "Today the spirit of evil has been unchained."

1947   World Revival Prayer League (National Christian Women's Prayer League) founded, based on Tokyo, Japan.

1948   Latter rain revival (New Order of the Latter Rain) erupts among classical Pentecostals in Saskatchewan, Canada, spreads rapidly to Europe, USA, and across world; emphasis on laying on of hands with prophecy, government by order of living apostles; begins Global Missions Boardcast; from 1965, merges into Charismatic Movement.

1949   2nd Pentecostal World Conference, Paris; plan to form an ongoing World Pentecostal Fellowship thwarted by Scandinavian Pentecostals.

1949   Cursillos de Cristianidad (short courses) movement begun in Spain by RC bishop J. Hervas; short three-day retreats to renew personal faith of Catholics; 1950s spreads to Latin America, then to USA, 1961 Britain, then globally; many leaders later become first Catholic charismatics.

1950   Full Gospel Business Men's Fellowship International (FGBMFI) founded in USA as an end-time ministry by dairy magnate D. Shakarian after a vision of the people of every continent; preachers and women excluded; grows rapidly by 1970 to 300,000 members in 700 chapters worldwide, and by 1986 to 700,000 regular attenders worldwide in 3,000 chapters (1,715 in USA) in 95 countries including USSR, Czechoslovakia, Saudi Arabia, and other closed countries.

1952   3rd Pentecostal World Conference, in London, on theme "Into All the World."

1952   Worldwide Revival Movement inaugurated in Ireland by W. E. Allen and Revival Publishing Company (Lisburn) to promote theme "Revival Is the Key to World Evangelization."

1953   India: massive growth of Pentecostalism evident, especially in south India.

1953   USA: Southern Baptists implement first nationwide simultaneous revival or evangelistic campaign, with 361,835 baptisms reported during the year.

1954   Argentina: USA Pentecostal evangelist Tommy Hicks travels uninvited to Buenos Aires; without advertising or outside finance, with free government radio and press coverage, conducts biggest single evangelistic crusade ever; in 52 days, audiences exceed 2 million (over 200,000 at final service); 1956, Oswald Smith campaign (25,000 attenders); 1962, Billy Graham crusades in three cities.

1955   4th Pentecostal World Conference, in Stockholm, Sweden, on "The Calling and Commission of the Pentecostal Movement: a Re-evaluation."

1955   Pentecostalism spreads rapidly throughout Europe's Gypsy population, especially in France, Italy, Spain, Portugal.

1955   Radio IBRA (Swedish Pentecostal) begins in Tangier in twenty languages.

1956   Catholic Bishop L. J. Suenens publishes *The Gospel to Every Creature*; considerable influence on Vatican Council II, becomes leading advocate of Catholic Charismatics.

1956   Christian Pentecostal Fellowship of Nigeria (CPFN) inaugurated;
        1987, holds first convention, uniting Christ Apostolic Church (CAC),
        the Apostolic Church (TAC), becomes major power bloc in Nigeria's
        CAN; 1990, 2nd Convention, in Ibadan, joined also by Saviour Apos-
        tolic Church (SAC).

1956   USA: charismatic (new-pentecostal) renewal begins among Episcopal
        and Protestant churches, first being at Trinity Episcopal Church,
        Wheaton, Illinois; rapidly increases to 10 percent of all clergy and 1
        million laity by 1970, and to 1.6 million active Spirit-baptized charis-
        matics by 1980; over these decades, vast new proliferation of "signs,
        wonders, and healings" arises worldwide accompanying expansion
        of charismatic movement.

1957   Nights of Prayer for World-Wide Revival (NPWR) launched in Lon-
        don by Anglican layman and CMS missionary to India, G. S. Ingram
        (c. 1881–1969); continues till his death.

1958   5th Pentecostal World Conference, in Toronto, Canada, on theme "The
        Purpose of God in the Pentecostal Movement for This Hour."

1958   Brazil: neo-pentecostal (charismatic) renewal termed Renovation be-
        gins among Baptist pastors.

1958   Latin America: Renovation charismatic movement spreads to several
        other major Protestant denominations; major clashes, leading to
        schisms.

1960   P. J. Farmer's novel *Flesh projects revival of ancient vegetation religions in
        the far future*; religion now interpreted as earliest form of science fiction.

1960   USA: charismatic renewal spreads in Episcopal Church under parish
        priest D. Bennett.

1960   World Missionary Assistance Plan (World MAP) founded (California,
        USA) as interdenominational, evangelical, charismatic service agency;
        inaugurates Leadership Spiritual Renewal Seminars "to create spiri-
        tual renewal among all the world's church leadership to bring change
        within all nations, hence worldwide evangelization, to be completed
        by the year 2000"; by 1987, claims 60 percent of that goal has been
        completed.

1960   Youth with a Mission (YWAM) begins as evangelical-charismatic
        sending agency, expanding as outgrowth of the Jesus movement in
        USA; at first, little church consciousness; 1977, outfits 10,000-ton evan-
        gelistic ship m.v. *Anastasis* for discipleship and mercy ministries; by
        1983, the world's largest evangelistic agency with 14,000 short-term
        young people sent overseas each year, in 56 countries; by 1987, 50,000;
        goal to field 100,000 a year by A.D. 2000.

1961   6th Pentecostal World Conference, in Jerusalem, on theme "Pentecost
        in Jerusalem—Then and Now."

1961   World Evangelism founded in USA by Pentecostal evangelist Morris
        Cerullo; 1967, World Evangelism Society of Great Britain.

Charismatic Renewal Expands in Anglicanism

1961   Kenya: charismatic movement Maria Legio of Africa splits from Catholic diocese of Kisii with 90,000 adherents (by 1980, 248,000 in 9 dioceses); largest secession to date from Roman Catholic Church in Africa.

1962   Charismatic renewal in Church of England recommences (after 1907 beginning had lapsed); rapid growth of Anglican charismatics to 1.7 million in 30 countries by 1985, and to 14 million by A.D. 2000.

1964   7th Pentecostal World Conference, Helsinki, Finland, on the theme "World Evangelism" (June).

1964   Germany: neo-pentecostal revival sparked in German Protestant churches in tour by USA Lutheran charismatic L. Christenson.

1965   Indonesia: Communist party (17 million members) prepares plan to massacre millions of Christians and missionaries, thwarted by army, 500,000 communists and sympathizers massacred; mass revivals begin, producing 2.5 million Protestant and Catholic converts within 15 months.

1965   Timor: spirit movement among the Atoni around Amanuban during major famine; more than 100 evangelistic teams of youths and women.

1966   Anglican theologian A. H. Dammers publishes A.D. 1980: a study in Christian unity: mission and renewal, envisaging organic union of all churches in Britain by 1980, but scarcely any progress happens, even by A.D. 2000.

1966   European Pentecostal Fellowship formed, in Rome; 1969 Pentecostal European Conference formed, in Sweden; 1987, EPF and PEC amalgamate as Pentecostal European Fellowship (PEF); 1978 also European Pentecostal Theological Association (EPTA); 1980 Pentecostal and Charismatic Research in Europe conferences held (Leuven 1980, 1981; Birmingham, UK, 1984; Gwatt, Switzerland 1987).

1966   USA: denominational charismatic bodies emerge: 1967, Consultation on Charismatic Renewal, first national meeting, Presbyterian and Reformed Renewal Ministries (PRRM), in Austin, Texas; followed in next 11 years by RC, Lutheran, Episcopal, American Baptist, Mennonite, Greek Orthodox, United Church of Christ, Methodist, and other bodies.

Charismatic Renewal Erupts in Catholicism

1966   National Cursillo Convention, Pittsburgh (USA): Duquesne students become interested in charismatic renewal, a year after Vatican II closes with prayer for a new Pentecost.

1967   Catholic charismatic renewal in USA suddenly erupts, first at
        Duquesne University (run by Holy Ghost priests), Pittsburgh, USA,
        and also in Bogota, Colombia; spreads to Notre Dame University,
        South Bend (intellectual capital of American Catholicism); active
        Catholic charismatics increase by 1985 to 7.5 million in 80 countries,
        with 50 million Catholics related or involved, and to 120 million by
        A.D. 2000.

1967   8th Pentecostal World Conference, in Rio de Janeiro, Brazil, on theme
        "The Holy Spirit Glorifying Christ."

1967   Logos Ministry for Orthodox Renewal founded for Greek and other
        Orthodox charismatics.

1967   South Korea: massive evangelistic campaigns held: 1965, 17-denomi-
        nation 80th anniversary of Protestantism (20,000 professions of faith);
        1967, Crusade for World Revival (30,000 attenders a night), linked
        with organization CWR begun in 1965 in Britain; 1973, Seoul crusade
        (3,210,000 attenders, 275,000 enquirers); 1974, EXPLO 74 training con-
        ference on evangelism and discipleship (323,419 workers from 78
        countries); 1977 National Evangelization Crusade; 1978 Here's Life
        Korea; 1980, 16.5 million attend 4-day World Evangelization Crusade,
        in Seoul; et al.

1968   1st Ecumenical Pentecost Assembly (Kirchentag) in Augsburg (Ger-
        many); Catholics officially join Protestants at Pentecost for joint wor-
        ship; subsequently, Protestant Kirchentag becomes biennial (30
        percent of attenders being RCs) alternating with RC Katholikentag
        (liturgical, processions, vast numbers).

1968   Australia: first conference on "Rediscovering the Holy Spirit" con-
        vened in Sydney by evangelist Alan Walker (June); 1970, charismatic
        renewal breaks out.

1968   Pentecostal evangelist Jimmy L. Swaggart begins USA radio ministry
        Camp Meeting Hour, then in 1972 television ministry; by 1987, Jimmy
        Swaggart Ministries air telecasts over 3,200 TV stations in 145 coun-
        tries weekly, raising donations of $150 million a year, and claim "The
        medium of television is the most expedient method of spreading the
        gospel the world has ever known. It is God's directive that the Great
        Commission be carried out by this means"; 1988, partial collapse due
        to sex scandal.

1970   Global status: Pentecostals now number 15,382,000, charismatics
        3,349,000, neo-charismatics 53,490,000; total living members in re-
        newal 72,223,000; total renewal believers since A.D. 1900, 117,004,000.

1970   USA: rise of Jesus people in California as a nationwide youth revival.

1970   Society for Pentecostal Studies (SPS) formed to coordinate rapidly ex-
        panding research interest in charismata; founded in USA to hold an-
        nual meetings each with 10–30 professional papers read; 1982, 12th
        Annual Meeting, SPS, held in Pasadena, Calif., with 12 papers pre-
        sented (18–20 November); 1996, 25th Annual Meeting, SPS, held in
        Wycliffe College, Toronto (7–9 March).

1970 9th Pentecostal World Conference, Dallas, USA (November).

1971 Final Advance of Scripture Translation (FAST) launched with WBT/SIL cooperation as computerized closure version to finally complete remaining task of translating Bible into every language; main purpose to galvanize denominational Bible translating agencies (Baptist, Pentecostal, Catholic, et al.), but finally terminates in 1983 despite over 5,000 languages still remaining untranslated.

1971 2nd Ecumenical Pentecostal Meeting, Augsburg (Germany), for Catholics and Protestants, at Pentecost (2–5 June).

1972 International Catholic Charismatic Renewal Office (ICCRO) founded as International Communications Office in Ann Arbor (USA); first two International Leaders Conferences (1973, 1975) held there; 1976 office transferred to Brussels; 1981 relocates as ICCRO in Rome, organizes five worldwide leaders conferences (4 in Rome, 1 in Dublin), 1985 relocates in Vatican "moving to the heart of the Church, by 1988" representing 63.5 million Catholic Pentecostals in over 160 countries; 1993 name changed to ICCRS ("Services"), by 2000, 119 million Catholic charismatics in 230 countries.

1972 Origin of European Charismatic Leaders Conferences (Protestants/Pentecostals/ Catholics) at Schloss Craheim, Germany after initial visits by David du Plessis and Rodman Williams; further ECLC conferences in 1973, 1975, then in Belgium by invitation of Catholic primate, Cardinal L. J. Suenens in 1976, 1978; 1982 Strasbourg Conference with 25,000 participants; then ELCs in 1982 Paris, 1984 Zurich, 1986 Birmingham UK (Acts '86); 1988 ongoing European Charismatic Consultation formed; 1989 in Dissentis, Switzerland, 1990 Bern '90; 1991 ECC organized and meets annually.

1972 Sri Lanka: Morris Cerullo charismatic campaign (140,000 attenders, 80 percent being Buddhists).

1972 World Pentecost editor Donald Gee writes article "World Evangelisation"; widely quoted throughout Pentecostal movement.

1973 10th Pentecostal World Conference, Seoul, Korea: "Anointed to Preach"; 3,000 delegates.

1973 ECCLA-I Conference (Encuentro Charismatico Latino Americano), planned to become first of annual series sponsored by Catholic Charismatic Renewal (ICCRO).

1973 Pentecostal missions executive D. A. Womack writes *Breaking the Stained-Glass Barrier,* urging church "to abandon its sanctuaries of security and return to the evangelistic strategy of the apostle Paul (the Ephesian Method of spontaneous lay evangelism)"; proposes mathematical formula measuring evangelization.

1973 Trinity Broadcasting Network launched in southern California as Pentecostal television station "to get the gospel to every living human being on planet Earth" before Jesus comes; by 1986, TBN owns 55 TV stations in USA with 26 affiliates, also stations in Guatemala, St. Kitts-Nevis, Italy, Ciskei.

1974   Catholic Charismatic renewal now has 2,400 prayer groups across world with 350,000 active adult participants (total charismatic community 1,540,000); 30,000 attend USA international annual conferences at Notre Dame, South Bend.

1974   Mission Renewal Teams begun (by D. Bryant, B. Goheen; and Fuller Theological Seminary, Pasadena) as seminarian teams teaching local churches through book *Ten Steps for World Evangelization*; wound down by 1979.

1975   Ireland: 2nd National Conference on the Charismatic Renewal, held in Dublin, led by Cardinal L. J. Suenens, 190 priests and 5,000 lay charismatics; at Dublin's 1978 International Conference, Suenens concelebrates on TV with 17 bishops and 1,500 priests in the presence of 20,000 laity.

1975   New Life International begun as evangelical charismatic service agency involved in TEE, literature, research; 1984, renamed Total World Evangelization Vision (Fresno, California), in 8 countries.

1975   ECCLA III: 3rd Latin American Catholic Charismatic Renewal Leaders Conference; 250 delegates from 25 countries, including 8 bishops; in Aguas Buenas, Puerto Rico (where Catholic Pentecostals number 40,000) (January).

1975   ALL Nagaland Congress on World Evangelization, in Dimapur (North East India), following Lausanne I Congress, to study revival and missions (1–9 March).

1975   International Catholic Charismatic Conference in Rome at Feast of Pentecost: 10,000 pilgrims addressed by Pope Paul VI in St. Peter's Basilica (May).

1975   Nairobi International Conference for Renewal, on "Unity in Christ"; first of series of interdenominational African conferences for charismatics (August).

1976   Full Gospel World Mission Association established (1 April) in Seoul, Korea, as sending body supporting 8 overseas churches and 22 Korean missionaries; by 1985, 143 missionaries in 21 countries.

1976   11th Pentecostal World Conference, Albert Hall, London: "The Spirit of Truth."

1976   Lausanne Intercession Advisory Group formed after ICOWE I; organizes conferences, annual day of prayer for world evangelization (Pentecost Sunday).

1977   First National Southern Baptist Charismatic Confrence (21–23 July), held in USA.

1977   Greece: Orthodox charismatics organize Crusade for Christ in Athens.

1977   ECCLA V, 5th Latin American Catholic Charismatic Renewal Leaders Conference, in Caracas, Venezuela; leaders from almost all Latin American countries (January).

1977   1st Conference on the Charismatic Renewal in the Christian Churches; ecumenical, at last embracing all pentecostal traditions; on theme "Jesus Is Lord"; in Kansas City, USA; 59,000 present (July); but after this ecumenical climax, charismatic conferences revert to monodenominational or monoconfessional status (15,000 Lutheran charismatics each year in Minneapolis, 10,000 RCs in Notre Dame, et al.).

1977   500 million hear or see one-hour radio/TV gospel service broadcast from Jerusalem on Christmas Eve in seven languages simultaneously (Pentecostal preacher Rex Humbard).

1978   4th Latin American Protestant Conference (CELA-IV), held at Oaxtepec (Mexico); decision to create ecumenical council CLAI (Latin American Council of Churches) with 100 denominations and agencies (some pentecostal); Conservative Evangelical opponents organize rival CONELA (Latin American Evangelical Confederation), claiming 20 million Evangelicals in 84 founding denominations (including Evangelical Council of Venezuela, CEV), mainly AG (Brazil).

1978   International Conference on the Charismatic Renewal in the Catholic Church, in Dublin: "You shall be My Witnesses"; 10,000 participants, led by L. J. Suenens cardinal primate of Belgium (June).

1979   Anglican renewal agency SOMA (Sharing of Ministries Abroad) founded, "dedicated to fostering Renewal in the Holy Spirit world wide so as to enable and equip the Church to fulfill the Great Commission of Jesus Christ, to proclaim the Kingdom of God and minister in the power of the Holy Spirit"; holds international conferences 1981 Singapore, 1983 Nairobi, 1984 Fiji; by 1987, its work in 50 countries covers 26 of the 31 Anglican provinces worldwide.

New Forms of Renewal Multiply Worldwide

1979   England: Alpha Course, an Anglican outreach introduction to Christianity, is begun at Holy Trinity Church Brompton; 1990, 100 participants regularly for 15-session home meetings; 1993, transformed into a powerful medium for evangelism; 1994, Youth Alpha introduced for 11- to 18-year-olds; 1998, mushrooms worldwide into 10,000 11-week Alpha courses running in 77 countries and in most cities across world, operated by Protestant/Catholic/Anglican churches from several hundred denominations; participants rise from 600 in 1991, to 4,500 in 1993, 30,000 (1994), 100,000 (1995), 250,000 (1996), 500,000 (1997), then to 1 million (1999).

1979   Over 10,000 pilgrims attend International Charismatic Pilgrimage to Lourdes on shrine's 100th anniversary (July).

1979   12th Pentecostal World Conference in Vancouver, Canada: "The Holy Spirit in the Last Days" (October).

1980   1st Asian Leaders Conference, Catholic Charismatic Renewal (ICCRO), on "Feed My Sheep," Manila.

1980   A large African indigenous charismatic church, World Evangelical Crusaders in Christ Ministries (Benin City, Nigeria), begins Operation World Begin From Here; other AIC denominations across Africa also advance similar global plans.

1980   Third wave of 20th-century renewal in the Holy Spirit begins in 40 major evangelical churches, emphasizing power evangelism, power encounters, power healing, et al.

1980   USA: new generation of charismatic TV evangelists arises, including Oral Roberts (who began Pentecostal TV preaching in 1953) and son Richard, Pat Robertson, Rex Humbard, Jimmy Swaggart, James Robison, Kenneth Copeland, Paul Crouch, Jim Bakker, et al.

1980   USA: "Washington for Jesus 1980" rally brings out 500,000 charismatics and evangelicals.

1981   8th World Council of YMCAs, in Estes Park, on theme "Christ: Renewal and Hope."

1981   International Leaders Conference, Catholic Charismatic Renewal (ICCRO) in Rome, addressed by Pope John Paul II (May).

1982   2nd Asian Leaders Conference, Catholic Charismatic Renewal (ICCRO), on "Evangelize Asia for Christ," Singapore.

1982   Institute for World Evangelism established in Atlanta, Georgia (USA), as major long-range achievement of World Evangelism Committee, World Methodist Council; its 1987 3rd biennial International Seminar, Atlanta, on theme "The Holy Spirit and World Evangelization" draws over 100 delegates from 33 countries; authentic Wesleyan evangelism, with twofold witness to personal salvation and social redemption, given a new credibility and acceptance in Methodism worldwide.

1982   1st Pan-European Charismatic Congress, "Pentecost over Europe," Strasbourg '82 (held at Pentecost); 25,000 attenders, 80 percent RCs and organized by RCs, scandal of Christian divisions discussed; 1998, 2nd Ecumenical Charismatic Meeting, in Paris with 12,000 participants.

1982   Asian Conference on Church Renewal, Seoul, Korea (18–22 August); results in inauguration at Hong Kong in July 1983 of Evangelical Fellowship of Asia (EFA) with 12 member bodies (8 being national fellowships).

1982   13th Pentecostal World Conference, Nairobi, Kenya; theme "Alive in the Spirit in Our World"; peak attenders 18,000 (September).

1983   Committee on the Holy Spirit & Frontier Missions (CHSFM) begun in conjunction with USCWM to involve charismatics in frontier missions among hidden peoples; defunct by 1985.

1983   SOMA Pan-African Conference (Sharing of Ministries Abroad) for Anglophone Charismatic Renewal Leaders, Nairobi, Kenya (October).

1984   Argentina: large-scale two-year revival originating with Assemblies of God evangelist Carlos Annacondia results in 2 million converts.

1984   Britain: major ecumenical venture "Not Strangers But Pilgrims" involving over 30 denominations including RCs, Anglicans, black Pentecostals, to formulate ecumenical policy for the future.

1984   5th International Leaders Conference, Catholic Charismatic Renewal, in Rome, attended by Pope John Paul II (May); also ICCRO Worldwide Priests Retreat, in Vatican attended by 6,000 priests and 80 bishops and cardinals (October); 1990, 2nd Worldwide Priests Retreat, in Rome (14–18 September).

1984   13th International Lutheran Conference on the Holy Spirit (ILCOHS), in Minneapolis; 12,000 participants (15–19 August).

1984   8th European Charismatic Leaders' Conference, Nidelbad, Switzerland (19 September).

1984   Mexico: 2nd National Youth Conference, Catholic Charismatic Renewal, with 18,000 young people, Guadalajara (November).

1985   Colombia: during International Year of Youth, Catholic Charismatic Renewal undertakes to proclaim Jesus to one-fifth of all Colombian youth; each RC diocese allocated large quotas as targets.

1985   R. Stark and W. S. Bainbridge write *The Future of Religion: Secularization, Revival and Cult Formation*.

1985   South Africa: Andrew Murray Consultation on Prayer for Revival and Mission Sending; 800 attenders in Cape Town and Pretoria.

1985   Third-wave/charismatic leader John Wimber writes *Power Evangelism: Signs and Wonders Today*, followed in 1987 by *Power Healing*, also in 1988 *Power Encounters Among Christians in the Western World*.

1985   USA: North American Full Gospel Missions Association formed to promote missions in charismatic churches; name then changed three times, finally to AIMS (Association of International Mission Services), with slogan "Unity in the Spirit for World Evangelization"; 75 member agencies.

1985   India: 6th National Convention of the Charismatic Renewal, with 15,000 attenders, bishops, 600 RC priests, 1,500 religious personnel, in Madras (January).

1985   Presbyterian Church (USA) sponsors Congress on Renewal (charismatic) in Dallas, Texas, with over 5,000 attenders (January).

1985   1st General Assembly, Evangelical Fellowship of Asia (EFA, formed 1983), in Manila (Philippines), on 'The Holy Spirit and the Church' (30 January–2 February).

1985   15th European Pentecostal Fellowship Conference, Naples, Italy (19–21 March).

1985   Italy: 8th National Charismatic Conference, in Rimini; 12,000 participants including several bishops, 500 priests (25–28 April).

1985   3rd Scandinavian Conference of Catholic Charismatic Renewal, Stockholm, with 150 delegates (16–19 May).

1985   11th Session, Roman Catholic/Classical Pentecostal theological dialogue (begun 1972), on topic "Communion of Saints"; at Riano, Rome (21–26 May); 1986, 12th Session, in USA (24–31 May).

1985   Charismatic Retreat for Priests (Polish Bishops Conference and ICCRO) in Czestochowa, Poland (June).

1985   9th Latin American Leaders Conference (ECCLA IX), Catholic Charismatic Renewal (ICCRO), for 200 leaders, Costa Rica (July).

1985   14th Pentecostal World Conference in Zurich, organized by World Conference of Pentecostal Churches; on "Jesus Christ—the Hope of the World"; 10,000 participants from 100 countries (2–7 July).

1985   Uganda: National Catholic Charismatic Leaders Conference, with 130 leaders (22–27 August).

1985   Anglican Renewal Leaders Consultation, sponsored by SOMA (Sharing of Ministries Abroad), in Chorleywood, UK, with 90 leaders (September).

1985   Britain: 5th National Charismatic Conference for clergy and Leaders (sponsored by Anglican Renewal Ministries), Swanwick (23–26 September).

1985   1st Pan-African Francophone Leaders Conference, Catholic Charismatic Renewal (ICCRO), on "A Holy People," with 100 headers, Kinshasa, Zaire (4–9 October).

1985   1st International Youth Leaders Consultation, Catholic Charismatic Renewal (ICCRO), held in Rome, with 500 participants from 100 countries (15–19 October).

1985   3rd Asian Leaders Conference, Catholic Charismatic Renewal (ICCRO), on "Discipleship in the Holy Spirit," with 100 leaders, Bangalore, India (9–12 November).

1986   LCWE/WEF Consultation on the Work of the Holy Spirit and Evangelization, in Oslo, Norway; more than 70 participants from 30 countries (May); results in published book *God the Evangelist*.

1986   Intercontinental Broadcasting Network (IBN) begun in Virginia Beach, USA, by independent charismatics linking up with European counterparts.

1986   Good News World (Operation World/Mass Scripture Distribution), a global plan announced by Southern Baptist Sunday School Board, Nashville, Tennessee, as: "Purpose: To place Scriptures in the hands of everyone in the world in 1994 to prepare for worldwide revival in 1995."

1986   Australia: Jubilee '86 United Charismatic Convention, in Adelaide; over 3,000 delegates, 10,000 attenders (7–11 January).

1986   Australia: 1st National Convention on the Holy Spirit (World

Methodist Council), in Sydney (February); followed by regional conferences, then 1987 2nd National Convention.

1986 Conference of Revival Evangelists for Inter-Africa (sponsored by CFAN, Christ for All Nations), Harare, Zimbabwe (April).

1986 1st Catholic FIRE Charismatic Evangelistic Rally, Providence, RI (relayed by satellite to 17 cities), on "I have come to cast fire on the Earth" (5 April).

1986 USA: International Conference for Equipping Evangelists (charismatic Pentecostal) in Sacramento, California, "training thousands of evangelists to equip millions of Christians to reach billions of unbelievers" (5–9 May).

1986 Scandinavian Oasis Conference (Oase; Lutheran Charismatic Renewal), based in Oslo, with 500 pastors and 10,000 others (July).

1986 2nd Pan-European Charismatic Congress—Acts '86 (European Festival of Faith), an all-Europe charismatic congress on Evangelism in the Power of the Holy Spirit,' in Birmingham (UK); 20,000 RC/Protestant/Anglican/Orthodox participants from East and West (100 from Eastern Europe), but without formal RC participation (23–27 July).

1986 14th International Lutheran Conference on the Holy Spirit (ILCOHS), Minneapolis; 12,000 attenders (5–8 August).

1986 USA: Aldersgate '86, 8th National Conference on the Holy Spirit (United Methodist, UMRSF), at Savannah, Georgia, on "Christ in You, the Hope of Glory" (7–10 August).

1986 3rd Chinese Congress on World Evangelization (CCOWE '86) sponsored by CCCOWE, held in Taipei (Taiwan), on theme "Renewal, Breakthrough and Growth"; 1,900 Chinese church leaders from over 20 countries (6–13 August); CCCOWE produces six-volume survey in Chinese (2 volumes in English) of whole Chinese diaspora across world.

1986 Korea: 10th Church Growth International Seminar (P. Y. Cho and Full Gospel Church) in Seoul and Osaka (Japan), with 3,000 attenders (September), bring total attenders since 1976 to 70,000 pastors and leaders from 30 countries; goal announced of winning 10 million Japanese to Christ by A.D. 2000.

1986 North American Leaders Congress on the Holy Spirit and World Evangelization (RC/Protestant charismatic renewal), New Orleans with over 7,500 pastors and leaders, also 4,000 other attenders (October); vast numbers of regional and denominational conferences and seminars proliferate.

1987 1st Africa's Deliverance Convention, Charismatics sponsored by Christian Missionary Foundation (CMF) begun in 1982 in Ibadan (Nigeria); then annually.

1987 Advance Ministries: Reaching the Unreached, a mission-sending agency serving the USA's 60,000 independent charismatic churches, begun with Mennonite support.

1987   Australia: 1st National Baptist Charismatic Conference held.

1987   Charismatic pastor D. Shibley writes *Let's Pray in the Harvest* on how to 'Discover the Missing Key to World Evangelization.'

1987   6th Annual All India Renewal Conference (charismatic), Kerala, with 300 church leaders and 2,000 attenders (27–30 January).

1987   Consultation on World Evangelization, Singapore, with 31 global charismatic renewal leaders (RC/Lutheran/SOMA-Anglican, et al.) (9–12 February).

1987   National Charismatic Leaders Conference (North American Renewal Service Committee, NARSC), related to global Charismatic Renewal in mainline denominations (100 million Christians, fielding 60,000 foreign missionaries), meets in Glencoe, Missouri (USA), appoints World Evangelization Strategy Committee with AD 2000 goal in mind (4–8 May).

1987   6th International Leaders Conference, Catholic Charismatic Renewal (ICCRO), Rome, on "The Spirit of the Lord is upon Me"; addressed by Pope John Paul II (11–16 May).

1987   Pentecost '87: National Satellite Celebration of Catholic Evangelization: one-day 7-hour USA-wide multimedia TV event (Pentecost Saturday, 6 June) by Paulist National Catholic Evangelization Association (PNCEA), training 60,000 lay, religious and clerical evangelizers in 200 auditoriums; to be repeated every Pentecost Saturday up to A.D. 2000.

1987   North American General Congress on the Holy Spirit and World Evangelization, in New Orleans (successor to 1977 Kansas City ecumenical charismatic rally); over 50,000 participants (RC/Protestant charismatic renewal), 51 percent RCs; theme "Power Evangelism" (22–26 July); launches magazine *AD 2000 Together* with front page motto "To Bring the Majority of the Human Race to Jesus Christ by the End of the Century."

1987   Pentecostal European Conference (PEC/PEK). Lisbon (22–26 July).

1987   Interdenominational Global Missions Conference (Dallas I) convened (17–18 September) by Southern Baptist FMB president R. K. Parks, with 20 mission agencies present; agreement on (1) prayer and fasting every Pentecost weekend up to A.D. 2000 as "focused intercession for global evangelization," and (2) sharing data, plans and strategies; 1988, Dallas II (February), followed by teleconferences.

1987   Ecuador: SOMA International Conference, Quito, on "Evangelism in the Power of the Holy Spirit in Latin America," for Anglican bishops, clergy, and lay leaders (8–11 October).

1987   1st Ibero-American Missions Congress (Congreso Misionero Ibero-Americano, COMIBAM '87), in Sao Paulo (Brazil), with 3,500 Evangelical representatives (70 percent pentecostal/charismatic) from across Latin America, and preceded by series of national missions consultations in 23 countries; goal of world evangelization, with 10,000 new Latin American foreign missionary vocations generated (23–28 November).

1988   Conferences on evangelization: since 145, some 5,510 conferences on mission and evangelism (at international, continental, regional or national level) have been held, via 5 groupings: 1,050 by Roman Catholic agencies; 1,100 by Ecumenical Movement agencies; 2,100 by Protestant and Anglican mission agencies; 840 by evangelical mission agencies; and 420 by charismatic renewal agencies.

1988   European Charismatic Leaders Conference, meeting in Berlin with 150 participants from 18 countries, organizes European Charismatic Consultation.

1988   Evangelist N. Krupp writes large volume *The Church Triumphant at the End of the Age*, characterized by revival, restoration, unity, world evangelization, and persecution; holds Great Commission will only be fulfilled by supernatural means of a global end-time revival.

1988   Evangelistic citywide mass campaigns: several hundred organized multidenominational campaigns (under Billy Graham, Luis Palau, et al.), and some 3,000 denominational campaigns, are held in 1,300 metropolises and cities across the world each year; also hundreds of mega-meetings (over 100,000 attenders) under Christ for All Nations and numerous other charismatic agencies, using slogan "The Great Commission to Each Generation."

1988   Explosive growth of charismatic, evangelical, and fundamentalist "video churches," video denominations and video mission agencies; vast rash of house church networks begins to spread in all countries where large denominations have grown up.

1988   '88 World Evangelization Crusade, Korea, led by charismatics (Methodists, Presbyterians) and Pentecostals.

1988   3rd International Conference on Russian Orthodox Liturgical Life and Art held in Leningrad; describes iconographic renewal, icons as windows on eternity (31 January–5 February).

1988   Singapore II Consultation on World Evangelization, with 65 global charismatic renewal leaders organized as CUWE, Charismatics United for World Evangelization with the new watchword "The whole church, bringing a whole Christ, to the whole world," "to consider the distinctive contribution that the charismatic renewal could make in spreading the Christian gospel in the years leading up to A.D. 2000" (February).

1988   2nd International Christian Zionist Congress, held in Jerusalem, sponsored by International Christian Embassy in Jerusalem (ICEF), European Charismatics (USA, Scandinavia, Holland, Germany, UK), and premillennial dispensationalists, the USA religious right, and Israeli government officials (April).

1988   Canterbury '88: Anglican Spiritual Renewal Conference, Canterbury
        (UK), organized by SOMA, for leaders of leaders on "The Church in
        the Valley of Decision"; 350 present including many bishops (3–7
        July).

1988   15th Pentecostal World Conference arranged to be held in Kuala
        Lumpur, Malaysia (5–9 October) but forced to cancel by Muslim
        opposition.

1989   Conference on Pentecostal and Charismatic Research in Europe, at
        Utretch University; reports published as *Experiences of the Spirit*.

1989   New religions arise based on psychobiological altered states of con-
        sciousness: ecstatic experiences, trance, dissociation, spirit possession,
        soul loss, astral projections, faith-healing, mysticism, glossolalia, oc-
        cult, shouting visions, out-of-body experiences, et al.

1989   3rd Gulf Churches Conference, held in Lamaca (Cyprus), with 50 rep-
        resentatives of 11 confessions: Anglican, United (CSI, CoPak),
        Lutheran, Coptic Orthodox, Syrian Orthodox, Pentecostal, Mar
        Thoma, Reformed/ Presbyterian, Roman Catholic (27 February–4
        March).

1989   Jerusalem Charismatic Leaders Meeting (Pentecost 89) convened for
        120 renewal leaders worldwide, dealing with power intercession,
        power evangelism, world evangelization; in Jerusalem over Pentecost
        weekend (7–14 May).

1989   15th Pentecostal World Conference finally opens in Singapore, on
        theme "Behold the Glory of the Lord"; over 6,000 delegates from 100
        countries, 30,000 attendees; emphasis on strategy for world evange-
        lization (27 September–1 October).

1989   Pakistan: 3rd Catholic Charismatic Conference held in Karachi with
        500 attendees, on theme "New Evangelization" (5–6 October).

1989   Northeast Asia Church Leaders Conference (NACLC-1), held in
        Hakone (Japan) with 50 attendees, on theme "Ministry in the Power
        of the Word of God"; 1991 NACLC-2 in Sorak (Korea) (28–31 Octo-
        ber); 1995 NACLC-3 in Kyoto (Japan) with 70 attendees, on "The
        Power of the Holy Spirit in Ministry"; 1997 NACLC-4.

1990   5th General Assembly, Middle East Council of Churches (MECC, now
        with 26 member churches and 14 million Christians including all 7
        Catholic bodies), held in Cyprus on theme "Keep the Unity of the
        Spirit in the Bond of Peace (Ephesians 4:3)."

1990   World Congress on the Holy Spirit and World Evangelization, in Indi-
        anapolis, on "Power Evangelism"; more than 25,000 attendees
        (Catholic/ Protestant charismatic renewal).

1990   13th National Convention of the Renewal in the Spirit, held in Rimini
        (Italy), with 50,000 Catholic attendees (28 April–1 May).

1990   3rd European Charismatic Consultation (ECC; ecumenical
        Catholic/Protestant megacongress) with theme "Jesus Hope for Eu-

rope," meets in Berne, Switzerland with 4,000 participants from 30 nations across Europe (2,000 from ex-Communist lands; 50 percent RCs; 50 percent under 35); "Praise March" across city releases 4,000 helium-filled balloons each with a participant's card attached (24–28 July).

Decade of Global Evangelization Begins

1991   Sudden growth and mushrooming worldwide of youth churches completely outside control by denominations: loosely organized churches begun and run by charismatic under-25s, meeting at lunch times in hotels, theaters, cinemas, shops, warehouses, anywhere; huge growth of converts.

1991   24th German Protestant Church Congress (Kirchentag), held in four cities in Ruhr (Dortmund, Essen, Bochum, Gelsenkirchen), with 125,000 attendees (10,000 from former East Germany), on theme "God's Spirit Liberates for Life" (5–9 June).

1991   International Charismatic Consultation for World Evangelization (ICCOWE), in Brighton (UK), to usher in decade of evangelization before A.D. 2000; 4,000 renewal leaders (8–14 July).

1992   2nd Pan-African Catholic Charismatic Renewal Conference in Brazzaville, Congo.

1992   17th Session, International Roman Catholic-Pentecostal Dialogue meets outside Rome, with theme "Evangelism and Culture."

1992   Launching of Charismatic Fellowship of Asia (CFA), and Asia Charismatic Theological Association (ACTA).

1992   Symposium on Oneness Pentecostalism (sponsored by United Pentecostal Church International, UPCI), held in St. Louis, Missouri (USA) (8–10 January).

1992   1st Latin American Encounter for Pentecostal Women, held in Costa Rica (11–14 August).

1992   16th Triennial Pentecostal World Conference convenes in Oslo, becomes largest religious meeting in Norway's history with 12,500 in evening services; theme "By My Spirit/Hope for a Changing World" (9–13 October).

1992   Encuentro Pentecostal Latinoamericano, held in Brazil, sponsored by WCC and CLAI (22–28 November).

1993   Asia Charismatic Theological Association (ACTA) meets in Singapore (12–14 April).

1993   ICCRO International Leaders Retreat (Catholic Charismatic Renewal) at Assisi, Italy, with 1,200 retreatants (13–17 September).

1994   3rd Annual Conference, Association of Pentecostal and Charismatic Bible Colleges of Australia (PCBC.).

1994   Final decade of 20th century proves to be greatest decade in Christian history for signs and wonders, miracles, conversions, evangelism, and evangelization: greatest sign or wonder being Christians loving one another and gathering in unity everywhere.

1994   Lebanon: large Catholic Charismatic Renewal Conference (and a second in 1995) attracting 30,000 attendees with live TV coverage watched by over a million viewers.

1994   Toronto Holy Laughter Revival: 250,000 pastors and other visitors from across world (i.e., party of 116 from Indonesia) visit Airport Vineyard Church to experience Holy Spirit phenomena; spreads to more than 10,000 churches in 50 countries within the year; large volume of information reported on global Internet.

1994   World Holy Spirit Conference in Seoul (Korea) with 30,000 attendees in 6 meetings.

1994   Malaysia '94 Charismatic Consultation, sponsored by ICCOWE at Port Dickson, Kuala Lumpur; 200 leaders of charismatic groups; on theme "Cooperation at a Time of Unparalleled Opportunity," call to Christian unity emphasized (March).

1994   European Pentecostal Theological Association (EPTA) meets in Portugal (26–30 July).

1994   Asian Pentecostal Theological Association (APTA) meets in Seoul (Korea) (September).

1994   "Memphis Miracle" in Memphis, Tennessee, witnessed by 4,000 attendees finally reconciling USA white Pentecostals (classical, in Pentecostal Fellowship of North America) with black Pentecostals (Church of God in Christ) after 100 years' estrangement, to form multiracial Pentecostal/Charismatic Churches of North America (PCCNA) (September).

1994   General Congress, Charismatic Fellowship of Asia (CFA) held in Manila (Philippines) (16–19 November), preceded by Asia Charismatic Theological Association (ACTA).

1994   XVIIth Annual Conference, Italian Charismatic Consultation (RC/Pentecostal/ Waldensian/Baptist) (9–11 December).

1995   4th Pan-European Charismatic Congress '95 (triennial), held in Vienna (Austria), discusses three difficult subjects: Toronto Blessing, Working Together, Church Planting/Community Building; 400 attendees.

1995   Revival erupts in an Assemblies of God church in Brownsville (Pensacola, Florida): in two years, 1,500,000 visitors attend services, with 100,000 professions of salvation.

1995   Orlando '95 Congress on the Holy Spirit and World Evangelization, held in Orlando, Florida, with more than 10,000 present (4,000 young persons), on theme "From Generation to Generation You Will Be My Witnesses" (26–29 July).

1995 17th Pentecostal World Conference (PWC) held in Jerusalem on theme "From Jerusalem . . . to All Peoples" (11–14 September); 10,000 attendees from 100 countries.

1995 1st General Assembly, Catholic Charismatic Council for Asia-Pacific (CCCAP), held in Sabah (Malaysia) with 63 delegates from 9 nations, on theme "We are God's Coworkers" (18–22 November); 1996, 1st Asia-Pacific Charismatic Leaders Congress, held at Kinasih (Indonesia) (7–12 October).

1995 European Charismatic Consultation, held in Prague with 400 participants (15–23 October).

1996 3rd Anglophone Africa Consultative Meeting, Catholic Charismatic Renewal, held in Johannesburg (South Africa).

1996 Biannual Meeting of National Service Committees of Europe (Catholic Charismatic Renewal), held in Bratislava (Slovakia), report declining numbers and aging membership in weekly prayer groups.

1996 XIXth Annual National Conference of the Italian Catholic Charismatic Renewal in the Holy Spirit, on *"iano uno, perche il mondo creda* (John 17:21)," in Rimini (Italy) with 65,000 attendees including 4 cardinals, ICCOWE and ECC executive committees, and 100 ecumenical guests; calls for Catholic/ Pentecostal reconciliation (25–28 April).

1996 7th Annual Koine-Research International, held in Feria di Roma (Rome fairgrounds) on "The Actuality of Sacred Space," a trade show majoring on physical, tangible implementation of Vatican II/renewal changes, for ecclesiologists, liturgists, church historians, architects, Vatican appointees, engineers, clergy, publishers, 600 retailers (8–11 June).

1996 3rd Pan-African Catholic Charismatic Renewal Conference held in Yamoussoukro (Ivory Coast) on theme "Evangelizing in the Power of the Holy Spirit: Go and Proclaim, Cast Out and Heal" (3–13 August).

1996 Ecumenical Charismatic Young Leaders Conference (ECC) in Berlin (6–8 September).

1996 17th National Catholic Charismatic Conference of Ecuador, held in Azogues with 300 leaders and 8,000 attendees, on theme "Towards the XXI Century" (October).

1996 7th International Meeting, Catholic Fraternity of Charismatic Covenant Communities and Fellowships (CFCCCF) held in Rome with 285 delegates from 40 communities, on theme "Prepare the Way of the Lord" (5–12 November).

1997 10th Meeting, Pentecostal European Conference (PEK) held in Frydek-Mistek (Czech Republic) with 3,000 attendees; 11th Meeting, A.D. 2000.

1997 International Consultation on Evangelism, Social Concern and Renewal in the Spirit, sponsored by ICCOWE.

1997   13th Assembly, Mennonite World Conference (MWC, representing 1 million Mennonites), held in Calcutta (India) on theme "Hear What the Spirit is Saying to the Churches" (January); meets as "Assembly Gathered" in Calcutta and "Assembly Scattered" in sites across India and Bangladesh, with 3,800 attendees.

1997   March for Jesus, held in Trinidad, organized by Catholic Charismatic Renewal, with 50,000 participants from Trinidad, St. Lucia, Dominica, Grenada, Guyana (5 January).

1997   Panama: 18th Catholic Charismatic Renewal Youth Meeting, in Llano Bonito, with 6,000 youths attending (20–23 January); preceded by CCR Priests Retreat, with 200 priests and 7 bishops from 15 countries.

1997   3rd Annual Conference on Pentecostal / Charismatic Care & Counseling, held in Atlanta (USA), on "The Family: Mending the Broken Circle" (27 February–2 March).

1997   46th Annual Eucharistic Congress, held in Wroclaw (Poland), with Pentecostal observers invited (May).

1997   10-yearly East African Revival Convention (in a tradition going back to 1927), with many thousands, held in Mbarara (Uganda), supported by Anglican and other leading churches (September).

1997   ICCOWE/ECC (European Charismatic Consultation) Prague '97 Consultation (Czech Republic), on "Building Bridges Breaking Barriers," with 340 attendees from 35 countries (10–14 September).

1997   At Prague 97, Theologians' Forum is sponsored by ICCOWE/ECC (European Charismatic Consultation)/EPCRA (European Pentecostal and Charismatic Research Association), with 55 Pentecostal/Charismatic theologians present (10-14 September).

1997   16th Annual Church Growth International Conference, in Seoul (Korea) at Yoido Full Gospel Church, with 100,000 intercessors present, on theme "The Son Is Rising" (30 September–9 October).

1998   22nd National Conference of RnS (Rinnovamento nello Spirito, CCR), held in Rimni, Italy, with 40,000 attendees under the theme "Guided by the Holy Spirit Towards the Jubilee of the Year 2000."

1998   Two Anglican charismatic conferences sponsored by SOMA and ARM, held in Canterbury to overlap 13th Lambeth Conference of Bishops: (1) Open Conference, with 754 attendees from 50 countries, on theme "The Church for the Healing of the Nation," in 20 seminars; and (2) Leaders Retreat, with 485 from 51 countries (96 bishops, 40 bishop's wives, 170 clergy, 179 lay leaders).

1998   France: 2nd Ecumenical Charismatic Meeting (after 1st in 1982), held in Charlety Stadium, Paris with 12,000 participants, organized by Fraternite Pentecote and the French Ecumenical Charismatic Consultation (Catholics, Orthodox, Protestants, ecumenical leaders).

1998   2nd Philippines National Catholic Charismatic Congress on the Holy Spirit, held in Manila with 300,000 attendees including 40 archbishops and bishops, 195 priests, 30 brothers and seminarians, 247 religious sisters and 3,883 lay leaders on theme "Holy Spirit, Renew the Face of the Earth!" (22–25 January).

1998   4th Annual Conference on Pentecostal / Charismatic Care & Counseling, held in Virginia Beach (USA) (26 February–1 March).

1998   Nordic Pentecostal Missions Conference (sponsored by Finnish Free Foreign Missions), held in Finland to mobilize for reaching unreached peoples (26–29 March).

1998   Haiti: 6th National Conference of Catholic Charismatic Renewal (begun 1973), held in Port-au-Prince on theme "Stir into Flame the Spiritual Gift That God Placed in You" (2 Timothy 1:6)"; 50,000 attendees including 100 priests, 10 Haitian bishops, 4,000 Protestants (17–19 April).

1998   8th International Conference of the Catholic Fraternity of Charismatic Covenant Communities, held in Rome (31 May–3 June).

1998   Mexico: 13th National Youth Gathering in the Holy Spirit (ICCRS), held in Aguascalientes with more than 14,000 youth (24-26 July).

1998   4th CCR Anglophone Africa Consultative Meeting, held in Harare (Zimbabwe), followed by open Catholic Charismatic Conference (4–9 August).

1998   18th Pentecostal World Conference (PWC), held in Seoul (Korea), with 100,000 attendees from 60 nations (22–25 September).

1998   17th Latin American Catholic Charismatic Conference (ECCLA XVll) organized by CONCCLAT, held in Monterrey, Mexico (10–14 October), followed by Leaders Conference, also International Priests' Retreat (12–16 October).

1999   Latin American Congress on Catholic Arts (CONLARTE, sponsored by Catholic Charismatic Renewal), held in city of Cachoeira Paulista (Brazil), aiming to evangelize through dance and theater (14–17 January).

1999   World Congress on Deliverance: Equipping the Church for Revival (A.D. 2000 Movement), held in World Prayer Center, Colorado Springs; 14 speakers on aspects of deliverance ministries (exorcism, powers, curses, the occult, healings) (29–31 July).

1999   Pan-African Congress of the Catholic Charismatic Renewal, held in Yaounde (Cameroon) in May, Bangui (CAR) in December, culminating in the Jubilee of the Year 2000 in Kinshasa (August 2000).

1999   New World Missions Congress for the Third Millennium (sponsored by Third World Missions Association / TWMA and Nippon Revival Association), held in Kyoto (Japan), with 2,000 delegates from 1,500 mission agencies worldwide (25–31 October).

Assessing the Decade of Global Evangelization

2000   Global status: Pentecostals (classical) now number 63,064,000; charismatics 175,856,000; neo-charismatics 295,405,000; total living church members affiliated to renewal 523,767,000; total all living believers in renewal (whether affiliated or unaffiliated) 619,894,000; total renewal believers dying since A.D. 1900, 175,728,000.

2000   Emergence of hundreds of new short-lived millennial religions or belief systems at local, national and global levels; ultra-fast-growing religious cults and revivals, millions joining and leaving in rapid succession.

2000   ICCOWE holds Consultation in Penang, Malaysia (27–31 March).

2000   29th Annual World Congress, Apostolic World Christian Fellowship (AWCF, with 161 apostolic/oneness Pentecostal member denominations, mostly black, with 12,000 fivefold-ministry pastors in 44 nations), held in South Bend, Indiana (3–5 May); including graduation ceremonies of Apostolic World Christian University (AWCU).

2000   Celebrate Jesus 2000 Millennium Congress (sponsored by NARSC), held in St. Louis, Missouri, with 8,000 registrants and 13,000 attendees, on themes "Reconciliation, Repentance, Revival, Release, Renewal" (22–25 June).

2000   4th Pan-European Charismatic Congress, sponsored by ECC and ICCOWE, held in Prague (23–27 August).

2000   During 20th century, believers in Pentecostal/charismatic/neo-charismatic renewal in the Holy Spirit have numbered 795 million since A.D. 1900, of whom 523 million are still alive as active church members, mainly in Africa (126 million), Asia (134 million) and Latin America (141 million).

2001   19th Pentecostal World Conference (PWC) and Centenary Celebration of Pentecostalism, held in Los Angeles (USA) (29 May–2 June).

Some Possible Future Events

(A small selection based on present trends and a large literature expounding each's possibility and significance).

2004   Massive Pentecostal/charismatic latter-rain revival sweeps across whole of Asia due to power evangelism with signs and wonders, with 150 million converts in Korea, Japan, China, Vietnam, Thailand, Malaysia, Indonesia, Burma, Cambodia, India, Sri Lanka, and Pakistan.

2008   Scientists at International Astronomical Union announce sun will go nova and explode in A.D. 3620; by 2553, 4 km-long seedships packed with data, life (species, DNA), technology and a million hibernating humans each depart for Alpha Centauri A and 50 other planetary systems with oxygen; 3450, quantum drive invented making perpetual travel without fuel possible; 40 seedship voyages fail but 10 succeed including Mormon "Ark of the Covenant" and other religious ones; 3617, starship *Magellan* leaves doomed Earth, 4135 arrives to begin life on planet Sagan Two (A. C. Clark, *The Songs of Distant Earth,* 1985).

2009   Total global charismatic worship of Christ introduced, in which at a fixed time each Sunday one billion living believers across world are holographically present visibly at same location; the ultimate in inspiration and evangelistic converting power.

2010   Rise of totalitarianism produces mass religious revivals; bogus robot evangelists seduce ignorant with promises of immediate salvation.

2010   Universal Christian Church Council (WCC-RCC-Orthodoxy-Pentecostals) convened to resolve main outstanding issues dividing confessions and churches, including a role for primacy of bishop of Rome; leading to a common confession of faith, sanctioning total communion, and celebrating Eucharist together.

2025   Churchmanship. Churches tend increasingly to combine three traditions or streams: (a) Catholic (liturgical or sacramental), (b) Protestant (Bible-based), (c) Pentecostal (Spirit-filled, charismatic).

2025   Christians. At world level, Christians are now 55 percent Third Worlders, 32 percent of whom are Pentecostals/charismatics, 12 percent in Pentecostal denominations, 33 percent charismatics, and 10 percent neo-charismatics in Chinese house churches).

2025   Spirituality. Widespread revival of monasticism both eremitic (hermits) and cenobitic (communities), among young people of all churches across world, especially in Third World countries.

2030   After World War III nuclear holocaust, Christianity spreads again around world in global revival led by "an ancient, black, and primitive church"; ascendancy of non-White indigenous Christianity.

2030   Conversion of China to Christianity through multitude of Chinese house-church evangelists and witnesses, resulting in 1.5 million zealous, neocharismatic, postdenominationalist Christians, who then launch their own global mission without reference to Western or Eastern churches and missions, or to historic Christianity, or to the 3,000 previously proposed world evangelization plans.

2050   50 percent of all Christians are charismatics (pentecostals, neo-pentecostals, neo-charismatics, apostolics, neo-apostolics, et al.), as are 70 percent of all church workers and 90 percent of all foreign missionaries.

2050   Christianity now dominated worldwide by Third World indigenous pentecostal-charismatic bodies, spreading like wildfire through unorganized self-replicating media churches.

3781   Monks of Order of Leibowitz, charismatics who have preserved

knowledge through Dark Ages after A.D. 2010 World War III nuclear
holocaust, eventually see civilization rebuilt by A.D. 3100 to point
where, again, a new industrial-scientific age culminates by A.D. 3781
in imminent nuclear World War IV; just before outbreak, discredited
order launches an ecclesiastical starship through which Church of
New Rome transfers authority of St. Peter from Earth to Alpha Centauri (W. M. Miller's novel, *A Canticle for Leibowitz*, 1960).

Notes

Chapter 2

1. Henry P. Van Dusen, "The Third Force in Christendom," *Life*, 9 June 1958, 113–24.
2. "But What About Hicks?" *Christian Century*, 7 July 1954, 814–15. Also see Tommy Hicks, *Millions Found Christ* (Los Angeles: Alberty Offset Printing, 1956).
3. Charles Sydnor Jr., "The Pentecostals," *Presbyterian Survey*, May 1964, 30–32; June 1964, 36–39.
4. Quoted in Warren Lewis, *Witnesses to the Holy Spirit* (Valley Forge, Pa.: Judson Press, 1978), 121.
5. Ibid., 122.
6. Phillip Schaff, *Nicene and Post-Nicene Fathers* (Grand Rapids: Eerdmans, 1956), 168–70.
7. Quoted in Lewis, *Witnesses*, 173.
8. Ernest R. Sandeen, *Roots of Fundamentalism: British and American Millenarianism 1800–1930* (Chicago: Univ. of Chicago Press, 1970), 7.
9. Ibid., 26–36.
10. The best treatment of Irving's Pentecostal tendencies is David Dorries' "Edward Irving and the 'Standing Sign,'" in *Initial Evidence: Historical and Biblical Perspective on the Pentecostal Doctrine of Spirit Baptism*, ed. Gary McGee (Peabody, Mass.: Hendrickson Publishers, 1991).
11. William S. Merricks, *Edward Irving the Forgotten Giant* (East Peoria, Ill.: Scribe's Chamber Publications, 1983), 179–80. Also see Christie Root, *Edward Irving, Man, Preacher, Prophet* (Boston: Sherman, French & Company, 1912), 70–112.
12. Thomas Carlyle, *Reminiscences* (New York: Macmillan, 1887), 58.
13. Gordon Strachan, *The Pentecostal Theology of Edward Irving* (London: Dartan, Longman & Todd, 1973), 193–201; also see Larry Christenson, *A Message to the Charismatic Movement* (East Weymouth, Mass.: Dimension, 1972); and "Pentecostalism's Forgotten Forerunner," in Vinson Synan, *Aspects of Pentecostal-Charismatic Origins* (Plainfield, N.J.: Logos International, 1975), 15–37.
14. Charles H. Spurgeon, *Spurgeon's Sermons* (Grand Rapids: Zondervan, reprinted from 1857), 129–30.
15. William Arthur, *The Tongue of Fire* (Columbia, S.C.: L. L. Pickett, 1891), 288, 315, 375–76.
16. Ibid., 376.
17. Vinson Synan, *The Holiness-Pentecostal Tradition: Charismatic Movements in the Twentieth Century* (Grand Rapids: Eerdmans, 1997), 25.
18. Donald Dayton, "From Christian Perfection to the Baptism of the Holy Ghost," in Synan, *Aspects*, 39–54. Also see Dayton's *The Theological Roots of Pentecostalism* (Grand Rapids: Francis Asbury Press, 1987).
19. Dayton, "From Christian Perfection," 46.
20. Ibid., 47.
21. Martini Wells Knapp, *Lightning Bolts from Pentecostal Skies, or the Devices of the Devil Unmasked!* (Cincinnati: Pentecostal Holiness Library, 1898).
22. Melvin E. Dieter, *The Holiness Revival of the Nineteenth Century* (Metuchen, N.J.: Scarecrow Press, 1980), 245. Also see Dieter, "Wesleyan-Holiness Aspects of Pentecostal Origins," in Synan, *Aspects*, 67.
23. Timothy Smith, *Called unto Holiness* (Kansas City, Mo.: Nazarene Publishing House, 1962), 25.
24. Reuben A. Torrey, *The Person and Work of the Holy Spirit* (New York: Revell, 1910), 176–210.

25. Richard K. Curtis, *They Called Him Mister Moody* (Garden City, N.Y.: Doubleday, 1962), 149–50.

26. See Synan, *The Holiness-Pentecostal Tradition,* 44–67.

27. Robert R. Owens, *Speak to the Rock: The Azusa Street Revival, Its Roots and Message* (Lanham, Md.: Univ. Press of America, 1998), 40–41; Stanley M. Burgess and Gary McGee, eds., *Dictionary of Pentecostal and Charismatic Movements* (Grand Rapids: Zondervan, 1988), 471–72.

28. Edward O'Conner, "Hidden Roots of the Charismatic Renewal in the Catholic Church," in Synan, *Aspects,* 169–92.

Chapter 3

1. Vinson Synan, *The Holiness-Pentecostal Movement in the United States* (Grand Rapids: Eerdmans, 1971), 84.

2. Frank Bartleman, *Azusa Street* (Plainfield, N.J.: Logos International, 1980), 26.

3. Synan, *The Holiness-Pentecostal Movement,* 97, 99; Stanley M. Burgess and Gary McGee, eds., *Dictionary of Pentecostal and Charismatic Movements* (Grand Rapids: Zondervan, 1988), 791; John Nichols, *Pentecostalism* (New York: Harper & Row, 1966), 34, 70; Robert Mapes Anderson, *Vision of the Disinherited: The Making of American Pentecostalism* (New York: Oxford Univ. Press, 1979), 70–71, 143.

4. *Yorkshire Post,* 27 December 1904, as quoted in, Synan, *The Holiness-Pentecostal Movement,* 99.

5. Eifion Evans, *The Welsh Revival of 1904* (Bridgend, Wales: Evangelical Press of Wales, 1969), 63–119.

6. For a biography of Charles Fox Parham, consult James R. Goff Jr., *Fields White Unto Harvest* (Fayetteville, Ark.: Univ. of Arkansas Press, 1988).

7. Anderson, *Vision of the Disinherited,* 48; Goff, *Fields White Unto Harvest,* 29.

8. Edith L. Blumhofer, *Restoring the Faith: The Assemblies of God, Pentecostalism, and American Culture* (Urbana: Univ. of Illinois Press, 1993), 50.

9. Goff, *Fields White Unto Harvest,* 37, 40, 45–46.

10. Ibid., 67; Synan, *The Holiness-Pentecostal Movement,* 101; Blumhofer, *Restoring the Faith,* 51; Eric W. Gritsch, *Born Againism* (Philadelphia: Fortress Press, 1982), 71.

11. Charles F. Parham, *Voice Crying in the Wilderness* (Joplin, Mo.: 1944), 31–32, as quoted in Synan, *The Holiness-Pentecostal Movement,* 102.

12. Goff, *Fields White Unto Harvest,* 89–90; Blumhofer, *Restoring the Faith,* 53.

13. Donald Dayton, *The Theological Roots of Pentecostalism* (Grand Rapids: Francis Asbury Press, 1987), 22–23.

14. Wayne E. Warner, "The Miracle of Azusa," *Pentecostal Evangel,* vol. 22 (September 1996), 11.

15. W. W. Robinson, *Los Angeles: From the Days of the Pueblo* (Los Angeles: California Historical Society, 1981), 61, 64–66.

16. Michael Engh, *Frontier Faiths: Church, Temple, and Synagogue in Los Angeles, 1846–1888* (Albuquerque, N.M.: University of New Mexico Press, 1992), 60, 190–92; Gregory H. Singleton, *Religion in the City of Los Angeles: American Protestant Culture and Urbanization, Los Angeles, 1850–1930* (Los Angeles: UMI Research Press, 1979), 54–56.

17. Nichols, *Pentecostalism,* 33.

18. Clara Davis, *The Move of God! The Outpouring of the Holy Spirit from Azusa Street to Now (As Told by Eyewitnesses)* (Tulsa: Albury Press, 1983), 20.

19. Synan, *The Holiness-Pentecostal Movement,* 106.

20. Anderson, *Vision of the Disinherited,* 66; Richard T. Hughes, ed., *The American Quest for the Primitive Church* (Urbana: Univ. of Illinois Press, 1988), 200–203; Walter J. Hollenweger, *The Pentecostals* (London: SCM Press, 1972), 22.

21. *Pentecostal Evangel,* vol. 6, no. 4 (1946): 6, as quoted in Hollenweger, *The Pentecostals,* 23.

22. Nickel, *Azusa Street Outpouring: As Told By Those Who Were There,* 6–7.

23. *Los Angeles Daily Times,* 18 April 1906, 1.

24. Vinson Synan, *In The Latter Days* (Ann Arbor, Mich.: Servant Publications, 1991), 50.

25. Bartleman, *Azusa Street,* 54.

26. *Los Angeles Daily Times,* 18 April 1906, 1.

27. Stanley M. Horton, "A Typical Day at Azusa Street," *Heritage* (Springfield, Mo.: Assemblies of God, Fall 1982), 6.

28. A. W. Orwig, "Apostolic Faith Restored," *Weekly Evangel,* 18 March 1916, 4.; A. G. Osterberg, interview by Jerry Jensen and Jonathan E. Perkins, tape recording, March 1966. Transcription by Mae Waldron, Assemblies of God Archives, Springfield., Tape one, 1293 075; Horton, "A Typical Day at Azusa Street," 6.

29. "Acting out of the flesh" refers to people who try to imitate the anointing of God either through ignorance or pride.

30. Martin E. Marty, *Modern American Protestantism and Its World,* vol. 11, *New and Intense Movements* (Munich: K. G. Saur, 1993), 207.

31. Orwig, "Apostolic Faith Restored," Article XII, *Weekly Evangel,* 8 April 1916, 4.

32. Ernest S. Williams, "Memories of Azusa Street Mission," *Pentecostal Evangel,* 24 April 1966, 7.

33. Bartleman, *Azusa Street,* 68, 84.

34. Sanders, *Saints in Exile,* 30.

35. Kimberly Wesley, "Bishop William J. Seymour: Father of the Modern Pentecostal Movement," *Whole Truth,* vol. 1, no.1 (Spring 1996), 18.

36. Blumhofer, *Restoring the Faith,* 19, 93, 80.

37. Bartleman, *Azusa Street*, 143; 150–52; Synan, *The Holiness-Pentecostal Movement*, 148–49.

Chapter 4

1. Jonathan Goforth, *By My Spirit* (Minneapolis: Bethany Fellowship, 1942), 137–38.
2. T. B. Barratt, "Baptized in New York," *Apostolic Faith* (Los Angeles), December 1906, 3, col. 2.
3. A. J. Tomlinson, *The Last Great Conflict* (Cleveland, Tenn.: Walter E. Rodgers, 1913), 31.
4. J. Roswell Flower, (untitled editorial), *Pentecost*, August 1908, 4.
5. Darrin J. Rodgers, "Spirit of the Plains: North Dakotan Pentecostalism's Roots in Immigrant Pietism and the Holiness Movement" (M.A. seminar paper, Assemblies of God Theological Seminary, 1997), 24–25.
6. James R. Goff Jr., *Fields White Unto Harvest: Charles F. Parham and the Missionary Origins of Pentecostalism* (Fayetteville: Univ. of Arkansas Press, 1988), 115.
7. "Beginning of World Wide Revival," *Apostolic Faith* (Los Angeles), January 1907, 1, col. 1.
8. Arthur Mercer, "Here and There," *South African Pioneer*, February 1907, 1. Mercer served as the secretary of the South Africa General Mission under Andrew Murray.
9. "The Pentecostal Revival," *Apostolic Faith* (Los Angeles), May 1908, 4, col. 2.
10. Paul Voronaeff, *My Life in Soviet Russia* (Tulsa: Christian Crusade, 1969), 33–34.
11. Nicolai J. Poysti, *With Christ in Russia & Siberia* (Chicago: Russian and Eastern European Mission, 1936), 4.
12. Gheorghe Bradin cited in Trandafir Sandru, *The Pentecostal Apostolic Church of God in Romania* (Bucharest: Pentecostal Apostolic Church of God, 1982), 26.
13. Janet Lancaster cited in Barry Chant, *Heart of Fire: The Story of Australian Pentecostalism* (Unley Park, Australia: House of Tabor, 1984), 36.
14. Cora Fritsch, *Letters from Cora*, comp. Homer and Alice Fritsch (n.p.: by the compilers, 1987), 6.
15. Grace C. Agar, "Tibetan Border of Kansu Province," 1940, 14. (Typewritten.) (Available at Flower Pentecostal Heritage Center, Springfield, MO 65802.)
16. See G. H. Lang, *The History and Diaries of an Indian Christian (J. C. Aroolappen)* (London: Thynne & Co., 1939); W. J. Richards, "The 'Six Year's Party' in Travancore," *Church Missionary Intelligencer and Record*, November 1882, 660–67.
17. Minnie F. Abrams, "The Baptism of the Holy Ghost and Fire," *Indian Witness*, 26 April 1906, 261.
18. "The Holy Spirit and Physical Manifestations," *Indian Witness*, 13 December 1906, 786.
19. "Pentecost in India," *Apostolic Faith* (Los Angeles), November 1906, 1, col. 4.
20. "A Late Report from Bombay," *Apostolic Faith* (Portland), July / August 1908, 3.
21. G. H. Lang, *The Modern Gift of Tongues: Whence Is It? A testimony and an examination* (London: Marshall Brothers, 1913).
22. Dana L. Robert, *American Women in Mission: A Social History of Their Thought and Practice* (Macon, Ga.: Mercer Univ. Press, 1996), 241.
23. Charles F. Parham, "The Story of the Origin of the Original Apostolic or Pentecostal Movements," in *The Topeka Outpouring: Eyewitness Accounts of the Revival that Birthed the 20th Century Pentecostal/Charismatic Movements*, ed. and comp. Larry Martin (Joplin, Mo.: Christian Life Books, 1997), 37.
24. *Eleventh Annual Report of the Christian & Missionary Alliance*, 27 May 1908, 143.
25. "Alleged Crank in Limelight," *Daily Oregon Statesman*, 7 January 1911, 1.
26. Fritsch, *Letters from Cora*, 42–43, 48.
27. Untitled news note, *Apostolic Faith* (Los Angeles), December 1906, 3, col. 5.
28. John G. Lake, "My Baptism in the Holy Spirit and How the Lord Sent Me to South Africa" (booklet) (Portland, Oreg.: Divine Healing Institute, n.d.), 14.
29. Willis Collins Hoover, *History of the Pentecostal Revival in Chile*, trans. Mario G. Hoover (Lakeland, Fla.: by the translator, 2000), 4.
30. Minnie F. Abrams, "The Baptism of the Holy Ghost and Fire," *Bombay Guardian*, 23 June 1906, 9. Although ten thousand copies of the first edition were printed, I have only found it in serialized form.
31. Dr. Stuntz cited in Hoover, *History of the Pentecostal Revival in Chile*, 62.
32. Fritsch, *Letters from Cora*, 16.

Chapter 5

1. Charles Harrison Mason, *The History and Life of Elder C. H. Mason* (Memphis: Church of God in Christ Publishing House, 1920). This book has been reprinted and revised several times since 1920, the latest version being J. O. Patterson, German R. Rose, and Julia Mason Atkins, *History and Formative Years of the Church of God in Christ with Excerpts from the Life and Works of Its Founder—Bishop C. H. Mason* (Memphis: Church of God in Christ Publishing House, 1969). The newest scholarly history is Ithiel Clemmons's *Bishop C.H. Mason and the Roots of the Church of God in Christ* (Bakersfield, Calif.: Pneuma Life Publishing, 1996).
2. Patterson, Rose, and Mason, *History and Forma-*

tive Years, 14–17; Otho B. Cobbins, ed., *History of the Church of Christ (Holiness) U.S.A.* (New York: Vantage Press, 1966), 1–27.

3. Klaud Kendrick, *The Promise Fulfilled* (Springfield, Mo.: Gospel Publishing House, 1961), 16. Also see Phillip Garvin, *Religious America* (New York: McGraw-Hill, 1974), 141–69; Cobbins, *History of the Church of Christ*, 117–20.

4. Leonard Lovett, "Black Origins of the Pentecostal Movement," in Vinson Synan, *Aspects of Pentecostal-Charismatic Origins* (Plainfield, N.J.: Logos International, 1975), 123–41; David M. Tucker, *Black Pastors and Leaders: The Memphis Clergy, 1819–1972* (Memphis, Tenn.: Memphis State University Press, 1974), 90–94; Patterson, Rose, and Mason, *History and Formative Years*, 17–20.

5. Cobbins, *History of the Church of Christ*, 16, 50–52.

6. Tucker, *Black Pastors and Leaders*, 97–99. Ithiel Clemmons, personal interview with the author, Oklahoma City, Okla., 29 January 1986.

7. Howard N. Kenyon, "Black Experience in the Assemblies of God" (paper read at the Society for Pentecostal Studies, 15 November 1986, Costa Mesa, Calif.); Vinson Synan, *The Holiness-Pentecostal Tradition: Charismatic Movements in the Twentieth Century* (Grand Rapids: Eerdmans, 1997), 178–79.

8. Ibid., 149–53. Also see William Menzies, *Anointed to Serve* (Springfield, Mo.: Gospel Publishing House, 1971), 370.

9. Arnor S. Davis, "The Pentecostal Movement in Black Christianity," *Black Church*, 2:1 (1972), 65–88. Also see the U.S. Bureau of the Census reports for 1926 and 1936 under "Church of God in Christ, Statistics, Denominational History, Doctrine, and Organization" (Washington, D.C.: U.S. Government Printing Office, 1929 and 1940).

10. Ithiel Clemmons, Synan interview; Patterson, *History and Formative Years*, 71–75.

11. Eileen W. Lindner, *Yearbook of American and Canadian Churches 2000* (Nashville: Abingdon, 2000), 342.

12. The two standard histories of the church are Joseph E. Campbell, *The Pentecostal Holiness Church, 1898–1948* (Franklin Springs, Ga.: Publishing House of the Pentecostal Holiness Church, 1951); and Vinson Synan, *The Old-Time Power: A History of the Pentecostal Holiness Church* (Franklin Springs, Ga.: Lifesprings, 1997). Also useful is A. D. Beacham Jr.'s *A Brief History of the Pentecostal Holiness Church* (Franklin Springs, Ga.: Advocate Press, 1983).

13. Synan, *The Old-Time Power*, 107.

14. Joseph H. King, *Yet Speaketh, The Memoirs of the Late Bishop Joseph H. King* (Franklin Springs, Ga.: Advocate Press, 1949), 111–21.

15. Synan, *The Holiness-Pentecostal Tradition*, 117–39.

16. N. J. Holmes, *Life Sketches and Sermons* (Franklin Springs, Ga.: Publishing House of the Pentecostal Holiness Church, 1920), 135–48.

17. G. F. Taylor, *The Spirit and the Bride* (Dunn, N.C.: Private printing, 1907); Joseph H. King, *From Passover to Pentecost* (Memphis, Tenn.: H. W. Dixon Printing Company, 1914).

18. See Synan, *The Holiness-Pentecostal Tradition*, 141–63.

19. Synan, *The Old-Time Power*, 165–71.

20. Ibid., 265–68. Also see David Harrell Jr's *Oral Roberts: An American Life* (Bloomington, Ind.: Univ. of Indiana Press, 1985), 8–55, 287–311.

21. Synan, *The Old-Time Power*, 225–28.

22. Ibid., 266–67.

23. Lindner, *Yearbook of American and Canadian Churches 2000*, 346.

24. See *Minutes of the Twentieth General Conference of the Pentecostal Holiness Church, Inc.* (Franklin Springs, Ga.: 1985), 92–99.

25. The standard history of the Church of God (Cleveland, Tenn.) is Charles W. Conn's *Like a Mighty Army: A History of the Church of God, 1886–1976*, rev. ed. (Cleveland, Tenn: Pathway Press, 1977). The history of the Church of God of Prophecy is given in Charles Davidson's *Upon This Rock*, 3 vols. (Cleveland, Tenn.: White Wing Publishing House, 1973–76).

26. Conn, *Like a Mighty Army*, 1–18; Synan, *The Holiness-Pentecostal Tradition*, 80–83.

27. A. J. Tomlinson, *Answering the Call of God* (Cleveland, Tenn.: White Wing Publishing House, 1942), 1–15.

28. See Homer Tomlinson, *The Shout of a King* (New York: Church of God, World Headquarters, 1965), 14–20; and Lillie Duggar, *A. J. Tomlinson: Former General Overseer of the Church of God* (Cleveland, Tenn.: White Wing Publishing House, 1964), 30–45.

29. Tomlinson, *Answering the Call of God*, 17.

30. L. Howard Juillerat, *Book of Minutes, General Assemblies, Church of God* (Cleveland, Tenn.: Church of God Publishing House, 1922), 15–19; Conn, *Like a Mighty Army*, 61–69.

31. Juillerat, *Book of Minutes*, 15–19.

32. See Homer A. Tomlinson, ed., *Diary of A. J. Tomlinson, 1901–1923* (New York: Church of God, World Headquarters, 1949–55), 68–72.

33. Charles E. Jones, *A Guide to the Study of the Pentecostal Movement*, vol. 1 (Metuchen, N.J.: Scarecrow Press, 1983), 271.

34. Conn, *Like a Mighty Army*, 175–90; Tomlinson,

Answering the Call of God, 8; Davidson, *Upon This Rock*, 573–610.

35. Tomlinson, *The Shout of a King*, 1–219; John Nichols, *Pentecostalism* (New York: Harper & Row, 1966), 139–43.

36. The record of Church of God (Cleveland, Tenn.) foreign missions is given in Charles W. Conn's *Where the Saints Have Trod* (Cleveland, Tenn.: Pathway Press, 1959).

37. Lindner, *Yearbook of American and Canadian Churches 2000*, 342.

38. Ibid.

39. H. L. Fisher, *History of the United Holy Church of America* (n.p., n.d.), 1–7.

40. Chester W. Gregory, *History of the United Holy Church of America, Inc.:1886–1986* (Baltimore: Gateway Press, 1986), 30–36, 231–32.

41. See Synan, *The Holiness-Pentecostal Tradition*, 65–66.

42. Margaret Moffett Banks, "Evangelist Speaks Before United Holy Church Following," *Greensboro News and Record*, 5 May 2000, 1.

Chapter 6

1. Major histories of the Assemblies of God include: Carl Brumback, *Suddenly . . . From Heaven: A History of the Assemblies of God* (Springfield, Mo.: Gospel Publishing House, 1961); Klaud Kendrick, *The Promise Fulfilled: A History of the Modern Pentecostal Movement* (Springfield, Mo.: Gospel Publishing House, 1961); William Menzies, *Anointed to Serve: The Story of the Assemblies of God* (Springfield, Mo.: Gospel Publishing House, 1971); and Edith Waldvogel Blumhofer, *The Assemblies of God: A Popular History* (Springfield, Mo.: Gospel Publishing House, 1985). Also useful for the Assemblies of God and other classical Pentecostal groups are Robert Mapes Anderson, *Vision of the Disinherited: The Making of American Pentecostalism* (New York: Oxford Univ. Press, 1979); and Vinson Synan, *The Holiness-Pentecostal Tradition* (Grand Rapids: Eerdmans, 1997).

2. Menzies, *Anointed to Serve*, 64–76, 48–49, 70–71; Anderson, *Vision of the Disinherited*, 188–94; Synan, *The Holiness-Pentecostal Tradition*, 149–52, 153–56. Also see William Menzies, "Non-Wesleyan Origins of the Pentecostal Movement," in Vinson Synan, *Aspects of Pentecostal Charismatic Origins* (Plainfield, N.J.: Logos International, 1975), 81–98.

3. Anderson, *Vision of the Disinherited*, 188–94; Synan, *The Holiness-Pentecostal Tradition*, 167–86.

4. Anderson, *Vision of the Disinherited*, 173–84; Richard A. Lewis, "E. N. Bell: An Early Pente-

costal Spokesman" (paper presented to the Society for Pentecostal Studies, 14 November 1986, in Costa Mesa, Calif.).

5. Brumback, *Suddenly . . . From Heaven*, 88–97; John S. Sawin, "The Response and Attitude of Dr. A. B. Simpson and the Christian and Missionary Alliance to the Tongues Movement of 1906–1920" (paper presented to the Society for Pentecostal Studies, 14 November 1986, in Costa Mesa, Calif.).

6. Synan, *The Holiness-Pentecostal Tradition*, 149–52; Brumback, *Suddenly . . . From Heaven*, 99–103.

7. J. Roswell Flower, "History of the Assemblies of God" (n.p., n.d.), 17–19; Menzies, *Anointed to Serve*, 92–105.

8. Menzies, *Anointed to Serve*, 80–105; Brumback, *Suddenly . . . From Heaven*, 151–71.

9. These reasons were listed in the "call" in *Word and Witness*, 10 December 1913, 1; see Brumback, *Suddenly . . . From Heaven*, 157, for a photocopy of the call.

10. Ibid., 168–69.

11. Ibid., 216–25; Menzies, *Anointed to Serve*, 129, 320.

12. Menzies, *Anointed to Serve*, 106–21. Also see Brumback's answer to the oneness movement in *God in Three Persons* (Cleveland, Tenn.: Pathway Press, 1959).

13. Synan, *The Holiness-Pentecostal Tradition*, 156–60; Menzies, *Anointed to Serve*, 384–90.

14. For the Assemblies of God statement on the charismatic renewal movement, see Kilian McDonnell, *Presence, Power, Praise: Documents on the Charismatic Renewal*, vol. 1 (Collegeville, Minn.; New York: Paulist Press, 1980), 318. Also see Blumhofer, *The Assemblies of God*, 113–17, 141.

15. Jae Bum Lee, "Pentecostal Distinctives and Protestant Church Growth in Korea" (Ph.D. dissertation, Fuller Theological Seminary, 1986), 169–228.

16. Eileen W. Lindner, *Yearbook of American and Canadian Churches 2000* (Nashville: Abingdon, 2000), 340. Also see *Assemblies of God: Who We Are and What We Believe* (Springfield, Mo., 2000); and *A/G Facts, Current Information About the Assemblies of God* (Springfield, Mo.: Office of Information, 2000).

17. *AG News*, Wednesday, 9 August 2000. Report of the World Assemblies of God Fellowship meeting in Indianapolis, Indiana, August 2000.

18. Sources for Aimee Semple McPherson's life and ministry include her autobiography, *In the Service of the King* (New York: Boni and Liveright, 1927); and *The Story of My Life* (Los Angeles: Echo Park Evangelistic Association, 1951). Critical works include Robert P. Shuler's *McPherson-*

ism (Los Angeles: n.d.); and Lately Thomas, *The Vanishing Evangelist* (New York: Viking Press, 1959).

19. McPherson, *The Story of My Life*, 15–79.

20. See *Historical Data of the International Church of the Foursquare Gospel* (April 1968), 1.

21. Synan, *The Holiness-Pentecostal Tradition,* 191–202.

22. *Facts You Should Know About the International Church of the Foursquare Gospel*, 5; Harold Helms, personal interview with the author, Los Angeles, 19 November 1986.

23. McPherson, *Personal Testimony*, 47–49; Thomas, *Vanishing Evangelist*, 1–319.

24. *Articles of Incorporation and By-laws of the International Church of the Foursquare Gospel* (Los Angeles, 1986), 20–28.

25. *Facts You Should Know*, 6; Aimee Semple McPherson, *This We Believe* (Los Angeles: n.d.), 7–35.

26. McPherson, *Story of My Life*, 75–42; *Personal Testimony*, 43.

27. See the *Articles of Incorporation*, 20–28.

28. *Yearbook, 1986, International Church of the Foursquare Gospel* (Los Angeles), 9.

29. Harold Helms, personal interview with the author, Oklahoma City, Okla., 19 November 1986.

30. Lindner, *Yearbook of American and Canadian Churches 2000*, 346.

31. Guy Duffield and Nathaniel Van Cleave, *Foundations of Pentecostal Theology* (Los Angeles: L.I.F.E. Bible College, 1983).

32. See Synan, *The Holiness-Pentecostal Tradition*, 195–96.

33. Wayne Warner, "Pentecostal Church of God," in Stanley Burgess, Patrick Alexander, and Gary McGee, eds., *Dictionary of Pentecostal and Charismatic Movements* (Grand Rapids: Zondervan, 1988), 701–2.

34. Ibid.

35. Lindner, *Yearbook of American and Canadian Churches 2000*, 348.

36. See Synan, *The Holiness-Pentecostal Tradition*, 221–22.

37. Ibid., 202–3. The best history of the church is R. Bryant Mitchell's *Heritage and Horizons* (Des Moines: Open Bible, 1982).

38. See Klaud Kendrick, *The Promise Fulfilled*, 164–71.

39. Wayne Warner, "Open Bible Standard Churches, Inc.," in Burgess, Alexander, and McGee, *Dictionary of Pentecostal and Charismatic Movements*, 651–53.

40. Lindner, *Yearbook of American and Canadian Churches 2000*, 348.

41. See David Reed, "Aspects of the Origins of Oneness Pentecostalism," in Synan, *Aspects of Pentecostal-Charismatic Origins*, 143–68.

42. Synan, *The Holiness-Pentecostal Tradition*, 156–64.

43. Edith Blumhofer, *The Assemblies of God: A Chapter in the Story of American Pentecostalism*, 221–39.

44. Synan, *The Holiness-Pentecostal Tradition*, 160–61.

45. A major study of the history of the Pentecostal Assemblies of the World is James L. Tyson's *The Early Pentecostal Revival* (Hazelwood, Mo.: Word Aflame Press, 1992).

46. J. L. Hall, "United Pentecostal Church, International," in Burgess, McGee, and Alexander, *Dictionary of Pentecostal and Charismatic Movements*, 860–65.

47. Lindner, *Yearbook of American and Canadian Churches 2000*, 351.

Chapter 7

1. See Dennis Bennett, *Nine O'Clock in the Morning* (Plainfield, N.J.: Bridge Publishing, 1970), 1–30.

2. Liston Pope, *Millhands and Preachers, A Study of Gastonia* (New Haven: Yale Univ. Press, 1946), 138.

3. Bennett, *Nine O'Clock*, 61.

4. See *Time*, 29 March 1963, 52; 15 August 1963, 52–55.

5. Michael Harper, *As At the Beginning: The Twentieth Century Pentecostal Revival* (London: Hodder and Stoughton, 1965), 34–39. Also see Harper's *Three Sisters* (Wheaton: Tyndale, 1979).

6. Richard Winkler, personal interview with the author, Maui, Hawaii, 11 January 1986.

7. See Kilian McDonnell, *Presence, Power, Praise: Documents on the Charismatic Renewal*, vol. 1 (Collegeville, Minn.; New York: Paulist Press, 1980), 10–20. For the report coming out of the Bennett case, see vol. 1, 1–21.

8. Frank Ferrell, "Outburst of Tongues: The New Penetration," *Christianity Today*, 13 September 1963, 3–7.

9. Vinson Synan, *In the Latter Days* (Altamonte Springs, Fla.: Creation House, 1991), 89–95.

10. McDonnell, *Presence, Power, Praise*, 96–104.

11. Bennett, *Nine O'Clock*, 73–90. Personal interview with the author, Kansas City, July 1977. Also see John Sherrill, *They Speak with Other Tongues* (New York: McGraw-Hill, 1964), 61–66.

12. Richard Quebedeaux, *The New Charismatics II* (San Francisco: Harper & Row, 1983), 58, 138-142, 156, 179.

13. Quebedeaux, *The New Charismatics II*, 78–81, 102–4, 151-173. Also see Jean Stone and Harald Bredesen, *The Charismatic Renewal in the Historic Churches* (Van Nuys, Calif.: Full Gospel Business Men's Fellowship International, 1963).

14. McDonnell, *Presence, Power, Praise*, 20.

15. For the Fountain Trust story see Quebedeaux, *The New Charismatics II*, 98–105.

16. Terry Fullam, personal interview with the author, 6 August 1986. See Steve Lawson, "Episcopal Renewal on the Move," *Charisma*, March 1986, 64; also see David Collins, *There Is a Lad Here: A Book of Gratitude* (Darien, Ga.: Darien News, 1996), 151–91.

17. Much of this description is based on the eyewitness experience of the author, who was present for the service. Also see Vinson Synan "The New Canterbury Tales," *Pentecostal Holiness Advocate*, 22 October 1978, 12. Also see Michael Harper, ed., *A New Canterbury Tale: The Reports of the Anglican International Conference on Spiritual Renewal Held at Canterbury, July 19, 1978* (Bromcote, Nottinghamshire: Grove Books, 1978).

18. Bob Slosser, *Miracle in Darien* (Plainfield, N.J.: Logos International, 1979).

19. Beth Spring, "Spiritual Renewal Brings Booming Growth to Three Episcopal Churches in Northern Virginia," *Christianity Today*, 13 January 1984, 38–39.

20. Harald Bredesen, *Yes, Lord* (Plainfield, N.J.: Logos International, 1972), 48–57.

21. See *Time*, 29 March 1963, 52.

22. Pat Robertson, *Shout It from the Housetops* (Plainfield, N.J.: Logos International, 1972), 65–79.

23. Larry Christenson, personal interview with the author, New Orleans, 1 April 1986. See also Christenson, *The Charismatic Renewal Among Lutherans* (Minneapolis: International Lutheran Renewal Center, 1975); and Erling Jorstad, *Bold in the Spirit: Lutheran Charismatic Renewal in America Today* (Minneapolis: Augsburg Publishing House, 1974). For Christenson's testimony see "A Lutheran Pastor Speaks," *Trinity* (Whitsuntide, 1962), 32–35.

24. For a brief treatment of Luther's view on the charismata, see Synan, *In the Latter Days*, 29–30.

25. Christenson, *The Charismatic Renewal Among Lutherans*, 13–31.

26. Herbert Mjorud, personal interview with the author, Pittsburgh, Pa., 21 May 1986.

27. John P. Kildahl, *The Psychology of Speaking in Tongues* (New York: Harper & Row, 1972). For early Lutheran official reports on Lutheran Pentecostalism, see McDonnell, *Presence, Power, Praise*, 21–566.

28. Christenson, Synan interview.

29. Donald Photenhauer, personal interview with the author, Minneapolis, 8 August 1986. See the *Minneapolis Tribune*, 4 February 1968, 14 A.

30. News reports of the 1972 conference were carried by the *Minneapolis Star* in an article by Wilmar Thorkelson, "God's Electricity Is Here,"

10 August 1972, 1–3. Also Norris Wogen, personal interview with the author, Pittsburgh, Pa., 20 May 1986.

31. Christenson, *Charismatic Renewal Among Lutherans*, 46–52. See Christenson's *Welcome, Holy Spirit* (Minneapolis: Augsburg, 1987). Also see Theodore Jungkuntz, *Confirmation and the Charismata* (Lanham, Md.: Univ. Press of America, 1983).

32. McDonnell, *Presence, Power and Praise*, 321–73.

33. Ibid., 369–73.

34. Ibid., 543–66.

35. Dennis Pederson, "Introducing . . . International Lutheran Center for Charismatic Renewal," *Lutheran Renewal International*, Spring 1980, 14–17.

36. Christenson, Synan interview.

37. Kenneth Kantzer, "The Charismatics Among Us," *Christianity Today*, 22 February 1980, 25–29.

38. C. Peter Wagner, "Survey of the Growth of the Charismatic Renewal" (unpublished report, 1985).

39. Herbert Mirly, personal interview with the author, Charlotte, N.C., 17 May 1986 (unpublished history and letter).

40. John Calvin, *Institutes of the Christian Religion*, John T. McNeill, ed., 4 vols. (Philadelphia: Westminster, 1960), vol. 1, 15–31; vol. 4, 1466–84. Also see Calvin's *New Testament Commentaries: 1 Corinthians* (Grand Rapids: Eerdmans, 1960), 258–73.

41. Benjamin B. Warfield, *Counterfeit Miracles* (Carlisle, Pa.: Banner of Truth Trust, 1918). Also see Ronald A. Knox, *Enthusiasm* (London: Clarendon Press, 1950).

42. See Bernard Weisberger, *They Gathered at the River* (New York: Little, Brown, 1958), 10–15; and Archie Robertson, *That Old-Time Religion* (Boston: Houghton Mifflin, 1950), 56–57.

43. Jonathan Edwards, *A Faithful Narrative of the Surprising Work of God* (1737); and *The Distinguishing Marks of a Work of the Spirit of God* (1741). This awakening is discussed in Richard Lovelace, *Dynamics of Spiritual Life* (Downers Grove, Ill.: InterVarsity, 1979), 35–46.

44. Synan, *In the Latter Days*, 25, 37, 52; Timothy Smith, *Revivalism and Social Reform* (New York: Abingdon, 1957), 114–34.

45. See William S. Merricks, *Edward Irving, The Forgotten Giant* (East Peoria, Ill.: Scribe's Chamber Publications, 1983), 179–80.

46. Holmes, *Life Sketches and Sermons* (Franklin Springs, Ga.: Publishing House of the Pentecostal Holiness Church, 1920), 9–97.

47. James H. Brown, personal interview with the author, Charlotte, N.C., 5 March 1986. Also letter from Brown to Synan, 27 January 1986.

48. George "Brick" Bradford, personal interview with the author, Oklahoma City, Okla., 6 December 1985.

49. Ibid.; "Charismatic Renewal in the Reformed Tradition," *Renewal News*, May-June 1981, 1–4.

50. Whitaker's story is given in his booklet, *Hang in There: Counsel for Charismatics* (Plainfield, N.J.: Logos International, 1974), 38–41.

51. Bradford, Synan interview. Letter from Whitaker to the author, 19 December 1985. The records of the case *The Reverend Robert C. Whitaker, Complainant, vs. The Synod of Arizona, United Presbyterian Church in the United States of America, Respondent*, may be found in the office of the Presbyterian and Reformed Renewal Ministries in Oklahoma City.

52. This report is published in McDonnell's *Presence, Power, and Praise*, 221–82. (The 1971 report of the Presbyterian Church in the United States is published on pp. 287–317.)

53. See Catherine Marshall, *Something More* (New York: McGraw-Hill, 1974); Quebedeaux, *The New Charismatics II*, 131, 133–34.

54. Ibid., 133, 146–47, 161. See J. Rodman Williams, *The Pentecostal Reality* (Plainfield, N.J.: Logos International, 1972); and *The Era of the Spirit* (Plainfield, N.J.: Logos International, 1971).

55. "Presbyterian Charismatic Communion Changes Name to Presbyterian and Reformed Renewal Ministries International," *Renewal News*, May-June 1984, 1–3.

56. Bradford, Synan interview.

57. Ibid.

Chapter 8

1. The standard early biography of Wesley is Robert Southey's *The Life of John Wesley*, 2 vols. (London: Longmans Hurst and Company, 1820). A recent edition of his journal, letters, and sermons is found in Thomas Jackson, ed., *The Works of John Wesley*, 14 vols. (Grand Rapids: Zondervan, 1959).

2. See John Leland Peters, *Christian Perfection and American Methodism* (New York: Abingdon, 1956), 19–20; and Vinson Synan, *The Holiness-Pentecostal Tradition: Charismatic Movements in the Twentieth Century* (Grand Rapids: Eerdmans, 1997), 1–21.

3. The definitive history of American Methodism is Emory Stevens Bucke et al., *History of American Methodism*, 3 vols. (Nashville: Abingdon, 1964).

4. Timothy Smith, *Revivalism and Social Reform* (New York: Abingdon, 1957), 123.

5. Delbert Rose, *A Theology of Christian Experience*

(Minneapolis: Bethany Fellowship, Inc., 1965), 23–78; Charles Edwin Jones, *Perfectionist Persuasion* (Metuchen, N.J.: Scarecrow Press, 1974), 16–21.

6. Donald Dayton, "From Christian Perfection to the Baptism of the Holy Spirit," in Vinson Synan, *Aspects of Pentecostal-Charismatic Origins* (Plainfield, N.J.: Logos International, 1975), 39–54. This theme is developed in Donald Dayton's important book, *Theological Roots of Pentecostalism* (Grand Rapids: Francis Asbury Press, 1987).

7. See "Interview with Tommy Tyson, Evangelist," *Your Church*, November/December 1973, 10–28.

8. For the Oral Roberts University story, see David Edwin Harrell Jr., *Oral Roberts: An American Life* (Bloomington: Indiana Univ. Press, 1985), 207–52.

9. Harrell, *Oral Roberts*, 287–311.

10. Ross Whetstone, personal interview with the author, Oklahoma City, Okla., 25 September 1986.

11. "Where Have We Been and Where Are We Going?" *Manna Ministries (UMRSF), Notes*, June 1985, 1–2.

12. Kilian McDonnell, *Presence, Power, Praise: Documents on the Charismatic Renewal*, vol. 2 (Collegeville, Minn.; New York: Paulist Press, 1980), 270–90.

13. Whetstone, Synan interview, and letter.

14. John Osteen, personal interview with the author, Tulsa, Okla., 24 June 1986.

15. Edward T. Hiscox, *The New Directory for Baptist Churches* (Philadelphia: Judson Press, 1984), 354–63, 536–37.

16. Synan, *The Holiness-Pentecostal Tradition*, 114–23.

17. "But What About Hicks?" *Christian Century*, 7 July 1954, 814–15; Vinson Synan, *In the Latter Days* (Altamonte Springs, Fla.: Creation House, 1991), 25.

18. David Manuel, *Like a Mighty River: A Personal Account of the Conference of 1977* (Orleans, Mass.: Rock Harbor Press, 1977), 117.

19. Gary Clark and Charles Moore, personal interviews with the author, Green Lake, Wisc., 9 July 1986; Gary Clark, "An Extra Dimension," *Christian Life*, August 1985, 36–39.

20. W. Leroy Martin, personal interview with the author, Tulsa, Okla., 7 June 1986.

21. Don Le Master, personal interview with the author, Fort Lauderdale, Fla., 23 August 1986.

22. Ras Robinson, "Who Are You Who Read *Fulness*?" *Fullness*, July-August 1986, 4.

23. Le Master, Synan interview.

24. Kenneth Kantzer, "The Charismatics Among Us," *Christianity Today*, 22 February 1980, 25–29.

25. Derstine's story is told in his autobiography *Fol-*

lowing the Fire, as told to Joanne Derstine (Plain-field, N.J.: Logos International, 1980).

26. Also see "Champion of the Faith, Henry M. Brunk, 1895-1985" (Bradenton, Fla.: Christian Retreat, 1985), 6.

27. Terry Miller, "Renewing the Anabaptist Vision," *Empowered*, Fall 1984, 8–9.

28. Roy Koch, *My Personal Pentecost* (Scottsdale, Pa.: Herald Press, 1977), 15–35.

29. McDonnell, *Presence, Power, Praise*, 285–87.

30. Roy Koch, personal interview with the author, Charlotte, N.C., 16 January 1986. "Mennonite Renewal Services Formed," *Mennonite Renewal Newsletter*, February 1976, 1.

31. Miller, "Renewing the Anabaptist Vision," 9.

32. Derstine, Synan interview.

33. Athanasius F. S. Emmert, "Charismatic Develop-ments in the Eastern Orthodox Church," in Rus-sell Spittler, *Perspectives on the New Pentecostalism* (Grand Rapids: Baker, 1976), 28–42.

34. Ed Plowman, "Mission in Orthodoxy: The Full Gospel," *Christianity Today*, 26 April 1974, 44–45; Eusebius Stephanou, *Charismatic Renewal in the Orthodox Church* (Fort Wayne, Ind.: Logos Min-istries for Orthodox Renewal, 1976).

35. William Hollar, "The Charismatic Renewal in the Eastern Orthodox Church in the United States of America with Emphasis on the Logos Ministry for Orthodox Renewal," (M.A. thesis, Concordia Theological Seminary, Fort Wayne, Ind.).

36. George Allen, "The United Church of Christ: A Pluralistic Church or a Liberal One," *Focus Newsletter*, August 1982, 7–8.

37. Robert K. Arakaki, "The Holy Spirit and the United Church of Christ," *Focus Newsletter*, May 1983, 1–4; see Vernon Stoop, *Fellowship of Charis-matic Christians in the United Church of Christ* (Sassamansville, Pa.: Self-published, n.d.).

38. The historic connection between the holiness and Pentecostal movements is traced in Synan's *The Holiness-Pentecostal Tradition*, 1–106.

39. Timothy Smith, *Called Unto Holiness* (Kansas City: Nazarene Publishing House, 1962), 118; Alma White, *Demons and Tongues* (Bound Brook, N.J.: Pentecostal Union, 1910); Jones, *Perfectionist Persuasion*, 121, 173.

40. John L. Peters, personal interview with the au-thor, Oklahoma City, Okla., 10 December 1986.

41. Warren Black, personal interview with the au-thor, Cincinnati, Ohio, 29 September 1986. See also Warren Black, "A New Dimension," in *The Acts of the Holy Spirit Among the Nazarenes Today* (Los Angeles: Full Gospel Business Men, 1973), 23–29.

42. See the *Journal of the Nineteenth General Assembly*

of the Church of the Nazarene, 240; and McDon-nell, *Presence, Power, Praise*, 220–21.

43. See "Evidence of the Baptism with the Holy Spirit," in the *Manual 1985 Church of the Nazarene* (Kansas City: Nazarene Publishing House, 1985), 284.

44. See the "Report: Study Committee on Glosso-lalia" (presented to the general assembly of the Church of God 18 June 1986); Paul Tanner, per-sonal interview with the author, Oklahoma City, Okla., 21 July 1986.

45. See *Acts of the Holy Spirit Among the Nazarenes Today*, 9–72.

46. See the *Wesleyan Holiness Charismatic Fellowship Newsletter* (Athens, Ga., n.d.); Wilbur Jackson, Synan interview.

47. Howard Snyder, *The Divided Flame: Wesleyans and the Charismatic Renewal* (Grand Rapids: Fran-cis Asbury Press, 1986).

Chapter 9

1. Patty Gallagher Mansfield, *As by A New Pente-cost: The Dramatic Beginning of the Catholic Charis-matic Renewal* (Steubenville, Ohio: Steubenville Univ. Press, 1992), 5–29.

2. Vinson Synan, *In the Latter Days* (Ann Arbor, Mich.: Servant Publications, 1984), 110–11.

3. E.g., Fr. Jos Biesbrouck of the Netherlands in 1965 through the ministry of David du Plessis; Barbara Shlemon at Trinity Episcopal Church in Wheaton, Illinois, in 1965; and some Catholics in the Seattle area through the min-istry of St. Luke's Episcopal Church led by Dennis Bennett.

4. Edward O'Connor, *The Pentecostal Movement in the Catholic Church* (Notre Dame, Ind.: Ave Maria Press, 1971). Also see Edward O'Connor, "The Hidden roots of the Charismatic Renewal in the Catholic Church" in Vinson Synan, *Aspects of Pentecostal-Charismatic Origins* (Plainfield, N.J.: Logos International, 1975), 169–91.

5. It was known for a short while as the Catholic Pentecostal movement, but this was changed in the 1970s to the Catholic charismatic renewal, which has remained the accepted designation.

6. Also influential was Fr. Heribert Mühlen of Paderborn, Germany, the author of major stud-ies on the theology of the Holy Spirit. Father Mühlen became active in the promotion of the renewal of the charisms of the Spirit as part *of Charismatische Gemeinde Erneuerung* (Charis-matic Parish Renewal) while objecting to the CCR pattern, which he saw as insufficiently in-tegrated into parish life.

7. The third document, *Charismatic Renewal and So-*

cial Action (1979) was jointly written by Cardinal Suenens and Archbishop Helder Camara.

8. Vinson Synan, *Charismatic Bridges* (Ann Arbor, Mich.: Word of Life, 1974), 25.

9. The others present were Michael Harper (Anglican) and Larry Christenson (Lutheran).

10. The twelve steps are: (1) Conversion, (2) Call, (3) Covenant, (4) Commitment, (5) Corporate Structures, (6) Catechesis, (7) Caring Shepherd-Leaders, (8) Ministries, (9) Communion, (10) Communal Witness, (11) Church Renewal, (12) Come, Lord Jesus!

11. International Catholic Charismatic Renewal Services.

12. The major gathering of half a million people was preceded by a World Congress of Ecclesial Movements and New Communities. Besides CCR and RnS, many other participating bodies were charismatic, as the major charismatic communities were invited to send their own representatives to the congress.

13. The members include: *Ligaya ng Panginoon* (Joy of the Lord); *Buklod ng Pag-ibig* (Bond of Love); *Bukas Loob sa Dios* (Open to God); Elim Community; Risen Christ Catholic Community; Loved Flock, the Lord's Flock; *Pag-ibig ng Dios* (God's Love); and *El Shaddai*.

14. Those that did included Msgr. Vincent Walsh (Philadelphia), Henri Lemay (ICCRS member from Quebec), Fr. Hal Cohen and Patti Mansfield Gallagher (New Orleans).

15. "Concerning Extraordinarily Bodily Phenomena in the Context of Spiritual Occurrences," Eng. trans. in *Pneuma* 18/1 (1996), 5–32.

Chapter 10

1. George Fox, *The Works of George Fox*, vol. 3 (New York: AMS Press, 1975), 13.

2. Robert Wearmouth, *Methodism and the Common People of the Eighteenth Century* (London: Epworth, 1945), 223.

3. Susan C. Hyatt, *In the Spirit We're Equal: The Spirit, The Bible and Women—A Revival Perspective* (Dallas: Hyatt Press, 1998), 140.

4. Benjamin St. James Fry, *Woman's Work in the Church* (New York: Hunt and Eaton, 1892), 1.

5. William B. Godbey, *Woman Preacher* (n.p., 1891), 1.

6. Phoebe Palmer, *The Promise of the Father* (Boston: Henry V. Degen, 1859), 14, 341–47.

7. F. Booth Tucker, *The Life of Catherine Booth*, vol. 1 (New York: Revel, 1892), 123.

8. Carol D. Spencer, "Evangelism, Feminism, and Social Reform: The Quaker Woman Minister and the Holiness Revival," *Quaker History: The Bul-*

letin of the Friends Historical Society, 80, no. 1 (Spring 1991): 39.

9. Perhaps the best documentation for this is Sarah Parham's book, *The Life of Charles F. Parham* (Joplin, Mo.: Tri-State Publishing, 1929).

10. Carl Brumback, *A Sound from Heaven* (Springfield, Mo.: Gospel Publishing House, 1977), 73.

11. Parham, *The Life of Charles Fox Parham*, 87

12. Edith Blumhofer, *Pentecost in My Soul* (Springfield, Mo.: Gospel Publishing House, 1989), 121.

13. Ethel E. Goss, "The Story of the Early Pentecostal Days (1901–1914)," in *The Life of Howard A. Goss* (New York: Comet, 1958), 56.

14. Mother Cotton, "Message of the 'Apostolic Faith,' 1," 1939.

15. B. F. Lawrence, *The Apostolic Faith Restored* (St. Louis: Gospel Publishing, 1916), 66.

16. Brumback, *A Sound from Heaven*, 331.

17. Yonggi Cho, *Successful Home Cell Groups* (Plainfield, N.J.: Logos International, 1981), 28.

18. Maureen Eha, "Aglow with the Love of Jesus," *Charisma*, December 1997, 43–47.

Chapter 11

This chapter is a revision of the article "Pentecostalism" in Larry Murphy, J. Gordon Melton, and Gary Ward, eds., *Encyclopedia of African American Religions* (New York: Garland Reference Library of Social Science, 1993), 585–95.

1. William A. Andrews, ed., *Sisters of the Spirit: Three Black Women's Autobiography of the Nineteenth Century* (Bloomington: Indiana Univ. Press, 1986); Paul R. Griffen, *Black Theology As the Foundation of Three Methodist Colleges: The Educational Views and Labors of David Payne, Joseph Price, and Isaac Lane* (Lanham, Md.: Univ. Press of America, 1984); Amanda Berry Smith, *An Autobiography: The Story of the Lord's Dealings with Mrs. Amanda Smith, The Colored Evangelist* (Chicago: Meyer & Brother, 1893); Adrienne M. Israel, *Amanda Berry Smith: From Washerwoman to Evangelist* (Lanham, Md.: Scarecrow Press, Inc., 1998).

2. *General Rules and Discipline of the Reformed Zion Union Apostolic Church* (Norfolk, Va.: Creecy's Good-Will Printery, 1966); Wardell J. Payne, ed., *Directory of African American Religious Bodies* (Washington, D.C.: Howard Univ. Press, 1991), 110.

3. *Christian Recorder* (Philadelphia), 9 September 1880, 2; *Christian Recorder* (Philadelphia), 28 June 1877, 2.

4. *Christian Recorder* (Philadelphia), 9 August 1877, 2; *Christian Recorder* (Philadelphia), 12 September 1878, 37.

5. *Christian Recorder* (Philadelphia), 9 September 1880, 3.

6. *Christian Recorder* (Philadelphia), 3 May 1882, 1; *Christian Recorder* (Philadelphia), 29 July 1880, 3; Israel, Ibid; *Christian Recorder* (Philadelphia), 14 August 1878, 3; *Christian Recorder* (Philadelphia), 26 August 1880, 3.

7. Chester W. Gregory, *The History of the United Holy Church of America, Inc., 1886-1986* (Baltimore: Gateway Press, 1986), 30–46.

8. Daniels, 6–7.

9. Charles Brown, *When the Trumpet Sounded* (Anderson, Ind.: Warner Press, 1951), 269; James Earl Massey, *An Introduction to the Negro Churches in the Church of God Reformation Movement* (New York: Shining Light Survey Press, 1957), 51.

10. Vinson Synan, *The Holiness-Pentecostal Tradition: Charismatic Movements in the Twentieth Century* (Grand Rapids: Eerdmans, 1997), 55, 176.

11. Lowell Barks Sr. et al., *Glorious Heritage: The Gold Book, Documentary—Historical, Church of the Living God, Motto: (CWF) 1899–1964* (n.p., 1967), 22; William Christian, *Poor Pilgrim's Work* (Texarkana, Ark.: n.p., 1896), 14.

12. Barks, *Glorious Heritage*, 17; Christian, *Poor Pilgrim's Work*, 4.

13. Josephine Washburn, *History and Reminiscences of the Holiness Church in Southern California and Arizona* (n.p., 1911), 88, 238, 18.

14. Ibid., 91–92.

15. David D. Daniels III, "The Cultural Renewal of Slave Religion: Charles Price Jones and the Emergence of the Holiness Movement in Mississippi" (Ph.D. diss., Union Theological Seminary in New York, 1992), 247–48.

16. Ibid., 263–66.

17. The United Holy Church of America family includes the United Holy Church of America; Mt. Sinai Holy Church; Mt. Calvary Holy Church; Mt. Zion Pentecostal Church; and the Original United Holy Church of America. The Church of the Living God family includes the Church of the Living God, Pillar and Ground of Truth; the First Born Church of the Living God; the House of God, Which is the Church of the Living God, the Pillar and Ground of the Truth. The Church of God in Christ family includes the Church of God in Christ, Inc.; Church of God in Christ, Congregational; and Church of God in Christ, International. The Church of God (Apostolic) family includes the Church of God (Apostolic); the Apostolic Church of Christ; and Apostle Church of God in Christ. The Fire-Baptized Holiness Church of America family includes Fire-Baptized Holiness Church of God of the Americas and the Universal Pentecostal Church. The Apostolic Faith Church of God family includes the Apostolic Faith Church of God.

18. Synan, *The Holiness-Pentecostal Tradition*, 96–98; Cecil M. Robeck, "Azusa Street Revival" in *Dictionary of Pentecostal and Charismatic Movements*, ed. Stanley M. Burgess et al. (Grand Rapids: Zondervan, 1988), 33.

19. Synan, *The Holiness-Pentecostal Tradition*, 98, 104–5.

20. Ibid., 89, 92–94; Douglas Nelson, "For Such a Time as This: The Story of Bishop William J. Seymour and the Azusa Street Revival" (Ph.D. dissertation, Univ. of Birmingham [UK], 1981), 9–54.

21. David D. Daniels, "'Everybody Bids You Welcome': A Multicultural Approach to North American Pentecostalism," *The Globalization of Pentecostalism: A Religion Made to Travel*, ed. Murray W. Dempster, Byron D. Klaus, Douglas Petersen (Oxford, UK; and Irvine, Calif.: Regnum Books International, 1999), 227–31.

22. Ibid., 229–30.

23. James C. Richardson, *With Water and Spirit* (Washington, D.C.: Spirit Press, 1980).

24. Ibid.

25. Theodore Kornweibel Jr., "Bishop C. H. Mason and the Church of God in Christ During World War I: The Perils of Conscientious Objection," *Southern Studies: An Interdisciplinary Journal of the South* 26, 4 (Winter 1987), 277.

26. Ithiel C. Clemmons, *Bishop C. H. Mason and the Roots of the Church of God in Christ* (Bakersfield, Calif.: Pneuma Life Publishing, 1996), 68–70.

27. Daniels, "'Everybody Bids You Welcome,'" 235; Cheryl J. Sanders, *Saints in Exile: The Holiness-Pentecostal Experience* (Oxford Univ. Press), 32–33.

28. Sanders, *Saints in Exile*, 71–78, 86–90.

29. Arturo Skinner, *Deliverance* (Newark, N.J.: Deliverance Evangelistic Centers, 1969).

30. Mary Sawyer, "The Fraternal Council of Negro Churches, 1934–1964," *Church History*, vol. 59 (March 1990), 51–64; C. Eric Lincoln and Lawrence H. Mamiya, *The Black Church in the African American Experience* (Durham and London: Duke Univ. Press, 1990), 191–94; Synan, *The Holiness-Pentecostal Tradition*, 186.

31. Smallwood E. Williams, *This Is My Story: A Significant Life Struggle: Autobiography of Smallwood Edmonds Williams* (Washington, D.C.: Wm. Willoughby Publishers, 1981); Arthur Brazier, *Black Self-Determination: The Story of the Woodlawn Organization* (Grand Rapids: Eerdmans, 1969).

32. Sanders, *Saints in Exile*.

33. Ibid., 118–21; William H. Bentley, "Bible Believers in the Black Community" in *The Evangelicals,* D. F. Wells, ed. (Nashville: Abingdon Press, 1975), 108–21; Bennie Goodwin, "Social Implications of Pentecostal Power," *Spirit,* 1:1 (1977), 31–35; Leonard Lovett, "Conditional Liberation: An Emergent Pentecostal Perspective," *Spirit* 1:2 (1977), 24–30; James A. Forbes, Jr., "Shall We Call This Dream Progressive Pentecostalism," *Spirit* 1:1 (1977), 12–15.

34. Stephen Strang, "The Ever-Increasing Faith of Fred Price," *Charisma* 10:10 (May 1985), 20–26; Lincoln and Mamiya, 385–88; Vinson Synan, "Paul Morton Organizes Full Gospel Baptist Fellowship," *Timelines* (Spring 1993), 1–4.

Chapter 12

1. David Stoll, *Is Latin America Turning Protestant? The Politics of Evangelical Growth* (Berkeley: Univ. of California Press, 1990).

2. David Martin, *Tongues of Fire: The Explosion of Protestantism in Latin America* (Cambridge, Mass.: Basil Blackwell, Inc., 1990).

3. Martin, *Tongues of Fire,* 284.

4. See Brian H. Smith, *Religious Politics in Latin America: Pentecostal v. Catholic* (South Bend, Ind.: Univ. of Notre Dame Press, 1998), 3–9.

5. Jeffrey Gros, "Confessing the Apostolic Faith from the Perspective of the Pentecostal Churches," *Journal for the Society of Pentecostal Studies,* 9 (Spring 1987), 12.

6. Elizabeth E. Brusco, *The Reformation of Machismo: Evangelical Conversion and Gender in Colombia* (Austin: Univ. of Texas Press, 1995).

7. Thomas Weyr, *Hispanic U.S.A.: Breaking the Melting Pot* (New York: Harper and Row, 1988), 193.

8. *Time,* 2 November 1963, 56.

9. Eugne A. Nida, "The Indigenous Churches in Latin America," in *Understanding Latin Americans* (Pasadena, Calif.: William Carey Library, 1974), 137–48.

10. Clifton L. Holland, *The Religious Dimensions in Hispanic Los Angeles: A Protestant Case Study* (Pasadena, Calif.: William Carey Library, 1974), 356.

11. Alice E. Luce, *Pentecostal Evangel,* 14 December 1918.

12. Manuel J. Gaxiola, *La Serpiente y la Paloma* (Pasadena, Calif.: William Carey Library, 1970), 157.

13. Luce, *Pentecostal Evangel,* 17 July 1917.

14. San Jose, Calif., *Mercury,* 9 January 2000.

15. *Newsweek,* 12 July 1999.

16. Thomas F. Coakley, "Protestant Home Missions Among Catholic Immigrants," *Commonweal* 28 (18 August 1933): 386.

17. Victor De Leon, *The Silent Pentecostals: A Biographical History of the Pentecostal Movement among the Hispanics in the Twentieth Century* (self-published).

18. Robert M. Anderson, *Vision of the Disinherited: The Making of American Pentecostalism* (New York: Oxford Univ. Press, 1979), 126.

19. Luce, *Pentecostal Evangel,* 21 April 1923.

20. Nellie Bazan, *Enviados de Dios* (Miami: Editorial Vida,1987).

21. Luce, *Pentecostal Evangel,* 9 February 1924.

22. Luce, "Pentecost on the Mexican Border," *Pentecostal Evangel,* 11 November 1939.

23. Luce, *Pentecostal Evangel,* 15 June 1918.

24. Gastón Espinosa, "El Azteca: Francisco Olazábal and Latino Pentecostal Charisma, Power, and Faith Healing in the Borderlands," *Journal of the American Academy of Religion* 67 (September 1999), 597–616.

25. Holland, *The Religious Dimensions in Hispanic Los Angeles,* 356.

26. Leo Grebler, "Protestants and Mexicans," in Leo Grebler, Joan M. Moore, and Ralph C. Guzman, eds., *The Mexican-American People: The Nation's Second Largest Minority* (New York: Free Press, 1973), 505.

27. Weyr, *Hispanic U.S.,* 218.

28. For a bibliography on Latin American Pentecostalism see: Walter J. Hollenweger, *The Pentecostals* (Peabody, Mass.: Hendrikson Publishers, 1972); and Charles Edwin Jones, *Guide to the Study of the Pentecostal Movement,* 2 vols. (Metuchen, N.J.: Scarecrow Press, 1983). See also David Martin, *Tongues of Fire: The Explosion of Protestantism in Latin America* (Cambridge, Mass.: Basil Blackwell, 1990); David Stoll, *Is Latin America Turning Protestant? The Politics of Evangelical Growth* (Berkeley: Univ. of California Press, 1990); and Cecil M. Robeck Jr., "Select Bibliography on Latin American Pentecostalism," *PNEUMA, The Journal of the Society of Pentecostal Studies* 13, 1 (Spring 1991), 193–97.

29. "Evangelical" is here the translation of the Spanish *evangélico,* the preferred self-designation of the many Christian groups in Latin America with some connection to Protestantism. Samuel Escobar, "Identidad, misión y futuro del protestantismo latinoamericano," *Boletín Teológico,* 3–4 (1977):2; Orlando E. Costas, *Theology of the Crossroads in Contemporary Latin America* (Amsterdam: Rodopi, 1976), 48n. 65.

30. Penny Lernoux, "The Fundamentalist Surge in Latin America," *Christian Century,* 20 January 1988, 51.

31. Assemblies of God Division of Foreign Missions, *1984 Annual Report: idem, 1985 Annual Report.*

32. Gary Parker, "Evangelicals Blossom Brightly Amid El Salvador's Wasteland of Violence," *Christianity Today* 25 (8 May 1981), 34.

33. Wagner, *Spiritual Power*, 29. Cf. also *Estudios Teológicos* 7 (January-June 1980):1–157.

34. See Christian Lalive d'Epinay, "Reflexiones a propósito del pentecostalismo chileno," *Concilium* 19 (January 1983), 87–105; Ignacio Vergara, *El protestantismo en Chile* (Santiago: Editorial del Pacífico, 1962); and Edward L. Cleary and Juan Sepulveda, "Chilean Pentecostalism: Coming of Age," chap. 6 in *Power, Politics, and Pentecostals in Latin America*, ed. Edward L. Cleary and Hannah W. Steward-Gambino (Boulder, Colo.: Westview Press, 1998).

35. Willis C. Hoover, *Historia del avivamiento pentecostal en Chile* (Santiago: Imprenta Excelsior, 1948).

36. Kessler, *A Study of Protestant Missions in Peru and Chile*, 288–330.

37. Vergara, *El protestantismo en Chile*, 246.

38. Louis Francescon, *Resumo de una ramificação da obra de Deus, pelo Espirito Santo, no seculo actual* (1942, 1953, 1958). Francescon's untitled autobiography was published in G. Bongiovanni, *Pioneers of the Faith* (1971). See also Walter Hollenweger, *The Pentecostals*.

39. Cf. Emilio G. Conde. *História das Assembléias de Deus no Brasil: Belem 1911–196l* (Rio de Janeiro: Casa Publicadora das Assembléias de Deus, 1960); Abroao de Almeida, ed., *Historia das Assembléias de Deus no Brazil* (Rio de Janeiro: Casa Publicadora das Assembléias de Deus, 1982).

40. Cf. Berg's autobiography, Daniel Berg, *Enviado por Deus: Memórias de Daniel Berg*, 3rd ed. (Rio de Janeiro: Casa Publicadora das Assembléias de Deus, 1973).

41. Cf. Ivar Vingren, *Pionjärens dagbok: Brasilienmissionären Gunnar Vingren* (Stockholm: Lewi Pethrus Förlag, 1968).

42. Read, *New Patterns of Church Growth in Brazil*, 119–21.

43. Roberto Domínguez, *Pioneros de Pentecostés en el mundo de habla hispana*, vol. 2: *México y Centroamérica* (Hialeah, Fla.: Literatura Evangélica, 1975), 25–29.

44. Peggy Humphrey, *María Atkinson: la Madre de México* (1967).

45. Willems, *Followers of the New Faith*, 86–89.

46. Mortimer and Esther Arias, *The Cry of My People: Out of Captivity in Latin America* (New York: Friendship Press, 1980), 8.

47. Lalive d'Epinay, "Reflexiones a propósito del pentecostalismo chileno," 104.

48. Juan Tennekes, *La nueva vida: el movimiento pente-*

costal en la sociedad chilena (Ámsterdam: published by the author, 1973), 130.

Chapter 13

1. An overview of the healing revival up to the mid-1970s is David Edwin Harrell Jr.'s *All Things Are Possible: The Healing and Charismatic Revivals in Modern America* (Bloomington: Indiana Univ. Press, 1975).

2. For a good overview of American Pentecostalism see Vinson Synan, *The Holiness-Pentecostal Tradition: Charismatic Movements in the Twentieth Century*, 2nd. ed. (Grand Rapids: Eerdmans, 1997).

3. The best biography of William Branham is C. Douglas Weaver, *The Healer-Prophet, William Marrion Branham* (Macon, Ga.: Mercer Univ. Press, 1987).

4. "The Gifts of Healing Plus," *Voice of Healing* (March 1950), 10.

5. An early autobiography of Lindsay is Gordon Lindsay, *The Gordon Lindsay Story* (Dallas: Voice of Healing Publishing Co., n.d.); see Harrell, *All Things Are Possible*, 53–58.

6. A good survey of the early missionary spirit in Pentecostalism is James R. Goff Jr., *Fields White Unto Harvest* (Fayetteville, Ark.: Univ. of Arkansas Press, 1988).

7. See Deborah Vansau McCauley, "Kathryn Kuhlman," in Charles H. Lippy, ed., *Twentieth-Century Shapers of American Popular Religion* (New York: Greenwood Press, 1989), 225–32.

8. See David Edwin Harrell Jr., *Oral Roberts: An American Life* (Bloomington: Indiana Univ. Press, 1985).

9. See Harrell, *All Things Are Possible*, 140–44.

10. See Ibid., 153–55. A good history of the FGBMFI is Vinson Synan, *Under His Banner: History of the Full Gospel Business Men's Fellowship International* (Costa Mesa, Calif.: Gift Publications, 1992).

11. Lee Braxton, "Millions See the First Oral Roberts Telecast," *America's Healing Magazine* (March 1955), 22. Also see Oral Roberts, "A Call to Action," *America's Healing Magazine* (June 1954), 12.

12. "Preacher's Timely TV Miracles Raise Questions of Station's Standards," *New York Times*, undated clipping in Oral Roberts University Archives scrapbook.

13. "Oklahoma Faith Healer Draws a Following," *Christian Century*, 29 June 1955, 749–50. See Ben Armstrong, *The Electric Church* (Nashville: Thomas Nelson , 1979), 44–52.

14. Taped Interview with W. V. Grant, Dallas, Tex., 15 December 1973.

15. "400,00 in Single Service," *Voice of Healing* (Au-

gust 1954), 19. See Thomas R. Nickel, "The
Greatest Revival in All History," *Voice of Healing*
(February-March 1955), 4–7; "But What About
Hicks?" *Christian Century*, 7 July 1954, 814–15.

16. T. L. Osborn, "World Missions' Crusade," *Voice of Healing*, July 1953, 10–11.

17. Ibid.

18. Taped interview with Daisy and T. L. Osborn, 6 September 1991, Tulsa, Okla.

19. See T. L. Osborn, "World Missions' Crusade," *Voice of Healing*, August 1953, 12–13.

20. "Concerning Our Association with the Voice of Healing," *Faith Digest*, June 1956, 17.

21. William Campbell, "God Has Spoken Again," *Faith Digest*, November 1959, 2–3.

22. Daisy M. Osborn, "Magnificent Revolution," *Faith Digest*, September 1971, 10–11.

23. T. L. Osborn interview.

24. Taped interview with Freda Lindsay, Dallas, Tex., 25 March 1991, and 7 December 1973; and with Gordon Lindsay 27 July 1972.

25. "Christ for the Nations in Dallas Celebrates 50 Years of Ministry," *Charisma*, 4 September 2000.

26. For an overview of Robertson's ministry see David Edwin Harrell Jr., *Pat Robertson: A Personal, Political and Religious Portrait* (San Francisco: Harper & Row, 1987).

27. Two books on the rise of televangelism are Quentin J. Schultze, *Televangelism and American Culture* (Grand Rapids: Baker, 1991); and Jeffrey K. Hadden and Anson Shupe, *Televangelism: Power & Politics on God's Frontier* (New York: Henry Holt and Company, 1988).

28. Chapel transcript, 14 October 1974, Oral Roberts Archives, 18.

29. For a discussion of the reasons for the television success of charismatic evangelists see David Edwin Harrell Jr., "Oral Roberts: Media Pioneer," in Leonard Sweet, ed., *Communication and Change in American Religious History* (Grand Rapids: Eerdmans, 1994), 320–34.

30. Probably the best way to find up-to-date information on the major independent ministries is by checking their Web sites. See the Kenneth Hagin Ministries Web site, http://www.rhema.org/khm.htm.

31. Interview with Jim Woolsey, director of missions, Jimmy Swaggart Ministries, 31 March 1991, Baton Rouge, La.; Paul G. Chappell, "Jimmy Swaggart," in Lippy, ed., *Twentieth-Century Shapers of Popular American Religion*, 417–24; Jamie Buckingham, "He Points 'Em to Heaven," *Logos* (September 1987), 16–20.

32. See Liz Szabo, "Robertson Recommits to Ministry," *Norfolk Virginian-Pilot*, 23 March 2000.

33. See Charles E. Shepard, *Forgiven* (New York: At-

lantic Monthly Press, 1989); Cecile Holmes White, "Jim and Tammy Bakker" in Lippy, *Twentieth-Century Shapers of American Popular Religion*, 14–20.

34. For a detailed description of the Bakker scandal, see Shepard, *Forgiven*.

35. See "Satellites and Scripture," *Orange County Register*, 31 May 1998, a01; Trinity Broadcasting Web site, http://www.tbn.org.

36. For an interesting description of this development, see Hanna Rosin, "White Preachers Born Again on Black Network," *Washington Post*, 3 September 1998, A1.

37. See Benny Hinn Web site, http://www.benny-hinn.org.

38. Deborah Kovach Caldwell, "TV Evangelist Will Move Growing Empire to Area," *Dallas Morning News*, 4 June 1999, 37A.

39. Bill Sherman, "Hinn Crusade Calls for Steady Rise in Holiness," *Tulsa World*, 7 August 2000, 1.

40. Joyce Meyer Web site, http://www.jmministries.org; Ken Walker, "The Preacher Who Tells It Like It Is," *Charisma*, September 2000.

41. See Fred Price Web site, http://www.faithdome.org.

42. See Creflo Dollar Web site, http://www.worldchangers.org; John Blake, "Dollar and the Gospel," *Atlanta Journal and the Atlanta Constitution*, 5 March 2000, G1.

43. See T. D. Jakes Web site, http://www.tdjakes.org.

44. For a brief description of Dinakaran's ministry, see "41 Years with the Lord Jesus," *Jesus Calls*, February 1996, 10–17.

Chapter 14

1. Vinson Synan, *The Holiness-Pentecostal Tradition: Charismatic Movements in the Twentieth Century* (Grand Rapids: Eerdmans, 1997), 186–211.

2. For more information on the FGBMFI see Vinson Synan's *Under His Banner:History of the Full Gospel Business Men's Fellowship International* (Costa Mesa, Calif.: Gift Publications, 1992).

3. Vinson Synan and Ralph Rath, *Launching the Decade* (South Bend, Ind.: North American Renewal Service Committee), 101–2.

4. David Moore, "The Shepherding Movement in Historic Perspective" (unpublished D.Min. dissertation, Regent Univ., 1999); Harold Hunter, "The Shepherding Movement" in Burgess, McGee, and Alexander, *Dictionary of Pentecostal and Charismatic Movements* (Grand Rapids: Zondervan, 1988), 783–84.

5. Peter Hocken, "Charismatic Communities," in

Burgess, McGee, and Alexander, *Dictionary of Pentecostal and Charismatic Movements*, 127–30.

6. Leonard Lovett, "Positive Confession Theology," in Ibid., 718–20.

7. For a full description of this wave see C. Peter Wagner, *The Third Wave of the Holy Spirit: Encountering the Power of Signs and Wonders Today* (Ann Arbor, Mich.: Servant Publications, 1988).

8. David du Plessis, *The Spirit Bade Me Go*, rev. and enlarged (Plainfield, N.J.: Logos International, 1970).

9. Bob Slosser, *A Man called Mr. Pentecost: David du Plessis* (Plainfield, N.J.: Logos International, 1977).

10. Moore, "The Shepherding Movement."

11. Vinson Synan, *In the Latter Days* (Altamonte Springs, Fla.: Creation House, 1991), 126–30.

12. David Manuel, *Like a Mighty River: A Personal Account of the Charismatic Conference of 1977* (Orleans, Mass.: Rock Harbor Press, 1977).

13. Synan and Rath, *Launching the Decade.*

14. Synan, *The Holiness-Pentecostal Tradition*, 267–70.

15. Pat Robertson, with Jamie Buckingham, *Shout It from the Housetops* (Plainfield, N.J.: Logos International, 1972); J. R. Williams, "Marion Gordon Robertson," in Burgess, McGee, and Alexander, *Dictionary of Pentecostal and Charismatic Movements*, 761–62.

16. See David Edwin Harrell, *Oral Roberts: An American Life* (Bloomington, Ind.: Indiana Univ. Press, 1985).

17. "The Rise of Pentecostalism," *Christian History*, Issue 58 (Vol.XVII, No. 2).

18. Mary Rourke, "Redefining Religion in America," *Los Angeles Times*, 21 June 1998, A1–A30.

19. See Vinson Synan, "The Apostle," a review in the *Journal of Southern Religion* (Vol. I, No. 1, January-June, 1998), [www.jsr.as.wvu.edu/synan.htm].

20. David Barrett, personal interview with author, 28 August 1998.

21. These figures were supplied by John Vaughan.

22. These figures were supplied by John Vaughan and Peter Wagner.

23. Harold Hunter, "Reconciliation Pentecostal Style," *Reconciliation*, Number 1, Summer 1998, 2.

24. Lesslie Newbigin, *The Household of God* (New York: Friendship Press, 1954); Van Dusen, "The Third Force," *Life*, 113–24.

25. Michael Harper, *Three Sisters* (Wheaton, Ill.: Tyndale, 1979), 9–15.

26. J. Lee Grady, "Denomination Blends Charismatic Spirituality with High Church Style," *Charisma* (September 1996), 25–27.

27. Calmetta Coleman, "A Charismatic Church Deals with a Preacher Who Finds New Faith," *Wall Street Journal*, 14 June 1996, 1–7. For his side of the story see: Charles Bell, *Discovering the Rich Heritage of Orthodoxy* (Minneapolis: Life and Light Publications, 1994), 1–7, 86–90. Also see Peter Gillquist, *Becoming Orthodox: A Journey to the Ancient Christian Faith* (Ben Lamond, Calif.: Conciliar Press, 1992).

28. See Randall Balmer, "Why the Bishops Went to Valdosta," *Christianity Today*, 24 September 1990, 19–24; and Robert Libby, "Newest Episcopalians are a Spirited Group," *Episcopal Life*, June 1990, 6.

29. See Michael Harper, *Equal But Different* (London: Hodder and Stoughton, 1993), 131, 171, 213. Letter from Michael Harper to Vinson Synan, 17 March 1995.

30. Peter Wagner, *The New Apostolic Churches* (Ventura, Calif.: Regal Press, 1998), 13–25.

31. Guy Chevreau, *Catch the Fire: The Toronto Blessing: an Experience of Renewal and Revival* (Toronto: Marshall Pickering, 1994); John Arnott, *The Father's Blessing* (Orlando: Creation House, 1996). For news of the Brownsville revival see the Brownsville Web site at www://brownsville-revival.org.

Index

Contributors

David B. Barrett is a leading Christian researcher and co-editor of the monumental *World Christian Encyclopedia* (Oxford University Press). He is head of the Global Evangelization Movement in Richmond, Virginia.

David Daniels III is an associate professor of Church History in the Modern Period at McCormick Theological Seminary in Chicago, Illinois. His articles in various scholarly journals, including the *Encyclopedia of African American Religions,* have made him an authority on American black Pentecostalism. He is an ordained minister in the Church of God in Christ.

Pablo Deiros serves as professor of the History of Christianity at the International Baptist Theological Seminary in Buenos Aires, Argentina. With a Ph.D. degree from Southwestern Baptist Theological Seminary in Fort Worth, Texas, and the author of many publications, Deiros is widely recognized as one of the leading authorities on Latin American Christian history.

David Edwin Harrell, Jr., serves as the Daniel F. Breeden Eminent Scholar in the Humanities at Auburn University in Auburn, Alabama. Author of *All Things Are Possible* and *Oral Roberts: An American Life,* Harrell is the definitive historian of the healing movement in America.

Peter Hocken is the Bishop's Chaplain and Chancellor at the Bishop's House in Northampton, England. A Roman Catholic charismatic scholar, he has written widely on the history and theology of the charismatic movement.

Susan Hyatt is the founding co-ordinator of the International Christian Women's History Project in Dallas, Texas. With a Doctor of Ministry from Regent University, she is author of *In the Spirit We Are Equal: The Spirit, the Bible, and Women.*

Gary B. McGee serves as Professor of Church History and Pentecostal Studies at the Assemblies of God Theological Seminary in Springfield, Missouri. A co-editor of the highly acclaimed *Dictionary of Pentecostal and Charismatic Movements,* he is a respected and well-published historian of Pentecostalism.

Robert Owens is the dean of the School of Christian Ministries at Emmanuel College in Franklin Springs, Georgia. He holds a Ph.D. degree from Regent University, and he is author of *Speak to the Rock: The Azusa Street Revival—Its Roots and Its Message.*

Vinson Synan is a highly regarded historian of the Pentecostal and charismatic renewal movements. He has written over ten books, including *Holiness-Pentecostal Tradition* (Eerdmans). He is dean of the School of Divinity at Regent University, and he earned his Ph.D. degree from the University of Georgia.

Everett A. Wilson serves as president of Bethany College of California, an Assemblies of God college located in Scotts Valley, California. Author of *Strategy of the Spirit: J. Philip Hogan and the Growth of the Assemblies of God, 1960-1990,* and a former missionary, Wilson is a recognized authority of the Hispanic Pentecostal movement in the U.S.

Photo Credits

Andaloro, Mike: 9, 211, 216, 218, 374
Bennie Hinn Ministries: 344
Billy Graham Evangelistic Association (BGEA): 367
Bradford, Brick: 170
CBN: 286, 340
CFNI: 253, 327
Christ for All Nations: 345
Christian Church of North America: 312
Dorries, David: 3, 23
Flower, J. Roswell: 4, 5, 30, 43, 44, 48, 50, 76, 84, 89, 100, 116, 125, 127, 128, 129, 133, 141, 142, 146, 242, 246, 247, 249, 257, 274, 279, 302, 310, 326, 352,
Joyce Meyer Ministries: 260
Kellar, Nancy: 226
Moore, David: 354
Oral Roberts Evangelistic Association (OREA): 11
Oral Roberts University: 328
Owens, Rosalee: 282
Pentecostal Holiness Archives: 271
Presbyterian and Reformed Ministries: 173
Ranaghan, Kevin: 214, 222,
Rhema Bible Institute: 359
Stoop, Vernon: 202
Synan, Vinson: 16, 26, 32, 77, 79, 92, 109, 155, 158, 159, 161, 181, 193, 212, 225, 240, 311, 318, 333, 337, 358, 366, 375, 380, 430
T.D. Jakes Ministries: 289
Williams, Rod: 173
Wilson, Aaron: 139